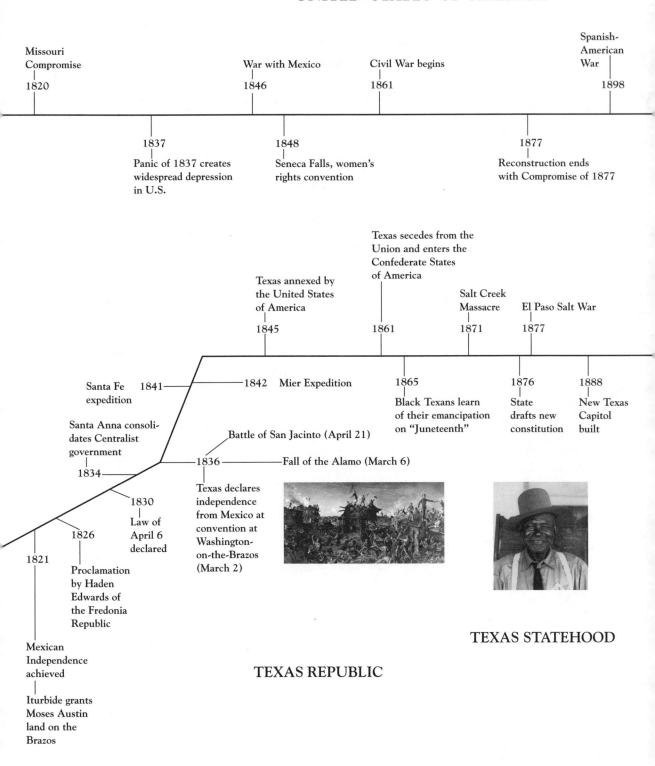

UNITED STATES OF AMERICA

Missouri
Compromise

1820

War with Mexico

1846

Civil War begins

1861

Spanish-
American
War

1898

1837

Panic of 1837 creates
widespread depression
in U.S.

1848

Seneca Falls, women's
rights convention

1877

Reconstruction ends
with Compromise of 1877

Texas secedes from the
Union and enters the
Confederate States
of America

Texas annexed by
the United States
of America

1845

1861

Salt Creek
Massacre

1871

El Paso Salt War

1877

Santa Fe
expedition

1841

1842   Mier Expedition

1865

Black Texans learn
of their emancipation
on "Juneteenth"

1876

State
drafts new
constitution

1888

New Texas
Capitol
built

Santa Anna consoli-
dates Centralist
government

1834

1830

Law of
April 6
declared

Battle of San Jacinto (April 21)

1836

Fall of the Alamo (March 6)

Texas declares
independence
from Mexico at
convention at
Washington-
on-the-Brazos
(March 2)

1826

Proclamation
by Haden
Edwards of
the Fredonia
Republic

1821

Mexican
Independence
achieved

Iturbide grants
Moses Austin
land on the
Brazos

TEXAS STATEHOOD

TEXAS REPUBLIC

MEXICAN TEXAS

THE HISTORY OF TEXAS

THIRD EDITION

Robert A. Calvert

Arnoldo De León
Angelo State University

Gregg Cantrell
University of North Texas

Harlan Davidson, Inc.
Wheeling, Illinois 60090-6000

Library of Congress Cataloging-in-Publication Data

Calvert, Robert A.
    The history of Texas / Robert A. Calvert, Arnoldo De León, Gregg Cantrell.—3rd ed.
        p. cm.
    Includes bibliographical references and index.
    ISBN 8-88295-966-2 (alk. paper)1. Texas—History. I. De León, Arnoldo, 1945– II.
Cantrell, Gregg. III. Title

F386.C26 2002
976.4—dc21

                                                                    2001051868

Cover photograph: The Rio Grande by Bill Wright.
Cover design: DePinto Graphic Design

Manufactured in the United States of America
04 03 02 1 2 3 4 VP

C O N T E N T S

PREFACE

Like its predecessors, the Third Edition of *The History of Texas* presents the fascinating story of the various peoples who have inhabited the land known as Texas. Readers of this book will gain an understanding of the forces of cause and effect that have shaped the disparate pasts of different groups within the state as well as the heritage shared by all Texans. They will also develop an appreciation for the dynamic interpretations that scholars give to historical movements and specific incidents.

In writing this book, we have retained those many features of the first two editions that appealed to both students and professors. All peoples make history; we have continued to honor that tenet by incorporating the many cultures embraced by the Texas experience. The same principle also drove our effort to give due attention to the lives of ordinary Texans, as seen in the continued and expanded coverage of topics such as agriculture, industrialization, urbanization, economic disparity, migration patterns, and demographic change. Also included are the unsung subjects who contributed to the Texas saga, among them plain white folks, women, and the leaders and members of local labor, agricultural, and other grass-roots organizations. Like the first two editions, this one also pays attention to the history of folklore, music, literature, sports, religion, and other aspects of Texas culture that help determine the flavor of Texas, past and present. Finally, once again we provide a comprehensive, unflinching analysis of twentieth-century Texas.

On the other hand, but just as important, in response to the feedback of instructors and students who used the earlier editions, as well as the recommendations of experts on particular periods of Texas history, we have made substantial changes to many parts of the text. These include the clarification of chronologies, the reorganization of topics, and the addition of entirely new sections and the deletion of others. We also felt compelled to incorporate into this edition new scholarship representing the cutting edge of historical research. For example, our expanded discussion of American Indians makes extensive use of scholarship published since the mid-1990s. Readers will also note that Chapter 14 has been completely rewritten in view of the rapid movement of events that occurred during the years since the publication of the Second Edition. The result is a comprehensive new account of Texas History from 1970 to the summer of 2001. A most obvious change in the Third Edition is the addition of Gregg Cantrell as a third author. He succeeds the late Robert A. Calvert, the senior author of *The History of Texas* and the person who initially conceptualized this textbook in the 1980s.

Like the text, the lists of suggested readings that appear at the end of each chapter have been updated. Space limitation permitted only a small selection of titles that have informed our writing or that we think must come to the attention of serious students of the state's past. Primary material also proved crucial to this writing. Most of the statistics not specifically cited come from U.S. Census Bureau reports and the Texas Almanac, although the thoroughly revised Chapter 14 also makes extensive use of data found in the Web sites of the U.S. Department of Agriculture, the Bureau of Labor Statistics, the Bureau of Economic Analysis, the Texas Agricultural Statistics Service, the Business and Industry Data Center, and the Texas Comptroller's Office, among others. New maps and photographs make the Third Edition even more useful and visually appealing than the earlier editions.

Beginning with the first edition and continuing to the present one, we have leaned heavily on the advice and input of numerous colleagues. These include Malcolm D. McLean, formerly of the Robertson Colony Collection of the University of Texas at Arlington, Charles Martin of the University of Texas at El Paso, Paul D. Lack of McMurry University, Alwyn Barr of Texas Tech University, Norman D. Brown of the University of Texas at Austin, Larry D. Hill of Texas A&M University, William Childs of Ohio State University, Dorothy DeMoss of Texas Woman's University, Fane Downs formerly of McMurry University, Ben Procter of Texas Christian University, Barry A. Crouch of Gallaudet University, Jesús F. de la Teja of Southwest Texas State University, Stanley Siegel of the University of Houston, Walter L. Buenger of Texas A&M University, and Robert Wooster of Texas A&M University-Corpus Christi. In preparing the Third Edition, we gratefully acknowledge the assistance of David La Vere of the University of North Carolina at Wilmington, who helped to improve our portrayal of American Indians, Ty Cashion of Sam Houston State University, who provided numerous suggestions for improving the coverage of frontier Texas, and the University of North Texas's Randolph B. Campbell, Charldean Newell, and Bernard Weinstein, who read and critiqued the new Chapter 14. Finally, we wish to thank photographer Bill Wright of Abilene, Texas, who was kind enough to contribute several new photographs, including the cover photo, for this Third Edition.

Arnoldo De León
Gregg Cantrell

CONTACT OF CIVILIZATIONS

CHAPTER 1

The story of Texas begins many thousands of years before the birth of Christ, when ice masses connected the continents of Asia and North America, between points in what we now know as Siberia and Alaska. Between 10,000 and 30,000 years ago, until the Bering Sea reclaimed this bridge of ice for good, Asiatic nomads of the same *Homo sapiens* group that became today's Mongoloid race trekked across it in a series of distinct migrations as they hunted for edible plants and animals.

Scientists now agree that American Indians descended from a relatively small number of parent migrants who contributed to the "founding" gene base. Once the broad ice fields of the Bering Strait had melted, the ancestors of the American Indian were cut off from other Asians. Thereafter, natural selection and genetic mutation helped to produce distinctive physical types.

Through the ages, these ancient nomads dispersed throughout the vast lands of North and South America. Different cultural and linguistic patterns appeared as bands struck out on their own in the search for fresh sources of game and vegetation, and as people sought to adjust to diverse habitats. Cultural patterns further evolved over time as New World peoples began to develop agriculture, around 7000 B.C. Once New World societies learned to till the soil and harvest plants, human beings began to exercise some control over nature and developed strong ties to the land. Family units eventually formed into complex social and political organizations. Religious figures emerged as leaders or spiritual advisers, and the roles of males and females became more clearly delineated. As each group sought survival from its local environment, regional distinctions developed, as evidenced by the different types of housing, aesthetic decoration, clothing, and tools used by the people of particular regions.

Right: White Shaman. Cave art of the prehistoric inhabitants of the Pecos River area. *Courtesy of Jim Zintgraff, San Antonio, Texas*

THE DIVERSITY OF
NEW WORLD CULTURES

Various groups and cultures spread throughout all regions of the New World. Though historians disagree over population estimates, most concur that more people lived in what we now know as Latin America than remained in North America. At the time of Columbus's voyage, roughly 12 million people lived north of the line dividing present-day Mexico and the United States; between this boundary and the Isthmus of Panama lived an estimated 35 million people; finally, some 60 million people inhabited the continent of South America and the Caribbean Islands.

Of the pre-Columbian civilizations, that of the Maya has generally been considered the most intellectually advanced. Situated in what are today the Yucatán Peninsula and Guatemala, the Maya, during the height of their civilization (about A.D. 300 to A.D. 900), made brilliant advances. For example, the Maya's discovery of the zero cipher, well before Arab mathematicians introduced the concept to Europe in the thirteenth century, allowed them significant achievements in architecture, astronomy, and calendrics. Speculation lingers as to why the Mayan civilization declined. A deadly disease may have spread throughout the population, natural catastrophes may have produced food shortages, or a social revolution to undermine the ruling class may have hastened their demise.

Another major civilization thrived for a time at Anáhuac (Valley of México), this of the Toltecs, who raised a mighty empire at Tula until drought and famine forced them to desert their capital city. In 1215, new barbarians named the México, but more commonly known as Aztecs, arrived from unknown parts in the north and built upon the collapsed Toltec empire by establishing themselves in Tenochtitlán, today's Mexico City. One of the cleanest and most populous cities in the world at the time of its "discovery" by explorers from the Old World, Tenochtitlán contained pyramids, royal palaces, and other large structures, homes for the several social classes, canals crafted from stone that served as waterways for canoes, botanical gardens and zoos, and causeways connecting the island city to the mainland. Although the Aztecs had a warlike disposition and a penchant for human sacrifice, they abided by strict codes of morality, esteemed education, adhered to an honest and efficient system of legal and political administration, and excelled in various branches of the arts.

In South America another civilization flourished at the time of the European conquest of the Western Hemisphere. Embracing an area extending from today's Ecuador to Chile, the Inca civilization had its headquarters in Cuzco, in present-day Peru, and ruled through a remarkably efficient system of civil administration. A road system superior to any in Europe at the time enabled government officials to carry out their responsibilities, laborers to travel throughout the empire to maintain public works, and soldiers to move quickly in order to protect the realm and suppress rebellions. Unsurpassed by other Native American civilizations in architectural skills, the Incas designed and built structures that flexed with the tremors of earthquakes, resuming their original forms after each jolt. The Incas also possessed advanced scientific skills. Amazingly, archaeological findings point to their apparent success in performing brain surgery.

The Indian tribes that inhabited the North American continent generally developed less sophisticated civilizations. The Northeast Woodlands Indians, found from the Ohio Valley to the Atlantic Ocean and southward to the Chesapeake Bay, lived in loghouse villages or in wigwams and survived by farming corn, squash, and beans nearby their homes, or by hunting deer and wild fowl and fishing from canoes. Among the most famous of the Woodlands tribes was the Iroquois, who despite their renown as warriors organized the famous League of the Iroquois. Considered the most effective Indian alliance north of the Aztec Empire, the League succeeded in ending the chronic bloody conflicts among its member tribes.

South of the Woodlands tribes, stretching from the Atlantic Coast to the Mississippi Valley and even into East Texas, lived a culture group that maintained ties to mound-building societies of a past age. These were the Choctaws, Seminoles, Chickasaws, Creeks, and Cherokees—later referred to by Anglo Americans as the "Five Civilized Tribes" because they adopted Euro-American ways. The most famous of the descendants of the mound builders were the Natchez. At the time of the European exploration of the area, trappings of the classic Natchez era remained evident in villages along the lower Mississippi River. These villages surrounded temple mounds and ceremonial council houses, the identifying traits of the ancient mound builders.

A third advanced culture group that flourished at the time of Europeans' arrival in the Western Hemisphere was located roughly from what is now West Texas to Arizona, and north as far as southern Colorado. Here the Hopi and Zuñi created a distinctive cultural heritage. These tribes, who belonged to a group that Spaniards referred to collectively as *Pueblos*, resided in planned towns consisting of stacked, apartment-type complexes, sometimes two or more stories high. For defensive purposes, the Pueblos built their adobe villages into rock walls or upon steep mesas and structured them so as to oversee the spacious streets and squares below. In the fifteenth century, the Pueblos cultivated corn and other crops, developed irrigation canals, used cotton to make clothing, and lived much in the same manner as did the European peasant of the same period.

THE INDIANS OF TEXAS

Anthropological evidence reveals that before the Europeans arrived, a number of distinct culture groups lived in the varied geographical areas of what is now Texas. Such pre-horse people shared numerous characteristics, certainly the result of evolutionary processes, adaptation to historical situations, and common responses to environmental factors. Generally, Native Americans bonded around self-reliant bands or extended families. Leaders rose through the ranks, gaining their positions by a proven display of bravery, wisdom, or special attributes. These culture groups recognized social distinctions among themselves, and relegated some of their members (in many cases women) to a lesser place in the social order. Early people in Texas held no concept of individually owned objects, such as elaborate dwellings or land. Their religion embraced the supernatural, while spiritual mentors among them tended to the piety of tribesmembers.

Certain shared traits notwithstanding, Native American civilizations before Europeans arrived in Texas were quite diverse. Several of the peoples had different places of origin, some tracing their lineage to culture groups in the modern-day U.S. South, northern Mexico, or the Rocky Mountain region. No common language united Native American groups in Texas. While some made war with or raided neighboring groups regularly, most preferred to avoid conflict and lived in terror of attacks by aggressors. Numerous peoples preferred a sedentary life, while others maintained a nomadic existence. Adaptation to local environment tended to separate one culture group from another. Thus, one Texas tribe might build villages (and reside in permanent dwellings constructed of cane and grass) and rely on farming, while another might stay on the move, living in portable shelters such as teepees as they migrated seasonally to gather wild vegetation or pursue game, trapping their prey and killing it with clubs and other crude weapons. Region also determined a group's economy, as livelihoods might turn on agriculture, hunting big game such as bison (buffalo), or perhaps a mixture of both combined with intertribal trade.

THE COASTAL INDIANS

Along the coast of southern Texas and in parts of the Trans-Nueces lived the Karankawa and Coahuiltecan people. Both groups had common roots in modern-day northern Mexico: the Coahuiltecans were tied linguistically and otherwise to the Native inhabitants of Coahuila. The Karankawas and the Coahuiltecans lacked formal political organization; social life revolved around the family, extending into small autonomous bands (related by kin) presided over by a chieftain. Their religious life was primitive and animistic: they believed that supernatural entities governed the cosmos.

Their respective environments of marshy terrain close to the Gulf Coast and the chaparral of the brush country were harsh ones. Karankawa territoriality extended along a thin area running down the coast from Matagorda (some archaeologists believe even as far north as the Lower Brazos River region) to Corpus Christi Bay, while the Coahuiltecans lived in the Gulf Coast Plain and much of what is today considered South Texas. Both tribes moved frequently, their migrations generally corresponding to the change of seasons. Over the years, the nomadic Karankawas and Coahuiltecans had learned the ecology of their respective regions well; they knew when nature produced its greatest yields and the precise grounds where such bounties lay. Indeed, they tended to live in the same general site during one part of the year before moving on to another favorite camp. To guarantee a reliable and abundant food supply, the Karakanwas during the fall and winter months stayed close to the coast, where they relied most heavily on shellfish, aquatic plants, and water fowl, but also hunted deer and even alligators. For life along the bays and lagoons, the Karankawas built small canoes from tree trunks and fashioned nets, an assortment of traps, lances, and bows and arrows. The Coahuiltecans also preferred to inhabit specific locations during the winter, places where they could expect to find abundant roots and other easily attainable foodstuffs. During the spring and summer, the Karankawas moved inland to the coastal prairies and woodlands. There they relied less on marine life (though numerous rivers and creeks still provided them with fish) and more on land animals—among them deer, rabbits, prairie fowl, and occasionally buffalo—and the annual offerings of nuts, beans, and fruits produced by indigenous trees and shrubs. During the warmer seasons, the Coahuiltecans foraged for nature's yields over the large expanse of South Texas. They took advantage of the spring rains, catching fish trapped in receding pools of water, and hunting deer, lizards, birds, fish, insects and gathering mesquite beans, prickly pears, pecans, and roots. Dome-shaped wigwams covered by animal skins or improvised windbreaks served as the most common type of Karankawa and Coahuiltecan housing. When it came time to move, they simply dismantled their shelters, taking them and other useful item with them.

The Northeast Texas Indians

In the section of Texas east of the Trinity River, tribes related to the Indians of the Mississippi Valley prospered, among them the Caddo. Many centuries before Europeans had realized the existence of the New World, people in the lower Mississippi River expanse roamed about the region in quest of edible flora and small game. About 500 B.C., however, these hunting-and-gathering peoples turned to farming, cultivating a variety of vegetables, among them corn, beans, and squash, but also tobacco for personal use. Around A.D. 1200, the Mississippian civilization reached its high point of cultural growth and tribal strength, then entered a gradual decline. The Caddo Indians of Texas constituted the westernmost flank of Mississippian culture, owing much to it in the way of farming, village life, and religion, though the Caddo had also borrowed from tribes to the west (in New Mexico) and the south (Mexico). While Mississippian culture at the time that Columbus sailed from Spain was in a state of deterioration, Caddoan civilization thrived.

[handwritten margin note: more civilized]

Caddo settlements extended from the Trinity River, due north past the Red River, and as far east as the Mississippi River. Stable communities—consisting of isolated rural villages as well as clearly outlined urban sites—were generally located on the best farming lands in the region. Close to sources of fresh water (primarily rivers and streams), the Caddo constructed dome-shaped homes from grass and cane. As many as four families shared one such domicile, for Caddo home life apparently revolved around multifamily dwelling. With fields sur-

This famous panther is an outstanding example of the prehistoric art of the Lower Pecos people.
Courtesy of Jim Zintgraff, San Antonio, Texas

rounding their settlements, the Caddo had easy access to their principal source of sustenance. Like peoples in the other parts of the world at the time, the Caddo planted twice a year—in the spring and early summer—tended the plants (generally corn, squash, beans and others native to East Texas) with the utmost attention, rotated the crops periodically, fertilized the soil (the Caddo used the droppings of animals native to eastern Texas), and stored the excess harvest carefully for use during lean times.

Chiefs known as the *xinesí* presided over Caddo society, both as political and religious leaders. Serving in a hereditary position, the xinesí (whose authority extended over several Caddo communities) mediated between his followers and a supreme deity—the world's creator who influenced both good and bad things in life—and led religious celebrations, ceremonies, and festivals. In Caddo society, the xinesí was a person demanding of respect from tribal members, who looked upon him as a powerful figure able to determine such phenomenon as a successful sowing; as such, the xinesís's wishes and directives were to be followed unquestionably. Under the supervision of the xinesí, the Caddo constructed impressive temple mounds (signature traits of their Mississippian kin) that served as storehouses and as places in which to conduct important meetings and ceremonies. Below the xinesí in the Caddo religious order were lesser medicine men who attended to the spiritual as well as the physical needs of the people. Quite adept in the use of medicinal herbs and various folk remedies, these healers treated a multitude of wounds and illnesses.

Governing single Caddo communities (also through hereditary right) were the caddí. Such rulers were members of the upper stratum; while mostly disqualified from holding office, a commoner might elevate himself to a leadership position through feats of bravery on the battlefield. Ostensibly, administrators proved adept at their roles, for at the time that Spaniards begin the exploration of Texas, the Caddo world apparently functioned quite efficiently. Lieutenants enforced the policies determined by the caddí, directing commoners in their tasks of tilling the soil, building shelters for all concerned, and seeing to the public good, which included defending the nation from outside threats. War, however, was not integral to Caddo culture. Indeed, they undertook attacks on neighboring tribes primarily as a form of release for young men craving to act out their bravado, or as opportunities for others wanting to rise in social status.

Although they primarily relied on farming for their sustenance, the Caddo supplemented their diet through other means. In addition to gathering roots, nuts, and fruits, a task usually performed by women, the Caddo hunted the wild game indigenous to eastern Texas: turkeys, rabbits, or quail in the summer; deer and bear (useful for lard, clothing, and shelter) in the fall and winter; and buffalo (present on the western rim of the Caddo confederacy) when the supply of other foods grew scarce during the colder months. Comfortable in their stability and self-reliance, the Caddo also engaged in extensive trade. Eventually the Caddo world served as a hub for those bringing goods from as far as New Mexico, northern Mexico, and the Mississippi Valley. The Caddos welcomed many trading partners, bartering their baskets, tools, ceramics, decorative art, and weapons for certain types of vegetables, furs, and other luxury items not otherwise available to them in East Texas.

The Jumano Indians

Another group inhabiting Texas in the final years of the fifteenth century was the Jumanos, who inhabited the Trans-Pecos area. The Jumanos still remain not well understood by ethnographers, and there continues disagreement as to the distinct features their culture comprised. Opinions also differ as to what specific peoples (or tribes) made up the Jumanos, what linguistic groups they derived from, and the precise regions they occupied. Some studies note that the term *Jumano*, as used by the first European observers, delineate those descendants of the Tanoan-speakers, a linguistic group from New Mexico, or those tribes that made their living as traders and traveled as far east as Texas's South Plains. To some anthropologists, the word *Jumano* identifies people of a shared cultural background, and not necessarily a general grouping of people with a common language or a specific livelihood.

More recent research presents the Jumanos as descending from the Jornada line of the Mogollon, a people indigenous to modern-day Arizona, New Mexico, and neighboring regions. Sometime in the mid-fifteenth century, part of the

Jornada tribe commenced migrating eastward towards the Trans-Pecos, ultimately establishing permanent settlements in the West Texas river valleys such as El Paso, but more specifically in the region that the Spaniards later referred to as *La Junta de los Ríos* (the confluence of the Rio Grande and the Concho Rivers). Quite plausibly, the whole of western Texas became the domain of the Jumanos—more fierce tribes such as the Apaches and Comanches would not enter the region until sometime in the seventeenth century—for what were most certainly Jumano settlements (many of them temporary) have been found beyond the fertile river valleys. In any case, the Jumano civilization stretched from eastern New Mexico and perhaps into Oklahoma, and south to northern Chihuahua in Mexico, with its easternmost appendage extending into the South Plains. In these hinterlands, they made a living by farming and hunting.

At La Junta de los Rios and other permanent settlements, the Jumanos worked produce gardens, cultivating traditional farm crops such as maize, beans, and squash. Their communities resembled those used by their kinspeople in New Mexico—clustered single-family dwellings constructed of reeds and grass formed villages over which a chief ruled. Such farm hamlets were indicative of the branch of the Jumano people that had opted for a sedentary life, though seasonably, certain village members left on hunting expeditions.

Hunting nearly full time became the unique trait of the nomadic Jumanos of the West Texas plains. Living in transient camps, this branch of the Jumanos roamed the vast grasslands throughout the spring and fall in pursuit of a variety of game: from snakes, fish, and birds, to deer, antelope, rabbits, and armadillos, and, naturally, to the indispensable buffalo, which furnished them with meat for

This is a recreation of a Caddo house typical of those built by the Wichita Indians in northeastern Texas. *Courtesy of the Caddoan Mounds State Historical Park, Texas Parks and Wildlife*

food and hides for shelter and clothing. During winter, the hunters relocated near the more permanent villages of their farming relatives, launching the hunting cycle anew in the spring.

Both the sedentary and nomadic Jumanos earned reputations as accomplished merchants (as noted above, some Europeans used the word *Jumano* synonymously with *trader*). The nomadic Jumanos, in particular, appear to have made commerce as much a part of their way of life as was hunting, establishing trading villages on the Plains as centers of exchange. In these posts, they bartered products manufactured or acquired by the tribespeople—bows and arrows, pearls, and animal furs and hides. But they also traveled widely to exchange buffalo products and foodstuffs for vegetables and fruits possessed by other tribes, for woolen textiles produced in New Mexico, or for wares manufactured in the Caddo world.

The Plains Indians

Strikingly different from the aforementioned Native American tribes were the Apaches, Comanches, Kiowas, and Tonkawas. None of these Indian peoples—who would play important parts in Texas history during the eighteenth and nineteenth centuries—lived in Texas in pre-Columbian times. Their origins may be traced to the northern Rocky Mountain region of the present-day United States. The Apaches, for instance, were related linguistically to tribes in Canada and Alaska, while the Comanches had originally made their homes in the valleys of the upper Yellowstone and Platte Rivers. No one knows when exactly these tribes commenced their pedestrian migration into the Great Plains (the geographical expanse immediately east of the Rocky Mountains) and into the Southwest in the pursuit of the buffalo. Historians do know that these Plains Indians found new power in the horse (acquired in the seventeenth century from raids upon fledgling Spanish settlements or by capturing wild herds), for they learned to ride horseback with great skill while hunting buffalo, conducting warfare, or relocating to newer locales.

A number of forces ultimately led the Plains Indians toward Texas. Mounted warfare produced winners and losers; the Comanches—the most successful because of their high mobility and unmatched riding skills—became such a terror on the Plains that the Apaches (namely the groups known as the Lipans and the Mescaleros) by the late seventeenth century began heading south to take refuge in Central and West Texas. In time, however, the Comanches expanded their nomadic hunting grounds southward, pursuing the buffalo on mounts, fighting the hated Apaches, and bolstering their pony herds by rounding up wild horses. By the early 1700s the Comanches had arrived in Texas and soon thereafter became the dominant force in the northern, central, and western regions of the province.

In Texas, the Apaches, Comanches, Kiowas, and Tonkawas depended on the buffalo for almost all their living essentials, including shelter, clothing, weapons, and tools. Using bows and arrows, the Plains Indians effectively hunted not only buffalo but also deer, antelope, turkeys, and other wild game. Small garden plots, however, provided a secondary source of food, and some of these bands raised maize and other vegetables including squash and beans. They also gathered berries and other domestic fauna like agave, from which they made intoxicating beverages. Additionally, wild plants gave them herbs, fruits, and other products that they consumed themsevles and used in barter.

The Plains Indians lacked any pan-tribal political structure, families forming the basic social foundation. Groups of families under a chief composed working units that served to defend the people or to retaliate against other groups for wrongs inflicted. In some cases, their livelihood depended as much upon preying on other tribes who had items they needed for sustenance as it did upon reaping nature's bounty. Fiercely independent, the Plainspeople held religious views that allowed for individual relationships with deities; their faith in a single, all-powerful being was only ephemeral. Shamans, or religious figures, exerted no great authority among the wanderers of the Plains, as they mainly served to heal the infirm.

THE FIRST EUROPEANS

The first white people that the indigenous inhabitants of Texas encountered came from the Iberian Peninsula—a part of Europe in which history had departed in substantive ways from that of the rest of the continent. The early history of Spain, however, does not belie this difference. Like the rest of Europe, the Iberian Peninsula had come under the rule of the Greeks and later was subsumed by the Roman Empire. From the Romans, Spaniards derived their language, law, customs, religious faith, and their country's name—*Hispania*. When Spain, along with the rest of Europe, fell to the barbarians in the fifth century, the Visigoths swept over the peninsula and superimposed their way of life over that which the Romans had instilled. Like other Europeans, the Iberians then began forging a new way of life that combined the Roman influence, the newer Germanic contributions, and evolving Christian beliefs, for in Spain, as elsewhere, the Visigoths ended up assimilating the religion, language, and form of government of the people they had conquered.

The Muslim Era and the Reconquista

What chiefly separated the history of the Iberian peoples from that of the rest of western Europe was the conquest of Spain by Muslims from northern Africa (Arabic or Berber peoples known loosely as the Moors) who sought to spread their Islamic faith. Partly because of the Muslim domination of the peninsula, which began in A.D. 711, feudalism did not attain maturity in Christian Spain. The constant state of warfare to oust the Muslim intruders equalized social distinctions, thereby blurring class differences such as those prevalent in northern Europe. In each Christian state, furthermore, the war bolstered the role of the king as the military leader responsible for the *reconquista*, the term generally used to refer to the centuries of struggle to regain Spain from the Muslims. Following a tradition used by the Moorish invaders, Christian fighters surrendered one-fifth of the spoils of their conquests to the monarch—a custom that granted further power and wealth to the king. Since the Muslims were among the world's best-connected merchants, their influence helped Spain enjoy brisk economic activity with the Islamic world. Numerous Spanish cities became commercial hubs as their merchants developed prosperous ties with their counterparts in Africa, the several Mediterranean countries, and the Muslim world of the Middle East. Even Iberians who earned their living from the soil participated in the economic good times, as they sold their produce in domestic as well as export markets.

Castile and the Legacy of the Reconquista

Efforts to resist the aggressors and reconquer the motherland molded Spanish culture during the Middle Ages. Of the several Christian states that individually or jointly sought to push back the Moors, none excelled Castile, the heartland of Spain stretching from the peninsula's northern lands southwardly to the central plateau. Castile's campaign to expel the Moslem interlopers turned into a way of life that accentuated the warrior hallmarks of valor, tenacity, intrepidness, and survival at any cost—traits embraced by the *conquistadores* (conquerors) whatever their social station.

Through time, moreover, the Castilian Reconquista assumed the aura of a religious crusade. The discovery in the year 900 of what Spaniards believed to be the burial site and body of the apostle Santiago (St. James the Great) in northern Spain, inspired Spanish religious fervor, for St. James supposedly had brought Christianity to Iberia. The reconquista prompted the Crown to bestow the role of ally upon the Catholic Church, and the Church's preachings in behalf of the war rendered numerous social and political privileges to the clergy. By the thirteenth century, Catholic religious orders such as the Franciscans and Dominicans engaged in proselytizing activity among the Spanish Moslems.

The reconquista also encouraged the raising of sheep in agrarian Castile, for the Castilians found that sheep produced higher and quicker profits than did their crops. And unlike crops, herds could be moved quickly out of harm's way during the constant warfare. When stockmen imported merino sheep from northern Africa in 1280, the Iberians bred them with their native stock. The new strain produced such a superior grade of wool that merchants in the international market eagerly sought the product, which brought handsome profits.

Cattle raising also flourished in the reconquered areas of southern Castile. In Andalusía, lords raised breeds of cattle that became widely known for the fine quality of their beef and hides. Seasonally, *vaqueros*, mounted herders, drove the stock cross-country from the northern summer grazing lands to winter in southern pastures. The vaqueros developed a distinctive dress and equipment, as well as cattle ranching traditions and practices such as the *rodeo* (round-up) and the branding of calves for identification purposes, that were later transplanted to areas that came under Spain's dominance.

Compared to other various European urban centers, which experienced economic downturns, Spain's cities witnessed a good deal of development, for in the process of reconquest, towns held down and consolidated the gains of battle. In return for their assistance in helping to regain territory from the Moslem "infidels," towns received charters by which the king guaranteed townspeople the protection of their individual possessions and privileges and permitted them a semblance of self-governance. During this period, city inhabitants came to belong to *ayuntamientos* (city councils), which elected town officials. Furthermore, they organized *hermandades* (brotherhoods) responsible for maintaining the peace. This new form of municipal government replaced the old Roman administrative structure that had broken down following the arrival of the Moslems.

Los Reyes Católicos

The two Iberian kingdoms of Castile and Aragón united in 1479, when Isabella of Castile and Ferdinand of Aragón, married since 1469, inherited the thrones of their respective dominions. Seeking to consolidate their power over the whole peninsula, the monarchs swiftly pressed for the pacification of the countryside and the subordination of the nobles, the Church, and the military orders, which had gained power during the final stages of the reconquista. The couple's strategy for accomplishing their plans proved shrewd, inventive—even cunning. In order to suppress criminal activity, for instance, Isabella co-opted the medieval institution of the hermandad, turning what had begun as municipal brotherhoods to defend mutual interests—ironically against the nobility—into a standing army for the Crown. Political gains made by individuals at the local level during the reconquista thus receded as *los reyes católicos* (the Catholic kings) began the task of molding Spain into a sovereign nation.

With a semblance of peace and unity restored domestically, the monarchs turned their attention to foreign policy. By the fifteenth century, technological advances enabled Spain to expand its commerce. Much of the new technology came from Portugal, where Prince Henry the Navigator had made brilliant strides in map making and ship building in an effort to see his own country be the first to probe the African coastline, establish sea routes to the Orient, and find a friendly ally for a besieged Christian Europe. As fate determined, it was Portugal's rival, Spain, that used Henry's inventions to discover a world completely unknown to Europe.

Columbus

In 1492 Isabella gave consent to the Italian mariner Christopher Columbus to sail under the flag of Spain in a westerly course to the East Indies. Columbus's principal motives were economic and political gain, but a desire to spread his religion also prompted him. If successful, he would achieve great things for Spain and Latin Christendom.

From the port of Palos in southern Spain, Columbus, in command of three caravels, steered toward the Canary Islands, already claimed and colonized by the Spaniards. After reprovisioning there, the crews headed into the strong Atlantic seas never before sailed by Europeans. The admiral reckoned he would reach the Orient in thirty days, tap its riches, and in the process establish new allies and trading partners for the Christian world and open vast new lands for religious proselytizing. On October 12, 1492, after more than a month at sea, Columbus sighted land. But he had not reached Asia, as he had assumed he had; rather he came ashore on the modern-day Bahamas. He named the first island on which he stepped *San Salvador* (Holy Savior).

The Conquistadores

Following Columbus's grand find, Spain proceeded swiftly to transform the "New World," as the Europeans had dubbed it, into colonies that would provide the Spaniards with the elusive riches they had hoped to reap by finding a shortcut to the Orient. Now a new wave of conquistadores, who in many ways resembled those who had reconquered the peninsula from the Moslems—by ousting the last of the Moors from Granada in 1492—took the initiative for the acquisition and subordination of new dominions. Characteristics of the traditional conquistador—courage and tenacity, but also callousness, a propensity toward violence, religious zeal, and a desire for gold and glory—thus typified those who led the conquest of the New World.

Columbus himself played a major part in the takeover of the Caribbean Islands, but the exploration, and exploitation, of the New World proved too vast for one man's energies. Numerous explorers thus left what had been labeled the "West Indies" for fresh explorations, among them was Vasco Nuñez de Balboa. Balboa ultimately crossed the Central American Isthmus, and in 1513 he claimed the Pacific Ocean on behalf of the king of Spain. In the same year, Juan Ponce de León reached Florida, bringing the North American peninsula into the Spanish sphere, though the Spaniards did not succeed in settling the region until the 1560s. The expedition to establish control over modern-day Mexico was spearheaded by several intriguing war campaigns led by Hernán Cortés, who by 1521 had conquered and plundered Montezuma's Aztec empire, paving the way for the ruthless domination of the rest of Mexico. In Peru, conquest of the Incas fell to an unlettered conquistador named Francisco Pizarro, who arrived there in 1532, eventually executed the emperor, and despoiled buildings and shrines of their treasures throughout Inca settlements. Blood, rapine, and plunder marked the Spaniards' path through Peru, as it had their swath through Mexico.

LOOKING FOR FORTUNES IN TEXAS

Just as the atmosphere of fifteenth-century Spain helped to mold the ruthless nature of the exploring Spaniards, so, too, did it shape their desire to find

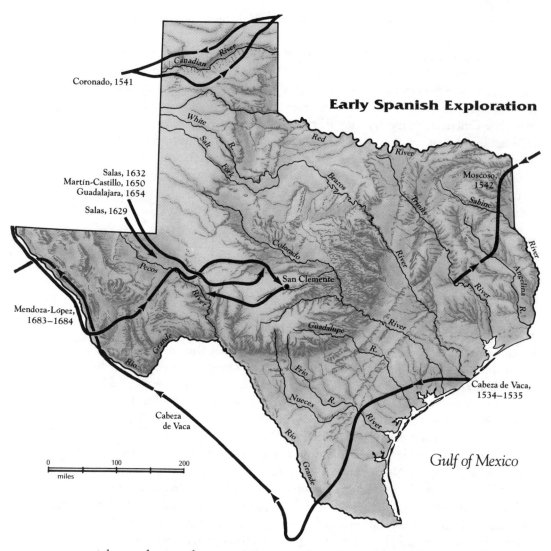

Early Spanish Exploration

Coronado, 1541

Salas, 1632
Martín-Castillo, 1650
Guadalajara, 1654

Salas, 1629

Mendoza-López,
1683–1684

Moscoso,
1542

San Clemente

Cabeza de Vaca,
1534–1535

Cabeza
de Vaca

0   100   200
miles

Gulf of Mexico

riches and amass fortunes. Many people in late medieval Europe still believed
in the romance of mythic adventure, and books telling of places of great riches
and enchantment stimulated Spanish hopes of finding the fabled land of the
warlike Amazon women, of the opulent Seven Cities, and the legendary Foun-
tain of Youth. The treasures that the conquistadores did find in Mexico and in
Peru only encouraged their people's convictions that the romantic dreams of lore
were indeed realizable in the New World.

It was this search for great fortune that led the Spaniards to the land now
known as Texas. The earliest European penetration of what was to become Texas
occurred accidentally in 1528, when Pánfilo de Narváez led 400 men into
Florida. After landing around today's Sarasota Bay, Narváez took three-fourths
of his crew ashore with him to investigate stories of a golden land. Narváez and
his men were left stranded on Florida's west coast, however, after miscommuni-
cations prompted his ships to depart for their home base without them.

Improvising, Narváez and his castaways killed their mounts, fashioning five small boats from the horse hides, in which they hoped to float along the Gulf Coast and eventually reach Mexico. But on a spit of land close to the western portion of modern-day Galveston Island, the Spaniards were shipwrecked and forced to brave the winter of 1528–1529. Enslaved by a band of coastal Indians, only a handful of the Spaniards, among them Alvar Núñez Cabeza de Vaca and Estevanico, a Moorish slave, survived into the spring. After years in bondage, and with their number now down to four, Cabeza de Vaca persuaded the others to escape and follow him. Posing as "medicine men" as they traveled, their remarkable odyssey led them across the Rio Grande, at a spot slightly northwest of present-day Roma, Texas, then on through northern Mexico and eventually back into Texas, near today's Presidio. From there they trekked along the east bank of the Rio Grande, towards a site some seventy-five miles below El Paso, then back across the Rio Grande into Mexico, and, finally, into the Spanish frontier town of Culiacán, in the western province of Sinaloa.

Upon his arrival in Culiacán in 1535, Cabeza de Vaca had much to tell, including tales of riches existing in the lands that he had traversed. To confirm his reports, the Crown in 1539 dispatched Friar Marcos de Niza to the northern lands, with Estevanico accompanying him as a scout. In present-day western New Mexico, the friar, supposedly viewing a Pueblo Indian town from a distant hilltop, reported upon his return of having seen a glittering city of silver and gold. Niza's fabulous vision may be accounted for by the reflective quartz imbedded in the walls of the adobe dwellings sparkling in the sunlight, but Spanish officials interpreted his testimony as evidence of the existence of the fabled Seven Cities. Their general location was deemed *Cíbola*, a term meaning buffalo, which the Spaniards had heard the Indians use and now applied as a place-name to the pueblos of the Zuñis.

Historians question whether or not Niza actually traveled as far as Cíbola, but, whatever the truth, Niza's report raised expectations among the Spaniards, and the viceroy assigned Francisco Vásquez de Coronado to lead a follow-up expedition. Coronado arrived in Zuñi country the next year, only to discover that Niza's glittering cities were, indeed, merely adobe complexes. Conflict soon brewed with the Pueblos, for Coronado and his troops imposed insensitively on the villagers, inflicted numerous indignities upon them, even burning some Pueblo people at the stake. After this, newly generated tales of a golden kingdom called *Gran Quivira* induced the Spaniards to venture out upon the Great Plains, but, as they crossed what is today the Texas Panhandle, they saw nothing of value to themselves or the Crown.

At first, Coronado refused to be disillusioned, continuing his search for Gran Quivira near the land of the Wichita tribes in Kansas. But two years of futile searching finally convinced him to return to Mexico, and his reports of the absence of riches in the lands he had traversed discouraged further explorations of the north for another half-century.

While Coronado was exploring the Plains, another expedition, this led by Hernando de Soto, made its way from Florida to Alabama and across the southeastern Mississippi Valley, tracking down rumors of gold treasures and civilized cities. But this quest also proved fruitless, and De Soto, despairing of his failure, took ill with fever and died in the spring of 1542. His party, now situated on the Mississippi River, was taken over by Luis de Moscoso de Alvarado, who opted to march west in hopes of reaching Mexico. In their trek, the Spaniards penetrated eastern Texas and may have traveled as far west as the Trinity River, near present-day Houston County. But, frustrated that they had not yet managed to reach Mexico, Moscoso and his men returned to the Mississippi, building crude boats and floating downstream and then westward along the Gulf Coast. Destiny forced the sailors ashore near present-day Beaumont. Two months later, the 300 men arrived in the Spanish town of Panuco, Mexico, with, of course, no news of finding riches. This report reinforced decisions to cease exploration into Texas.

Competition for the North

By the early part of the seventeenth century, Spain's New World dominion extended nearly 8,000 miles, from southern California to the tip of South America. But Spain could claim no monopoly over the world discovered by Columbus, for several other European countries now competed for their share of colonies in the Western Hemisphere. The Dutch laid claim to the Hudson Valley and New Netherlands, the settlement that later became part of the En-

Coronado on the High Plains by Frederic Remington. Copied from a reproduction in *Collier's Magazine*, Dec. 9, 1905. *The UT Institute of Texan Cultures, No. 68-2015*

glish colony of New York. The French, meantime, founded Quebec in Canada and launched the occupation of Nova Scotia. As time passed, French traders pushed southwestwardly into the Great Lakes area, and by the 1650s they had infiltrated the general region around what is today the state of Wisconsin.

Most determined of the seventeenth-century efforts were those of the English, who explored along the Atlantic Coast north of the lands chartered by Ponce de León, Pánfilo de Narváez, and Cabeza de Vaca. By the 1640s, the English empire had established solid possession of the Atlantic seaboard between northern Florida and New England. Britain now prepared to expand its mainland North American empire west, toward areas that the Spaniards regarded as exclusively their own.

Colonizing Baggage

The edge Spain had over its competitors were the skills of colonization, for by the seventeenth century the trappings of Spanish civilization (much of it a legacy of the reconquista) were well in place throughout much of Latin America and ready for relocation to North American frontiers. Responsible for coordinating settlement was an autocratic king, who since the conquest of the Aztecs had passed along royal orders to political bureaucracies responsible for the day-to-day affairs in Spain's respective New World colonies. Although these field officials tended to mold royal directives and laws to fit local circumstances, they implicitly recognized the king's right to set policy and their duty to acknowledge his decisions.

The king, however, did not act haphazardly in bringing Indian lands under the Spanish flag. To the contrary, he oversaw an orderly process of expansion and settlement by employing those agencies already proven effective against the Moslems or tested on the frontiers of the New World. The military garrison and fort called the *presidio*, the roots of which lay in the Roman concept of *praesidium* (meaning a militarized region protected by fortifications), for example, was initially employed in the last half of the sixteenth century as protection against the Chichimeca Indian nations that inhabited the north-central plateau of New Spain. From the Indian frontier north of Mexico City, the core government deployed the presidio into other regions, each fort under the direction of a presidial commander acting in behalf of the governor and whose authority outweighed that of local civilian officials. The presidio served many functions. It was a place for prisoners to complete their sentences, and it provided a walled courtyard in which to conduct peace talks with representatives of restive Indian tribes. More important, as a garrison for soldiers trained and equipped for frontier warfare, the presidio protected another frontier institution—the mission—guarding the friars in the mission compounds as they attempted to pacify and instruct newly converted congregations of Native peoples.

The practice of conducting missionary activity among the Moslem occupiers had been used during the reconquista in Spain, and it evolved into the sys-

Mission San José, San Antonio, Texas. *Prints and Photograph Collection, The Center for American History, The University of Texas at Austin, CN08004*

tem found in the Mexican north in the 1580s. Priests of different Catholic religious orders (such as the Franciscans or the Dominicans) staffed the missions, performing various functions relevant to exploration, conquest, and Christianization. The missionaries sought to convert the Indians to Catholicism, establish friendly relations with hostile tribes, and, by their fortified presence at the mission, assist in retaining conquered territories for the Crown.

Missionaries acted for the government in a tradition traceable to medieval times, when the reconquista became a joint enterprise between the Crown and the Church. As Ferdinand and Isabella acquired the right to make appointments to religious positions (the *patronato real*) in the 1480s, furthermore, the alliance between the king of Spain and the pope was even more closely welded. By the time of the conquistadores, the Crown had won the right to regulate the Church (including making such decisions as where Church edifices would be erected), sponsor evangelical forays into pagan lands, and decide which religious order would take priority in missionizing particular regions. With these powers, the Crown controlled the pattern of Church activities in the New World, though doctrine and dogma still remained strictly the domain of the clergy.

In their further efforts to Europeanize new lands, the Spaniards also used the civilian settlement, another institution employed during the reconquista to hold recently reconquered territory. As the Spaniards advanced northward from Anáhuac, they used the civilian settlement to populate frontier regions and integrate the hinterlands and their resources into the kingdom. By this time, the Spaniards had devised extensive laws governing the location, layout, and defense of urban outposts. Again, these laws generally derived from previous experiences in urban settlement during the reconquista. According to these plans, the town plat was square and included one or more rectangular plazas, the main one constituting the town center, with outlying streets crossing one another at right angles. The east side of the central plaza was designated for church edifices, the west side for government and public buildings. This arrangement facilitated daily routines: the idea was to use the morning light for mass and other church operations, then allow government officials to work late into the evening using the afternoon sun. Lots allocated to residents also conformed to the pattern of perpendicular streets oriented to the four cardinal directions. Lands surrounding the new urban sites were designated as public property that all residents could use to sustain themselves and their livestock. Other ordinances stipulated that sites for new municipalities be chosen only after thought had been given to matters of sanitation, the proximity of food resources, local weather patterns, and the prospects afforded for self-defense against raids by hostile Indians. *Pobladores* (settlers) made every effort to adhere to these regulations, but the contingencies of the moment many times dictated otherwise. In Texas, therefore, plans did not always follow the letter. Officials who belonged to a bureaucratic structure, the roots of which went back to the reconquista, governed these new municipalities.

The Spaniards also utilized the *rancho* (ranch) to help them claim unsettled areas. Stockmen and farmers invariably accompanied frontier expeditions, and, over the course of time, they played supportive roles in the Christianizing of the Indians and the defense of settled territories. *Rancheros* (ranchers) provided settlements with resources otherwise absent on the frontier, such as beef, pork, wool, and useful byproducts such as hides and tallow. This helped the missionaries retain Indian convertees who otherwise might have chosen to run off in search of wild game more palatable to their diet than the friars' normal fare. The ranchers also helped presidial soldiers, not only by providing them with meat but by furnishing them with live animals necessary for farm work, freighting, and, of course, military expeditions of all kinds.

These, then, were the traditional institutions that Spain employed, albeit in a modified form, to settle the contemporary American Southwest, while the Dutch, English, and French sought footholds in the region east of the Mississippi River. Spain renewed its efforts to colonize New Spain's Far North because of the prospects of finding wealth, a persistent desire to Christianize the settled Indians reported by Coronado, and the need to protect the expanse from foreign encroachment, for by the late 1570s and 1580s, English pirates such as Sir Francis Drake began sailing along the California coast. In 1598, therefore, Don Juan de Oñate led an expedition into what would become *Nuevo México;* this operation resulted in the founding of Santa Fe in 1609. The establishment of this permanent settlement started the Spanish activity that led to the domination of Texas.

Western Texas

For years, Jumano Indians had traveled to the Pueblo country in New Mexico to conduct trade. In 1629, the Jumanos asked the Spaniards they met there to visit them in their West Texas lands and instruct them in the religion to which they had been introduced by the "Lady in Blue." According to some Church historians, this personage was the Spanish nun Madre María de Agreda, who asserted that she had spiritually visited New World lands through miraculous bilocation. Whatever the truth to the mystery surrounding this figure, the Spaniards responded to the invitation with an expedition to Jumano country in 1629 commanded by Fray Juan de Salas, and another one in 1632 led by the Franciscans.

Their desire to proselytize notwithstanding, the Spaniards also held interests in more mundane things in Jumano country: namely, freshwater pearls (found in mollusks living in the western tributaries of the Colorado River) and the countless buffalo on the West Texas plains. Also appealing to them was the possibility that Jumano country might become a base for trading with the Caddo Indians; the eastern tribes, according to the Jumanos, comprised a wealthy population of many villages. In 1654, therefore, Diego de Guadalajara returned in search of pearl-bearing *conchas* (shells) in the present-day forks of the Concho River of West Texas. At that time, however, Spanish officialdom lacked the resources to pursue their plans to trade with East Texas Indians through the Jumanos.

Finally, approaches to West Texas were made in 1683 and 1684. By now, the Spaniards resided a bit closer to the Jumanos, for the Pueblo Revolt of 1680, in which the Pueblo tribes attacked and destroyed the Spanish settlements of the upper valley of the Rio Grande, had caused much of the New Mexico population to take refuge in El Paso (modern-day Juárez), where a Franciscan mission, which sheltered a small band of Jumanos, had existed since 1659. From this civilian settlement the Spaniards returned to West Texas when the Jumano Chief Juan Sabeata asked that priests be sent to his land in West Texas, and, parenthetically, for assistance in countering threats from the Apaches. Responding to Sabeata's request, Spanish authorities dispatched a missionary expedition led by Juan Domínguez de Mendoza and Fray Nicolás López down the Rio Grande from El Paso to today's Ruidosa, Texas, then into the San Sabá River area, where they established themselves at Mission San Clemente. From temporary quarters there, the expedition's men slaughtered some 4,000 buffalo. In fact, Sabeata's primary motive in luring the Spaniards into Jumano country may have been to get the Spaniards to protect his people from the Apaches while the Jumanos hunted buffalo. The Jumanos then planned to carry Spanish goods and trade them with the Caddos of East Texas. After about six weeks at San Clemente, the Spaniards left for El Paso with several thousand buffalo hides, promising the Jumanos to return at a later date.

Eastern Texas

The Spaniards did not revisit the Jumanos in West Texas, however, because they became preoccupied with increased French activity close to the Gulf of Mexico. By the early 1670s, the French actively explored the middle of the

North American continent from their bases in Canada, and they now planned to install a string of trading stores and forts to stretch from the Great Lakes region to the mouth of the Mississippi. They made important headway in doing so when, in 1682, Robert Cavelier, Sieur de La Salle, traveled down the Mississippi and asserted title to all of the lands drained by the great river for France.

Promptly, La Salle made plans to lay more than symbolic claims to the Mississippi River basin: this he intended to accomplish by building garrisons, civilian settlements, and trading posts. He arrived from France to the Gulf of Mexico in late 1684 (the same year that the Spaniards were active among the Jumanos in West Texas) but, betrayed by the meager technology of the era—faulty navigational equipment, poorly drawn maps, lack of familiarity with Gulf currents— he missed the mouth of the Mississippi and ended up on the Texas coast in Matagorda Bay (or Espíritu Santo, as the Spaniards called it). In an unexpected turn of events, part of his crew sailed back to France, and La Salle found himself marooned on the Texas coast with some 180 of his would-be settlers.

At Garcitas Creek (in the vicinity of today's Vanderbilt, Texas), La Salle erected Fort St. Louis, but the travails of living in such an inhospitable area greatly undermined the settlers' well-being. Seeking help, in October 1685 the Frenchman undertook an exploration of the Texas interior; this brought his party toward the Rio Grande and near today's Langtry, Texas. But the expedition produced no beneficial results. As a last resort, La Salle turned towards the Mississippi in hopes of meeting other Frenchmen coming down from the Illinois posts he had established earlier. This strategy also proved unsuccessful and resulted in La Salle's death at the hands of his own frustrated men in 1687. Indians, in the meantime, had wiped out the survivors at Fort St. Louis and destroyed the garrison.

As unimpressive as it was, the French activity in the area nonetheless alerted the Spaniards to the dangers of losing Texas and prompted them to reimplement the exploration of the eastern periphery of their northern frontier. Starting in 1686 and continuing until 1690, the Crown dispatched Alonso de León on several expeditions, his fourth one in 1689 taking him to the remains of Fort St. Louis on the Garcitas. The next year, the Spaniards explored past the location of the ill-fated settlement and made contact with the Caddo world, long regarded by the Spaniards as "the great kingdom of the Tejas" due to legends regarding prosperity and magnificence among the Caddo.

Actually, the Caddos of what is now East Texas consisted of about 10,000 people; among those belonging to the Caddo nation were the Hasinai Indians, whom the Spaniards referred to as the *"Tejas,"* the Spanish rendition of the Hasinai word for *friend*, from which the state of Texas is named. Encircled by tribes hostile to their way of life, the Caddos stood prepared to defend their territory against any group that might try to encroach upon it. However, the Caddos freely accepted the Europeans upon their arrival, for they saw them as potential allies and trading partners.

De León and *Fray* (Father) Damián Massanet thus encountered no problem in setting up two missions (one of them being San Francisco de los Tejas, the first Spanish mission in Texas) among the Caddo when they entered their territory in 1690. The Spanish perceived the Tejas (Caddos) as a particularly stable tribe that adhered to religious beliefs that recognized the existence of but one supreme being. Moreover, they ascertained that the Caddos traded widely, exchanging their bows and pottery, as well as salt and other goods, with representatives of other bands, among them the Jumanos. So many Indians from such great distances arrived in the Caddo villages in order to barter that the priests quickly envisioned the Caddo kingdom as the ideal setting for disseminating the Christian message in New Spain's Far North.

Despite these seemingly ideal circumstances, the Caddos did not prove to be willing converts. For one thing, Christianity actually clashed with their religious beliefs. For another, the Spaniards had disrupted their traditional way of life. When Domingo de Terán, who had been named governor of what became the province of Texas, visited the Caddo in 1691 intending to found additional missions, his livestock indiscriminately trampled and fed upon the Caddos' new farm harvests. This, along with the actions of "unruly" soldiers and imprudent overtures by the missionaries who violated Caddo protocol, made the Caddos resentful, leading the tribesmembers to retaliate by attacking the interlopers' domesticated stock. Finally sensing hostility, the Spaniards retreated to Coahuila, leaving behind only a few missionaries to continue the work of Christianizing. But those few persons could no longer convince the Caddos of their good intentions, so, by 1693, the Spanish had departed from East Texas.

The departure proved temporary, for events from within and without New Spain forced a return to Caddo land. Father Francisco Hidalgo, who had worked with Massanet among the Tejas, desired to resume the work he had helped begin in East Texas. In addition, the French renewed their activity along the mouth of the Mississippi to thwart English plans to move westward from the Atlantic to the middle of the continent. When the French established themselves at Mobile Bay in 1702, then farther west at Natchitoches, in what is now western Louisiana, it gave the Spaniards cause for alarm.

While several motives had brought the French to the border of Texas, trade ranked high on their list. This became evident when in 1713 a French Canadian named Louis Juchereau de St. Denis, who had been trading successfully with Indians in Louisiana, appeared in Natchitoches with an array of merchandise and determined to seek markets among the Spaniards.

Setting out across Texas, St. Denis and a small detachment of traders headed for New Spain proper. They arrived at San Juan Bautista on the Rio Grande (some thirty miles downriver from today's Eagle Pass on the Mexican side) on July 19, 1714, where Captain Diego Ramón quickly arrested them, detaining the encroachers until word arrived from the viceroy early the next year that the Frenchmen should be taken to Mexico City for official interrogation. Once in New Spain's capital, St. Denis gave a revealing account of his purpose: the French had received a letter from Father Francisco Hidalgo the previous year describing the Tejas and asking if the French would support a mission for the Indians. St. Denis disclosed that the Tejas yearned for a continuation of Christian missionary work, especially that of Father Hidalgo. As for trade, St. Denis declared that he saw no legal bans against commercial intercourse between French and Spanish territorial possessions.

Whatever the pretext, the viceroy saw no real justification for the French intrusion, so he immediately ordered Captain Domingo Ramón (the son of Diego Ramón) to make preparations to convert East Texas into a buffer zone by rebuilding the Spanish missions there. Assigned as second-in-command of this expedition was none other than St. Denis, who had adroitly persuaded the Spaniards that he now planned to set up stead on the Texas frontier and assist the Spanish in the work of Christianizing the Tejas. While room for distrust existed between the Spanish viceroy and the Frenchman, both found mutual benefit in their alliance. The Spaniards hoped to take advantage of St. Denis's knowledge of the Texas terrain, his command of Indian languages, and his knack for befriending certain Indians nations, for developing friendly terms was essential for establishing a prosperous trade. However, according to some historians, St. Denis's subsequent marriage to Captain Diego Ramón's step-granddaughter at San Juan Bautista lay at the heart of his defection from the service of France.

Settlements

Such was the course of events in the early eighteenth century that placed the Spaniards permanently in Texas. In February 1716, Captain Domingo Ramón and St. Denis crossed the Rio Grande headed for East Texas at the head of about seventy-five people, among them twenty-six soldiers and several Franciscan priests (including Father Hidalgo). Upon the Europeans' arrival, the Tejas and other Caddos greeted them warmly (they regarded St. Denis as their friend, after all), and in late June the explorers set up base at a site close to the Neches River. They immediately constructed a temporary presidio, then four missions close by it, among them Nuestra Señora de Guadalupe de los Nacogdoches, situated near present-day Nacogdoches. With the erection of the missions and presidio by the summer of 1716, the Spaniards had succeeded in accomplishing two objectives: revitalizing missionary work among the East Texas Indians, which Father Hidalgo had sought; and laying claim to the region, the objective pursued by the Spanish government in order to ward off French encroachment.

But this was not the end of New Spain's Texas enterprise, for now New Spain's central government pushed ahead with plans to solidify the Spanish position on the northern periphery. At the beginning of 1717, Captain Ramón and Fray Antonio Margil de Jesús established two more missions farther east of the original foundations, inching the missionaries closer to the French post of Natchitoches. Another expedition, led by Martín de Alarcón, marched from Mexico City toward the Río San Antonio in 1718 to found a military post called San Antonio de Béxar and a mission they named San Antonio de Valero. The new presidio and mission would serve the purpose of Christianizing the Coahuiltecan Indians, who had long eked out a marginal existence in their ancestral territories and who were presently under attack by marauding bands of Apaches coming down from the plains. Additionally, the presidio-mission complex midway between the Rio Grande and the East Texas frontier line would become a supply station. The result was the peopling of what became the original municipality of San Antonio. Around this site the Spaniards constructed the Mission San José y San Miguel de Aguayo in 1720 and three others in the 1730s. In 1721, the Spaniards secured control of the Bay of Espíritu Santo (or *La Bahía*) by building a fort that they hoped would serve as a Gulf Coast deterrent to Frenchmen desiring to initiate sea trade west from Louisiana. They also reasoned that the garrison would temporarily store provisions to be brought into Texas from Vera Cruz by ship. In 1749, however, the Crown moved the presidio and mission (built in 1722) of La Bahía inland toward the San Antonio River at the site of modern-day Goliad (the site kept the name of La Bahía) as part of a plan to found two civilian communities there. The towns did not thrive, but the presidio-mission-settlement complex of La Bahía remained.

Despite the entrenchment, the French chased the Spaniards out of East Texas in 1719, when war broke out in Europe between Spain and France. In a countermove, the Spanish Crown sent the governor of the province of Coahuila and Tejas, the Marqués de Aguayo, to regain the lost East Texas lands. The governor discharged his assignment by restoring the old missions among the Tejas and establishing a new presidio in July 1721 named Nuestra Señora del Pilar de los Adaes, just twelve miles west of Natchitoches, near the present-day town of Robeline, Louisiana. Returning to San Antonio in early 1722, Governor Aguayo issued directions for finishing the San Antonio de Bexár presidio started in 1718, then headed for La Bahía, where he established a mission to protect and Christianize the Karankawas and other coastal tribes. By the time Aguayo returned to his home in Coahuila in May 1722, he had increased the number of military posts and missions in Texas, repopulated the region with civilians, and established a much stronger Spanish hold on the entire province.

A new reconnoitering expedition in 1728 partly undermined Aguayo's work when it ascertained that the French were no longer the threat they once had been and concluded that a reduction in the number of Texas presidios, missions, and civilian settlements would make sense financially. But the friars remained committed to working among the Indians; hence some of the missions continued functioning as before. Moreover, the imperial government still desired to reinforce the halfway station at San Antonio. A villa, or civilian settlement, called San Fernando de Béxar, was built there in 1731, when sixteen families (somewhere between fifty-five and fifty-nine individuals) arrived from the Canary Islands. In that same year, the friars from East Texas relocated to San Antonio. So, by the 1730s, a presidio, a municipality, and five missions constituted the San Antonio, or Béxar, complex.

The Spaniards also pushed to settle the country along the Rio Grande. Don José de Escandón took charge of this expedition, and by the early 1750s he had colonized the south bank of the Rio Grande and also planted the seeds of modern-day Laredo, Texas. The lands of the lower Rio Grande Valley proved conducive to farming and ranching, and the region up to the Nueces River became pasture land for feral cattle and horses. The settling of this territory on both sides of the Rio Grande proved to be one of Spain's most successful ventures in the Far North.

Church efforts to win converts also begot expansion, although attempts to broaden the mission system proved disappointing. In 1746, the Church established a mission (and the viceroy authorized the construction of a presidio in 1747) on the San Gabriel River (near present-day Rockdale, Texas) to assist the Tonkawas, who were then being victimized by the Apaches and Comanches, and it added two more missions in the vicinity in 1749. But the Crown never fully attended to these assignments. Demoralization among the presidial soldiers and even the missionaries set in, and the Indians became dissatisfied due to what they felt was a lack of proper attention. The project on the San Gabriel thus died in 1755.

An attempt to convert the dreaded Apaches also failed. Since the establishment of the San Antonio complex, these Indians had made periodic attacks on the settlements there, but, by the 1740s, their own hostilities with the Comanches had made the Apaches receptive to an alliance with the Spaniards. Seeing the opportunity to Christianize the Apaches finally present itself, the Spaniards in 1757 established a mission and fort along the San Sabá River (near modern-day Menard, Texas); prospects of finding silver deposits also encouraged the enterprise. However, a broad group of tribes allied against the Apaches (among them the Comanches) almost immediately attacked the new mission. Furthermore, the Apaches showed indifference to the Spaniard's proselytizing overtures. Therefore, following futile attempts to carry out their missionary objectives, the viceroy ultimately abandoned the San Sabá enterprise in 1769.

Incorporation

What Spain sought by its efforts at settlement and missionization in Texas was the annexation of its far northern territory into the national core. Incorporation would involve transplanting the accoutrements of Spanish civilization to the frontier and ensuring the defense of the region from foreign threats by linking it to social and political systems in New Spain's interior. Ties to the center of Spain's New World empire would be established and maintained through the presidio, the mission, the rancho, and the villa, for these institutions had been successful in the process of incorporating former frontier regions throughout New Spain. But as in all such efforts, settling the periphery of the empire entailed dealing with the indigenous Indian peoples by either assimilating or annihilating them.

READINGS

Books

Bannon, John Francis, *The Spanish Borderlands Frontier, 1513–1821* (New York: Holt, Rhinehart, and Winston, 1970).

Carlson, Paul, *The Plains Indians* (College Station: Texas A&M University Press, 1998).

Chipman, Donald E., *Spanish Texas, 1519–1821* (Austin: University of Texas Press, 1992).

Chipman, Donald E. and Harriett Denise Joseph, *Notable Men and Women of Spanish Texas* (Austin: University of Texas Press, 1999).

Cruz, Gilbert R., *Let There Be Towns: Spanish Municipal Origins in the American Southwest, 1610–1810* (College Station: Texas A&M University Press, 1988).

Driver, Harold E., *Indians of North America*, 2nd ed. (Chicago: University of Chicago Press, 1973).

Hickerson, Nancy Parrott, *The Jumanos: Hunters and Traders of the South Plains* (Austin: University of Texas Press, 1994).

Jennings, Jesse, *Prehistory of North America*, 2nd ed. (New York: McGraw Hill, 1974).

John, Elizabeth, *Storms Brewed in Other Men's Worlds: The Confrontation of Indians, Spanish, and French in the Southwest, 1540–1795* (College Station: Texas A&M University Press, 1975).

La Vere, David, *The Caddo Chiefdoms: Caddo Economics and Politics, 700–1835* (Lincoln: University of Nebraska Press, 1998).

Moorhead, Max L., *The Presidio: Bastion of the Spanish Borderlands* (Norman: University of Oklahoma Press, 1975).

Newcomb, William W., Jr., *The Indians of Texas: From Prehistoric to Modern Times* (Austin: University of Texas Press, 1961).

O'Callaghan, Joseph F., *A History of Medieval Spain* (Ithaca: Cornell University Press, 1975).

Ricklis, Robert A., *The Karankawa Indians of Texas: An Ecological Study of Cultural Tradition and Change* (Austin: University of Texas Press, 1996).

Smith, F. Todd, *The Caddo Indians: Tribes at the Convergence of Empires, 1542–1854* (College Station: Texas A&M University Press, 1995).

Spencer, Robert E., et al., *The Native Americans: Ethnology and Background of the North American Indians*, 2nd ed. (New York: Harper & Row, 1977).

Weber, David J., *The Mexican Frontier, 1821–1846: The American Southwest under Mexico* (Albuquerque: University of New Mexico Press, 1982).

Bibliographies

Cruz, Gilberto Rafael, and James Arthur Irby, *Texas Bibliography: A Manual on History Research Material* (Austin: Eakin Press, 1982).

Cummins, Light Townsend, and Alvin R. Bailey, Jr., *A Guide to the History of Texas* (Westport, CT: Greenwood Press, 1988).

Jenkins, John H., *Basic Texas Books: An Annotated Bibliography of Selected Works for a Research Library* (Austin: Texas State Historical Association, 1988).

General Reference Books

Branda, Eldon S., *Handbook of Texas*, Vol. III (Austin: Texas State Historical Association, 1977).

Tyler, Ron, ed., *The New Handbook of Texas*, in 6 vols. (Austin: Texas State Historical Association, 1996).

Webb, Walter Prescott, and H. Bailey Carroll, eds., *Handbook of Texas*, in 2 vols. (Austin: Texas State Historical Association, 1952).

The Texas Almanac and State Industrial Guide (Dallas: *The Dallas Morning News*, published yearly).

Surveys

Connor, Seymour V., *Texas: A History* (Arlington Heights, IL: Harlan Davidson, Inc., 1971).

Richardson, Rupert N., et al., *Texas: The Lone Star State*, 8th ed. (New York: Prentice Hall, 2001).

Geographies

Jordan, Terry G., et al., *Texas: A Geography* (Boulder, CO: Westview Press, 1984).

Stevens, A. Ray, *Historical Atlas of Texas* (Norman: University of Oklahoma Press, 1989).

SPANIARDS IN A FAR NORTHERN *FRONTERA*

CHAPTER 2

The king's plans to solidify control of New Spain's Far North do not fully account for the development of Spanish settlements in Texas. While the new communities may have acted as buffers against possible French and British incursions into the province, other motives prompted frontierspeople to make their way into the Far North. The expanding *frontera* (frontier) gave some an outlet for escape—from natural disasters, ecological hardships, or unemployment in another province of New Spain. In addition, pulling up roots offered common folks restrained by ethnic prejudice a fresh start, for social distinctions tended to blur on the frontera. Frontier liv-

ing also gave respite from oppressive taxation and miscellaneous duties imposed on the lower classes in some well-established communities. Moreover, the cattle and mining industries that thrust outwardly from New Spain held out the prospects of improvement through gainful employment. The northern lands even extended the possibility of achieving a livelihood in landholding or some modest business venture. Finally, unsavory types visualized the frontier as a wide-open place in which to escape the authorities and continue to engage in smuggling and banditry.

Such motives have propelled migratory movements in other places and times, and they played themselves out in New Spain. By no means, however, did pobladores inundate Texas. Several factors explain why the migrational flow northward never swelled beyond a trickle. Diseases had so severely reduced New Spain's population in the sixteenth century that overcrowding pressures that generally uproot people did not build for quite some time thereafter. Even in the early eighteenth century, European immigration was so slight that few people already in New Spain felt crowded enough to brave adventure by relocating to the unknown hinterlands. Landowners in New Spain, furthermore, faced a labor supply severely reduced and sought mightily to retain control of their workers. Lastly, concerted efforts by royal officials to populate Texas entered a lull during the last half of the eighteenth century. After

Above: Detail from *Corrida de la Sandía* (Watermelon Race), part of the celebration of the Día de San Juan. *Painting by Theodore Gentilz. Yanaguana Society Collection, Daughters of the Republic of Texas Library*

Spain acquired Louisiana in November 1762, Texas no longer had to serve as a frontier defensive outpost. Accordingly, the Crown shifted its concerns to other, more-pressing problems.

At the same time, Texas was hardly a place with many immigrational "pull" factors. The region lacked an infrastructure, hostile Indian tribes threatened the lives of many a settler, and fruitless searches had convinced people that no great deposits of precious metals lay in the land to fulfill their hopes. Indeed, at the close of the eighteenth century, Texas remained one of the least-inhabited territories of New Spain.

Never, however, did isolation degenerate into imperial neglect. Orders from the viceroy and lesser officials filtered down systematically to colonial officials, primarily the governor of the province. As the king's appointee, the governor (his assignment was to reside in the presidio of Los Adaes, but he sometimes took up residence in Béxar) held a range of duties that included ensuring the execution of military assignments, dealing with the Indians, and tending to law enforcement and various other civic affairs. Settlers were expected to abide by the governor's commands. Benign neglect, however, allowed the Tejanos to carry out Crown directives in their own way or to modify royal mandates to meet the exigencies of frontier life. Therefore, society in Spanish Texas emerged as a compromise between policy prescribed by imperial and national goals and the survival instincts that served the colonists trying to build decent lives in an uncompromising land.

After the 1730s, the Crown made no concerted effort to recruit and dispatch new settlers to Texas. Population increases in the province derived from the voluntary arrival of more settlers (and the periodic assignment of soldiers to the province), most of whom arrived from Coahuila and Nuevo León. On the frontier, the newcomers joined their predecessors in a process of demographic change, cultural growth, and economic activity revolving around the centers of socialization: the missions, presidios, ranchos, and civilian settlements.

FRONTIER INSTITUTIONS

Missions

In the Far North, Catholicism remained the sole religion, disseminated by missionaries belonging to ecclesiastical orders (regular clergy) who labored both for the Crown and the Church in the tradition of the patronato real. The king provided the ecclesiastics with government subsidies; the priests reimbursed the monarch by guarding the frontier line and ministering to the un-Christianized Indian flocks, whom the king wanted brought into "civilized life." In such an accord, the king retained title to the plot upon which the friars built their missions. The Church, in turn, owned the mission compound, which included the edifices that the friars erected, the surrounding gardens, the mission pasture lands and livestock, and the holy burial ground (*campo santo*). In the mission compound the friars introduced the Indians to Christianity and instructed them in

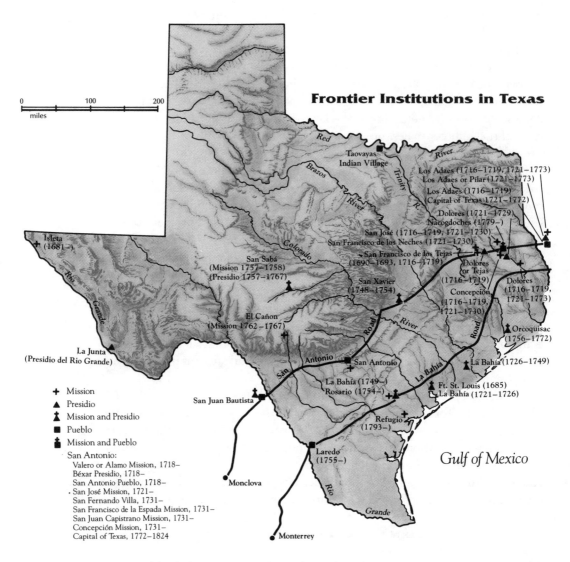

Frontier Institutions in Texas

Taovayas
Indian Village

Los Adaes (1716–1719, 1721–1773)
Los Adaes or Pilar (1721–1773)
Los Adaes (1716–1719)
(Capital of Texas 1721–1772)
Dolores (1721–1729)
Nacogdoches (1779–)

San José (1716–1719, 1721–1730)
San Francisco de los Neches (1721–1730)
San Francisco de los Tejas
(1690–1693, 1716–1719)

Isleta
(1681–)

San Sabá
(Mission 1757–1758)
(Presidio 1757–1767)

San Xavier
(1748–1754)

Dolores
or Tejas
(1716–1719)

Dolores
(1716–1719,
1721–1773)

Concepción
(1716–1719,
1721–1730)

El Cañon
(Mission 1762–1767)

Orcoquisac
(1756–1772)

La Junta
(Presidio del Rio Grande)

San Antonio

La Bahía (1726–1749)

La Bahía (1749–)
Rosario (1754–)

Ft. St. Louis (1685)
La Bahía (1721–1726)

San Juan Bautista

Refugio
(1793–)

Gulf of Mexico

+ Mission
▲ Presidio
♟ Mission and Presidio
■ Pueblo
♟ Mission and Pueblo
San Antonio:
   Valero or Alamo Mission, 1718–
   Béxar Presidio, 1718–
   San Antonio Pueblo, 1718–
   San José Mission, 1721–
   San Fernando Villa, 1731–
   San Francisco de la Espada Mission, 1731–
   San Juan Capistrano Mission, 1731–
   Concepción Mission, 1731–
   Capital of Texas, 1772–1824

Laredo
(1755–)

Monclova

Monterrey

"acceptable" behavior, using the Indians' own language at first before gradually switching to Spanish. The friars held their charges to a rigid routine that included daily mass, the recitation of prayer and the rosary, as well as lessons on the mysteries of the holy faith. Corporal punishment often was used to enforce this regimen. Once the neophytes had been deculturized and converted into faithful subjects (and, incidentally, tax-paying citizens), the state-subsidized missionaries left for new grounds, turning responsibilities for the preservation of the faith over to parish priests (secular clergy).

For the *gente de razón* (literally translated as "the people of reason" but meaning members of Spanish colonial society), the missions provided needed services, the friars tending to the people at baptism, marriage, and death. While most people professed to adhere to Catholicism, the institutional Church did not exert the influence in the province that it did in the parent state. Indeed, in the mid-eighteenth century, only one house of worship of any significance stood in Texas, the Church of San Fernando in San Antonio, the building started in 1738 and completed twenty years later. Most Tejanos practiced a type of popular religiosity, as did other people living in frontier settings where churches existed only sparsely. They slighted the more restrictive tenets of Catholicism and violated certain of its scriptures, as evidenced to by the enactment of laws designed to curtail blasphemous behavior. In the town of Nacogdoches, for example, authorities arrested a citizen in 1805 for publicly criticizing the Church by placing "indecorous" posters on trees. Notwithstanding such irreverence, the missionaries sought to minister to families, soldiers, and government representatives throughout the colonial era.

Presidios

Presidios functioned as agents for defense by extending the velvet glove to hostile Indian tribes, such as the Apaches, or serving as trading centers and camps where friendly tribes might take refuge among their new Spanish allies. The frontier garrisons also assisted with missionization. Presidio troops tracked down runaway mission subjects, such as the Karankawas in La Bahía, and even undertook expeditions to replace runaways by kidnapping Indians to work in the missions' households and fields. In such a role, the presidial staffs helped discipline the Indians and keep them in submission, thereby helping the missions maintain a sufficient labor force.

The presidio also served as the scene of much social and economic development. The presidial payroll influenced local economies. Moreover, the forts provided work for common laborers, purchased produce and finished goods from farmers, ranchers, and merchants, and hired the services of artisans. Furthermore, they helped entice people to the frontier by holding out prospects for steady employment and upward social mobility, especially for the poverty-stricken or the lower castes. Many of the important Tejano families in the early nineteenth century were descendants of presidial servicemen. Those presidios built in territories far remote from civilian settlements attracted pioneers seeking refuge from an isolated or dangerous life. Sometimes extralegal (unofficial, or unauthorized) settlements sprang up near the more remote forts.

Ranchos and the Cattle Trade

On the frontier, civilians made their living off the land, with ranching becoming the principal livelihood of settlers in Texas. The amount of acreage the pobladores worked varied, for the size of the parcel given to individuals varied according to how they planned to use it. For the keeping of large range animals and beasts of burden, the king granted one league of land, or 4,428.4 acres. Those grantees intending to raise sheep, goats, or hogs received approximately 1,920 acres. Cattle breeders received a unit of approximately 1,084 acres. Normal procedure for land concessions called for the completion of an application and the payment of a fee. But in Texas, as in other regions of the Far North, more flexible standards prevailed, as well as a tradition of informal land granting. In

Nacogdoches, for example, families acquired land simply by making a verbal agreement with a local official.

The assets of the frontier ranches stemmed from the first *entradas* (expeditions) into Texas. According to records, in 1689 Alonso de León brought to Texas 200 head of cattle, 400 horses, and 150 mules for the sole purpose of propagation. As he returned to Coahuila, he left a male and a female of each species on the bank of every stream he crossed in between the Neches River and the Rio Grande. In 1716, Domingo Ramón's expedition imported 64 oxen, 500 horses and mules, and over 1,000 sheep and goats into Texas. Aguayo's entourage had included nearly 4,800 cattle, some 2,800 horses, and about 6,400 sheep and goats. José de Escandón and his colonizers marched toward the Rio Grande in 1748 driving herds of equine and bovine stock. Over the years, the animals that survived these entradas roamed throughout Texas, their numbers augmented over time through natural reproduction and unintentional release, such as during a stampede.

The first persons to enter the ranching industry were the missionaries, those who had received the first land grants in Texas. But their stock soon multiplied beyond their control, with many individual animals straying off mission lands to join free-ranging herds. The frontier people referred to all unclaimed wild stock as *mesteños*. And just as they had laid claim to the roving herds descendent from the animals imported through the early entradas, the settlers were quick to claim the missionaries' livestock as soon as the animals had wandered into open pastures. As time passed, civilians who received land grants started their own ranches, often stocking their new enterprises with these "found" cattle.

The plains west of San Antonio to the Guadalupe River proved ideal for stock raising—one scholar refers to the area as the "cradle of Texas ranching"— and the mission ranches in this area enjoyed success. At La Bahía, the number of cattle increased from 3,000 head in the year 1758 to 16,000 head by 1768. In the 1760s, the five San Antonio missions herded close to 5,000 cattle, 1,100 horses, and 10,000 sheep. Naturally, Béxareños engaged in the livestock business to provide for numerous local needs, among them mounts for the military, sheep and goat products, and draft animals, including oxen. The settlers of Nacogdoches (a community surrounded by rich grasslands) after the 1780s also turned to ranching for their sustenance, and they earned a reputation throughout Louisiana and Texas for breeding fine horses. South of the Nueces River to the Rio Grande roamed another concentration of thousands of cattle, sheep, and horses. At the end of the eighteenth century, livestock raising flourished in Texas, the seeds of future, large-scale cattle raising already sowed.

The proliferation of the cattle ranches disguises the tremendous amount of energy that people exerted to wrest a living from a harsh environment. Generally, ranchers made their own corrals and other ranching necessities with the assistance of only their immediate families. They lived in homes better known for their function than their good looks. And because frontier people made their living working the land, they placed little emphasis on indoor living space. Usually, they built small houses with few modern amenities. Furnishings were homemade and often of an improvised design, among them furniture, bedding, and modest decorations. These conditions applied equally to the wealthier members of Tejano society, who also lived a fairly plain material existence. Although they had beef, poultry, and swine, most pobladores still cultivated a garden plot to supply their households with vegetables and fruits; usually, gardening fell to the women of the family.

While most ranches amounted to no more than one-family ventures, some comprised paid servants and slaves—in some cases Indians served as virtual slaves. The notion that the colonial ranching elite was composed of romantic gentlemen of leisure is misleading. According to lore, these grandees refused to perform any work they considered demeaning, devoting themselves instead to gambling and the chase. In reality, the rancheros, as well as their wives and children, labored long, hard hours.

Nevertheless, the ranchos displayed the Spaniards' ability to adapt to the new land's topography. The ranchos were well suited to the semi-arid plains, where farming was difficult. Furthermore, even with a shortage of labor the rancho might be very productive. Lastly, the rancheros could move their source of livelihood (their livestock) on short notice in order to save it from an impending raid or attack, a feat which a farmer with a field full of crops could not even contemplate.

During the early 1750s, livestock markets developed in the neighboring provinces of Nuevo León and Coahuila. Before long, Tejano settlers annually journeyed to the fair in Saltillo (in Coahuila), taking with them cattle and horses, suet, and tallow, which they bartered for supplies, implements, and manufactured goods that were scarce in their own settlements.

In the 1770s, Texas ranchers also entered into a fairly regular commercial association with markets in Louisiana. When, in 1780, the Spanish Crown issued a concession permitting Tejanos to trade cattle with merchants in Louisiana (which, though acquired by Spain in 1762, was tied to the administrative structure of Cuba), it proved fortuitous for the stockmen. In the next ten years, Tejanos drove countless herds of cattle east. But because this newly legalized trade required a tax on cattle and horses exported from Texas, smuggling continued alongside the extensive legal trade. Furthermore, rancheros established a pattern of marketing animals in the United States, taking their stock from Béxar or Goliad through the Piney Woods of East Texas. Such trade with the outside world strengthened the province's capitalist orientation, for it encouraged the concentration of private property, contributed to varying degrees of individual wealth, and abetted the division of labor. This interstate commerce eventually forged Texas's ties to the capitalist economy of the United States.

Farms

While settlers on the frontier planted a number of crops, in Texas farming did not flourish. Most grantees intending to farm received relatively meager parcels of land, usually as a *labor*—approximately 177 acres—and too many other factors worked against farming at this time to make it a major means of support. The setbacks included: the Tejanos' reliance on ranching and commerce in livestock; the lack of available workers to undertake the labor-intensive tasks of clearing land, digging irrigation ditches, and tending crops; the scarcity of and the difficulties in transporting farm equipment to the frontier; the threat of Indian raids on standing crops; and, perhaps most important, the absence of accessible markets that might have fostered commercialization. Ordinarily, then, farms in colonial Texas were of a hardscrabble, subsistence type that enabled their owners to eke out a living.

In the San Antonio settlements, farmers used the waters of the San Antonio River and San Pedro Creek to irrigate their fields. They raised pumpkins, melons, corn, beans, and peppers—crops raised by the Béxar mission Indians as well. While some in the East Texas community of Los Adaes undertook farming, early settlers there constantly faced natural disasters, usually in the form of crop-destroying floods, so that they often called on the nearby French settlements in Louisiana for needed provisions. In Nacogdoches, farmers nurtured small, town lots or harvested a variety of vegetable products from nearby fields. La Bahía was located in an infertile area before 1749; but neither did its permanent site in modern Goliad (to which it was moved) lend itself to farming, the local garrison forced to rely on San Antonio for its grain supplies.

Towns

As the eighteenth century waned, only four civilian settlements dotted the ranching province. In East Texas, Nacogdoches held 350 settlers as of 1783.

The pobladores turned to the environment for materials with which to build homes in the Texas frontera. *From "Mexicans in San Antonio, Texas, 1887" series, E. K. Sturdevant, photographer, Daughters of the Republic of Texas Library*

South towards La Bahía, approximately 450 pobladores lived in and around the mission and presidio that year. San Antonio, meanwhile, counted 1,248 inhabitants. On the Rio Grande, the population of Laredo comprised 700 residents as of 1789. Attempts to establish other civilian units in the early nineteenth century faltered.

These (relatively) urban sites acted in consort with the other frontier institutions, but they were civilian settlements. Townsfolk included the families of presidial soldiers, Indian neophytes, and even persons on the dodge or those engaged in contraband commerce. Those in charge of town government came from the civilian sector; the *alcalde* (mayor) cared for a *municipio*'s (the settlement proper plus outlying areas) numerous needs through the ayuntamiento. The ayuntamiento further held responsibility for executing imperial plans, building government structures, protecting the urbanites' property, maintaining law and order, boosting town growth, enforcing morality, and organizing community functions. Like other administrative bodies on the frontier, the ayuntamiento often interpreted royal directives loosely, bending them to meet local and immediate considerations.

Townspeople made a living in a variety of ways. Artisans served presidios and missions, vaqueros did seasonal work on ranches, teamsters transported goods and materials on carts pulled by livestock (horses, mules, donkeys, or oxen), and day laborers performed a range of unspecialized tasks. Merchants, bakers, tailors, shoemakers, blacksmiths, and barbers met the needs of an urban populace. But rancheros also took residence in town, diversifying and changing the economy. In Béxar, some ranchers used their livestock to produce essential commodities—soap and candles, but also hides, from which leathered body armor and shields were fashioned. In Laredo, rancheros exchanged livestock products and horses for tools and garments brought in from the interior of New Spain. People in other Rio Grande settlements also exported south a wide selection of products native to the area, from fish to mutton to hides. Money remained scarce throughout the province, but urban-based economic activity, like that on the ranchos, contributed to the nascent Texas economy.

Town living posed numerous problems, but the pobladores managed a crude survival. To make homes, they took advantage of materials readily available in wilderness areas, their domiciles ranging from the undistinguished to the attractive. Masons quarried stone for use in the construction of important buildings. Common people living around San Antonio and southern Texas constructed homes of mud, the type of soil essential for adobe found locally. Mesquite trees, grass, and other natural products were used to build *jacales* (huts): slender mesquite posts placed in vertical rows served as walls, thatched coverings functioned as roofs. Waterworks to serve a town and its adjacent fields had to be constructed communally. In Béxar, citizens contributed their tools and materials to this end. By their own labor, they built the dams, *acequias* (irrigation canals), and aqueducts for the town and the neighboring network of missions. As time progressed, even the Canary Islanders, who had once sought to remain aloof from the rest of Béxar society, came to terms with fellow residents; community and family ties impelled them to pull their own weight and deal cooperatively with the adversities of the frontier.

While town living was in some ways safer than life in a rural setting, numerous blights plagued the urbanites. Lack of proper sewage facilities and the concentration of rotting animal waste and carcasses and other litter contributed to the spread of deadly epidemics (such as smallpox and cholera), as did muddy streets (good breeding grounds for mosquitoes during rainy weather). Doctors, drugs, and hospitals rarely made their way to the Far North (the only hospital, which operated for less than ten years, was founded in San Antonio in 1805). Crime committed by vagrants, smugglers, prostitutes, and other social nonconformists became an undeniable aspect of urban life. Finally, attacks by Comanches and other Plains Tribes remained possible.

Despite such difficulties, townspeople managed to live reasonably well. Diversions, often in the way of cultural traditions brought from the interior of New Spain, took several forms. In leisure time, family members gathered to tell folktales or sing *corridos* (story-telling ballads). Religious holidays were observed with a combination of Catholic solemnity and frontier-charged enthusiasm, and they afforded welcome opportunities for entertainment. These and other special occasions might see the holding of a *fandango* (festive dance), those with a talent for playing the guitar or the fiddle providing the music. In a ranching culture, favorite amusements included horseracing and the *carrera del gallo*, a contest that took several forms; in one, mounted vaqueros raced at full gallop to be the first to reach down to pull off the head of a rooster buried up to its neck in the ground.

Though sparse, intellectual life existed on the frontier. A few books made their way there, though only the well to do could afford them. Writing was the domain of the literate, which certainly included government officials and the clergy, but most communities comprised a few settlers and soldiers with the necessary skills. Indeed, much of the earliest knowledge of the Texas landscape and its original inhabitants comes from the diaries and chronicles of the conquistadores. Missionaries, also, told their accounts of working with the neophytes and left to posterity careful records of early Native American civilizations. Historians have used these writings to enhance their knowledge of the colonial era. Especially valuable for this is Father Juan Agustín Morfi's *History of Texas, 1673–1779*, written by the clergyman after an official visit to Texas from 1777 through 1778.

Some of the province's leaders sought out, albeit with mixed success, good teachers within the community to instruct the young. Factors such as poverty, the uncertainty of frontier life, a belief in the general "uselessness" of an education in the hinterlands, and the dearth of books partly account for the absence of an educational system. But by the early nineteenth century, all the urban settlements had established some type of rudimentary educational facility.

The funeral of an "angel" or baptized infant. Infant mortality rates were high on the frontera. *Theodore Gentilz, Entierro De Un Angel, Yanaguana Society Collection, Daughters of the Republic of Texas Library*

Communications, however crude, connected Texas with Mexico over the *Camino Real* (the King's Highway, also called the San Antonio Road). This artery traversed the province from San Juan Bautista, on the Rio Grande, to Béxar, and on to the East Texas settlements. A second route extended from Laredo to La Bahía, then connected to the Camino Real at the Trinity River. Mounted couriers regularly carried mail from throughout New Spain to Texas towns.

FRONTIER SOCIETY

Mestizaje

The nonindigenous population of Texas stood at about 500 persons in 1731. It grew to about 3,000 during the 1770s and 1780s, and then leaped to about 4,000 in 1800. Despite high birth rates, many factors kept the population from growing rapidly. The adversities of frontier life included a high infant-mortality rate, continual warfare with the Indians, farming methods that yielded only a paucity of agricultural foodstuffs, traditional (and by modern standards improper) notions of diet and hygiene, a lack of doctors and hospitals, and periodic waves of virulent diseases. Epidemics such as cholera, which swept through

San Antonio in 1780 and took the lives of three people daily, also kept the population's growth in check.

Other forces, nonetheless, do account for demographic growth. Immigration from the interior of New Spain, much of it sporadic, played a part, as resolute settlers struck out for the Far North. In addition, convicts were at times dispatched to the region to help build presidios; in time, the former inmates intermixed with the indigenous population. Still, natural propagation accounted for most of the Tejano population growth.

Those who peopled Texas in the eighteenth century had a range of ethnic makeups, and they lived with a degree of sexual imbalance, with males outnumbering women. This led presidial soldiers and *mestizos* (mixed-bloods who descended from European-Indian parents) to mix with assimilated Indians, especially those around San Antonio. The process of *mestizaje* (racial and cultural union involving Europeans, Indians, and some Africans), which dated back to the earliest years of Spain's contact with the New World civilizations, continued in Texas unabated.

Although the censuses of the 1780s show that *españoles* (Spaniards) made up about one-half of the population of the province, those figures are misleading, for the term did not designate undiluted Spanishness. Rather, it served as an all-embracing label that described relative wealth, social and occupational standing, degree of cultural assimilation, and even the attitudes of the census takers. In reality, few European Spaniards lived in Texas, and those classified as such really belonged in the mestizo category. Even the Canary Islanders had mixed with the rest of the Tejano population within two generations of the founding of San Fernando de Béxar, so that none of them could truly speak of their own racial purity.

Classification regarding "Spanishness" derived from the accepted feeling on the frontier that people of darker skin hues and of mixed blood could "pass" as Spaniards, especially when they had come to achieve some sort of social standing as ranchers, government officials, or military personnel. Thus, on the frontier, economic success tended to override racial makeup in one's classification. Lower-class mestizos and other people of color such as mulattoes and slaves, however, almost always encountered difficulties in achieving the more prestigious status of "Spanish." At another level, Hispanicized Indians, African-descent people who had attained their freedom, and mulattoes might break through the mestizo stratum.

Social Differences

The social structure of Texas, therefore, did not mirror the stratified order of New Spain's interior, which placed the *peninsulares* (European-born Spaniards who dominated the higher political offices) at the top, ranked the *criollos* (American-born Spaniards who ordinarily inherited their European-born parents' possessions) next, and relegated the mestizos, Indians, and Africans to the bottom. In Texas, as in other frontier regions, the routine mixing of races mitigated ethnic divisions.

Degrees of wealth nonetheless separated some Tejanos from the majority. Government officials and military commandants enjoyed more secure incomes, although they hardly earned enough to claim prosperity. Entrepreneurs in towns and rancheros and farmers working peons or slaves constituted part of the emerging capitalist sector in colonial society. This group owned the nicer homes, and they had the capacity to derive a better standard of living from their tracts of land. But this upper stratum represented no corporate interest or any attempt to perpetuate and protect specific privileges of a social order. Moreover, their distinction from other Tejanos remained tenuous. In education, racial makeup, cultural heritage, speech, and dress, the "upper class" largely resembled the rest of society. Their status hinged mainly on their material holdings and not on deference owed them because of their skin color or place of birth or noble family background. The above qualifications applied equally to the Canary Islanders, who eventually became part of the overall Texas population, although some of them did manage to remain at the top of the social hierarchy.

Beneath the small upper crust representing the well to do in Tejano society lay the remainder of the Tejano population, comprising common laborers, semiskilled workers, and Hispanicized Indians. Once again, their social categorization had less to do with their ethnic makeup than their lack of material assets.

Slavery

The nature of slavery in colonial Texas has yet to be studied adequately. According to the censuses conducted in the latter part of the eighteenth century, the number of black persons in the province barely exceeded fifty, the majority of which resided in East Texas, the region closest to Louisiana, from which some had run away. Most blacks were not slaves; whether they had arrived in Texas as fugitives or as free persons, they integrated themselves into colonial society, adopting Spanish surnames and learning the Spanish language. At least a few Tejano rancheros, however, did acquire slaves in New Orleans, exchanging cattle for bondspeople or through barter with the French living in neighboring Louisiana communities. And in the latter years of the century, some farmers living around Nacogdoches held slaves. Although Spain did not follow a pattern of exporting Africans to the Far North, the Crown did extend its official policy on slavery to Texas. This prohibited Africans from congregating, lest they plan insurrection, and from possessing firearms. Given the dire need for free laborers to perform so many menial tasks on the frontier, however, doubt exists that colonials stringently enforced such regulations. More plausibly, Africans worked alongside other day laborers in an integrated workforce.

Tejanas

Women's place in Spanish Texas probably resembled that of other women in similar colonial societies. Living far from the interior, Tejanas escaped some of the sexual limitations more strictly outlined in New Spain proper. The rigors of frontier life tended to soften gender discrimination, as they did that of race, and women engaged in such duties as fighting Indians, helping with ranch and farm chores, including herding, and entered into mercantile activity. Still, women's chief role was that of providing the best possible domestic setting in an isolated place. The drudgery of dragging in water and wood, preparing food, making, repairing, and washing clothes, cultivating local plants, making household necessities such as soap, and passing on to the children the morals and values of Spanish-Mexican culture all crammed their way into a woman's busy life.

Although frontier life may have featured certain democratizing tendencies, it posed severe problems for women. Isolation limited social mobility—improvement for women could occur only through fortuitous changes, such as marriage to a rising businessman or rancher. The region offered little opportunity for women to establish their own vocations, though some women practiced midwifery as a profession. Indeed, most of the responsibility for taking care of the ill (such as treating snakebites, setting bones, or tending to rheumatism) fell on the shoulders of women. It was women who primarily practiced *curanderismo* (folk healing). In addition, on the frontier, women often were treated as objects. Fathers might arrange marriages for their young daughters, unscrupulous military officers sexually exploited their subordinates' wives, and shameless husbands abused their spouses with impunity.

The law denied colonial women certain rights. Women could not vote or hold elective office. Moreover, a man could legally prevent his wife from leaving him. On the other hand, Tejanas enjoyed certain rights under Spanish law. Women could use the judicial system and be parties to suits, either as plaintiffs or defendants. They could hold material assets and investments independently of their spouse. Additionally, they could negotiate on their own for the sale of such goods. Finally, legal tradition did not bestow upon husbands the control of property that a wife possessed before marriage. In short, women in Spanish Texas enjoyed more legal rights than did their contemporary counterparts in French or British North American colonies.

The historical record shows that women played constructive roles in colonial society. Doña María Hinojosa de Ballí, sometimes hailed as Texas's first cattle queen, enlarged the South Texas ranch she inherited from her husband; the estate eventually covered much of the lower Rio Grande Valley as well as Padre Island. Other women similarly experienced success as ranch managers, merchants, or community activists.

INDIAN ACCOMMODATION AND RESISTANCE

No one knows exactly how many Native Americans lived in Texas during the colonial era, for government officials found it difficult to ascertain a correct count of unsettled tribes. One census in the late 1770s placed the number of Indians (excluding those in the missions) in excess of 7,000.

The Indians who came from the hunter-gatherer bands inhabiting the areas east and south of San Antonio to the Gulf Coast displayed the most interest in the teachings of the missionaries. In many cases, however, reasons other than a true desire for conversion to Catholicism explain their cooperation. For the Coahuiltecans, a move to the mission represented protection from neighboring tormentors. For other Indian bands afflicted with disease or starvation, the mission centers simply offered an alternative to death. Furthermore, once under the tutelage of the friars, the neophytes learned numerous usable skills; prospective converts learned to farm, herd stock, manufacture cotton and woolen products, and make such useful items as bricks, soap, adobe, and footwear. Those in San Antonio helped erect the town's complex of missions by digging irrigation ditches, building beamed bridges and other structures, planting vegetables and cotton, and pasturing horses, sheep, goats, and pigs that the friars then sold at modest profits locally. By the end of the eighteenth century, many of the converts had accepted aspects of Catholicism into their lifestyle, as well as new attitudes toward work and certain other tenets of European civi-

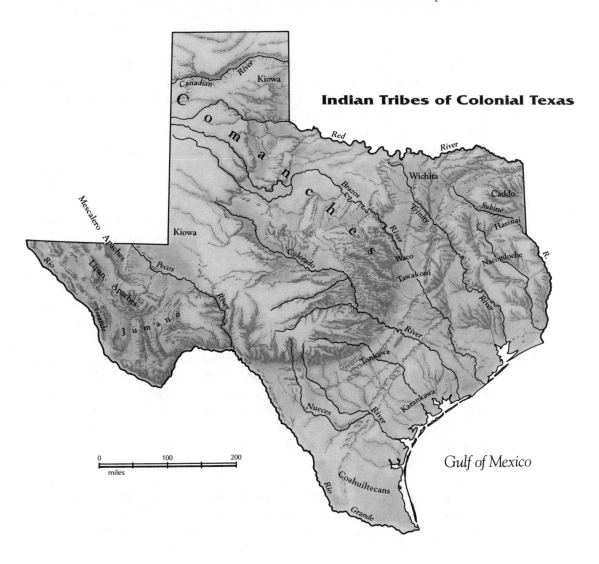

Indian Tribes of Colonial Texas

lization. Some in Béxar even had intermarried or become Hispanicized to the point that they became part of the local labor force. Tribes such as the Coahuiltecans, on the other hand, ceased to exist as a distinct people during the eighteenth century due to displacement by Spaniards, the unceasing hostilities of warlike tribes, and the scourge of Old World plagues.

But most other Texas tribes had no desire to submit themselves to the disciplined life that was the mission routine. This fierce independence was displayed by the Karankawas of the Gulf Coast, whom the curates once had seen as likely recruits for conversion. Failure to assimilate occurred with other tribes who remained faithful to their way of life by maintaining economic independence. The Jumanos, for all their clamoring for Christian teaching, sought to use the Spaniards as temporary guards who might protect them as they conducted trade with the East Texas Caddos. The Caddos themselves resisted missionary overtures due to their ability to provide for themselves, both as skilled farmers and traders, the commerce that they had developed with the neighboring French proving favorable.

Ultimately, Native American peoples in Texas suffered irreversibly from such factors as frontier warfare, disease, and foreign violation of their territory. The Jumanos, whose fortunes suffered from a disruption of trade as they had long known it—their old trading partners the Caddos by the 1690s preferring to trade with French Louisiana, and incessant Indian attacks made commerce across Texas dangerous—were absorbed by the Apache nation, and little is known of them after the 1770s. The Karankawas, on the other hand, remained at odds with the Spaniards until the last decades of the eighteenth century—bitter towards the Europeans over the diseases they imported and the attacks the outsiders made upon Karankawa camps (in retaliation, it must be noted, for the cattle rustling undertaken by the Karankawas)—and made common cause with the Apaches by supplying them with arms acquired from Louisiana. Not until the 1790s did the Karankawas become receptive to the idea of missionization. By then, they were under constant attack by other tribes, namely the Comanches, and experiencing rapid population losses brought on by the ravishes of warfare and pestilence. From 8,000 in 1685, the Karankawa population had been whittled down to approximately 3,000 by 1780. It was, therefore, in the 1790s and early 1800s that the Karankwas finally turned to the missions (at least to *Nuestra Señora del Refugio* Mission, in present Calhoun County, established for them in 1793) and integrated the religious institutions into their survival patterns. Missions provided them a source of refuge from the Comanches and extended them sustenance, at least during those seasons of the year when the ecology of the coastal areas made traditional lifeways difficult.

The Caddo civilization in East Texas weathered the calamities of the colonial era better than did the Coahuiltecans, Jumanos, and Karankawas. Although suffering a decline in numbers due to the destructive forces mentioned above, Caddo society remained stable. In the latter decades of the eighteenth century, the great chief Tinhiouen (the Elder) played an influential role in the interna-

tional trade conducted in Caddo country, with Spanish, French, and Indian traders seeking his favor. Commercial links with the French became so intimate that
they modified Caddo society during the eighteenth century. In exchange for
their own farm goods as well as buffalo skins, bear fat, and mustangs acquired
in bartering with nearby tribes, the Caddos received weapons, work tools, hunting equipment, blankets, and clothing from the French. This symbiotic relationship made the Caddos more successful hunters and improved their standard of
living, but it had a downside. Old skills atrophied as tribe members no longer
needed to produce bows and arrows, traditional crafts, or weave clothing. Their
close relationship also brought the Caddo new diseases and an over-reliance on
the French for protection. When France left Louisiana in 1762, the Caddos were
suddenly on their own to face hostile Indian tribes, the encroachment of Spaniards from the west, and the threat of American settlers from the east. At the
end of the colonial era, the Caddos struggled for their very survival, but they
managed to remain in their homelands until the 1850s.

Many other tribes known as out-and-out hostile, belligerent, and nomadic
(the *indios bárbaros*), survived well into the latter years of the nineteenth century. These Native peoples realized that the foreigners represented a serious
threat to their traditional lifeways. Europeans arrived in Indian Country with
different ideas about religion and land, speaking a strange language, and laying
claim to Indian lands through "right of discovery," and subjugating Indian
peoples through assimilation and violence. With the newcomers also came diseases responsible for taking more Indian lives than bullets and swords ever did.

Resistance, therefore, characterized relations between whites and the more
independent Natives. Tribes such as the Apaches and the new converts to Plains
culture, the Wichita (called *Norteños*, or Nations of the North, by the Spaniards) from the Red River area, openly rejected the presence of the interlopers
and responded with vicious attacks upon the European settlements, stealing livestock, horses, weapons, tools, and supplies—items useful for
living off the land and waging war. Periodically, the Apaches
would dabble in missionary life, but they principally did so
to dodge the dreaded Comanches. The Norteños entertained no such plans; with firearms and other supplies acquired through the Caddos from the French in the
Mississippi region, they were content to keep up their raids
on enemy tribes, livestock ranches, and Spanish missions.
Similarly, the Comanches launched awesome military campaigns against Native American competitors and frontier
communities alike. Generally, the Plains Indians seemed to
have had the better war strategies—at times playing the
Spaniards off against enemy tribes—and the winning battle

Buffalo Hump, a Comanche Indian. *Caldwell Papers, The Center for
American History, The University of Texas at Austin, CN10934*

plans, and they struck daringly at and swiftly escaped from the stationary out-posts of European civilization. In turn, they had no villages as such to protect or a formal military to surrender. Moreover, a treaty signed with one Plains band might mean nothing to other groups within the same tribe, a concept that the Spanish, and later the Americans, never seemed to grasp.

THE BOURBON REFORMS

In the second half of the eighteenth century, New Spain's fear of the invasion of Texas by foreign powers diminished. The French threat to the province dissolved when, in 1762, France ceded Louisiana west of the Mississippi River to Spain during the War for the Empire, known in Britain's New England colonies as the French and Indian War (1754–1763), hoping to prevent the province from falling into British hands. Though the 5,700 Frenchmen in Louisiana did not welcome the prospect of becoming Iberian subjects and sought to undermine Spanish rule by forcing their first Spanish governor to depart for Cuba in 1768, the next year a Spanish fleet reestablished Spanish sovereignty over the new acquisition. The British settlements situated along the Atlantic coast were too far away to cause many problems for Texas. And after 1783, even the new country of the United States suffered from too many internal problems to pose much of a menace. It was the indios bárbaros who continued to present the pobladores and Spanish officials with the most immediate difficulty.

But dramatic changes, with potentially adverse implications for New Spain and its northern frontiers, were taking place in Spain under the new Bourbon king, Carlos III (1759–1788). An admirer of the Enlightenment philosophies then current throughout Europe, Carlos moved to bring about important reforms to make the Crown's administration of the Latin American colonies easier and to restore Spain's diminished great-power status. To Mexico, Carlos dispatched José de Gálvez to investigate the colony and recommend reform policy. Gálvez's fact-finding tour, which lasted from 1765 to 1771, produced a series of changes. The Crown replaced native Mexican lower-level administrators (who allegedly were guilty of institutionalized graft, inefficiency, and flouting the laws) with trusted and efficient officers from Spain who would preside over intendancies, or districts, in the interest of better government. Other edicts lowered the amount of taxes but ensured their collection by an efficient corps not known for corruption, as the old officials had been. Free trade was established in 1778 within most of the Spanish kingdom. Subsequent directives opened more New Spanish ports for trade and lowered custom duties to encourage intercolonial commerce. These reforms brought about a fabulous development within the empire.

In the meantime, the king entrusted the Marqués de Rubí with carefully inspecting the military organization and the state of defenses of the Far North frontier. Rubí spent from 1766 to 1767 gathering information for his report, touring the frontier from the Gulf of California to East Texas. In the process, he entered Texas from San Juan Bautista, on the Rio Grande, first inspecting the fledgling presidio complex at San Sabá. From there, his party headed for San Antonio, then to Los Adaes, the designated capital of the province, and to other stations in East Texas, thence to La Bahía, and from there back to San Juan Bautista. After this 700-mile swing, Rubí submitted his recommendations for presidial system reform.

Rubí's recommendations laid the groundwork for the New Regulations of Presidios of 1772. In consideration of the post-1762 conditions, in which Spanish-owned Louisiana now shielded Texas from European enemies, the new regulations directed several maneuvers: pulling back the military and missionary presence in East Texas; the relocation of the settlers of East Texas to San Antonio, so as to strengthen the latter city (the provincial capital would also be moved to Béxar); and the implementation of a velvet-glove policy toward the Comanches and other northern tribes and an iron-fist one toward the Apaches. The last suggestion derived from Rubí's understanding of Indian affairs. The Comanche and Norteño attacks upon Spanish institutions were not directed at the whites specifically; instead, the two tribes sought retaliation for the Spanish practice of coddling, through missionization, their common Apache enemy. Rubí reasoned that peace in Texas might be achieved through an alliance with the Comanches and Norteños against the Apaches.

While the new policy against the Apaches alienated few Spanish colonists, such was not the case with the directives to uproot the people of East Texas. The East Texas pobladores living around the presidio and mission—approximately 500 persons, including Spaniards, Indians, blacks, and some French-descent people who had transferred in from Louisiana—were enjoying relative prosperity and had no wish to leave their homes. The governor of Texas, Juan María de Ripperdá, sympathized with the pobladores but had his orders to oversee the evacuation. In June 1773, the departure of 167 Los Adaes families, along with soldiers and friars, began. The group reached San Antonio after three months of suffering due to illness, floods, poor equipment, and few riding stock. Within a few weeks after arriving in Béxar, some thirty Adaesaños had perished from the hardships they had endured on the march.

Once in San Antonio, the Adaesaños asked the governor for the right to return to their homes, which they already missed. The governor, still sympathetic to their situation, received their supplication without protest and gave them his personal approval to return as close to their former home sites as the Trinity River. Later, the viceroy approved the governor's decision, as there now seemed to be a need to defend the East Texas region from land-hungry British settlers pushing west.

A momentous march in the fall of 1774, led by Antonio Gil Ybarbo, who longed to return to his ranch, resulted in the founding of Bucareli on the Trinity River in September. Named after the viceroy, the little settlement increased in population (347 in 1777) but faced numerous problems, among them dismal harvests, rampant disease, and attacks by Comanches. Consequently, in the spring of 1779, some 500 people left Bucareli and pushed farther east, closer to where their homes once had been. Settling near the abandoned mission Nuestra Señora de Guadalupe de los Nacogdoches, they founded a new town that they logically named Nacogdoches.

Nacogdoches survived to become the only successful civilian settlement in East Texas. Significantly, it owed its origins to actions other than those that had determined the establishment of San Antonio de Béxar and La Bahía. In violation of official settlement policy, the Tejanos had trusted their own instincts and successfully launched what is today one of the oldest municipalities in Texas history.

Throughout Texas, the settlers had continued to have their hands full with fighting the Apaches and Comanches. José de Gálvez thus pursued strong measures, in accordance with the New Presidio Regulations of 1772. Now assuming the powerful post of minister-general of the Indies for Spain, Gálvez created in 1776 the *Provincias Internas* (the Internal Provinces), an administrative entity that comprised the present north Mexican states as well as Texas, New Mexico, and California. The commandant-general who headed this unit oversaw its military and civil administration. He answered to the king, and the governor of Texas reported to him.

Teodoro de Croix, an experienced military man in Europe and a veteran administrator in New Spain, was designated as the first commandant-general of the Provincias Internas. He received instructions to give priority to Indian pacification. Carefully considering which tribes were the principal threat, which alliances with which tribes would prove most effective, and what troop strength would be needed in the overall campaign, Croix concurred with Rubí that the Apaches were the main enemies and that collusion with the Comanches and other Norteño bands would best serve Spain's purposes. But just as Croix was about to implement his offensive initiative in 1779, higher authorities recommended a new plan to contend with the Apache foes. Spain was at the time readying for renewed warfare in Europe and found it difficult to allocate precious resources for frontier campaigns. Croix was thus forced to forego his planned military drive against the Apaches and instead offer them small commissions and inexpensive presents in an effort to conciliate them, a strategy that hardly induced the Indians to cease their raids.

TEXAS TOWARDS THE END OF THE SPANISH ERA

Towards the late eighteenth century, the Crown began the secularization of the Texas missions. Secularization involved converting the missions from financial dependency on the government into parishioner-supported institutions; the process assumed that the Indian converts had been transformed into productive citizens and could now function adequately as Spanish subjects. Although a couple of missions remained under the care of the friars towards the end of the Spanish period, the process of secularization proceeded, not culminating until the 1820s.

Several factors contributed to the desertion of the missions. Certainly, the last years of the eighteenth century tried Spanish tenacity. Carlos III was succeeded by a son lacking in wisdom, and political affairs on the European continent, starting with the French Revolution of 1789, soon engulfed Spain in shifting alliances with France and England. War with both Great Powers distracted attention from Spain's commitment in the New World and diverted monies from New Spain back to the mother country.

Working alongside these developments were newer philosophical trends that questioned the program of missionization. Since the sixteenth century, Christianization had posited the equality of Indians with the rest of humankind. On that premise, Spain had sought to convert indigenous New World populations. The anti-church sentiment buoyed by the Enlightenment, however, wrought bad times for the missionaries. By the late eighteenth century, the Franciscans and the other regular clergy found themselves facing new demands for the secularization of missions. Despite protests from the friars, the intellectual currents of the late eighteenth century undermined efforts to continue missionary work in the name of the state.

Even at the local level, several factors worked against missionary activity in Texas. First, the economic stability of the province depended on a steady, marketable commodity, and livestock seemed to fit the bill closely. As their numbers grew, however, the pobladores began to covet the mission cattle, and government officials simultaneously saw the potential for increased tax revenue in transforming mission lands into private property. Second, the neophytes played a part in the breakdown of the religious institutions. From the beginning, the mission concept did not make for a happy arrangement between Europeans and Native Americans. Priests and presidial soldiers lorded over literally hundreds of charges, disciplining them with intimidation and cruelty. Mission life for the Indians meant dehumanization and the abandonment of traditional lifeways and religious beliefs, not to mention their shameless exploitation by ranchers and presidial officials. Assimilation offered little hope, as it never entailed full acceptance into Spanish society. Some mission Indians rebelled by resisting the work expected from them by the missionaries, responding as other forced laborers have by feigning illness, turning to gambling or abusing alcohol, sabotaging work implements, intentionally showing up late for work, destroying sacred articles, and deriding the priesthood. Escape seemed the best alternative, and it became the most visible sign of resistance. Actually, by the late eighteenth century, few potential Indian converts remained. As the program of secularization ended, the friars, despite all their work and numerous accomplishments for the Church and the Crown, could claim to have Christianized or Hispanicized only a small fraction of the total Native American population in Texas.

As for the indios bárbaros, they gave the settlers little respite. The presidial soldiers, upon whose shoulders lay the responsibility of maintaining the peace, never effectively devised successful tactics to ward off the Texas Indians. In many ways, their inability to carry out their purpose emanated from the design of the presidio system itself. Troops in command of large forts were not effective against such highly mobile enemies as the mounted Comanches and Wichita, who attacked farmers in the fields, struck civilian settlements, raided ranches for horses which they exchanged for guns available from westering U.S. citizens, and harassed the neophytes who took refuge among the Spaniards. Moreover, many presidial installations were in constant need of repair, and their commanding officers often lacked good administrative skills. Militarily, the posts were understaffed, under equipped (with weapons not upgraded regularly), and often outfitted with horses unfit for service. Shortages of food and proper uniforms and the meager salaries awarded soldiers became perennial problems. Amid such conditions, morale among presidial personnel understandably remained low.

Finally, in the 1780s, the Crown returned to its earlier policy of trying to appease the Apaches by giving them gifts and rewards, applying this as well to the Comanches and Norteños. Actually a tactic to divide and rule by playing one tribal band against another, this official bribery aimed to reduce the Indian forces, create animosity among them, and way-lay intertribal alliances. And for a time it worked, as a semblance of peace, albeit punctuated by destructive clashes, ensued for roughly the next three decades.

Notwithstanding the tribulations of the frontier, the three civilian settlements that traced their origins to the 1710s remained in place as the nineteenth century dawned. San Antonio, now the provincial capital, had a population of 2,500 near its chain of five missions and in the town of Béxar. Some 1,200 persons lived in Goliad's surroundings, and about 500 lived in Nacogdoches. A few more pobladores populated two new towns erected to counter the threat of Anglo-American aggression from the United States: Salcedo, founded in 1806, was situated on the Trinity River near the old outpost of Bucareli; and San Marcos de Neve, established in 1808, was located north of today's city of Gonzales. Neither community thrived. Salcedo's population was listed as ninety-two inhabitants in 1809, but no one lived there by 1813. San Marcos de Neve had a population of sixty-one in 1808, but a flood in June of that year, followed by Indian attacks, persuaded the luckless settlers in 1812 to relocate.

Trade with other frontier areas remained brisk, giving a needed boost to the province's fledgling market economy. Residents of Nacogdoches continued to violate government trade regulations, swayed by the demand for their goods east of the Sabine River; indeed, contraband trade seemed for the isolated community a necessary mode of survival. Natchitoches, Louisiana, was scarcely 100 miles away, seducing men like Gil Ybarbo, who carried on such a lucrative extralegal business that the government ultimately investigated and arrested him. Military troops dispatched to Nacogdoches in the mid-1790s hardly discouraged the contraband ventures, however. Neither were commandants able to prevent foreigners from migrating into the area. Soon after its founding, Nacogdoches had a population composed of various ethnic groups engaged as merchants, Indian traders, and ranchers, many of whom took Spanish wives and acclimated themselves to Spanish-Mexican culture. There, the only American trading company in Spanish territory functioned. With the endorsement of the royal government, the enterprise of Barr and Davenport sought to pacify the neighboring Indians and supply the needs of local soldiers.

For people in the interior, economic activity remained agrarian based, with ranching persisting as the most secure means of making a living. The business of trading horses and mules picked up within the province as well as between Louisiana and Texas during the 1770s, in part due to the success of the British colonies in their struggle for independence. Texas rancheros around San Antonio and La Bahía engaged in illegal intercolonial trade by exchanging their livestock for tobacco and other finished goods that made their way into Louisiana from the newly independent United States or from European countries. A new opportunity for those on the make appeared when the United States bought the Louisiana Territory from France, a move that brought Anglo-American settlers to the New Orleans region. The proceeds of clandestine commerce were not equitably distributed among all segments of Texas society, however, as the large rancheros benefitted primarily.

The king had ever prohibited such international trade, but during the 1770s he passed decrees regulating access to wild herds (including the levying of fees upon those rounding up mesteño stock), cattle branding, and the exportation of livestock. Then, he appointed governors who proved unduly firm in enforcing these laws. Furthermore, legal restrictions upon the rancheros and the reduction of the wild herds due to slaughtering and exportation by Tejanos produced economic difficulties, further angering the ranching elite. Over the years, the pobladores of Texas had developed an identity tied more to their daily necessities than to imperial designs that the authorities sought to implement. During the colonial era, they had survived almost on their own, living by their wits, even ignoring the king's decrees when they conflicted with immediate concerns. They had come to appreciate their semiautonomous relationship with the heartland, and now they resented what seemed an unnecessary intrusion into their personal affairs.

INDEPENDENCE FROM SPAIN

The Bourbon Reforms of the Enlightenment, which helped Spain make a remarkable recovery, produced resentment and discontent toward the mother country in New Spain. Over the centuries, Mexico had come to perceive itself as something greater than a mere colony. Thus, Mexicans resented the newly appointed peninsular administrators who practically monopolized the intendancy and tax-collection positions enacted by the reforms. Furthermore, they disliked the arrogant attitudes of the peninsulares, who insisted upon deference and even subservience to their positions. Naturally, the people resented these developments, but vexation did not signify a wish to overthrow the system, rather a desire to replace a bad government that denied them full participation.

It was, then, an imperial crisis that ultimately led the people of Mexico, already alienated by the Bourbon Reforms, to talk of doing something about their dependent status. Spain's European wars after 1789 sapped the colonies; stepped-up taxation and other forced contributions to the Crown produced financial distress. Mexicans denounced the injustices but, in the traditional manner, continued to pay homage to the king.

The drive for Mexican autonomy mounted following Napoleon's conquest of Spain in 1808. Spaniards resisted the French occupation on May 2 (*Dos de Mayo*), then organized a *Cortes* (parliament) to hold the land while the deposed King Ferdinand VII remained in exile. Copying the Iberian example, the Latin American colonies established *juntas* (committees) to protect the New World empire until Ferdinand could reassume the throne.

In New Spain, criollos in Querétaro (in the state of Querétaro) established a similar junta. Most had felt the pinch of Spain's money-raising measures during the era of the Napoleonic wars, among them a priest from Dolores, Guanajuato, named Miguel Hidalgo y Costilla. Suddenly exposed as a plotter to overthrow the peninsular officials who had been running Mexico since Napoleon's invasion of the Iberian Peninsula, Hidalgo opted for a war against bad government. Skirmishes broke out in Hidalgo's parish at Dolores on September 16, 1810 (*Diez y Seis de Septiembre*), and developed into the unexpected: a social revolution between the colony's elite and the downtrodden lower classes, many of the former being the criollos who themselves had planned to gain their independence from the peninsulares.

The revolt rippled into far-off Texas. Despite the distance between the core government and the frontier, the province never was so isolated that political winds blowing in the interior did not earn the notice of Tejanos. In Texas, one

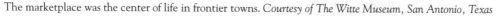

The marketplace was the center of life in frontier towns. *Courtesy of The Witte Museum, San Antonio, Texas*

Juan Bautista de las Casas, a military veteran, took up Hidalgo's cry, garnering the support of some of the soldiers in the Béxar presidio, members of the lower class in the city, and local rancheros who had been alienated by recent Crown policies. On January 22, 1811, Las Casas displaced the few official representatives of royalist government still living in Béxar. From the capital, the insurrection widened to other parts of the province. But Las Casas's rebellion had not gained the support of all Béxareños, and it soon encountered opposition from proroyalist forces in the city who ousted Las Casas on March 2, 1811. Given a trial in Coahuila, Las Casas received a death sentence and was shot in the back for treason; to remind would-be rebels of the penalty for challenging the status quo, royal officials sent his head to Béxar for public display. Meanwhile, Father Hidalgo, who was defeated in battle on March 21, 1811, also suffered execution.

The sympathy Tejanos displayed for the limited independence movement brought destruction to the province, for civil war did not end following the defeat of Las Casas. One Bernardo Gutiérrez de Lara assumed Hidalgo's revolutionary mantle. Apparently encouraged by U.S. officials wanting to develop an appropriate foreign policy toward New Spain once that country had achieved its independence, Gutiérrez de Lara worked to wrest Texas from royalist control. Accompanied by Augustus W. Magee, a former U.S. Army officer at Natchitoches, Louisiana, Gutiérrez forded the Sabine River in August 1812 at the head of the Republican Army of the North and captured Nacogdoches. Soon, the expedition exceeded 700 in number, attracting recruits from among Anglo volunteers in Louisiana and members of the local militia. From East Texas, the expedition marched toward Central Texas, captured San Antonio and La Bahía, and proclaimed Texas as an independent state in the spring of 1813. But in August, a royalist force led by José Joaquín Arredondo crushed the rebels south of San Antonio at the Battle of the Medina River. It was the bloodiest battle ever fought on Texas soil, with some 1,300 rebel soldiers killed. Soon thereafter, the royalists shot 327 suspected rebel sympathizers in San Antonio, and Nacogdoches became the scene of another bloody purge committed by one of Arredondo's lieutenants. The royalists now ravaged the ranchos, compelling many Tejanos to flee across the Sabine River into Louisiana. For the next several years, these agents of peninsular and criollo power dominated the region, living off the land and harassing the frontier people, most of whom sympathized with the insurgents. By 1821, when Spanish rule came to an end with New Spain achieving its independence, Nacogdoches, with much of its populace having fled, faced extinction as a community.

R E S I L I E N C E

Throughout the colonial era, the number of people who lived in Texas fluctuated, reaching the aforementioned figure of about 4,000 early in the nineteenth century, then dwindling to 2,240 (excluding soldiers) by 1821. Remarkably, these few thousand pobladores succeeded in transporting traits of their heritage into the next era. Numbers by themselves, therefore, are deceptive: they do not testify to enduring aspects of the Tejanos, among them a unique character as a people of the frontier. As already indicated, the central government of Spain did not strictly dictate life in the Far North. Relative isolation had always guaranteed a modicum of independence and honed the development of attitudes and skills necessary for survival in an unforgiving environment. Even the governor and other royal officials pursued a compromise with viceregal rule, adhering to the old dictum of *obedezco pero no cumplo* (I obey but do not comply). Military officials behaved no differently. And the Church, burdened as it was with debt and commitments to missionary work, could hardly have acted as an arm of the state.

The atmosphere in colonial Texas, therefore, encouraged informal community building. Tejanos sought their own economic ends by selecting the most convenient and profitable markets for their livestock; this meant turning to Louisiana and even to the United States to engage in contraband trade. The ayuntamiento at times acted as a legitimizing agent when local necessities clashed with imperial dictates. Such adjustments to circumstances at hand permitted Tejanos to survive quite well as a community after the end of Spain's presence in their land.

The Far North also produced traits of ruggedness that traversed cultures and nationhoods. Spaniards in the hinterlands carried the task of establishing roots and the responsibility of perpetuating their civilization hundreds of miles from previous settlements. On the range, settlers had to perfect their skills in handling horses to exact a livelihood from a predominantly ranching culture. This "Norteño" variety of Mexican culture, some historians hypothesize, resulted from these experiences. The north fostered egalitarianism, the will to work, an implied strength and prowess, as well as determination and courage in the face of danger.

At the end of its war for independence, which ended in 1821, then, New Spain effectively preserved traditions with origins in the Iberian Peninsula, which Tejanos transmitted past 1821. Some customs applied to the ranching economic order. Spanish-Mexican terminology, riding gear, and methods of working the range became etched into Anglo-American culture. Among familiar ranch terms are "buckaroo" from *vaquero*, "cinch" from *cincha*, "chaps" from *chaparejos*, "hoosegow" from *juzgado*, and "lasso" from *lazo*. The rodeo, a semiannual roundup of livestock to determine the ownership of free-ranging animals, evolved into a highly competitive sport in the Anglo period.

Also perpetuated were legal practices that had derived from Spanish precedent. Iberian laws, revised for application to frontier situations, allowed outsiders to become part of a family unit. Long-standing rules applicable to community property also lingered: couples shared jointly any assets they had accumulated while married; a woman could keep half of all financial gains the couple earned; and a husband could not dispose of the family's holdings without his wife's consent. Women also retained the right to negotiate contracts and manage their own financial affairs.

Corrida de la Sandía (Watermelon Race), part of the celebration of the Día de San Juan. *Theodore Gentilz,* Corrida de la Sandía, *Yanaguana Society Collection, Daughters of the Republic of Texas Library*

Furthermore, the Spanish tradition protecting debtors prevailed. Over the centuries, neither field animals nor agricultural implements could be confiscated by creditors, and in the subsequent era this safeguard applied to a debtor's home, work equipment and animals, and even his or her land.

The legacy of Spain to the Texas experience thus makes for an extensive list that runs the gamut from the esoteric, such as legal influences concerning water laws, to the prosaic. Among the latter are contributions to a bilingual society in various sections of the modern state of Texas, Spanish loan words (for example, mesquite and arroyo), delectable Spanish-Mexican foods, styles of dress, geographical nomenclature (every major river in Texas bears a Spanish name, for example), and architecture. Empires might wane, but their cultures endure.

While Spain's rule over Texas left a lasting imprint on the outpost, few Tejanos mourned its replacement in 1821 by an independent Mexico. Communities had valued their relative autonomy on the hinterland, but they had wanted better administration and military protection. Simultaneously, Tejanos resented the bureaucratic restrictions they believed discouraged profit making in ranching, farming, and other forms of commerce. Spain had not convinced many people to relocate into the wilderness region; a hard enough task given the fact that frontiers hold out few migational pull factors, nor did sufficient population pressures exist in the interior to push Mexicans northward. Yet some Tejanos saw the solution to their myriad problems—among them Indian depredations and economic underdevelopment—in the arrival of new settlers, in the spread of urban settlements, and in the growth of the pastoral industries. Thus, while Spain retained sovereignty over Texas for three hundred years and Hispanic culture endured there past 1821, Spain had left a community of people still groping to devise their own survival strategies, political and otherwise. Therefore, in the era of Mexican rule in Texas, 1821–1836, the pobladores would continue to pursue political solutions more appropriate to their local conditions and less relevant to their national government's political aims.

READINGS

Books and Dissertations

Almaráz, Félix D., *Tragic Cavalier: Governor Manuel Salcedo of Texas, 1808–1813* (College Station: Texas A&M University Press, 1992).

Bannon, John Francis, *The Spanish Borderlands Frontier, 1513–1821* (New York: Holt, Rinehart, and Winston, 1970).

Bolton, Herbert E., *Texas in the Middle Eighteenth Century* (1915; reprint Berkeley: University of California Press, 1977).

Castañeda, Carlos E., *Our Catholic Heritage in Texas, 1519–1936* (7 vols; Austin: Von Boeckmann-Jones Co., 1936–1958).

Chipman, Donald E., *Spanish Texas, 1519–1821* (Austin: University of Texas Press, 1992).

Chipman, Donald E., and Harriett Denise Joseph, *Notable Men and Women of Spanish Texas* (Austin: University of Texas Press, 1999).

de la Teja, Jesús F., *San Antonio de Béxar: A Community in New Spain's Northern Frontier* (Albuquerque: University of New Mexico Press, 1995).

Faulk, Odie B., *A Successful Failure* (Austin: Steck-Vaughn Co., 1965).

Hickerson, Nancy Parrott, *The Jumanos: Hunters and Traders of the South Plains* (Austin: University of Texas Press, 1994).

Hinojosa, Gilberto M., *A Borderlands Town in Transition: Laredo, 1755–1870* (College Station: Texas A&M University Press, 1983).

Jackson, Jack, *Los Mesteños: Spanish Ranching in Texas, 1721–1821* (College Station: Texas A&M University Press, 1986).

John, Elizabeth, *Storms Brewed in Other Men's Worlds: The Confrontation of Indians, Spanish, and French in the Southwest, 1540–1795* (College Station: Texas A&M University Press, 1975).

Jones, Oakah L., *Los Paisanos: Spanish Settlers on the Northern Frontier of New Spain* (Norman: University of Oklahoma Press, 1979).

La Vere, David, *The Caddo Chiefdoms: Caddo Economics and Politics, 1700–1835* (Lincoln: University of Nebraska Press, 1998).

MacLachlan, Colin M., and Jaime E. Rodríguez-O, *The Forging of the Cosmic Race: A Reinterpretation of Colonial Mexico* (Berkeley: University of California Press, 1980).

McReynolds, James Michael, "Family Life in a Borderlands Community: Nacogdoches, Texas, 1779–1861" (Ph.D. diss., Texas Tech University, 1978).

Moorhead, Max L., *The Presidio: Bastion of the Spanish Borderlands* (Norman: University of Oklahoma Press, 1975).

Myers, Sandra L., *The Ranch in Spanish Texas, 1691–1800* (El Paso: Texas Western Press, 1969).

Newcomb, William W., Jr., *The Indians of Texas: From Prehistoric to Modern Times* (Austin: University of Texas Press, 1961).

Poyo, Gerald E., and Gilberto M. Hinojosa, *Tejano Origins in Eighteenth-Century San Antonio* (Austin: University of Texas Press, 1991).

Ricklis, Robert A., *The Karankawa Indians of Texas: An Ecological Study of Cultural Tradition and Change* (Austin: University of Texas Press, 1996).

Smith, F. Todd, *The Caddo Indians: Tribes at the Convergence of Empire, 1542–1854* (College Station: Texas A&M University Press, 1995).

Tijerina, Andrew Anthony, "Tejanos and Texas: The Native Mexicans of Texas, 1820–1850" (Ph.D. diss., University of Texas at Austin, 1977).

Weber, David J., *The Mexican Frontier, 1821–1846: The United States Southwest under Mexico* (Albuquerque: University of New Mexico Press, 1982).

————, *The Spanish Frontier in North America* (New Haven, CT: Yale University Press, 1992).

Weddle, Robert S., *San Juan Bautista: Gateway to Spanish Texas* (Austin: University of Texas Press, 1968).

Wintz, Cary D., "Women in Texas," in *The Texas Heritage*, 3rd ed., edited by Ben Procter and Archie P. McDonald (Wheeling, IL: Harlan Davidson, Inc., 1998).

Articles

Bannon, John Francis, "The Mission as a Frontier Institution: Sixty Years of Interest and Research," *Western Historical Quarterly* 10 (July, 1979).

de la Teja, Jesús F., "Indians, Soldiers, and Canary Islanders: The Making of a Texas Frontier Community," *Locus* 3 (Fall, 1990).

Faulk, Odie B., "Ranching in Spanish Texas," *The Hispanic American Historical Review* 45 (May, 1965).

Poyo, Gerald E., and Gilberto M. Hinojosa, "Spanish Texas and Borderlands Historiography in Transition," *Journal of American History* 75 (September, 1988).

Tjarks, Alicia V., "Comparative Demographic Analysis of Texas, 1777–1793," *Southwestern Historical Quarterly* 77 (January, 1974).

MEXICAN TEXAS, 1821–1836

CHAPTER 3

The execution of Miguel Hidalgo in 1811 by royalist forces did not end New Spain's rebellion against the mother country. Another priest, José María Morelos, assumed command and committed the movement to a repudiation of the Spanish past. In Spain, meantime, the liberal *Cortes* (parliament) that had fought off Napoleon wrought changes upon the country. Heeding the ideals of the Enlightenment, Spaniards penned the Constitution of 1812; the document forced King Ferdinand to acknowledge the will of the Cortes and provided the means by which people could gain better representation at all levels of government. An absolutist, Ferdinand suspended the constitution upon returning from exile in 1814, and Morelos's capture and execution in 1815 spawned a royalist resurgence. Guerrilla bands carrying the Hidalgo/Morelos banner went underground for the next five years. Then, surprisingly, in 1820 liberalism returned to Spain when a military revolt coerced the king into reinstating the Constitution of 1812.

Alarmed, conservatives in New Spain—who had envisioned a nation retaining the basic foundations of the colonial era, but with themselves presiding over the society—considered independence preferable to living under a liberal rule that might well encourage the lower classes to challenge the social order. Agustín de Iturbide surfaced as the leader of this conservative faction, but he successfully recruited among the liberal resistance fighters, who shared with him and the other conservatives the belief that liberation would be for the common good. In 1821, New Spain's viceroy, realizing that the power of this expedient conservative/liberal coalition meant that the colony could not now be subordinated, recognized Mexico's independence.

Finally free from the Old World's yoke, Mexico confronted the task of forming its own kind of government. Liberals wished to mold a republic based on the liberal precepts of the Enlightenment and on the Constitution of 1812. The conservatives, however, disliked the egalitarian ideas that Enlightenment thinking put into the minds of the lower classes. In a conservative countermove,

Above: Detail from *Dawn at the Alamo* by H. A. McArdle. *Courtesy of The Texas State Library and Archives Commission*

Iturbide, who had been responsible for uniting all classes and political elements in Mexico behind the rallying cry of independence, centralized rule by establishing himself as emperor of Mexico. No sooner had he taken the throne, however, than he was denounced in the *Plan de Casa Mata* (February 1823), a liberal edict issued by a young military commander named Antonio López de Santa Anna. After successfully removing Iturbide from power in March 1823, the liberal supporters of the Plan de Casa Mata sought to solidify their victory by establishing a federalist republic.

Besides ideological differences over class distinctions, several other issues plagued the newly independent Mexico. These included economic chaos, the desire of military and Church officials to preserve their traditional standing alongside government, and the political inexperience of Mexico's new leaders.

Equally pressing was the need to defend the Far North from the United States. Texas, especially, had been the scene of an increased amount of activity by American adventurers since the close of the eighteenth century. In 1801, Spanish soldiers caught the mysterious Philip Nolan, an American who claimed to be looking for mustangs for subsequent sale in Louisiana. Nolan had no official permission to be in the area (present-day Hill County, historians believe), and the Spanish soldiers, suspecting Nolan of conspiring to acquire Texas and perhaps other parts of the Crown's northern empire, killed him. In 1806, the Spaniards repelled two U.S. encroachments into East Texas. One was a scientific expedition dispatched by President Thomas Jefferson to clarify the boundaries of the Louisiana Territory acquired by the United States in 1803; royal troops turned back the small party at Spanish Bluff in today's Bowie County. The second was an intrusion made by General James Wilkinson over the same disputed eastern boundary of Texas. Wilkinson and a Spanish commander avoided a major dispute when they mutually agreed to recognize a neutral ground between the Arroyo Hondo (a branch of the Red River close to where the presidio of Los Adaes once stood) and the Sabine River.

Then, in 1819, the Spaniards faced an attempt by Dr. James Long and a force of fellow filibusters to wrest Texas from Mexico. This endeavor apparently had the backing of a group of Natchez entrepreneurs who were upset over the passage of the Transcontinental Treaty of 1819. Under the terms of the Louisiana Purchase of 1803, many Americans believed, the United States had bought lands that extended west from Louisiana into Texas. But the Transcontinental Treaty established the Sabine River as the dividing line between the United States and Spanish Texas. The agreement led many land-hungry southerners to make the argument that the United States had "surrendered" Texas in order to acquire Florida from Spain. Taking it upon themselves to "reclaim" Texas from Spain, Long's small army of filibusters was not quelled until October 1821, when Spanish troops apprehended Long and took him to a prison in Mexico City. The whole Long incident created enormous distrust of Americans by Spanish (and later Mexican) officials.

IMMIGRATION

Past trespasses into Mexico's Far North amounted to relatively little compared to new threats in the 1820s from expansionists in the United States. Defense of the Texas frontier appeared urgent for Mexico, and a government-directed colonization of the area seemed to be the best way to deter the land-hungry Americans. After careful consideration, the short-lived Iturbide government turned to plans that would entice European and Anglo-American settlers into Texas, hoping they would serve as Mexican-citizen buffers against the indios bárbaros as well as the citizens of other nations then threatening the province.

Mexico decided to allow the formal immigration of Americans to Texas for at least three reasons. First, the Spanish government had already set precedent. In 1788, for instance, Spain had experimented with a defensive immigration policy to attract Anglo frontierspeople from the American West into Louisiana, but it suspended the plan in the 1790s when the newly arrived Americans resisted accepting Spanish customs and traditions. Then, following the Transcontinental Treaty, when the United States abandoned all claims to Texas, Spain once more turned to its previous policy of defensive immigration. In January 1821, the Spanish government agreed to a proposal by Moses Austin to let him oversee the settlement of American citizens in Texas. According to the contract, Austin was to relocate 300 Catholic families from the United States to Texas in exchange for a huge personal grant of Texas lands. Since the start of the nineteenth century, Austin had prospered in lead mining in Missouri (once part of Spanish Upper Louisiana). Then the Panic of 1819 had wiped him out, and now he hoped that the Texas venture would help him recover financially. Second, by this time, Mexican liberals had come to regard the missions as liabilities that added to the power of the Church and encouraged its intervention in governmental affairs. Since the liberals no longer wished to support the missions as colonizing institutions, they looked for alternative ways to people the North. Third, security in Texas and the Far North appeared to rest on foreign immigration. With about 6 million inhabitants settled over an expanse reaching from California to Central America, Mexico lacked the manpower to occupy its vast territory. The war for independence, moreover, had deprived Mexico of many of its younger people.

Upon Moses Austin's death (in Missouri) on June 10, 1821, his son, Stephen F. Austin, assumed the Austin contract, the Spanish-born

Stephen F. Austin. *The Center for American History, The University of Texas at Austin, CN 01436*

governor of Texas, Antonio Martínez, having recognized its legality. Prospective colonists (some of them slave owners) began to arrive in the settlement by the end of 1821, as authorized. However, in March 1822, Martínez received word that independent Mexico no longer recognized Austin's colonization contract. Compelled to press his claim in the nation's capital, Austin journeyed to Mexico City.

On January 3, 1823, the tottering government of Iturbide approved the Imperial Colonization Law. Though it lasted only as long as Iturbide remained in power, the legislation authorized Stephen F. Austin to proceed with his plans to import families under the original agreement made between his father and the Spanish government.

His right to locate the full complement of 300 families in Texas established, Austin left Mexico City in April 1823 and returned to his colony to find the settlers he had left there in a state of uncertainty. Attacks by the Karankawas, food shortages, and other misfortunes had convinced many of the first wave of settlers to depart. Those who had "toughed it out" awaited word on the recognition of the Austin contract. Others who had moved into the colony since early 1822, when Mexico had ceased to recognize Austin's right to settle families, similarly hoped that Austin would get his concessions officially sanctioned by the government in Mexico City, so that their presence in Texas might be legalized. Austin regrouped and renewed his call for colonists to fill his contract's allotment. By the end of the summer of 1824, the land commissioner, Baron de Bastrop, who originally had helped Moses Austin get his contract, had approved most of Stephen F. Austin's remaining land titles. Some historians refer to the settlers who helped Austin complete his first contract as the Old Three Hundred. San Felipe de Austin, on the Brazos River, became Austin Colony's principal settlement; it lay some eighty miles from the Gulf, or about sixty miles from today's Houston (and should not be confused with Austin, the present-day capital of Texas).

The Colonization Laws of Mexico

Of all the empresarios who applied for contracts, only Austin profited from the law of 1823, for Iturbide's downfall in March of that year annulled the program. The peopling of Texas, therefore, occurred mainly under the National Colonization Law of August 18, 1824, which, though establishing certain restrictions for colonization, left the individual states of Mexico with complete control over immigration and the disposal of public lands. The legislation instructed the states, however, to remain within the limits of the national constitution. Even though general sentiment in Mexico scorned human bondage, the law did not directly prohibit the importation of slaves or outlaw slavery.

The National Colonization Law of 1824 emanated from a developing federalist-liberal philosophy advanced by men who planned the creation of a republic based on the principles of the American Revolution and the Spanish Constitution of 1812. Their leaders included Valentín Gómez Farías of Zacatecas and Lorenzo de Zavala of Yucatán. Conservatives, supported by the clergy, major landholders, and the military—all of whom espoused a strong central government—opposed the rising Federalists. Using the unfulfilled dream of establishing a republic and the abdication of Iturbide to their advantage, the liberals created the Federal Constitution of the United States of Mexico on October 4, 1824. The republican document sought to satisfy regional interests by giving states control over their own internal affairs and by diluting the power of the national government. As its framers had hoped, the new document resembled the U.S. Constitution in many ways as well as borrowed from the Spanish Constitution of 1812. Among those signing the new constitution was the forty-two-year-old Tejano ranchero Erasmo Seguín.

In the north, the national government united the two old Spanish provinces of Coahuila and Texas into one state (*Coahuila y Texas*). Via a decree issued in early 1825 by the state constitutional congress at Saltillo, then functioning as a legislature while it drew up a constitution for the new state, Texas from the Nueces to the Sabine River became a *departamento* (called the "Department of Texas"). It was to be presided over by a *jefe político* (political chief) appointed by the governor of the state. This jefe politico was responsible for overseeing Texas's defense (including the command of local militias), education, taxes, censuses, and elections, as well as for enforcing the laws and supervising the ayuntamientos. When, on March 11, 1827, the congress finally promulgated the new constitution, this agreement was incorporated into the Coahuiltejano government. Furthermore, the legislature allowed two deputies for Texas, with provisions to add more as the population of the province grew.

Also decreed by the provisional state constitutional congress was the State Colonization Law of March 24, 1825. Through this measure, the legislature sought to achieve several goals, namely the peopling of Coahuila and Texas, the encouragement of farming and ranching in the state, and the stimulation of commercial activity. The plan permitted the immigration of Anglo Americans into Texas, but it tried to prod Mexicans into moving north by giving them priority in land acquisition. For modest fees, heads of families qualified to obtain a league or *sitio* (4,428.4 acres) of grazing land and a *labor* (177.1 acres) of farming land. Immigrants were temporarily exempted from paying tariffs or custom duties. Provisions required all new residents of Coahuila and Texas who were not already Mexican citizens to take an oath declaring that they would abide by the federal and state constitutions and promise to observe the Christian religion. The legislature made no explicit mention of Catholicism: it was simply understood that the people of Mexico practiced no other religion. After agreeing to said conditions and establishing residence by obtaining lands, the land grantees were regarded by the government as naturalized Mexicans. The wording of the Colonization Law of 1825 was so vague, however, that it did not immediately prohibit the importation of slaves.

Negotiations for land titles could be handled individually or through immigration agents, or *empresarios*, who acted in behalf of the state government to select colonists, allocate land, and see to the enforcement of the laws in the colonies they helped to found. As compensation for their work, empresarios qualified personally to receive five leagues and five labores (a total of 23,027.5 acres) for each 100 families they settled in Texas.

Empresario Contracts

Between 1821 and 1835, a total of forty-one empresario contracts were signed, permitting some 13,500 families to come to Texas. Anglo Americans from the United States entered into most of these contracts.

By 1825, Stephen F. Austin had nearly completed the terms of his first contract, and that year the government made a second agreement with him to settle

Published in *The Historical Atlas of Texas* by A. Ray Stephens and William Holmes. *Copyright © 1989 by the University of Oklahoma Press. Reprinted by permission.*

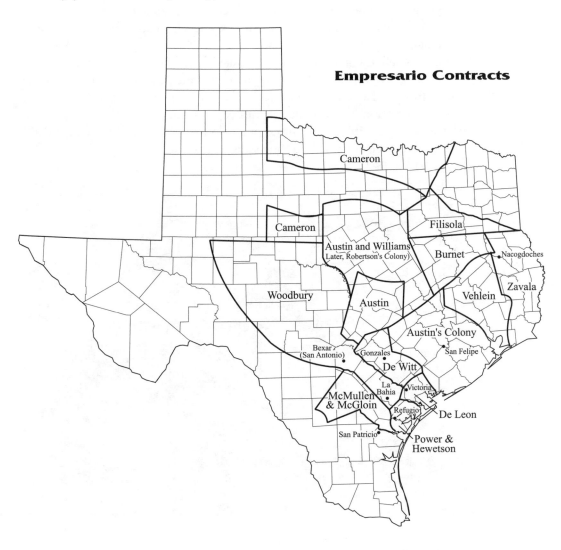

500 families. Two years later, he negotiated to locate another 100 families in what is today Bastrop County. In 1828, Austin obtained another land deal, and in 1831 he received his last contract. Actually, Austin only complied fully with his first contract and never came close to meeting his obligations on the other four. He used part of his grants for speculating purposes, but for that matter, so did the other land agents and even some settlers who sought to turn a profit from the Mexican government's generosity.

To the west of Austin's original lands, between the Guadalupe and Lavaca Rivers, Green DeWitt planted a colony with its center at Gonzales. This contract expired in 1831, however, by which time DeWitt had settled only about one-third of the 400 families he had pledged to bring. Bordering the DeWitt colony to the southeast lay the tract belonging to the rancher Martín de León. Issued at San Antonio in 1824 (even before the enactment of the Colonization Law of 1825), this grant had ill-defined boundaries, which caused some disputes between de León's and DeWitt's settlers, at least until DeWitt's land became part of the public domain in 1832. De León's colony, with its principal settlement at Victoria, remained small, though titles had been issued to 162 families by 1835.

Most other empresarial colonies achieved only moderate success in the 1820s. In 1825, Robert Leftwich received (for a cooperative venture called the Texas Association of Nashville, Tennessee) a contract to settle lands situated northwest of Austin's lands, but no one colonized them until the early 1830s, when a Tennessean named Sterling C. Robertson took over as empresario for

Martín de León. *The UT Institute of Texan Cultures, No. 72-1799, San Antonio Light Collection*

the Texas Association. Farther east, Haden Edwards's colonization contract called for 800 families to settle around the Nacogdoches region, but following his armed uprising in 1826 against government officials (the so-called Fredonian Rebellion, discussed below) his vacated land reverted to the state. Part of Edwards's tract went to David G. Burnet, and another portion of it went to a German merchant named Joseph Vehlein in 1826. Lorenzo de Zavala, one of the framers of the Mexican Constitution of 1824, received land along the Sabine River in 1829, but he never colonized it.

THE NATIVE MEXICANS OF TEXAS

As Anglo settlers arrived in East Texas, the native Mexicans were, according to historian Andrés A. Tijerina, experiencing a resurrection in fortunes following the devastation of the war for independence. Ranches between Béxar and La Bahía (called Goliad after 1829—from an anagram of the name Hidalgo) were reestablished in the mid-1820s along the entire stretch and on both sides of the San Antonio River and its tributaries. These ranches belonged to Texas Mexicans of wealth and status, like Martín de León of Victoria, Erasmo and Juan N. Seguín of Béxar, and Carlos de la Garza of Goliad. In Nacogdoches, a few brave souls had held the town together throughout the upheaval of the 1810s, and by 1823 a steady flow of the Mexican population into Nacogdoches and the surrounding district was apparent. In the 1830s, Nacogdoches consisted of a small town surrounded by approximately fifty founding ranchos. In South Texas, the Trans-Nueces ranching frontier spread northward from the Rio Grande in the 1820s to cover the present counties of Willacy, Kenedy, Brooks, Jim Hogg, Duval, Jim Wells, and Kleberg, with its northern point at Nueces County. Ten years later, approximately 350 rancherías (small family-operated concerns) existed in this region, many of which provided the foundations for future Texas towns.

ANGLOS AND THE MEXICAN GOVERNMENT

Anglos, whether they had entered Texas legally or illegally (most of those fleeing debts or the law in the United States arrived in Texas independently rather than under the guidance of an empresario), began to worry the Mexican government. For one thing, many of the Anglos were not taking their Mexican nationality seriously. Situated mainly in the eastern areas or the predominately Tejano settlements and ranchos of San Antonio and Goliad, the Americans went about conducting their affairs in ways that made the Mexican government uneasy: squatting on unoccupied lands; engaging in smuggling; applying American practices to local situations; speculating with their properties, and otherwise violating the conditions (and oath) under which they had been allowed to settle. Their independent attitude manifested itself at Nacogdoches as early as 1826, when the empresario Haden Edwards proclaimed the independence of the region, his so-called Fredonian Republic. For months, disputes had developed between the old settlers in Nacogdoches and Edwards's colonists over land titles; a break from Mexico, thought Benjamin Edwards—Haden's brother and the actual leader of the insurrection—would resolve the conflict in favor of the newcomers. But the armed revolt collapsed when more successful, foreign-born colonists denounced the affair and Austin led his colony's militia, along with Mexican officials, to Nacogdoches to suppress it. Nonetheless, the episode heightened concerns in Mexico that further American immigration might dissolve Mexico's hold on Texas; meanwhile in Texas, immigrants became distrustful of a government that voided an empresario contract without due process of law.

In order to evaluate how the national government might best deal with the troubles in Texas, Mexico dispatched Manuel de Mier y Terán, a high-ranking military officer and trained engineer, to the north. Crossing into Texas in 1828, Mier y Terán reported that the province was flooded with Anglo Americans, that Nacogdoches had essentially become an American town, that prospects for assimilation of the Anglos into Mexican culture appeared dim, and that the Anglo settlements generally resisted obeying the colonization laws. Once back in Mexico, his concerns over American immigrant loyalty mounted, and his fear that Mexico might indeed lose Texas to the newcomers intensified. Mier y Terán's recommendations spurred the drafting and implementation of the Law of April 6, 1830.

The Law of April 6, 1830, intended to stop further immigration into Texas from the United States by declaring uncompleted empresario agreements as void, although Mier y Terán let stand as valid those contracts belonging to men who had already brought in 100 families. Thus, Americans could still immigrate to Texas legally, but only into colonies such as those of Austin or DeWitt; these were about the only two empresario grants that met the general's requirement, and neither was filled to capacity. Furthermore, future American immigrants must not settle in any territory bordering the United States. New presidios, garrisoned by convicts serving out their prison sentences through military service, were established to check any such illegal immigration. Finally, the Law banned the further importation of slaves into Texas.

Actually, on September 15, 1829, President Vicente Guerrero had issued a directive abolishing slavery throughout the country. (Guerrero's gesture notwithstanding, slavery in Mexico would continue until the 1850s, though never as a legal institution.) Concerned about an immigration policy that seemed to be going astray, Guerrero had sought to dissuade Anglos from further colonization altogether by depriving them of their enslaved workforce. Political resistance from various quarters in Coahuila and Texas, however, ended up persuading Guerrero to except Texas from his national emancipation decree. Now, only seven months later, the Law of April 6, 1830, reinstated the ban on bringing human chattel into Texas—a point not lost on the American immigrants.

José Antonio Navarro. Painting by Dee Hernández, *The UT Institute of Texan Cultures*, No. 68-465

MEXICAN AND AMERICAN CAPITALISTS

It was a rising class of capitalists from Coahuila and Texas who had convinced Guerrero to excuse their state from the antislavery law. Leaders of this coalition were the statesmen from Parras and Monclova in Coahuila, José María Viesca and his brother Agustín. In the 1820s, the Viesca faction belonged to the liberal Federalist party struggling to maintain control in Mexican politics. Their leaders at the national level were revolutionary veterans such as Guadalupe Victoria, Lorenzo de Zavala, and Vicente Guerrero, as well as intellectuals like Valentín Gómez Farías. Their antagonists were members of the Centralist party, who were usually conservatives bent on securing the traditional power of the military and the Catholic Church.

According to Tijerina, the Viesca faction was committed to achieving economic prosperity through the state colonization program of 1825 and other means. Through legislation, they obtained exemptions from taxes on cotton, foreign imports, and domestic items for use by colonists and residents of Coahuila and Texas. They granted citizenship and special concessions to many Anglo Americans, among them the entrepreneur James Bowie, who acquired a textile mill permit. These liberals posited that slave labor was necessary for the economic advancement of the state.

Meanwhile, Stephen F. Austin's plan for developing the cotton industry in Texas paralleled the ambitions of the liberal Coahuiltejanos, who, seeing their own prosperity in the cultivation of cotton, worked strenuously to have slavery legitimized. An early victory came in a decree passed on May 5, 1828, that validated contracts of servitude made in foreign countries by immigrants to Coahuila and Tejas. Sponsored by the Texas delegate José Antonio Navarro, the new law provided for Anglo-American colonists to bring slaves into Texas as permanently indentured servants. Support for passing this legislation was generated by the same coalition of Coahuiltejanos and Anglos that had mobilized in 1829 to have Texas exempted from the Guerrero decree.

THE LAW OF APRIL 6, 1830, RESISTED

The Law of April 6, 1830, passed by Centralists following a conservative coup in late 1829, posed a dilemma for the liberal Coahuiltejanos, for they now fell out of step with both national and state politics. Committed to stopping

Anglo-American immigration and slavery, the Centralists preferred counter-colonization from the Mexican interior or from Europe. Stepping up their initiative, the conservatives reinforced presidios at San Antonio, Goliad, and Nacogdoches and commissioned the building of more garrisons, among the most important of which were Velasco, at the mouth of the Brazos River, and Anahuac, founded just above Galveston Bay. Situated near the Gulf Coast, these two were to discourage the infiltration of illegal immigrants by sea.

The liberals resisted these conservative policies. When the state congress expelled one of the Texas delegates in September 1830, the ayuntamientos of Béxar, Goliad, and San Felipe de Austin proclaimed that only the appropriate constituents would determine whether their deputy would serve. In this way, the Tejanos were committing themselves to the liberal, Federalist standard and the Viesca faction.

Among Anglos, a radical faction of the Federalists, which has come to be known in Texas history as the "war party," emerged from the outrage over the Law of April 6. In the summer of 1832, friction between settlers and authorities trying to enforce recently instituted policies regulating commerce in the Gulf ports and the collection of new tariffs reached a high pitch at the military post in Anahuac. Colonel Juan Davis Bradburn, an Anglo-American adventurer who had joined the Centralist cause in Mexico, arrested the lawyer William Barret Travis when the latter attempted a ruse to secure the release of two runaway slaves that Bradburn had in protective custody. In response to Travis's arrest, vigilantes gathered to call for his release. When Bradburn refused to surrender his prisoner, the colonists, accustomed to the Anglo-American tradition of the separation of military and civilian law, and to trial by jury, labelled Bradburn a despot.

Consequently, in June of 1832, a party of Anglo Texans from around Anahuac and the port town of Brazoria marched on Bradburn's garrison. A full-scale battle seemed imminent, but, while waiting for reinforcements, the Anglos issued a document known as the Turtle Bayou Resolutions on June 13, 1832, which cleverly argued that their actions at Anahuac were not an uprising but a demand for their constitutional rights as Mexican citizens, adding that their cause was in sympathy to that of the Federalists and their leader, Antonio López de Santa Anna, then attempting to overthrow the Centralists, the party to which Bradburn belonged. Higher military officials avoided further bloodshed at Anahuac by replacing Bradburn and releasing Travis and others whom Bradburn had arrested.

At this time, however, the radical war party failed to garner popular endorsement; indeed, many Texans condemned the group as adventurers. Most Texans belonged to a "peace party," led by Austin, which preferred to work for solutions to settlers' grievances via established political channels. Hence, on October 1, 1832, delegates from several Anglo settlements met at San Felipe de Austin and drafted petitions requesting certain concessions from the national government, among them the removal of the article in the Law of April 6, 1830, that severely limited immigration.

This meeting, or consultation, was out of order and was so identified by Ramón Músquiz, the political chief in Béxar, though he sympathized with the protesters. Regardless of their grievances, he admonished, such meetings were outside the law; in the Spanish-Mexican tradition, protests originated in the ayuntamientos, not in extralegal conventions of citizens. Músquiz therefore refused to forward the peace party's petitions to the governor, so its convention of 1832 bore no fruit.

In late 1832, leading citizens of Béxar, among them Juan N. Seguín and José María Balmaceda, met in San Antonio to express their own grievances to Saltillo, the state capital. They complained about the constant intervention of the national government in the state colonization program and contended that the Law of April 6, 1830, threatened to dissuade useful capitalists from moving into Texas. They further demanded bilingual administrators, more judges, better militia protection from hostile Indians, and certain tax exemptions for businesses. These complaints, along with the October petition from Austin's group, were part of the groundswell of federalism pervasive throughout Mexico in 1832.

The Tejanos' petition was endorsed by the ayuntamientos of Goliad, Nacogdoches, and San Felipe, and Political Chief Músquiz submitted it to the governor, explaining that the Tejanos' boisterous tone was designed to remedy a situation that might otherwise lead the Anglos to try to separate Tejas from Coahuila. What Tejanos wanted, he assured the governor, were reforms, not the creation of their own state. The Tejanos understood that should Texas become a separate state with its own legislature, Anglo Americans, who already outnumbered the native Mexicans, would dominate politics.

Since little had come out of the Anglos' consultation of 1832, another was held at San Felipe de Austin the next year. But those attending the second meeting included new leaders who opposed Austin's position of caution and conciliation with Mexico. Among the new group were the brothers William and John Wharton, David G. Burnet, and the former governor of Tennessee, Sam Houston, who had arrived recently in Texas. Scholars attribute different motives to Houston's immigration, from attempts to buy up all the stock remaining in the Leftwich contract (he had been among those investing in the Texas Association in 1822), to an honest desire to start anew in Texas, perhaps as a landholder, a lawyer, or a politician. Overall, this second consultation desired the division of Coahuila y Tejas, maintaining that a separated Texas would enjoy political autonomy to make decisions affecting its own well-being. As things stood, Coahuila had nine times the population of Texas, and its representatives in the legislature could easily checkmate the Texans on crucial issues. Upon adjourning, the second consultation entrusted Erasmo Seguín, Stephen F. Austin, and Dr. James B. Miller of San Felipe with taking the grievances to Mexico City. Of the three, only Austin made the long journey to the capital.

LIBERALS IN POWER

In January 1833, Santa Anna ushered in a brief liberal era in Mexican politics when he was elected president as a Federalist. Back in favor, the liberals in Coahuila y Tejas and the Viesca brothers immediately arranged for the state legislature to petition the national government for the repeal of the Law of April 6, 1830. Now they had more helpful allies in Mexico City, among them Gómez Farías, whom Santa Anna appointed as his acting president before retreating to his hacienda in Vera Cruz, and Lorenzo de Zavala, the legislator from Yucatán who still held interests in Texas lands for which he sought settlers from the United States. Working alongside the Federalists in Mexico City was Stephen F. Austin, who had arrived there following the consultation of April 1833. Ultimately, effective May 1834, Mexico's senate revoked the section in the Law of April 6, 1830, that had curtailed the immigration of Anglos into the Mexican nation.

Austin failed, however, to gain the separation of Coahuila and Texas. And when officials discovered letters between him and the San Antonio ayuntamiento encouraging Texas's separation from Coahuila, they threw Austin in prison (early in 1834). Nonetheless, the state and national governments abided by their previous stand on colonization, and liberal legislation continued to emanate from Coahuila. New acts recognized the acceptance of English as a legal language of the state, permitted the extension of empresario contracts, expanded the number of local courts, and provided for trial by jury. The Coahuilan legislature also raised Texas's representation in the state congress and increased the number of departments in Texas to three. Actually, the district of Nacogdoches, which extended from the watershed between the Brazos and the Trinity Rivers to the Sabine, had been created in 1831 to accommodate the rise in the Anglo population. In order to allow more self-autonomy in the province, the legislature in 1834 established the department of Brazos, with its capital at San Felipe de Austin, which extended from the Nacogdoches district to a north-south line from the coast to the Red River, just east of the Béxar and Goliad settlements. The third zone, the department of Béxar, included San Antonio and extended to the Nueces River.

THE INEFFECTIVENESS OF THE LAW OF APRIL 6, 1830

These changes point starkly to the ineffectiveness of the Law of April 6, 1830. Since Mexican officials had not been strict in interpreting the provisions of the decree, Anglos had continued to come into those colonies whose empresarios had imported the minimum 100 families by the time the Centralists enacted the Law. Also, two empresario groups from Ireland persisted in their efforts to complete contracts they had acquired in the late 1820s; Centralists, after all, looked favorably upon European immigration as a way to people Texas. James McGloin and John McMullen brought several Irish families to the Nueces River area and founded San Patricio in 1831. Three years later, James Power and James Hewetson located colonists in the place that became modern-day Refugio, Texas.

Furthermore, the Galveston Bay and Texas Land Company, a land-speculating corporation from the eastern United States that the empresarios Vehlein, Burnet, and de Zavala had commissioned to complete their contracts, continued to advertise the availability of its properties in Texas, even though the Law of April 6, 1830, had prohibited the further disposal of such lands. Thus, the company sold invalid land certificates to buyers. Despite the company's fraudulent activities, it brought several European families into Texas in the early 1830s, whom, since they were not Americans, Mexican officials ultimately accepted and resettled elsewhere in Texas.

In addition, Sterling C. Robertson, still representing the Texas Association of Nashville, continued to claim ownership of the original Leftwich contract. Though Stephen F. Austin contested the contract, convincing the legislature at one point that the Robertson contract was invalid and that it should therefore be allotted to himself, Robertson persuaded the authorities in 1834 that he had brought to Texas the required 100 families before the Law of April 6, 1830, had been effected. Despite the dispute, Robertson successfully settled numerous families while the Centralists remained in power.

Finally, many immigrants had arrived in Texas illegally during the early 1830s, hoping to start afresh as merchants, lawyers, land speculators, politicians, squatters, trappers, miners, artisans, smugglers, or as jacks-of-all trades. But with the dilution of the Law of April 6, 1830, the stream of Anglo American immigration into Texas became a torrent. By 1834, it is estimated that the number of Anglo Americans and their slaves reached over 20,700. This figure might well have represented the doubling of the number of Americans in Texas just since 1830.

A Multicultural Society

Anglos

As one would expect, the number of towns in Texas increased—from three in 1821 to twenty-one by 1835, most of them inhabited by the Anglo newcomers. The principal towns included San Felipe de Austin, in Stephen F. Austin's first colony, Gonzales, in Green DeWitt's grant, Velasco, on the Brazos (near present-day Freeport), and Matagorda, on the mouth of the Colorado River.

For all Texans, life consisted of a battle for survival, largely against the same odds the pobladores had faced before 1821. Basic goods such as clothing, blankets, and footwear were not readily available in Texas, but many immigrants had known enough to bring such items with them. Material for homemade apparel came either from animal skins or from cloth made on a spinning wheel, which a few persons had managed to import. Necessarily, the colonists used local resources such as stones, mud, or timber to construct log cabins or other types of shelter that ordinarily consisted of no more than two rooms (with dirt floors). Pioneers similarly lived off the land, hunted wild game, fished, planted small gardens, and gathered natural produce such as nuts and berries.

Anglos managed to convert parts of their grants into farmsteads, though agriculture as a gainful enterprise in Texas developed sluggishly. Early on, farming earned one barely the minimum standard of living, but by the late 1820s, cash-crop farming in Austin's colony and sections of East Texas began reaping better rewards. With slaves and imported technology at their disposal, some Anglos planted and processed cotton for new markets outside the province. One prominent scholar estimates that Anglos' farms by 1834 shipped about 7,000 bales of cotton (to New Orleans) valued at some $315,000.

Because hard currency did not circulate in the province, people bartered to obtain needed commodities and services, using livestock, otter and beaver pelts, and even land to complete their transactions. Improvising, Anglos found numberless ways to earn an income, among them smuggling. The tariff laws that exempted Anglo products during the 1820s had not applied to all imports (generally, codes excluded household goods and implements), so Anglos brought merchandise illegally into Texas. From there, some even brazenly shipped the products south to Mexican states or west to New Mexico.

Goods moving out of the province included corn, the skins of deer and bears, salted meats, and even timber from East Texas. The latter enterprise amounted to no more than a local activity undertaken to meet the needs of the people around Nacogdoches, but some of the lumber found its way to buyers as far away as Matamoros.

To further their education, the foreigners established numerous schools in the 1820s and 1830s. They patterned the schools after institutions similar to ones they had known in the southern United States. Private enterprise provided the funds for children's education (public schooling did not exist during that era), both at the elementary and secondary levels. Older students attended academies or boarding schools, which were private institutions established by religious groups, local residents, immigrant teachers (often women) of certain communities who wanted a place in which to practice their profession, or by individuals seeking a profit. In Texas, education suffered the limitations of the frontier. Instructors were never plentiful, private homes usually had to serve as makeshift educational facilities, and schoolhouses, where they existed, were often little more than simple structures constructed from pine logs. Colonists who could afford to do so sent their children to schools in the United States.

Printing in Texas had started in the 1810s with the first and probably the only issue of *La Gaceta de Tejas*, printed to spread republican ideas that might help Mexico liberate itself from Spain. But the first successful press in Texas was established in 1829 in Austin's colony by Godwin Brown Cotten. His newspaper, named the *Texas Gazette*, served Austin in his determination to assure the host country of Anglo American loyalty and to remind the colonists of the gratitude they owed to Mexico. Although the *Gazette* ceased publication in 1832, other papers continued to spread the news to Anglo Texans.

Although Anglos had agreed to observe the Catholic religion in order to qualify as Mexican citizens, the Church neglected them because of, among other things, a shortage of priests. Hence, many Anglo settlers held illicit church services and (religious) camp meetings. Lacking priests, the people in Austin's colony conducted their own civil ceremonies when necessary, though in 1831 and 1832 the Irish-born Father Michael Muldoon did tend to the community as the resident clergyman. He reported the colonists as faithful to Catholicism, but he wed couples who had already been living together outside of Church-sanctioned marriages. For a brief time after 1834, at least, the settlers did not have to be so cautious about their religious practices, for the state government conceded them freedom of conscience.

Anglos defended themselves by organizing local militias, ready volunteer companies authorized by the Mexican government as alternatives to standing armies. These were necessary given the government's inability to provide the settlers adequate protection. In 1825, the garrisons at San Antonio and Goliad had only 59 men; by 1832 the government had managed to raise that number to about 140, but only half of these Texas soldiers were formally prepared for military action. Unlike Austin's, most of the colonies failed to establish their own militia as was prescribed by law. Instead, they relied on volunteer companies of a temporary nature; such units evolved into the organization of the Texas Rangers by July 1835.

Blacks

For black people, life on the Mexican frontier differed radically from that of their counterparts during the Spanish colonial era. As already noted, Anglos had, in the guise of contract labor, been able to perpetuate slavery despite Mexican disapproval. Neither the Law of April 6, 1830, nor a state decree issued in 1832 to weaken negotiated servant contracts deterred some of the immigrants from bringing slaves into Texas surreptitiously. Anglos argued that the economic development of the province depended on slave labor, and both Tejano oligarchs and liberal politicians in Coahuila seconded this position. While many Mexican officials genuinely believed in the cruelty and immorality of the institution, they somehow consistently accepted the argument that the province could not grow and prosper without it.

By 1836, the number of slaves in Texas numbered about 5,000. Most slaves lived on the Anglo plantations located in the productive lands adjacent to the Brazos, Colorado, and Trinity Rivers, although slavery did exist around Nacogdoches and in other fledgling Anglo communities along the Red River.

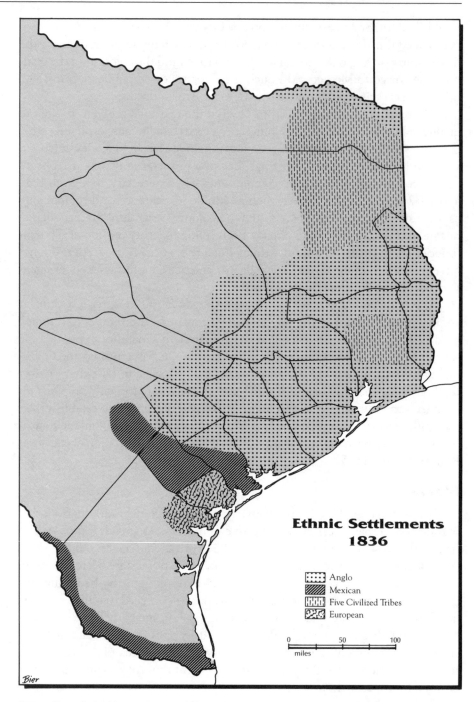

**Ethnic Settlements
1836**

Anglo
Mexican
Five Civilized Tribes
European

0   50   100

miles

Bier

*Source: Terry G. Jordan, "A Century and a Half of Ethnic Change in Texas." Southwestern
Historical Quarterly, 89 (April, 1986). Courtesy Texas State Historical Association, Austin, Texas*

The peculiar institution arrived in Texas with all its southern trappings, for whites sought to recreate it just as it existed in the United States. As in the South, where society delineated strict roles for the disparate races, in Texas many Anglos considered blacks a racially inferior people suited to a life of strenuous labor and servitude. As far as these people were concerned, black persons could be bought and sold, hired out, counted as part of one's assets, and bequeathed to relatives. To control the slave population, whites followed tried and tested policies, including the liberal use of the lash. Slaves attempted to alleviate their condition by running away when possible, often seeking refuge among the Indian tribes of East Texas or in the Mexican settlements of the nation's interior.

Tejanos

Hispanic Texans, many of them descendants of the first colonizers and presidial soldiers assigned to garrisons throughout the Spanish period, lived in the ranching areas of Central and South Texas. In the latter area, they occupied lands granted to them since the 1770s but also ones acquired from the state of Tamaulipas as late as the early 1830s. Most Tejanos, however, continued living in the older cities established in the eighteenth century. The Tejano urban settlements included: San Antonio, which had a Hispanic population of 2,500 in 1835; Goliad, with 700 in 1834; and Nacogdoches, reporting a figure of 537 Mexicans in 1835. Additionally, Tejanos resided near Goliad, in the nascent town of Victoria founded in 1824 by the empresario Martín de León. By 1830 the population of Victoria had grown to 248, and to 300 four years later. On the Rio Grande, Laredo consisted of about 2,000 predominately Hispanic residents in 1835.

In the towns, people tried to make a living in a variety of ways. Merchants, especially in San Antonio, sojourned to the Mexican states below the Rio Grande to acquire finished goods such as clothing and household items for resale in the province. Tradespeople met both civilian and military needs as tailors, blacksmiths, and barbers. Poor people, most of them *peones* (commoners), did whatever task people would pay them to perform, including work on nearby ranches.

In the countryside, rancheros still took to the open range to round up mesteños, though by this time government regulation impeded efforts to make a profitable living in this way. Nonetheless, the rancheros around San Antonio clandestinely captured wild horses and cattle and invented clever ways to sell the stock to soldiers, fellow Béxareños, and even Anglo Americans. Alternatively, as rancheros had done in the Spanish era, they drove their stock into other Mexican states or into Louisiana.

Generally, farming continued to provide only a subsistence-level existence. The people in San Antonio generally limited themselves to working family plots, though larger landowners tried harvesting vegetables and fruits on a grander scale. Some of the farmers in Béxar and Goliad who possessed irrigable lands did experiment with growing cotton. Farming did at times yield slight surpluses, most of which was consumed locally.

As was the case before Mexico gained independence, Mexican society in Texas continued to be a divided one, the emerging opportunities in commerce, ranching, and politics during the 1820s and 1830s fueling the fragmentation. Government bureaucrats, successful merchants or rancheros, and others who came from prominent families made up a small elite. Among its members were Erasmo and Juan N. Seguín, José Antonio Navarro, Ramón Músquiz, and retired soldiers such as José Francisco Ruiz and José María Balmaceda.

The status of Hispanic women reflected both liberties and restrictions. Women sued for military survivors' benefits and engaged in the sale of lands, from which some achieved financial standing equal to or surpassing that of some men. But women also suffered from serious disadvantages. Law and tradition barred them from voting or the holding of political office. Religion discouraged divorce, dooming many women to endure unhappy marriages. Furthermore, societal conventions at the time demanded the ostracism of adulteresses, while turning a blind eye to the philandering of men. As was common practice in other western societies at the time, women often ate their home-cooked meals apart from (and sometimes only after) their spouses.

As in the Anglo sector, education was an area of concern for the Hispanic community, and, in the traditional Mexican way, Tejanos supported it locally through fund-raising drives. In Laredo, citizens opened a school in 1825. In Nacogdoches, Mexicans began a determined drive in 1828 to establish a similar facility, and by 1831 they had a school building and a teacher. San Antonio had two teachers in the late 1820s and early 1830s, though education there seems to have had its ups and downs according to prevailing economic conditions. Béxar and Nacogdoches boasted the highest proportion of students per capita in Texas. Generally, education declined with the turmoil of the mid-1830s.

Militia units remained the primary form of defense, as had been common during the period before 1821. Different from the Anglo volunteer companies, which were basically retaliatory, the Tejano militia, led by locally elected officers, followed an offensive strategy that conducted forays into Indian camping grounds. By the early 1830s, militia squadrons had developed into highly efficient, ranging cavalry units with the capacity to strike and pursue the enemy. Leaders of these companies included Martín de León, Juan N. Seguín, and Carlos de la Garza.

Catholicism remained the primary religion among the Mexican Texans. As during the Spanish era, the Tejanos carried on the practices of their colonial forefathers. The Church had all but given up its work in the Far North during the period, and the two priests responsible for Texas Catholicism during the period had earned disgraceful reputations. Displaying their own independence from religious dictates, Tejanos pleaded poverty and refused to pay the fees that the clergymen requested for performing the sacraments and other priestly functions.

Indians

The Indian peoples of Texas, still seeking to maintain their independence, now contended with Tejano militias and Anglo rifle companies instead of Spanish priests and royal armies. Those tribes that the Spanish had targeted for conversion had by the 1820s either perished due to wars and (European) diseases, been displaced from their native lands and driven into the western regions, or had integrated successfully into Spanish/Mexican communities. Only vestiges of the tribal Coahuiltecans remained by the 1830s, some of them having managed to melt into Goliad's population following the last phase of mission secularization in the 1820s.

With *Nuestra Señora del Rosario Mission* no longer operative, the Karankawas lost one of their last sources of refuge near their old hunting grounds; at the same time, they became the targets of Anglos with designs on obtaining Karankawan lands. In 1824, settlers from Austin's colony launched hostilities to drive nearby Karankawas from the vicinity. By 1827 the antagonistic whites had succeeded in forcing the tribe to relocate farther south along the coast. But the move only produced new problems for the Indians, as it placed them closer to the Tejano settlements at La Bahía, where local ranchers tolerated no threats to their livestock. During the 1830s, the Karankawas numbered less than 800 persons, but desperately clung to survival by preying on Tejano-owned cattle, or, in the case of those who gradually drifted back to their previous homeland, by "hiring out" to Anglo settlers as casual laborers or domestic servants.

Meanwhile, the fierce Indian tribes of the plains—such as the Comanches, Apaches, and Norteños—remained faithful to their traditional lifeways, relying on a combination of the hunt and small-scale farming. Women tended gardens, cultivating and harvesting corn, pumpkins, and beans, while the Plains warriors sabotaged settlements in an effort to halt the encroachment on their land and to take livestock, especially horses. Developing new entrepreneurial skills, some Plains bands traded with unscrupulous Anglo Americans, exchanging the very horses, mules, and other property they had stolen from the settlements for coveted American-made weapons.

The Caddos of East Texas, who had long lived in farming communities, now contended with problems that threatened to unravel their civilization. Alcohol, provided them by American traders, enfeebled many tribespeople almost at the same time outsiders began penetrating long-held Caddo territory. Interlopers included other Native American peoples from the U.S. South as well as Anglo empresarios bearing contracts to establish colonies in Caddo land. By the late 1820s, the Caddos numbered no more than 300 families; they attempted to survive by farming, but also by using beaver, deer, and otter pelts to trade for weapons and household and other personal items in Louisiana.

The cultural diversity of Indian society was enhanced in 1819–1820 when a band of Cherokees, bowing to legal and extralegal pressure by Anglos to abandon their homelands in Georgia and Alabama, arrived in northeastern Texas near Caddo land with members of other southern tribes. Their leader, Duwali (known also as Chief Bowles), located the Cherokees on the Trinity River, in the proximity of present-day Dallas. But friction with the Plains Indians soon forced the Cherokees to relocate in today's Van Zandt, Cherokee, and neighboring counties. During the late 1820s, the Cherokee settlement in Texas included about eighty families that made their living from a combination of farming, livestock raising, and trade with nearby Nacogdoches. From the time of their arrival until the mid-1830s, Duwali and his people actively sought to acquire legal title to their new homeland from the Mexican government, never to receive anything other than vague promises.

THE CENTRALISTS BACK IN POWER, 1834–1836

Santa Anna returned from retirement in May 1834 to remove Gómez Farías, his acting president, whose liberalism had thoroughly alienated the Church and the established military. Surfacing now as a reactionary, Santa Anna abolished the Federalist Constitution of 1824 and held elections for a new congress composed of conservatives: that is, Centralists and others supportive of the powers of the military and the Catholic Church. In October 1835, the new congress took steps to create a Centralist state in Mexico. It dissolved all state legislatures and turned the former states into military departments, over which presidential appointees would now govern.

The dissolution of federalism produced revolts in several states. Zacatecas opposed the new order most resolutely, but Santa Anna crushed an uprising there unmercifully. The people in Yucatán, however, broke with the government at this time, managing to retain their separatism until 1846. Meanwhile, in Monclova (which had become the capital of Coahuila y Tejas in 1833), liberal politicians denounced Santa Anna's new government in the summer of 1834. The legislature refused to obey Centralist orders, and, in March and April of 1835, it passed two laws designed to raise money for resisting the Centralists. The decrees authorized the governor to sell up to 400 leagues of public land in order to meet the "public exigencies" that the state then faced with Santa Anna, and designated another 400 leagues with which to compensate militiamen willing to take up arms against hostile Indians.

Many in Texas disapproved of investors acquiring real estate for the sake of profit, but Anglo Texans present in Monclova acquired grants during the crisis by promising to raise and equip 1,000-man companies on these lands, though most of these agents beat a swift retreat back to Texas determined to sell their newly acquired property. Fearing that some of these speculators might in fact raise a militia to be used against the central government, Domingo de Ugartechea, the principal commandant in Béxar, called upon General Martín Perfecto de Cós to muster reinforcements. Cós, the commanding general of the northeastern Mexican states, relayed the request to President Santa Anna.

Responding to reports that Mexico was preparing to send troops into Texas, a band of men (historians provide different numbers, anywhere from twenty-five to fifty) led by William Barret Travis and armed with cannon descended on Anahuac on June 30, 1835, forcing the surrender of the forty-four Mexican troops stationed there. The immediate cause behind the assault on the Mexican installation dealt with the old grievance regarding import tariffs, which people could ill afford to pay on needed goods. But the war party, which traced its origins to 1832, banked on the assumption that the episode would rally people in support of their cause of seeing Texas achieve its independence from Mexico. However, committees of (political) correspondence, which had organized by the early summer of 1835, still held divided views on what stand Texas should take in its relationship with Mexico. Some even assured Mexican officials that Texans, overall, had nothing to do with the acts that had induced troop movements into Texas.

But to Mexican political and military figures long wary of the Texans, the Anahuac incident represented the beginning of a revolt, and the refusal of Texan authorities to arrest the Anahuac agitators, primarily Travis, as the government wished, pointed to a widespread opposition. Moreover, the speculators stayed at large, mainly because by August they had either left Texas or gone into hiding. Among those lying low was Lorenzo de Zavala, once one of Mexico's most prominent Federalists, who had fled to Texas not only to escape the Centralist regime but to be closer to his East Texas land possessions, which he had been using for speculative purposes from afar.

Meanwhile, other, more radical committees of correspondence called for another consultation but resolved not to surrender the fugitives to the authorities. By August, stories circulated that Mexico's troops were on the move into Texas; communities reacted by calling general meetings to decide their best course of action: reason with the government, or openly resist it. Then, in early September 1835, Austin arrived newly freed from jail in Mexico City and threw his prestige behind the ideals of the war party. On the twentieth of that month, Cós landed with men and materiel at Copano Bay, whence they marched into the interior, reinforcing Goliad before heading toward Béxar. Reports that the Centralist forces intended to free the slaves, oppress Texans, and lay waste to the region influenced communities to take necessary measures for an expected confrontation.

Above: Lorenzo de Zavala. *The UT Institute of Texan Cultures, No. 76-31*

Even before the Centralist armies from Mexico skirmished with the Texans, the first episode between Anglos and the Mexican military occurred at Gonzales, where Lieutenant Francisco de Castañeda arrived on September 30, 1835, to request the transfer of a cannon that the Mexican government had given to the colonists four years earlier to help them protect themselves from Indians. Because he feared provoking a fight should he cross the Guadalupe River into Gonzales, Castañeda found himself negotiating for the surrender of the artillery piece in a rather awkward manner—he on one side of the river, and local officials, determined to retain possession of the cannon, on the other. Without much hope of success and still reluctant to start a conflict, Castañeda retreated. Then, on the morning of October 2, the rebels fired upon the government forces in their camp, some four miles upriver from Gonzales, using the very cannon in question: on the artillery piece the Anglos had draped a white banner bearing the combative phrase "COME AND TAKE IT." A brief and minor encounter ensued. Shortly, the Anglos called for Castañeda's surrender, resuming their fire with the cannon when the lieutenant refused. With orders from his superior to withdraw "without compromising the honor of Mexican arms," Castañeda left Gonzales without further ado, and the Anglos proclaimed victory.

The insurgents claimed another triumph a week later when Goliad fell to them. With the capture of the presidio and the soldiers Cós had left there, the Texans obtained a new cache of military goods recently brought in by Cós; more important, they could now prevent the general from using the Gulf to import additional troops or to escape in case of an impending defeat.

By the end of the month, Texas volunteers under the command of Stephen F. Austin began moving into San Antonio. In late October, they quarantined the city, which was by then under the control of some 800 to 1,200 troops under Cós. On December 5, some 550 men led by Ben Milam and Edward Burleson (Austin by this time had been sent on a diplomatic mission to the United States) attacked. Isolated from reinforcements and resupply for his army, Cós, having defended Béxar in door-to-door combat, succumbed to the assault on December 11. Now the attackers, less Ben Milam, who had been killed by a Mexican sharpshooter, forced Cós to begin a retreat into the interior of Mexico and to promise to respect the Constitution of 1824.

Meanwhile, fifty-eight delegates from a dozen Texas communities had assembled in what is called the Consultation of 1835 at San Felipe de Austin. Meeting between November 3 and November 14, they elected Branch T. Archer president of the Consultation and, after lengthy discussion, declared their commitment to federalism as embodied in the Constitution of 1824. By this strategy, the delegates hoped to win support from liberals in Mexico and gain time in which to acquire assistance from the United States; in fact, Texans already wanted independence from Mexico. Delegates further created a provisional government and elected Henry Smith as governor, James W. Robinson as lieutenant governor, and established a general council (a legislative body like a parliament) to be composed of representatives from the various settlements.

Among other things, the Consultation empowered the new government to seek funds to finance the expected war (to that end, it dispatched Austin, Archer, and William H. Wharton to the United States) and selected Sam Houston as commander of the regular army.

By early 1836, President Santa Anna himself was on the move toward Texas to crush the rebellion. In February the Mexican army, consisting of some 6,500 soldiers, half of them "recruited" hastily for the war in Texas, crossed the Rio Grande. The recently conscripted troops included reluctant draftees from the lower classes, political opponents of the Centralists, and about 300 Mayan Indians from the isolated regions of Yucatán. Santa Anna led one column towards San Antonio while General José Urrea took another towards Goliad.

Texas troops in the field, meantime, proved difficult to manage. Officers faced problems imposing order and discipline. Enlisted men tended to show more allegiance to their immediate leaders, as opposed to those higher up the chain of command. For the most part, the Texan army consisted of volunteers willing to fight when needed but ready to leave the ranks in order to care for their families and property once an immediate crisis had passed.

The disorder in the military was symptomatic of problems besetting Texans in general, for into the winter of 1835 and 1836 they still faced much political division. Their own individualism inhibited agreement on the best path to pursue toward independence. Some still held conflicting feelings about their relationship to Mexico and agonized over whether to join the peace or the war party. Others took issue with their fellow Texans over land claims or denounced them for shirking military duty.

As to the government, it faced such confusion and dissension that in December 1835, the general council called for the election of men to meet in early March 1836 for the purpose of adopting an ad interim government and framing a new constitution. When delegates to the convention convened at Washington-on-the-Brazos on March 1, sentiment had crystallized in favor of independence from Mexico. On March 2, the delegates endorsed a committee document, a declaration of independence, stating that Santa Anna had overthrown the Constitution of 1824 and substituted it with tyranny, that the Mexican government had subjugated Texas to Coahuila and thereby had diminished the voice of the people of Texas, that it had denied them the right to trial by jury, the right to religious freedom, and the right to bear arms, and that Mexico had failed to establish a system of education. It further denounced Santa Anna's regime for employing the military to enforce the law instead of utilizing civilian justice, for inciting the Indians against the colonies, and for mustering an army of mercenaries which was even then on its way to exterminate the colonists. All fifty-nine delegates to the convention signed the document, among them three Mexicans: Lorenzo de Zavala and the Tejanos José Antonio Navarro and José Francisco Ruiz, the latter two belonging to that group of Coahuiltejano capitalists who had profited from Anglo-American colonization.

THE WAR FOR TEXAS INDEPENDENCE

Causes

How can this move for independence be explained when just fifteen years earlier, Anglo American immigrants to Texas had pledged their loyalty to Mexico and agreed to conform to Mexican tradition? Traditionally, historians viewed the Texas rebellion as a courageous act of liberty-loving Anglo Texans against the intolerant and undemocratic government of Mexico: in this light, Anglos were simply following in the footsteps of their ancestors who had rebelled against the autocratic British. Over time, other interpretations gained acceptance. One depicted the Texas rebellion as part of a southern slavocracy conspiracy to take over Texas. Another cited collusion between President Andrew Jackson and Sam Houston. Nevertheless, the original democracy versus tyranny thesis remained the most tenacious.

Recent interpretations, however, depart from the above explanations. One line of analysis takes a narrow political view, arguing that the uprising was primarily a constitutional conflict against the Centralist party, which consistently followed a discriminatory course against the Texans, and that the abrogation of the Constitution of 1824 explains the move for independence.

Another alternative view asserts that economic incentives, such as land speculation, lay behind the revolt. The land-trafficking thesis sees several of the influential men in Anglo Texas having migrated from the United States to the Mexican north with the intention of turning a profit in land transactions. This argument links these individuals to speculators in Texas, Coahuila, and Mexico City, as well as to financial centers in New York and Philadelphia. When Mexico moved against Texas in 1835, the leading men in the colony threw their influence behind rebellion in an effort to maintain opportunities in land speculation.

Other historians attribute more subtle economic reasons for the uprising, seeing the rebellion as one launched by Texans to preserve long-standing political values and recently achieved economic gains. For years, Anglos had lived under the auspicious climate created by the Constitution of 1824—federalism had fostered further immigration, political liberty, slavery, and economic progress. Santa Anna's effort in 1835–1836 to impose stricter rule over the province threatened the Texans' notions of government by the people and of an individual's right to make a living through inventive entrepreneurship. The rebellion, then, intended to protect individual liberty and the agricultural and commercial advances Anglos had made in Texas, as well as slavery.

Still other historians focus on Anglo American contempt for Mexico's rule. According to these views, Anglo Americans throughout the 1820s and up to the outbreak of the war refused to assimilate or conform to Mexican rules or convert to Catholicism. Relatively isolated in their East Texas settlements, the foreigners practically governed themselves and refused to pay duties, meanwhile objecting to troop increases designed to enforce Mexico's laws, even as they maintained their own militias. They constantly viewed the Mexicans as a politically and culturally inferior people living under a tumultuous government.

Ethnocentrism or racism as causes of the conflict have also received attention from scholars, with some arguing strongly that racial prejudice acted as a guiding force (though not the sole one) in the break with Mexico; others sincerely contest this analysis. The first school would note that Anglo Americans arrived in Texas already conditioned to think negatively of Mexican people: the Mexicans' darker skin and their adherence to Catholicism helped racially biased Anglos view Mexicans as biologically inferior and morally flawed. Believing, as past generations of Anglos did (and future ones would) that the United States had a special purpose in the world (a "Manifest Destiny" to bring order and discipline to "untamed" and "uncivilized" hinterlands), they arrived in Texas bent on "rescuing" the underdeveloped region from a backward people and a government enmeshed in instability.

Critics of such an interpretation argue that racism truly was not manifest in Texas before 1836, and thus should be discounted as a primary cause in the independence movement. In fact, Anglos and Tejanos coexisted fairly well, sharing similar economic and political interests. Settlements were so removed on the frontier that large-scale contact between the two peoples hardly aroused ill-feelings. But once begun, the war itself, one group of scholars observes, spurred anti-Mexican prejudice. During the conflict Anglos came to see Mexicans as decadent, brutal, and subhuman, the reality of the events that transpired during the conflict hardening such perceptions. Still other scholars note that not until after 1836, when new conditions entered the scene, among them the desire to turn Mexicans into a tractable labor force, competition for land, and control of the frontier, did feelings that may be classified as racist develop. Prejudice evolved from a need to justify the violent domination of the Tejanos, in short, from anxiety, distrust, fear, conflict, and competition.

Each of the above viewpoints, advanced by historians who have studied the era carefully, has some validity. Santa Anna's efforts to install a Centralist government threatened values and interests dear to Anglo Texans and engendered fears of political despotism or a reversal of those policies that until 1835 had facilitated commercial expansion, land speculation, and slavery. Ingrained racial attitudes toward Mexicans (both in Texas and Mexico) made Anglos uneasy about an indefinite submission to a people they considered inferior, but they may have chosen to minimize their differences since coalitions with Tejanos had served them well by bringing about favorable political and economic programs.

Independence Won

Santa Anna arrived in Béxar on February 23, 1836, to find the Alamo (the popular name of the old mission of San Antonio de Valero) fortified by a contingent led by William Barret Travis. Laying siege to it, Santa Anna prepared for a final assault, as those inside mobilized for defense.

On March 6, sometime around 5:00 A.M., 1,800 of Santa Anna's troops began a trot toward the walled compound as the *degüello*, a bugle call that signals the taking of no quarter, sounded. The old mission would not fall easily; its lo-

Dawn at the Alamo by H. A. McArdle; this romantic painting is exhibited at the Texas State Capitol Building. *Texas State Library and Archives Commission*

cation on a slight rise afforded those inside it a clear view of their attackers. Moreover, the defenders (historians place their number anywhere from 182 to 189) had already armed the compound with twenty-one heavy artillery pieces, and many of those inside were expert riflemen, including foremost the Tennessee marksmen led by the recently arrived volunteer Davy Crockett. Using grapeshot and long rifles, the Alamo's defenders felled the lead soldiers who were carrying ladders; thus officers and more-seasoned fighters rushing behind the first wave could only try to claw their way up and over the compound's eight- to nine-foot walls. Now fighting for their lives, the Mexicans contended with small handweapons and Bowie knifes used with deadly effect against them. Within ten minutes of the battle's start, the assault appeared to have miscarried, and Santa Anna committed his reserve unit to the engagement. As this new wave of soldiers dashed toward the fortress, their bullets hit many of the hapless conscripts who still lay bunched up at the base of the walls. Frantic effort finally overtook the attackers inside the Alamo, where the volunteers fell back to find cover within the compound. The actual battle ended within twenty minutes, but the carnage followed for another hour, as the Mexicans ferreted out soldiers still resisting from makeshift secondary lines of defense. Amazingly, the assault had cost Santa Anna 500 to 600 men.

Even though Santa Anna gave orders to spare no one's life, several who had stood in the Alamo survived. Among them were Susannah Dickinson, her small child, and a black slave belonging to Travis. Many of the survivors were Mexicans, most of them family members of (what recent research reveals were) nine

Tejanos who chose to fight with those inside the Alamo. About six or seven volunteers, among them Davy Crockett, were captured and were executed within minutes after the battle by orders of Santa Anna.

While Santa Anna scored his victory at Béxar, Texans under the command of Colonel James W. Fannin protected Goliad from advancing Mexican forces that were coming up the coast from Matamoros under Urrea, who had already disposed of Anglo resistance his forces had met at San Patricio, Agua Dulce, and Refugio. Though well fortified at the old presidio in Goliad, Fannin decided on the morning of March 19 to abandon the garrison and make a run for Victoria, reasoning that the lack of adequate provisions at Goliad undermined a capable defense. As Fannin and his men retreated, Urrea intercepted them, deterring the Texans from taking refuge at Coleto Creek, the ravined terrain of which might have allowed Fannin to dig in to mount a spirited resistance. Therefore, at the "battle of the prairie," some two miles from the timber of Coleto Creek, Urrea forced Fannin to surrender on the morning of March 20, and then marched the enemy force back to Goliad. A week later, Urrea, despite his personal pleas for clemency for the prisoners, slaughtered the Anglos at Santa Anna's insistence. Some 340 persons met their death, but close to 30 men who had not been fatally wounded by the executioners' first volley managed to escape into the woods.

The defeats at the Alamo and Goliad eliminated the old allegiances that Texan military units had felt towards their immediate leaders and handed Houston (who had been reaffirmed as commander of all Texas forces on March 4 following the declaration of independence) unity of command—an element essential to fighting a war. Houston, who had been at Gonzales training troops in mid-March, now headed away from Santa Anna's advancing force, toward more familiar territory. While this maneuver may have been undertaken in order to engage the Mexican army on the Texans' own ground, many perceived it as a mindless retreat and panic spread quickly among the plainfolk of the area. Resultantly, an exodus Texans called the "Runaway Scrape" ensued, as people deserted their Central Texas communities, fleeing in family groups or with neighbors, taking only those belongings and livestock that they could transport easily and seeking refuge along the Texas-Louisiana border. Cold weather, floods, and deep mud intensified the frightened people's hardship as they scrambled to stay ahead of the Mexican military.

Santa Anna, by now, felt confident that his conquest of the Texan army was near at hand. When he later caught up with Sam Houston at the San Jacinto River, he audaciously made camp on April 20 in a location that defied the rules of engagement. Although Santa Anna had the Texans boxed in, he, too, was shut off on three sides, with the enemy less than a mile in front and already poised for an attack. The San Jacinto River on Santa Anna's right and swampy terrain behind him would make a disciplined retreat impossible.

Sometime between 3:30 and 4:00 P.M. on April 21, 1836, Sam Houston's forces of approximately 900 troops (made up of volunteers from the Anglo settle-

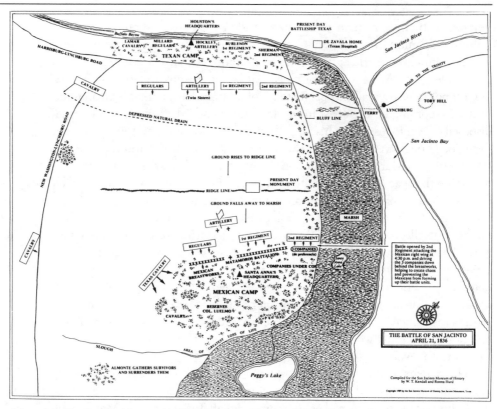

Map of the Battle of San Jacinto by W. T. Kendall and Ronna Hurd. *Courtesy San Jacinto Museum of History, Houston, Texas*

ments, recent arrivals from the United States, as well as a detachment of Texas Mexicans led by Juan N. Seguín) attacked Santa Anna's army of about 1,300 to 1,500 personnel. Caught by surprise, Santa Anna's forces attempted to beat back the Texans, even killing a horse out from under Sam Houston and wounding the general, but their resistance proved inadequate. Within eighteen minutes after the first shot had been fired, Houston's men had full control of the enemy camp. The Mexican army, by this time already deserted by Santa Anna, had become disorganized and gave ground, with the Texans chasing them as they fled into the river and the marsh, killing the Mexican troops as they came upon them. The slaying of Santa Anna's men continued until nightfall. Casualty figures showed 630 Mexicans dead and 208 wounded. Additionally, the victors took 730 prisoners. The Texans had suffered only eight or nine killed and somewhere between seventeen and thirty injured.

Captured the day following the Battle of San Jacinto, Santa Anna succeeded in negotiating an agreement whereby Houston spared his life in return for a concession that the Mexican leader order his army's retreat into Mexico. On May 14, in the Treaties of Velasco, Santa Anna acknowledged Texas independence, vowed again to remove all of his forces into Mexico, accepted Texas's southern boundary as the Rio Grande, and promised to see an independent Texas receive full diplomatic recognition by the Mexican government. Although the Mexican congress refused to accept the general's accords, by this time Mexico lacked the means to attempt a reconquest of the lost land. Texas's independence had been won.

READINGS

Books and Dissertations

Alonzo, Armando, *Tejano Legacy: Rancheros and Settlers in South Texas, 1734–1900* (Albuquerque: University of New Mexico Press, 1998).

Barker, Eugene C., *The Life of Stephen F. Austin: Founder of Texas,1793–1836* (Nashville and Dallas: Cokesbury Press, 1925).

Campbell, Randolph B., *An Empire for Slavery: The Peculiar Institution in Texas* (Baton Rouge: Louisiana University Press, 1989).

Cantrell, Gregg, *Stephen F. Austin: Empresario of Texas* (New Haven, CT: Yale University Press, 1999).

Castañeda, Carlos E., ed. and trans., *The Mexican Side of the Texan Revolution* (Dallas: P. L. Turner Co., 1928).

Crisp, James E., "Anglo-Texan Attitudes toward the Mexican, 1821–1845" (Ph.D. diss., Yale University, 1976).

Friend, Llerena, *Sam Houston: The Great Designer* (Austin: University of Texas Press, 1954).

Glaser, Tom, "Victory or Death," in *Alamo Images,* edited by Susan P. Schoelwer (Dallas: DeGolyer Library and Southern Methodist University Press, 1985).

Gracy, David B. II, *Moses Austin: His Life* (San Antonio: Trinity University Press, 1988).

Hardin, Stephen L., *Texian Iliad: A Military History of the Texas Revolution* (Austin: University of Texas Press, 1994).

Hensen, Margaret Swett, "Hispanic Texas, 1519–1836," in *Texas: A Sesquicentennial Celebration,* ed. Donald W. Wisenhunt (Austin: Eakin Press, 1984).

Himmel, Kelly F., *The Conquest of the Karankawas and Tonkawas, 1821–1859* (College Station: Texas A&M University Press, 1999).

Jenkins, John H., *The Papers of the Texas Revolution, 1835–1836* (10 vols., Austin: Presidial Press, 1973).

Kilgore, Dan, *How Did Davy Die?* (College Station: Texas A&M University Press, 1978).

Lack, Paul D., *The Texas Revolutionary Experience: A Social and Political History* (College Station: Texas A&M University Press, 1992).

Long, Jeff, *Duel of Eagles: The Mexican and United States Fight for the Alamo* (New York: Morrow, 1990).

Lord, Walter, *A Time to Stand* (New York: Harper and Row, 1961).

McDonald, Archie P., *Travis* (Austin: Jenkins Press, 1976).

McLean, Malcolm D., *Papers Concerning Robertson's Colony in Texas* (19 vols.; Fort Worth: Texas Christian University, 1974–1976; Arlington, Texas: The UTA Press, 1977–1993).

McReynolds, James Michael, "Family Life in a Borderlands Community: Nacogdoches, Texas, 1779–1861" (Ph.D. diss., Texas Tech University, 1978).

Pohl, James W., *The Battle of San Jacinto* (Austin: Texas State Historical Association, 1989).

Reichstein, Andreas V., *Rise of the Lone Star: The Making of Texas* (College Station: Texas A&M University Press, 1989).

Ricklis, Robert A., *The Karankawa Indians of Texas: An Ecological Study of Cultural Tradition and Change* (Austin: University of Texas Press, 1996).

Santos, Richard G., *Santa Anna's Campaign Against Texas, 1835–1836* (Waco: Texian Press, 1968).

Smith, F. Todd, *The Caddo Indians: Tribes at the Convergence of Empire, 1542–1854* (College Station: Texas A&M University Press, 1995).

Tijerina, Andrew Anthony, "Tejanos and Texas: The Native Mexicans of Texas, 1820–1850" (Ph.D. diss., University of Texas at Austin, 1977).

Vigness, David, *The Revolutionary Decades* (Austin: Steck-Vaughn, 1965).

Weber, David J., *The Mexican Frontier, 1821–1846: The American Southwest under Mexico* (Albuquerque: University of New Mexico Press, 1982).

Articles

de la Teja, Jesús F., and John Wheat, "Béxar: Profile of a Tejano Community, 1820–1832," *Southwestern Historical Quarterly* 89 (July, 1985).

Lack, Paul D., "Slavery in the Texas Revolution," *Southwestern Historical Quarterly* 89 (October, 1985).

Miller, Thomas Lloyd, "Mexican Texans in the Texas Revolution," *Journal of Mexican American History* 3 (1973).

Pohl, James W., and Stephen L. Hardin, "The Military History of the Texas Revolution: An Overview," *Southwestern Historical Quarterly* 89 (January, 1986).

LAUNCHING A NATION, 1836–1848

CHAPTER 4

At Washington-on-the-Brazos, the men who declared Texas independent from Mexico on March 2 also established an ad interim government under a constitution drafted by the time they adjourned on March 17, 1836. They also selected as leaders of the infant nation men who had been in the vanguard of critical attacks against the Centralists—among them David G. Burnet, who was chosen president, and Lorenzo de Zavala, the new vice-president. To carry on the independence movement, the framers of the Constitution of 1836 empowered the temporary government to solicit loans, issue promissory notes, negotiate treaties, begin to develop a navy, and recruit men and provide supplies for the army. This government would serve until constitutional elections scheduled for December 1836.

Santa Anna's defeat at San Jacinto had solved one of the new nation's problems, but many remained. First, the Mexican commander's fate became a source of discord. Some counseled holding him hostage until Mexico complied fully with the Treaties of Velasco, so-called because the seat of the ad interim government had been moved from Galveston Island to Velasco, but, after he and Santa Anna signed the Treaties, on May 14, Burnet released him, holding Santa Anna to his word of returning to Mexico and seeing to it that Mexico duly recognized Texas as an independent country. The military displayed a similar divisiveness, its condition resembling the preindependence disorder in that volunteers remained faithful to their own company commanders—many of whom thirsted to inflict further vengeance on (any) Mexicans for the atrocities committed at the Alamo and Goliad and resisted acknowledging the new commander of the army, Thomas Jefferson Rusk.

(Sam Houston had left for New Orleans to seek medical assistance for a leg wound suffered at San Jacinto.) Worse yet, the government languished in dire financial straits, much of the land was devastated, and the Plains Indians still roamed the hinterlands preying on settlements. Furthermore, the fear of a Mexican invasion to regain the lost territory hovered over the nation.

Above: Detail from "6 o'clock a.m. Military Plaza." *The UT Institute of Texan Cultures, No. 83–85*

In an effort to speed up the institution of a permanent government, Burnet in July 1836 implemented plans to hold a general election in September, instead of December as was previously planned. Citizens were to vote on the constitution drafted during the March convention at Washington-on-the-Brazos, express their feelings on the possible annexation of Texas to the United States, and elect officials for their new government. Sam Houston's victory at San Jacinto had made him immensely popular, and in the September contest he won easily for president over Henry Smith and Stephen F. Austin. Voters chose Mirabeau B. Lamar as their vice-president.

In the plebiscite, Texans also approved the constitution overwhelmingly and gave a mandate for annexation to the United States. By so doing, the majority revealed the deep-seated connection they felt to their country of origin. They wished to keep part of what they had left behind them (the Texas constitution resembled the one written in Philadelphia in 1787 and those of other American states) and their vote exhibited an unmistakable endorsement of the transplantation of U.S. institutions to a region that for generations had been dominated by Native Americans, then by Spaniards, and then by Mexicans.

REPUBLICANISM

Exactly what type of culture came to the forefront in 1836? Although people of different backgrounds inhabited the republic, the Anglo-American way of life dominated all others, and English became the nation's primary language. As Protestants, Anglo Texans subscribed to the notion of religious toleration, though they harbored a distrust toward Catholics. The right of free enterprise—the freedom to compete in the marketplace without governmental interference—was taken wholesale from the United States and reigned as Texas's chief economic tenet. Just "redeemed" from the Mexicans and Indians, frontier Texas offered boundless opportunities—to be pursued, perhaps, on the backs of the people deemed unworthy of the republican triumph.

Politically, Texans believed in republican system of government like the one many had known in the United States. Unlike the more aristocratic governments that existed in Europe, republicanism bestowed sovereignty upon the masses. In this political model, a constitution stipulated the duties of government, carefully divided the government into three branches, which regulated one another through a permanent system of checks and balances, and ensured the rights of citizens before the law. Regularly scheduled elections of public officials guaranteed that the will of the people would be paramount.

The political figures who took office to lead the Republic of Texas, on October 22, 1836, were themselves products of the Anglo American political tradition. The president, Sam Houston, was a veteran of American politics, most prominently serving as a U.S. congressman from 1823 to 1827, then as governor of Tennessee from 1827 to 1829. The vice-president, Mirabeau B. Lamar, had served in the Georgia legislature. Stephen F. Austin, appointed to the post of secretary of state, had been a member of the Missouri territorial legislature for several years before coming to Texas, while Henry Smith, assigned the position of secretary of the treasury, had acted as provisional governor following the Consultation of 1835. Other important figures who would serve as the architects of the young nation include Thomas J. Rusk, as secretary of war, and William H. Wharton, as minister to the United States, both of whom had lengthy credentials as political activists.

Houston's first administration included a mixture of political allies and opponents, a development Houston relished for at least two reasons. First, he sought to create national harmony by integrating the most prominent prewar political factions into the government (Austin had led the peace party, while Wharton represented the war party). Second, displaying further political insight, he had determined to have his political enemies in the capital, where he could keep an eye on them.

THE POLITICS OF CAUTION

One of President Houston's most immediate concerns was securing diplomatic recognition of the Republic of Texas by foreign powers. Without it, Texas was no more than an errant province within a legitimate nation (for Mexico still had not recognized Texas's independence), and as such it could not secure credit in order to seek financial aid from other countries, sell land, or even legislate its own affairs with any kind of credibility. Since the days of the Consultation of 1835, leaders of the independence movement had taken steps toward legitimizing their government; lobbying efforts in Washington, D.C., had been underway since the spring of 1836. With independence won and a mandate for annexation to the United States already expressed, recognition by President Andrew Jackson was a necessary first step toward joining the country from which so many Texans had descended; the United States could annex an independent country, but it could not even consider annexing a part of Mexico. In the fall of 1836, however, Jackson feared northerners' reaction to a simmering but potentially explosive issue: abolitionists saw talk of annexing Texas as part of a southern conspiracy to add new slave states to the Union. Washington, therefore, rebuffed the overtures of the Texas minister, and Jackson delayed appointing a chargé d'affaires to the republic until the last day of his term in 1837. The United States thereby became the first country to recognize the Republic of Texas; it would be another two years before any European countries responded similarly.

Aside from the question of recognition, Houston's government grappled with numerous internal problems, among them financial distress. The Texas Congress, which had assumed power with the September elections of 1836, lacked the resources to pay its bureaucrats and elected officials, its army, or any part of the $1.25 million debt that had accrued since the formation of the provisional government. To raise money, congress passed acts imposing taxes on imports, property, and livestock and levied other types of duties, but such gestures yielded little revenue since most Texans had very little cash and faced high obstacles to economic development. The government's efforts to borrow money largely met with failure.

President Houston attempted to alleviate the financial crisis through a policy that combined gamble with austerity. So desperate was congress to pay the governmental bureaucracy, foreign diplomats, the military, and sundry creditors, that in June 1837 it commenced printing paper money in the form of promissory notes but, as ordinarily happens when governments take such chances, depreciation weakened the currency. Houston believed strongly in a strict economy, however, and his politics quickly turned towards frugality. Along with other essentials, defense became a major target of budget reductions. In May 1837, Houston dealt with the problem that the army of volunteers posed to civilian order and to the budget by furloughing all but 600 soldiers (the others could be recalled to duty upon notice), offering them a paid return to New Orleans if they wished to leave for the United States, or 1,280 acres of land apiece if they opted to make the republic their home. Houston also saved money by avoiding campaigns against the Indians whenever possible. But even with the budget cuts in place, when Houston left office in 1838, the public debt stood at close to $2 million.

Despite its problems, the Houston administration set the new country on its feet and pushed it away from the Mexican past and into an American future. The First Congress fixed the boundaries of the Republic of Texas at the Rio Grande, from its mouth at the Gulf of Mexico to its source in the Rockies, then northward to the forty-second parallel. It also began to readjust the (Mexican) political hierarchy at the local level into one more in keeping with the U.S. tradition. The Mexican municipios became county units, and the district courts assumed the function of the alcaldes.

The Houston administration also passed legislation to encourage immigration and raise revenue; for this it turned to land, the government's most tangible resource. The ad interim government had provided headrights (grants of land that obliged grantees to comply with certain conditions, such as improving the land) in order to entice volunteers into the Texas army. Laws passed by the congress now established a similar land policy to reward veterans and to populate the vast region of the republic—under the least generous of these headrights, heads of families received entitlements as large as 640 acres; single men qualified for 320 acres. Officials hoped to attract other colonists to Texas who would purchase the public lands and thereby provide needed revenue for the treasury, but few people could afford to buy real estate. Therefore, the government continued to people the republic by holding out offers of free land. Generally, provisions of the grants required citizens to live in Texas for three years and to make improvements on the land before their titles became official. This measure obviously was an attempt to attract well-intentioned settlers as opposed to speculators or shady newcomers fleeing the law, creditors, or familial responsibilities elsewhere. Between 1836 and 1841, the government apportioned close to 37 million acres.

Another accomplishment of the Houston government was the development of new forms of defense. Congress allocated funds for the establishment of a small navy, and local militias composed of citizen-soldiers now replaced the disbanded volunteer army. To protect the settlements, congress in May 1837 created a law enforcement corps that would later take on the name Texas Rangers. During the period of the republic, however, most of the "Texas Rangers" were ordinary citizen-soldiers who volunteered to complete a specific mission and, upon accomplishing it, usually returned home to resume their private lives. Some of these men, however, did patrol the range for more prolonged periods. In concept and in practice, these roving companies duplicated the "strike and pursue" tactics of the Tejano militia, upon which defense of the frontier had rested in the 1820s and 1830s. Not until later did a law enforcement outfit constituted of "elite" recruits take on the official name of Texas Rangers. By then, the unit was perceived of as a unique Texas invention.

THE POLITICS OF ACTION

The Constitution of 1836 stipulated that chief executives of the republic were to serve three-year terms, except for the first president, whose initial term was limited to two years. Furthermore, although presidents could serve alternate terms, they could not succeed themselves. Thus, in 1838 Houston searched, with limited success, for a candidate (and possible successor) whose politics resembled his own.

During this period in Texas history, formal political parties did not exist, but factions, mainly pro- or anti-Houston and his policies, had already formed. Vice-President Lamar, who expressed dissatisfaction with many of the president's programs, headed the opposition to Houston. Whereas Houston counseled acceptance of a treaty he personally had negotiated in February 1836 for the provisional government's recognition of Cherokee claims to Northeast Texas lands in return for a pledge of neutrality during the upcoming war for independence, Lamar recommended the treaty's rejection to the republic's senate and denounced Houston for failing to eliminate the Indian danger on the western frontier. Furthermore, Lamar faulted Houston for his lack of success in foreign relations: the president had not gotten Mexico to acknowledge the independence of the republic, and he had pur-

Above: Mirabeau Buonaparte Lamar, from a painting by C. B. Norman. *Texas State Library and Archives Commission*

sued U.S. annexation as a major goal. Lamar, on the other hand, rejected incorporating the republic into the United States, for he envisaged Texas remaining an independent republic that might one day be a great power. Lastly, the vice-president blamed the financial condition of the republic on Houston's fiscal ineptness. Campaigning on remedies for the incumbent's mistakes, and with little opposition from the Houston faction, Lamar easily took the presidency.

Lamar's politics differed from his predecessor's, especially in his management of the nation's finances. The new president sought to alleviate the republic's financial woes through a $5 million loan, which he never managed to secure. Undaunted, he issued nearly $3 million of noninterest-bearing promissory notes. Other forms of legal tender followed, but with little reserves in the treasury and only the public honor and the public lands to back it, Texas money cheapened. By one estimate, a dollar of the republic's paper money in 1841 equaled no more than 12 to 15 cents in U.S. currency.

Despite such setbacks, Lamar spent extravagantly. Relying on the new currency the government had printed, what credit was still available, revenue from business licenses (such as those levied on taverns), taxes levied on slaves, the expectation of acquiring a $5 million loan in Europe, and $457,380 that the republic managed to borrow from a bank in Philadelphia in 1839, Lamar built up the navy and increased the size of the staffs of frontier garrisons in order to launch a campaign against the Indians—an effort that cost the nation $2.5 million. In addition, the republic's capital was transferred at some expense from Houston to a small settlement (renamed Austin) on the Colorado River; the move made in 1839 sought to lure people to the west but also to lash out against Sam Houston's power, as his political following centered along the Houston-Galveston axis. Furthermore, under Lamar, the cost of maintaining the postal service increased, as did the expense of expanding the bureaucracy. Recognition of the republic in Europe was pursued with vigor, and Lamar's plans to build Texas into an empire of some standing led him to subsidize a military excursion into New Mexico in 1841–1842 in order to expand the republic, what became known as the Santa Fe Expedition. Some historians see the above agenda as visionary or foolish, but others perceive it as part of a well-thought-out plan to secure the survival of a nation ostensibly unwanted, at least until the mid-1840s, by the United States.

More sensible policies helped the republic along the road to permanence. The Homestead Act passed in 1839 protected citizens from seizure of their homestead, tools, and work animals for any debts they might have incurred; this legislation had its antecedents both in the Hispanic tradition and in a decree passed by the congress of Coahuila y Tejas in 1829. An empresario system instituted in 1840–1841 and modeled on the Mexican colonization program of the 1820s and 1830s called for issuing contracts to immigration agents entrusted with settling colonists in specified areas within a stipulated number of years. Here, again, the congress attempted to attract upstanding families to the republic. In respect to education, Lamar in 1839 and 1840 signed bills credited with laying the groundwork for the system of public education in Texas. The provisions set aside four leagues (17,714 acres) of land in each county for the establishment of a primary school, and they designated that a good amount of the public land be retained for the establishment of two colleges. Funds generated from the sale or rental of these lands or profits derived from the sale of minerals extracted from them would fund the institutions of higher learning. Again, Lamar's programs had precedents in a plan laid out by the Coahuiltejanos. In 1826, Béxar and Saltillo had submitted a proposal by which the state would donate land to create two colleges, and, in 1832, Nacogdoches had proposed that the state set aside four leagues of land in that municipality for the establishment of a permanent fund to erect a school. The Coahuila y Tejas legislature had in fact decreed these proposals in 1833.

RETRENCHMENT

By 1841 the republic's debts—the nation owed money to bureaucrats and military personnel who had not received their appropriations, the American lender of the $457,380 loan, and still other creditors—amounted to nearly $7 million. The country seemed to be on the verge of a complete financial collapse. The Houston partisans had watched much of Lamar's doings with dismay, none moreso than Houston himself, who as a congressman from San Augustine County had continued to perpetuate political factionalism. Deciding to recapture the office he had yielded by law in December 1838, he publicly attacked Lamar for the woeful economic standing of the nation. But Houston raised other salient political points for the Lamar faction to answer as well. On the stump, he criticized Lamar's relocation of the capital from Houston to Austin as too expensive, and he claimed that the new site was too vulnerable to Indian depredations. He reproached Lamar for the unsuccessful, costly, and embarrassing episode known as the Santa Fe Expedition. The issues, however, became subordinated to vicious negative campaigning, as both sides stooped to gossip, charges of scandal, and invective. At election time, Houston easily defeated David G. Burnet, the Lamar camp's candidate, and he served as president for the second time from December 1841 to December 1844.

With Houston back in office, bureaucratic retrenchment ensued. Congress terminated dozens of offices, lowered the salaries of public officials, and reduced the republic's military forces to a few companies of Rangers. Peace initiatives with the Indians again replaced a policy of active confrontation. Fiscal policy was also redirected. Houston's government overturned laws passed by the Lamar administration authorizing the printing of money and the pursuit of foreign loans. Only about $200,000 of new money was printed, and Houston spent less than $600,000, borrowing from the future—when, presumably, tax revenues would be greater, the public lands would be sold, and better and larger loans would be negotiated.

In December 1844, Anson Jones, secretary of state under Houston, won the presidency on a platform to stay the course his predecessor had set. He did just that, but, like Houston, he could never rein in the republic's debt, which, since the government had made no payments on it, by 1846 had increased to more than $10 million.

DEMOGRAPHIC GROWTH

Fundamental to the stability of the republic was an increase in the number of its citizens. Though difficult to determine precisely, the population grew rapidly during the republic's existence, to about 162,500 in 1848, according to one estimate. At this time, most Texans made their homes in the eastern sections of the republic, though the majority of Texas Mexicans continued to reside in the more familiar cultural milieu of what had been the Department of Béxar.

Several factors explain the population growth. Natural reproduction accounted for it in part, but more substantial was a renewed flow of immigration. From the United States came people enticed by the republic's headrights. Others arrived to escape the depression of 1837 then gripping the United States; in the late 1830s and 1840s, Texas offered limitless opportunities to start afresh, both for those wanting to wrest their living from the soil and for land speculators. So many debtors and destitute Americans fled their hometown sheriffs for the Lone Star during this era that one historian claims that "the debtor-fugitive element of Texas was substantially higher than that of mature American communities." Equally responsible for population increases during the period of the republic was the empresario system introduced by the Lamar administration in 1840–1841 to replace the ineffective land policy that used headrights as inducements.

The Peters Colony became the most successful enterprise to grow out of Lamar's new immigration program. Established in 1841 in the upper fringes of the republic, west of a line from the modern-day counties of Grayson and Dallas, empresario W. S. Peters and his associates brought to the colony 10,000 to 12,000 people by the early 1850s. These newcomers to northern Texas had descended primarily from the Ohio Valley and the northeastern United States, and they established a cultural atmosphere reminiscent of their Yankee and midwestern origins, founding successful towns such as Dallas.

The immigration policies of the 1840s also attracted Europeans to Texas. Tired of facing economic distress at home and lured by the seemingly boundless opportunities in North America, an array of groups responded to the glowing accounts of Texas as a land of promise. Illiterate peasants mixed with literate political refugees and skilled artisans as Irish, French, English, Scottish, Canadian, Swiss, Scandinavian, Czech, and Polish arrivals established colonies in Texas in the 1840s and 1850s.

This supply of European immigrants fueled an already culturally diversified republic as at least two communities of Old World people made successful new beginnings in Texas's western regions. Castroville, a French-speaking community founded by Henri Castro with some 2,134 immigrants, took root on a land grant near the Medina River, west of San Antonio, from 1843 to 1847. In 1844,

Prince Carl von Solms-Braunfels led Germans to Texas under the auspices of an organization called the *Adelsverein* (Society of Noblemen). In 1845, they founded New Braunfels in present-day Comal County.

THE RISE OF TOWNS

New prospects for the republic, new and different types of immigrants, and new venues of commerce acted as stimuli for the growth of existing towns and the birth of new ones. Preindependence communities such as Gonzales, Victoria, Brazoria, Velasco, Liberty, Nacogdoches, Goliad, Washington, Refugio, and Jonesborough kept their vitality, while new cities such as Shelbyville, Richmond, La Grange, Columbus, Independence, and Clarksville grew with the republic.

To be sure, the above list includes the "lesser" towns of the republic—the major cities during the period were Houston, Galveston, Austin, and San Antonio. Of the four, Houston had an edge in importance. Its origins lay in the grand plans of two brothers, Augustus C. and John K. Allen, who had scrupulously searched for a strategic town site in the rich cotton and timber lands between the Brazos and Trinity Rivers, where transportation by water would be convenient. Having located the spot at the confluence of Buffalo and White Oak Bayous, the founders of Houston energetically laid out streets and reserved plots for a school, churches, a courthouse, and even the nation's capitol. Through shrewd lobbying, the Allens convinced lawmakers that Houston was the ideal spot for the seat of government, and on November 30, 1836, an act of the legislature so recognized the city. Although its stead as the capital of the republic lasted only until 1839, the city evolved into a commercial entrepôt. Steamboats navigating Buffalo Bayou brought travelers, entrepreneurs, prospective settlers, and goods and supplies directly into town; they departed with raw materials from the area's plantations and farms. By 1845, some 14,000 bales of cotton left Houston on steamships and sloops bound for outside markets.

The nearby community of Galveston, blessed with one of the best natural harbors on the Gulf of Mexico west of New Orleans, similarly grew out of its prospects as a center for trade. Established by the Galveston City Company of Colonel Michel B. Menard, Samuel May Williams, Gail Borden, and others, the town by the late 1830s rivaled Houston in the cotton trade.

The town of Austin originated under unique circumstances. Planned by President Lamar as the capital of the fledgling republic in 1839, the government laid out the settlement on the Colorado River, and by October of that year republic officials occupied crudely built structures there. After its shaky start, Austin began to receive acceptance as the capital site, despite its location in what in those years represented the westernmost line of the frontier.

While Houston, Galveston, and Austin sprung directly from Anglo American enterprises, the fortunes of San Antonio and Laredo differed. In the 1830s and 1840s, Béxar was recovering from the destruction caused by the sieges of 1835 and 1836, and it remained vulnerable to Indian attacks and (reoccupation)

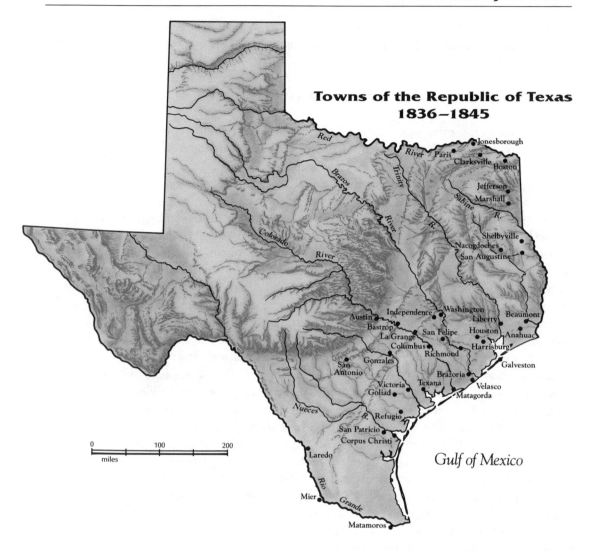

**Towns of the Republic of Texas
1836–1845**

expeditions from Mexico. Laredo, meanwhile, faced periodic occupations by Mexican armies and Texas volunteers. Both towns remained isolated from the Anglo settlements, though Anglo outsiders began drifting into San Antonio in the late 1830s, creating friction with the dominant population of Mexicans.

Despite the ruggedness of frontier living and the hard economic times, urbanites looked with anticipation at the advantages that city living offered them: as a marketplace, the city brought people, resources, and ideas together. For the literate public, the larger cities featured professional theatre performances, social organizations, newspapers, and opportunities to obtain a private education. Businesspeople, lawyers, and doctors walked alongside blacksmiths, gunsmiths, wheelwrights, tanners and saddlers, tailors, and carpenters. Some urban workers agitated for improved conditions in their trade. In 1838, printers in Houston formed the Texas Typographical Association and, in what is considered the first work stoppage in Texas, struck that year and won a slight wage increase. Conversely, businesspeople in Houston, Matagorda, and Galveston founded organizations that they termed "chambers of commerce," apparently for settling legal disputes arising among themselves, without resorting to litigation.

FARMS, PLANTATIONS, AND RANCHES

The liberal land policies of the republic helped numerous Texans begin new lives as farmers. Cotton and corn remained the common staples in most agricultural areas of the republic. In spite of bad weather, crop-destroying insects, and other difficulties, small farmers and slaveholding planters helped advance cotton as the traditionally most-reliable export commodity, though by no means was the crop their material salvation. Farmers supplemented their earnings by raising domesticated animals and planting side plots of vegetables and fruit trees. Most provided their own services—blacksmithing and the like—frequently with the assistance of the entire family, or, as in the case of plantation owners, with the help of slaves.

The slave plantation, generally situated in southeastern and eastern Texas, stood during this time as an important part of the agrarian sector. With impediments to slavery removed following independence, Texans immediately acted to define the institution. The Constitution of 1836 guaranteed the legality of human property by providing that persons in bondage at the time of the document's writing would continue in that status. Subsequent laws passed by the republic's congress augmented constitutional provisions. Legislation specified various punishments for those found guilty of stealing slaves, encouraging slaves to run away, giving refuge to fugitive slaves, or abetting slave insurrection. With such official support, slavery as an institution experienced brisk expansion in the republic. The number of plantations increased, as did the slave population, from 5,000 black persons (all but a handful of whom were enslaved) in 1836, to 38,753 in 1847, according to a state census taken that year.

The sorry lot of blacks in Texas rested on racial prejudices and discrimination that went all the way back to Elizabethan England, and plantation owners saw blacks as innately inferior. Slave codes carefully defined the status of blacks as chattels in perpetuity. Laws imposed the most severe penalties on blacks found guilty of assaulting or murdering a white person, sexually assaulting a white woman, or committing arson, though the white community easily could and often did turn to lynch law to avenge anything it considered a heinous act against a white person. Because of the cruelty of slavery, whites desperately feared slave plots against them, and companies of volunteers patrolled the countryside to try to squelch any possible trouble and to look out for runaways. Slaves lived out their days without the possibility of relief from arduous field work, which

"6 o'clock a.m., Military Plaza," San Antonio.
The UT Institute of Texan Cultures, No. 83–85

in Texas usually meant the planting, care, and harvesting of cotton, corn, and sugar. Furthermore, slaves could expect beatings and even death as punishment for failing to meet the work expectations of their owners, for being insolent, or for attempting to escape.

Although a failed escape would bring them severe penalties, in the 1830s many slaves attempted to gain their liberty by escaping and then joining the East Texas Indians, such as the Cherokees. In the 1840s, however, other runaways turned south, finding assistance from Texas Mexicans who escorted them through the sparsely settled, semi-arid frontier between Central Texas and the Rio Grande, and on into Mexico. That country soon became a haven for runaway slaves; an estimated 3,000 fugitive slaves found refuge in Mexico by the early 1850s.

Not every black person in the republic was a slave, for there was a very small number of free blacks, about 300 according to the above-mentioned census of 1847. These people held a tenuous status, however, for both the government and society refused to acknowledge their freedom. Whites discouraged free blacks from living as full citizens of the republic, applying the same negative attitudes and laws toward them that they did to bondspeople.

Cattle and horse raising remained the traditional pursuits in East Texas. Long a Spanish and Mexican enterprise in the region, Anglos added a new dimension to livestock raising when they imported ranching traditions from the South, primarily South Carolina. Although large cattle herds were raised in the various Anglo-American settlements of the republic, the most successful ranches lay in the Coastal Prairie, a grassland region stretching from near the mouth of the Sabine River and running along the Gulf Coast (extending for some 75 to 100 miles inland) before reaching its western limits near Victoria.

Anglo Americans who brought their sheep to Texas cross bred them with Spanish sheep, which had been raised in the region since the colonial era. During the 1830s and 1840s, moreover, Mexicans drove flocks of sheep out of the northern Mexican states and into the Republic of Texas, and European immigrants brought sheep from their native lands, too. Despite the wide interest in the sheep-raising industry, this aspect of agribusiness did not exactly thrive during this period.

THE TEXIANS

Texian was a term that expressed the people's identity with and pride in the new land, and indeed the republic was fertile soil for the emergence of a strong nationalism. Texans, after all, had a revolutionary past to glorify, one replete with war heroes who symbolized a tradition of fighting against tyranny. By the 1840s, the Alamo emerged as a symbol of the Texian's valor and martyrdom for liberty, and citizens toasted its place in Texas lore upon appropriate occasions. Independence Day and San Jacinto Day became dates for firecrackers, patriotic speeches, parades, and all sorts of outdoor festivities. Leaders of the era proclaimed the nation's uniqueness and encouraged the perpetuation of the values and ideas expressive of "Texian culture," traits such as resiliency, self-reliance, courage, and faith in the promise the future of the Republic held.

However, as was already suggested, some of the people that the republic received from both the United States and Europe were not exactly upstanding and law-abiding citizens. Consequently, in its early years the republic was a more-or-less undisciplined society in which individualism sometimes was expressed without much inhibition. In the fledgling towns of the republic, wild, vulgar, sometimes even violent and brutal behavior flourished, and the substantial consumption of alcoholic beverages fueled the general lawlessness. Bowie knives were commonly toted by folks whose habit of constantly swearing seemed to reinforce their ruggedness, while "gentlemen" turned to the duel to settle insults and disagreements.

Often descended from remote areas of Kentucky, Alabama, or Tennessee, where wilderness violence was common, many immigrants to the republic carried with them a heritage of fending for themselves. These people often chose to settle private quarrels without the assistance of legal authorities, who mostly resided a long way from the frontier anyway.

Social pressures emanating from the persistent threat of danger, under which many Texans lived, further fed the population's general belligerence. Texans valued manly prowess and displays of courage in the face of danger—Indians, Mexican soldiers or bandits, the dueling opponent, a wild animal, or whatever hostile force came their way. Not surprisingly, the most highly esteemed members of society were military heroes.

The very bravado that led people to stand up and fight against their enemies, however, nourished a disorderly society. A violent feud involving the so-called "Regulators" and "Moderators" (labels traceable to feuds that originally started in Appalachia) erupted in East Texas over land titles in the late 1830s. In 1840, there was a series of public shootings and murders, and a reign of terror spread over Shelby County until President Houston sent the militia in to end the lawlessness. Smaller feuds, however, continued to spin off from this disorder for the rest of the century.

Of course, there were honest, principled citizens to balance those of violent temperament; and the vast majority of immigrants were decent, law-abiding folks who basked proudly in the "Texian" label.

THE INDIANS

The government of the Republic of Texas had no Indian policy to inherit. As of 1836, it had no standing treaties to honor, as old ones made between Mexico and the hostile tribes were now void. The Constitution of 1836 said nothing of recognizing Indian rights to the land, and the government was too new to have judicial precedent to guide it.

By this time, many of the old tribes from the colonial era barely clung to life. Their fortunes during this period came to be touched further by inexorable population expansion on the part of Anglos, as well as the alternating Indian policy of Houston, with its attempt at conciliation, and that of Lamar, which emphasized displacement and extinction. The Karankawas, for one, suffered further setbacks as Anglo pioneers founded new towns and ranches along the coastal lands that once had been Karankawa hunting grounds. Debilitated by sickness, alcoholism, and malnutrition, the Karankawas seemed unable to stop the encroachment or the attacks leveled against them by the settlers during the mid-1840s. By then, the Karankawas teetered near extinction as a recognizable tribe. The Caddos, meanwhile, saw only a slight interlude from their own misery of poverty and displacement. Lamar's plan to expel Indians had led Caddos to retreat into Oklahoma, but Houston's re-election as president had proven fortuitous, and they had returned to Texas and established themselves along the northwestern stretches of the Brazos River. As of 1845, the Caddos believed they had found safety in their new camps located some distance away from the westernmost Anglo settlements.

As early as 1823, a delegation of Cherokees had journeyed to Mexico City seeking land titles for their people. Mexico had never honored their requests, but, as noted, the Cherokees and Sam Houston consummated a treaty in February 1836 acknowledging Cherokee rights to certain lands in East Texas. The First Congress rejected the agreement, however, reasoning that the treaty had been negotiated by the ad interim government and thus did not obligate the republic to honor it, that the lands inhabited by the Cherokees had never been awarded by the Mexican government, that the Indian lands actually belonged to the empresario contract given to David G. Burnet, who had already settled several families therein, and that Indian attacks on the settlements had continued despite the treaty.

Duwali, the Cherokee leader, had expected approval of the treaty, for Houston had supported it unswervingly. But with the election of Lamar, Cherokee hopes for becoming recognized landowners vanished. The new president harbored fixed attitudes against Indians—he had been in Georgia when Creek Indian lands there had been expropriated by the whites—and persistent attacks across the republic committed by the most hostile tribes, together with his belief that some of the Cherokees were part of a multitribe conspiracy to destabilize the republic, produced his hard-line policy toward all American Indians, and, most prominently, his push for the expulsion of the Cherokees. Despite Duwali's logical argument outlining the Cherokees' legitimate claims to the East Texas lands promised them, Lamar pressed his demand for their removal: either the Cherokees would leave peacefully or they would be forcibly evicted. The Indians chose to resist, and at the Battle of Neches, in present-day Van Zandt County, regular troops and two volunteer companies defeated the Cherokees and killed Duwali on July 16, 1839. Cherokee resistance died with the chief, and the remainder of his people departed across the Red River into the Indian Territory (Oklahoma) or dispersed into Mexico.

To the west, hostile tribes, as independent as ever, roved the plains. Especially fierce were the Comanches, who had fought off, and even raided, Apaches, Spaniards, and Mexicans for years. Unlike the Cherokees, the Comanches in the mid-1830s had yet to feel pressure from land-hungry whites, but soon enough farmsteads were being established close to their hunting grounds, a foreshadowing of wholesale intrusion. Simultaneously, those settlements tantalized the Comanches with items that the Indians found quite useful for survival. Consequently, the Comanches consistently breached the treaties that the Houston government had negotiated. Furthermore, the Comanches had no real tribal government: principally functioning as nomadic, autonomous bands, agreements reached with one group meant little to the majority of the Comanche people.

In the first encounters, Anglo Texans found the Plains Indians as formidable as had the Spaniards and Mexicans before them—the Texans' Kentucky rifles proving largely ineffective against mounted warriors on the open plains. But by the late 1830s, the Texans began to find more successful methods of fighting the Comanches. The "strike and pursue" tactic of the ranging companies, endorsed by Lamar, was one such technique.

By 1840, it seemed as if both sides might be ripe for a truce; the Comanches expressed a willingness to talk in order to end the Ranger strikes, while numerous other problems plagued Lamar's government. Comanche raids, furthermore, had left the destruction of property, murder, and a pattern of hostage taking in their wake.

In March, Comanches met with Texans at the Council House in San Antonio to negotiate for the release of captured white women and children. The Indians brought with them a young white prisoner by the name of Matilda Lockhart, but they had purposely left the remainder of their white captives behind. Texas authorities, who had planned to take the Comanche chiefs into custody and ransom them for the return of all the whites, attacked the Indians upon learning from Lockhart that the Indians did not intend to release their prisoners all at once. Most of the Indians present were killed, as were several Texas troops. The Comanche tribe retaliated for the episode by torturing their prisoners to death. They also implemented a plan of attack upon the settlers. In August 1840, close to 1,000 warriors plundered Victoria and Linnville. But Texas Rangers under Ben McCulloch gave chase, and upon engaging the Indians they served them two punishing defeats.

Subsequently, the Rangers kept the Indians on the run. Among the leaders in these campaigns was John Coffee "Jack" Hays, a Tennessee immigrant in charge of a San Antonio outpost. Armed with the revolver patented by Samuel

Colt in the eastern United States in 1836, Hays launched a tactical war that used the element of surprise and a policy of giving no quarter. Effective as Hays's tactics proved, periodic raiding of settlements by the Indians continued throughout the era of the republic. In October 1844, Houston successfully negotiated a treaty of peace and commerce with the Comanches and other western tribes at Tehuacana Creek (in modern-day McLennan County), and even though the pact produced a time of relative tranquility for the republic, the Indians' marauding never stopped completely.

THE TEJANOS

Texas Mexicans had found themselves caught between two worlds during the independence movement. A few had assumed prominent roles alongside Anglos, and their presence had been conspicuous at Washington-on-the-Brazos, the Alamo, and San Jacinto. While some had envisioned their destinies tied to the capitalist economic order being furthered by Anglo Americans in the 1820s, others were cautious toward a people who expressed disgust and contempt for them as Mexicans.

For Tejanos, the post-1836 reality presented a departure from a way of life rooted in the Texas frontera: they were at a numerical disadvantage, business was conducted in a different language, and they were not completely familiar with the new form of politics. Despite guarantees in the Constitution of 1836, Tejanos seemed defenseless against a people who freely expressed their dislike for them and openly desired retribution against their race for Santa Anna's carnage at the Alamo and Goliad. The wrath of whites was strong and swift: throughout the old Department of Béxar, Mexican families were banished from their homes immediately after the Battle of San Jacinto, and rancheros later had great difficulty recovering their scattered stock. In the late 1830s, the Mexicans of San Antonio felt like "foreigners in their native land," as increasing numbers of Anglos moved into the area. According to Juan Seguín, who served as mayor of the city in 1841–1842, Béxareños came to him seeking protection from harassment by white antagonists. "Could I leave them defenseless, exposed to the assaults of foreigners, who on the pretext that they were Mexican, treated them worse than brutes?" he asked. By the summer of 1842, Seguín had become a refugee in Mexico, seeking to flee the enmity of whites who considered him an accomplice in Mexican efforts to reconquer Texas.

Notwithstanding their quandary, Tejanos molded a place for themselves within the new society. While remaining faithful to the tenets of their cultural past, they adopted many of the new customs and habits. Anglo American institutions with which they interacted, moreover, eventually acculturated them into embracing many of what would become mainstream concepts, values, judgments, and patterns of behavior.

Therefore, in the Tejano communities continuity accompanied change. The old upper class, which traced its origins to the colonial era, endured, although

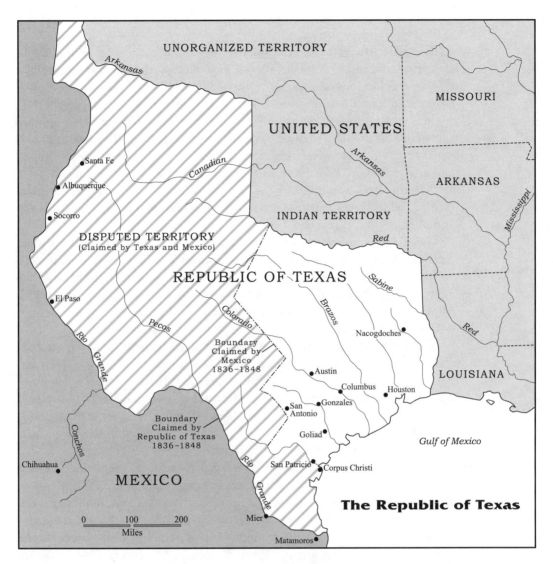

The Republic of Texas

precariously. It was most visible in the Béxar area, where the Navarros, the Seguíns, and other prominent families had been entrenched—indeed, some of these oligarchs went on to serve as members of the Texas congress. The majority of Tejanos were less fortunate in finding a niche in Anglo society; most supported themselves by carrying on, as their people had done for many years, in the ranching and freighting enterprises.

LEARNING AND PLAIN FOLKS

As colonists, Anglo Texans had complained, somewhat unjustifiably, of Mexico's failure to provide adequate educational opportunities for them. Once independent, however, Texans faced so many problems in improving the general welfare that they themselves failed to remedy the situation they had decried on the eve of independence.

Education, therefore, did not improve much under the reign of the republic. Lamar's ambition for educational grandeur produced only one public school—this in Houston during the year 1839–1840—but citizens improvised in creating informal learning institutions. In the rural areas, mothers taught their children in makeshift classrooms. Whenever possible, communities employed teachers (who usually received payment in produce), most of whom lacked proper training and saw teaching more as a way to supplement their livelihood than as a profession. Education thus remained rudimentary; the unpredictable weather, the crops, and raids by the Indians all interfered with the routine of learning. Educational reforms such as those Horace Mann popularized in the United States hardly reached Texans.

Well-to-do families were able to educate their children by dispatching them to private schools. Female academies, also known as "seminaries," were numerous but usually short-lived; they emphasized courses designed to provide the "appropriate instruction" for young women—basic reading and writing skills with a smattering of math, history, or geography. Parents with enough money to do so sent their children to schools in the United States.

The lamentable condition of education and the travails of living on a demanding frontier naturally impeded the advancement of the arts, and few artists of merit emerged from the republic. Jefferson Wright achieved recognition as the semiofficial painter of the republic, and he painted famous portraits of President Sam Houston and other notables. Literary pieces, some of them historical, found their way into print, but citizens of the republic produced little literature that could be claimed as their own.

What frontier people did have was a knack for relating a more folksy literature—namely, colorful tall tales and yarns of exaggerated humor. The literature of the republic, thus, was largely in the oral tradition of common folks, one difficult for scholars to trace and preserve. Topics of this genre included humankind's struggle with nature and exploits of such heroes as Davy Crockett and even "Old Sam" the president. Houston's affinity for whiskey, his unhurried drawl, and his fondness for whittling made him a subject with whom plain people could identify.

But there existed enough of a reading public that newspapers prospered. The *Telegraph and Texas Register,* founded during the days of independence, led the way in respectability and staying power. From its headquarters in Houston, it kept citizens of the republic abreast of the issues of annexation, real-estate promotions, immigration, presidential campaigns, and local politics.

Competition for the Houston paper came principally from Galveston, but a number of papers also developed in Texas's interior. When Austin arose as the new capital, at least two significant newspapers started publication there to cover political matters at the seat of government and to carry news of frontier affairs. Once development spread to northeastern Texas in the 1840s, newspapers emerged there also, covering such episodes as the ongoing local feud between the Regulators and the Moderators.

TRANSPORTATION

The intellectual condition of citizens of the republic—indeed just about everything that touched the lives of people, including the economy—was hampered by the retarded state of transportation. During the days of the republic, Texans remained dependent on existing waterways and crude roads for mobility. People commonly traveled down the several rivers to the Gulf, but with great difficulty, since boat captains had to navigate around numerous obstacles and seasonally deal with water levels that were alternately too low or too high. Outlets into the Gulf presented similar problems—river mouths could be shallow, erratic (because silt and sandbars can shift), or simply impassable. Land travel was no less convenient. Since country roads did not drain well, downpours could hamper commerce for months, the standing water and thick mud stalling stagecoaches, freight wagons, and mail service and shutting down trade between the interior and Gulf ports. Consequently, different parts of the country remained isolated from one another, and practically no funds to subsidize internal improvements in the infrastructure were forthcoming from the financially strapped government.

RECOGNITION IN EUROPE

At the same time that Texans were pursuing annexation to the United States, their agents in Europe petitioned for diplomatic recognition and loans that could assist the republic with its pecuniary difficulties. Eminent among the envoys was James Pinckney Henderson, who tempted the English with the opportunity to acquire prime access to Texas cotton and the chance to sell British manufactured goods in the republic. But England wished to maintain cordial relations with Mexico, and strong abolitionist sentiment in Great Britain opposed recognizing a country committed to nourishing slavery. The British, therefore, could only consent to a trade agreement in 1838. The French balked at formally recognizing a country whose independence might be short-lived, and they, too, would concede only to a temporary commercial arrangement.

With the all-important European recognition eluding the republic, Lamar commissioned James Hamilton, a former governor of South Carolina and an enthusiastic backer of the Texas experiment, to assist Henderson. Hamilton also had the assignment of negotiating Lamar's desired $5 million loan. With a need to acquire new friends in North America and the prospect that Texas would remain independent of the United States, the French government directed the secretary of the Washington legation, Count Alphonse de Saligny, to inspect the republic. The count's favorable impression, verified by other observers, finally led France, on September 25, 1839, to become the first European nation to recognize the Republic of Texas. His work accomplished, Henderson returned home, but Hamilton traveled to other countries seeking similar treaties. In September 1840, he convinced the Dutch to acknowledge Texas's sovereignty.

In due time, Hamilton returned to Britain. He reminded the British that friendly relations could indeed produce mutually beneficial commercial windfalls; diplomatic ties might also give England the clout it needed to thwart the United States' westward expansion. Convinced that a treaty would serve their interests, the British in November 1840 also extended diplomatic recognition to the republic.

However commendable Hamilton's achievements, he had not been able to procure the $5 million desired by President Lamar to buoy the Texas economy. The traditional story, however, that Hamilton failed in France due to the "Pig War" in Texas is not true. According to this often-repeated explanation, while in Austin, the Count de Saligny became embroiled in an undignified altercation with his innkeeper after the Count's servant shot and killed some pigs that had been eating corn being stored for the Count's own consumption. When the Texas government failed to support the Count against the enraged innkeeper, the owner of the derelict hogs, Saligny left in a huff and recommended to his government that the loan not be extended. Actually, this trifling episode had little bearing on France's decision. The French were worried about their own economic problems, and they could ill afford risking a large sum on an economy as unsteady as that of Texas. Indeed, Hamilton never blamed Saligny for the failure to get the loan approved. Britain had reasons similar to those of France for rejecting Hamilton's financial appeals as well.

FRICTION WITH MEXICO

Mexico still refused to honor the Treaties of Velasco, so even as European countries recognized the new republic, Mexico sought to return Texas to the fold. To that end, it assigned saboteurs to Texas to undermine the government in the hope of reconquering the wayward province. An alliance discovered in 1838–1839 between Vicente Córdova and Manuel Flores—two Tejanos with ties to Mexico's military in Matamoros—and the Cherokees seemed part of a design to prevent Texas from maintaining its independence. Recent research portrays Córdova and Flores as leaders of discontented Tejanos in the Nacogdoches area who turned to the Mexican government in a desperate gesture to alleviate their oppressed status under the new Anglo government.

While Houston had tempered his policy towards Mexico—militarily and economically, he reasoned, Texas could not afford another war with the erstwhile mother country—Lamar risked provocation by talking up his plans for expansion to the south and the west. Diplomatically, he offered to buy the disputed region between the Nueces River and the Rio Grande, but privately he prepared to carry out his grand illusions of empire. Such dreams led to the ill-fated Santa Fe Expedition of 1841.

Lamar posited that if Texas were to incorporate New Mexico (he just assumed that the New Mexicans would prefer to live under the Texas republic than under the sovereignty of Mexico), the acquisition would enhance Texas's destiny in several ways. First, it could help the nation share in the trade between Santa Fe and Missouri (such commerce had begun in the 1820s) collecting specie at custom houses that would aid the struggling economy. Second, it would give Texas persuasive leverage in its position in the middle of the continent. Lastly, it might even be a stepping stone for further expansion towards the Pacific. Along this train of thought, if Texas were to annex California, it would enjoy strategic and commercial benefits on two oceans.

Without the congress's consent, Lamar assembled an expedition of 320 armed men for his expansionist campaign and dispatched them to Santa Fe, New Mexico, on June 20, 1841. After a trying and desperate march of about 1,000 miles, the Texans, under the command of Hugh McLeod, arrived in New Mexico in October only to be intercepted by soldiers who subdued them without difficulty. The invaders quickly realized that the people of Santa Fe did not welcome their proposal of annexation, and the Texans were escorted all the way to Mexico City, where they were promptly imprisoned. Back in Texas, the congress did not take Lamar's blunder lightly. It censured him and might have commenced impeachment proceedings against him had his tree-year term not been drawing to a close.

Mexico responded daringly to Lamar's gamble. In February 1842, President Santa Anna ordered General Rafael Vásquez across the Rio Grande and into San Antonio. The Mexicans captured the city on March 5, in an apparent gesture to reassert Mexico's claim to territory as far north as Béxar (or, conversely, to negate the Texans insistence that the republic extended to the Rio Grande). Though Vásquez lowered the Mexican flag and returned to Mexico after only two days, San Antonio fell to the Mexicans once again, this time to troops under the command of General Adrián Woll, who took some sixty prisoners with him when forced to retreat by Texan volunteers arriving at the scene. Texans, who had been on edge since the Vásquez raid, now felt inspired to vindicate their country's honor. Houston thus commanded General Alexander Somervell to lead a volunteer expedition of about 750 men toward the Rio Grande: its mission was to patrol the border to prevent further invasions. The general reached the river without incident in early December and took Laredo. Part of his force then marched downriver in the direction of the Mexican village of Guerrero, where Somervell decided to go no farther.

But approximately 300 of the volunteers ignored the general's decision, opting to press a counteroffensive deeper into Mexico. At the little town of Mier, on Christmas Day 1842, Mexican infantrymen that had been occupying the town for the last two days overpowered some 260 of the intruding Texans. The surviving members of what became known as the "Mier Expedition" were taken prisoner and then marched toward Mexico City. On February 11, 1843, the Texans managed to escape, though only four of them actually made it back to

Shooting of the 17 designated prisoners from the "Mier Expedition," at El Salada, Mexico. *Painting by Theodore Gentilz. Courtesy of Mr. J. Laurence Sheerin*

the republic, for Mexican troops recaptured 176 of them. At this point, the would-be escapees were forced to draw from a pot containing 159 white beans and 17 black ones. Those unfortunates who had drawn the black beans were lined up against a wall and shot to death. The authorities confined the remaining prisoners in the capital.

ANNEXATION

The Mier Expedition jarred Texans into rethinking their Lone Star status. Annexation to the United States, though loudly rejected by Lamar, had ever been the dream of most Texans, and the ignominious defeat at Mier now heightened many people's preference for statehood. Joining the Union, in so far as Texans saw things, would bring benefits in the form of financial and military security. People's distrust of the republic's currency and the ever-increasing public debt seemed to be taking Texas toward possible bankruptcy. Militarily, the republic stood vulnerable to Mexico's hostilities—some feared a massive invasion from the south—while the Indians continued threatening those settlers on the frontier. To many in the United States, the annexation of Texas also was appealing. Those with an eye for Texas lands, among them real estate speculators and southern slaveholders who hoped to profit from an increase in land values once Texas entered the Union, displayed particular interest.

Public debate in the United States during 1843 and 1844 revived hopes of Texas's annexation. Following the Mier Expedition, Houston had begun making overtures toward England and France regarding closer commercial ties, especially if they persuaded Mexico to concede independence to Texas. Diplomatic recognition by Mexico, Houston hoped, would end Mexico's harassment of the republic. By early 1844, sentiment in the United States was shifting toward annexation, for some U.S. citizens worried that Britain, which now offered Texas assistance, ostensibly in defense of its commercial treaties, might gain undue influence in North America, but also because the spirit of Manifest Destiny—the concept that the United States' fate was to occupy the entire continent, from the Atlantic to the Pacific—still captivated many Americans.

But the annexation of Texas faced solid resistance from northern abolitionists and Free Soilers (those who opposed the expansion of slavery) who argued against adding another slave state (the South's foremost spokesperson, John C. Calhoun, had argued publicly for the annexation of Texas so that slavery could be expanded), and from the Whig party, which direly predicted a war with Mexico should the United States acquire Texas. An annexation treaty negotiated in April 1844, therefore, proved abortive: the U.S. Senate rejected it by a vote of thirty-five to sixteen. Meanwhile, Houston renewed his courtship of the British and the French while simultaneously sympathizing with the pro-annexation camp. He later likened his strategy to that of a woman playing off two suitors in order to gain a commitment from the one she loved.

When James K. Polk, the Democratic party candidate for U.S. president, won election on an expansionist platform in November 1844, the U.S. Congress again took up the matter of incorporating Texas into the Union. The next month, outgoing president John Tyler proposed the annexation of the Lone Star republic through a joint resolution. This maneuver required only the majority approval of both houses of Congress, instead of the approval of two-thirds of the Senate, which the annexationists previously had failed to win. Congress expedited the annexation resolution, and on March 3, 1845, President Tyler signed the bill. According to the terms of the act, Texas won admission to the Union as a single state (though as many as five states could be carved out of the former republic) and retained title to its public lands, as a means of repaying its debts. Annexation helped neutralize British influence in the middle of the continent, satisfied the U.S. voters' endorsement for continental expansion, and opened new opportunities for more people who wanted to speculate with the rich lands of Texas.

For Texans, annexation meant relief from public debt and a new measure of military security. When the new (and last) president of Texas, Anson Jones, called a special session of congress in June 1845, the annexation offer met little resistance. Meantime, a constitutional convention produced a state constitution that the voters approved overwhelmingly in October. A few weeks later, the U.S. Congress accepted it. President Polk then signed the Texas Admission Act on December 29, 1845. In February of 1846, James Pinckney Henderson was the first to assume the office of governor of Texas.

THE WAR WITH MEXICO

As many had feared, Mexicans expressed indignation that the United States should annex land that Mexico considered its sovereign territory. The Mexican minister in Washington immediately protested the approval of the joint resolution, and diplomatic relations between the two nations deteriorated rapidly. The Mexican minister prepared to return home, as did his American counterpart in Mexico City. War appeared to be the next step.

Polk aimed to pressure Mexico into formally ceding the coveted lands in its Far North. To this end, he assigned General Zachary Taylor and his forces to a post near the Rio Grande, but he also made a last effort to reconcile differences through diplomacy. The most crucial issue preventing compromise was the disputed territory between the Nueces River and the Rio Grande. Throughout New Spain's colonial era, the Nueces had been considered the northern boundary of the state of Tamaulipas and the southern extreme of Texas, but the Texans argued that the Treaties of Velasco had recognized the Rio Grande as the republic's southern border. John Slidell, the U.S. special envoy sent to Mexico City in December 1845 to resolve the issue, was to press for the Rio Grande as the boundary line, but also to offer the Mexican government $5 million for the New Mexico territory and $25 million for California. Mexico rejected his offers, and by March 1846 Slidell was homeward bound.

As Slidell was on his way back to Washington, Polk pondered his next move. Fate seemed to favor the president, for on May 9, 1846, news arrived from Taylor that he had skirmished with Mexican cavalry near modern-day Brownsville on April 25 and incurred casualties of sixteen men killed or wounded. At this point, Polk delivered a war message to Congress, reasoning that "Mexico has passed the boundary of the United States, has invaded our territory, and shed American blood on American soil. She has proclaimed that hostilities exist and that the two nations are now at war." Congress approved the war resolution a few days later.

Causes

Several historical interpretations seek to explain the causes of the war with Mexico. One school of thought sees Mexican belligerency and irrationality in failing to act in good faith towards resolving the boundary question as a causal factor, compelling Polk to declare war. In 1846, the Centralists, the same party that had issued the Law of April 6, 1830, and had expressed anti-American feelings on numerous occasions, once more ruled Mexico. Irreconcilable Anglophobes, the Centralists had initiated the hostilities by ordering troops across the Rio Grande to attack Zachary Taylor's camp on the north bank of the river. A counterview holds that Polk simply manipulated the United States into the war. In this interpretation, the United States provoked the conflict as a means of acquiring Texas and California. An expansionist fervor, with capitalism as its driving force, motivated ambitious Americans to take whatever steps necessary to acquire Mexico's Far North: Mexico was a quiescent player. Most scholars from Mexico subscribe to this point of analysis; they see their country as a pawn in the game of U.S. imperialism.

But recent historiography has presented a more objective treatment of the war with Mexico. One body of thought maintains that national preservation forced Mexico to fight. The Mexican people would have revolted against any leader who had not resisted U.S. designs on their territory. Thus, politicians of every persuasion in Mexico publicly advocated war with the United States—to do less would have invited popular censure and internal rebellion. However, recent revisionist historians from Mexico suggest another motive for the bravado: a military victory would have permitted the prevailing political party to maintain power in the country for years to come. Whatever the case, Mexican leaders considered retreat impossible, so the government opted to face the United States head on rather than risk self-destruction.

In the same vein, yet another recent interpretation says Polk pursued a provocative plan of bluster and intimidation. In the United States, Mexicans were regarded as a degenerate Indian race unable to exert a stable influence over their own land. Faced by a people regarded as feeble and lacking in self-respect, Polk's administration hoped to annex all of Mexico's Far North without resorting to military force. But when Mexico was ultimately backed into a corner at the Rio Grande, Polk was forced to prosecute his intrigue.

The War

The U.S. offensive involved a three-pronged attack: the invasion of New Mexico and California, northern Mexico, and central Mexico through Vera Cruz on the Gulf Coast. Some 6,000 Texans participated in the U.S. campaigns, though the mounted volunteers gained the most notoriety. The Texas Rangers, as they now preferred to be called, became the "eyes and ears" of Zachary Taylor's army. Under such figures as John Coffee "Jack" Hays, Ben McCulloch, William A. "Big Foot" Wallace, Mustang Grey, and Samuel H. Walker, in battle Ranger companies and regiments earned a reputation as being second to none, prompting Taylor to single them out for commendation. But the activities of the Rangers in the war campaigns created bitter memories in Mexico, for in many cases the Rangers carried their frontier individualism to extremes: they wreaked havoc on innocent civilians and cold-bloodedly disposed of those suspected of abetting the resistance movement. When Texas Rangers went on expeditions in search of Mexican guerrilla forces, they brought back no prisoners, shooting the guerrilleros on the spot. After Taylor won a decisive victory at Buena Vista in February 1847, the Rangers received orders to reinforce General Winfield Scott's command, already in Mexico City by September 1847. Assigned to protect Scott's supply line from the coast, the Rangers cleared the jungles of guerrilleros and again earned praise for their courage. But their reputation for committing atrocities preceded them when they arrived in Mexico City on December 6 to join Scott. People murmured their fears of *Los Diablos Tejanos* (the Texas Devils), and

William A. "Big Foot" Wallace in San Antonio. *Western History Collections, University of Oklahoma Library*

the Rangers did little to allay such dread, continuing their practice of abusing Mexicans until the war's conclusion with the signing of the Treaty of Guadalupe Hidalgo on February 2, 1848.

The treaty confirmed the United States' title to Texas and turned over California and New Mexico to the *norteamericanos*. Under the agreement, the United States paid Mexico $18,250,000 for these regions, which constituted almost half of the Mexican nation. According to the treaty, those of Mexican descent living on the newly taken lands would acquire all the rights of U.S. citizens and their property rights were to be respected inviolably.

The conflict left a hostile legacy between Mexico and the United States. Mexico began to blame all of its ills on the imperialists and vigorously condemn all things Yankee. For the United States, the war brought the issue of slavery's expansion to the forefront: would the new territories be organized on a "slave" or "free" basis? In this issue, Texas would play a vital part, for its acceptance into the Union had strengthened the South's hand in the fiery debate over the future of slavery in the United States.

END OF THE LONE STAR REPUBLIC

Swift and significant changes had transpired in the course of Texas history between 1836 and 1848. During this time, the claim over Texas once held by Native Americans, then Spaniards, and finally Mexicans ended. For those who had lived through the transformation, a look back showed a world at once different and familiar.

Most markedly distinguishing the mood of people in 1848 from that of the preindependence period was the conviction that they now commanded their own destiny. An unpopular dictatorship had been removed, "backward" rule had been replaced by "enlightened" politics, and a "wilderness" had been rescued for "civilized" humanity. Texans toasted their triumph on national holidays and on other patriotic occasions, their beliefs in American ideals reinvigorated now that they were United States citizens. Could anyone question the success of the government founded by Washington, Adams, Hamilton, Jefferson, Madison, and Monroe?

Other differences were not difficult to discern. A new population had replaced Texas's old inhabitants, though Anglo Americans had outnumbered the native Tejanos as early as the mid-1820s. By 1836, Texas was home to only a few settlers from overseas; by 1848, European colonies dotted the terrain. Cities had taken different forms. New urban layouts resembled those typical of cities in the United States—individual promoters and developers now determined a city's appearance, the newcomers largely abandoning the old Spanish tradition of urban planning. Cultural influences now defined the state's geography: East Texas contained many transplanted folks from the Old South; North Texas, in the vicinity of modern-day Dallas, was settled by pioneers from Missouri, Arkansas, Kentucky, Tennessee, and Illinois; Central Texas had attracted southerners who owned successful plantations, and European settlers, especially Germans, on its western fringes; while South Texas remained the stronghold of Tejanos, especially the regions around San Antonio and Laredo. Occupations, leisure-time activities, and styles of architecture and dress were only a few of the many things that now set apart the world of Texans in 1848 from that of Mexicans in 1836.

But the Texas of 1848 was too closely tied to the preceding historical era to have rejected the Mexican legacy completely. However much Texans might associate Mexico with ignorance, their fifteen-year experience under Mexico left its imprint upon them, and Anglos carried that influence into the period of the republic. The Hispanic tradition continued in the laws that the Texans decided to keep, the empresario systems of Mexico and the Republic of Texas, the approach towards financing education, and even the strategy behind the organization of law enforcement groups such as the Texas Rangers.

Material conditions were more or less the same in 1848 as they had been a dozen years earlier. Obviously, the Texans had not been exceptionally successful in creating a vibrant economy (though they did ensure its capitalist basis), work days still lasted from sunup to sundown in rural regions, the state of transportation was only slightly better than it had been in Mexican days, and daily hardships of struggling against diseases and Indians, of fetching water and disposing of waste, were just as severe.

The general class structure of the republic also had carried over from the 1830s. Anglos dominated society, of course, but the majority of black Texans still served as slaves, Mexicans occupied the lower stratum, and whites persisted in regarding the Indians as irremediable savages.

As the 1850s began, all who resided in the State of Texas were caught up in the same historical currents as other Americans. People disagreed over the meaning of republicanism, had different material ambitions, and each of the various cultural groups desired to retain its special identity while enjoying the benefits of being American. The electoral process gave Americans an avenue for arriving at some consensus, but conflict and violence remained alternatives for defending deeply held convictions. Indeed, within a dozen years after the signing of the Treaty of Guadalupe Hidalgo, Texans found themselves seceding from the nation they had fought so hard to join.

The Republic of Texas is No More—President Anson Jones conducts the Annexation Ceremony, February 19, 1846. Drawing by Norman Price. *The Center for American History, The University of Texas at Austin, CN 03085-A*

READINGS

Books and Dissertations

Barr, Alwyn, *Black Texans: A History of Negroes in Texas, 1528–1971* (Austin: Jenkins Publishing Co., 1973).

Campbell, Randolph B., *An Empire for Slavery: The Peculiar Institution in Texas, 1821–1865* (Baton Rouge: Louisiana State University Press, 1989).

———, *Sam Houston and the American Southwest* (New York: HarperCollins, 1993).

Clarke, Mary (Whatley), *Chief Bowles and the Texas Cherokees* (Norman: University of Oklahoma Press, 1971).

Connor, Seymour V., *Adventure in Glory* (Austin: Steck-Vaughn, 1965).

Everert, Dianna, *The Texas Cherokees: A People between Two Fires* (Norman: University of Oklahoma Press, 1990).

Fehrenbach, T. R., *Comanches: The Destruction of a People* (New York: Knopf, 1974).

———, *Lone Star: A History of Texas and the Texans* (New York: McMillan Publishing Co., 1968).

Haynes, Sam W., *Soldiers of Misfortune: The Somervell and Mier Expedition* (Austin: University of Texas Press, 1990).

Himmel, Kelly F., *The Conquest of the Karankawas and Tonkawas, 1821–1859* (College Station: Texas A&M University Press, 1999).

Hogan, William R., *The Texas Republic: A Social and Economic History* (Norman: University of Oklahoma Press, 1946).

Jordan, Terry G., *Trails to Texas: Southern Roots of Western Ranching* (Lincoln: University of Nebraska Press, 1981).

Lack, Paul, "The Córdova Revolt," in *Tejano Journey, 1770–1850*, ed. Gerald E. Poyo (Austin: University of Texas Press, 1996).

Nackman, Mark E., *A Nation Within A Nation: The Rise of Texas Nationalism* (Port Washington, NY: Kennikat Press, 1975).

Nance, Joseph M., *After San Jacinto: The Texas-Mexican Frontier, 1836–1841* (Austin: University of Texas Press, 1962).

———, *Attack and Counterattack: The Texas-Mexican Frontier, 1842* (Austin: University of Texas Press, 1965).

Oates, Stephen B., *Visions of Glory: Texans on the Southwestern Frontier* (Norman: University of Oklahoma Press, 1970).

Pletcher, David M., *The Diplomacy of Annexation: Texas, Oregon, and the Mexican War* (Columbia: University of Missouri Press, 1973).

Reichstein, Andreas V., *Rise of the Lone Star: The Making of Texas* (College Station: Texas A&M University Press, 1989).

Reps, John W., *Cities of the American West: A History of Frontier Urban Planning* (Princeton, NJ: Princeton University Press, 1979).

Schmitz, Joseph, *Texan Statecraft, 1836–1845* (San Antonio: Naylor Co., 1941).

Sibley, Marilyn McAdams, *Lone Stars and State Gazettes: Texas Newspapers Before the Civil War* (College Station: Texas A&M University Press, 1983).

Siegel, Stanley, *Political History of the Texas Republic, 1836–1845* (Austin: University of Texas Press, 1956).

———, *The Poet President of Texas: The Life of Mirabeau B. Lamar, President of the Republic of Texas* (Austin: Pemberton Press, 1977).

Smith, F. Todd, *The Caddo Indians: Tribes at the Convergence of Empires, 1542–1854* (College Station: Texas A&M University Press, 1995).

Spellman, Paul N., *Forgotten Texas Leader: Hugh McLeod and the Texan Santa Fe Expedition* (College Station: Texas A&M University Press, 1999).

Tijerina, Andrew Anthony, "Tejanos and Texas: The Native Mexicans of Texas, 1820–1850" (Ph.D. diss., University of Texas at Austin, 1977).

Wheeler, Kenneth W., *To Wear A City's Crown: The Beginnings of Urban Growth in Texas, 1836–1865* (Cambridge, MA: Harvard University Press, 1968).

Woolfolk, George R., *The Free Negro in Texas, 1800–1860* (Ann Arbor, MI: University Microfilms International, 1976).

Articles

Barker, Nancy N., "Devious Diplomat: Dubois de Saligny and the Republic of Texas," *Southwestern Historical Quarterly* 72 (January, 1969).

Benjamin, Thomas, "Recent Historiography of the Origins of the Mexican War," *New Mexico Historical Review* 54 (July, 1979).

Downs, Fane, "'Tryels and Trubbles': Women in Early Nineteenth Century Texas," *Southwestern Historical Quarterly* 90 (July, 1986).

Dysart, Jane, "Mexican Women in San Antonio, 1830–1860: The Assimilation Process," *Western Historical Quarterly* 7 (October, 1976).

Nackman, Mark E., "The Making of the Texan Citizen Soldier, 1835–1860," *Southwestern Historical Quarterly* 78 (January, 1975).

UNION AND DISINTEGRATION

CHAPTER 5

Following annexation, Texas remained a magnet for immigrants seeking new beginnings. The first federal census taken in Texas, 1850, revealed that 212,000 persons (including slaves) inhabited the state. This population was ethnically and culturally diverse, but as Table 5.1 on population origins shows, Anglo Americans from the southern United States accounted for more than half of all Texas residents.

Actually, the South provided two different streams of immigrants. People from the Lower South—meaning those states from South Carolina west to Louisiana along the Gulf Coast—clustered in eastern and southeastern Texas. Not surprisingly, this section of the state hosted commercial farms that used slave labor to raise cotton, sugar, and rice. In contrast, inhabitants from the Upper South—those border states separating the Deep South from the North, ranging westward from Virginia to Missouri and Arkansas—gravitated towards the north and north-central counties of Texas. Most of these people ran family farms, depending less on cotton and more on the production of foodstuffs, primarily corn and wheat.

The 1850 census also enumerated Anglo Texans who had come from states outside the South—some 10,000 of them. The largest number of these persons hailed from the Midwest; fewer had arrived from New England or the mid-Atlantic states.

Ironically, Texas Mexicans already were relegated to numerical insignificance, constituting only about 5 percent of the total population in 1850. They remained concentrated in their original cultural strongholds of the Béxar-Goliad region and South Texas (on the rancherías along the Rio Grande).

The Germans who had arrived in Texas in the mid-1840s as part of colonization programs such as the Adelsverein Society added to the diversity of the state's peoples. By 1847, the society had transported 7,000 Germans to Texas, and John O. Meusebach had founded Fredericksburg. Henri Castro brought some 2,000 immigrants (many

Detail from photograph of Leñeros. *Texas State Library and Archives Commission* of them experienced farmers) from various parts of Germany, including a good many German-speaking settlers from Alsace in northeastern France. Other Germans had come to Texas on their own initiative, and by 1850 the German-descent population stood at around 11,500. By this time, German rural communities stretched along an ethnic corridor extending from the coast, at Galveston, through the towns of San Antonio and Austin, and on to western counties such as Gillespie, Mason, and Kerr.

Other European groups added to the growing pluralism of the state's population. Irish settlements along the coastal counties of San Patricio and Refugio, which traced their origins to Mexican land grants, were prospering as of 1850. Immigrants from the United Kingdom at midcentury totaled approximately 2,900. Norwegians, numbering about 100 in 1850, lived in north-central Texas in counties such as Kaufman, Van Zandt, and Henderson, and in a little colony they founded in Bosque County in 1854.

By the eve of the Civil War, the Texas population had tripled to over 604,000. Its growth since 1850 had been dramatic, and the cultural diversity and ethnic regionalism of the population were marked. During the same era, however, slavery and the politics of sectionalism fused many of the diverse elements of Texas society to life in the Deep South. In 1861, the majority of Texans would side with the seceding Confederate states despite their disparate group affiliations.

THE TEXAS ECONOMY AT MIDCENTURY

Rural Growth

Under Mexico, Texas had been shaped by the basic premise of Mexican federalism: the state and not the federal government should administer the state's public domain. Desiring to perpetuate that tradition, Texas had insisted upon retaining its public lands under the terms of annexation. As a state, therefore, Texas perpetuated the land policy of the republic and thereby continued to attract immigrants. In 1854, the legislature passed the Texas Preemption Act, through which the state offered homesteaders 160-acre parcels of land for as little as fifty cents an acre (as compared to the concurrent U.S. price of $1.25 an acre).

Throughout the 1850s, indeed, Texas remained primarily an agrarian society. In 1850, there were 12,107 farms in the state; this number leaped to 35,563 by 1860. During that same decade, the number of improved acres rose from 639,821 to 2,590,895. The production of cotton increased from about 58,000 bales in 1849 to 431,463 bales in 1859. While sugar and wool increasingly became cash commodities raised in Texas, cotton remained the state's staple.

And cotton thrived on plantations, the largest units located in the territory extending from the lower valley of the Colorado River to the Sabine, a region populated by settlers from the Lower South. Between 1848 and the eve of the Civil War, lands worked by slaves produced lucrative returns for planters, the profits auguring cotton's and the slave system's westward expansion. It must be

TABLE 5.1 Origins of the Texas Population, 1850

GROUP	NUMBER	PERCENT OF STATE TOTAL	PERCENT OF GROUP LIVING IN URBAN AREAS[a]
Southern Anglo-American[b]	114,040	53.7	3
Northern Anglo-American	9,965	4.7	11
Negro[c]	58,558	27.5	3
Spanish-surname[d]	11,212	5.3	13
French-surname[d]	1,071	0.5	29
German element[e]	11,534	5.4	32
Other foreign elements	3,900	1.8	23
Other[f]	2,312	1.1	—

SOURCES: *The Seventh Census of the United States, 1850*
[a] *"Urban" includes towns of 1,000 or more population that were listed in census.*
[b] *Includes the Texas-born children of northern Anglo-Americans.*
[c] *Includes both slave and free colored.*
[d] *Includes American-born with Spanish or French surname.*
[e] *Includes foreign-born persons and their American-born offspring.*
[f] *Includes all persons who were born in California and the Territories or whose origins could not be determined.*
SOURCE: *Terry G. Jordan, "Population Origins in Texas, 1850," Geographical Review, 59 (January, 1969), p. 85.*

understood, however, that only about one-third of all Texas farms at midcentury had slaves as part of their workforce and that Texans constituting a planter elite (landholders who owned more than 100 slaves) amounted to only a small minority. In reality, the 20 percent of planters heading the list of slaveowners monopolized 96 percent of the entire Texas slave population. Most Texas slave owners held fewer than five bondspeople.

And not all of those who wrested their living from the soil relied on cotton. As mentioned, north and north-central Texas farmers grew wheat, oats, and other foodstuffs, an agricultural pattern resembling that of the Upper South. In the part of the state extending from the Brazos River west to the frontier beyond San Antonio, Anglo landowners using slave labor coexisted with small farmers (mostly European) who cultivated vegetables, grains, and fruits, engaged in viticulture (wine making) and delved into ranching. However, many of the small farmers of this region, among them Germans, slowly accepted the nuances of southern culture and began to support chattel slavery.

The ranch retained its economic importance, primarily along the Coastal Prairie but also in the southern portions of the Piney Woods and northeastern counties. Tejanos continued to ranch along the Rio Grande border, but as Anglos drifted into the area in the wake of the war with Mexico, disputes over the ownership of cattle and ranch lands arose between the two peoples. Among the newcomers who built cattle-ranching empires in the region were H. L. Kinney, Richard King, and Mifflin Kenedy.

From the three early settings of Anglo cattle ranching in eastern Texas, ranchers during the 1850s migrated southwest toward the Guadalupe, San Antonio, and Nueces river valleys—rich pasturelands dominated by Tejano ranchers as late as 1836. Ranching also pushed into the central-western frontier of the state towards the counties of the western Cross Timbers, among them Eastland, Erath, Comanche, and Palo Pinto, as well as into the Upper Hill Country counties of San Saba, Lampasas, Llano, and Mason. With this spread, ranching traditions originally imported from the southeastern seaboard of the United States made their way westward.

Urban Industrialization

As of 1850, Galveston was the largest town in Texas, with a population of 5,000. Its location on the Gulf made it a natural center for shipping, storage, and wholesale commerce, though the port city also sustained itself through manufacturing, banking, and cotton compressing. Only four other towns had a population of more than 1,000 at this time. In order of size they were: San Antonio, which acted as a point of departure for passenger stage coaches and freight-company wagons heading for Mexico and California; Houston, an inland port that acted as a conduit to the Gulf; New Braunfels; and Marshall. Austin, the seat of government, had barely 600 inhabitants at midcentury. But even the largest Texas towns lacked the comforts and conveniences generally associated with urban living. Crudely built or improvised one- or two-room structures acted as stores or municipal buildings, and such urban amenities as libraries, theaters, and recreational facilities were conspicuously absent.

By 1860, the number of Texas communities boasting a population of more than 1,000 had increased to twenty, and San Antonio, with 8,000 inhabitants, had surpassed Galveston as the state's largest city. North Texas still had no major city by the onset of the Civil War; not even Dallas showed prospects of its eventual role as a commercial and financial center.

Urban economics reflected the state's agrarian basis. Cotton, sugar, and wool constituted the main urban exports. Industry was in its infancy. The iron foundries of Galveston and Houston ranked among the major industrial employers in Texas, yet neither employed more than forty people. At the beginning of the Civil War, therefore, the state's economy more closely resembled the South's than that of the urbanized industrial North. In comparison to New York and Pennsylvania, each of which boasted more than 22,000 manufacturing establishments, Texas had few industrial plants—only 983, which averaged about four workers each.

TRANSPORTATION

Conditions for travel remained as poor as they had been during the period of the republic, which slowed a nonetheless growing economy. The state government entrusted internal improvements to the counties, but inadequate resources compelled local authorities to let bad roads languish. Besides the sorry shape of the roads, few bridges existed. Water travel was also quite arduous, for the rivers were shallow and narrow in sections and often clogged with debris. Navigation into the Gulf remained treacherous.

Travel by stagecoach was not much better. In the early period of statehood, it continued mostly as an intrastate mode of transportation, moving passengers, mail, and light freight, though by the time of the Civil War, thirty-one lines handled stage traffic inside the state. After the discovery of gold in California, entrepreneurs founded stagecoach lines between San Antonio and far-off El Paso, but not until 1857 did the first interstate line, the San Antonio–San Diego (California) Mail Line, begin business, though its coaches usually experienced horrendous difficulties along the way to the coast. To cross the 100 miles of the Colorado Desert (in southeastern California), for example, passengers had to transfer from the coaches to muleback. For obvious reasons, the company quickly earned the epithet of the "Jackass Line." In 1858 the dependable Butterfield Overland Mail Company followed up with another stage line from Texas to California. However, stagecoach operations between Texas and the West Coast ceased regular service during the Civil War.

Freight haulers battled inclement weather and other obstacles as they attempted to move goods on their mule- or ox-drawn wagons between San Antonio or Austin and the Gulf Coast. Nonetheless, hundreds of freighting teams operated during the 1850s, many of them handled by Tejanos who forged a reputation as excellent *arrieros* (teamsters). Because of their skill and lower charges, Texas Mexicans briefly dominated the transportation of food and merchandise between the interior and the Gulf.

Railroad building in Texas lagged behind that of other states in the 1850s. At midcentury, when the total railroad mileage of the United States stood at 9,021, Texas had virtually no tracks. A modest start was made in 1853, when the Buffalo Bayou, Brazos & Colorado Railway Company commenced operation on thirty miles of track between Harrisburg and Richmond in central Fort Bend County; the line continued expanding until 1861, by which time it had reached Brazoria County. Then, in 1854, the state government sought to further railroad building by passing a law that offered railroad construction companies sixteen sections of public land (or 10,240 acres) for every mile of track they laid. This effort proved ineffectual. By 1860, the state still only had about 400 miles of track, much of this stretching from Houston to inland terminals along the Brazos, Colorado, and Trinity Rivers.

TEXAS SOCIETY AT MIDCENTURY

Inequality

Judging from the pace of immigration and the increase in population, many many people perceived Texas as a land of opportunity. Not everyone's expectations were fulfilled, however. Recent studies on antebellum Texas indicate that

Land Forms of Texas

the egalitarian ideal in Texas was mythical, though this condition was not atypical of the South or the nation in general.

The census of 1850 disclosed a sharp inequality in the distribution of wealth among the free population of Texas, and the pattern persisted until the next decennial period. In the 1850s, most of the state's real and personal property (including slaves) and total wealth lay concentrated in the hands of a small elite that constituted less than 10 percent of all Texans; this group seems to have expanded slightly by 1860. On the eve of the Civil War, 7.1 percent of the population held 56 percent of state's wealth. Slaveowners in particular were among the wealthiest Texans, given their high investment in cash-crop farming. Moreover, they exerted undue political influence, for they held a disproportionately large number of political offices.

Obviously, there also existed a large body of Texan plain folk who did not share the available wealth. Protest against economic inequalities was apparently neutralized, however, by opportunities for upward advancement, the ability of free adult (Anglo) males to express opinions at the ballot box, and the equalizing forces of the frontier, which, as mentioned, tended to deemphasize class consciousness.

Labor organizations, one traceable indication of widespread discontent, surfaced only faintly. Several workingmen's associations appeared during early statehood, but no labor unions were founded in the state between 1838 and 1857. Then, in 1857, pressmen employed by two Galveston newspapers unionized and asked for pay increases. In 1860, Galveston carpenters organized Carpenters Local No. 7, but they primarily concerned themselves with altruistic activities such as mutual assistance, as did the printers' union (which had not received its requested wage hike). Otherwise, labor unionism hardly existed in Texas by 1860. The relative absence of industrial development, the small number of workers concentrated in manufacturing enterprises, and the faith that many workers had in upward mobility made Texas infertile ground for the growth of labor unions.

On the other hand, there remained as part of the cultural landscape those people whom modern-day social scientists classify as minorities; many found their opportunities to acquire property restricted, their chances for upward mobility limited, and avenues for legitimately expressing their discontent firmly blocked. Black slaves (and free blacks), Mexican Americans (Tejanos), and the people of the Indian nations then being forcibly removed from their ancestral lands comprised the state's minorities.

Black Texans

Free blacks enjoyed no better standing during the early era of statehood than they had during the days of the republic. Only about 350 free blacks resided in the state according to the 1860 federal census, though one newspaper put the figure unofficially at about 1,000. The status of these people remained ill-defined—they possessed no civil rights before the law—and their presence continued to be unwelcomed by the white majority.

Although only a handful of blacks lived as free persons, the number of blacks in Texas increased rapidly. In 1850, the U.S. census counted 58,161 blacks in Texas; the next decennial enumeration listed 182,566. The increase made slaves the fastest-growing segment of the population; indeed, slaves constituted more than 30 percent of the state's inhabitants by 1860. Most enslaved persons lived in the East Texas area inhabited by people originally from other parts of the South. Three identifiable regions—the bottoms of the Brazos and Colorado Rivers east towards the Houston area, the counties along the Sabine and (middle) Trinity Rivers, and the fertile lands along the Red River—contained large concentrations of slaves on the eve of the Civil War.

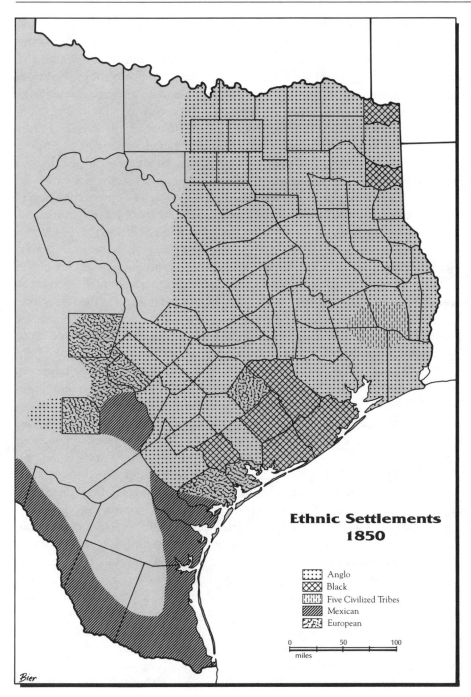

Ethnic Settlements 1850. *Source: Terry G. Jordan, "A Century and a Half of Ethnic Change in Texas." Courtesy Texas State Historical Association, Austin, Texas*

In the fifteen years before 1860, slavery in Texas persisted for various reasons, among them the fact that it proved profitable. Indeed, Texans during the 1850s considered slavery as essential to the economic survival of the state and even predicted for Texas a future as a slave empire. Throughout the state, bondspeople were considered a form of capital. Texas society recognized slaves as valuable assets, to the extent that they could be converted to cash even more readily than could real estate. Planters used slaves to earn extra income (by hiring their work out), to negotiate loans (by using them as collateral), to acquire currency in emergency situations, to pay off debts, to exchange for land, or to bequeath to heirs. The government, moreover, turned to slaves as a source for raising revenue, since the law considered slaves a species of property. Masters paid taxes on their slaves, just as they would on their land and range animals.

Slave labor, indeed, brought planters great wealth during the 1840s and 1850s. In the eastern third of the state, slaves annually picked cotton crops that yielded substantial financial dividends, and cotton production as part of the state's market economy far exceeded the value of other commodities such as corn, wheat, oats, vegetables, cattle, hogs, mules, and horses. At the same time, slavery and the cotton harvest stimulated related sectors of the economy, for planters needed grains, slaughter animals, and certain manufactured goods to run their plantations.

But Texans, like their counterparts in the Lower South, also saw slavery as a necessary means to restrain a people of color. Whites in antebellum Texas viewed themselves as virtuous, compassionate, and pious; they viewed slaves in the other extreme, as a people inclined to be dirty, evil, lascivious, paganish, depraved, and bestial—connotations associated with the color black in European culture. These attitudes, reinforced by racist thinking that Africans were an inferior and inassimilable people, helped slaveowners rationalize the need for a system of repression and justify their abhorrent treatment of other human beings. In the eyes of many Texans (and other southerners), slavery even benefited those enslaved, by uplifting them from the "primitivism" of life in the African homeland. Hence, slavery necessarily fueled racism as long as it existed.

As to the legality of slavery, the Constitution of 1845 considered Texas slaves personal property that could be bought, sold, and separated from their families at the owner's will. The document defined slavery as a perpetual condition, and it forbade blacks from marrying or forming a family, bearing arms, assembling, or using the courts in a case involving a white person. To control slaves, the law specified the allowance of whippings for those found guilty of crimes such as petty theft or violating the rules of "proper" public behavior, such as insulting a white person. If a slave committed a heinous crime, the law called for the administration of the death penalty, and whites often used lynch law in retribution for a host of real or suspected infractions.

While bondage revolved around the exploitation of human beings, the peculiar institution was never, neither in urban areas nor on the plantations, so totalitarian that it denied slaves the ability to develop their own social identity. Conversely, African American culture capably dealt with the cruelty of slavery. From Christianity, slaves borrowed those tenets that assured them that all humankind was equal before the Lord and worthy of God's forgiveness and redemption. The hope that they, along with the white master, had an equal chance for achieving God's reward lessened the worldly burden that slavery cast upon them. In death, at least, they would find the freedom that eluded them in life.

In their family structure, slaves arranged social units. While not recognized by law, family ties were legitimized within slave society in a variety of ways, including the common ritual of having an engaged couple symbolize their marriage by jumping in unison over a broomstick. The slave family was an important source of defense (offering individuals love, kinship support, and self-worth) against the dehumanizing evil of slavery, including the physical and sexual abuse of their family members by white masters. And blacks were quick to take advantage of slave owners' attitudes toward certain facts of the human condition: planters allowed marriages and encouraged the creation of families, for this led to reproduction (and hence to more valuable property for the owner), gave masters greater control over their slaves (by instilling in them the fear that something bad might befall—at the master's behest—a loved one should they disobey), and made workers tractable, dutiful, and more productive (because familial relationships naturally made them happier). Within slave family arrangements, fathers and mothers sought to assert their respective roles. Husbands supplemented the family meal by hunting and fishing or taking on odd jobs, when the master permitted it. Wives tended to the many (and demanding) domestic duties in the slave household, although only after having finished their assigned work.

Many slaves did not resign themselves to complete submission to slavery. To be sure, some coped by not resisting at all, even accepting the scriptures of slavery and respecting the wishes of their masters. Others compromised with the institution but worked out personal understandings of life that helped them preserve a sense of self-worth. But most bondspeople displayed their discontent in several subversive forms. Thousands ran away from Texas plantations, some of them heading south to Mexico, others to the southern states—their place of birth—to look for loved ones. Others sabotaged the institution by causing mischief, purposely breaking tools, burning sheds, maiming or killing the plantation's domesticated animals, or simply slowing down on the job.

The most desperate display of slave discontent was the slave rebellion. Although there exists no record of major slave uprisings in antebellum Texas, a wave of insurrection hysteria passed over the state in the 1850s, culminating in 1860 with what is known as the "Texas Troubles." This episode, instigated during the summer of 1860 by a string of suspicious fires in northern Texas (including blazes in Dallas and Fort Worth), led whites to fear that slaves, encouraged by abolitionists, were fomenting a widespread insurrection. Scholars have yet to prove the actual existence of an organized plot, but about ten white men

Leñeros, Tejano wood hauler, with donkeys. *Texas State Library and Archives Commision*

(many of them from the northern United States) and over thirty African Americans were executed for their alleged roles in the so-called conspiracy before the statewide paranoia subsided.

Mexican Americans

Also largely excluded from wealth and opportunity in midcentury Texas were persons of Mexican descent, who, according to some estimates, numbered anywhere from 13,900 to 23,200 (including those in the El Paso area). Since 1836, Tejanos had tried to find a niche in Anglo Texan society by accepting elements of the new order. But because of racial prejudice and the dominant group's need to maintain them as part of a pliable and inexpensive labor force, Tejanos faced constant obstacles in their quest for equality.

Harassment and violence such as had occurred in the aftermath of the war for independence continued into the period of statehood. From several towns of Central Texas, Mexicans were banished on suspicion of having assisted runaway slaves in reaching freedom in Mexico. In 1857, Anglo-American freighters launched hostile action against Mexican American teamsters, their major competitors in transporting goods from the interior to the Gulf. In what became known as the Cart War, Anglos destroyed the arrieros' carts, confiscated their cargo, sabotaged their equipment, and murdered some of the drivers. The violence only ended after the Mexican government, the U.S. secretary of state, and volunteer Texas companies interceded to restore order. Following the epidsode, the Mexicans recovered a share of their old business, although the technology of the post–Civil War era would soon make traffic by cart an outmoded concern.

Similar episodes of interracial friction occurred in South Texas between the Nueces River and the Rio Grande, an area that ambitious Anglos began entering in force following the war with Mexico, displacing Tejanos from their lands and traditional positions of influence. Resentment against the interlopers finally produced violent conflict in Brownsville, sparked by an encounter in 1859 at a city cafe between the town's marshall and Juan Nepomuceno Cortina, a local ranchero and the descendant of old grantees on the border. Cortina resented whites for their racist sentiments toward Mexicans, for the way they used the courts to dispossess Mexican Americans of their rightfully owned land, and for their determined drive to supplant the local Mexican American leadership of the South Texas political structure. When on the morning of July 13 the marshall hurled racial epithets at Cortina as he came to the defense of an elderly ranch hand whom the marshall was in the process of beating, the rancher drew his gun and shot and wounded the lawman. Things simmered down for a while, but Cortina returned to Brownsville on September 29, bent on avenging old wrongs inflicted on the Mexican people. He killed two whites (whom Cortina believed had been involved in the deaths of Mexican Americans), then in two proclamations, issued from his mother's ranch upriver from Brownsville, denounced all those engaged in persecuting Tejanos. Mexican Americans rallied to his cause (and others to his banner), viewing Cortina as a champion fighting the injustice of the whites. But Texas Rangers and federal troops finally suppressed the so-called Cortina War early in 1860. The whole incident, however, resulted in a number of tragic deaths, some property damage, and an enduring residue of racial distrust and antagonism.

American Indians

Also existing on the fringes of white society were the state's Native Americans. White Texans did not exactly deny Indians admission into the mainstream—they did not have to, for the people of the tribes hardly wished a place among those they regarded as intruders and mortal enemies. But white Texans did enfeeble Indians by keeping them from making their living on their traditional hunting grounds. Settlers continued to encroach upon the Indians', especially the Comanches', territorial space; by the late 1840s, whites had pushed the line of settlement so far west that the federal government, now responsible for protecting what had become U.S. frontiers, established in 1849 a cordon of military forts stretching from modern-day Tarrant County to Eagle Pass in southwestern Texas. Westward expansion moved so swiftly, however, that in the early 1850s, the military established another line of defense even deeper into Indian lands, this one composed of forts Belknap (in Young County), Phantom Hill (north of Abilene), Chadbourne (in today's Coke County), McKavett (in what is now Menard County), Terrett (midway between the present-day towns of Junction and Sonora), and Clark (near Brackettville). In order to guard travelers en route to El Paso, Forts Lancaster, Stockton, Davis, and Quitman were erected in extreme West Texas. As of 1860, the westernmost boundaries of the state extended for more than 500 miles, from the Red River (the settlement of Henrietta) to the Rio Grande border (the village of Eagle Pass).

To guarantee Indian autonomy on some of the Comanche land, the U.S. Indian agent in Texas, Major Robert Simpson Neighbors, recommended establishing reservations; this, he reasoned, would allow westering settlers to bypass the Indian farm communities. The state legislature concurred, and in 1854 it made as much as 53,136 acres available to the federal government for the foundation of two such reservations that were to become the new "homelands" for about 1,500 Texas Indians. The Brazos Reservation was established in present-day Young County (close to Fort Belknap) for some of the old semisedentary Norteños such as the Tawakonis, Wacos, and Tonkawas, and the Clear Fork Reservation, for the Comanches, was founded farther west, on the upper Clear Fork of the Brazos River in what is now Throckmorton County.

While the idea of living on a reservation appealed to some Comanches, most had no desire to live penned up as the whites' dependents, and they continued to raid farmsteads. The settlers' encroachments (which were fast ruining Comanche hunting grounds) imperiled the way of life to which these Indians

clung. Angry at the holdouts, the state and the federal governments pursued a more aggressive policy toward the marauders, mustering Texas Rangers and civilian volunteer units for a new Indian offensive. These forces took the fight north of the Red River to the very camping grounds of the Plains people. Captain John S. "Rip" Ford, for one, led an expedition into the Comanche strongholds in northwestern Oklahoma, his forces decisively winning a battle at the Canadian River on May 12, 1858. The victory, the first in which whites had shown the power to damage the Comanches, infuriated the warriors and only hardened their resolve to resist. Subsequently, Texas settlers experienced frightening retaliation for Ford's triumph and for other battles won by federal troops in the Comanche ranges north of the Texas border.

Clashes between Indians and whites continued even more frequently, as the experiment with reservations proved unsuccessful. Some of the Indians found it difficult to adjust to changes from their traditional nomadic lifestyle. Whites, suspecting the nearby reservation Indians—instead of the hostile northern tribes— of stealing their horses and livestock and scalping and murdering whites on the western and northern regions of the state, began to call for the eviction of the Indians from the reservations. Carrying their threats further, they waylaid and killed those Indians who ventured out of the sanctuaries. Its hand forced by the wave of lawless hostility, the federal government closed down the Texas reservations in 1859 and transferred the internees to western Indian Territory (Oklahoma). On the eve of the Civil War, however, the north and western frontier line of settlement continued to scorch, as Kiowa and Comanche raiding parties stepped up their strikes, inflicting more attacks on Texans than they had in the prior decade.

Women

The Texas population at midcentury consisted predominately of youthful individuals, a characteristic generally associated with frontier environments; some 77 percent of resident Texans were under forty years of age according to the census of 1850. Also indicative of a frontier setting were skewed sex ratios: men in 1850 outnumbered women by 15,704, and in 1860 by 36,000. This sexual imbalance could not help but influence the nature of midcentury Texas society. In part, the disparity explains why interracial mixing between white men and Mexican and black women occurred more commonly in the antebellum period than it did after the Civil War, and why women, who worked to ensure such things as the efficient functioning of the farm, were permitted to cross into decidedly male roles.

Indeed, women faced a hard lot that included starting a family at a young age and then caring for it through sickness and all manner of misery. Simultaneously, women tended to household chores and helped perform those tasks essential for frontier survival, including the construction of the family dwelling (which at midcentury generally consisted of little more than four make-shift walls, a roof, dirt floors, and improvised accommodations), hunting and fishing,

Batting cotton. Frontier women were responsible for every step of the clothes-making process. *The Center for American History, The University of Texas at Austin, CN 00939C, Taulman Collection*

working stock, clearing fields, cultivating crops, and fighting off raids by Indians and desperadoes.

Despite the liberating tendencies of the frontier, the Texas heritage remained basically masculine and discriminatory. The male-dominated culture held firmly to the belief that women should remain subordinate to men, and thus it restricted women's political, legal, social, and economic activities. Although the women of Texas enjoyed certain legal rights based on the U.S. legal system as well as the (more equitable) Hispanic tradition that persisted following 1836, the norms of the period limited their privileges. Women still could not vote or sit on juries, nor were they permitted to take the pulpit or speak in public forums. Nonetheless, a handful of women during the 1850s participated in such reform causes as the abolitionist and women's rights movements, among them Melinda Rankin, a New England Presbyterian missionary working in South Texas, whence she denounced slavery, and Elise Waerenskjold, an immigrant from Norway who became an activist for abolition and the rights of women. Married women could not be assured of the guardianship of their children in cases of divorce, and they lacked full control of their own earnings, though the Constitution of 1845 did declare that properties acquired by women before and after marriage were theirs—and not the husband's—to claim. Texas law during this period also provided that property and income accrued by a couple during marriage became community property. Consequently, a few Texas women went on to amass sizable fortunes during the antebellum period.

Education

Public education in Texas at midcentury remained in its nascency, with no overwhelming improvements having been made over Lamar's efforts during the period of the republic. The Constitution of 1845 entrusted the legislature with reserving one-tenth of tax revenues for a "perpetual" school fund, but efforts toward carrying out the constitutional mandate of establishing a statewide system of free public schools moved slowly. Finally, in 1854, Governor Elisha M. Pease (1853–1857) signed into law an educational measure with several provisions. One created a permanent education endowment of $2 million to be derived from the $10 million that the United States had given Texas as a part of a settlement in 1850 whereby the state surrendered its claim to territory in New Mexico. Another section of the law provided that schools be made available to all Texas children in common (from which concept the label "common schools" is derived) and mandated the creation of schools for the hearing and visually impaired in 1856. Another act of the legislature in 1858 provided for the creation of a university (which ultimately became the University of Texas) by appropriating for the institution, among other things, 3 million acres of public land.

Little of substance came from these efforts. The permanent fund grew slowly and never amounted to enough to pay teachers' salaries and construct school buildings. Although the facilities for the handicapped opened in 1857, these institutions progressed but slowly. The government maintained the university endowment, but it took little action to establish a university campus until much later.

Newspapers and Literature

Although the condition of public education remained weak, newspapers, at least, helped perpetuate literacy, keeping the public abreast of political controversies and current events. Indeed, the number of presses increased measurably during the 1850s. While only nine papers actively reported before 1845, the U.S. census of 1860 counted eighty-nine Texas-based newspapers and periodicals. The *Telegraph and Texas Register* remained the state's best-known newspaper, but few frontier communities lacked access to a local newspaper. In the ethnic communities, German and Spanish presses published papers in the native language of their readership. Among these were the *New Braunfels Zeitung* and *San Antonio El Bejareño*.

Literature produced in the 1840s and 1850s mirrored the rural and frontier nature of the state. Instead of the Romanticism that characterized the literature of the northern United States, mundane themes marked Texas writing: travel logs, histories, and journals of personal adventure are thus overrepresented. Out of this era, however, came the state's first major resident historian, Henderson

K. Yoakum. In his *History of Texas* (1855), Yoakum portrayed Texans as a people nourished by American democratic institutions and possessed of an industry and energy then breaking a path for civilization and republican institutions. To Yoakum, Texans were ably helping to fulfill the United States' manifest destiny.

Ethnic and women writers also contributed to the early development of Texas literature. Melinda Rankin's *Texas in 1850*, Juan N. Seguín's *Personal Memoirs of John N. Seguín, From the Year 1834 to the Retreat of General Woll from the City of San Antonio, 1842*, and Ferdinand Roemer's *Texas*, first published in German in 1849, all possess historical significance. Several Europeans also wrote books about their impressions of midcentury Texas.

Religion

Religious activity at midcentury, while lacking the force of those religious movements that overtook the northern United States during the 1830s and 1840s, sustained an evangelical impulse. Since the 1820s, Protestant preachers had seen in Texas a society of sinners in dire need of spiritual rescue, a place ripe for the establishment of institutions to carry on the struggle against Satan. By the time of annexation, the largest denominations in terms of size of congregations were (in descending order) Methodists, Baptists, Presbyterians, Catholics, and Episcopalians.

The Protestants taught a southern and conservative brand of religion that stressed humankind's imperfections and the need for individuals to improve themselves and develop a personal relationship with God. More concerned with people heeding the precepts of the Christian faith, Protestants in Texas did not generally call on their flocks to address social issues or engage in reform crusades. Consequently, Protestantism in Texas differed from the evangelical Protestantism in the North, which emphasized the amelioration of society.

As part of their work in Texas, churches established Sunday schools and other educational institutions. Most of the latter had short lives, but some survived the era of early statehood. Among those founded during the period that have proved durable are: "Old Baylor," opened by the Baptists in 1845 in the small town of Independence and then moved in 1887 to its permanent site in Waco; Austin College, established in 1849 by the Presbyterian church in Huntsville but relocated to Sherman in 1878; and St. Mary's University, a Catholic facility that began operation in 1852 in San Antonio.

Although it might be presumed that clergymen of the time would have tended to shy away from public discussions of the morality of slavery, to the contrary, most chimed in with the majority opinion that regarded slavery as a necessary institution and one beneficial to an "inferior" race. Actually, very few Texans dared denounce the peculiar institution, although a few Tejanos (as mentioned already) took matters into their own hands and escorted fugitive bondspeople to Mexico. Most Texans joined the proslavery camp that upheld the institution's necessity, its righteousness, and its benefit to those enslaved.

TEXAS POLITICS AT MIDCENTURY

Sectional Troubles

For Texans in the 1840s, there was reason for confidence and optimism. Their state had been newly accepted into the Union, the former diplomat James Pinckney Henderson had been elected governor, and no less than Sam Houston served as one of their two United States senators. Furthermore, Texas had reason to share in an expanding national pride. The United States now stretched to the Pacific Ocean, and gold from California swelled the national money supply.

But annexation also held pitfalls, for the issues that threatened to tear the Union asunder also garnered attention in the new state. In the late 1840s, the entire country wrangled in debates over a host of divisive matters. The North desired to see slavery and the slave trade abolished in Washington, D.C., while the South demanded a stronger fugitive slave law that would permit southerners to retrieve runaway slaves who had fled to the North. Issues created by the war with Mexico burned more portentously. Was slavery going to exist in the territories acquired from Mexico? Southerners said yes, northerners said no. The expansion of California following the gold rush of 1849 forced another related question: Should California join the Union as a free or a slave state? Connected also to the aftereffects of the war with Mexico was the question of the western boundary of Texas: Was it to be the Rio Grande, as Texans and southerners argued, or was much of New Mexico to be excluded?

In January 1850, Henry Clay proposed a compromise bill in the Congress. According to Clay's settlement offer: the slave trade should be ended in the nation's capital; a strong fugitive slave law should be passed; the territories acquired from Mexico should be organized without prohibiting the importation of slaves into those regions; and California should be admitted into the Union as a free state. On the issue of Texas and New Mexico, Clay recommended that Texas be denied

Sam Houston in the latter years of the 1850s. Elected governor in 1859, it was Houston's last political position. *Daughters of the Republic of Texas Library, CN 96.101*

claims to lands extending westward to the Rio Grande in New Mexico, but that it be compensated for relinquishing those claims. At first, Texans denounced the idea of giving up any part of New Mexico, but reason replaced misgiving when negotiators proposed that Texas's western boundary would extend due east from the Rio Grande along the 32nd parallel to the 103rd line of longitude and up along this meridian to the 36° 30′ line. To indemnify the state for relinquishing its New Mexican claims, the federal government would give Texas $10 million (this plan established the state's modern boundaries in that area). In this offer, the state saw the opportunity to receive money that finally would erase the public debt incurred during the period of the republic. Texans endorsed the plan in a referendum in November 1850, thus supporting the measures that President Millard Fillmore had signed into law in September as part of Clay's Compromise of 1850.

Throughout the first half of the 1850s, at least, Texans had reason to expect a sanguine future. Removed from the rest of the country by a long distance traversable only by a rudimentary infrastructure, and preoccupied with their own internal problem of defense against the Indians, Texans did not feel as much of the era's turmoil as did the rest of the slave states. In other words, location, geographic peculiarities, demographic diversity, and other factors distinctive to the state acted to blunt the severity of the sectional issues then sizzling throughout the rest of the nation.

Whigs, Democrats, Know-Nothings, and Republicans

Although the controversies of the 1850s influenced the Deep South more than they did Texas, the state was not immune to its own political discourse. Traditionally, Texans had adhered to the principles of the Democratic party, though before 1848 candidates ran more on their personality and reputation than on party platform. Texans had always associated the Democrats with Andrew Jackson and Sam Houston, both men war heroes and both embodying the ideology of the triumph of the common man.

Although the Democratic party would remain well-entrenched as the party of the majority in Texas, in the mid-1850s it began to depart from its Jacksonian foundation. This restructuring owed its impetus to numerous factors, the foremost of which was reaction to the newly resurgent Whig party. Though active only temporarily in the 1850s, the Whig party's strength lay in East Texas, North Texas, and urban and commercial areas, where southern Whiggery found support among the planter and mercantile class, as well as professionals. Economic expansion, internal improvements, banking to enhance a business climate, loyalty to the Union, an emphasis on nationhood, and a call to heed core American and Protestant values served as the rallying points for Texas Whigs.

While successful in local elections, doing well in 1848 and 1852, the state Whig party was handicapped by the stand the national party had taken against annexation and the war with Mexico, by President Zachary Taylor's and then

President Millard Fillmore's (both Whigs) hostility to the claims Texas made to territory in New Mexico, and by the northern wing's support for abolition. Indeed, the slavery issue of the 1850s ultimately undid the Whig party. Though it declined, the party had for the moment mobilized those Texas Democrats fearful of the Union's breakup.

A second factor prodding the restructuring of the Democratic party was the appearance of an upstart organization called the Know-Nothings. Like the national American party to which it belonged, the Texas wing of the Know-Nothings (a sobriquet that had lingered from earlier times when many Know-Nothings had belonged to a secret fraternal order that admonished them to reply "I know nothing" when asked to divulge the order's secrets) drew its backing from nativists, anti-Catholics, Democrat-haters, Unionists, and other nationalistic elements. Obviously, natural opponents of the Know-Nothings included Mexicans and Germans, whom the nativist party perceived as culturally un-American because of their Catholic religion and foreign origins (the Know-Nothings also saw these groups as radicals due to their stand against slavery). The Know-Nothings also distrusted Democrats, whom they believed had threatened the structure of the Union by inflaming sectional passions in the territories following passage of the Kansas-Nebraska Act (1854). Viewing itself as the defender of the Union, the Know-Nothing party painted the Democrats as perpetrators of the internecine conflict.

Other, disparate groups alarmed by the events of the 1850s found elements of the Know-Nothing platform attractive. Many persons in the commercial centers of East Texas switched over, for businesspeople feared that the current partisan rivalry would imperil the region's economic stability. Furthermore, Know-Nothing support for state banks and federally subsidized programs of internal improvements attracted planters, lawyers, and merchants. The presence of the federal military in such western areas as San Antonio financially benefited local businesspeople and added strength to Know Nothingism, for if Texas left the Union, the federal troops would be withdrawn. Finally, others sympathized with Know-Nothing sentiments without formally joining the party. In the election of 1854, the party won mayoral offices in San Antonio, Austin, and Galveston. Even Sam Houston, concerned over increased talk of the breakup of the Union, came to endorse and support some of the party's beliefs in 1855. But Know-Nothingism proved to be a temporary phenomenon, for the slavery question divided the national Know-Nothing party just as it had the Whigs. The party's presidential defeat in 1856 dealt it a blow from which it never recovered.

A third factor dividing the Democratic party related to the increased influence of the Lower South culture in Texas. Know-Nothings had siphoned off Unionist Democrats such as Sam Houston, thereby leaving southerners in control of the state party. This in part had allowed Hardin R. Runnels, who favored reopening the slave trade, to overcome Houston's challenge for the governorship in 1857. Deep South Democrats, a few of them "fire-eaters," those advocating immediate, unconditional secession from the Union, defended the peculiar institution as essential to the preservation of the southern way of life, championed white supremacy as a standard of race relations, guarded the doctrine of southern states' rights, endorsed the ambitions of the Knights of the Golden Circle (a group based in Texas but committed to founding a slaveholding empire in the United States, the Caribbean, and parts of Latin America), and condemned the upstart (northern) Republican party.

Certainly, the growing vigor of the national Republican party weakened the Democrats' cohesiveness. Born from the controversy surrounding the passage of the Kansas-Nebraska Act—which in 1854 opened the question of expanding the southern lifestyle into Kansas and Nebraska by allowing settlers there to decide whether their respective territories would permit slavery—the Republican party assailed the legislation for having produced "Bleeding Kansas," a regional civil war wherein pro- and antislavery forces inflicted violent acts on one another. The Democrats, the Republicans contended, were responsible for the bloodshed. Stern Republican opposition to slavery in the new territories and heated rhetoric about the immorality of the institution aroused fears that the Republicans had only northern, and abolitionist, interests at heart and therefore might stop at nothing to overturn slavery and disrupt southern civilization. In response, many Texans turned to the ultrasouthern wing of the Democratic party, seeing it as a vehicle for defending cherished traditions.

Therefore, increasing numbers of Texas Democrats drifted away from Jacksonian nationalism, believing that the best interests of the state lay in protecting slavery at all costs. By 1858, the Democratic party in Texas had edged closer to the Secessionist Democrats of the plantation South.

1859: A Tumultuous Year

Despite this realignment, Texans worried about disunion—and many of them were put off by the Secessionist Democrats' rhetoric. The extent of disaffection allowed Unionist Democrats (that wing of the Democratic party committed to the preservation of the Union) to defeat the Secessionists in the election of August of 1859, installing Sam Houston as governor. In the campaign, Houston put Runnels on the defensive by criticizing the latter's inadequate protection of the frontier, highlighting Runnels's wishes to see the slave trade renewed, and reminding voters of the governor's preference for secession. Houston now distanced himself from the Know-Nothings and claimed to be the same supporter of national democracy that he always had been. By so doing, Houston attracted non-slaveholding voters in the Rio Grande country, in western Texas, and North Texas. Yet he still appealed to former Know-Nothings and Whigs and successfully enticed into his camp several thousand voters who had not participated in the election of 1857. Furthermore, he won the support of two other elements: those eligible to cast ballots for the first time and voters recently arrived in Texas. Houston's 1859 victory was hailed as a tribute to Unionism, but it turned out to be only a partial success, for the Secessionist Democrats, determined to redeem the party from the Unionists, selected Louis T. Wigfall, a fire-eater, for the U.S. Senate.

Political differences in the fall of 1859, however, gave way to tumultuous historical events. John Brown's attempted slave rebellion at Harpers Ferry, Virginia, in October of that year reaffirmed southern fears that northerners would employ violence to curtail or even end slavery. Juan Cortina's attack on Brownsville in South Texas at about the same time made many Texans question the federal government's willingness and ability to defend the state's southern frontier; Comanche attacks on the northern and western settlements raised similar questions. Then, when members of the House of Representatives in Washington, D.C., wasted two months debating the selection of a Republican Speaker between 1859 and 1860, thereby delaying defense measures for the Texas frontier communities, it convinced many Texans that the Republicans held their immediate party concerns above all others.

Disintegration

On April 23, 1860, the Democrats met in Charleston, South Carolina, to nominate their candidate for the upcoming presidential election. Failing to agree on a platform, the party reconvened in Baltimore in June but again could not reach a consensus. In frustration, southern Democrats split from the national party and held their own nominating convention, in which they chose John C. Breckinridge as their presidential candidate. In their own convention, the northern Democrats picked Stephen A. Douglas. Afraid that the splintering of the Democratic party signalled disunion, a border states' coalition of Unionist Democrats, former Whigs, and ex-Know-Nothings fused to form the Constitutional Union party, running John Bell as their standard-bearer on a patriotic platform emphasizing the preservation of the Constitution and the Union. Meanwhile, the Republican party, meeting in Chicago, turned to Abraham Lincoln of Illinois; Lincoln felt that slavery was morally wrong and should be kept out of the territories, although he did not advocate its abolition where it already existed.

Texas Democrats faced an excruciating decision over which Democrat to support. By summer, however, most Texans began to swing over to Breckinridge, who most closely mirrored the sentiments of pro-slavery Texans and seemed most likely to win. But the election returns brought grim news to all Texas Democrats: a Republican, Abraham Lincoln, would be the country's next chief executive. As president, they feared, Lincoln would ignore the state's frontier problems, push for tariffs and internal improvement programs that southern states resisted, campaign to bar slavery from the territories (and future states), and, notwithstanding his assurance that he would respect slavery where it already existed, agitate for its dissolution. News of South Carolina's secession from the Union on December 20 helped to advance the cause of Texan secessionists. Democratic party leaders now requested that governor Houston convoke a special session of the legislature, in order that the body could then legally convene a secession convention.

Texas Democrats by no means unanimously chose secession, and Unionists within the party, such as Sam Houston, fought to avert the nation's disintegration. But time favored the pro-slavery elements. One after another, states from the Lower South continued to issue ordinances of secession, and moderate politicians in Texas supported the trend. The very preservation of the state's way of life seemed to make secession essential, and the deep-seated understanding many held of republicanism only committed them to the belief that their lives should be run as they, and not the federal government, defined it. Secession, therefore, received broadening popular support. Recent historical thought discounts the belief that the Knights of the Golden Circle were responsible for the increase in secessionist sentiment in Texas.

Although Governor Houston resisted scheduling a special legislative session, Democratic party leaders responding to the growing public pressure summoned Texans to a People's Convention. Then Houston, on December 17, finally did call the legislature into session, thereby legalizing the secession convention; still, he asked that the decision of the secessionists be submitted to a public referendum. Meeting on January 28, 1861, convention delegates voted overwhelmingly to sever ties with the North: 166 for, 8 against.

Who Wanted War?

Scholars disagree on the reasons for secession, but they have offered a lengthy list of explanations. Among the causes they identify are: alleged conspiracies by a southern Slave Power and perceptions of a plot by northern Republicans to overturn southern culture; the denunciation of slavery as immoral or its defense as a positive good; constitutional issues of states' rights versus the inviolability of the Union; the incompatibility of the South's and the North's economic systems (one agrarian and primitive, the other industrial and modern); and conflicting value systems that revolved around religion, immigration, cultural conformity, or sectional prejudices. In Texas, certainly, the increased economic viability of slavery from 1850 to 1860, the racial prejudices and fears upon which slavery rested, and the increased connection of the state to the Lower South linked all of these causes together, and they explain the fervor for secession in the state and why Texans chose to fight with the Confederacy. Texans' justification for leaving the Union, enunciated by the secession convention in a "declaration of causes," was in part a response to the Republican party's opposition to slavery in the territories and its alleged advocacy of the doctrine of racial equality. Texas intended to go to war, the declaration stated, to preserve a southern way of life that made racial distinctions, in part, by maintaining blacks in a condition of servitude.

One last step to secession remained following the vote cast by the delegates to the secession convention: the people had to be called upon to speak on the issue. To reach ethnic voters, the delegates had the secession resolution printed in Spanish and German as well as in English. On February 23, by a statewide referendum, Texas ratified secession, with 46,188 votes for and 15,149 against it. Texans did so because they feared northern Republicans, viewed the South as the only protector against the growing abolitionist movement, and because secession seemed a last alternative for upholding social and economic institutions. As the vote totals revealed, cultural pluralism and economic reality shaped Texans' views. Expectedly, eastern and southeastern Texas voted heavily for secession. Half of the voters living in counties that drew their settlers from the Upper South, on the other hand, expressed less enthusiasm for the breakup, mainly since North and north-central Texas had few slave owners. On the West Texas frontier, four German-populated counties were overwhelmingly opposed to secession. To a large extent, the vote reflected western fears, similar to those prevalent in the northern counties, of the cessation of federal protection from Indians should Texas leave for the Confederacy. At the same time, this vote may have pointed to an inherent cultural bias that Germans had against slavery, though by the 1850s many Germans had become indifferent to the peculiar institution or even defended southerners' right to own slaves. The fact remains that where the demographic composition did not resemble that of the Lower South, Texans more noticeably opposed secession.

A short time following the referendum, the secession convention reconvened, announced that the state no longer recognized the Union, and pursued the necessary protocol to enter the Confederate States of America. But Governor Houston refused to concede, proposing that the state instead restore the Republic of Texas and in that way avoid entering the Confederacy. When he declined to swear allegiance to the South, the convention proclaimed the office of governor vacant and replaced Houston with Edward Clark, the lieutenant governor. Refusing to stay in office through the use of force, Houston rejected President Lincoln's offer to dispatch federal troops to try to keep Texas in the Union. Rather, the sixty-eight-year-old Sam Houston relocated with his family to Galveston. He died in Huntsville in 1863.

TEXAS AND THE CIVIL WAR

The Texas Front

Texans took up the southern cause without hesitation. Acting under the instructions of the secession convention, Ben McCulloch on February 16 went to San Antonio, compelled Brigadier General David E. Twiggs, commander of the Department of Texas, to surrender all U.S. forces there and to evacuate federal property in Texas, then raised the Lone Star flag over the Alamo. A few days later, Colonel John S. "Rip" Ford, with some 500 volunteers, captured Brazos Island, at the mouth of the Rio Grande, from its twelve U.S. Army defenders. By the time that news of the shelling of Fort Sumter arrived in South Texas, Ford had taken Fort Brown and secured the lower Rio Grande country, gaining a foothold on the Mexican port city of Matamoros across the Rio Grande.

With the withdrawal of federal troops from posts on the northern and western frontiers, the responsibility of protecting citizens from Comanche hostility fell upon state and special volunteer companies. By the summer of 1861, these units appeared in Indian country along the Red River, chasing away Comanche war parties. By 1862, Texas forces occupied eighteen military stations roughly from the 97th meridian at the Red River, thence southwestwardly toward Eagle Pass in South Texas. But the Comanches were too masterful and resourceful to be deterred from conducting their raids, and they continued to wreak havoc upon settlers throughout the Civil War.

As the westward wing of the Confederacy, Texas served as a launching point for campaigns against Union forces along the upper Rio Grande. An expedition under Lieutenant Colonel John R. Baylor subdued Fort Bliss in El Paso in July 1861, and the next month Baylor's men assumed control of southern New Mexico. Another campaign under Henry Hopkins Sibley left San Antonio in November 1861, marched through the El Paso Valley, and moved into New Mexico, where it met up with Baylor and his men. Then, on February 21, 1862, the Sibley Brigade, temporarily under the command of Colonel Tom Green, encountered Union soldiers at Valverde, and in an all-day battle defeated the Unionists. Sibley then continued toward Upper New Mexico and brought it, too, under Confederate rule. In late March, the Union launched a counteroffensive and repelled the southerners, forcing them back to Fort Bliss. Sibley and what remained of his force retreated to San Antonio by summer 1862.

The Texas coast had ever remained vulnerable to Union attacks, but in late 1862 John Bankhead Magruder took steps to secure this vital area. Of extreme value was the port city of Galveston, which had fallen to Union guns in October of that year. In a daring night assault on New Year's Day 1863, Magruder's unit (which included troops under Colonel Tom Green of New Mexico fame) attacked the city by both land and sea. Fierce fighting ensued, resulting in a spectacular Confederate win that reestablished their control of Galveston. A few days later Union gunboats returned to regain the port and to shell other fortifications along the coast, but the Confederates repelled the strike. Nevertheless, Magruder and the Texans knew that the federals would return, and they duly prepared for an all-out Union invasion of the state, though they did not know when or where the Union troops would land.

In the middle of 1863, the war's current turned against the South following Union victories at Gettysburg (Pennsylvania), Vicksburg (Mississippi), and Chattanooga (Tennessee). For Texans, the task of defending the state's three frontiers remained. In the north and west, the Indians persisted in their attacks upon homesteaders, and not until late 1864 did volunteer regiments repel the Comanches and drive them toward the southern High Plains.

On the eastern coastline, the long-anticipated Union offensive against the state occurred in September of 1863, when a Union fleet of four gunboats and twenty-two troop transport vessels carrying approximately 4,000 men attacked

Sabine Pass. Though outnumbered, the Confederates led by Lieutenant Richard W. Dowling repulsed the attack. Recoiling, the Union troops turned their invasion plans to the region of the lower Rio Grande Valley. On November 2, 1863, Nathaniel P. Banks and some 7,000 Union troops took Brownsville, interrupting the important Confederate supply line through Matamoros. Now the Union sought to secure the Nueces region, but ultimately it decided to hold Brownsville and concentrate on plans for another northeastern invasion of the state.

Not until the next summer (of 1864) did Rip Ford regain the lower Valley and restore the supply lines from Matamoros to Texas (and from there to the rest of the Confederacy). The expected counterattack upon South Texas came in May 1865; this time Ford rebuffed the enemy. But the Unionists proved to be members of the regular garrison at Brazos Island, which Ford had failed to take in 1864. From a prisoner of war, Ford learned that the South had surrendered over a month earlier. As fate would have it, this was the last land battle of the Civil War.

The Confederate Front

No one can accurately state the total number of Texans who contributed to the war effort, either on the Texas or the Confederate front; historians generally accept the estimated figure of 68,500, though some argue that the total was closer to 90,000. (Similarly, determining the number of casualties remains elusive; a commonly accepted fact is that some 24,000 Texans perished during the four years of fighting). Many Texans distinguished themselves in the fighting as part of Texas units. Among those companies winning praise for valor were Terry's Texas Rangers, named for the unit's organizer, Benjamin Franklin Terry. The Rangers saw constant action in the Kentucky-Tennessee-Mississippi region, and then, carrying out their reputation for swift and daring attacks, they assisted in efforts to delay Sherman's march through Georgia in 1864. Also earning kudos for bravery was Ross's Texas Brigade, named for its commander, Lawrence Sullivan "Sul" Ross. This cavalry brigade conducted hit-and-run strikes in the Alabama-Mississippi-Tennessee theater and participated in several major battles and numerous small engagements—in a three-month period in 1864, Ross's unit engaged the enemy almost daily. Another outfit that won renown for its audacity and bravery was Hood's Texas Brigade, named for John Bell Hood, who succeeded the brigade's original organizer, Louis T. Wigfall. This unit fought in the Army of Northern Virginia and participated in such significant engagements as the Second Battle of Manassas (Second Bull Run) and Antietam in the late summer of 1862, as well as in the Battle of Gettysburg in July 1863. Numerous other Texas units, which fought on both sides of the Mississippi River, were singled out for praise by Confederate commanders.

Thirty-seven Texans went on to lead important Confederate brigades as high-ranking officers. Albert Sidney Johnston, who fell at the Battle of Shiloh, had been commissioned a general by the Confederate government; John Bell Hood, in 1862, earned a promotion to lieutenant general; and Samuel Bell Maxey, John A. Wharton, and Tom Green led forces as major generals. Addi-

Albert Sidney Johnston. From a painting by E. F. Andrews. Exhibited at the Texas State Capitol. *The UT Institute of Texas Cultures, No. 68-245*

tionally, Texas furnished the Confederacy with thirty-two brigadier generals and about one hundred colonels.

Aside from the military aid Texas rendered to the Confederacy, the state also assisted the southern cause economically. Until the very end of the war, Matamoros remained a center for Confederate trade, primarily through the port town of Bagdad. From the commencement of hostilities, the Confederacy had utilized Brazos Santiago, a small island near the mouth of the Rio Grande, as a way station for the export and import of goods, but following the arrival of the Union navy in early 1862, the suppliers removed across the Rio Grande into Mexico in order to conduct commerce under the guise of neutral trade. Bagdad, located about thirty-five miles from Matamoros, emerged as a boom port, as cargoes destined for Matamoros were first unloaded there. To Bagdad flowed cotton hauled from the plantations of Texas, Louisiana, Arkansas, and even states east of the Mississippi River, for export to British and French markets. From Bagdad left manufactured goods and war munitions, which were then distributed throughout the Confederacy.

Despite the close association that existed between the Confederate government of Texas and that in Richmond, relations between the two were not always amiable. From the beginning of the war, Texans, along with citizens of other western Confederate states, had felt neglected by the Confederate authorities. This had led the governors of Texas and Arkansas in 1862 to complain emphatically about the lack of protection they felt their states, as well as Missouri and Louisiana, were receiving. In July 1862, therefore, Jefferson Davis, President of the Confederate States of America, sanctioned a meeting in Marshall, Texas. The results of this conference appeased the two governors attending, Texas Governor Francis R. Lubbock and the governor of Missouri; Richmond Confederate leaders created the Trans-Mississippi Military Department and assigned Edmund Kirby Smith as its commander. A subsequent conference in August 1863, again held at Marshall and chaired by Lubbock, however, produced little relief for the western states, for the Confederacy had become increasingly concerned with the state of affairs east of the Mississippi.

Behind the Lines

Besides defending the state, Texas officials also were responsible for outfitting their own troops. State-run arsenals produced small arms, ammunition, and cannons, but shortages of all sorts of matériel remained throughout the conflict. A scarcity of labor forced women and children to toil in the munition factories. Unable to collect taxes and place confidence in the paper money it issued, the state found it difficult to purchase weapons elsewhere. Troopers had to supply their own gear, and in the latter stages of the war, fighting men faced such difficulties finding mounts, firearms, food, and other provisions that they frequently confiscated goods from civilians.

Recruitment also plagued the military mobilization. The wartime governors, Francis R. Lubbock (1861–1863) and Pendleton Murrah (1863–1865), found filling army ranks a difficult and thankless responsibility. Disdain for military discipline and tradition, the necessity of having to care for family members, contempt for the rule that permitted planters and other members of the elite to exempt themselves from military service by finding (hiring) a substitute, and despair over the Confederacy's lack of progress in the war all hindered recruitment efforts. After the calamitous defeats suffered by the Confederacy in 1863, desertions increased. Decent men weary of battle and losing hope of victory departed for home upon learning that their families were hungry and unable to fend for themselves. Less honorable deserters made common cause with gangs of slackers and even Unionists on the run.

Additionally, Confederate Texans contended with dissent against the Southern Cause, especially in the Red River counties of North Texas, where several factors had fueled strong antisecessionist sentiment in 1861: such factors included the relative absence of slavery, regional dependence on the federal government which from neighboring Oklahoma purchased wheat and corn from North Texas farmers, fears that the section would be exposed to Indians and Union attacks in case of war, and the influence of anti-secessionists such as Collin McKinney, who propagandized against the fragmenting of the nation. In Cooke County, citizens who had voted against secession in February 1861 formed the Peace Party in the summer of 1862 to protest secession, resist taxation, defy the conscript law, and, according to rumors, prepare the way for a Union invasion into North Texas from Kansas. By the winter of 1863–1864, other parts of north-central Texas seemed openly to contest the war effort; men in the regions between Dallas and the Red River engaged in such lawlessness that the Confederates feared losing the section.

Less blatant but no less serious was opposition posed from Unionist Democrats. One faction of the party, which had found the Texas Whigs attractive in the 1850s or had been Know-Nothings, had disapproved of secession but, valuing Texas more than the nation, had reluctantly submitted to the people's referendum of February 1861 and fought for the Confederacy. A smaller element within the ranks of the Unionist Democrats, those of the Jackson-Houston persuasion or former Know-Nothings, revered the Union and the federal constitution and, placing nationhood above sectional concerns, had gone on to join Union military forces or become government officials in the North.

In addition, minority groups of diverse ethnicity also expressed disapproval with the majority cause of their state. Many blacks took the opportunity to run

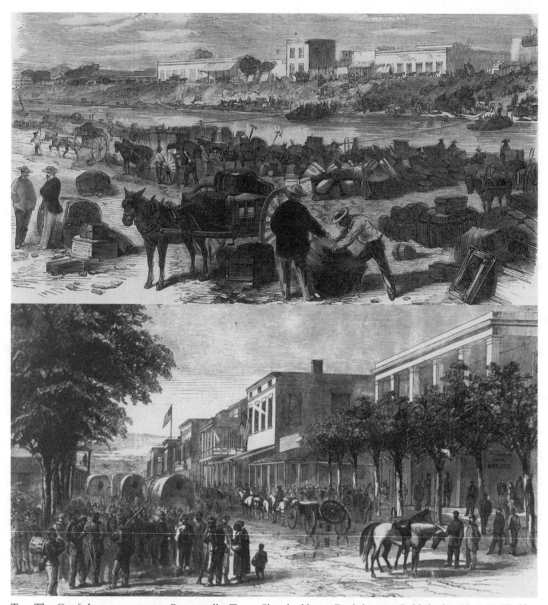

Top: The Confederates evacuating Brownsville, Texas. Sketched by an English artist. Published in *Harper's Weekly*, Feb 13, 1864. *The UT Institute of Texan Cultures, No. 72-328*; Bottom: Union soldiers on Elizabeth Street in Brownsville, Drawing from a photograph, published in *Harper's Weekly*, Dec 16, 1865. *The UT Institute of Texan Cultures, No. 72-330*

away from plantations, or, if possible, flee to Union lines. Indeed, some fifty black Texans fought in the Union Army. German Americans (especially those concentrated in West Texas beyond San Antonio and Austin), while not vociferous in their opposition to slavery and secession, tended to harbor antislavery attitudes and sympathize with the Union. Actions in the German-populated Hill Country during the war, such as shielding Union sympathizers and draft dodgers, revealed German Texan displeasure with the South's cause. In South Texas, anti-Confederate resistance was evidenced by the 950 Texas Mexicans who fought for the Stars and Stripes. Unionist sympathizers led by Cecilio Valerio and guerrilleros such as Juan N. Cortina harassed Confederate troops throughout the war, seizing cotton and livestock for Union forces.

But it should be emphasized that most Texans steadfastly supported the South, and few of them committed themselves to the defeat of the Confederacy. Their devotion to the war effort periodically took dastardly turns, manifesting itself in intolerance, harassment, and violence in the form of vigilante justice against suspected traitors.

Ethnic Unionists confronted repression by angry Confederates. Slaves suspected of sedition or treason received swift physical punishment. German Texans became especially targeted for any outward sign of disloyalty or subversion, even as hundreds of German Texans from West Texas enlisted in the Confederate ranks. Authorities kept an especially keen eye on West Texas Counties such as Gillespie, Kerr, Kendall, Medina, and Comal, some of which acted as a sanctuary for the Union Loyal League. Through this organization, German Unionists endeavored to destabilize the Texas Confederacy and hopefully reinstate Union authority, by military means if necessary. Expectedly, Austin officials considered the Union Loyal League a danger to Southern security, so in July of 1862, they ordered a company of Confederate cavalry and Texas state troopers into the Hill Country entrusted with suppressing League activities. Many Germans found the Confederate effort to establish law and order through arrest, detention, and violence so odious, however, that some sixty-one of them opted for flight into Mexico on August 1. Convinced that those fleeing the country were part of the seditious sentiment overrunning the German counties, Confederate troops gave pursuit, overtaking the Unionists on August 10 near modern-day Bracketville, on the West Nueces River. In what came to be known as the "Battle of Nueces"—a brief skirmish resulting in fatalities on both sides—the Confederates forced the Germans into surrendering. Subsequently, on their own initiative, a handful of Confederates foully murdered some of the German survivors.

As to Mexican Americans, only the relative isolation of the border country protected them from attacks such as those Anglos had leveled against Germans, even though 2,500 Tejanos served in the Confederate ranks, including officers like Santos Benavides. But Texans held those Tejanos disputing the Southern cause in contempt, referring to them at one point during the war as an assortment of abolitionists, outlaws, Mexicans, and fugitive slaves.

But ethnic background was not a criterion for victimization by vengeful Rebels. In Gainesville (Cooke County), for instance, North Texas Confederates—responding to reports of a plot by members of the Peace Party to take over local ordnance depots and to revolt at the same time that Unionists forces invaded Texas from Kansas and Galveston—executed some forty-two alleged conspirators (most of them innocent) in October 1862 and proclaimed martial law in the county. The imposition of lynch law followed, and more men in Cooke and neighboring counties fell victim to beatings, imprisonment, or hanging without a trial. Luckier ones made for the brush, successfully warding off Confederate detachments sent to bring them to "justice."

At War's End

Following Confederate General Robert E. Lee's surrender at Appomattox Court House, Virginia, Texans looked to the future with a mixed sense of remorse, satisfaction, and uncertainty. Pride could be taken in the significant role Texans had played in the major battles of the Civil War and in the number of highly regarded officers the state had furnished the Confederacy. Gratifying as well was the fact that the war either furthered or launched the political careers of many Texas veterans. Among those ex-Confederates who resumed their antebellum political careers were Governor Oran M. Roberts and Senator Samuel Bell Maxey. Many began a political career based on their participation in the war; this group included Governors Richard Coke and Lawrence Sullivan "Sul" Ross, Senator Roger Q. Mills, and Congressmen David B. Culberson and George W. "Wash" Jones. Also of consequence was the contribution of John H. Reagan, who served throughout most of the war as Confederate Postmaster General. But the hard truths remained that Texas and the South had lost the war, that legal slavery was a thing of the past, and that before the state could once again enjoy its membership in the United States, it would have to tread the rugged road of Reconstruction.

READINGS

Books and Dissertations

Ashcraft, Allan C., *Texas in the Civil War: A Resume History* (Austin: Texas Civil War Centennial Commission, 1962).

Barr, Alwyn, "Change and Continuity in Texas During the Civil War and Reconstruction," in *The Texas Heritage*, 3rd ed., eds. Ben Procter and Archie P. McDonald (Wheeling, IL: Harlan Davidson, Inc., 1998).

Baum, Dale, *The Shattering of Texas Unionism* (Baton Rouge: Louisiana State University Press, 1998).

Buenger, Walter L., *Secession and the Union in Texas* (Austin: University of Texas Press, 1984).

Campbell, Randolph B., *An Empire for Slavery: The Peculiar Institution in Texas, 1821–1865* (Baton Rouge: Louisiana State University Press, 1989).

————, *Sam Houston and the American Southwest* (New York: HarperCollins, 1993).

Campbell, Randolph B., and Richard G. Lowe, *Wealth and Power in the Antebellum South* (College Station: Texas A&M University Press, 1977).

Collins, Michael L., "Statehood, 1845–1860," in *The Texas Heritage*, 3rd ed., eds. Ben Procter and Archie P. McDonald (Wheeling, IL: Harlan Davidson, Inc., 1998).

Daddysman, James W., *The Matamoros Trade: Confederate Commerce, Diplomacy, and Intrigue* (Newark: University of Delaware Press, 1985).

De León, Arnoldo, *The Tejano Community, 1836–1900* (Albuquerque: University of New Mexico Press, 1982).

Eby, Frederick, *The Development of Education in Texas* (New York: The Macmillan Co., 1925).

Jordan, Terry G., *Trails to Texas: Southern Roots of Western Ranching* (Lincoln: University of Nebraska Press, 1981).

Lowe, Richard G., and Randolph B. Campbell, *Planters and Plain Folk: Agriculture in the Antebellum South* (Dallas: Southern Methodist University Press, 1987).

Marten, James, *Texas Divided: Loyalty and Dissent in the Lone Star State, 1856–1874* (Lexington: University Press of Kentucky, 1990).

McCaslin, Richard B., *Tainted Breeze: The Great Hanging at Gainesville, Texas, 1862* (Baton Rouge: Louisiana State University Press, 1994).

Meinig, Donald W., *Imperial Texas: An Interpretive Essay in Cultural Geography* (Austin: University of Texas Press, 1969).

Moneyhon, Carl and Bobby Roberts, *Portraits of Conflict: A Photographic History of Texas in the Civil War* (Fayetteville: The University of Arkansas Press, 1998).

Nackman, Mark E., *A Nation Within a Nation: The Rise of Texas Nationalism* (Port Washington, NY: Kennikat Press, 1975).

Peters, Robert K., "Texas: Annexation to Secession" (Ph.D. diss., University of Texas at Austin, 1977).

Smith, David Paul, *Frontier Defense in the Civil War: Texas Rangers and Rebels* (College Station: Texas A&M University Press, 1992).

Storey, John W., "Battling Evil: The Growth of Religion in Texas," in *Texas: A Sesquicentennial Celebration*, edited by Donald W. Wisenhunt (Austin: Eakin Press, 1984).

Thompson, Jerry Don, *Vaqueros in Blue and Gray* (Austin: Presidial Press, 1977).

Utley, Robert, *Frontiersmen in Blue: The U.S. Army and the Indians, 1848–1865* (New York: MacMillan, 1967.

Wheeler, Kenneth W., *To Wear A City's Crown: The Beginnings of Urban Growth in Texas, 1836–1865* (Cambridge, MA: Harvard University Press, 1968).

White, Michael Allen, "History of Education in Texas, 1860–1884," (Ed. D. diss., Baylor University, 1969).

Wooster, Ralph A., *Civil War Texas* (Austin: Texas State Historical Association, 1999).

————, *Texas and Texans in the Civil War* (Austin: Eakin Press, 1995).

Articles

Campbell, Randolph B., "The Whig Party of Texas in the Election of 1848 and 1852," *Southwestern Historical Quarterly* 73 (July, 1969).

Friend, Llerena B., "The Texan of 1860," *Southwestern Historical Quarterly* 62 (July, 1958).

Jordan, Terry G., "Population Origins in Texas, 1850," *Geographical Review* 59 (January, 1969).

Ledbetter, Bill D., "White Over Black in Texas: Racial Attitudes in the Ante-bellum Period," *Phylon* 34 (December, 1973).

McGowen, Stanley M., "Battle or Massacre?: The Incident on the Nueces, August 10, 1862," *Southwestern Historical Quarterly*, CIV (July 2000).

Oates, Stephen B., "Texas Under the Secessionists," *Southwestern Historical Quarterly* 67 (October, 1963).

Wooster, Ralph A., and Robert Wooster, "'Rarin' For a Fight': Texans in the Confederate Army," *Southwestern Historical Quarterly* 84 (April, 1981).

REPUBLICANISM AND REUNION

CHAPTER 6

What was to be the agenda for the country's future now that the Civil War had ended? Even the victorious Republican party of the North held divergent views. One element within the party gave uppermost importance to granting citizenship to the newly manumitted slaves. These Radical Republicans, as they came to be called, advocated extending full civil rights to ex-slaves, among them the franchise, education, and, possibly, ownership of confiscated Rebel-owned land. Another faction within the Republican party, known as the Conservative Republicans, principally pursued economic development. During the course of the war, Conservative Republicans succeeded in enacting a protective tariff, a plan of internal improvements, a national banking system, and a homestead law that permitted the rapid settlement of the West. Backers of this agenda sought to keep southerners from undermining the vibrancy of an expanding national economy by their opposition

to the new programs, their insistence on states' rights (the cornerstone of southern politics) and their demands for other concessions. More moderate Republicans and northern Democrats, not to be dismissed from determining the course of the nation, held still other views on the future of the postbellum United States. Nevertheless, conservative and moderate Republicans alike believed that African Americans should, at the very least, have legal equality.

In April 1865, the war moved from the battlefield to the political arena. Texans, as did other southerners, sought to reestablish the Democratic rule redolent of that before the war. Most urgent, for them, was to find a way to keep a newly freed black population (estimated by scholars to have numbered about 250,000) in subordination. In the differing goals of Republicans and southern Democrats lay the seeds of division and confrontation that would mark the era of Reconstruction.

AFTERMATH OF THE WAR

News of the Confederate surrender in April 1865 resulted in the disintegration of the army and government in Texas. Servicemen deserted in large num-

Above: The 9th Cavalry at Fort Davis. *The UT Institute of Texan Cultures, No. 68-1139*

bers, and as the army dissolved, chaos erupted. Disbanding soldiers sacked arsenals and government buildings and confiscated Confederate public property of every sort. Scoundrels capitalized on the general disorder to rob and recklessly kill innocent civilians. Unidentified persons pillaged the state treasury on the night of June 11. Simultaneously, government at the state and local levels staggered. Courts were disrupted and prominent Confederates, among them the governor, Pendleton Murrah, fled to Mexico to escape Union forces. This was the situation when the occupation army (U.S. troops), commanded by General Gordon Granger, arrived in Galveston on June 19, 1865. Granger declared all acts of the Texas government since 1861 illegal, the parole of members of the Confederate army, and all slaves free. The day of emancipation in Texas thenceforth was known as "Juneteenth," a traditional holiday among black Texans ever since.

In comparison to other southern states, Texas emerged from the Civil War relatively unscathed. Seeing Texas as a haven from federal attacks, a number of slaveholders from every southern state "refugeed" their chattel in Texas, to prevent federal troops from expropriating their bondspeople or to keep slaves from absconding to Yankee lines. No one knows the exact number of slaves relocated to Texas, but historians estimate it to have been about 50,000. The increasing labor pool led to the opening of new cotton lands and in some cases greater production of the staple. Trade with Mexico during the war had also proved fortuitous. Since commerce in the international market demanded specie, gold currency was more common in Texas than it was in other parts of the Confederacy, and its presence served to mitigate the effect that the southern defeat had on a number of businesses in the state.

Furthermore, Texas had been spared the kind of wartime devastation the rest of the Confederacy suffered. Federal armies never undertook a significant invasion of the state; Union troops did not level Texas towns or demolish roads and bridges. Civilian deaths resulting from combat in no way compared to casualties incurred in other states, such as Georgia. Community life, moreover, had not been disrupted as it had in other regions of the Confederacy. Despite the absence of so many male heads of household, society had functioned more or less routinely. Women "made do," caring for their families by improvising in the kitchen, in clothing their loved ones, and in educating their children. Women also had assumed certain male roles and responsibilities and thereby maintained social stability. They had defended their homes from Indian raids and other threats, assumed the management of plantations where needed (in some cases, slave overseers performed the duties of an absent owner), and took over farm tasks such as plowing, planting, and tending livestock. A few women had contributed to the war effort by running supply wagons within the state; some even smuggled guns in from Mexico.

Nonetheless, Texans came out of the war needing to regroup. The accrued expenses had landed the state back in financial distress. Property values and the worth of farmsteads and ranches had depreciated. The war, furthermore, left a legacy of deep personal hatreds. Unionists and northern sympathizers, who had been harassed and denied liberties for four years, now sought vengeance. Ex-Confederates, on the other hand, despised and vented their hatred of anything symbolizing the North: Unionists, soldiers in blue, and ex-slaves, who desired to exercise their new freedoms.

PRESIDENTIAL RECONSTRUCTION

President Andrew Johnson (1865–1869), who succeeded to the presidency on April 15, 1865, after Abraham Lincoln was assassinated, appointed Andrew Jackson Hamilton, a former U.S. congressman from Texas and a Unionist who had fled to the North, as provisional governor of Texas on June 17, 1865. As part of his ongoing plan to implement what historians call Presidential Reconstruction, Johnson instructed Hamilton to call a convention and undertake the necessary steps to form a new civil government in the state. Johnson's terms of Reconstruction were mild: he was, after all, a Unionist Democrat from Tennessee whom fate had placed on the Republican ticket as Lincoln sought to gain Democratic votes in 1864. Now Johnson called on the seceded states to declare secession null and void, to cancel the debt accumulated while fighting the war (repudiating the debt acknowledged the wrongfulness of the struggle), and to approve of the Thirteenth Amendment, which ended slavery, though he did not press further to guarantee the rights of African Americans. Most persons who took the oath of loyalty (to the United States), as required by President Johnson's amnesty proclamation issued on May 29, 1865, could participate in the restoration of home rule. This lenient policy permitted the majority of Texans to assume previous civil rights. Ineligible to take part in reestablishing the postbellum order were high-ranking ex-Confederates and those owning property valued at more than $20,000.

Given Johnson's rather lenient plan of Reconstruction, Hamilton and his supporters worried that those tied to the Confederate past would attempt to regain their former prominence, and duly block efforts to realize civil rights for black persons. The governor's efforts to neutralize these former Secessionist Democrats, now known as Conservative Democrats, and launch a new unionism unfettered by slavery (and perhaps even form a Republican party in Texas) were apparent in the provisional appointments Hamilton made to state and local offices.

But even as Hamilton sought to consolidate his authority, divergent political philosophies on the status of the ex-slaves were splintering the Democratic party in Texas into two distinct factions. Hamilton Unionists, on one hand, proposed basic civil rights for the freedmen

Andrew Jackson Hamilton. *Texas Collection Library, The Center For American History, The University of Texas at Austin, CN 01000*

TABLE 6.1 Phases of Reconstruction

	PROVISIONAL GOVERNMENT	PRESIDENTIAL RECONSTRUCTION	CONGRESSIONAL RECONSTRUCTION	RADICAL RECONSTRUCTION	REDEMPTON
Dates	1865–1866	1866–1867	1867–1870	1870–1874	1874–1876
Constitution	——	1866	——	1869	1876
Leaders	A. J. Hamilton	J. W. Throckmorton	Elisha Pease	E. J. Davis	Richard Coke
Political Supporters	Unionist Democrats (pre–Civil War Anti-Secessionists)	Conservative Democrats (pre–Civil War Secesionist Democrats)	Unionist Democrats	Radical Republicans and Moderate Republicans	Conservative Democrats
Ideology	basic rights for freedmen	no rights for freedmen	basic rights for freedmen	full equality for freedmen, strong governor, increased taxes, state-supported school system, bonds for railroads, state police/state militia, attractive homestead policy	white supremacy, weak governor, low taxes, locally controlled school system, land grants for railroads, anti-state police/state militia, weak homestead policy

before the law; in such sentiments they resembled congressional Republicans at the national level. On the other hand were the Conservative Unionists and Conservative Democrats, both of whom opposed granting any freedoms to blacks beyond emancipation; they favored new legislation specifically restricting the rights of African Americans.

Yielding to pressure from President Johnson, who pressed for a rapid reinstatement of the former Confederate states, Hamilton, on November 17, 1865, called for an election on January 8, 1866, for the purpose of selecting delegates to a constitutional convention. The campaign to choose these delegates found Hamilton's followers, the Unionist Democrats, competing against the Conservative Unionists and the Conservative Democrats. All white Texans could participate in the contest, save those excluded by President Johnson's amnesty proclamation of the previous year, so when the convention assembled at Austin on February 7, 1866, both factions of Democrats were reprsented. The Unionist Democrats quickly suffered a defeat, however, when James W. Throckmorton, a Conservative Unionist, was chosen as convention chairperson.

Then the delegates proceeded to the business of considering the legal status of secession, the controversy over the state war debt, and slavery. While Hamilton's Unionist Democrats argued that the U.S. Constitution did not permit states the right to secede from the Union, and that freedmen deserved to be given basic rights, the Conservative Unionists and Conservative Democrats defended the state's right to leave the Union and strenuously opposed extending rights to the ex-slaves. In the end, the convention reluctantly declared secession illegal and the debt repudiated. It also accepted slavery's demise; although Texas did not approve the Thirteenth Amendment until 1870. As on the first two questions, the delegates awarded to blacks only those freedoms federal policy forced them to concede. The constitution they drafted extended to the freedmen the right to purchase and sell property, to sue and be sued, to enter legally binding contracts, and to testify in court cases involving other African Americans. But the document purposely deprived blacks of the franchise and access to public office, jury participation, and public schools—leaving to the legislature that would meet later in the year the responsibility of more precisely detailing the civil rights of black persons. Before adjourning, the convention called for a statewide election that summer. On June 25, 1866, the voters would approve the Constitution of 1866, which essentially consisted of an amended Constitution of 1845, and elect a new slate of state officials.

The two factions of the Democratic party moved quickly to galvanize public support, placing their respective platforms and candidates before the people. Governor Hamilton's supporters, now simply using the Union party label, reminded the voters that their rivals did not reflect the true demands established by President Johnson and the national Congress, that in fact the opposition was a throwback to the sentiments of the 1850s. The path to the state's readmission into the Union, they urged, lay in the philosophy of the Unionists. This party endorsed Johnson's Reconstruction policy, believed secession illegal, concurred with abolition, and consented to a semblance of equality for the freedmen. The Unionists' choice for governor, Elisha M. Pease, headed their campaign.

A formidable opposition led by Throckmorton, a prewar member of the Texas legislature who voted against (although he did not reject) secession in 1861 but had gone on to rise to the rank of brigadier general in the Confederate army, appealed to Conservative Democrats in Texas. These old Secessionist Democrats saw in Throckmorton a leader who could assist them in their comeback. Understandably, Throckmorton's position on denying blacks the franchise appealed

Elisha M. Pease. *Texas Collection Library, The Center for American History, The University of Texas at Austin, CN 03883*

to the conservatives as an opportunity to regain the former power structure of the state. Indeed, in October 1865 they had denounced John H. Reagan, the former member of Jefferson Davis's cabinet, for a public letter he sent to Texans from imprisonment in Fort Warren (Massachusetts) advocating black suffrage, though limited to those with some schooling or who had managed to acquire property. (Reagan had seen the need for such a concession in order to expedite the state's readmission into the Union). This camp of Conservative Unionists and Conservative Democrats stressed the "radical" tendencies of the Pease ticket and took a stand against elevating blacks politically. A "radical" victory, they electioneered, would lead to a new racial order in the South, the political disarmament of ex-Confederates, and the denial of a place for the former Confederate states in the Union.

In the election, Texans opted for Throckmorton, giving him 49,314 votes to Pease's 12,694. Texans had decided to go with the candidate who called for the least amount of change from the prewar days. While Pease promoted fundamental equality for blacks and refused to return to the prewar society, the majority of voting Texans believed, like Throckmorton, that states should have the right to determine internal political matters, among them the power to relegate black people to a marginal citizenship.

THE EX-CONFEDERATES COME TO POWER, 1866–1867

With Throckmorton as governor, the legislature that convened in August 1866 acted with dispatch to empower the Conservative Democratic leaders of the state. For example, the legislators chose as one of Texas's U.S. senators Oran M. Roberts, the same man who had presided over the secession convention in 1861. Moreover, the legislators were inclined to support the programs being advanced by the ex-Confederates. Lastly, the lawmakers worked to limit civil rights for blacks.

In the stand they took against black equality, the Conservative Democrats certainly reflected the sentiments of most Texans on the central issue of Reconstruction: the status of the freedmen, who, as mentioned, numbered about 250,000 as of 1865. In the wake of emancipation, some slaveholders procrastinated in releasing their chattels until the year's crops had been harvested. Other planters simply postponed informing their charges of emancipation, so that in some extreme cases African Americans remained in bondage three years after the Union victory. Some ex-slaves who took matters into their own hands and fled East Texas plantations immediately after the war were ambushed and killed as they attempted to cross the Sabine River or were hanged as whites came upon them.

In general, townspeople were not inclined to accept African Americans as free persons among them. Many municipalities viewed the former slaves' arrival with fear, believing they would become an economic and social burden. Typically, whites refused to countenance the conduct of some freedmen. Black Texans now shunned the old standards of social decorum that demanded that they stand deferentially when addressing a white person or get well out of the way of white women when encountering them on city streets. Whites deemed blacks' refusal to continue such submissive practices as defiant, impudent, and insolent behavior.

White Texans insisted that blacks should remain submissive because they still firmly believed in their own racial superiority. The paranoia of whites concerning retribution by the former bondspeople and especially over sexual congress between black men and white women, helped refuel old racial hatreds, though neither fear ever materialized as a major social phenomenon.

In order to regulate the lives of African Americans, the 1866 state legislature enacted a "black code" resembling those adopted in other ex-Confederate states. This body of laws did not mention race specifically, but it clearly intended to dictate the way the freedmen would earn their living. The black code, for example, included a contract labor law specifying that laborers wanting to work for more than thirty days would have to enter a binding agreement. A child apprenticeship law provided employers with the easy opportunity to indenture black children until they reached adulthood or until they married. Other segments of the black code stipulated that workers suspected of being truant from their jobs could be arrested and put to work on public projects without pay until they agreed to return to their "proper" employer. Further legislative acts clarified what the Constitution of 1866 had failed to enumerate: blacks were prohibited from interracial mixture, holding public office, serving on juries, voting, or pressing claims or bearing witness against white defendants in the courts (though blacks, as noted previously, could testify against other blacks). Through such measures, the Conservative Democrats sought to reestablish, as nearly as possible, the social conditions that had existed for African Americans in Texas before the Civil War, including serving as a cheap and controllable labor force.

As both races struggled to redefine their roles within an atmosphere of bitterness, frustration, and resentment, white violence against blacks mounted. Several peculiarities about Texas at this time enabled acts of terrorism against blacks to flourish: U.S. Army troops tended to be assigned to the western frontier regions instead of the interior, where they might have safeguarded the freedmen, and Texas was too big and northern government agents were too few to protect the freedmen in every place where whites and blacks commingled, whether it be the fields, the streets, or on the political circuit. Numerous situations provoked acts of violence by whites against blacks: political events (historians find a correlation between political setbacks for anti-Unionist Texans and an increase in violence), disagreements over labor relations, violation of social codes by blacks, or a sense of defeatism within the white population. In other cases, nothing short of mindless hatred or sadism can explain the murders of African Americans by whites. One murderer explained that he had wanted to "see a d—d nigger kick," another that he meant to "thin the niggers out and drive them to their holes." One historian has estimated that close to 1 percent of black men in Texas between the ages of fifteen and forty-nine met a violent death at the hands of whites in the three years following the end of the war.

NORTHERN INSTITUTIONS
IN A VANQUISHED STATE, 1865–1867

During Presidential Reconstruction, Texans also resisted the efforts of the Bureau of Refugees, Freedmen, and Abandoned Lands, commonly known as the Freedmen's Bureau. Established by the U.S. Congress in 1865 to help African Americans across the South make the transition from slavery to freedom, the Freedmen's Bureau dispatched bureau agents (those in charge of bureau offices in the various counties) to Texas in September 1865 to discharge its functions. No sooner did the agents arrive, however, than trouble began. White Texans detested the outsiders from the North, looking upon bureau men as "carpetbaggers" who wanted to render the South powerless, as intruders bent on interfering with race relations, and as opportunists working only for the money they derived from their offices. Moreover, the bureau suffered internally from its own inability to fill offices and build administrative centers at the grass-roots level—most of its appointees were recently retired Union soldiers. With only about seventy field agents and subordinates at its full manpower level, the bureau lacked the personnel to help ex-slaves successfully enter society as free persons.

Many Texans saw the bureau as an institution thrust upon them by the Radical Republicans of the North, and the devotion of the bureau representatives to their duties may have confirmed attitudes Texans entertained about the agents' radicalism. General E. M. Gregory, the first head of the bureau in Texas, for one, attempted to integrate the freedmen into the new order. Although he called upon freedmen to retain the jobs they currently held and enter into labor contracts, which were subject to review by the bureau, he simultaneously asserted that the freedmen had full legal rights and demonstrated a sympathetic attitude toward their aspirations. This partisanship incurred so much protest from Texans that bureau officials transferred Gregory to Maryland.

Despite the hostility, the bureau pressed ahead with its commitments, among them the education of the former bondspeople. But it found teachers difficult to recruit, school supplies hard to secure, and instruction no easy task in an atmosphere in which the white majority opposed black education. Notwithstanding such drawbacks, the bureau began operating sixteen schools for freedmen in Texas in 1865. With the assistance of philanthropic organizations, as well as the Texas black community itself, the bureau made significant strides in the field of education during this period. Its achievements served as a foundation upon which a later Reconstruction administration would build.

On other fronts, the bureau took steps toward ameliorating conditions for the freed persons. Bureau commissioners adjudicated countless cases dealing with diverse facets of the black community, and black Texans looked to the bureau courts to rectify wrongs perpetrated against them, often by whites. In addition, the bureau attempted to provide relief to the former slaves; it offered aid and health care to those who needed it, for example. But as in the case of education, the bureau faced white resistance and inadequate funding from the federal government.

Disgruntled Texans also resisted the occupation army, which was responsible for executing myriad duties. Military tasks included protecting the western and southern frontiers from Indians or foreign threats, as well as the more unpopular duties of seeing to the protection of the civil rights of both the former slaves and former Unionists. Furthermore, the U.S. Army personnel found themselves having to perform many nonmilitary duties, such as escorting cattle herds on drives north to Kansas, censoring the press (most Texas newspapers were anti-North), performing inspections and enforcing quarantines at ports (to keep contagious diseases from entering the state through the coast) and enforcing other types of sanitation programs, as well as preserving the peace by tracking down lawbreakers. For many Texans, the military presence touched so many aspects of their lives that it seemed to violate the brand of republicanism to which they were accustomed.

In retaliation, Texans openly condemned the men in blue. Brutality and violence became byproducts of the people's dislike of U.S. Army soldiers, who suffered numerous assaults in the years immediately after the war. To vent their frustration further, Texans turned to hit-and-run tactics, attacking supply trains and bushwhacking military details.

In some cases, however, the soldiers brought trouble upon themselves. Their public drunkenness offended many citizens' sensibilities, and some soldiers stole or callously destroyed farm goods and livestock, their wanton destruction and violation of private property only exacerbating the touchy situation. Furthermore, some federal troops were openly contemptuous of the ex-Confederates. Therefore, Texans not only saw the military as an arm of the tyrannical North but also as an oppressive force whose presence they would have to endure until the Secessionists regained control of the state's destiny. Amazingly, despite certain attitudes on both sides, some individual friendships did develop between citizens and army personnel, and there are even records of marriages between soldiers and civilians.

CONGRESSIONAL RECONSTRUCTION

Their loss to Throckmorton in the state election of 1866 and the subsequent actions of the Conservative Democrats solidified an affinity that had existed between Texas Unionists and the national Republican party since the end of the war. Like the Unionists, the Republicans rejected Conservative rule.

Johnson's conservative Reconstruction had never gone over well with northern congressmen. To be sure, various ideological opinions floated around in Congress regarding the direction Reconstruction should take, even within the Democratic and Republican parties themselves. Radical Republicans believed that southerners should take an oath of allegiance before being allowed to vote or serve in government, that the states should be treated like conquered provinces, and that all means should be taken to guarantee the freedpersons equality with whites. Conservative Republicans, meanwhile, mostly concerned themselves with mainstream Republican ideology, including endorsing tariffs and internal improvements. The views of moderate Republicans rested somewhere between the two extremes. But the Republican party overall stood aghast at Johnson's lenient policy toward the South, feeling that the war had been fought in vain if the South rejoined the Union with its prewar social structure basically intact.

But Johnson's refusal to cooperate with congressional wishes, especially with those of the Radicals, who articulated their policy most succinctly, unified the several Republican groups. Under Presidential Reconstruction, governments in the South remained in the hands of ex-Confederate leaders and military men, voters used their powers to maintain the antebellum status quo, states placed restrictions on their former slaves, and violence continued to plague Union soldiers stationed in the South. Such developments enhanced the influence of the Radicals as time passed, and in the congressional election of the fall of 1866, Radicals and Moderates gained strength as voters endorsed Radical Republican alternatives to Johnson's brand of Reconstruction.

Between March and July of 1867, the legislative branch managed to dismantle Johnson's Reconstruction policies and redesign them, imposing what historians call Radical Reconstruction on the defeated South. A series of new Reconstruction Acts divided the ex-Confederacy into five military districts (each under a federal military commander whose authority exceeded that of state governments), suspended existing state governments, and demanded that the ex-Confederate states write new constitutions with all races participating in the selection of delegates to the constitutional conventions (these constitutions must grant suffrage to black males and permit them to hold public office). All prospective voters were subjected to the restrictions of the Reconstruction Acts, which barred from voting former Confederate office holders who had earlier sworn (and therefore broken their promises) to uphold the Constitution of the United States. Nevertheless, some 59,000 white Texans still were able to register to vote, among them ex-Confederate soldiers, for the prohibitions of the Reconstruction Acts did not apply to those who had never taken an oath to support the U.S. Constitution. Therefore, only between 7,000 and 10,000 Texans were disfranchised for having held office before 1861 and then actively engaging in the rebellion.

The passage of the Reconstruction Acts and the overturning of Presidential Reconstruction led to the establishment of the Republican party in Houston on July 4, 1867, as Texas Unionists now joined Congressional Republicans in the repudiation of the Conservative Democrats. Texas Republicans included those from moderate factions committed to Congressional Reconstruction policy, to enacting projects that might improve underdeveloped parts of Texas, and to the betterment of the lives of the state's black citizens. But while moderate Republicans agreed to granting basic freedoms for the ex-slaves, the radical camp within the Republican party supported complete civil and political rights for African Americans.

A major question asked of Congressional Reconstruction has been: Was its "radicalism" a sincere attempt to help the freedmen, or did it seek merely to boost the numbers within the Republican party? Until a few decades ago, scholars argued that selfish motives accounted for the Republican moves; that is, Republicans recruited blacks into their ranks in order to neutralize the strength of hostile white southerners. More recently, however, scholars have seen Radical Republicans as truly desiring to bring about a meaningful change in the South and to allow blacks the chance to achieve equality under the law. Many scholars now maintain that Republicans sincerely believed that blacks should be given the vote and legal rights so that the freedmen might be better able to help themselves.

Texas Republicans received their chance to implement their platform when General Philip Sheridan, commander of the military district that included Texas, removed Governor James W. Throckmorton from office as an impediment to Reconstruction on July 30, 1867, and replaced him with Elisha M. Pease as interim governor. The commander of the subdistrict of Texas followed up by dismissing the incumbents of state and local officials and recruiting Republicans to fill the vacant offices. Military authorities then announced an election for February 1868 to choose delegates to another constitutional convention scheduled for the coming summer.

Having taken over state government, the Republicans invited black political participation, and black Texans became co-agents in giving direction to Texas Reconstruction. In the campaign to mobilize the freedmen at the grass-roots level, blacks achieved leadership roles, the most prominent among them George T. Ruby of Galveston. As a teacher and traveling agent for the Freedmen's Bureau, Ruby had already organized local chapters of the Union (or Loyal) League in the areas he had visited. Throughout the South (and therefore in Texas) the Union League after 1867 was the vehicle utilized to integrate the enfranchised freedmen into the political process. The League also served African Americans in efforts of self-help and self-protection.

Among other things, black leaders now demanded, successfully, that voter registration boards include black members. Freedmen hosted strategy meetings and used the Union League to assert their political goals. About 48,000 freedmen registered to vote for the upcoming convention charged with framing a new state constitution.

In the face of violent threats, 82 percent of the registered blacks cast ballots in February 1868. The black vote and the refusal of whites to participate (they had hoped to scuttle the convention by not going to the polls, for the Reconstruction Acts stipulated that at least one-half of the registered voters had to cast ballots in favor of the convocation before it could convene) resulted in the election of delegates (among them ten blacks) sympathetic to Radical Reconstruction. But the sentiments of the chosen delegates were no means monolithic: of the seventy-eight Republicans present, only about half of them could have been regarded as radicals; the rest would have to be categorized as moderates. Ironically, some white Republicans jealous of black power and unwilling to share the fruits of postwar gains now dominated the leadership of a party that consisted largely of black constituents. Overall, the Republican party of the era was a frail organization of blacks, native white Unionists, and a few northerners.

At the convention, which met in Austin on June 1, 1868, delegates engaged in contentious debate. Disagreements arose between followers of Edmund J. Davis, a former district judge in Texas who became a brigadier general in the Union Army, and those of former Governors Pease and Hamilton. The Davis faction supported *ab initio* (the belief that all official acts passed under secession to help the Confederacy were null and void) equality for the freedpersons, the state financing of public schools, the use of eastern railroad interests to build new lines in Texas, the disenfranchisement of the ex-Confederates, and the division of the state (as the different regions of the state desired a government sensitive to their particular needs). The moderate supporters of Pease and Hamilton rejected *ab initio*, the effort to partition the state, the movement to extend complete civil rights to African Americans, and the use of eastern railroad companies to further internal improvements. By late August, the money allotted for the session ran out, so the delegates disbanded until December with no document ready to put before the electorate.

While the Republicans continued to debate, the Democratic opposition launched a vigorous campaign to undermine the power of black voters. Arsonists victimized centers in which blacks assembled, including offices of the Freedmen's Bureau and Bureau-run schools. And increased numbers of whites joined the Ku Klux Klan, which made its appearance in Texas at about this time; vicious activity became the hallmark of the Klan's conspiracy against African Americans. Black sections of towns witnessed violence. On June 7, 1868, some fifteen Klansmen rode into the black quarter of Millican, in Brazos County, intent upon disrupting the local meeting of the Union League. But the blacks mobilized and fired back, driving away the intruders. The next month witnessed a riot in which two of Millican's black leaders (among other persons) were killed. Fear infused the Millican black community, and the disquiet spread throughout black communities in other sections of the state.

Weakening the Republicans further was persistent intraparty conflict. During the four-month adjournment of the constitutional convention, the state party came to enunciate two discernible positions, and Texans started to label the Davis faction "Radicals," while regarding Governors Pease and Hamilton's followers as "Moderates." But the two groups reached compromise when they returned to Austin for the second session of the constitutional convention on December 7, 1868. The *ab initio* issue no longer was a point of contention, as a decision was pending in the U.S. Supreme Court (in *Texas v. White*, March 1869, the court ruled that a state's secession from the Union was unconstitutional). Regarding issues that had split the convention during the summer, the delegates concurred that the next state legislature should determine whether to partition the state, arrived at an amiable settlement regarding railroad building, and addressed the question of civil rights guarantees by barring from office holding only those specifically restricted by the U.S. Constitution. The Constitution of 1869, which resulted from the convention when it adjourned in early February, departed from the Texas political tradition in a number of ways. It granted suffrage and general civil rights to black Texans, extended enthusiastic support for the opportunity of all Texans to receive a public education, sought to check local- and county-level interference with state laws by increasing the power of the governor (who could appoint people to executive and judicial posts), and attempted to keep the railroads from plundering the state's most valuable asset (its public lands) by prohibiting land grants for internal improvements. Recently, some historians see this document as one that augured a social, political, and economic transformation.

THE FREEDMEN'S BUREAU, AND THE UNION ARMY, 1867–1870

From the time Congressional (Radical) Reconstruction began in Texas until 1868, when the Freedmen's Bureau ceased operations in the state (except for its efforts in education, which continued until 1870), bureau agents faced formidable opposition in carrying out their work. For example, they had to contend with thugs such as the northeastern Texas (Bowie and Cass counties) desperado Cullen Montgomery Baker, whose self-proclaimed enemies included all carpetbaggers, Texas Unionists, and freedmen; Baker killed several such persons before being murdered himself in 1869. The continued efforts of bureau agents between 1868 and 1869 to provide education for freedmen were impeded by hostile whites who abused the northern teachers that staffed many of the black schools. But the bureau made schooling a priority, and by 1870 the state managed some sixty-six schools, with an enrollment of more than 3,000 black children; approximately 300 black students even engaged in "higher" learning. Black illiteracy had been reduced in the process, and the groundwork for black education in the state had been established.

The southerners' view that bureau agents were opportunistic carpetbaggers is not substantiated by recent, balanced studies of the Texas bureau. True, some of the agents were inept and disinterested in their work, but many, such as William G. Kirkman, who was stationed in Bowie County in 1867 (and who was murdered by Cullen Montgomery Baker the next year), and Charles E. Culver, who took command of a subdistrict in east-central Texas, defied such classification. These two northerners carried out exemplary service in rendering needed assistance to the areas' black communities. They enforced the laws equally for blacks and whites, refereed labor and apprenticeship contracts, mediated disagreements between the races, and encouraged blacks to be self-sufficient and independent. Overall, agents who served in Texas tended to be men of high principles who worked towards carrying out the intentions of the bureau despite the limitations imposed upon them. The general lack of success in executing bureau mandates owed less to the agents' determination and more to white opposition to the enforcement of freedmen's rights.

The bluecoats, meantime, continued to bear the stigma of outsiders who were propping up an unfriendly government. Union Army soldiers performed such duties, upsetting to Texans, as helping to register voters of all races, filling offices when local citizens could not take the loyalty oath, trying lawbreakers in military courts (because civilian tribunals at the grass-roots level could not be trusted to rule impartially), protecting freedmen and Freedmen Bureau agents from the Ku Klux Klan, and enforcing martial law. While Texans resented the power wielded by the occupation army, military rule cannot be rigidly depicted as capricious and despotic. Only about 4,500 federal troops served in Texas between 1867 and 1870, 40 percent or less of which saw duty in the more heavily populated areas where they might enrage Texans; the majority guarded against Indians in the western frontier forts. Many of the officers who served in Texas at the time were able and devoted men who discharged their duties impartially.

THE 1869 ELECTION

By the time of the state election in December 1869, the Republicans had split and consequently fielded two candidates. The Radical Republicans chose Edmund J. Davis, who supported the principle of *ab initio* and the Thirteenth and Fourteenth Amendments. Seeking to attract disaffected Democrats, the Moderate Republicans ran A. J. Hamilton, even though he did not believe in much of their program. This, they felt, was their best hope of defeating Davis. Democrats did not nominate a separate candidate for a variety of reasons. Some whites could not take the loyalty oath required by Congress and thus were disfranchised. Second, some Democrats feared that a Democratic victory at the state level would only prolong Reconstruction should the Congress then reject the state's readmission into the

Portrait of Edmund J. Davis. Exhibited in the Texas State Capitol Building. *Texas State Library and Archives Commission*

Union. Third, some Democrats decided to boycott the election and stayed away from the polls.

Nevertheless, Hamilton's Moderate Republicans sought to entice old-guard Conservative Democrats. Such a strategy presented the possibility of stealing the election from Davis, but several factors undermined Hamilton's campaign. For one thing, Democrats refused to endorse a man who during the war had fled to the North—while there Hamilton had cemented his relationship with national politicians—and who had criticized them while serving as provisional governor. More important, the opposition marshaled the black vote through the efforts of the Union League, in which Ruby's registration efforts had paid dividends. Approximately 37,375 blacks cast ballots in 1869, and with their support and the utmost participation of the Republican electorate, Davis edged out Hamilton: 39,838 to 39,005 (voters also approved the Constitution of 1869 by the wide margin of 72,366 to 4,928). At this point, General Joseph J. Reynolds, Texas military commander, who was in effect governor since Pease had resigned in September 1869, appointed Davis governor on January 8, 1870, before Davis's constitutional term officially began.

The results of the election then went to the U.S. Congress. With few problems, the Congress produced a bill to restore Texas to the Union, which President Ulysses S. Grant signed on March 30. General Reynolds thereupon transferred civil authority to the slate of Republican winners on April 16, 1870. This measure terminated Congressional Reconstruction in Texas.

Although the state now had a Republican-controlled legislature, its membership consisted of diverse elements. While several Radicals had been victorious, Democrats and their allies won more than 40 percent of the seats in both

Watercolor of Matt Gaines and G. T. Ruby in the Senate Chambers, Twelfth Legislature, 1870, by Milton Emanuel. *The UT Institute of Texan Cultures, No. 75-730, San Antonio Light Collection*

houses. Moderate Republicans, furthermore, held enough seats to sway legislation in either chamber.

Additionally, two black senators and twelve black representatives sat in the Twelfth Legislature (1870–1871); they constituted about 12 percent of the body's entire membership. Of these men, George T. Ruby is the best known. Born, raised, and educated in the North, Ruby came to Texas in 1866 via Louisiana, where he did educational work among blacks. As a teacher for the Freedmen's Bureau in Galveston, Ruby cultivated close ties with the city's black community and established a solid political base, which he enhanced by becoming an agent for the bureau. As he traveled throughout the state in this capacity, he established chapters of the Union League. By 1868, he captured the presidency of the League and molded it into an efficient Republican political machine. His influence in Republican party circles became evident when he performed the duties of vice president at the first state convention the Republicans held, in Houston in 1868. Between 1869 and 1873, Ruby served as state senator from Galveston and contributed significantly to the work of several influential committees.

The other black state senator was Matt Gaines, a self-educated former slave who became a lay preacher of the Baptist church after the Civil War. In the legislature, he gained attention as an advocate for African American causes and as a persistent critic of those colleagues who remained temperate on issues pertinent to blacks. Although he alienated the opposition in the legislature, he won the grateful support of his African American constituents.

Although less strident than Ruby and Gaines, the twelve black representatives in the Twelfth Legislature nonetheless served with competence. Richard Allen, a former slave who during Reconstruction earned a reputation as an accomplished bridge builder but who also held various public offices locally, has been judged to have been a very capable representative. Another colleague, Benjamin F. Williams, a minister and land speculator, wielded such influence among his black associates in the house that he was nominated for speaker.

Overall, black legislators who served during the era of Reconstruction in Texas amassed political savvy and performed as well as did their black counterparts throughout the South. To win office, they had acquainted themselves with the new politics and functioned adequately within it. In carrying out their work, they displayed allegiance to the Republican party and their black supporters, but they also responded ably to the diverse needs of the districts they represented.

THE DAVIS ADMINISTRATION AND RADICAL RECONSTRUCTION

Governor Edmund J. Davis initiated what scholars refer to as Radical Reconstruction. He made the reestablishment of law and order, the funding of a statewide school system for both blacks and whites, the subsidization of internal improvements, and the protection of the frontier some of his top priorities.

In executing these provisions under the new state constitution, Davis was aided primarily by scalawags, and only minimally by the carpetbaggers of lore. The terms *scalawags* and *carpetbaggers* were born out of the animosity toward Reconstruction; both labels were invented by southerners and used pejoratively, the former to identify southern whites allied with the Republican party, and the latter to refer to northerners who participated in Radical Reconstruction. Southerners despised both groups because of their alleged collusion with Radicals, but in Texas, carpetbaggers hardly influenced Reconstruction.

With scalawag help, therefore, the governor moved vigorously, and in his first two years in office he made successful strides towards accomplishing his legislative goals. Davis organized a state police (a law enforcement body empowered to assist local peacekeeping officials) as well as a state militia (a military force composed of volunteers between the ages of eighteen and forty-five who would help guard the frontier and the border with Mexico but who also could assist in handling internal problems or upheavals), both to be under the governor's oversight. Further legislation established an attractive homestead program designed to settle the state and encourage farming: the plan offered several options, among them providing heads of households 160 acres of land so long as the family worked its grant for three years. The legislature also created a Bureau of Immigration to attract European settlers. In April 1871, Davis signed a bill financing a public school system with such progressive features as a state superintendent and compulsory attendance. Higher taxes were imposed on property to finance these efforts, and the state issued bonds (redeemable at maturity) to railroad companies to subsidize railroad construction projects, a necessary move given the proscriptions under the Constitution of 1869 against awarding land grants (Texas, once again, retained its public domain) to interstate railroad interests.

Actually, these reforms harmonized with most people's conventional politics. Texans always had desired some kind of public school system. Since the 1850s, government had tried to bring about internal improvements, but a program for an updated infrastructure was now sought across the state, not only for the old plantation region. Radical Reconstruction, therefore, did not seek to overturn long-standing economic, political, and social mores. Land reform was not attempted, labor did not receive protective legislation, and blacks, the backbone of the Republican party, did not achieve political equality. Davis did make a place for African Americans in his administration, but no black person held a high-level position such as a cabinet post. Key openings in the Republican party continued to elude black Texans.

Overall, the Davis administration succeeded in establishing a creditable record. Concededly, the state government's expenses almost tripled between 1860 and the end of the Davis administration, but several unusual factors justify the increase. Population grew (and with emancipation, a new sector needing services such as education suddenly appeared) and the expanded frontier broadened the need for defense. Crime increased during the period, and the militia and state police had to contend with all kinds of criminal activity and public disturbances (some of which erupted out of the era's myriad political differences). Service in the state police, incidentally, proved beneficial to the careers of some of its members who went on to fame with the Texas Rangers after Reconstruction. Finally, the state had indeed needed a public school system and new plans for railroad construction.

Nevertheless Davis's opponents, who included some Republicans and the Conservative Democrats, managed to mold public opinion into associating the Radical administration with corruption and extravagant spending. Recent research suggests that the greatest percentage of the state's revenue went to law enforcement, the common school system, and frontier defense and that the Radicals were not in fact wasteful with the taxpayers' money. But Texans (among them members of the planter class, allies of the Democrats), opposed what they considered arbitrary taxation, while others condemned what they believed to be a central government's usurpation of local autonomy. Critics of the administration attacked Governor Davis for cozying up to northern railroad companies, even though the governor vetoed some bond aid bills to save money for the state. Nonetheless, Davis's critics maneuvered to wrest power from him at the first opportunity. As Democrats campaigned in the special congressional election of October 1871, they stressed the issues of high taxes, corruption, fraud, and misgovernment. Their propaganda hit responsive chords. When the results were in, the Democrats had elected all four of their candidates to the U.S. Congress.

The assault on Texas Republicanism spilled over into the general legislative election of November 1872, in which the Democrats won majorities in both chambers of the Thirteenth Legislature (1873). As a result, for the remainder of his term, Davis fought in vain to preserve the programs he had enacted. Democrats overthrew his public school system. They abolished the state police. Their changes to the homestead policy made public lands less affordable. Finally, a constitutional amendment in 1873 permitted the government to use land grants as an enticement to railroad buildings, since bond aid had become a financial burden on the state.

FREEDMEN DURING RECONSTRUCTION

The former slaves, whose status was the central issue of Reconstruction, in reality found themselves only partially liberated. Generally, Texans had retained their old racial attitudes, and during Reconstruction they found ways to deny the freedmen equal protection under the law. Social segregation, for one thing, arose immediately after the war, not towards the latter part of the century, as has been generally assumed. This practice followed social customs rather than legal dictates, for no state law required racial separation during Reconstruction.

Devising methods of labor control, white farmers effected tenancy or sharecropping arrangements, the latter used more commonly. In return for land, seed, fertilizer, tools, food, farm animals, and other essentials, black sharecroppers delivered a good portion of their year's crops to the landowner. Freedmen at first liked the arrangement, as it actually permitted them a degree of independence and provided a release from gang labor and direct supervision by whites. And for the first time in their lives, black sharecroppers established their own work schedules, something that meant a great deal to former slaves.

But sharecropping (for blacks and whites) seldom led to prosperity, and most freedmen faced chronic indebtedness. By the mid-1870s, many rural blacks had become tenants, with their families destined to work together under a white landlord. Those who labored for salaries on the old plantations experienced other kinds of miseries, and urban blacks, vying with discrimination and competing with new laborers arriving from the countryside, had little choice but to take the most undesirable and lowest-paying jobs.

These economic conditions drove black Texans into dismal living standards. Although many African Americans expressed the desire to acquire their own land and build their own dwellings, most found shelter in one- or two-room shanties with dirt floors. Illnesses such as smallpox and cholera ravaged black communities, food scarcities lingered, and segregation forced many former slaves into districts lacking potable water. And, without access to proper medical attention, blacks faced high rates of mortality especially infants.

Amidst such travail, blacks did their best to forge normal and decent lives for themselves and their families. They turned to the family as a means of coping. Viable African American family structures had existed for some time, and blacks moved to legitimize these arrangements immediately following the war. From its appearance in Texas in March 1865, the Freedmen's Bureau had outlined a policy regarding family organization, including the stipulation that blacks having lived together outside of wedlock (during slavery) were now legitimate spouses. Many black couples, however, lived in an uncertain marital state until 1870, the year in which Texas formally legalized black marriages. In any case, recent studies derived from census data point to a certain stability within the black family in Reconstruction Texas and to a resemblance to the white family in its patriarchal structure.

The internal cohesiveness of the black community also was manifest by

"Uncle" George Glenn, an honored life member of the Trail Drivers' Association of Texas (the emblem is pinned on his shirt). In 1870 he drove back from Abilene, Kansas, alone with the body of his dead trail boss, John Folts, beside him. *The UT Institute of Texan Cultures, No. 0347-A, San Antonio Light Collection*

the emergence of leaders at the local level who sought to assert their people's newly won rights. Besides Ruby, the activist from Galveston who was so instrumental in the development of the Union League, other black organizers for the League included Richard Allen and D. W. Bryant of Houston. By 1867, black leaders had succeeded in encouraging their communities to take a stand in behalf of their civil rights. Through such efforts of the Union League, blacks had been able to choose delegates to the Republican convention in 1868. After Davis became governor, African American participation increased in local and state politics. Blacks acted to promote community aspirations and protect their cultural autonomy.

The struggle for self-help led blacks to organize benevolent agencies to aid the less fortunate members of their communities. But self-improvement fell primarily on individual initiative, and black Texans pursued every viable form of employment. Some became cowboys on the ranches of East Texas or worked in the region's burgeoning lumber industry. Some wanting to contribute towards Radical Reconstruction joined the state police or militia in the early 1870s. Army service took other freedmen to patrol duty on the frontier. Black women sought employment in white households—washing clothes, cooking meals, cleaning house, and raising children. Despite the fact that labor practices of the day confined most blacks to performing menial tasks for substandard wages (as compared to the compensation offered whites who performed the same jobs), some black Texans managed to found successful businesses, these persons forming an entrepreneurial elite during Reconstruction.

Aware of the importance of education, black communities built their own schools, at times with the help of the Freedmen's Bureau. Several black religious institutions also made efforts to provide fundamental education. Those fortunate enough to have acquired some education as free persons or as slaves, before 1865, taught in early schools, passing on to children their own knowledge, and black soldiers who had acquired some reading and writing skills while in the military tutored illiterate adults.

Religion also aided blacks in resisting oppression. As freed people, black Texans established their own centers of worship—structuring their respective institution's hierarchy and Christian message to fit their own experience. As a focal point in the community, the independent black church became a place in which to hold religious services, social activities, educational instruction, political planning, and an office for such miscellaneous services as helping to place black workers in available jobs. From the church came reinforcement of the people's sense of morality and proper behavior. A large percentage of African Americans joined the Baptist Church.

That black Texans found the wherewithal to stave off the onslaught of white racism by their own initiative was demonstrated by their ability to transfer their ideas of justice to their new status as freedpersons. They had learned something of Texas law during slavery and recognized that courts could be used for self-protection. While the Freedmen's Bureau functioned in Texas, blacks brought their grievances before bureau courts, seeking redress for numerous wrongs.

168 ❖ The History of Texas

While civilian courts offered blacks little sympathy, once the Freedman's Bureau left in 1868, African Americans did find sympathetic understanding from Republican district court judges appointed by Governor Davis between 1870 and 1873.

THE DEMOCRATS REGAIN CONTROL OF STATE GOVERNMENT

Following their legislative victory in 1872, the Democrats bided their time until the next general election, when they hoped to regain full control of the state government. When the gubernatorial race came around in December 1873, Davis again ran on the Republican ticket, while Richard Coke, an ex-Confederate, campaigned as a Conservative Democrat. During the campaign, Davis highlighted the programs he had initiated, while Coke and his followers talked of "redemption," of restoring strong states' rights and of overthrowing the coalition of Republicans and freedmen. Even as Texas Democrats tried to keep blacks from the polls, the Republicans got out even more votes than they had in the earlier gubernatorial race of 1869. But even these efforts were insufficient to fend off a Democratic victory. Coke took the election, outdistancing Davis in the vote count 100,415 to 52,141.

Davis readied to transfer his office to Coke, but on January 5, 1874, the state's Supreme Court in the case of *ex parte Rodríguez* declared the election illegal. The decision had stemmed from an arrest involving a Mexican American named Joseph Rodríguez whom authorities in Harris County accused of voting twice in the December election. Rodríguez's lawyers maintained their client's innocence, asserting that a law passed by the Thirteenth Legislature in March 1873 (designating only one day for elections) conflicted with the state Constitution. The 1869 document stipulated, generally speaking, that "all elections shall be held at the county seats until otherwise provided by law; and the polls shall be open for four days." The court argued that the semicolon in the sentence made the two clauses independent and, consequently, the legislature was not empowered to alter the length of the voting period. Thereafter, the court earned the epithet of the "Semicolon Court."

Now, Davis was in a bind. One option was to disregard the Supreme Court's decision and abide by the results of election, but to do so would be to discount the judicial system's role in governance. Instead, he wired President Ulysses S. Grant for direction. Coke and the Democrats, meanwhile, made it plain they would not abide by the court's ruling, and pursued plans to take over the government immediately. On January 13, 1874, they convened the Fourteenth Legislature, and two days later they swore in Coke as governor. And when Grant's reply arrived, informing Davis that he refused to get involved in the Texas controversy, Davis assumed the president was telling him to disregard the Supreme Court decision. The Radical governor thus formally resigned the executive seat on January 19, 1874. The Democrats' resurrection and Coke's victory spelled the end of Reconstruction in Texas.

The bearded and slightly balding Coke possessed a booming voice and often sported floppy felt hats and long-tailed coats. The new governor appealed to business interests, who recognized his moderate endorsement of railroad and industrial expansion, but also to a rural constituency. His perceived support for some agrarian goals won for him the undying loyalty of the Patrons of Husbandry, a farmers' society better known as the Grange.

Coke and his Democratic supporters represented a group of politicians that has been described as southern Redeemers, for their goal was to "redeem" the South from Republican rule. According to their thinking, Republicans had destroyed southern prosperity and upset the region's traditional racial relationships. They suggested that the agricultural depression of 1870, which grew into the industrial Panic of 1873, was the fruit of Republican misrule. The Redeemers' solutions for the future included the endorsement of the New South, the concept that the South should emulate the North in some ways in order to industrialize. And the way to industrialize, according to New South advocates, was to hold down the expenses of government, lower taxes, and create an inexpensive labor supply. Such measures would attract northern investment and industry into the southern states.

THE CONSTITUTION OF 1876

With the conservative Democrats back in power, a majority of the state's citizens wanted to erase all vestiges of Reconstruction, and they demanded the replacement of the Constitution of 1869. A new document, they figured, would overturn Republican successes on behalf of blacks and let the state return to the limited concept of government that had prevailed before the Civil War. Coke delayed calling a constitutional convention until 1875, citing lack of adequate financing. But after an 1874 legislative commission failed to revise the Constitution of 1869, Coke asked the legislature to submit a proposal to the citizens for the calling of a constitutional convention. In August 1875, voters approved the proposal, which called for a convention to meet in September, and selected three delegates from each of the thirty senatorial districts to write the new constitution.

Of the ninety delegates who gathered in Austin, seventy-five professed allegiance to the Democratic party. Six of the fifteen Republican delegates were black. None of the delegates had participated in the constitutional convention of 1869. Forty-one farmers composed the delegation's largest single bloc, with twenty-nine lawyers constituting the second largest group. Overall, however, the conventional delegation was not a particularly distinguished one.

Several of the delegates would, however, go on to have distinguished political careers. John H. Reagan, who by 1875 had recovered from rebuke cast upon him following the uncovering of his Fort Warren letter, belonged to the Grange and endorsed the organization's moderate concept of reform. Already elected in 1875 to the U.S. House of Representatives, he would carve out a reputation for himself there and later in the Senate as an expert on railroad regulation. Other well-known delegates included Lawrence Sullivan "Sul" Ross, a hot-tempered frontiersman and hero of the pre–Civil War Indian wars who would go on to become governor of the state and then president of the Agricultural and Mechanical College of Texas. Also present at the convention were the distinguished Texas Rangers John S. "Rip" Ford and Thomas Lewis Nugent. The latter would follow a different political path than most others present. Nugent, a deeply religious man committed to social activism, received the nomination for governor on the Populist party ticket in 1892 and 1894.

The majority at the constitutional convention wished a general return to what might best be described as Jacksonian concepts of limited government and frugality. The delegates set the tone for the convention by authorizing salaries of $5 per day for themselves, as opposed to the $8 per day then received by legislators. In addition, the convention voted to keep no official record of its proceedings in order to save the costs of hiring a stenographer and printing the minutes. For a model constitution the delegates relied upon the Texas constitution of 1845, which in turn had been heavily influenced by the earlier constitution of Louisiana and other similar documents written by Jacksonian Democrats. The concepts of frugality and antimonopoly appealed to the Granger bloc, which had a major influence on the form of the final document. Consequently, the Constitution of 1876 included provisions that prohibited the state from chartering banks, empowered the state (if it should choose to do so) to regulate corporations and railroad companies, established a state debt ceiling of $200,000, put a strict limit on the maximum *ad valorem* tax rate, and all but abolished the public school system.

The Grangers also became embroiled in one of the more heated controversies of the convention. Some delegates, particularly those from East Texas, wished a poll tax as a suffrage requirement, ostensibly to disfranchise black people (most of whom could not afford to pay a poll tax). But a combination of Republicans and Grangers defeated the proposal. The convention then went on to strike down voter registration and to deny women, but not aliens, the right to vote. The new constitution recognized the Jacksonian concept of universal manhood suffrage.

The distrust of central and expensive government, heightened by the depression of the 1870s and the skewed perception of Republican misrule, permeated the majority of the articles of the new constitution. The executive received the traditional constitutional charge of responsibility for overseeing the execution of the laws but no real authority to do so; control of the executive branch rested with the electorate. The office of secretary of state was still a governor-appointed position, but voters would choose the other five members of the executive branch: lieutenant governor, comptroller, treasurer, commissioner of the land office, and attorney general. The governor could, of course, veto legislation, subject to the legislative powers of a two-thirds vote override, and was empowered to call special sessions of the legislature. The salary of the governor was lowered to $4,000 per year, and the term of office was cut from four to two years.

The general pattern of austerity in government and direct responsibility of public officials to the electorate was continued in other articles of the constitution. The term of the thirty-one senators was reduced from six to four years, and the 150-member house of representatives served two-year terms. The framers chose biennial rather than annual legislative sessions, and they cut the pay of lawmakers to $5 a day for the first sixty days of each session and $2 a day thereafter. All judicial positions became elective rather than appointive, with district judges and those from lower courts serving for four years and appellate court justices serving for six. (The issue of partisan election of judges continues to be debated with regularity.) The Texas Supreme Court would accept appeals in civil cases, and the court of appeals would conduct criminal ones.

Most significant, the demands for economy in government and what was a backlash against Reconstruction led to two controversial decisions that shaped the future for Texas. Upset with the centralization and the expense of the public school system, many delegates to the constitutional convention argued that parents should bear sole responsibility for the education of their children. The argument came in part from those who rejected the idea that white landowners should pay taxes for the education of black children. Others, in particular Grangers and other family farmers, favored local educational control as a way to save money and to establish community schools with terms that corresponded to crop cycles. Both groups opposed compulsory attendance. Consequently, the new constitution authorized a $1 tax on males between the ages of twenty-one and sixty to state support education, but it made no provision for local taxes to fund community schools. While the new document eliminated the office of state superintendent and compulsory education, it mandated segregated schools. The Texas school system, already inadequate even by nineteenth-century standards, had received a weakening blow.

The convention did endow a permanent school fund with revenue from lands previously set aside for the support of the public schools and added to this fund monies derived from the sale of one-half of the unreserved sections of the public domain. In a like measure, the convention took from The University of Texas the 3 million acres granted to it in 1858 and replaced it with 1 million acres of unclaimed land farther west. As luck would have it, this move placed some of the university's property over pools of oil, and this and later additions of acreage helped the permanent school fund accrue considerable monies.

The convention delegates adopted the new constitution in November 1875 by a vote of fifty-three to eleven. Few of them seemed very enthusiastic about the document they had created, and the campaign over its ratification sparked little enthusiasm. Those who defended the document justified the public school provisions as necessitated by poverty and prior Republican extravagance. Nevertheless, the state Democratic convention avoided endorsement of the constitution by tabling a motion that affirmed the party's support of it, while the Republican party condemned outrightly the proposed document. The Grange and most state Democratic leaders and newspapers did campaign for its ratification, however. Voters ultimately approved the new constitution by a better than two-to-one margin.

Despite the contemporary and later criticisms of the Constitution of 1876, it reflected fairly well the current political views of most white southerners. Shortly after their own "Redemption," Alabama (1875), Arkansas (1874), Georgia (1877), Louisiana (1879), North Carolina (1876), Tennessee (1870), and Virginia (1870) adopted new constitutions. These documents differed in particulars, but all displayed a general distrust of activist government and a desire to limit its powers. Moreover, they all called for retrenchment in government services and expenses and placed ceilings on taxes. In Texas, checks on the state government were written into the Constitution of 1876, so that most changes in government services and legislative powers can only be effected by an amendment reported out by two-thirds of the legislature and approved of by the voters. Consequently, more than a century later, the state's citizens still serve as an awkward check on the legislative process by approving or disapproving amendments to the constitution that deal with matters that could best be handled by legislative action. Critics have maintained that the nineteenth-century constitution is one poorly suited to cope with the evolving industrial and urban society of present-day Texas. Texans seemed satisfied, however, with the awkward amending process and the archaic constitution. Two serious attempts to write a new and modern constitution, in 1919 and 1975, were vetoed by the electorate.

READINGS

Books and Dissertations

Barr, Alwyn, and Robert A. Calvert, eds., *Black Leaders: Texans for Their Times* (Austin: Texas State Historical Association, 1981).

Baum, Dale, *The Shattering of Texas Unionism* (Baton Rouge: Louisiana State University Press, 1998).

Crouch, Barry A., *The Freedmen's Bureau and Black Texans* (Austin: University of Texas Press, 1992).

———, "'To Enslave the Rising Generation': The Freedmen's Bureau and the Texas Black Code," in eds. Paul A. Cimbala and Randall M. Miller, *The Freedmen's Bureau and Reconstruction's Reconsiderations* (New York: Fordham University Press, 1998).

Foner, Eric, *Reconstruction: America's Unfinished Revolution, 1863–1877* (New York: Harper & Row, 1988).

McPherson, James M., *Ordeal by Fire: The Civil War and Reconstruction*, 2nd ed. (New York: McGraw-Hill, 1992).

Moneyhon, Carl H., *Republicanism in Reconstruction Texas* (Austin: University of Texas Press, 1980).

———, "George T. Ruby and the Politics of Expediency in Texas," in *Southern Black Leaders of the Reconstruction Era,* ed. Howard N. Rabinowitz (Urbana: University of Illinois Press, 1982).

Moore, Richard R., "Reconstruction," in *The Texas Heritage,* eds. Ben Procter and Archie P. McDonald (Wheeling, IL: Harlan Davidson, Inc., 1980).

Owens, Nora Estelle, "Presidential Reconstruction in Texas: A Case Study" (Ph.D. diss., Auburn University, 1983).

Pitre, Merline, *Through Many Dangers, Toils and Snares: The Black Leadership of Texas, 1868–1900* (Austin: Eakin Press, 1985).

Ramsdell, Charles W., *Reconstruction in Texas* (New York: Columbia University Press, 1910).

Richter, William L., *The Army in Texas During Reconstruction, 1865–1870* (College Station: Texas A&M University Press, 1987).

———, *Overreached on All Sides: The Freedmen's Bureau Administration in Texas, 1865–1868* (College Station: Texas A&M University Press, 1991).

Smallwood, James, *Time of Hope, Time of Despair: Black Texans During Reconstruction* (Port Washington, NY: National University Publications, 1981).

Wooster, Ralph A., *Texas and Texans in the Civil War* (Austin: Eakin Press, 1995).

Articles

Barr, Alwyn, "Black Legislators and Reconstruction Texas," *Civil War History* 32 (December, 1986).

Campbell, Randolph B., "Scalawag District Judges: The E. J. Davis Appointees, 1870–1873," *The Houston Review* 4, No. 2 (1992).

Cantrell, Gregg, "Racial Violence and Reconstruction Politics in Texas, 1867–1868," *Southwestern Historical Quarterly* 93 (January, 1990).

Cooper, Lance A., "'A Slobbering Law Thing': The Semi-colon Case," *Southwestern Historical Quarterly*, CI (January 1998).

Crouch, Barry A., "'All The Vile Passions': The Texas Black Code of 1866," *Southwestern Historical Quarterly* 97 (July, 1993).

———, "A Spirit of Lawlessness: White Violence, Texas Blacks, 1865–1868," *Journal of Social History* 18 (Winter, 1984).

———, "Black Dreams and White Justice," *Prologue* 6 (Winter, 1974).

———, "Self-Determination and Local Black Leaders in Texas," *Phylon* 39 (December, 1978).

———, "'Unmannacling' Texas Reconstruction: A Twenty-Year Perspective," *Southwestern Historical Quarterly* 93 (January, 1990).

Crouch, Barry A., and Leon J. Schultz, "Crisis in Color: Racial Separation in Texas During Reconstruction," *Civil War History* 16 (March, 1970).

Hornsby, Alton, Jr., "The Freedmen's Bureau Schools in Texas, 1864–1870," *Southwestern Historical Quarterly* 76 (April, 1973).

Moneyhon, Carl H., "'Edmund J. Davis in the Coke-Davis Election Dispute of 1874: A Reassessment of Character," *Southwestern Historical Quarterly*, C (October 1996).

———, "Public Education in Texas Reconstruction Politics, 1871–1874," *Southwestern Historical Quarterly* 92 (January, 1989).

Pitre, Merline, "A Note on the Historiography of Blacks in the Reconstruction of Texas," *Journal of Negro History* 66 (Winter, 1981–1982).

Richter, William L., "'It is Best to Go in Strong-handed': Army Occupation of Texas, 1865–1866," *Arizona and the West* 27 (Summer, 1985).

———, "Spread Eagle Eccentricities: Military-Civilian Relations in Reconstruction Texas," *Texana* 8, No. 4 (1970).

Shook, Robert W., "The Federal Military in Texas, 1865–1870," *Texas Military History* 6 (Spring, 1967).

Smallwood, James, "The Freedmen's Bureau Reconsidered: Local Agents and the Black Community," *Texana* 11, No. 4 (1973).

———, "When the Klan Rode: White Terror in Reconstruction Texas," *Journal of the West* 25 (October, 1986).

Woods, Randall B., "George T. Ruby: A Black Militant in the White Business Community," *Red River Valley Historical Review* 1 (Autumn, 1974).

A FRONTIER SOCIETY IN TRANSITION

CHAPTER 7

Signs of a new modernity in Texas during the remainder of the century following the Civil War included a rise in the number of towns, a marked increase in the amount of railroad track laid, the growth of labor unions, and educational innovations. But several forces tied the state to its frontier roots. Most people still lived in rural areas. Towns remained basically small and agrarian—no city in Texas compared to any of the urban giants of the North such as New York City or Chicago. Transportation services and facilities left much room for improvement. And the lack of good roads and modern forms of communication kept many people isolated; even the inhabitants of the most densely populated regions, in the eastern half of the state, endured relatively primitive conditions.

Furthermore, the state's population remained predominately male. In 1880, the ratio of men to women was 111 males for every 100 females; this had barely changed by 1890, when it stood at 110 men for every 100 women. The median age of Texans was 18.7 in 1900, and the census of that year reported that 41.6 percent of the population was under fifteen years old. This demographic reality helped fuel a frontier mentality. The persistence of a horse and gun culture, for example, led men to settle scores extralegally. Violence against lawbreakers and hated minorities (including Indians) continued much as it had in prewar days.

Although the unsettled regions of the state now lay in West Texas (and to some degree in South Texas), the frontier ethos pervaded the entire state. The values of an older Texas, vis-à-vis the community, the family, the church, and ethnic groups, were as prevalent in the populations of the more stable regions of East Texas as they were in West Texas, where settlers still fought off Indians and raised cattle and sheep. This frontier society was in transition, to be sure, but even as more modern trends came to predominate by the 1890s and early twentieth century, Texans continued to honor the old heritage. That legacy (in conjunction with the nationalism spawned by the republic period) manifests itself today in a unique nationalist solidarity visible throughout several Texas regions, and in various other tenets of Texanism, including distinctive styles of dress, art and literature, music, and speech patterns.

Quanah Parker—Comanche Chief. *Gibbs Memorial Library, Mexia, Texas*

Top to bottom: Stagecoach at Concho Mail Station, Tom Green County, 1879; Mail station in Concho Country, West Texas, ca. 1870s; San Angelo's first jail. *Fort Concho National Historic Landmark*

THE TEXAS POPULATION, 1870–1900

Texas grew dramatically in the last several decades of the nineteenth century. In 1860 the population of the state was 604,215, but by 1900, 3,048,710 persons called Texas home.

In-migrants to the state were mainly white southerners, who relocated in large numbers to Texas. Residents of states that had been devastated by the Civil War and post-1865 economic stagnation sought out a fellow ex-Confederate state with cotton lands and similar racial attitudes in which to resettle. Texas had retained its public lands, and now it generously opened vast tracts of it to settlers willing to move. Thus (in descending order) Arkansas, Alabama, Mississippi, Tennessee, Missouri, Louisiana, and Georgia sent the majority of the in-migrants to Texas. Only 2.5 percent of the newcomers to Texas had arrived from New England.

The state actively encouraged immigration in 1871 by establishing the Texas Bureau of Immigration. The superintendent of the agency, which experienced chronic budget problems, relied upon railroad guides to extol the beauties of Texas, but never with much success. The bureau was identified with Radicals and Reconstruction, and the Redemption government of 1876 prohibited the use of state funds for the recruitment of immigrants. However, other solicitations of immigrants continued. Private companies such as railroads, agricultural organizations such as the Grange, and local societies sent brochures to the Old South and to Europe to recruit whites, whom they assumed would become independent farmers. W. W. Lang resigned as Worthy Master of the Grange in 1880 in order to accept the presidency of the Southwestern Immigration Company, and from 1881 to 1884 he remained in Europe trying to recruit immigrants to Texas, though his success, and that of other immigration companies, was limited.

The influx of new people did little to alter the previously formed cultural regions that had determined the course of prewar politics—North and north-central Texas with settlers from the Upper South, and East and southeastern Texas with people from the Lower South—for most new arrivals tended to assimilate into existing regional cultures. From these areas, people eventually made their way into West and South Texas.

Numerous factors played a part in pushing and pulling people into the state's sparsely populated sections. The end of the Civil War, of course, permitted the previous expansionist tendencies to resume. The pacification of the Indian

TABLE 7.1 Makeup of the Texas Population

YEAR	TOTAL	URBAN	RURAL (%)	BLACK (%)
1860	604,215	26,615	577,600 (96.4)	182,921 (30.0)
1870	818,579	59,521	764,058 (95.6)	253,475 (31.9)
1880	1,591,749	146,795	1,444,954 (93.7)	393,384 (25.0)
1890	2,235,521	349,511	1,886,016 (90.5)	488,171 (21.8)
1900	3,048,710	520,759	2,527,951 (84.5)	650,722 (20.0)

peoples and their confinement on reservations (almost all of which lay outside the Lone Star State's borders) removed a formidable obstacle for settlers pushing farther west. Cattlemen found new grazing areas in the range lands of West Texas. Farmers followed the ranchers, bringing with them families and social institutions that gave the new settlements a degree of permanence. Railroad lines went hand in hand with the push southward and westward, helping to give birth to urban sites, which, in turn, furthered the stability of the transplanted culture.

THE GROWTH OF SOUTH TEXAS

South Texas is a case in point. In the aftermath of the war with Mexico, a small but meaningful influx of American and European civilians arrived in the region seeking to divest Mexicans of the land they held. Fraud played a part in the dispossession of Mexican grantees, but so did other factors such as Tejanos' inability to pay newly imposed taxes or to ride out declines in the price of beef or prolonged droughts, and a reluctance on the part of independent ranchers to commercialize. Meantime, migration from other parts of Texas and Mexico into the area continued apace.

In the postbellum era, as wealthy markets in the northern United States spurred the demand for beef, ranching proved lucrative. Large enterprises, such as the Kenedy Ranch in Kenedy County and the famous King Ranch founded by Richard King, came to specialize in cattle raising, while other estates turned to raising sheep on the Rio Grande Plain. Close relationships developed between the successful ranchers and their employees. In return for work, ranchers provided their Mexican hands with essentials such as clothes, food, shelter, and ammunition. On especially large ranches such as King's, wherein resident employees came to be called the Kineños, a permanent workforce developed a close loyalty to the ranch.

In the 1880s and 1890s, however, a slow transition towards commercial farming began, and increasingly South Texas acreage was converted from ranchland to farmland; the process reached fruition in the early part of the twentieth century, one result of which was the deterioration of the former system of labor relations, as ranch hands became displaced wage workers. Meanwhile, new railroad connections to the region in the 1880s furthered its urban development. Corpus Christi, Laredo, and Brownsville all profited from the expanded lines.

THE INDIAN DISPLACEMENT

Comanches, and their Kiowa allies, still lorded over the plains. They remained fierce defenders of the West Texas plains for several reasons. For one, their society traditionally valued warfare as a means of gaining prestige and honor. For another, the Plains Indians had finally honed their military tactics—Comanches and Kiowas preferred (because of their dwindling forces) hit-and-run strikes, the raiders quickly inflicting damage on the enemy then fleeing with booty, scalps, and additional horses. Third, westering Texans stopped short of Comanche and Kiowa territory, realizing the deep enmity the Plains Indians held for white intruders, hate displayed in the sadism both tribes extended to new interlopers. Because they believed wounds inflicted on victims during or immediately after combat tormented the deceased for eternity, warriors of both tribes tortured prisoners or mutilated their corpses. Comanches and Kiowas, further, often abducted white women and children, another horror that deterred families from venturing too far from settled regions. Finally explaining the Comanches' and Kiowas' hold on the plains was their nomadic lifestyle; the Indians maintained no stationary farms, store houses, or munition stockpiles that an adversary might attack in order to diminish their ability to sustain quick raids.

The Civil War and the turmoil that followed permitted the Comanches—who by then had gained control of the territory from southern Kansas, west to the Pecos River in New Mexico, south to the German-descent populated town of Fredericksburg, then north up the 98th meridian—the opportunity to sweep into the northern and western lands and devastate settlers' livestock and farmsteads. In 1866 and continuing until 1868, the U.S. War Department reestablished a line of defense in the West and replaced with U.S. Army troops the militia units and regiments of Indian fighters that had tried to protect the frontier during the Civil War. This line of posts consisted both of prewar forts and new ones and included Fort Richardson (near Jacksboro, the county seat of Jack County), Fort Belknap (in Young County), Fort Griffin (in Shackelford County), Fort Chadbourne (in today's Coke County), Fort Concho (at present-day San Angelo), Fort McKavett (Menard County), Fort Clark (opposite Brackettville), and Fort Duncan (above Eagle Pass). Farther west lay Fort Stockton (near the present-day town of the same name), Fort Davis (neighboring today's Fort Davis), and Fort Bliss (close to El Paso). Despite the soldiers' reconnaissance missions undertaken under a full moon (known to westerners as a "Comanche moon" because the Comanches themselves used the light of the full moon to carry out their fiercest raids), the Indians proved resourceful and cunning, easily avoiding the forts, which were spaced too far apart to effectively cordon off the raiders.

Offensive attacks against the Comanches and Kiowas (the only tribe that had been able to negotiate any type of survival arrangement with the Comanches) did not begin until the early 1870s, for during the early administration of President Grant the U.S. government followed a peace policy patterned after that used by the early Quakers in their effort to assimilate the Woodlands Indians into American culture. But the Salt Creek Massacre, committed in May 1871 in Young County by the Kiowa chief Satanta and between 100 and 150 followers from the Fort Sill Reservation in the Indian Territory, changed Indian policy. In the incident, Satanta and his Kiowas, who considered relinquishing control of their West Texas lands unthinkable, set upon a train of supply wagons, killing and mutilating seven of the twelve drivers. When news of the attack reached the general of the army, William T. Sherman, then on an inspection tour of the area, he ordered the arrest of Satanta and the other Kiowa chiefs upon their return to the reservation. Authorities did indeed apprehend the wanted Kiowas and return them to Texas, where they were tried as murderers. A jury in Jacksboro found the Indians guilty and sentenced them to death by hanging. But Governor Davis, persuaded by certain Washington officials still committed to the peace policy, reduced the Indians' sentences to life imprisonment, and in 1873 Davis granted them parole. Once free again, Satanta resumed his old ways, but the law soon rearrested the chief and sent him to the Huntsville state penitentiary, where he died in 1878. (It is not clear whether the chief killed himself or was forcibly pushed out of a window.)

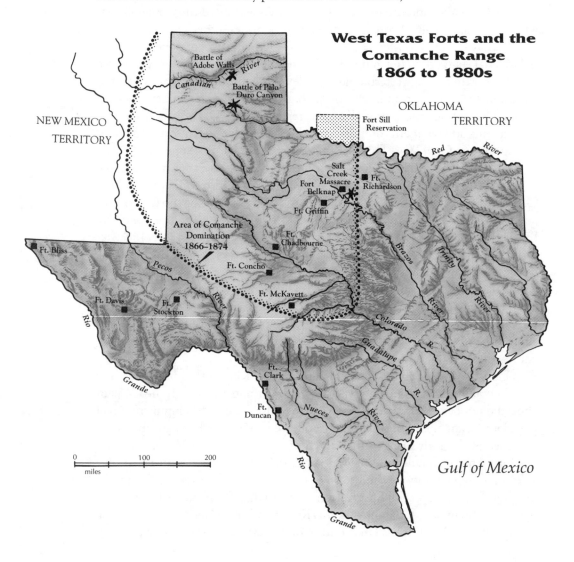

West Texas Forts and the Comanche Range 1866 to 1880s

The new U.S. Army military offensive following the Salt Creek Massacre was led by Colonel Ranald Slidell Mackenzie, assisted by Benjamin H. Grierson, commander of the all-black Tenth Cavalry, William R. Shafter, and John L. Bullis of the Twenty-fourth Infantry, also an African American unit. By the fall of 1871, Mackenzie was conducting search-and-destroy missions on the Panhandle Plains against Comanche bands—among them warriors under Quanah Parker, son of a (white) Comanche woman named Naduah, who was actually Cynthia Ann Parker, taken prisoner in 1836 from "Parker's Fort" in Limestone County. Other commanders pursued the offensive with similar conviction. The objective of the campaign was the forcible removal of the Indians to the reservations, a feat best accomplished by first luring the Indian bands into open combat. But since the Indians refused to fight under circumstances and in locations not to their advantage, officers resorted to ruthless measures. Soldiers consequently slaughtered the Indians' pony herds, razed entire Indian villages, and confiscated food, weapons, utensils, and blankets, which the Indian people needed to survive. By 1873, the frequency of Comanche raids had decreased discernibly. Mackenzie therefore was assigned in April 1873 to Fort Clark to deal with Kickapoos, Apaches, and Mexican bandits then wreaking havoc along the Mexican border. The next month, Mackenzie, with the acquiescence of his superiors, led a four-hundred-man cavalry unit across the Rio Grande near Eagle Pass. Some seventy-six miles into Mexico, Mackenzie's unit attacked and destroyed three Kickapoo and Apache villages, in the process wounding several of the warriors involved in the Texas raids.

Whites launched a final military operation against the Indians in northwestern Texas following a Comanche, Kiowa, and Cheyenne attack of a buffalo hunters' camp at Adobe Walls, in modern-day Hutchinson County, in June 1874. Called the Red River War, since the actual engagements took place close to the tributaries of the Red River in the Panhandle, this campaign for Indian removal involved a multipronged assault from New Mexico, Kansas, Oklahoma, and West Texas. In September 1874, Mackenzie came upon a Comanche village at Palo Duro Canyon, and after dispersing the Indians following a brief skirmish, he ordered the destruction of the tribe's pony herd. Afoot, the Indians could not escape, and the soldiers had little difficulty subduing them. Finding it increasingly difficult to live off the land, remnants of the Plains Tribes by mid-1875 turned for their survival to the Oklahoma reservations, among them was Quanah Parker.

The extermination and relocation of Texas Indians was not solely the result of defeat on the battlefield. The same way of life that made the Plains peoples superior fighters also had a downside. While Comanches and Kiowas had no permanent bases to be attacked, they also lacked a system of supply depots and armories essential for protracted warfare. Nor did the Indians build a support network of factories, farms, or an efficient infrastructure necessary to stem what seemed an inexorable tide of white pioneers moving West. Similarly, the weapons the Indians employed served them well in sneak attacks and brief battles, but not in prolonged conflict against well-armed, well-organized, and well-financed opponents. Even casual contact with whites had potentially disastrous results, for those selling the tribes rifles and other needed supplies might well spread devastating diseases into Indian camps, if not abet alcoholism. And a new reliance on consumer goods acquired from whites often had the effect of eroding age-old skills and traditions.

Perhaps most disruptive of the Plains peoples' traditional lifestyle was the thinning of the great buffalo herds by the 1870s and 1880s. Historians today advance a multitude of causes for the decline of the American bison population. New tribal migrations into the Plains at midcentury produced increased slaughtering, not solely because the nomads hunted buffalo for sustenance and essen-

tial byproducts, but also for its trade value: buffalo products fetched finished goods from the white world, among them alcohol. In addition, range animals such as horses, cattle, and sheep imported by westering Anglos contaminated the wild buffalo with fatal diseases. European livestock and new settlers further upset the ecology of the region, taxing the flora such as grass or reducing the timberlands that sheltered the buffalo during winter weather. Seasonal dry spells further reduced the herds. Another contributing factor in the decimation of the buffalo was the whites' intentional killing of the beasts. In their trek west, tourists and "sportsmen" shot buffalo from trains as the animals grazed near the rail line, and railroad contractors laying track across the plains freely shot buffalo as a cheap source of food for their crews. Then, by 1871, trade in buffalo hides became profitable, as people found that buffalo leather made durable straps and belts for factory machines. Hide hunters using high-powered rifles and accompanied by skinners appeared in the Texas Panhandle around 1873, and the wholesale slaughtering of

the buffalo began by 1875. Buffalo hunters loaded the pelts on wagons, leaving skinned carcasses behind to rot in the sun. By the early 1880s, less than two hundred buffalo were left on their old Texas feeding grounds, where untold thousands had once roamed.

Upper left: Satanta—Kiowa Chief. *The Center for American History. The University of Texas at Austin, CN 04948, Frank Caldwell Collection.*

Lower left: Quanah Parker as whites perceived him in highly stylized dress. *Library of Congress, Prints and Photographs Div., Washington, D.C.*

THE CATTLE KINGDOM

Before the Civil War, longhorn cattle still roamed free in Texas, where they mixed with other varieties of cattle that had been brought into Texas from the United States, drifting randomly from South Texas and the ranches of the Cross Timbers in search of more grazing land as their numbers swelled. Eventually, the animals spread into the open ranges of West Texas, running wild from the South Texas country to the Panhandle Plains. Some 5 million of the beasts grazed throughout Texas in 1865, the majority of them "mavericks," which would belong to the first person to brand them.

The era of the Texas Cattle Kingdom commenced even as the Civil War drew to a close, and it lasted until about the mid-1880s. In the North, people needed new animals to restore their war-depleted herds, the new demand for beef pushing up the price of cattle in Texas. Beeves that sold for $3 or $4 a head in Texas might bring $30 or $40 in the upper Mississippi Valley. Within a year after the cessation of hostilities between North and South, therefore, the Texas cattle boom was in full swing.

Those taking advantage of the situation were stockmen from the two cattle regions of prewar days—the Guadalupe, San Antonio, and Nueces River valleys and the ranches founded during the 1850s in the western Cross Timbers and the upper Hill Country. The earliest "long drive," undertaken in 1866, began in the northern Nueces Valley and passed through the Austin area, Fort Worth, and the North Texas town of Denison, through the southeastern part of the Indian Territory, and then on to the newly established railhead at Sedalia, Missouri. From there, meat dealers shipped the cattle north to reap handsome profits. On the trail to Sedalia, however, cattle drivers faced bandits and Indians who preyed on the herds. Also, Missourians made the Texas cowboys unwelcome—shooting cattle, trying to turn the herds back, and generally doing anything to keep the drives out of Missouri—charging that the cattle carried Texas Fever, to which the Missouri stock had no resistance. With so much trouble attached to it, the Sedalia route was hardly a popular one with Texas cattlemen after 1866.

A preferable (rail) shipping point, therefore, became Abilene, Kansas: the town's location on the wide-open plains gave herds more room on the trail and allowed cowboys to circumvent the troublesome areas in Missouri. Developed in 1867 by an Illinois entrepreneur named Joseph G. McCoy, Abilene became a veritable cattle exchange for transporting steers to the stockyards in Chicago. Texans reached Abilene via the Chisholm Trail, named after the Scots-Cherokee trader Jesse Chisholm, who in 1867 used a route through the Indian Territory and Kansas that McCoy had already marked and posted. The Chisholm Trail went from the South Texas range, past the state capital, thence Lampasas, north through a corridor between Fort Worth and Weatherford, then through the Indian Territory to the town of Caldwell, in southern Kansas. From there, spokes of the trail led to several points, including north to Abilene. Some 35,000 cattle were driven from Texas to Abilene in 1867, and the number increased

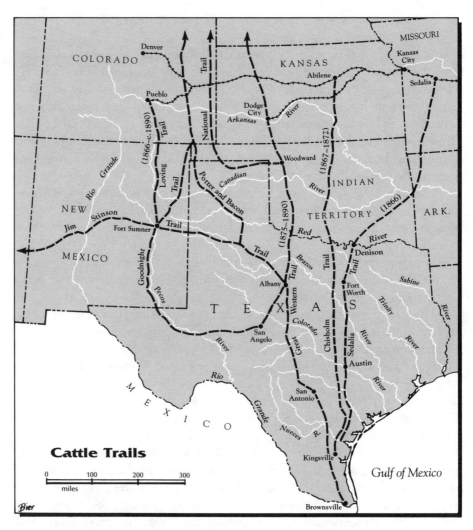

Cattle Trails

0   100   200   300
miles

Gulf of Mexico

Bier

thereafter; the 1880 census recorded the number of beeves taken to the Abilene yards in the years between 1867 and 1871 at 1,460,000.

Equally successful long drives—which generally consisted of about 2,000 head of cattle driven by a dozen or so cowhands—from South Texas set out for other stockyards in the western plains. Ellsworth, Kansas, west of Abilene, became a more attractive destination during the early 1870s, as the line of farm settlements in Kansas forced cattlemen to veer west to go around them. After 1875, when the Indian tribes on West Texas lands had been relocated, Texas cattlemen often chose to take the Great Western Trail, which ran north from San Antonio, to Kerrville and Mason, through Coleman and Fort Griffin, then across the Indian Territory to Dodge City, Kansas, located even farther west than Ellsworth.

Cattle (most of them born and raised on the ranches established in north-central Texas during the 1850s) were also driven during the late 1860s into Colorado Territory along the so-called Goodnight-Loving Trail. Who exactly blazed the trail is open to dispute—one account claims a beef contractor named James Patterson founded it in 1865. In any event, the trail was named after cattlemen Charles Goodnight and Oliver Loving, who in 1866 braved brushes with dangerous Indians to drive a herd from the western Cross Timbers along the Middle Concho and Pecos Rivers to New Mexico, then north to Colorado.

Cattle driven north through the Goodnight-Loving Trail heralded, by only a few years, the large-scale westward movement of Texas cattle herds from the Cross Timbers and upper Hill Country into the Great Plains. By the early 1870s, Texas longhorns thrived in Colorado, Nebraska, Montana, and Wyoming, and in the Dakotas by the 1880s. Following the suppression of the Comanches and Kiowas by the mid-1870s, Texas cattlemen also thrust into West Texas past the 100th meridian via two discernible courses. Ranchers from the Guadalupe, San Antonio, and Nueces River valleys headed towards the Trans-Pecos region in the 1870s, founding new ranches along the Rio Grande in the Big Bend and Davis Mountain region. Now, Mexican vaqueros transported traditional Mexican herding practices into this area, mixing them with new ones adopted from Anglo American cowboys. Ranchers from the north-central counties who had led the advance of the cattle frontier into the Great Plains, meantime, also pushed into the Texas South Plains, the Texas Panhandle, and the Concho Valley during the 1870s.

Into the South Plains and Panhandle came cattlemen who made free use of the grasslands on the open range, from which the Indians had been banished. These so-called "free rangers" by the 1870s included John Chisum, Charles Goodnight, C. C. Slaughter, George Littlefield, Abel H. (Shanghai) Pierce, and Oliver Loving. Customarily, these stockmen squatted on the open range, grazing their cattle over vast stretches of public lands and using the water resources thereof as they saw fit. These men often proved ruthless, asserting their "range rights" by resorting to arms to drive away intruders . They justified their actions by arguing that they had occupied the pastures first and had continued to use them. Once the government put the public lands on the market, the free rangers obtained legal title to as much of their domains as possible. In some cases, they leased the grazing rights to adjacent public lands, which they did not own but still controlled.

Several gigantic ranches emerged out of the need of speculators to legalize the claims they had assumed on the open range. In some cases, eastern and European investors eagerly subsidized a cattleman's purchase of open range land and cattle, or financed the amalgamation of smaller ranches into one huge ranchstead. Under this arrangement, ranchers provided the labor and shared the profits with their financial sponsors. By the late 1870s, "land and cattle companies" dominated more than half the rangeland and livestock in the South Plains and Panhandle. Charles Goodnight's JA Ranch by the late 1880s consisted of 700,000 acres in Palo Duro Canyon, as well as enough fences, houses, corrals, and water tanks to maintain a ranch boasting 40,000 head of cattle. Thomas Sherman Bugbee enlarged his Shoe Bar Ranch in the Panhandle to 450,000 acres. In 1882, the Matador Land and Cattle Company of Dundee, Scotland, put up the capital to procure some 300,000 acres and a herd of 60,000 cattle in Motley County, and the enterprise grew into an immense empire. Across Dickens, Crosby, Garza, and Kent counties stood the Spur Ranch, a 439,000-acre spread owned by the Espuela Land and Cattle Company of London. The largest of the Texas ranches was the XIT, situated along the western boundary of the Panhandle, owned by a Chicago-based syndicate that received 3,050,000 acres from the state in payment for having built the new capitol in Austin in 1888.

During the mid-1880s, the cattle boom waned. By this time, the long drives were proving less than cost effective: cattle lost weight on the trail and thus did not command a handsome price upon arrival to the railheads, the cost of provisioning the cowboys on the trail kept rising, and Kansans began to enact laws that prevented Texas cattle from passing through their state—because they, too, hoped to deter the spread of ticks that caused Texas fever. Furthermore, the long drives had upset the land's ecological balance; the range could only support so many cattle, but ranchers continually overstocked it. Yearly, the pastures grew thinner and quantities of good grass dwindled. Then, after stockmen imported barbed wire into the West in about 1874, fencing the range further reduced its grazing capacity. Finally, calamitous freezes and droughts in the mid-1880s dealt cattle ranchers a devastating blow from which some never recovered.

Its heyday past, the cattle industry in Texas changed. Now ranchers divided the entire range with barbed-wire fences, carefully calculated how many cattle each pasture could sustain, supplemented their herds' dietary needs with special feeds, controlled the animals' breeding, and took a new interest in ranching methods then being introduced by stockmen's associations.

In its wake, the reign of the cattle kings left a settled region. Farmers had followed closely behind the ranchers, pushing forward the line of settlement. New railroads expanding west also lured many people, giving rise to towns planned by railroad promoters in blatant attempts to create new centers of commerce or get already established settlers to make financial contributions to their lines. Abilene (Texas), Sweetwater, Big Spring, Midland, and Odessa grew out of ventures negotiated by railroad executives and townsfolk wanting access to railroad facilities for their communities. On the northern frontier, similar agreements between railroad lines and groups of people either directly or indirectly produced such towns as Amarillo, in the Panhandle, and Lubbock, in the South Plains. El Paso, in extreme West Texas, increasingly attracted new arrivals from other parts of Texas and the United States following the completion in the early 1880s of four major railroad lines.

SHEEP AND GOATS

The first effort to make sheep raising a viable concern in the State of Texas were undertaken by George Wilkins Kendall, a New Orleans journalist, who in

1857 entered the sheep-raising business in the Central Texas county that today bears his name. But the sheep ranching industry—centered in the Rio Grande plain, known by contemporaries as the Wild Horse Desert, and the section west of the 100th meridian—did not thrive until the decade after the Civil War. In the Rio Grande plain, an area of several counties encircled by the San Antonio River, the Gulf of Mexico, and the Rio Grande, supported more than 3.5 million Mexican and Mexican-cross sheep and 323,000 goats by 1885, their products ready for market in Mexico, Europe, and the interior of Texas. Then, swiftly, the bottom fell out. Overgrazing, prolonged droughts and hard freezes, and drops in the price of wool combined to weaken the sheep industry in South Texas.

Simultaneous with the expansion of the sheep and goat industry in the Rio Grande plain, sheep ranchers and cattle ranchers moved into West Texas. In addition, by the late nineteenth century, the Edwards Plateau—a 24 million-acre tableland in southwest Central Texas that extends from the Colorado River at Austin southwest to the Rio Grande at Del Rio—had surged ahead as a major producer of sheep (mutton) and wool; it also became known as an ideal region in which to raise Angora goats. Overall, there were more than 4,750,000 sheep in Texas in 1886, ranking it second only to California.

After the boom years following the Civil War, the sheep and goat industry entered a period of reorganization and consolidation. In the twentieth century, it experienced alternating periods of decline and improvement, and investors succeeded in reaping considerable revenues from the sale of wool and quality mohair.

Child shepherds with Angora flock in the early twentieth century. *Texas State Historical Association, Austin*

VIOLENCE AND LAWLESSNESS

Patterns of violence, manifest since antebellum days, only worsened during Reconstruction and persisted through the 1890s. In efforts to explain this phenomenon, historians have cited several factors. Bitterness arising from the Civil War and Reconstruction has been advanced as a cause, as have been Indian warfare, new waves of banditry, regional conflicts stemming from the cattle industry, agrarian discontent, political difficulties, tensions related to modernization, race relations, and the final drive to close the frontier. According to the famous Texas historian Walter Prescott Webb, Texas in the 1870s could be a perilous place in which to live. "Where all men are armed," Webb quipped, "conflicts among them are inevitable and the violent death of some is certain."

Indicative of postbellum violence was the rise of vigilante movements in the 90,000-mile triangular expanse framed by Houston near the Gulf Coast, the Hill Country west of San Antonio, and to the north by the Dallas–Fort Worth region. From 1865 to the end of the century, the area witnessed some fifty or sixty violent incidents involving vigilantes, most of them occurring in the 1870s.

In addition to vigilantism, feuding erupted. While some of these protracted conflicts were strictly family affairs, most of the major feuds in Texas (about eight) have been identified as "community feuds," that is, the larger community rallied behind the core group that had originated the conflict, forming a coalition of immediate and more-distant relatives, sympathetic acquaintances, and others linked by a common or vested interest in the outcome of the feuds. Probably the most notorious of these conflicts was the so-called Sutton-Taylor feud waged in DeWitt and surrounding counties. It began in 1867–1868, when two ex-Confederates, Hays and Doboy Taylor, murdered five blue coats who were enforcing military rule. To avenge the deaths of the Yankees, Bill Sutton (a Unionist sympathizer) and his followers killed two members of the Taylor clan in 1868. That this qualified as a community feud is seen in the fact that Bill Sutton was the only member of the Sutton family to become embroiled in the conflict in any leadership capacity. Though the Taylors had closer ties to the community leadership, their faction included a number of devil-may-care gunslingers. Indeed, by the summer of 1874, some 2,000 men from the community prepared to do battle in DeWitt County. The arrival of Texas Rangers put a halt to the conflict, but beyond the eyes of the authorities, the feuding factions continued their vendetta.

Also responsible for the violence during the turbulent frontier era were several notorious gunfighters, the most prominent and dangerous of which was John Wesley Hardin, a Texas native who killed more men than Billy the Kid, Jesse James, or Wild Bill Hickok. During the ten-year span after 1868, Hardin slew more than twenty men, and he is acknowledged to have sent more rivals to their grave in one-on-one shootouts than any other western desperado. A master of the quick draw, Hardin ranked among the select group of shootists capable of drawing second and still dropping a challenger. As a hateful racist, he terrorized blacks, as an unrelenting supporter of the Confederate cause, he vented his anti-northern rage on the state police (that Governor Davis had organized), as a rancher, he had countless clashes with rustlers and competing cattlemen, and as a hired gun, he shot down many a man, as he did on behalf of the Taylors in the Sutton-Taylor feud. The legal system in 1878 sent Hardin to the Texas state prison for murdering a deputy sheriff. In 1895, only a year after his release from prison, another Texas gunman named John Selman shot and killed Hardin in El Paso.

Other gunfighters of the period came close to matching Hardin in notoriety. And several of the other famous outlaws in western history built their reputations in Texas (and died in Texas shootouts), among them Ben Thompson, Jim Miller, John Selman, Dallas Stoudenmire, King Fisher, Cullen Montgomery Baker, Jim Courtright, John Hughes, and Bill Longley. This last brigand became known as "the nigger killer" for his arbitrary murder of blacks. But Longley amassed a record of killings that included men of every color and persuasion; by the time the law hanged him in 1878, his list of crimes included thirty-two murders.

All racial and ethnic groups in Texas felt the effects of the rampant violence. Blacks living in East Texas communities experienced it in vicious forms. In the "Black Belt" counties (among them Washington, Matagorda, Fort Bend, Brazoria, and Wharton) white men in the 1880s used a variety of pretexts— among them the desire to dilute the strength of the black vote or drive black office holders from power—to persecute blacks. Lynching or a threat of it by "white cappers" (white racist vigilantes) and loyalists to the defunct Ku Klux Klan was common practice.

Rape or other heinous crimes allegedly committed by blacks against whites also motivated wanton and savage cruelty. Although accurate figures on the lynching of blacks are lacking, one study estimates that in Texas between 1870 and 1900, extralegal justice was responsible for the murder of about 500 blacks— only Georgia and Mississippi exceeded Texas's numbers in this grisly record. So fiendish was some of the racially motivated sadism—in two cases in particular during the 1890s, victims were tortured and burned alive before hundreds of onlookers—that the legislature in 1897 passed an antilynch law, which, unfortunately, was ineffective.

Equally gruesome forms of violence visited the Tejano community, especially in South and West Texas as more whites moved into the regions. Whites lynched Mexicans on mere accusation of having murdered a white person, frequently in the charged atmosphere of the 1870s and 1880s. Suspicion of collusion with raiders from Mexico also proved reason enough to bring the wrath of whites down upon Tejanos. When Mexican bandits raided Corpus Christi in 1875, vigilante committees took to the countryside and brutally terrorized and murdered peaceable Mexican farmers and ranchers. Then, in 1891–1892, when Texas-raised

Catarino Garza used South Texas as his base for launching a revolution against Mexican President Porfirio Díaz, Texas Mexicans once more felt the sting of harassment, persecution, and violence.

Perceived threats to white supremacy also provoked whites to antagonize Tejanos. In numerous instances, Mexican Americans amassed to protest some misdeed or injustice perpetrated against their people. Such demonstrations, which in whites' eyes assumed the proportions of "riots" or "wars," also invariably invited vindictive retaliation. In the El Paso Valley, for example, racial friction heightened in the 1870s over the nearby Guadalupe Salt Lakes, which Mexicans had historically mined for salt to support their livelihoods but which Anglo entrepreneurs sought to monopolize following their arrival in the region during the 1860s. Animosity over the ownership of the lakes peaked near San Elizario in the fall of 1877, when residents arrested Charles Howard, the principal Anglo claimant to the salt deposits, whom they released after he promised to permit Tejanos to continue to use the lakes. Hostility subsided following the initial skirmish, but disputes erupted anew in December, resulting in the deaths of Howard, four other Anglos, and the surrender of a Ranger group that had been dispatched to the site. Then U.S. Army troops, Ranger reinforcements, and volunteers from New Mexico descended on the valley, and, through indiscriminate killings and atrocious acts committed against innocent people, put down what came to be called the Salt War and ended further Mexican access to the salt beds. Similar episodes involving this type of white reprisal against Mexican Texans include the Alpine Riot of 1886, the Rio Grande City Riot of 1888, and two riots in Laredo, one in 1886 and the other in 1899.

Meanwhile, out on the western range, lawlessness presided. Clashes between cattlemen and sheepmen broke out frequently. Cowboys looked down on sheepherders—especially on Mexican *pastores*, who performed much of the work. Cattlemen contended that sheep trampled and ruined (because of their sharp hooves) the range grass as they crowded to graze, that they chewed the grass to the roots thereby permanently damaging the range, and that the "woollybacks" emitted a certain odor that deterred cattle from feeding over the same grassland.

Cattle and sheep rustling intensified the lawlessness. Although it occurred throughout the state, rustling seemed most prevalent along the Mexican border. The so-called Cattle Wars, which followed the Civil War and lasted until the late 1870s, grew out of raids by Mexican nationals upon thousands of unbranded cattle that roamed the area between the Nueces River and the Rio Grande. Anglo Texan ranchers who moved into the region after midcentury claimed the free-roaming cattle and sheep as their own and incorporated them into their existing herds. Clashes between the Mexicans and the newcomers inevitably ensued. Lawlessness also existed in what contemporaries deemed "the bloody peninsula"—the lower part of Presidio County lying along the Rio Grande for a distance of sixty miles. In both regions, Mexican nationals and a motley array of white ranchers, cattle rustlers, and cowboys repeatedly fought over the ownership of unbranded mavericks.

The Growth of the Texas Rangers

In 1874, the Democratic legislature resurrected the Texas Rangers to replace the state police force that they had eliminated the previous year. New laws established two units of Rangers: the Special Force under the command of Captain L. H. McNelly; and the Frontier Battalion led by Major John B. Jones. Routine assignments now given to the Rangers included collecting taxes, ensuring the safety of prisoners from vigilante mobs, maintaining the peace during sensational court cases, monitoring elections, acting as mediators in labor strikes, and enforcing quarantines against contagious diseases such as smallpox. Their more adventurous law enforcement tasks included protecting the frontier by fighting Indians and tracking down outlaws. In the latter endeavors, they added to their reputation for bold courage in the face of danger.

Too often overzealous in enforcing the peace, however, the Rangers frequently overstepped the very laws they sought to enforce. On more than one occasion, they violated international law by entering Mexico illegally. The Mexican tradition of *ley de fuga* (law of flight) became a standard practice, as Rangers killed many a prisoner who allegedly had attempted to escape. Society, however, tacitly consented to the Rangers' use of "all reasonable means" to effect arrests. Texas law also allowed the Rangers to exercise "justifiable homicide" when attempting to thwart heinous crimes.

Notwithstanding their penchant for extremism, the Rangers became a legendary force in state law enforcement. On several occasions, citizens called the

"5 Captains and 1 Major" of the Texas Rangers. Among them (lower l. to r.) Capt. Sicken, Maj. John Armstrong, and Capt. Bill McDonald, ca 1880. *Texas Ranger Hall of Fame and Museum, Waco, Texas, P.80.342*

Rangers out to suppress riots, as in the case of the El Paso Salt War of 1877, the Laredo Election Riot of 1886, and the Rio Grande City Riot of 1888. As they had before, in all of the cases cited above the Rangers used extralegal methods (including beatings and indiscreet shootings) to restore order, but the white majority nonetheless placed great faith and confidence in them.

The Rangers also rode out to bring peace to the most notorious lawless regions. In 1877, three Ranger companies of the Frontier Battalion under Jones rode into Kimble County, a stronghold of cattle rustlers in West Texas, and initiated a general dragnet; they arrested thirty-seven bandits and cleared the area of desperadoes. Equally bold in implanting justice was Captain McNelly. Despite his lean, 135-pound frame, McNelly stood up to the most feared bad men of Texas as commander of the Special Force of Rangers. He is credited with breaking up the organized cattle rustling across the Texas-Mexico border in the 1870s.

The Rangers also showed their steel in the face of the vigilantism of the last quarter of the nineteenth century. It was they who in the summer of 1874 intervened in the Sutton-Taylor feud in DeWitt County. The Rangers successfully defused the situation and maintained order while the courts dealt with the leading antagonists.

Despite their accomplishments, the Rangers have received kudos out of proportion to those bestowed upon other peace officers in Texas. Local agencies generally tended to disorder without requesting aid from the Rangers. Uncounted numbers of sheriffs and deputy sheriffs in Texas undoubtedly distinguished themselves in the line of duty as they sought to bring law and order to their communities.

CITIES IN THE LATE NINETEENTH CENTURY

Table 7.1 (at the beginning of this chapter) reveals important characteristics of the state's population growth during the post–Civil War era. As mentioned, the state started out and remained overwhelmingly agricultural. In 1860, 4 percent of the population lived in urban areas; this increased modestly to 17 percent by 1900. Only San Antonio, which grew from a population of 12,256 in 1870, had more than 50,000 residents in 1900 (53,321 to be exact). The four other largest cities were situated in the eastern half of the state: in descending order they were Houston, Dallas, Galveston, and Fort Worth.

San Antonio's antebellum role as a center of military installations and the point of departure for western expeditions continued into the last decades of the nineteenth century. The iron rail reached the city in 1877 and proved a catalyst to economic growth. By 1880, San Antonio had more than 20,000 inhabitants; a decade later the old Spanish municipality had almost doubled in size to 38,000 residents. By the end of the century, modern architectural structures had spread outwardly from the central commercial district, detracting from the aura given to San Antonio by some of its old Spanish-Mexican and German-style buildings.

Houston, with a population of a bit over 9,000 in 1870, began to surge ahead of other towns when, in 1869, the Buffalo Bayou Ship Channel Company initiated major dredging operations in Buffalo Bayou. With cotton still king in Texas, Houston in the 1870s became a mecca for exporting the staple to manufacturing plants in the northeastern United States and Great Britain. By the 1890s, several rail lines replaced much of the shipping traffic through Buffalo Bayou, earning the city the motto, "Houston, Where Seventeen Railroads Meet the Sea." In 1900, Houston's population stood at 44,000.

Galveston, the largest town in Texas in 1870, with a population of 14,000, continued to grow. In the 1880s, it remained a major point of departure, as inland railroad networks expedited the conveyance of various raw products for export to overseas destinations and to factories in the eastern United States. However, a tragic hurricane in 1900 devastated the port city, and not until years later did Galveston recover.

The city of Dallas was transformed into a modern entrepôt in the early 1870s, when railroads came to town. With improved facilities for transporting goods to market, Dallas attracted farmers and ranchers from throughout North Texas, who hauled their goods to the city for shipment to out-of-state destinations. Soon, Dallas evolved into a thriving hub of financial and cultural activity.

In prewar days, Fort Worth had survived as a minor trading station and stopping point on the way west, but the cattle trade of the 1860s and 1870s energized it. By 1870, some 300,000 head of cattle en route to Kansas passed through the outskirts of the fledgling community, and the arrival of the railroads there in 1876 enhanced Fort Worth's prospects for major-city status. By 1900 it was the fifth-largest city in the state.

As late as 1900, Texas cities lagged behind other U.S. towns in urban and industrial development. Still crude towns in many respects, they lacked the fixtures of northeastern cities, such as tenement housing, distinct suburbs inhabited primarily by the wealthy, and systems of mass transportation (elevated trains, streetcars, and subways). Factories specializing in the mass production of clothing, shoes, and textiles also did not abound. Modern conveniences associated with urban living, however, appeared by the late 1890s, with some metropolitan areas maintaining telephone lines and a telegraph system. Some cities even had electric power, but not enough to provide modern lighting.

In the latter part of the nineteenth century, Texas towns generally lacked the visible (European) ethnic enclaves like those in northern cities. Of course, Texas drew immigrants from all over Europe, but its frontier orientation and the infancy of its cities restricted the growth of "Little Irelands" or "Little Polands." Immigrants coming into the larger Texas urban sites were subjected to Americanizing tendencies even as they sought to retain their native languages and customs. Germans, for instance, who consituted the largest European ethnic group in

Texas cities, made their presence felt in Houston and San Antonio, operating German-language schools and newspapers even though they did not live in exlusively German neighborhoods. Other Europeans persisted in cooking favorite dishes and honoring traditional customs of their homelands, but the small concentration of any one group of immigrants (except Germans) forestalled the rise of ethnic enclaves.

Missing also in Texas cities at this time were self-sustaining black communities with their own business district and professionals to serve them. As late as 1910, even Houston, with its geographical position and economy tied to the Old South, had no district clearly identifiable as a black one. Mainly black neighborhoods began to take shape during the late nineteenth century, but none of them were fully segregated until later in the twentieth century.

More fully segregated by ethnicity, however, were Mexican Americans, who lived in Hispanic neighborhoods called *barrios*. Predominately Anglo towns such as San Antonio and Corpus Christi had sections referred to as "Chihuahuita" or "Laredito." Although they were largely poverty-stricken communities, barrios helped Mexicans perpetuate their own cultural traditions in ways that European immigrants could not, for the barrios were solidly Mexican, with new arrivals from nearby Mexico increasingly buttressing their numbers and linking them to the homeland. Small business districts existed in the barrios, though in many cases the dire poverty of the enclaves prevented professionals from sustaining needed services, such as those of doctors and lawyers. In Hispanic South Texas towns such as Laredo and Brownsville, and in West Texas towns like El Paso, larger barrios displayed a semblance of self-sufficiency.

PLAIN LIVING

In the post–Civil War era, Texans relied both on their adaptive capabilities and the surrounding physical environment to wrest a hard livelihood from what was basically still a frontier society. People turned to the woodland, thicket, and brush for essential materials that could be used as fuel (for heating and cooking), or to make homes and useful household items such as kitchen utensils and furniture. They also looked to the environment for wild game such as turkeys, rabbits, quail, and deer, and fish from streams and rivers added variety to their table fare. Domesticated animals further enhanced diets. Chickens provided country folk with eggs; cows with milk, cheese, butter, soap, candles (from tallow), rawhide, and beef; hogs with ham, bacon, and lard; and sheep with wool and mutton. Garden plots yielded potatoes, peas, beans, and an assortment of other vegetables, while the fields they cultivated bore the cotton they needed to make clothing and useful items such as bedclothes and curtains.

Even in the settled regions of the state, isolation prevailed, and it was even more pronounced in West Texas, where modern means of transportation hardly existed. But wherever they resided, settlers did find ways to socialize and thereby mitigate the effects of the distance between communities. Popular occasions for interacting with neighbors or newcomers to an area included quilting bees and house-raisings. In the former, women gathered to sew patchwork quilts, for personal use or as a contribution to some worthy cause. Men, on the other hand, might volunteer their labor to build a house for a newlywed couple or a recently arrived family in the region.

Settlers also found relief from their general isolation in religious gatherings. In remote areas, people traveled by wagon or on horseback to the nearest service, whether that be held in a tent put up by an itinerant pastor or a community schoolhouse in which the teacher doubled as a minister. Town churches might have offered parishioners relatively comfortable seating, but the usual amenities elsewhere consisted of makeshift pews constructed from logs or rough lumber. Church picnics or dances also afforded Texans the opportunity to get acquainted with neighbors, to court a prospective spouse, and generally, to take a sorely needed break. Overall, Texans apparently found the conservative Protestant sects most attractive. By the last three decades of the nineteenth century, the Baptists and Methodist churches exceeded others in the number of members and congregations.

WOMEN IN POSTWAR TEXAS

The legal status of women in postwar Texas had changed little since antebellum times. The law still deprived married women the right to purchase property in their own name or dispose of it without the consent of their husband. And no woman could bring suit, sit on a jury, vote, or hold public office. In addition to these legal constraints, social norms continued to place women at a disadvantage. In the ambience of the West, a double standard of morality persisted: men permitted themselves certain freedoms that they denied to women.

Society also restricted women in the range of employment, and most women themselves thought that their responsibility to their children and husbands came first. Married women were not expected to work for pay outside the home, and single women did so only until they married and became homemakers. Census data bear out the latter point. The federal schedules for 1870 listed only some 5 percent of women aged ten years or over engaged in gainful employment. Almost one-half of those employed performed agricultural tasks, expectedly so given the state's agrarian economy and the fact that women worked beside men on farms, though nearly 25 percent of said rural laborers were adolescents, girls aged ten to fifteen years. The next decennial census, of 1880, indicates little change in the percentage of female agricultural hands, but the proportion of agricultural workers had increased from 25 percent to 33 percent.

In rural areas women often performed tasks considered to be "men's work," but their roles as wives and mothers prescribed set duties. Household chores included fetching all the water that the family used in the home. Furthermore, women often had to combine their domestic obligations with work outdoors that included tilling fields and maintaining the household garden, the products of which they often canned and stored for the family's later consumption. Women also assisted in slaughtering farm animals, dressing wild game, as well as in salting or smoking fresh meat. Additional burdens included clothing the family, a responsibility that entailed making the clothes from scratch and then keeping them clean and in good repair.

Aside from agricultural work, women took up domestic service most frequently. According to the 1870 and 1880 censuses, more than 40 percent of employed women worked as household servants. Many having to support themselves or supplement the family income earned pay as laundresses, seamstresses, waitresses, and cooks. Others took in washing and ironing or put up boarders.

While men largely monopolized positions of authority, the 1880 census does show some women engaged in such traditional male occupations as ministers, lawyers, physicians, and bankers. In the nursing and teaching professions, however, Texas women had not gained the same level of representation as had their counterparts in the rest of the country. In 1870, men generally dominated the teaching positions: of the 1,621 individuals listed as teachers, only 431 were women. Ten years later the census listed 2,710 male teachers and 1,624 female teachers. Some of the latter, by their example as professionals or mothers working outside the household, helped temper attitudes male culture harbored toward women working outside the home. Indeed, women's careers as educators influenced society to lift some of its more restrictive rules and traditions, and new opportunities for achieving meaningful goals ensued.

Women's efforts in Texas to acquire jobs dominated by men shows the human will to improve the self and perhaps an equal desire to contribute to the improvement of the social order. There are numerous examples in late-nineteenth-century Texas history of organizational activity by women in behalf of social reform. Women's pledge to prohibition, for example, led to the founding of the earliest chapter of the Women's Christian Temperance Union (WCTU) in Paris, Texas, in 1882. The larger towns in North Texas soon organized their own affiliates, and one year later the organization had spread statewide. As a political organization, the WCTU afforded women the opportunity to campaign for political issues besides prohibition, among them restrictions on child labor, improved educational opportunities for children and women (in 1901 the WCTU succeeded in getting the state legislature to found what later became Texas Woman's University), and women's suffrage. The women's suffrage movement crested during the World War I years, but in its early phase, it spawned two associations, both of them short-lived: the Texas Equal Rights Association in 1893 and the Texas Woman Suffrage Association in 1903.

During the 1890s, also, a women's club movement in the larger cities of the northern and eastern sections of the state began. Initially focusing on literary studies, women's clubs—membership generally derived from the middle class—turned increasingly to public activism, addressing issues that male society regarded as within the women's sphere. In the 1890s, white women's clubs endeavored to enrich the cultural life of their communities and improve social conditions, enhance education, promote child welfare, beautify municipalities, and modernize sanitation. In 1897, several community groups involved in such civic work founded the Texas Federation of Women's Clubs (TFWC) in Waco. By the early years of the twentieth century, thousands of white women belonged to the TFWC and were engaged in promoting numerous social and political reforms.

By the latter half of the 1890s, women also had taken an interest in the idea of preschool education. By the early twentieth century women had founded several kindergartens in several of the state's larger urban communities. The drive to organize kindergartens in part gave impetus to the formation of mothers' clubs, which in turn produced the organization of the Texas Congress of Mothers (later the Parent-Teacher Associations, or PTAs).

ETHNIC GROUPS IN THE POSTWAR ERA

Black Texans

Black Texans, still concentrated in East Texas, continued to experience the travails dating back to the years of slavery and Reconstruction. Violence, Jim Crow segregation, discrimination, and political suppression all remained facts of daily life for black Texans toward the end of the nineteenth century. Despite these conditions, African Americans courageously pressed ahead in efforts to build racial solidarity and carry out their daily activities as meaningfully as possible. Several social and cultural institutions played important roles in sustaining a viable black community, which was almost powerless to extract essential services from the white establishment. Benevolent associations and mutual aid societies, for example, offered charitable and other humanitarian aid, such as insurance and death benefits, to members during times of crises. Between 1870 and 1900, some sixty black-oriented and black-edited newspapers were published in the state. Most suffered from a shortage of paying advertisers and low subscription rates, due to a largely illiterate public, but they did serve the function of disseminating news and information of particular interest to black Texans.

Among the most influential social force within the black community was the church. Aside from being a place where blacks could worship free from the surveillance of whites, the church also evolved into an institution in which blacks could develop leadership qualities and learn the techniques of independent planning and the execution of group agendas. Some of the most accomplished black Texans received such leadership training in the church, among them Meshack Roberts, who in the 1870s served Harrison County for three terms in the state legislature.

The Methodists, Presbyterians, and Episcopalians were well represented among blacks, but the Baptists seemed to have been the most successful in winning loyal parishioners. Perhaps the theology and the autonomy of the Baptist church made it especially appealing to African Americans. In any case, by 1890, black Baptists claimed a membership of over 111,000.

Forms of entertainment also served as a force to reinvigorate the black community, often maintaining old traditions and allowing a respite from daily conditions. Days for leisure were numerous, but the most meaningful celebration

Freed slaves celebrate Juneteenth. *Austin History Center of the Austin Public Library, PICA #05476*

remained "Juneteenth," the anniversary of June 19, 1865, the day on which General Gordon Granger declared the slaves in Texas freed. On Texas's Emancipation Day, therefore, every black community sponsored a big to-do. The festivities often included a parade, inspiring speeches, barbecues and picnics, horseracing, and music and dancing.

While social forces brought cohesion to black communities in the more settled areas of the state, it was military life that brought black men together on the West Texas frontier. In the forts of South and West Texas, African Americans served as U.S. Army regulars with the infantry and cavalry, albeit in segregated regiments. Most renowned of these black troopers were the "buffalo soldiers" (a name given to black soldiers by Indians in Kansas: the Indians associated the troopers' curly hair with buffalo fur, but the term also implied an admiration for their courage and tenacity in battle). These particular units were responsible for scouting, charting, and recommending routes for linking the frontier to the settled areas of the state. On numerous occasions the buffalo soldiers proved gallant in combat, in particular Emanuel Stance, who won the Medal of Honor in 1870 for bravery against Apache foes near Fort McKavett. At the Battle of Rattlesnake Springs (north of Van Horn in far West Texas) on August 6, 1880, buffalo soldiers forced the Apache chief Victorio to abandon Texas for Mexico. When the last of the frontier troopers left in the mid-1880s, black regulars had been serving in Texas for nearly two decades and had made significant contributions to the peace, security, and settlement of West Texas. Among those who had served in the region from 1878 to 1882 was Lieutenant Henry O. Flipper, the first black man to graduate from the U.S. Military Academy and the first black officer in the regular U.S. Army.

Mexican Americans

Unlike blacks, many members of other ethnic groups were born outside the United States. Foreign-born Texans in 1890 numbered 152,956, or not quite 7 percent of the total population. The 1890 census lists only 710 Chinese and 3 Japanese and 704 "civilized" Indians. But the great majority of immigrants were Mexican or European.

In 1890 the Mexican American population stood at approximately 105,000 (49 percent of which was foreign born), and it increased ten years later to as many as 164,000 (43 percent of which was foreign born). Primarily, Tejanos were dispersed throughout three areas in the state, though preeminently in South Texas, in which Mexican Americans overwhelmingly outnumbered Anglo Americans. More balanced ethnically was West Texas, wherein the number of Tejanos roughly equaled the size of the Anglo American population, though Anglos dominated the urban centers while Mexicans remained in the majority in the border counties such as El Paso, Presidio, and Val Verde. In complete contrast was Central Texas, where Anglos and European immigrants outnumbered Tejanos by more than two to one in 1900.

As a community, Tejanos fashioned a bicultural world that borrowed tenets from white society yet retained familiar Hispanic cultural forms. The maintenance of the Mexican past was manifest in the language they spoke, the secular and religious holidays they observed, the foods they consumed, the curative herbs they turned to when ill, and the familial structures they honored. As a way of helping themselves, they organized mutual societies such as the Sociedad Benito Juárez. To keep abreast of local matters and current events in Mexico they read Spanish-language newspapers, of which there were several in Texas in the latter part of the nineteenth century.

That Tejanos familiarized themselves with the Anglo world about them was apparent by their ability to function within mainstream institutions when permitted to do so. Ranchos in South Texas owned by Tejanos were few, but some, such as Don Macedonio Vela's Laguna Seca, Hipólito García's Randado, and Dionisio Guerra's Los Ojuelos, operated successfully. The same applied to small business ventures in urban areas. Politics also drew Tejanos into participation in mainstream culture. Mexican American political activity was evident during Reconstruction and continued throughout the rest of the century. In those areas in which Tejanos predominated, such as Laredo, Brownsville, and the El Paso Valley, fervent political involvement secured the election of Tejano mayors and other local government officials. Election of Tejanos to the state legislature remained rare in the years after the Civil War, although G. N. García of El Paso, Santos Benavides of Laredo, and T. A. Rodríguez of Pleasanton did serve in the capitol.

European and Other Ethnics

European immigrants, except for those who settled in Galveston and Houston, joined in a fragmented "German Belt" of settlements clustered in three areas of Central Texas in which Germans predominated. From 30,000 to 35,000 Germans lived in Texas in 1860, about 60 to 70 percent of whom were of foreign birth. In the post–Civil War era, Germans who made their way into Texas primarily landed in the eastern end of the "German Belt," where they purchased land from railroad companies, former plantation owners, and restless folks itching to move farther west. A stream of new immigrants coupled with natural reproduction strengthened existing German communities throughout the region or created new ones. By 1887, the number of Germans had increased dramatically, to 130,000. Their numbers represented more than half of all European immigrants in the state.

Diverse groups composed the rest of the European element. Slavic migrations to Texas began in the 1850s and continued into the postbellum era. Czech migration spanned out from the primary settlement located at Fayetteville, in Fayette County. Serbin, in Lee County, was the home base for the Wends; from there they dispersed throughout the remainder of the county, but also into the South Texas town of Corpus Christi and the north-central settlement of Vernon in Wilbarger County. In Karnes County, Silesian Poles in 1854 established Panna Maria, said to be the mother of Polish settlements in Texas, and these Poles went on to found sister communities along the San Antonio River. After the Civil War, Galician Poles arrived to complement the Silesian colonies. The new Polish immigrants founded settlements in the valleys along the Brazos River. Bremond (Robertson County), for example, became the headquarters for extensive Polish immigration in the 1870s.

Other immigrant groups made Texas their home in the last quarter of the nineteenth century. Italian immigrants gathered in Montague County or in mining towns such as Thurber, in Erath County. The Dutch headed for southeastern Texas, establishing Nederland in Jefferson County. Greeks gravitated towards coastal towns in which they could make a living as fishermen. They also founded enclaves in several Texas cities. Of the small contingent of Asians, the Chinese were the most visible. During the 1870s, they arrived in Texas, namely in El Paso and Robertson Counties in Central Texas, to meet demands for railroad hands, but they left practically no imprint since most of the immigrants were males who did not intermarry. In Robertson County, the Chinese did wed local black women, begetting the "black Chinese" found in modern-day Calvert.

The contributions that each of these ethnic groups made to Texas created a pluralistic society that encompassed a diversity of languages, folkways, and modes of behavior. Distinctive features of each subculture, such as favorite foods, dances, and music, blended into Texas culture. Despite their cultural differences, the immigrants gave their civic involvement, military service, labor, and allegiance to the common good of the state. They may have chosen to retain elements of their distinctive ways of life, but residence in Texas also involved them in a process of cultural synthesis that simultaneously made them Americans.

Source: Terry G. Jordan et al., A Geography (Boulder, CO: Westview Press, 1984)

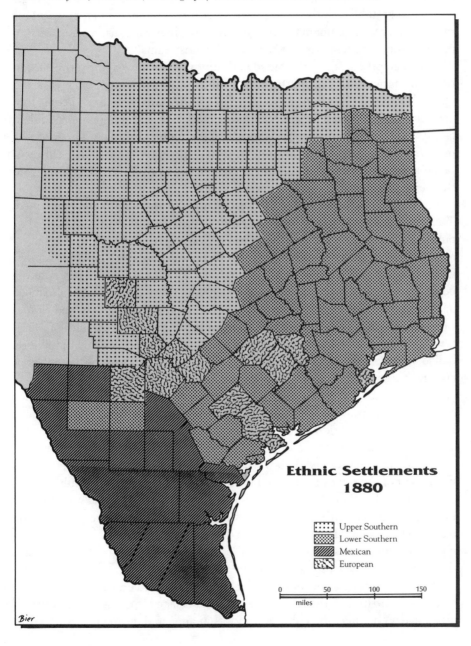

Ethnic Settlements 1880

Upper Southern
Lower Southern
Mexican
European

0   50   100   150
miles

Bier

THE LEGACY OF THE FRONTIER

The last quarter of the nineteenth century witnessed a tremendous transformation after which Texas no longer was a frontier region. Since the time of prehistoric peoples, those of different cultures had seen Texas as a land of promise. The struggle for territorial supremacy took on international overtones as Spaniards, then Mexicans, and then Americans intruded into the province and waged the fight to displace the land's indigenous groups. By the 1880s, Anglo Texans had established their hegemony over the state once and for all, having removed all other claimants to the region through warfare, usurpation, or simply by absorbing them into the new social mainstream.

Demographic factors, combined with innovations in weaponry, transportation, and agriculture, had by the end of the nineteenth century effected a dramatic shift in the older frontier society. The new technology pushed people into unsettled lands, assisted them in exploiting land and natural resources, and then facilitated the transportation of crops and products to market. The forces of modernity were so potent that neither inhospitable terrain nor the stiff resistance of its Native inhabitants could forestall the frontier's consolidation into the new sovereignty.

Nevertheless, the legacy of the nineteenth-century adventurers remained. The self-confidence and individualism that emerged during the era of the Republic of Texas persisted into the post–Civil War period. Entering the wilderness and deriving a livelihood from it, building cities and large ranching estates, and suppressing the Indians had instilled Texans with a sense of power and a belief that courage and hard work could overcome great odds. The saga also made a lasting imprint on American culture, as Texans are regularly depicted (sometimes stereotypically) as products of the nineteenth century. A wealth of literature, as well as a long list of films, depicts Texas as a frontier setting. In folklore, ballad, and story the legends of Davy Crockett, Sam Houston, the Texas Rangers, and outlaws such as John Wesley Hardin still fascinate.

Yet the legacy of the frontier is not entirely positive. With self-confidence came an arrogant attitude that often expressed itself at the expense of others, namely racial minorities. As already discussed, African Americans, Mexicans, and Indians were many times the targets of white Texans' hatred. Furthermore, Texans sometimes revealed their worst characteristics in the westward push. Development of the state was accomplished through courage, resourcefulness, and commitment, but their concomitants included violence, greed, and wastefulness. Intruders into the frontier often recklessly ravished the natural resources of the region. This resulted in the decimation of the great buffalo herds, the overgrazing of the range, the stripping of forest lands without regard for the future, and the pollution of rivers, streams, and the Gulf.

Although a rough-and-tumble epoch had come to an end at the turn of the century, the attitudes attached to the frontier persisted into the new industrial/urban age. Economic and cultural trends that appeared during the last quarter of the nineteenth century were to have an undeniable impact on the century to come.

READINGS

Books and Dissertations

Barr, Alwyn, *Reconstruction to Reform: Texas Politics, 1876–1906* (Austin: University of Texas Press, 1971).

Billington, Ray Allen, and Martin Ridge, *Westward Expansion: A History of the American Frontier,* 5th ed. (New York: MacMillan Publishing Co., 1982).

Brown, Richard Maxwell, *Strain of Violence: Historical Studies of American Violence and Vigilantism* (New York: Oxford University Press, 1975).

Carlson, Paul H., *Texas Woollybacks: The Texas Sheep and Goat Industry* (College Station: Texas A&M University Press, 1982).

Cashion, Ty, *A Texas Frontier: The Clear Fork Country and Fort Griffin, 1849–1887* (Norman: University of Oklahoma Press, 1996).

De León, Arnoldo, *They Called Them Greasers: Anglo Attitudes Toward Mexicans in Texas, 1821–1900* (Austin: University of Texas Press, 1983).

Downs, Fane, "Texas Women at Work," in *Texas: A Sesquicentennial Celebration,* ed. Donald W. Wisenhunt (Austin: Eakin Press, 1984).

Frantz, Joe B., and Julian Ernest Choate, *The American Cowboy: The Myth and the Reality* (Norman: University of Oklahoma Press, 1955).

Holden, William C., *Alkali Trails, or, Social and Economic Movements of the Texas Frontier, 1846–1900* (Dallas: Southwest Press, 1930).

Jordan, Terry G., *North American Cattle-Ranching Frontiers: Origins, Diffusion, and Differentiation* (Albuquerque: University of New Mexico Press, 1993).

———, *Trails to Texas: Southern Roots of Western Cattle Ranching* (Lincoln: University of Nebraska Press, 1981).

Malone, Ann Patton, *Women in the Texas Frontier* (El Paso: Texas Western Press, 1985).

Martin, Robert L., *The City Moves West: Economic and Industrial Growth in Central West Texas* (Austin: University of Texas Press, 1969).

Prassel, Frank Richard, *The Western Peace Officer: A Legacy of Law and Order* (Norman: University of Oklahoma Press, 1972).

Reps, John W., *Cities of the American West: A History of Frontier Urban Planning* (Princeton, NJ: Princeton University Press, 1979).

Rice, Lawrence D., *The Negro in Texas: 1874–1900* (Baton Rouge: Louisiana State University Press, 1971).

Schubert, Frank N., *Black Valor: Buffalo Soldiers and the Medal of Honor, 1870–1898* (Wilmington, DE: SR Books, 1997).

Seaholm, Megan, "Earnest Women: The White Woman's Club Movement in Progressive Era Texas, 1880–1920," (Ph. d. Diss., Rice University, 1988).

Utley, Robert, *The Indian Frontier of the American West, 1846–1890* (Albuquerque: University of New Mexico Press, 1984).

Webb, Walter Prescott, *The Texas Rangers: A Century of Frontier Defense* (Boston: Houghton Mifflin, 1935).

West, Elliott, *The Way to the West: Essays on the Central Plains* (Albuquerque: University of New Mexico Press, 1995).

Wintz, Cary D., "Women in Texas," in *The Texas Heritage*, 3rd ed., eds. Ben Procter and Archie P. McDonald (Wheeling, IL: Harlan Davidson, Inc., 1998).

Wooster, Robert, *Soldiers, Suttlers, and Settlers: Garrison Life on the Texas Frontier* (College Station: Texas A&M University Press, 1987).

Articles

Cuthbertson, Gilbert M., "Catarino E. Garza and the Garza War," *Texana* 12, No. 4 (1974).

Hunt, Sylvia, "Women Educators in Texas, 1850–1900: Were They Feminist?" *East Texas Historical Journal* 27, No. 1 (1989).

Jordan, Terry G., "The German Settlement of Texas after 1865," *Southwestern Historical Quarterly* 73 (October, 1969).

——, "A Century and a Half of Ethnic Change in Texas, 1836–1986," *Southwestern Historical Quarterly* 89 (April, 1986).

McClung, Donald R., "Second Lieutenant Henry O. Flipper: A Negro Officer on the Texas Frontier," *West Texas Historical Association Yearbook* 47 (1971).

McKay, S. S., "Social Conditions in Texas in the Eighteen Seventies," *West Texas Historical Association Yearbook* 14 (1938).

Nackman, Mark E., "The Indians of Texas in the Nineteenth Century: A Cross-Section of American Indian Culture," *The Texas Quarterly* 18 (Summer, 1975).

Weiss, Harold J., Jr., "The Texas Rangers Revisited: Old Themes and New Viewpoints," *Southwestern Historical Quarterly* 97 (April, 1994).

TEXAS IN THE AGE OF AGRARIAN DISCONTENT

CHAPTER 8

Between 1870 and 1900, industrialization transformed the United State from primarily an agrarian nation to an industrial and urban one. Americans wrestled with how they would redefine their society in their new environment of commercial farms, growing cities, increasing foreign immigration, and industrial consolidation. The ways in which they coped with these changes outlined the history of the period. The South did not undergo an industrial boom similar to that experienced by its northern and western counterparts, for the new southern industries such as ginning and textile mills tended to rely on extractive farm products. Therefore, the South remained an agricultural region with a society dominated by the indigenous majority culture, which was white and homogeneous. Although it was the poorest section of the nation—and despite the intentions of white southerners to preserve their racial supremacy—the South underwent tremendous social and political upheavals during the last decades of the nineteenth century.

Of all the southern states, Texas changed the most. Still largely unpopulated by whites west of the 100th meridian in 1870, with settled areas composed mostly of subsistence farms and small communities that more often than not used barter as the medium of commercial exchange, the state nevertheless stood on the brink of a major economic revolution. Over the next thirty years, railroads criss-crossed Texas, and more persons moved westward. Commercial agriculture followed the tracks, as cotton replaced cattle as the dominant factor in the economic growth of the state. New industries grafted themselves onto commercial agriculture, changing Texas from a preindustrial, rural state into one with modern transportation facilities that linked producers of raw materials to regional, national, and international markets (over which Texans had little control). Most Texans considered themselves Democrats, but the rise of the commercial economy threatened party unity. Landless farmers did not hold the same economic and political goals as did those who owned their farms. Nor did commercial cattle ranchers always endorse the same ends as did sheep ranchers, while both feared the threat of farmers who wished to close off open grazing land. Merchants, bankers, lumber-

Above: Horse-drawn plow. *Courtesy Texas State Historical Association, Austin*

205

men, and railroad entrepreneurs all might have considered themselves Democrats and yet disagree over railroad regulation or inflation. All business interests, however, opposed agrarians who wished to raise taxes on businesses. In
short, commercial expansion tore apart the consensus politics that had defeated
the Republicans and "Redeemed" Texas in 1874, opening the way for new battles
as the century came to a close.

THE RAILROADS AND ECONOMIC DEVELOPMENT

Texas lacked wide, navigable rivers and had only 583 miles of railroad tracks
in 1870. Except for coastal seaports and the town of Jefferson in northeastern
Texas, reachable by steamboat via the Red River, most of the state remained
landlocked. Inland farmers and merchants still relied on wagons and stagecoaches to move freight and supplies and for contact with the outside commercial world. The high freight rates and the slow service of ox wagons retarded the
growth of commercial farming and related businesses. Most Texans knew that
economic development of the state depended on the building of a railroad network.

Largely at the urging of Granger delegates to the constitutional convention,
Article X of the Constitution of 1876 defined railroads as "public" carriers. But
at first, most farmers and merchants hardly wished to regulate the railroads.
Rather, they sought to encourage railroad building through state, local, and private subsidies. The Land Grant Law of 1876 authorized the granting of sixteen
sections of land to railroad companies for every mile of main-line track they completed. Under the provisions of this act and three special grants awarding certain companies twenty sections per mile of track, forty railroads received a
combined total of 32,153,878 acres of land in return for building 2,928 miles of
track. Before the repeal of the Land Grant Law in 1883, the Texas and Pacific
Railroad garnered over 5 million acres of land, more than any other entity. Local communities also subsidized the construction of railroads by donating to
railroad companies sites for depots and holding pens, giving them rights-of-way,
paying bonuses to companies in return for choosing their town as a railroad stop,
and granting them tax exemptions. Although prohibited by the state constitution from doing so, five counties and cities combined to appropriate almost $1
million in public bonds for aid to railroads. Often, local civic organizations raised
money through private subscriptions to entice railroads into their communities.

Railroad entrepreneurs promised almost instant prosperity to the communities that subsidized a route through their town, and local governments and citizens needed little urging to grant bonuses to railroads. A railroad siphoned off
business from all areas not directly served by it, and local residents saw lower freight
rates and expanding markets as a key to both economic and population growth.
Indeed, the threat of a railroad to bypass a town might spell its economic doom.

Historians continue to debate the wisdom and effect of the land grants to
railroad companies. Certainly, private investments of eastern and foreign capi-

Locomotive on freshly built railroad near Houston, 1922. *Courtesy Houston Metropolitan Research Center, Houston Public Library*

talists played an important role in the development of Texas's railroad network, but this, coupled with the generous policy of public aid, allowed the expansion of railroads without the supervision of any state agency or any master plan for growth. Consequently, some areas of the state were overbuilt, while others lacked any railroad facilities. Moreover, most transportation companies never prospered from the sale of the granted land. Many of them lacked sufficient capital, went into receivership, and ended up selling the land for a few cents an acre. And since railroad land had been awarded in alternate sections, the companies often had difficulty selling their lands to prospective buyers, many of whom preferred to buy contiguous tracts of public land. This forced some of the railroads to sell land at below the cost of surveying it. Indeed, through agents recruiting prospective settlers and massive advertising campaigns, railroad and land companies played a major role in the settlement of the West. Nevertheless, the Texas Pacific Land Trust, created in 1888 from the holdings of the Texas and Pacific Railroad, remained in 1994 the state's largest landowner.

Regardless of who financed their growth, the railroads quickly laid tracks throughout the state. In 1872, Texas ranked twenty-eighth among the states in total railroad mileage; by 1880, it had jumped to twelfth; by 1890, it ranked third; and by 1904, it had over 10,000 miles of track, more than any other state in the nation. As predicted, population growth corresponded to the expansion of transportation services; in 1870, the population of Texas ranked nineteenth in the country; in 1880, eleventh; in 1890, seventh; and at the turn of the century, it ranked sixth.

The Missouri, Kansas and Texas (Katy) Railroad reached Denison in 1872, and the next year, through the Houston and Texas Central, linked the Gulf Coast to North Texas. Now farmers received goods quickly from the Gulf Coast, and after the Texas and Pacific (T&P) Railroad entered the state (by 1875) they could ship their cotton through St. Louis and on to the East Coast. The Katy and the T&P spelled the end for Jefferson as a commercial center and strengthened the young and vibrant Houston's chances to replace Galveston as the major Gulf port. The railroads moved west as the buffalo disappeared and whites displaced the Plains Indians. By 1881, Southern Pacific tracks linked El Paso to the rest of the state, and the Gulf, Colorado, and Santa Fe Railroad connected Galveston to Fort Worth, and eventually to the Panhandle. Finally, by 1900 the Great Northern Railroad linked Laredo to Marshall. This network of tracks united the Texas economy.

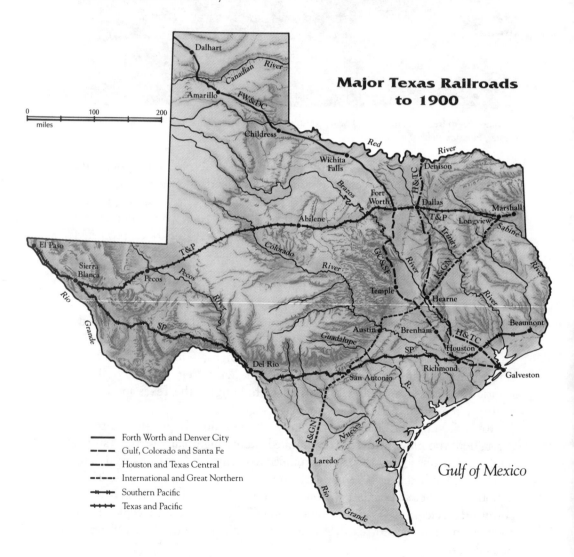

Major Texas Railroads to 1900

Legend:
- ———— Forth Worth and Denver City
- – – – Gulf, Colorado and Santa Fe
- —·—·— Houston and Texas Central
- - - - - International and Great Northern
- —||—||— Southern Pacific
- ++++ Texas and Pacific

Railroad building spurred the development of other industries. In the heyday of railroad construction, companies bought vast amounts of lumber for ties, bridges, stations, temporary housing for workers, holding pens, cotton wharves, and freight platforms. The T&P alone in 1880 ordered 500,000 crossties. That year it also purchased 2,000 tons of rails and spikes and employed 8,000 laborers, who along with thousands of draft animals consumed tons of agricultural products. Cotton gins and agricultural industries followed the tracks, with many a Texas city owing its origin to once having been a railroad terminus.

But railroads proved a mixed blessing in Texas, as they did elsewhere in the nation. The developing commercial and trade network that followed industrial growth broke up old and familiar patterns of trade, which frequently had been community- and kinsmen-oriented. Now farmers and local businesspersons dealt with markets far removed from their region and with agents of trade and transportation who seemed both impersonal and impervious to local concerns. Even as the rail network neared completion, criticism of the railroad companies increased. Critics asserted that railroads discriminated between shippers, often charged more for short than for long hauls, granted free passes to political friends, gave rebates to preferred customers, signed pooling and monopolistic agreements, frequently gave poor or inadequate service, and used their considerable economic and political resources to prevent any legislation that would attempt to stop their abusive practices. Public funds had subsidized the railroads, and now that they had fallen short of the promised economic panacea, proponents of the New South and the railroads themselves became politically suspect.

And the monopolistic policies of railroad management from 1882 to 1890 only fueled these suspicions. Collis P. Huntington of the Southern Pacific and Jay Gould of the T&P in 1882 organized a pool by signing an agreement to fix rates. Between their railroad holdings and lease arrangements with other lines, the two men controlled more than half the railroad mileage in Texas. Now they agreed publicly to joint use of the Sierra Blanca–El Paso line. Secret parts of the agreement, however, included possible joint purchase of competing lines, an understanding that the lines would not compete with each other, and a pooling of receipts. (The secret provisions of the agreement would not become public until 1893, when the Railroad Commission acquired a copy of the agreement and released its contents.)

A number of trunk lines or main rail routes organized the Texas Traffic Association in 1885, which announced as its purpose the control of rates for traffic that originated in Texas. Attorney General James Hogg won a court decree in 1888 dissolving the Association, which simply reorganized as the International Association, with its headquarters outside the state. For the next forty years, this monopoly or one of its successors would try to fix rail rates. This pooling device, along with a lengthy list of other abuses, explains shippers' charges of railroad corruption, which only increased in intensity as southern farmers became less prosperous. Particularly from 1882 on, farmers demanded that the state create an agency to regulate railroads. Not until the rise of James Hogg to the office of attorney general in 1887, however, would that proposition receive an able political spokesman.

Public Land

In 1876, Texas had a public domain of 61,258,461 acres. The land fell into two categories. First was the land assigned to the Permanent School Fund. As specified by the Constitution of 1876, this included half of all existing public lands, plus the alternate sections of the grants previosuly made to railroads, for a total of over 42 million acres. The remaining half of the unappropriated public domain could, at the Redeemers' discretion, be sold to retire the public debt or allocated to corporations (in practice, railroads) to encourage economic development. Governor Oran M. Roberts, concerned about the slow sale of land and citing the need to raise state revenue, encouraged the legislature to pass two laws in 1879 revising the method of dispensing public land. The price was set at $1 an acre for school land, of which a purchaser could acquire up to four sections. The second act permitted the sale of all unappropriated public domain for fifty cents an acre, with no limit on quantity purchased.

The so-called Fifty Cent Law did less damage to prospective settlement of the frontier than its critics estimated. During the law's tenure, the state sold less than 2 million acres. And Land Commissioner W. C. Walsh blocked the sale of much of the land by interpreting the law to its narrowest possible definition. Indirectly, the Fifty Cent Law had a different influence on land settlement than expected: by depressing the cost of land, it forced some railroads and land-holding companies into receivership, allowing speculators to purchase tracts at deflated values.

Nevertheless, immediately after passage of the Fifty Cent Law, critics charged Roberts with selling off Texas's heritage to corporations and syndicates. Speculators heightened the controversy by claiming land, holding it for ninety days with no interest charges, and then, if they failed to a find buyer, simply turning the land back to the state with no penalties. Political dissatisfaction in 1883 led to a revision of the law. No more land was to be granted to railroads, and the public domain was reclassified according to agricultural, timber, or pastoral values: the former two sold for $3 an acre and the latter for $2 an acre. Now the legislature created the State Land Board to reclassify public land and to ensure that settlers received priority over speculators. But the need for a general reorganization of public land laws led to the abolition of the State Land Board in 1887. From then on, the commissioner of the General Land Office administered the public land.

Some historians argue that Oran Roberts's unwillingness to try for a third term as governor stemmed from public discontent with his land policies. But his successor, "Ox Cart" John Ireland, who won his sobriquet as well as the gubernatorial nomination from his opposition to railroad land grants, had similar problems with the administration of the public domain. Indeed, the issue of the leasing of public lands generated quarrels between ranchers and the Land Board that led to, or at least intensified, the fence-cutting wars.

Technology had changed the western environment. The building of railroads into West Texas allowed the rapid transport of barbed wire into the area. Windmills, another technological innovation, made possible the utilization of shallow supplies of groundwater. Consequently, by 1883, cattlemen were fencing off their surface water sites in South and Central Texas and enclosing their pastures with barbed wire. In some cases, owners of large ranches also fenced off portions of the public domain, which they then leased or simply used as they saw fit. Settlers also used barbed wire to protect their crops and (any existing) water supplies. As a result, fence-cutting wars spread across the agricultural areas of Texas in 1883 and 1884, occurring in more than one-half of the organized counties in the state. The wars were waged by cattle ranchers against neighboring or competing cattlemen, between cattlemen and sheepmen, and by farmers who opposed the practices of both the cattlemen and the land-holding companies.

Law enforcement officers could do little to quiet the rampant destruction of property and violence. Governor Ireland called a special session of the legislature to address the problem, and lawmakers responded with an 1884 law that made fence cutting a felony and required the building of a gate for every three miles of fence line. Furthermore, the law prohibited the enclosure of public land. Better law enforcement and public opinion that decried the lawlessness brought an end to the wars by 1890. But the fence-cutting strife had added to the perception that monopolies were closing off the public domain. In the Cross Timbers region, for example, poor farmers organized community networks of secret organizations that saw fencing as a threat to traditional republican values of land use and democracy. These fence-cutting, vigilante organizations may well have developed a class consciousness in their members that emerged later as third-party revolts.

The general policy of encouraging settlers to purchase land continued until the end of the century. By 1895, the price of land was reduced to $1 an acre. Thus, from time to time, settlers could purchase tracts of from 40 to 640 acres (and in West Texas, four sections) with interest rates of 3 to 10 percent. Until 1899, a married man could claim a 160-acre homestead, a single male one-half that amount. The homestead provision was designed for settlers who could prove three years' residence and some improvement of the land.

The success of public land legislation was debatable. The actual number of settlers who claimed land in West Texas for themselves, rather than in behalf of large ranchers, was relatively small, for individual sales of land certainly exceeded the number of settlers in the area. Income from the sale of public lands did not solve Texas's debt problems. Speculators could purchase land from railroads and holders of Confederate veteran bonus certificates for fifteen cents or less an acre. The loss of land seemed a betrayal of the public school fund. And,

212 ❖ The History of Texas

finally, even if public land policies succeeded in encouraging settlement of the frontier and produced revenue for the government, the state failed to exercise careful management of its public domain.

As railroads opened public land for farming and other development, management of the land and the railroads' influence over it became political issues. East Texans, who held land in fee simple, would not ordinarily care what happened to West Texans or the western lands. But the fence-cutting wars and adverse publicity had made large ranching concerns, particularly those with foreign investors, seem to represent predatory, out-of-state monopolies. Although the geography of the area precluded the migration of small farmers to West Texas, the combination of large ranching enterprises and railroad land ownership there seemed to seal off the frontier as a potential safety valve. In short, so much land went to railroads and large ranches that the state's land policy seemed a hostage of the corporations and punitive to small farmers.

LUMBER AND OTHER INDUSTRIES

The rail network enabled the development of the lumber industry in Texas. The great yellow pine forests of East Texas grew on some 20 million acres of flat to gently rolling terrain that extended westward from the border of Louisiana. The area's mild climate and ready availability of cheap labor made it ideal for a lumbering industry. Although small-scale lumbering had been carried on in the region since its early settlement, up to this point the industry had relied on rivers to transport logs and rarely produced more finished lumber products than could be used locally. The 1870 census recorded slightly more than 100 million board feet of lumber cut in Texas, principally around Orange and Jefferson Counties. Lumbermen floated the cut logs from the Piney Woods down the Neches and Sabine Rivers to large commercial mills at Beaumont, Orange, or Houston. Boats then carried the finished lumber to coastal towns. Ox wagons took lumber into the Texas interior. In any case, the cost of such products for the average family was prohibitive. But railroad expansion changed the Piney Woods' economy. Pine trees, which farmers had always considered a nuisance, suddenly became a valuable commodity, as the arrival of cheap transportation coincided with the waning of eastern U.S. pine sources.

The white pine forests in the nation's Upper Midwest had fallen to overcutting and a ruthless exploitation that left them depleted by the 1880s. Lumbermen now turned to the South for new sources of timber. Many consumers considered the yellow pine inferior to its white counterpart, but the short supply of the latter and the increased use of southern timber soon eroded such prejudice. Indeed, the resulting timber bonanza pushed lumbering in Texas from a cottage industry into one that ranked first in the state's manufacturing economy. Lumber products led all other freight in tonnage transported by Texas railroads from 1875 to 1900, and by the twentieth century, lines carried 6 million tons of lumber products annually. The number of lumber-manufacturing plants in

Texas almost doubled in the period, with the 1900 census reporting 637 establishments that produced more than 1 billion board feet of lumber. Most of these products were used domestically until 1880, but thereafter entrepreneurs sent them to other states and overseas. The growing demand for Texas lumber moved the state to rank always in the top ten of lumber-producing states in the late nineteenth and early twentieth century. Texas lumber production peaked in 1907, when a record 2,197,233,000 board feet were logged. The rapid cutting and the lack of care for the forest destroyed much of the East Texas timberlands, but no drive for conservation of resources occurred until later.

The burgeoning lumber industry lured eastern capital and experienced lumbermen into the state. Henry J. Lutcher and G. Bedell Moore came to Texas from Pennsylvania in 1877 and built sawmills near Orange. Their company continued as an economic force in the area well into the twentieth century. Other capitalists followed. Foremost among them was John Henry Kirby, who organized in 1901 what became the first multimillion-dollar firm in Texas, the Kirby Lumber Company. Kirby grew up in poverty on an East Texas farm. He briefly attended college, read law with a local state senator, and gained entrance to the bar in 1885. With the aid of eastern capital and consultants, he made a fortune buying and selling timberlands. He eventually joined with Nathan D. Silsbee, namesake of the Texas town, and other easterners to acquire more than 250,000 acres of pine forests. In short order, a symbiotic relationship developed between railroads and lumber companies, one that encouraged lumbermen to build trunk lines to their bases of operation as well as to invest in railroad companies that transported their products to market. For example, Kirby built the Gulf, Beaumont, and Kansas City road to open untapped lumber sources before selling it to the Santa Fe Railroad, with which he established a long and friendly relationship. Railroads also acquired timberlands. By 1910, the Southern Pacific owned 117,000 acres of Texas forest.

Until 1883, Kirby and other entrepreneurs sometimes acquired their extensive timberlands at less than $2 an acre. Land Commissioner Walsh and others forced the reclassification of pine forests from unproductive farm acreage to that of timbered acreage, but their assigned value still was only $2 to $5 per acre. The reclassification also did not solve the problem of cutting timber on school lands, a practice that continued throughout the nineteenth century. In 1905, the state finally established competitive bidding for the right to exploit school lands. But only 31,978 acres of public land were then still available, so the new system had little impact on the timber industry. By that time the industry had undergone a concentration into the hands of a small number of corporations. Individuals still owned half of the lumbering plants in 1910, but one-third of the corporations hired three-quarters of the workforce and produced 75 percent of both the value and the value added by manufacture of lumber products.

As a group, the larger lumber entrepreneurs ruled over their domains as if they were fiefdoms. They built company towns, complete with churches, schools, housing, and stores. Up to 75 percent of the workforce were unskilled laborers who earned only $1.50 to $2 a day until 1917. The companies frequently paid their workers with merchandise checks spendable only at company stores, which charged higher prices than other local establishments. The workers, who lived in company houses and relied on company benevolence in times of illness or economic hardship, could do little to overturn the control of local mill owners.

The industry's laborers ordinarily came from the mills' surrounding areas. Of the 6,400 wage earners in the lumber industry in 1910, only 336 were foreign born. About one-third of them were African Americans, who usually held the lowest-paying jobs with no chance of advancement. Women seldom worked for wages in the lumbering industry, and child labor in the mills was rare. The 1890 census recorded only thirty-one boys between the ages of ten and fifteen working as skilled or unskilled operatives. Census figures did not report the number of women and children who did contract labor for lumber companies, such as marking trees and clearing brush, or those engaged in piece work; they might have fallen under the general census classification of unpaid family workers. In all cases, the average workday lasted a little over twelve hours.

Unions recruited few workers in the Piney Woods, but even without the leadership of organized labor, a few work stoppages did occur. Workers at the Elyan sawmill struck in 1886 for a lowering of the workweek from sixty-six to sixty hours with no decrease in pay, and four years later strikers shut down the mills in Orange. African American workers at Harrisburg threatened to burn down the town over what was probably a labor grievance, but a militia from nearby Houston quelled the potential violence.

The timber magnates vigorously opposed any labor organization. They used blacklists, antiunion contracts, paid informers, private police agencies, and other instruments to prevent the logging and sawmill workers from joining unions. Texas lumber manufacturers, moreover, organized themselves into trade associations (the largest being the Southern Pine Association) that exchanged information and colluded to set prices and wages. The Southern Pine Association also served as an effective lobbying force, making its wishes known to state legislators and circulating lists of suspected labor organizers or unruly workers to association members. In short, the lumber owners successfully avoided antitrust actions, maintained company towns, issued merchandise warrants, and prevented union organization until the New Deal in the 1930s.

Other industries in the state in 1870 consisted of small shops or plants that served self-contained villages or surrounding agricultural areas. Smaller villages usually supported such enterprises as saw and grist mills, gun and saddlery shops, blacksmiths, dry goods and grocery stores, and sometimes cotton gins and presses. These industries resembled the modern craft shops and mostly drew on easily processed raw materials.

Larger communities might additionally support light industries such as foundries, which made plows, or have more than one flour mill that sold to regional markets. But even relatively major industries such as flour milling used a single process to convert a raw material into a finished product. Flour mills and sawmills fit into the frontier economy in that they could easily be packed up and moved in order to exploit new sources of raw materials or untapped markets. Railroads settled down these migratory industries, for transportation links allowed larger plants to erect permanent shipping sites, using the cheap transportation to integrate supply and marketing facilities. An integrated economy also applied economic pressures to local industries as larger, more efficient, urban establishments threatened to drive even their far-flung, small competitors out of business.

Growth figures emphasize the changes in the Texas economy. In 1870, the average state industrial establishment had an investment of $2,200 and employed 3.5 workers; by 1900, the numbers were $7,200 and 4. The more than 300 percent increase in investment capital with no appreciable gain in workforce cataloged the expanded use of machinery. Statistics further demonstrate the rapid growth of Texas manufacturing. In 1870, the total value of industrial products was $11.5 million, less than one-fourth of the value of the state's agricultural products, and 2,400 shops employed 8,000 workers, or 1 percent of the state's population. Thirty years later the value of manufacturing rose to $119.4 million, and 12,300 establishments employed 48,150 workers, or 1.5 percent of the population. Finally, the value of manufacturing products that year roughly equalled one-half that of farm products.

This rapid growth, however, hardly placed Texas in the front rank of industrial states. The national per capita value of manufactures was $171 in 1900, as compared to Texas's $39.99. One-third of the value of Texas manufacturing in 1870 was represented by flour and grist mills or local productive manufacturing units. The next-largest industries were lumbering, beef processing, carpentry, blacksmithing, and slaughtering. Lumber became the number-one industry by 1900, followed by cottonseed mills, which now shipped their oil by rail in tank cars, and flour milling, now concentrated in large mills in urban areas. The 4,514 cotton gins in the state produced an average of 589 bales that year, or 34 percent of the nation's total cotton crop. The increase in gins corresponded to a similar increase in cotton compresses, with the 1890 census listing over

Cotton bale at Galveston before compression. *Courtesy of Robert A. Calvert*

forty compress companies. Cottonseed byproducts, which had no commercial value in 1860 and were still not listed as a significant industry in the 1870 census, ranked second ($14 million) only to lumbering enterprises ($16.2 million) in the 1900 census. Railroad car and general shop construction, liquor and malt distilling, foundry and machine shop production, planing mills, and clay product manufacturers rounded out the top-ten Texas industries at the turn of the century.

The cities that dominated industrial development pointed to later urban growth. A 1905 U.S. Census on Manufacturing listed Dallas as the leading industrial center in Texas, with flour and grist milling and printing and publishing as its major industries. Houston ranked second, with railcar construction and cottonseed as its principal sources of income. Those two were followed by San Antonio, which led the state in the distilling of malt liquors. Next came Fort Worth, which built a meat-packing plant that failed to survive the depression of 1893. Cowtown's development as a major packing center lay in the future. By 1905, Forth Worth's major industry was flour and grist milling. Galveston led Texas in industrial development in 1870 but had fallen to fifth place by 1900. The turn of the century still witnessed Galveston handling 4 million bales of cotton a year; over 90 percent of which went into the export trade. Waco, Sherman, and Beaumont completed the 1905 listing. The former two served as agricultural marketing centers, and the latter was already enjoying the advantages of economic gains produced by the Spindletop oil strike of 1901.

The concentration of agricultural wealth in shipping centers bothered farmers. As they became less prosperous during the period, they saw the growth of cities as being at their expense. When agricultural reformers condemned middle men, saying "neither do they reap nor do they sow, but grow rich off the toil of others," they were referring to the railroad corporations, large land companies, processing industries, and commission and furnishing merchants, as well as crossroads merchants, who profited from the transporting, grinding, compressing, ginning, and selling of agricultural crops.

Minerals

Oil, of course, became the mineral that eventually made Texas prosperous. In 1896, oil was struck at Corsicana, the field peaking in production in 1900 with 829,554 barrels. This relatively minor discovery, however, did not significantly affect the Standard Oil monopoly or change the Texas economy. Spindletop would do that the next year.

Industrialization in the late nineteenth century demanded coal and iron, of which Texas had little of high quality. Nevertheless, inferior grades of coal (with high slate and sulfur content) lay in the state, and as railroads in Texas increased in number, they often used local coal to stoke their engines. The first important ore discovery came in Stephens County in 1879. The next year, railroads purchased coal in Coalville in Palo Pinto County. A labor strike there in 1885 prompted railroads to concentrate their coal production at Thurber in Erath County, where the T&P coal company ran a company town. Work stoppages occurred there, however, in 1889, 1890, and 1903. The value of coal production per year rose from $1 million in 1870 to over $5 million in 1900, making coal the state's most valuable mineral until the oil strike at Spindletop.

Salt ranked second among minerals in the Texas economy at this time. Salt works or mines had dotted the Texas landscape and served local communities from the time of early settlement. When the Grand Saline plant opened in 1889 in northeast Van Zandt County, it tapped a solid vein of rock salt and soon dominated Texas's production.

Prospectors discovered some iron ores in East Texas, and entrepreneurs built foundries there. The Kelly Plow Company, near Jefferson, smelted iron to manufacture agricultural implements. The state prison at Rusk produced a limited amount of iron. With the help of British investors, New Birmingham in Cherokee County touted itself as a manufacturing center. Its furnaces turned out 50,000 tons of pig iron annually. Because of unfavorable transportation rates and the withdrawal of the British capital in 1905, however, the furnaces shut down and the town virtually died.

LABOR UNIONS

Labor unions developed in response to the industrialization process. As large corporations grew and the anonymity of the workplace pushed aside traditional laborer-employer relationships, workers turned to collective bargaining. Early unions, then, represented more than traditional labor grievances. Workers joined unions to preserve some independence and control of their lives in the newly forming commercial-industrial world. Most immediate causes of work stoppages or strikes emanated from disputes with employers over wages and hours. On average, wage earners put in twelve-hour days, earning about $12 a month for unskilled labor and upwards of $100 a month for skilled or craft work. The workweek totaled six days, seven in certain industries. And when economic downturns such as the depressions of 1873 and 1893 occurred, management tended to cut wages without a corresponding drop in workers' hours. Usually, employees either accepted employers' terms or left for other jobs. Such strikes as did occur often failed, leaving workers dispirited or unemployed.

Organized labor made little headway either in Texas or in the nation during this period because certain cultural assumptions limited the growth of unions. Most Americans considered a plant owner's right to control wages and hours as an inherent right of property ownership. Strikes frequently fomented violence, and as such, they represented a threat to stability and order. Detractors of unions identified them with radicalism, which they classified as downright un-American, surely the work of foreigners. In addition to these negative views, union organizers in Texas encountered other obstacles. The state's frontier traditions had fostered a cult of individualism that distrusted interference with private property. Furthermore, the type of industrialization that took place in Texas re-lied on agricultural and extractive businesses, difficult to unionize because of their heavy use of unskilled labor. Finally, the state leadership exhibited an an-tiunion spirit fostered by the New South creed that sought to attract industry to the region by guaranteeing incoming businesses a stable and inexpensive la-bor force. Such a view allowed corporations, like those in lumbering or mining, to carry on such union-busting tactics as blacklisting, the hiring of strikebreak-ers, and relying on public officials to forcibly break strikes.

Although union activities in Texas dated back to the days of the republic, the first major labor organizations entered Texas shortly after the Civil War. In 1866, longshoremen organized the Screwman's Benevolent Association, a group of specialized workers who combined to request health benefits and financial aid for ill workers. The organization took a moderate stance, avoiding strikes and only calling one work stoppage, and that to protest the employment of black workers. Black longshoremen, under the tutelage of black businessman Norris Wright Cuney, formed their own union in 1882. By that time, the major Texas cities had typographical unions, some of which were probably affiliated locals of the International Typographical Union. The United Mine Workers entered the state in the 1890s, and it remained active in Erath County until the increased use of oil drove the coal mines there out of business in 1921. Local unions made little headway into the lumbering camps.

The Knights of Labor began nationally in 1866, and from 1878 to 1886, the organization enjoyed spectacular national growth. The *Dallas Morning News* reported in 1885 that the Knights claimed 30,000 Texas members. The union advocated boycotts and economic cooperatives rather than strikes, and it ac-cepted women and African American members. Black people usually founded separate lodges of the Knights of Labor, but locals in some Texas cities accepted blacks into the main organization. David Black, an African American, served on the union's state executive board. The Knights were a true industrial union, admitting persons of all occupations except bankers, speculators, gamblers, law-yers, and liquor dealers. Therefore, some of its members were farmers and were not necessarily committed to labor union goals. Most farmers, however, had no difficulty endorsing the union's call for such political reforms as a graduated income tax, the direct election of U.S. senators, and other democratic measures.

Between 1881 and 1885, more than a hundred strikes took place in Texas, one of which involved 300 cowboys employed on big West Texas ranches. De-spite their stated policies to avoid work stoppages, the Knights led most of these strikes. They won a dockworkers' strike against the Mallory line in Galveston, but they had a mixed success in the Capitol Boycott, which originally began when the state agreed that convict labor could be used to aid in quarrying stone for the new Texas State Capitol and in building a railroad from the quarry in Burnet to the construction site in Austin. The contractors, an out-of-state syn-dicate, also had turned to Aberdeen, Scotland, to recruit stone cutters. The Knights warned the immigrant workers not to come to Texas, but some did anyway. The union then agreed to furnish money for the prosecution of the contractors under the 1885 federal Alien Contract Labor Law, an act originally passed in response to union demands that immigrant workers be prevented from competing with domestic labor. Charges were filed against the Capitol Syndicate in federal court in Austin, and the contractors were fined. Republican President Benjamin Harrison, however, scaled down the amount levied against the syndicate on his last day in office, and immigrant workers continued quarrying stone for the capitol until the work was completed.

In the Great Southwest Strike (March–May 1886), the notorious Jay Gould seemed determined to break the Knights of Labor. The railroad magnate paid off federal and local public officials and employed spies in the union halls to look after his interests. After identifying a foreman in Marshall as a member of the Knights, the T&P company fired him. The union responded with a strike that spread across the American Southwest. Violence occurred all along the line, particularly at switch junctures, where workers and strikebreakers clashed. At Buttermilk switch, in Fort Worth, Governor John Ireland sent in the militia and the Texas Rangers to maintain order and break the strike. Court injunctions, criminal proceedings against 1,000 workers, and a public opinion that rapidly moved from a pro-union stance to associating the Knights with wanton violence, augmented with the use of state-mandated force. In May, the strike ended, with many of the Knights losing their jobs to nonunion workers.

The experience of the Knights in Texas in many ways paralleled that of the national labor movement: strikes occurred; public opinion at first supported the workers, but as the strikes lingered on and violence erupted and consumer services stopped, it swung against the strikers; governmental powers (injunctions, national guard, or federal troops) were used to break the strike; and the union declined.

On May 4, 1886, at Haymarket Square in Chicago, police intervened to stop a protest meeting of anarchists and labor groups. During the melee, someone threw a bomb, killing seven policemen. Now, organized labor in general, and the Knights in particular, became labeled as radicals. Although no substantial connection ever was made between the Knights and anarchy, one member of the union, Albert R. Parsons, who had moved from Texas to Chicago, was unjustly accused of conspiracy to commit murder. He and three others were subsequently convicted and executed for having incited the Haymarket riot. Continued bad press and the failure of the Great Southwest Strike discredited the Knights, and by 1893 the union had only a few thousand members nationally.

The general failure of "reform unionism" encouraged labor leaders to move toward "business unionism," wherein unions remain apolitical and seek realizable, short-term gains of higher wages and fringe benefits. This decision eliminated most unskilled workers from the ranks of labor organizations, and it concentrated on the formation of craft unions, which relied on the inability of employers to replace skilled workers during walkouts. The American Federation of Labor (AFL), which began in 1886, advocated business unionism and first appeared in Texas in 1891. As the Knights collapsed, the craft unions attempted unsuccessfully to organize a statewide union. The Texas State Labor Union, agricultural and industrial in base, sought to organize a new labor coalition in 1895; it lasted four years. In 1900, the trade councils of six Texas cities (Austin, Corsicana, Dallas, Gainesville, Hillsboro, and Sherman) acquired AFL chapters. The Texas State Federation of Labor (TSFL) officially organized that year, claiming 8,475 members from seven unions. The TSFL advocated moderate social and political reforms, which linked it philosophically as much to the older reform unionism as to the business policies of the AFL. Overall, in a rural state suspicious of labor organizations, the dawn of the new century did not bode well for organized labor.

AGRICULTURE

The expansion of railroads encouraged Americans to leave other southern states to settle what remained of Texas's frontier. This migration bypassed the fertile, well-watered lands of East Texas for the marginal farmlands of the Cross Timbers and farther west to the Panhandle, an area which never seemed to get enough rain.

This westward migration testified to the commercialization of agriculture. At first glance, an observer might have categorized the economic change as one of expanding the farming frontier. But it signified more than that: it was the triumph of commercial over subsistence agriculture and of cotton over all rival crops. Table 8.1, which follows, best illustrates the story of commercial farming in Texas in the final decades of the nineteenth century.

Now, agricultural reformers urged Texas farmers to diversify. Theirs was a typical New South argument: diversification would lead to self-sufficient farms, which would allow landowners to be politically independent; scientific farming and crop rotation would preserve a family farm, avoid soil depletion, and prevent white sharecropping. The argument assumed that African Americans would not prove successful small farmers (thus the push for white immigration) and that nonspecialized farms would recapture the prosperity of the 1850s, a boom period in agricultural history. The New South reformers blamed the poor agricultural prices from 1870 to 1877 on Reconstruction, and they promised a return to prosperity once Democrats restored economic stability. The problem with this scenario, however, lay in the new technology. Better access to markets (through railroads) and improved agricultural implements and techniques soon led to overproduction, which naturally caused the world prices for staple crops to drop during the period.

Nevertheless, many farmers wished to produce a commercially viable commodity, and growing cotton seemed their best bet. Cotton was less susceptible than were other crops to drought; it exhausted the soil the least; it brought the

TABLE 8.1   Dollar Value of Texas Crops

	1870	1880	1890	1900
Wheat	$391,886	$2,441,918	$3,589,442	$7,592,852
Corn	10,153,941	11,509,808	34,940,748	39,259,415
Oats	297,439	1,761,609	5,334,496	6,241,192
Cotton	21,212,994	39,458,916	63,263,400	107,510,010

highest cash price; and it was the most adaptable to extensive agriculture. It fit the already existing farming habits of new settlers from the Upper and Lower South. And it coincided nicely with the national drive for agricultural specialization.

But growing cotton brought prosperity to very few Texans; instead, the rate of tenant farming increased. Tenancy had existed on a limited scale in the South before the Civil War, as there always had been a capital shortage in farming. But the severe lack of financial resources after the Civil War necessitated bringing together an abundance of land with a cheap labor source, and the number of tenants exploded. Originally, cotton planters assumed that only African Ameri-

Jesse Boyd plowing Charlie Swenson's farm in late 1890s or early 1900s. *The UT Institute of Texan Cultures, No. 71-443, courtesy of Mrs. Sadie Hoel*

cans would work the cotton fields, and sharecropping (one form of tenancy) effectively bound the freedpersons to the land. Ironically, many recently emancipated blacks opposed the wage system, seeing sharecropping as an alternative for advancement and a way to avoid the constant supervision of whites that they had endured under slavery.

Sharecropping, simply defined, was the exchange of labor for supplies or the use of land. In this arrangement, the rent for the land and the cost of the supplies (plus interest) would be paid for by the profits on the cotton crop. The crop lien, a mortgage on the growing crop, guaranteed the furnishing merchant, the person who *furnished* the supplies and foodstuffs for the farm family, a percentage of the crop grown plus the right to market the crop until all the costs of the supplies were repaid to him. One common sharecropping arrangement, "farming on halves," meant that half of the revenue the yearly crop produced went toward the rent, while the other half was pledged to pay off charges rung up with the local store owner or landlord, who might well be the same person. The difference between the bills owed to the furnishing merchant and the cotton sold was the sharecropper's profit, which, of course, might actually be a negative sum.

For this system to work well for the sharecropping family, the price of cotton had to rise. Instead it dropped, from 16.5 cents per pound in 1869 to a low of 5.7 cents per pound in 1898. Yet the rate of tenant farming went up, constituting 37.6 percent of Texas farming in 1880, 41.9 percent in 1890, and 49.7 percent in 1900. Under this system, independent farmers mortgaged their land to furnishing merchants and lost their land once bills for supplies exceeded money paid for crops. Tenancy was also biracial; in the age of agrarian discontent, white folks and black folks were becoming impoverished together. Probably no crop could have broken the tenant-farming cycle. In order to improve their condition, farmers needed long-term credit, controlled markets, larger farms, low interest rates (it has been estimated that interest rates on some sharecrop liens may have been as high as 150 percent), and some way to control the prices of machinery and land.

EDUCATION AND OTHER PUBLIC SERVICES

The reform of public education and other badly needed social services in Texas required a dynamic government, one capable of cooperating with the marketplace to raise revenue and fund public projects. But the philosophy of the state government from 1876 to the mid-1880s supported no such action. Citing the $3,167,335 state debt in 1874, the New South advocates argued that only economically conservative government could erase it, and that prosperity would come only after the state escaped from Republicanism and had attracted more corporations. Meanwhile, revenue realized from the sale of the public land was largely squandered, and the need for charitable and benevolent institutions, which cost money to found and operate, was ignored in the first several years following Reconstruction. The state, however, did establish the Terrell State

Prisoners, mostly black, at the stone dressing area of the quarry at Marble Falls, ca.1880. The Texas State Capitol was built from this rock. *Texas State Library and Archives Commission*

Hospital for the mentally ill in 1883, and shortly thereafter the legislature authorized the State Orphans School (1887), The Texas Blind, Deaf, and Orphan School for Negroes (1887), and the San Antonio State Hospital (1889) for mental patients.

Prisons

This minor gain in state services was not matched by one in the state prison system. Governor Oran Roberts believed that pardoning convicts and making prisons self-sufficient might solve the problems of overcrowded and inadequate correctional facilities. But self-sufficiency was difficult to achieve. The general population of the state had quadrupled by 1900, and efforts to end lawlessness in West Texas contributed to a rapid growth in the potential number of prison inmates. No one came forward with a comprehensive plan on how to handle the increased number of prisoners. From 1871 to 1883, the state used a form of convict leasing whereby private individuals leased and operated the Huntsville penitentiary and could employ the convicts in whatever economic endeavor the lessee desired. State inspectors were to see to it that the prisoners were not abused, but there were always too few inspectors and too many convicts working on far-flung farms, railroads, and other enterprises for effective oversight. Meanwhile, the death rate of prisoners increased markedly, as did the number of escapes. The system was modified in 1883 to contract leasing, whereby the state controlled the prisons but hired out its shops and convicts to private entrepreneurs. This system, too, was inefficient, if self-supporting, and agricultural and union organizations opposed it because it drove down wages. Although some citizens and lawmakers complained of the brutality of the lease system, the main question was one of profits. Many felt that instead of leasing out the convicts to private entrepreneurs, who then reaped handsome profits from the cheap labor, the state should be using convict labor directly in state-run enterprises, where the state would make the profits. Therefore, in the 1890s the prison system began acquiring land for state-owned and -operated prison farms and establishing prison workshops, where convicts would work under state supervision. But although a growing number of prisoners were now working for the state, the convict lease system continued to be used as well, with all its attendant inhumanity. There seemed to be no overall plan or guiding philosophy for the criminal justice system, except that it not impose a burden on the state's taxpayers.

Education

Education fared slightly better. The Constitution of 1876 turned the matter of education over to local communities. These communities had no direct taxing powers, but they could draw upon their share of the common school fund, composed of monies realized from the sale of assigned lands and a $1 annual tax on adult males. The schools were segregated by law, which until 1890 specified that black schools must have equal access to the school fund. But there are records of too many complaints of poor training and supplies for African American students for there to have been equal distribution of funds to black schools. Although illiteracy figures for blacks did drop from 75 to 45 percent in the period, Texas ranked fifth among southern states in enrollment of black schoolchildren.

Reform groups attacked the inadequate schooling of all children and asked that the state take control of education. The matter boiled to the surface in 1879 when, citing public debt, Governor Roberts vetoed the school appropriations bill. Public indignation followed, forcing a constitutional amendment in 1883 that allowed the state to support public schools and authorized local school districts to levy taxes. The next year the legislature passed the Law of 1884, which completely reorganized the public school system. The law mandated a partial return to a centralized education system with an elective state superintendent, county school districts under the supervision of county judges, teacher certification, and regular record keeping. It further provided that local districts could tax themselves to support the common schools. However, some fifty-odd school districts were exempt from this law. These "independent" districts already had successfully functioning schools, frequently maintained by a local civic organization. Under the new law, the period of required school attendance for Texans was raised from ages eight to fourteen to ages eight to sixteen.

The success of the Law of 1884 was debatable. The rural character of the state and its rapid increase in population created a scattered settlement pattern, and small farming areas had trouble establishing educational leadership or a viable tax base. City schools, with a permanent population base behind them, offered a much better education than did rural ones. In 1900, urban school districts spent an average of $8.35 per child, while rural school districts appropriated less than $3.34 per child. The school year for urban children consisted of 162 days, compared to 98 days in rural districts; and city teachers earned almost twice as much as their country counterparts. Nevertheless, the Law of 1884 laid a basis for the school system that had been dismantled in 1876. The legislature, urged on by citizens and such reformers as Barnas Sears (the first general agent of the Peabody Fund, a northern philanthropic agency) and O. N. Hollingsworth (secretary of the State Board of Education) would continue to grapple with educational problems.

Higher education in Texas enjoyed better success. The first public college, the Agricultural and Mechanical College of Texas, opened its doors in 1876 as a result of the Morrill Act of 1862, by which each state received funds from the sale of federal public lands in order to establish a college for practical training in agricultural and mechanical arts. Authorized by the legislature on April 17, 1871, and located near Bryan, the college originally was designated as a branch of the not-yet-born University of Texas. The Morrill Act required that the all-male school provide military training. Farmers complained early on that the school taught too many liberal arts courses and too much military drill. Led by A. J. Rose, worthy master of the state Grange and chair of the board of directors of the college, the proponents of A. and M. College eventually won the support of rural Texans. The Texas Agricultural Experiment Station began in 1888. It aided Texas agribusiness and helped validate scientific agriculture for farmers. Lawrence Sullivan Ross, the former governor of the state, took over the college presidency in 1891. His political acumen earned higher appropriations for the college and increased its credibility.

The University of Texas was chartered in 1839, when the Republic passed an act that set aside 231,400 acres of land for two universities, but the Civil War, Reconstruction, and controversies over public lands delayed the university's opening. In 1880, the State Teachers' Association sent a report to Governor Roberts with a plan of organization for the university. The legislature responded the next year and provided for the establishment of the school. Voters picked Austin as the site of the main university and Galveston for the medical school. The former commenced classes in 1883 and the latter in 1891, when it replaced Texas Medical College. Ashbel Smith, a pioneer in Texas education, served as the first president of the U.T. board, and O. M. Roberts, the former governor, as professor of law and the first head of the department. The university was to be financed by general revenues as well as the permanent fund, which derived from the sale or lease of fifty of the leagues granted in 1839, 1 million acres granted by the Constitution of 1876, and a second million in 1883. The legislature appropriated no maintenance funds for the school until 1889. By the end of the century the university had both academic and law departments.

By law, Texas A. and M. could admit no black students. The legislature provided for a Negro agricultural college in 1876. However, a lack of demand for an agricultural education for blacks prompted it to become a college for training teachers. Named the Prairie View Normal Institute, it opened in 1879 under the control of the Agricultural and Mechanical College's board of directors. Ten years later, industrial arts had been added to the school's curriculum.

Sam Houston State Normal School, restricted to white students, began operation in 1879 in Huntsville, Texas. When the Peabody Board offered the state $6,000 in matching funds to establish a model teacher-training college, Huntsville donated the site. Sam Houston State served as the institutional guide to the other normal schools, which were governed until 1949 by a single board of regents appointed by the governor.

TEXAS POLITICS, 1876–1890

A number of factors explain the conservative control of Texas from 1875 to 1891 and the supremacy of the Democratic party. Past allegiance to the Confederacy blended with the New South's creed of celebrating the past to create an almost religious devotion to "The Lost Cause." The period featured the rise of fraternal organizations based on Confederate symbols, and these organizations and their local communities sponsored ex-Confederate picnics, holidays, and funerals—all designed to honor the Confederate dead and their cause. To choose a Republican or a third-party candidate over the official Democratic nominee in an election meant for white voters a repudiation of the party of their fathers. And the cultural heritage of the Democratic party lingered long after this period.

Furthermore, party machinery and election laws worked for the benefit of Democratic conservatives. Democratic nominees for state and national offices were chosen by state nominating conventions composed of local party members. Political power brokers sought compromise candidates who would appeal to these delegates, usually local elites, and thus Texas's nominees were frequently even more conservative than the constituencies at large. The party leadership would then use party unity as a rallying cry to defeat any Republican or third-party candidates who challenged the Democratic nominees in the general elections for state or federal offices. Local elites usually controlled regional politics and captured local offices. They could meet as an unofficial group and nominate a slate of delegates to county party conventions, which, in turn, sent the delegates to state nominating conventions.

Sometimes, either through lack of party organization or because an independent or third-party challenger actually bothered to run, these Democratic machines lost a contested election to an outsider. The elites, however, usually kept a tight reign on the election process by occupying the offices that certified voter eligibility and vote-count totals. The state had no voter registration law until 1891—which originally applied only to cities of 10,000 or more people—and no secret ballot until the twentieth century. This skewed setup encouraged local Democratic bosses to use fraudulent methods to fix elections for themselves and their flunkies.

Finally, the agrarian wing of the Democratic party, which called for extensive reforms such as railroad regulation and expanded state services, was sympathetic also with the idea of low taxes. Consequently, Texas farmers were divided over how much reform legislation was needed and whether to achieve their goals within or outside of the Democratic party.

CONSERVATIVE DEMOCRATIC DOMINANCE, 1876–1886

Governor Richard Coke was unanimously renominated by the Democratic state convention in 1876. He won support from rural progressives, who saw him as the man who had defeated Reconstruction, as well as from entrepreneurs, for his promise to entice more railroads and corporations into the state. Citing, as usual, the need for party unity, the convention renominated Lieutenant Governor Richard B. Hubbard, who lacked the personal appeal and popularity of Coke. The general election to choose state officers was a landslide for the Democrats. When the newly elected legislature convened in Austin, it turned first to selecting a U.S. senator to replace the Republican incumbent, Morgan C. Hamilton, who had completed his term. Coke announced his candidacy and, upon his selection, resigned the governorship in 1877 to serve as one of Texas's U.S. senators (until 1895). The other U.S. senator, Samuel Bell Maxey, who openly bragged of his support for secession, held office until 1887. Then Congressman John H. Reagan, who had fought for years for a law to establish a federal Interstate Commerce Commission (ICC), saw legislation enacted that year to do so, and he announced that he was ready to move to the Senate. In a close campaign, Reagan garnered enough support in the legislature to unseat Maxey. Reagan served in the upper house until 1891, when he resigned to serve as the head of the newly created Texas Railroad Commission.

Although Lieutenant Governor Hubbard had ascended to the governorship after Coke's departure, he soon faced criticism for his failure to pay off the state debt, and several challengers came forward to contest him at the 1878 nominating convention. Now the delegates turned to a compromise candidate, nominating for the gubernatorial spot Oran M. Roberts, chief justice of the state supreme court. Roberts, representing the conservative wing of the Democratic party, handily won the general election. He served two terms as governor but refused to try for a third. Nevertheless, the conservative Democrats continued to control state politics through the successive administrations of Governors John Ireland (1883–1887) and Lawrence Sullivan Ross (1887–1891). These conservative chief executives brought no substantial reform to the state's economic system.

Possibly the major accomplishment of this time occurred during the Ireland administration, when the Texas State Capitol in Austin was completed. The legislature appropriated 3,050,000 acres of land in 1879 to finance the building of a new capitol. The state then awarded the construction contract to an English company, which hoped to profit from its work through the sale of its appropriated lands. In May 1888, the beautiful new building opened officially. Modeled on the capitol in Washington, D.C., the structure is classical in design and shaped like a Greek cross. Meanwhile, the English syndicate, unable to find buyers for the vast public lands it had acquired, eventually used the grant to establish the famous XIT Ranch.

For the poor and the dispossessed, the conservative Democratic governors failed even to raise any issues of significance. In order to find anyone who would fight for meaningful political changes for the underclass, one needs to turn to the period's opposition parties—the Republicans and the Greenbackers.

THE CHALLENGERS, 1876–1886

The Republican party reached its zenith of power, if not size, during Reconstruction. Black voters composed the majority of the party's constituency. No suffrage restrictions came out of Redemption, and approximately 50,000 blacks voted in 1886. After the death of E. J. Davis, Norris Wright Cuney, an African American from Galveston, claimed the headship of the party because of his influence over black voters. Cuney, an able leader, served as sergeant-at-arms in the Twelfth Legislature (1870–1871) and as collector of customs for the Port of Galveston, 1889–1893. Political patronage and shrewd leadership protected his position in the party. Some white Republicans resented black Texans' domination of the party and organized so-called lily-white factions, which hoped to seize the patronage plums that the national Republican party dispensed. The lily-whites, therefore, favored no fusion with any other party.

But the strength of the state Republican party lay in the Black Belt of East Texas and Gulf Coast. From Redemption to 1898, voters from those regions elected approximately sixteen state legislators and numerous local officials. Whites modified the election code in 1879 to forbid the use of colored paper ballots, thereby eliminating the Republican party's identification of a straight ticket for illiterate blacks and whites. By the mid-1880s, too, various counties organized white men's associations, which often used intimidation and election fraud to preclude the election of African Americans to local offices.

The Greenback party was the first third-party challenge to the Democrats' political hegemony. The new party was organized in response to federal monetary policies that were causing a drastic contraction (or deflation) of the nation's money supply. The roots of the problem lay in the Civil War. During the war, the U.S. government had taken the radical step of taking the country off the gold standard. To meet wartime needs for money, the government had issued paper money, nicknamed "greenbacks," which were not backed by gold in the U.S. treasury. The greenbacks had caused some inflation, but they had also allowed for a rapid expansion of the economy. When the war was over, Wall Street bankers, who had financed much of the war effort, wanted to be repaid not in greenbacks but in gold, which was more valuable. Indeed, they owned millions of dollars in greenbacks, which they hoped to be able to redeem at face value in gold. In 1875, Congress responded to their demands by passing the Specie Resumption Act, which would return the nation to the gold standard by 1879. When the country returned to the gold standard, the amount of money in circulation declined precipitously, which caused interest rates to skyrocket. Farmers were particularly hard hit by these developments. High interest rates were only part of the problem; ongoing deflation of the currency also causes dollars to become more valuable over time. Since most farmers must borrow money at the beginning of the year to finance the coming year's operations, they found that at the end of each year they had to repay their loans in dollars more valuable than the ones they had borrowed. In essence, on top of the already high interest rates, there was an additional hidden interest rate caused by deflation. The Greenback party's goal was to reverse these policies that were leading farmers to the brink of financial disaster.

The Greenbackers recruited from the more-radical farmers in Texas and courted fusion with the Republican party. The party specifically proposed that the federal government issue greenbacks until at least $55 per capita were in circulation. Greenbackers argued that this inflation of the currency (then estimated at $35 per head) would drive the price of agricultural commodities up by about one-third. Nationally, the party also advocated an income tax, an Australian or secret ballot, direct election of U.S. senators, and, in Texas, railroad regulation, a better school system, elimination of convict leasing, a reduction in the salaries of government officials, and the wholesale elimination of useless offices in state government.

The party held its first convention in 1878 in Waco, with the delegates nominating William H. Hamman for governor. Roberts easily defeated both Hamman and the Republican nominee, A. B. Norton. Greenbackers did, however, win ten seats in the legislature and elect George W. "Wash" Jones of Bastrop to Congress. Hamman received the Greenbacker nomination again in 1880. E. J. Davis, who had supported fusion with the Greenbackers in 1878, agreed to head a separate Republican ticket in 1880. The Democrats simply renominated Roberts, who won again by a wide margin.

Greenbackers, now a distant third in voter support, retained some strength in East Texas, the Cross Timbers, and other poor, white farming counties; Republicans, meanwhile, continued to run well in the Black Belt. Increasingly, an alliance of the Greenbackers and the Republican forces made political sense,

Top: Norris Wright Cuney (R); Bottom: George W. "Wash" Jones (Grnbk.).
Both at The Center for American History, The University of Texas at Austin,
CN 01074A & CN 07326

and the two parties fused in support of "Wash" Jones's race for governor in 1882. Jones, an excellent campaigner known for his oratorical skills, put some excitement and personal charisma into an otherwise drab political period. Having always been a political maverick, a Unionist who served in the Confederate army, a Democratic lieutenant governor from 1866 to 1867, and now an independent, Jones ran on an appeal to economic and racial out-groups. Although he lost the general election to Ireland, it was the closest such contest of the decade. Nevertheless, the Greenback party strength peaked that year, and attempts to continue the fusion between the Greenbackers and the Republicans failed. Although Jones again ran for governor in 1884, this time he lost by a wider margin to Ireland.

Shortly thereafter, the Greenback party faded away, and the next Democratic governor, Lawrence Sullivan "Sul" Ross, faced little political opposition. His success partially rested upon his record as an Indian fighter and Civil War general, and the lack of any coherent third-party challenge. The most divisive issue now was prohibition. A united front of prohibitionists asked by 1884 that the legislature replace the local option law with one that outlawed the sale of alcoholic beverages throughout the state. The United Friends of Temperance and its juvenile affiliate, the Bands of Hope, joined the powerful and recently arrived (in Texas) Women's Christian Temperance Union (WCTU) to mount a persuasive and powerful political campaign to force the Democratic party to comply with their wishes. The prohibitionists could count on the support of J. B. Cranfill, the important Baptist editor and minister, S. A. Hayden of the *Texas Baptist Herald*, Senators John B. Reagan and Sam Bell Maxey, and many members of the Grange and the newly organized Farmers' Alliance.

In 1886, the prohibitionists decided that they could not rely upon the Democratic party to overcome the antiprohibition stance of such leaders as Ross, James S. Hogg, and Congressman Roger Q. Mills. Therefore, the ardent prohibitionist E. L. Dohoney called for a convention at Dallas to organize a third party. Dohoney, an ex-Greenbacker who would later help organize the Populist party, garnered the gubernatorial nomination. Now the Democratic party closed ranks, and Dohoney received only 20,000 votes for governor. The next year, prohibitionists and their supporters forced the legislature to submit a prohibition amendment to the voters of Texas. The antiprohibitionists continued with a platform of governmental restraint in private affairs. In the end, the amendment failed to pass by over 90,000 votes, but the issue of prohibition would resurface in the twentieth century.

The voices of reform swirled about Texas in the mid-1880s, but no clear-cut consensus emerged on how reform organizations should identify and carry out their priorities. Greenbackers, prohibitionists, Knights of Labor, Grangers, progressive Democrats, black Texans, and the Farmers' Alliance all wanted a more responsive state government. Their demands meant that Ross would be the last of the New South conservatives to control Texas politics. Yet the issues of reform still needed some vehicle to articulate them. The farmers' organizations served as that instrument, pushing the Democratic party into accepting moderate reforms and mobilizing a third party that wanted more-radical solutions to the problems facing the state.

Agrarian Organizations, 1878–1890

In 1867, Oliver H. Kelley, an employee of the U.S. Department of Agriculture, founded the Patrons of Husbandry, commonly called the Grange. He conceived of the Patrons as a secret fraternal society that would offer social and educational benefits to its membership, composed mostly of family farmers. The Patrons of Husbandry had a loose national governing board, but each state Grange formulated most of the policies for its local lodges. As with many such organizations in the period, state officials had little control over the actions of the subordinate Granges. The local lodges, acting under broad national and state guidelines, selected their own membership and defined their own priorities. Consequently, the agricultural depression of the 1870s spurred state and local Granges into changing the major goals of the parent organization from social and educational ones to the establishment of economic cooperatives for farmers. The state lecturers, persons paid by the governing board to organize subordinate and local Granges, soon discovered that potential members asked first about the financial benefits that members of the order could expect to enjoy and second about the organization's social trappings. Since the lecturers received pay based on the number of new members they recruited, they soon spoke of economic cooperation to the near exclusion of any other topic. The Grange had been more or less moribund until the downturn in farm prices, but its new focus on monetary benefits to its members spurred 800,000 men and women to join the national fraternity. Even though the national Grange rules specified that the fraternity was apolitical, it encouraged its newly membership to take political action. Indeed, the subordinate Granges in the Midwestern states spun off viable third parties that advocated reform and successfully combined with small shippers to establish state railroad regulatory commissions.

Because of the lack of a centralized, national control, state Grange leaders quarreled among themselves over the exact direction that state Patrons should take. William Lang, the conservative worthy master of the Texas State Grange, wanted the organization to remain distinct from third parties, work within the traditional political system, and do nothing to antagonize merchants or railroads. Progressive farmers within the organization listened to Long's political appeals but rejected his economic ones. They insisted that the creation of economic cooperatives that featured pay-as-you-go rules would enable members to rise above poverty and become prosperous, middle-class farmers. After Lang left the organization, the progressive wing of the Grange seized the initiative and did indeed create cooperative ventures. Led by Archibald J. Rose, the Grange founded the Texas Cooperative Association in 1878. The Association's sales aggregated

$560,282.16 in 1883, handling 16,045 bales of cotton for 150 Grange stores. Since the cooperative's stores could not operate without credit, the Association extended credit to them and bought on credit from wholesalers. When the fierce drought years from 1885 to 1886 came along, farmers could not pay their stores, which in turn could not pay the Association, and the whole thing collapsed. The Association limped along until the 1890s, but it did not affect the lives of many farmers after 1887. Although individual Patrons may have joined such third-party movements as the Greenback party, the subordinate lodges never mobilized their collective membership into vehicles of political protest, as had occurred elsewhere. Instead, A. J. Rose and his Grange following exercised a moderately progressive agrarian influence within the Democratic party. And even after Grange membership declined, the organization's political philosophy proved helpful in mobilizing support for James Hogg.

By the mid-1880s, a new organization, the Texas Farmers' Alliance, was re-placing the Patrons of Husbandry as the mouthpiece for agrarianism. From its beginnings, this organization differed radically from the older Grange. The lat-ter had come to the South from a national organization, which had garnered its leaders from a higher economic class of farmers. The Alliance, on the other hand, was a grass-roots organization that first formed in the marginal farmlands of the Cross Timbers and drew its membership from voluntary associations that varied from vigilante groups to such social institutions as schools, churches, Ma-sonic lodges, old Grangers, and newly organized local farmers' clubs. Although it also emphasized the social and economic advancement of farmers, the Alli-ance never denied an interest in influencing politics. Yet this forced an inter-nal division within its ranks, with movement toward a third-party nomination driving the more-conservative members out of the organization.

The Farmers' Alliance had originated as a local organization in Lampasas, Texas, in 1877. This lodge had disbanded in 1878 ,when some of the Lampasas alliancemen threw their support to the Greenback party. At this point, Will-iam T. Baggett, a schoolteacher and member of the Grange as well as the Lampasas Alliance, moved to Parker County, taking with him the constitution of his defunct alliance, and immediately organized a school for farm children and a suballiance. Converts recruited converts, and in 1881 and 1882, local lecturers, compensated out of organizational fees, recruited more members throughout the Cross Timbers region. In 1884, this so-called Texas Farmers' Al-liance funded a traveling lecturer, S. O. Dawes, to move across Texas restoring flagging Alliances and organizing new ones. Dawes's rhetoric was more politi-cal than that of Grange organizers, as he attacked monopolies and unrespon-sive politicians.

By 1886, the Texas Farmers' Alliance claimed a membership of 100,000, and other organizations began to flirt with it. The president of the Alliance and two of its newspapers supported prohibition, suggesting to the *Dallas Morning News* that the Alliance and the "Drys" might unite into a viable third-party platform.

Moreover, some local lodges had cooperated with the Knights of Labor during the Great Southwest strike, implying a possible farmer-laborer party. Now, local third parties, such as the Commonwealth Party in Jack County, ran candidates against the establishment Democratic party. The Alliance members constituted the majority votes of the local groups. That year, too, black farmers in Houston organized the Colored Alliance and elected Robert M. Humphrey, a white minister, as its superintendent. The Colored Alliance posed no social threat to whites; it professed to want economic independence for its members, not social equality. Any melding of dissatisfied poor whites and blacks into a third party threatened Democratic hegemony; thus, the Populist party would later make overtures to the Colored Alliance membership.

By this time, the Democratic party fully realized the political dangers afoot. Its concern was heightened by the 1886 drought. That summer a bill to aid stricken Texas farmers passed Congress only to be vetoed by President Grover Cleveland, a Democrat. The president deemed such aid an unwarranted central government action. Some Texas farmers, mostly members of the Alliance, now argued that the time had come to challenge the federal and state political structures. Dawes, anxious to avoid the collapse of the Texas Farmers' Alliance, as had occurred in Lampasas, proposed the "Dawes Formula": the Alliance as an organization would only foster farmer education and cooperation, but individual Alliancemen were free to combine with their neighbors for political action.

The Dawes Formula set the stage for the 1886 state Alliance convention at Cleburne, where the majority endorsed a platform that began each statement with "We demand!" These "Cleburne Demands" included recognition of labor unions, regulation of railroads, a revision of the banking system, inflation, an interstate commerce commission, prison reform, and legislation that would outlaw speculation in agricultural futures and land. Conservative Alliancemen, who saw these demands as a challenge to the Democratic party, left the convention and split into an educational organization calling itself the Grand State Alliance.

In 1887, therefore, the new Farmers' Alliance president, Charles W. Macune, a moderate, presided over a divided organization. A self-read lawyer and physician, Macune announced that he had contacted the Louisiana Farmers' Union and that a merger with that union and the Arkansas Wheel would herald the beginnings of a national organization, The Farmers' Alliance and Cooperative Union of America, commonly called the Southern Alliance. Macune maintained that the new Southern Alliance would pressure Congress to bring relief to southern farmers, and he proposed that Texas farmers create an Alliance Exchange that would revolutionize marketing by having all members sign joint notes—essentially I.O.U.'s—to borrow money from banks, then purchase goods and supplies from a half-million-dollar corporation located in Dallas. The Exchange was to replace the middlemen in the chain of trade and extend credit, consequently addressing, unlike the Grange, the problems of tenant farmers. Macune accepted the post of manager of the Exchange, and it opened for business in September 1887.

But banks refused to accept joint notes, and within a year Macune's plan for large-scale economic cooperation had failed, convincing him only the federal government could solve the problems of poor farmers and their need for credit. At an 1889 national Alliance convention, he outlined a proposal he called the Subtreasury Plan, which called for Congress to build a nationwide network of warehouses where farmers could deposit their crops at harvest time and then receive low-interest government loans. The government would store the crops and only release them onto world markets when prices were sufficiently high. The loans would essentially be made in greenbacks, which would expand the money supply nationally, further easing the credit crunch.

The problem, of course, with the Subtreasury Plan, was that it called for an even larger role for government than the Alliance had previously envisioned with its other demands. The Democratic party promptly repudiated the idea, and many Alliancemen turned directly to third-party politics, where some of them had meant to be all along. As farmers' hard times turned to outright depression in the 1890s, these men organized the Populist party, a national third-party movement that, as will be seen, became the most serious political challenge to Democratic control of Texas between Reconstruction and the rise of the modern Republicans.

Politics, 1886–1900

The bellicosity of the Cleburne Demands and the growing third-party inclination of Texas farmers finally encouraged Democrats to respond politically to the agrarians' needs; that response, however, was a moderate one. Nationally, Texas Democrats took the lead in reform. Congressman Roger Q. Mills fought for lower tariffs to reduce the price of imported products and force domestic manufacturers to lower their prices in order to compete. Then, as mentioned, Senator John H. Reagan coauthored the Interstate Commerce Act of 1887, the first federal regulation of railroads. The Texas Democrats moved away from President Cleveland and endorsed the free coinage of silver, a measure to mint silver coins and thereby inflate the currency. Beginning in 1886, the progressive wing of the state Democratic party advocated legislation to encourage farmers to settle western lands, correct railroad and corporate abuses, and change the banking system into something resembling the later federal reserve system. Clearly, reform elements demanded that the Democratic party favor an active rather than a passive state government. Leading these demands for reform into action was James S. Hogg.

Hogg won his first statewide office in 1886. As early as 1889, the young attorney general was rumored as a potential gubernatorial candidate. His tenure as attorney general (1887–1891) and then as governor (1891–1895), represented a change in Texas politics. The son of a Confederate general, Hogg had not fought in the Civil War and seemed less bound by tradition than his contemporaries. He read the law, farmed some, and had worked as a printer and typesetter. The thirty-five-year-old attorney general identified with the common people, and his understanding of and sympathy with their plight made him very popular with moderate progressive farmers. A fierce debater and a good campaigner, Hogg was a formidable political opponent who enjoyed shedding his coat at rural picnics and gatherings in order to take to the stump to decry the avarice of corporations and monopolies. Undoubtedly, the rise of the Alliance and the threat posed by third parties forced Hogg and other progressive Democrats to the left. Certainly, he accepted traditional southern fears of the coercive powers of the federal government. Yet he led a new group of young Democrats who would use state powers to regulate railroads and trusts and prevent foreign ownership of Texas public lands.

As attorney general, Hogg wielded the powers of his new office vigorously. He fought to protect the public domain and set it aside for public institutions and school funds. As the state's lawyer, he instituted suits against railroads, large corporations, and ranchers who leased public land. He forced the return of 1.5 million acres to the public domain and compelled land companies to sell their land to settlers within a certain time limit. He won fame and notoriety by demanding that out-of-state insurance companies comply with Texas law, and he drove "wildcat" insurance companies from the state. Commissioner of Agriculture, Insurance, and Statistics L. L. Foster estimated that Hogg's stance saved Texas citizens $250,000 a year. Hogg's battles against monopolies and unscrupulous companies earned him widespread support from farmers and legitimate businessmen.

The majority of agriculturalists' enthusiasm for Hogg, however, emanated from his attacks upon what farmers saw as monopolies—railroads and trusts. Farmers believed that the railroads, cotton processors, and manufacturers of farming supplies transferred the rightful profits of their labor from them to middlemen. They demanded that state agencies interfere in their behalf. The young attorney general complied by assisting in the writing of antitrust legislation (the second such law in the nation) that outlawed corporate combinations in restraint of trade, either by fixing prices or limiting production; farm cooperatives and labor unions were exempted from prosecution. He activated the constitutional definition of railroads as public carriers, breaking up the Texas Traffic Association, and he compelled Jay Gould to resume operating the East Line Railroad, then in receivership. He also coerced railroads to establish or restore their headquarters within the state and to keep depots and tracks in good repair. Finally, judging the powers of the state inadequate to protect public interest, Hogg ran for governor in 1890 on a platform of "Hogg and a Commission," a promise to establish a railroad regulatory agency.

The constitutional legality of such an agency, however, remained in question. In 1889 the legislature had decided that a constitutional amendment should be submitted to the voters. Hogg campaigned for the amendment's passage, and in 1890 easily won the Democratic party convention's nomination for governor, and trounced the Republican, Webster Flanagan, in the general election. After voters ratified the constitutional amendment by more than 100,000 votes, Hogg moved quickly to create the Railroad Commission. The legislature established the Commission in 1891 and empowered it to set rates and fares and, as Hogg advocated, made its members appointive rather than elective. Hogg personally selected the three railroad commissioners, including John H. Reagan, without consulting the Farmers' Alliance. His actions outraged the Alliance, which now campaigned for an elected Commission, and spurred the left wing of the organization to move toward third-party action. By a subsequent constitutional amendment, therefore, offices of the Railroad Commission became elective in 1894. Seven railroads sued in 1892 to prevent the Commission from enforcing its rate-making powers. The trial immobilized the Commission until the U.S. Supreme Court upheld its constitutionality in 1894 in *Reagan v. Farmers Loan and Trust Co.*

As governor, Hogg championed five major pieces of legislation. In addition to the Railroad Commission, the "Hogg laws" included: the railroad stock and bond laws, authorizing the Commission to regulate how much stock a railroad could issue; a law forcing land corporations to sell off their land within fifteen years; the Alien Land Law, forbidding land grants to foreign corporations; and an act that restricted the amount of bond issues undertaken by county and municipal authorities, a measure to hold down indebtedness. But Hogg's influence extended past these economic reforms. He promoted prison reform, advocated longer school terms, supported the University of Texas and the Agricultural and Mechanical College of Texas, and, unfortunately, forced the railroads to segregate their facilities. He could have become a U.S. senator in 1896. Instead he left office in debt and resolved to go into business to guarantee financial security for his family. Through wise land and petroleum investments and his work as a corporate lawyer, Hogg accomplished that goal, too.

POPULISM

Political factions challenged Hogg during his successful tenure in office. His reputation as a reformer and his general popularity with rural populations subdued any potential political threat from the Alliance. Within that organization, however, militant radicals wanted more than regulatory reform; they thought that the economic system needed surgery, not palliatives, and they advocated government ownership of railroads, abolition of the national banking system, and establishment of the subtreasury system. The Subtreasury Plan, as mentioned, would have allowed farmers to store staple crops in government warehouses and receive loans against the market value of these crops in the form of government notes that could circulate as currency. As such, the subtreasury was an attack upon national banks and an endorsement of earlier Greenbacker ideology. In addition, the Alliance's militant radicals campaigned for a wide variety of reforms that would make the political and economic system more open, democratic, and fair. Among these were an income tax, an eight-hour workday, the direct election of U.S. senators, the free coinage of silver, the secret ballot, referendum, and recall. Texas Populists took no stand on woman suffrage and prohibition, probably fearing the divisiveness of the issues.

But the issues did not tell the whole story. The Democratic party could and did endorse some of the planks in the Populist platform. It could not or would not accept the Subtreasury Plan; in 1891 it specifically rejected it. After Hogg turned down an elective Commission and denied the Alliance a seat on an appointive one, future Populists used that issue against the governor. Although Hogg then compromised on an elective Commission, he could not compromise on the subtreasury, for the idea signified the intent of the dispossessed to use the government to correct economic injustices. In this sense, Populism was more than a political platform; it represented a crusade of rural Americans and a class awareness that appealed to the have-nots, persons who felt that the American economic system had failed them and that the existing parties offered no means of redress. Populism was a complex mix of old and new ideas. Populists believed that they were being true to the democratic ideals of Jefferson and Jackson, who had championed the "common man" and denounced monopolistic banks and corporations. In this sense, their movement was conservative and in keeping with American traditions of republicanism. At the same time, though, the Populists believed that the rise of large-scale industrial capitalism since the Civil War had enabled the monopoly power of banks and corporations to grow so great that in order to fight back, the common man had to turn to the only powerful institution that the people could control: the federal government. Hence their demands that the government create credit, inflate the currency, curb the abuses of banks and railroads, and make the political system more responsive. The ends were the same as those of the old Jeffersonians or Jacksonians—protecting the freedom of the common man—but the means—using the power of government— were radical, if not revolutionary. Through its experiments with economic cooperatives, its lecturers, newspapers, and meetings, the Farmers' Alliance had been the institution most responsible for preparing farmers to make this radical break with political tradition. The Subtreasury Plan became the most powerful symbol of the new party and of its political radicalism. Those who agreed with it voted Populist. Those who did not remained Democrats.

The Populist crusade relied on stump speakers and party newspapers to turn its goals into a secular religion. Its leaders used the Bible as the touchstone of their speeches and recruited in camp-meeting style, changing the words of familiar hymns to sing their political cause. They used rhetoric to identify themselves as being of the people, choosing to use the language, dress, and manners of the country folk. Among those able men were H. S. P. "Stump" Ashby, a former Methodist minister; W. R. Lamb, a leader of the Texas State Federation of Labor; Thomas L. Nugent, a Democratic judge; James H. "Cyclone" Davis, a spellbinding orator with strong Protestant religious affiliations; Ben Terrell, a national lecturer for the Southern Alliance; and Jerome C. Kearby, an old Greenbacker candidate for Congress. Nugent ran for governor in 1892 and 1894, as did Kearby in 1896.

For Texas Populism to succeed it had to gain the support of black voters, concentrated in the Black Belt of East Texas and the poor-soil region of central West Texas. To create a statewide coalition, the Populists formed a biracial party. While they did not profess a belief in racial equality, they did promise a parity in economic matters that affected social classes, such as education and relief from tenant farming. J. B. Rayner, a black Texan and an ex-Republican from Calvert, served on the state executive committee of the party and spoke to integrated audiences. Other blacks staffed local executive committees and held local offices. The Populist platform promised both equal protection under the laws and a guaranteed right of suffrage, regardless of race, color, or creed.

The campaigns of the 1890s grew increasingly strident as conservative Democrats, Hogg reformers, and Populists warred for control of the state. George Clark, a former Confederate officer from Alabama who had served both as attorney general and secretary of state for Texas, led the conservatives. He was closely identified with the railroads and big business interests. At the famous "street car barn convention," Clark led a group of anti-Hogg Democrats, or Gold Democrats, out of the party and declared his candidacy for governor in 1892. Black leader Norris Wright Cuney endorsed Clark rather than the Populist candidate, in an attempt to keep blacks from leaving the Republicans in order to join the third party. Hogg reclaimed the Democratic nomination, and Nugent led the Populist ticket. Both the Populists and the Democrats appealed to black voters through such promises as (Populism's) economic improvement or (Hogg's) antilynching bill, but the Democrats used violence and vote fraud to counteract the appeal of Populism to black voters. Nonetheless, in the election of 1892 Populists won eight seats in the state house of representatives, one in the senate, and numerous local offices. In the governor's race, Nugent (108,483 votes) lost to Hogg (190,486) and ran behind Clark (133,395).

By this time the Alliance had recruited 200,000 members, many of them potential Populist voters. To counteract the appeal of the third party, Governor Hogg now sought to fulfill his political promises and reconcile the division within the Democratic party, and an uneasy truce between the party's warring factions was fashioned in 1894. Edward M. House, an adroit party organizer who never held public office but had effectively managed Hogg's campaigns, now threw his support behind Charles A. Culberson, the state's attorney general. Culberson agreed with Hogg on state politics but was neither as inclined toward free silver nor as anti-Cleveland as was the governor, who preferred Reagan as the party's next gubernatorial nominee. House shrewdly led Culberson to the nomination and served as a behind-the-scenes leader of the party for the next twenty years. The Populists renominated Nugent. Although Culberson won the gubernatorial election by close to 60,000 votes, the Populists elected to state office twenty-two house members and two senators in 1894. In addition, the Republican and Prohibitionist candidates collected enough votes to make the new governor a plurality victor.

Two years later, with Republican support, the Populist gubernatorial candidate Kearby came the closest to unseating the Democrats, losing to Culberson by less than 60,000 votes. The campaign of 1896 on the state level was a particularly bitter one. Democrats charged Populists with racial betrayal, attempting to restore black Reconstruction, anarchism, and communism. Local Democratic party supporters intimidated voters, stuffed ballot boxes, and threatened and actually shot Populist organizers. On the national level, the Democratic party's move towards free silver and low tariffs encouraged some national Populist party leaders "to fuse" with the Democrats to endorse William Jennings Bryan for the presidency. Most Texas Populists, who came from the tradition of organizing the Alliance along the frontier and supported the subtreasury, were "midroaders" and not "fusionists." These men wanted to nominate national candidates specifically for the Populist party, but they lost out in the 1896 national Populist convention to those fusionists who gave the Populist party's presidential nomination to Bryan. Bryan's subsequent loss to Republican William McKinley left the Populists with no national leader, since their chosen candidate, Bryan, headed the Democrats, and with no national platform, since Bryan did not endorse the subtreasury.

Populists attempted to regroup after the 1896 election, but a measure of prosperity returned to the nation briefly after 1896, relieving some degree of agrarian discontent. Furthermore, the contentious campaign left both local and national Populist leaders disorganized and with no real political vehicle with which to begin another crusade. The Democracy of Bryan endorsed many of the old demands of Grangers, Greenbackers, and Alliancemen—although not the Subtreasury Plan or government ownership of the railroads. After a period of political alienation, some of the Populists returned to the state Democratic party and along with reform Democrats forged a "progressive" coalition that fought the political battles of the twentieth century. Other former Populists dropped out of politics permanently or joined the socialist movement.

The residue of the political contests of the 1890s shaped Texas politics for the next fifty years. The Populists had enjoyed some success in local campaigns. As a result of these bitter, often illegal, contests, white men's associations were organized in counties with large black populations. These associations attempted to remove the black voter from politics. Following this example, all-white primaries developed throughout the state. These devices allowed local county Democratic executive committees to force prospective voters in the Democratic party primaries and conventions to swear "I am a white Democratic voter. . . ." Obviously, those who could not do so were thereby disenfranchised. By 1903 it was accepted that the county executive committee could define who could and who could not qualify to vote in their county in the statewide primary, which was mandated by the Terrell Election laws (1903, 1907). In most counties in Texas, African Americans could still vote in the general election—which was meaningless in a one-party state—but not in the Democratic party primaries, which effectively chose state office holders. In 1902, Texas voters approved of a poll tax that disenfranchised many poor whites and blacks and further limited the possible third-party challenges to Democratic hegemony. Texans did not resort, as did most southern states, to literacy tests, grandfather clauses, and property requirements to prevent a reoccurrence of Populist-like challenges to the Democratic party. Probably the heterogeneity of the state's population by this time made such a course politically unworkable. But the legislature did continue to pass Jim Crow laws after it mandated segregated railroad facilities. By the twentieth century, Texas, like many southern states, had erected an elaborate legal code that racially segregated public and private facilities.

TEXAS AT CENTURY'S END

The political battles of the late nineteenth eroded much of the New South's concept of a passive state. During Culberson's four-year tenure as governor, he blended Hogg's reform tendencies with conservatism. Governor Culberson vetoed more legislation than did any other previous governor, including new reform measures, citing government economies as the reason for the vetoes. On the other hand, he enforced the 1889 antitrust act against Waters-Pierce Oil Company, a Standard Oil Company subsidiary based outside the state and one that would return illegally in 1900 and star in a famous political controversy. He also sponsored tax relief for victims of the 1893 depression, supported an increase in the powers of the Railroad Commission, and signed laws regulating labor relations and public lands.

Edward M. House, who later won national fame as an adviser to President Woodrow Wilson, gained considerable control of the state Democratic party. Texas may not have yet seen his equal as a political manager. House shared his power with Joseph Weldon Bailey, a congressman from 1891 to 1901 and then a U.S. senator from 1901 to 1913. More conservative than Hogg, House and Bailey represented moderate business views, as did Culberson, who in 1899 went on to the U.S. Senate, where he served until 1923. The next two governors of Texas, Joseph D. Sayers (1899–1903) and S. W. T. Lanham (1903–1907) might also be described as moderate Democrats. However, as the last two ex-Confederates to serve as the state's chief executive, they shared many of the conservative outlooks of the governors of the 1880s and thus, like Culberson, were reluctant to embrace Hogg-style progressivism.

The decline of agricultural influence on politics followed national trends. Progressivism, as it was emerging at the turn of the century, addressed urban as well as rural problems. Overall, Texans went along with the general course of other agricultural states and accepted the commercialization of agriculture and its growing interdependence with national markets. Texas farmers moved toward specialization, but most of them never overcame their economic dependency to escape poverty. Railroads had spread across the state, unifying it, closing the frontier, and encouraging the growth of cities. The new political battles over how to deal with an increasingly urban environment would be fought within the Democratic party. By endorsing segregation and one-party politics, Texas remained at the end of the nineteenth century as it had begun it, more southern than western in its political and social outlook.

READINGS

Books

Allen, Ruth A., *East Texas Lumber Workers* (Austin: University of Texas Press, 1961).

————, *The Great Southwest Strike* (Austin: The University of Texas Bulletin No. 4214, 1942).

Barr, Alwyn, *Black Texans* (Austin: The Pemberton Press, 1973).

————, *Reconstruction to Reform: Texas Politics, 1876–1906* (Austin: University of Texas Press, 1971).

Cantrell, Gregg, *Feeding the Wolf: John B. Rayner and the Politics of Race, 1850–1918* (Wheeling, IL: Harlan Davidson, Inc., 2001).

Cotner, Robert, *James Stephen Hogg* (Austin: University of Texas Press, 1951).

Goodwyn, Lawrence, *Democratic Promise: The Populist Movement in America* (New York: Oxford University Press, 1976).

Green, James R., *Grass Roots Socialism: Radical Movements in the Southwest, 1865–1943* (Baton Rouge: Louisiana State University Press, 1978).

Hare, Maud Cuney, *Norris Wright Cuney: A Tribune of the Black People* (New York: Crisis, 1913).

Martin, Roscoe C., *The People's Party in Texas: A Study in Third Party Politics* (Austin: University of Texas Bulletin No. 3308, 1933).

McMath, Robert C., Jr., *Populist Vanguard: A History of the Southern Farmer's Alliance* (Chapel Hill: University of North Carolina Press, 1975).

————, *American Populism: A Social History, 1877–1898* (New York: Hill and Wang, 1993).

Procter, Ben H., *Not Without Honor: The Life of John H. Reagan* (Austin: University of Texas Press, 1962).

Rice, Lawrence, D., *The Negro in Texas, 1874–1900* (Baton Rouge: Louisiana State University Press, 1971).

Spratt, John S., *The Road to Spindletop: Economic Change in Texas, 1875–1901* (Dallas: Southern Methodist University Press, 1955).

U.S. Bureau of the Census. *Abstract of the Twelfth Census of the United States, 1900* (Washington, D.C.: Government Printing Office, 1904).

————. *Ninth Census of the United States, 1870* (Washington, D.C.: Government Printing Office, 1894).

————. *Report on Statistics of Churches in the United States at the Eleventh Census: 1890* (Washington, D.C.: Government Printing Office, 1894).

————. *Tenth Census of the United States: 1880* (Washington, D.C.: 1883).

Wintz, Cary D., *Texas Politics in the Gilded Age* (Boston: American Press, 1983).

Articles

Abramowitz, Jack, "The Negro in the Populist Movement," *Journal of Negro History* 38 (1953): 257–89.

Barr, Alwyn, "B. J. Chambers and the Greenback Party Split," *Mid-America* 49 (1967): 276–84.

———, "Ben Terrell: Agrarian Spokesman," *West Texas Historical Association Yearbook* 45 (1969): 58–71.

Calvert, Robert A., "A. J. Rose and the Granger Concept of Reform," *Agricultural History* 51 (1977): 181–96.

———, "Nineteenth Century Farmers, Cotton and Prosperity," *Southwestern Historical Quarterly* 73 (1970): 509–21.

Calvert, Robert A., and William A. Witherspoon, "Populism in Jack County, Texas," *Southern Studies* 25 (1986): 67–84.

Dugas, Vera, "Texas Industry, 1860–1880," *Southwestern Historical Quarterly* 59 (1955): 151–83.

Ellis, L. Tuffly, "The Revolutionizing of the Cotton Trade, 1865–1885," *Ibid.*, 73 (1971): 151–83.

Griffin, Roger A., "To Establish a University of the First Class," *Ibid.*, 86 (1982): 135–60.

Macune, Charles W., Jr., "The Wellsprings of a Populist: Dr. C. W. Macune Before 1886," *Ibid.*, 90 (1986): 139–58.

Maxwell, Robert S., "The Pines of Texas: A Study in Lumbering and Public Policy, 1880–1930," *East Texas Historical Journal* 2 (1964): 77–86.

Reese, James V., "The Evolution of an Early Texas Union: The Screwmen's Benevolent Association of Galveston, 1886–1891," *Southwestern Historical Quarterly* 75 (1971): 158–85.

EARLY TWENTIETH-CENTURY TEXAS

CHAPTER 9

In 1901, wildcatters discovered oil at Spindletop, near Beaumont, an event that would dramatically influence the course of Texas history. The boom that Spindletop triggered would ultimately see oil surpass both cattle and cotton to become the linchpin of Texas prosperity. Indeed, the 1920s ushered in one of the more prosperous times that most Texans could recall. Yet as late as the end of the 1920s, the state seemed mired in the past; agriculture still dominated the economy, and segregation still defined race relations. The census recorded 3.9 million persons living in Texas in 1910; that number increased to 4.7 million in 1920, and to 5.8 million in 1929. Two-thirds of all Texans lived in rural areas when the period opened, with less than 20 percent of them residing in cities of more than 10,000 people. As late as 1930, the population was still classified as 60 percent rural. Most Texans were native born, with nearby southern states furnishing the highest percentage of newcomers. And while the state's values

and economy remained more like those of other Southern states than those of the industrial East or the West, the early twentieth century witnessed a beginning of the transition from a rural to an urban Texas.

OIL

Texans knew oil lay underground long before Spindletop. Indeed, in the 1500s Luis de Moscoso's men caulked their boats with a gummy petroleum substance they found near Sabine Pass, and even before that, Texas Indians used oil for various purposes. Periodically, in one section of the state or another, people drilled for water and instead hit oil. Never highly valued, oil and its byproducts served as lubricants or as ingredients in patent medicines or as curiosities. Nineteenth-century Texans never dreamed that oil and the state would become permanently intertwined in myth and economics. They had considered themselves as cotton farmers and cattle ranchers, but Spindletop changed that,

Above: Boulevard and bath houses, Galveston, Texas. *Courtesy Texas State Historical Association, Austin*

243

ushering Texas into the twentieth century with a bang and making the state ultimately different from its southern neighbors.

The first commercial oil well in Texas was struck in 1894, not near Beaumont but at Corsicana, in North Texas. An artesian water company hit oil sand at 1,035 feet, sealed off the oil with casing, and continued to drill deeper to find water. Subsequently, real estate developers persuaded James M. Guffey and John H. Galey of Pittsburgh, Pennsylvania (associates of millionaire Andrew W. Mellon) to come to Corsicana to join them in a search for more deposits of oil. Two years later, this team drilled a twenty-two-barrel-a-day well, and by 1900, their Corsicana field was producing 836,000 barrels a year. Soon this oil glutted the local market. Producers stored petroleum in open tanks and spilled a good amount of it, allowing it to become a hazard to the environment and to public

Oil Fields of Texas and Date of Discovery to 1918

safety. Corsicana's civic leaders even had oil sprayed on roads to keep dust down and filled potholes with petroleum by-products. Then, in 1897, the town's leaders asked J. S. Cullinan of Pennsylvania to come to Corsicana in order to exploit the resource better. In doing so, Cullinan founded the first successful commercial refinery in Texas. The J. S. Cullinan Company later merged with two other firms to form the Magnolia Petroleum Company (now known as Mobil, which merged with Exxon in 1999). As it expanded, the refinery needed new markets for its petroleum products, and Cullinan convinced the Cotton Belt Railroad in 1898 to run an experimental locomotive on steam created by an oil burner. Soon thereafter, most railroads began the switch from coal- to oil-burning locomotives.

Although the modern petroleum industry originated in North Texas, it was a discovery in Jefferson County that pointed out its true potential. Patillo Higgins of Texas believed that the salt dome three miles south of Beaumont known as Spindletop would be a good site to drill for petroleum. Captain A. F. Lucas, a mining engineer, deduced from his work in Louisiana that Higgins was probably correct and decided to join him, even though most experts of the day disputed the validity of their theory. Indeed, one executive of the Standard Oil Company of New Jersey (which controlled 90 percent of the nation's oil supply) stated categorically that no oil deposits existed west of the Mississippi River. In the face of such skepticism, Higgins and Lucas had a difficult time raising money for their drilling project. Finally, the Mellon men, Guffey and Galey, joined the Spindletop venture. These wildcatters then hired the Hammill brothers of Corsicana, users of a revolutionary rotary drilling process. The blending of technological expertise and Mellon money tapped the Spindletop pool on January 10, 1901.

For nine days Spindletop spewed oil unchecked, with between 70,000 and 100,000 barrels flowing from it daily. Before Spindletop, the largest oil well had produced 6,000 barrels a day. As word of the big strike spread, speculators of all stripes rushed to Beaumont. In 1901, the State of Texas chartered 491 oil companies. Houston Oil Company, in which John H. Kirby was the major stockholder, was capitalized at $30 million and quickly replaced the Kirby Lumber Company as the largest corporation in Texas. All told, that year oil companies issued $239,639,999 of capital stock, or six times that of all corporations, excluding railroads, in the previous decade.

A few other oil companies that were organized in the early days of Spindletop became giants. The J. M. Guffey Petroleum Company, owned by the Mellon interests, bought out Anthony F. Lucas's share of the original Spindletop oilfield in 1901 and later became Gulf Oil. J. S. Cullinan left Corsicana and joined investors James S. Hogg, Hogg's partner Jim Swayne, and barbed-wire entrepreneur J. W. "Bet a Million" Gates to create the Texas Company (later known as Texaco) in 1902. Other companies that can trace their roots to Spindletop include the Humble Oil Company (later Exxon), the Magnolia Petroleum Company, as mentioned, and the Sun Oil Company.

"Hogtown"—Desdemona, Texas, ca.1911. *Courtesy Houston Metropolitan Research Center, Houston Public Library*

Perhaps more important than the discovery of oil itself were the numerous oil-related spin-off industries that soon came into existence, for these spin-offs created a framework from which the industrial base of Texas would grow. Within a year of the Spindletop strike, Gulf constructed a refinery at Port Arthur. The Texas Company did the same in 1905. Both companies built pipelines connecting their refineries to the huge Glenn Pool field in Oklahoma, so that Oklahoma oil could now be processed in Texas. The Texas Company also built a refinery at Port Neches to make asphalt, another petroleum product. Tank cars were soon being fabricated to move oil by rail to great ocean-going tankers, which sailed out of new port facilities in recently dredged harbors. Machine shops turned to the making of oilfield equipment. Oil and gas law, petroleum engineering, and petroleum geology developed into important professions. Real estate firms especially designed for oil leasing and speculation spread throughout the state. Increasingly, Texans drove gasoline-powered automobiles over roads paved with asphalt. By the 1910s, natural gas, which was produced along with oil in most of the fields, was being transported to the major cities via pipeline. The construction of a carbon black plant in Stephens County in 1923 signaled the birth of the petrochemical industry in Texas.

In 1896, Texas had produced approximately 1,000 barrels of oil; in 1902, it produced 21 million barrels. The optimism and experience gained by increasing the production of this seemingly endless natural resource continued to send wildcatters scurrying through Texas looking for new fields. One obvious place to look was other salt dome areas, searches that yielded productive fields at Sour Lake (1902), Batson (1903), Humble (1905), and Goose Creek (1908), to list only the major ones. North Texas fields included Electra (1904); Mexia (1912, 1921); Burkburnett (1913); Hall, Barbers Hill, Ranger, and Desdemona (1918); Breckenridge (1920); and Big Lake (1923). From North Texas, oil exploration spread into Central Texas, turning up fields at Powell (1923) and Luling (1922). The rotary drills and improved bits made deeper drilling possible and expanded the industry in 1926 to West Texas, where the Yates, Hendricks, and Borger fields started production. Back in the drilled salt-dome areas, the loss of underground gas pressure had slowed the flow of oil to a trickle, but output was revived by new scientific methods of secondary recovery, the new, deeper drilling capabilities reactivating old wells and reaching new ones. The oil industry moved down the Texas coast, and by 1928 the Greta field, near Refugio, was a major producer. As the decade closed in 1929, the Texas oil industry produced 293 million barrels of oil annually, employed 13,726 persons in its refining, and had a value of $429.5 million. Oil and the industries it spun off added an entirely new tax base for the state.

The oil frontier rivaled the cattle frontier for boomtowns and wild times, as in one oil hamlet after another, sharpsters, oil-lease hustlers, drillers, and day laborers rubbed elbows with bootleggers, pimps, gamblers, and prostitutes. Oil fever swelled the population of Breckenridge in 1918 alone from 800 to about 30,000. People rented cots by the hour or slept on floors; city services ceased; chains hung between trees served as ancillary jails. In the 1920s, things got so bad in boomtowns such as Desdemona, Mexia, Wink, and Borger, that the Texas Rangers had to be sent in to tame lawlessness and expel troublemakers.

Texans were ill-prepared to deal with the physical and environmental problems posed by oil booms. Sudden rainstorms or simply the marshy qualities of the land often turned dirt roads into deeply rutted bogs, as heavy oilfield cars and trucks transported people and equipment over arteries designed and built for rural-village use. Entrepreneurs drilled as close to existing rigs as was physically possible, each fortune-seeker trying to extract a maximum share of the limited pools. In Breckenridge, some 200 derricks rose within the city limits of the town, and several thousand more derricks sprouted up in the immediate area. In such places, fire and health hazards abounded. In the aftermath of the boom at Corsicana, where the municipal water supply had been ruined by oil seeping into the water table, the legislature had passed an act requiring that casing be used in oil sands and that abandoned wells be plugged. But apart from this first step, matters of conservation and safety were left in the hands of the oil industry, which established voluntary standards that were too often ignored. Only after World War I would the Railroad Commission be empowered to enforce more stringent regulations, including rules governing the spacing of wells.

Other Industries

Besides petroleum refining, the other leading Texas industries in the 1920s (by rank) were extractive ones: slaughtering, oil drilling, coke mining, cottonseed pressing, flour milling, and lumbering. On the eve of the Great Depression, Texas was not yet an industrial state. Its per capita income ranked thirty-fifth nationally, its average earnings per employee, thirty-seventh. Nevertheless, industrial growth had begun, and Texans could point optimistically to an increase in the number of manufacturing establishments, from about 3,000 in 1900 to over 5,000 in 1929. More important, the value of these industries had risen from under $40 million to more than $450 million in the same period, while the number of industrial workers had grown from 38,604 to 134,498. The expansion of the economy led to a boom period in the late 1920s that constituted one of the more prosperous times in Texas's history.

But the growth had not been steady. World War I spurred on ship-building and oil and petrochemical industries, but it did not substantially increase Texas's industrialization. The depression of the early 1920s hit the state particularly hard, and it recovered slowly. Most industrial establishments in the state remained small, with more than half of them producing less than $50,000 annually. The popularity of automobiles and urbanization stimulated the construction industry. By 1928, Texans owned 250,000 motor vehicles, and businesses that serviced these vehicles would become a major industry.

URBAN GROWTH AND WORKERS

As the new century progressed, each decade saw a higher percentage of Texans living in metropolitan areas: 17.1 percent in 1900; 41 percent by 1930. Texas's five largest cities—Houston (292,352), Dallas (260,475), San Antonio (231,542), Fort Worth (163,447), and El Paso (102,421)—enjoyed a spectacular population surge of between 40 and 111 percent in the 1920s. By this time, each city had taken on specific characteristics. Fort Worth had become known as "Cowtown," a place dependent on its busy railroad and stock yards. Dallas, which had acquired one of the twelve national branches of the Federal Reserve System in 1913, built upon its railroad-induced marketing base to take on the air of a financial and business center. It had also achieved the image of a city of fine arts and culture. San Antonio, which drew on manufacturing enterprises as well as numerous military bases for its prosperity, prided itself on its Spanish heritage and began to emerge as a well-known tourist center. Houstonians boasted of living in the eye of the developing oil business, and the leadership of the city had committed early in century to the building of a channel that would accommodate ocean-going vessels. In 1914, the fifty-five-mile-long, thirty-foot-deep Houston Ship Channel opened and began to attract industries along its banks, turning the Bayou City into one of the nation's major ports. El Paso served as the commercial hub of the Trans-Pecos region and as a smelting and mining center. The Beaumont–Port Arthur area grew with the oil and petrochemical industry, as did a number of West Texas towns. Increased barge traffic encouraged the growth of Corpus Christi and other Gulf ports.

Brackenridge Park Swimming Pool, San Antonio, Texas, ca., 1912. *Courtesy Texas State Historical Association, Austin*

Meanwhile, Galveston was enjoying its status as the third-largest city in Texas, a major port, and a cotton compressing center when, on September 8, 1900, the greatest natural disaster ever to strike North America hit the "Island City." That night a massive Gulf hurricane slammed into Galveston, killing approximately 6,000 of its citizens and impoverishing more than half of the island's population, leaving its government and business community in utter disarray. Houston was already replacing Galveston by 1901 as the economic giant of the Texas Gulf Coast, but the storm hastened the latter's demise. By 1930, a rebuilt but economically diminished Galveston had begun to advertise itself as a vacation spot of scenic boardwalks and beaches.

In the wake of the disaster, the city leadership of Galveston adopted a new form of municipal government in 1901, the so-called commission plan. Under this setup, commissioners replaced the elected representatives from specific geographic wards, who in turn had selected the mayor. This scheme, designed to bring efficiency to the rebuilding of the devastated city, put individual commissioners in charge of specific municipal departments. When assembled, the commission acted as a policy-making and legislative body. Houston adopted this form of government, which came to be known as the Galveston Plan in 1905; Dallas, Fort Worth, and El Paso did so in 1907, and by 1920, seventy other Texas communities had followed suit. The plan underwent some modifications in 1913, when Amarillo adopted a council-manager form of city government. Under this arrangement, the council hired a city manager to oversee the administration of city services. The preceding year, the Texas legislature accorded cities the right of home rule (the authority to draw up their own charter without the legislature's approval). Critics charged that the commission form of government, which abolished ward representation through at-large voting, diluted the strength of minorities and secured the political control of cities by their respective elites. Progressives, however, did not disapprove of elites' control of local government, and the Galveston Plan, by this time also known as the Texas Idea, served as a model for city reform that spread across the nation.

After the turn of the century, Texas cities began to develop modern amenities. Most urban areas quickly developed telephone exchanges. In 1913, Texas Power and Light connected Waco, Fort Worth, and Dallas with high-tension electric lines. Oil producers supplied natural gas to urban areas. The growth of streetcars, interurban lines, and individual automobile ownership moved families from downtown to the newly forming suburbs. The League of Texas Municipalities, organized in 1913, advocated "city beautiful" movements. Some urban planners envisioned wide boulevards and areas of grass and foliage that would improve the aesthetic appearance of the unseemly urban sprawl. Most large cities had designated space for public parks before World War I, and Fort Worth, Waco, El Paso, Dallas, Houston, and San Antonio all had zoological gardens. As their residents sought new forms of recreation, cities responded by building public facilities. By 1910, Dallas, Houston, and San Antonio had public swimming pools, and these as well as other communities constructed baseball diamonds, football fields, and fairgrounds. The residents of these newly modernized cities were largely in-state immigrants, so the cities retained a rural, southern character. And the values of the urbanites harmonized with those of their rural counterparts, as all Americans responded with an equal uneasiness to the social changes the United States underwent in the 1920s.

Texas City oil refineries, 1911. *Courtesy Houston Metropolitan Research Center, Houston Public Library*

The expansion and linking of urban areas attracted more workers into the cities. The length of the average workweek dropped, and by 1929, forty-eight hours was becoming the norm, although some industries, such as slaughtering and cotton processing demanded longer hours. In 1929, the annual earnings of Texas wage workers averaged about $1,129, roughly 80 percent of the national average. Salaried employees in corporations earned roughly double that amount; while wage workers in skilled industries—petroleum, machine shops and foundries—received about 25 percent more. At the low end of the scale, those working in slaughtering and the cotton industries made about 30 percent less than the state average.

A comparison of cost-of-living expenses in major U.S. cities in 1920 reported that Houston's approximated those of other like-sized cities, though housing and heating were generally cheaper in the South. Yearly wage scales compared favorably throughout the urban areas in Texas, except that El Paso County's fell below the median ($1,052), while Harris County's exceeded it by about $100. On average, rural workers earned about one-third less than did their urban counterparts. The average Texas worker earned $540 per year in 1909. The increase in cost of living, however, which doubled between 1913 and 1920, offset any real increase in wages. Nevertheless, the rapidly growing number of industrial jobs continued to make urban areas more attractive than the countryside.

The expansion of job opportunities also affected women. The shortage of male workers during World War I lent respectability to female employment, and women's successes in the workplace encouraged male employers to continue to hire them. Slightly more than 400,000 Texas women worked outside the home in 1930, an increase of about 25 percent over 1920. A higher percentage of urban women than rural women were employed, a fact reflected by the decrease of female agricultural workers by nearly one-half, as more women moved to cities and the demand for agricultural labor in general dropped. During the same period, the percentage of women employed in domestic and personal services decreased slightly, with two-thirds of domestic jobs held by black and Hispanic females. In addition, over 50 percent of all divorced and widowed women worked in those occupations. Other divorcees and widows worked as seamstresses, lunchroom operators, and unskilled laborers in disproportionately high numbers as compared to other working women: a testimony to the lack of marketable skills among women who suddenly found themselves the heads of household.

The growth of large cities and new technologies offered Texas women increased employment in such occupations as telephone operators, clerical workers, and salespeople. Some occupations even became stereotyped as "women's work"; as professionals, Texas women accounted for 80 percent of the teachers, 90 percent of the nurses, and 90 percent of the librarians, but under 2 percent of the lawyers and physicians. Approximately 12 percent of married women worked in 1930, comprising more than one-third of the total female workforce. The increasing number of white married women in the workforce contributed to the concept of the "New Woman": the vibrant and independent woman who made her own decisions, free from male restrictions and advice. The New Woman was a product of the early twentieth-century social activism, an image amplified by urbanization and the activities of women in support of World War I.

The growth of an urban economy also aided in the decrease of child labor, as fewer children were now hired as farmhands. The percentage of employed children aged ten to fifteen years dropped from 20 percent in 1900 to 7 percent in 1930. Of the employed children in 1930, 90 percent worked in agriculture, usually on the family farm. In Texas cities of over 100,000, only 3.2 percent of children were employed. Twice as many boys as girls entered the job market, with black and Hispanic males the largest grouping and white females the smallest. The majority of employed boys sold newspapers or delivered goods for businesses. Most employed girls worked in the minority-dominated domestic services, which helped explain why three times as many black and foreign-born female children than white girls worked. Although Texans steadfastly refused to ratify a proposed child labor amendment to the U.S. Constitution, state regulatory laws effectively decreased the number of children in the labor pool, as did a 1915 law mandating compulsory school attendance.

LABOR UNIONS

As mentioned, labor unions never enjoyed a strong base in Texas. In the early twentieth century, the Texas State Federation of Labor was the strongest union, with 512 local chapters (simply known as "locals") at the union's peak of strength in 1918. By 1931, the organization had fallen to 135 locals. The United Mine Workers exhibited a modicum of strength until 1921, but as oil replaced coal as industry's and transportation's principal source of energy, the union's membership base declined. Meanwhile, oil workers in Texas and Louisiana, who had organized in 1905, called a strike during World War I that failed completely, temporarily ending unionism in the oil fields. This oil-workers' affiliate of the American Federation of Labor did, however, remain strong along the Gulf Coast. Although numerous other unions actively recruited members, a vigorous, unified voice for Texas industrial workers never materialized, and union membership in the state, as in the nation, dropped during the 1920s.

Some observers claimed that the lack of dynamic labor leadership underlay the decline in union membership. Others cited the open hostility of various businesses and chambers of commerce toward unions. Indeed, shortly after World War I, the nation experienced its first "Red Scare." The anticommunist hysteria led public opinion to link union activity with socialism and the Russian Revolution of 1917, a perception of "un-Americanism" that further limited the expansion of organized labor. Furthermore, the state's political leaders seemed to endorse the prevalent antiunion spirit. When dockworkers in Galveston joined a national strike in 1920 for higher wages and the exclusive employment of union workers, Governor W. P. Hobby declared the strike an illegal disruption of commerce, imposed martial law, and dispatched the National Guard to the area to force the longshoremen back to work. The troops were withdrawn after three months and replaced by Texas Rangers, who helped the local police maintain law and order. Meanwhile, a special session of the legislature passed an Open Port Law that officially prohibited any activities that might interfere with the free passage of trade within the state. In 1922, railroad shopmen in several Texas cities went out on strike. Responding to clashes between strikers and strikebreakers, Governor Pat Neff activated the Open Port Law and sent the National Guard to Denison to control strike-related violence there. He sent Rangers out to railyards at Amarillo, Big Spring, Cleburne, Childress, Dalhart, DeLeon, Gainesville, Kingsville, Lufkin, Marshall, Palestine, Sherman, Texline, and Waco, as well as other cities, to enforce the act. The courts held later that the Open Port Law contravened both the national and state constitutions. Although Hobby and Neff denied that the law was antilabor, union officials cited it as an example of Texas public officials' opposition to unions.

AGRICULTURE AND RURAL LIFE

Agriculture remained the major occupation and source of revenue for Texans into the 1920s. In 1927, for example, the value of Texas agriculture was three times that of oil and of manufacturing. And in Texas, cotton remained the king. Texas far outdistanced other southern states, producing one-third of all the cotton picked in 1922, a position held through the end of the decade. No other crop rivaled cotton in either acreage planted or value yielded.

Historically, the vast West Texas ranges had always provided new farmlands, and the early twentieth century saw commercial agriculture move into the Panhandle and High Plains, suitable ground for both cotton and wheat, and to the Rio Grande Valley, where the cultivation of cotton joined a nascent citrus industry. Although Central and East Texas still grew the most cotton, in 1894 the boll weevil arrived in South Texas from Mexico and proceeded to spread throughout the state, By 1922, the destructive insect had reached its westernmost limits, for the Panhandle climate was inhospitable to the weevil. This development coupled with the cultivation of early-maturing strains of cotton, which developed before the weevils had a chance to overtake the fields, encour-

TABLE 9.1 Ranking of Texas Crops by Acreage, 1909–1929

	1909	1919	1929
Cotton	9,930,000	11,523,000	16,813,000
Corn	5,131,000	4,748,000	4,075,000
Grain Sorghum	572,000	1,484,000	1,701,000
Wheat	325,000	2,414,000	2,969,000
Oats	459,000	1,864,000	1,148,000
Rice	207,000	964,000	106,000

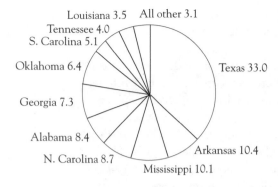

Louisiana 3.5　All other 3.1
Tennessee 4.0
S. Carolina 5.1
Oklahoma 6.4
Georgia 7.3
Alabama 8.4
N. Carolina 8.7
Texas 33.0
Arkansas 10.4
Mississippi 10.1

FIGURE 9.1 Percent of Cotton Grown in each State, Crop of 1922. *Source: U.S. Census Bureau*

aged the expansion of cotton-growing westward. Nevertheless, crop reporters estimated that in 1921 alone, boll weevils cost Texans one-third of their crop. Grain sorghums, used as stock feed, proved more drought-resistant than did corn, and they, too, spread to the High Plains. Corn, however, remained the principal cultivated food source for animals in north Central and East Texas.

The period from 1900 to 1929 witnessed a sizable change in livestock ratios, as the number of beef cattle and horses in the state dropped dramatically. Meanwhile, the number of Texas dairy cows, mules, sheep, and goats rose sharply. This transformation clearly demonstrated the passing of the Old West, as sheep and goats in the Hill Country and cows and mules or farm stock outnumbered both cattle and horses, the backbones of ranching.

As in the decades before the onset of the twentieth century, agriculture brought prosperity to few Texans. In particular, cotton failed many farmers. In 1900, the price of cotton stood at 9.78 cents per pound; in 1919, boosted by the demands of World War I, the price rose to 20.9 cents; however, with the agricultural depression of 1921, the price of cotton fell to 11.60 cents; and by 1929 it had retreated all the way back to 10.9 cents per pound. As mentioned, the cost of living doubled between 1913 and 1920, yet the farm family was earning about the same off its cotton in 1920 as it had at the beginning of the century. As destitute farmers saw their mortgaged land foreclosed, the rate of increase in farm tenancy increased. In 1910, 51.7 percent of Texas farmers were tenants; by 1930, 61 percent, or over 50 percent of white farmers and over 70 percent of black farmers, tilled someone else's land.

Cotton farming stayed largely unmechanized; cheap labor and land generally discouraged mechanization. But Texas farm values, including the value added by mechanization, did rise. In 1910, the average Texas farm had $85 invested in machinery; by 1930, the average was $367. Texas also led the South in the value of farms and farm buildings, and in the average per farm of acres harvested in the period from 1900 to 1930. Once again, the inflation that resulted from 1913 to 1919 must be taken into account, but, more important, the move of agriculture to the High Plains and Rio Grande Valley partially accounted for the increase in the value of farms and machinery. Those vast areas invited large, mechanized farms (with extensive acreage and expensive buildings). A more accurate gauge of mechanization, therefore, might be the number of tractors in the state, which between 1925 and 1929 increased by over 20,000. Almost one-half of this increase came from farms that had two or more tractors. The reported value of farm machinery included automobiles and trucks, inflating said value per farm. In the early twentieth century, East and Central Texas cotton farmers worked in much the same fashion as had those of the late nineteenth century: they plowed with mules, hoed one-half to one acre a day, and picked cotton by hand. Their lives still tightly conformed to the agricultural seasons of planting, weeding, and harvesting.

Tenant farmers and their families remained the poorest of the farmers. As in the nineteenth century, one's tenancy arrangements depended upon one's bargaining powers. Share tenants, who furnished some portion of animals, tools, implements, seed, and their own food, and then bargained what percentage of crops they paid to the landlord, were also termed "third and fourth" renters (one-third of the cotton and one-fourth of the corn going to the landlord). "Halfers" or "croppers," those who furnished nothing but their labor, divided their crops equally with the landlord. In addition, all tenants borrowed against their expected income. In 1914, an economist concluded that one-half of tenant farmers annually borrowed 100 percent of their gross income. In better years, they might mortgage one-third to three-quarters of their prospective earnings. In any case, tenants were not borrowing to invest in a productive process but simply to purchase food, clothing, and essential supplies. Interest rates varied depending upon the source: merchants, landlords, banks, etc. But the same economist concluded that the actual interest rate (from the date borrowed until repaid) for at least one-third of those farmers who acquired bank loans was 33.3 percent. (Bankers naturally extended the more favorable rates to the more secure farmers.) Regardless of the interest rates, in a very real sense, sharecroppers borrowed money on their own labor and then paid interest on it.

Rice farmers, Beaumont, Texas, 1920. *Courtesy Texas State Historical Association, Austin*

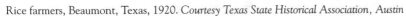

Texas farm income per family led the South in 1929 but trailed that of the agricultural areas of the Midwest. Agricultural reformers and educators continued to urge farmers to diversify their crops and aim for self-sufficiency. But limited access to urban markets and poor roads kept most Texas farmers from taking a chance on diversification. The income of farm families was determined by the size of the farm and the type of tenancy in which they were engaged, as well as by the family's race. Croppers, blacks and whites, farmed the smallest areas. Black croppers on average tilled 37 acres, as compared to 78 for white croppers; white farm owners and tenants worked 364 and 197 acres respectively, while black owners and tenants ran operations of 71 and 55 acres, respectively. The value of the respective farms (buildings, machinery, and land) also emphasized the differences in prosperity. Black owners had property worth an average of $2,195, black croppers, $196, as compared to $10,061 and $514, respectively, for white owners and croppers.

Farm Laborers

The 1929 census reported that 347,996 Texans worked in the fields for some period of the year. About 43 percent of these laborers toiled on their home farms; the figures include children aged ten years and higher who, as family members, may not have received a wage for their work. The remainder of farm workers were classified as wage earners. The number of farm laborers dropped after the peak agricultural year of 1919, even though the number of farms increased. Several factors probably explain this disparity. After 1920, there was a decrease in the yield per acre of cotton and an increase in the use of machinery. Fewer women worked in the fields, and more migrant Hispanic workers followed the harvest, lessening the number of local day laborers. Black female farm wage earners outnumbered white ones by two to one in 1929, and more white males hired out than did black ones. The major increase, however, was in the number of male and female Hispanic farm laborers, who were listed as nonwhites in the 1930 census.

The hours worked by day laborers depended on the chores at hand. In South Texas, cotton picking began in July and ended in December, as the crop only began to mature in colder weather. It was essential that the mature bolls be gathered quickly, before rain or wind damaged the exposed cotton; therefore, cotton pickers worked long hours, five and one half days a week. They were paid by the hundredweight. When labor was in short supply in 1919, pickers were paid from $3.50 to $4 per hundredweight. By the late 1920s, the wages per hundredweight had fallen to under $1. Townspeople, local farm families, and urban wage earners sometime joined field hands and migratory laborers in harvesting cotton. By 1929, a good picker earned around $4 a day. Additional wage scales were set by the acre for hoeing and chopping cotton, $1.50 to $1.75 per day being the norm, and roughly the same amount was earned for topping corn. The average Texas agricultural wage earner worked between nine and eleven hours a day for 165 days, or 27 weeks, and earned a yearly wage of $485.35, which fell

The boll weevil decimated southern cotton crops prompting many failed techological experiments such as the one pictured here. *Courtesy Texas State Historical Association, Austin*

slightly below the United States Department of Agriculture's estimate of $27 per week for seasonal wage work.

Equal employment opportunities, however, cannot be measured by averages. Black farm workers continually faced the pressures of segregation, which left them with little room for wage-scale bargaining. After World War I, for example, both the Ku Klux Klan and some local law enforcement officers pressured blacks to work in the fields in times of agricultural labor shortages. Women seemed to have earned equal pay, but most farm labor income was piecework, which meant that laborers were paid for the total amount of crops picked or the total number of acres or rows hoed. Therefore, many women were not physically capable of matching men's wages. At times, black and Hispanic women hired out on a family contract, whereby the arranger, frequently the eldest male, received the pay for the total family production. Migrant workers sometimes contracted with employers through a labor negotiator, who took a percentage of their pay. Consequently, their individual wages may have been less than those workers who arranged independently with farmers.

Farm Women and Families

Women probably faced the greatest hardships in the southern cotton culture. Their work included the arduous work of caring for the family as well as farm labor: studies in the 1920s pointed out that even though more blacks and foreign-born women than whites worked in the fields, nearly one-half of all white farmers' wives peformed field work as well. Changes in technology in the twentieth century improved farm women's lives, but not as much as one might have hoped. A study of 811 women in Central and East Texas in 1930 reported that of the white women sampled, 57 percent still cooked on wood stoves, 80 percent used oil lamps, and 63 percent washed clothes in tubs of boiling water and rubbed them clean on washboards. Black women fared worse. Ninety-nine percent of them used oil lamps and wood stoves. Simple amenities were rare for all farm families. In 1929, less than 5 percent of Texas farms had electricity, less than 8 percent had indoor plumbing, and less than 15 percent had water piped into the kitchen. Therefore, such duties as washing dishes or bathing children were time-consuming projects, necessitating hauling water in buckets and heating it on wood-burning stoves. Single women and children, and in some cases wives, were expected to work in the fields with the men, hoeing and picking cotton, and doing some plowing.

New technology in the twentieth century should have changed the rural woman's social life, lessening the isolation and loneliness that nineteenth-century Texans faced; in most cases, however, it had little effect. But the automobile did bring the village closer to the farm. In 1929, about three-fifths of farm families reported owning an automobile. The rate of telephone access was not as good; that same year, only 32 percent of all farms reported having a telephone. Radios were a rarity found only in 2.5 percent of rural homes in 1925. To make matters worse, poor roads limited access to the village in bad weather. Of the nearly 450,000 miles of Texas roads in 1929, 204,531 of them were described as unimproved and 186,644 as improved dirt ones. Nevertheless, 82 percent of the white women surveyed went to town about once a week. Besides trips to town for recreation, approximately 50 percent of the white women went to church, and 22 percent attended club meetings for social interchange. Probably, the lives of tenant and cropper women were worse than those of white women living on family-owned farms. Many croppers moved every two or three years, so they seldom enjoyed the traditional stability of rural-community life. The falling cotton prices of the first three decades of the twentieth century furthermore must have been psychologically debilitating to farm women, especially as they saw village and urban women acquire more luxuries and achieve a higher standard of living during the same period.

Patterns of Childbearing, Marriage, and Divorce

The lives of farm wives, like those of most women, centered on their family and child-care responsibilities. The average family size in Texas dropped from over 4.6 in 1910 to 3.5 in 1930, signaling a possible lessening of child-care labor. Although many women knew of contraceptive methods and abortifacients and could exercise some control over family size, in rural areas, children remained an economic asset, for they were able to do hand labor and chores at a very early age.

The ratio of children under the age of five to women of childbearing age reveals differences between urban and rural lifestyles. Women between 20 and 44 years of age who lived in cities of over 25,000 inhabitants bore fewer children than did their rural counterparts. And foreign-born women bore more children than did native whites. The census also reported that Slavic and Italian women in rural areas tended to have the largest families. San Antonio and El Paso, with large Hispanic populations, exceeded other cities' average of children under five years of age per thousand. But second-generation Americans did not necessarily follow their parents' lifestyles. In both Dallas and Fort Worth, women

This photograph of fig-shipping employess in the early twentieth century is testimony to the large number of women agricultural workers during this period. *Courtesy Houston Metropolitan Research Center, Houston Public Library*

of mixed parentage (having one foreign-born parent) had about the same percentage rate of marriage and of children under five years of age per thousand as did native whites. Except for blacks and Hispanics in Texas, urban life probably eroded ethnicity.

The black population figures were lower in every category. The high infant-mortality rate of black children partially explains this difference. The Census Bureau in 1929 estimated that one in four black children died within their first year. Texas, the last continental state to pass a birth and death registration law (in 1933), had no figures to verify that, but life-expectancy tables seemingly support the estimate. A white male born in 1905 in Texas had a life expectancy of 47.5 years, his female counterpart, 50.2; in 1929, the rates were 59.7 and 63.5 years, respectively. Conversely, a black male born in Texas in 1905 had a life expectancy of 29.6 years, a black woman 33.1; in 1929 those averages were 47.3 and 49.2, respectively.

Census takers also reported that 60 percent of the rural population was aged fourteen and under in 1920, while 32 percent of village and 27 percent of urban inhabitants fell within that age group. Young adults, particularly young women, tended to move from farms to urban areas during this period. In 1920 the gender ratio in Texas stood at 106.9 males for every 100 females. However, for young adults (aged fifteen to twenty-four), females outnumbered males in urban areas. That did not mean that more single women than single men lived in cities. On average, women married earlier (21.2 years of age) than did males (24.6), and all urban communities in 1920 had more bachelors than single, young adult females. Women who did remain on the farm married earlier, in a higher percentage, and had fewer divorces than did their urban counterparts.

Although the number of divorces in Texas rose steadily from 1890 to 1930, Texas granted more divorces than did any other state from 1922 to 1926, and by 1930 it trailed only Nevada, Oklahoma, and Oregon in having the highest divorce rate in the country.

Rural Life in an Era of Change

Certain qualities of rural life cannot be quantified, and some Texans genuinely preferred rural to urban living. The variation in farm work might have been more attractive to them than the monotony of unskilled labor on an urban assembly line. The durability of the farm family and a long familiarity with the pastoral life promised a measure of stability in an era of rapid change. At this time, the cities were by no means the great employment meccas they would become—once World War II triggered the state's massive industrialization—and for some Texans the farm might truly have seemed to offer the better chances for eventual prosperity.

Nevertheless, farmers genuinely resented the circumstances that prevented them from obtaining economic security. Before World War I, the Renters' Union of North America founded some two hundred locals in Texas. This socialist organization attempted to establish rules for tenancy as well as to improve methods of marketing crops. The Farmers' Union, organized in 1902 in Emory, Texas, grew into the 140,000-member Farmers' Educational and Cooperative Union of America. A Colored Farmers' Union formed in emulation of its white counterpart. Although the National Union suspended the Texas Farmers' Union for one year for its political activities, the goals of the latter closely mirrored earlier Alliance goals. It was best known for its "plowup campaign of 1908" (creating a planned shortage by destroying one-third of its cotton) and its some 1,300 cotton warehouses and marketing cooperatives. The Texas Farmers Congress and Farmers' Institutes at the Agricultural and Mechanical College stressed improvement through rural education, the use of scientific farming techniques, and cooperative marketing. The more conservative Farm Bureau, which became the dominant rural organization, also supported self-help ventures. All sought ways to expand credit availability to agriculturists, none of which succeeded for the average farmer. Instead, the condition of Texas farmers only worsened as the Great Depression approached, their economic plight explaining much of the rural sector's support for "Farmer" James E. Ferguson, governor from 1914 to 1917, and its later endorsement of President Franklin Roosevelt's New Deal.

ETHNIC TEXANS

Blacks in Texas

Historians have described the early twentieth century as the nadir of race relations in this country. Ironically, Populism, which tried to create a biracial political coalition, helped to encourage segregation in the South. Attempting to prevent the formation of any coalition of blacks and poor white farmers, establishment Democratic politicians frequently demonstrated their Negrophobia by accusing blacks of being genetically inferior to whites and claiming that such "innate" flaws made blacks a threat to society. There began a move to make African Americans outsiders, governed by political leaders for whom they could not vote and segregated by law and custom into a separate society. The movement largely succeeded. In rural areas of Texas, most blacks did not vote, the casualties of all-white primaries. In 1910, the Democratic state house of representatives urged a repeal of the Fifteenth Amendment, a clear indication that the majority of white Texans outrightly opposed black political participation.

But as increasing numbers of black Texans migrated to cities, they nevertheless acquired some voting power. White city bosses needed the support of the new arrivals to guarantee their control of political offices in close elections, and black organizers such as Charles Bellinger of San Antonio and organizations such as the Independent Voting Leagues in Dallas and Houston did gain some political participation for their constituencies. In 1923, the legislature acted to formalize black exclusion in the Democratic primary, but Lawrence A. Nixon, a Wiley College graduate and physician, challenged the law: in *Nixon* v. *Herndon* (1927) the U.S. Supreme Court ruled that all-white primaries violated the Fourteenth Amendment. The next year, however, the state defined political parties as "private organizations"—and therefore not subject to federal voting requirements—effectively skirting the federal law anyway. In short, until 1944, most black Texans simply did not vote.

SEGREGATION

Excluded from political participation, black Texans watched as white officials segregated public facilities. The state legislature in 1910 and 1911 ordained that railroad stations must have separate waiting rooms and that trains be furnished with designated employee compartments to prevent black porters from resting in unoccupied Pullman berths. Soon, virtually all public facilities had separate water fountains and restrooms. In 1916, the Dallas city council passed ordinances requiring residential segregation. The U.S. Supreme Court ruled against these types of laws, but the state legislature authorized cities to pass creative zoning regulations that effectively segregated neighborhoods. Consequently urban ghettos where poor black residents were made to concentrate developed in all Texas cities. Needless to say, health and recreational facilities and governmental services such as paving and road repair, lighting, sewage, and police protection were inadequate in these black neighborhoods and hardly equal to the level of city services provided to white neighborhoods. By 1930, it was virtually impossible for black citizens to stay at major hotels, eat in better restaurants, or attend most cultural or sporting events unless the venue provided segregated, usually inferior, seating sections.

White individuals employed vigilante-style violence to keep blacks "in their place," and even law enforcement agencies helped uphold the separate and unequal society. Sadly, Texas ranked third nationally in the lynching of black persons, as mobs murdered more than 100 black people between 1900 and 1910. In 1916 at Waco, approximately 10,000 whites turned out in a holiday-like atmosphere to watch a mob mutilate and burn a black man named Jesse Washington. In this violent atmosphere, race riots erupted periodically. In 1908, at Beaumont, whites burned down two black amusement parks. In 1919, clashes between whites and blacks in Longview culminated with the burning of the African American section of town. Similar experiences occurred at various times in Sherman, Port Arthur, Houston, and other cities. White prejudice included animosity toward black troops in the U. S. Army. Brownsville whites, for example, objected to the stationing of the all-black Twenty-fifth Infantry at Fort Brown. In anger, they charged that the troops had raided the city in 1906 in protest of discriminatory practices. Later evidence demonstrated the unfairness of the charges, but by that time President Theodore Roosevelt had dishonorably discharged 160 of the troops. In Houston, black soldiers' resentment of segregation flamed into a clash with white citizens in 1917. The riot, during which sixteen whites died, ended with the execution of nineteen of the black soldiers for murder and life imprisonment of fifty-three more.

Without recourse to political power, blacks in Texas, as in the rest of the nation, chose either accommodation or resistance to segregation. In 1912, the National Association for the Advancement of Colored People (NAACP) founded a chapter in Houston, and by 1930 the NAACP had organized thirty more chapters in the state. White hostility toward the NAACP surfaced in the 1919 beating in Austin of John R. Shillady, the organization's white executive secretary.

Finally, white reformers began to join blacks in their call to end the violence. A Texas Committee on Interracial Violence was formed in 1928 to fight extra-legal acts against blacks. By this time, both the *Dallas Morning News* and the *San Antonio Express* had openly condemned lynching. Meanwhile, African American newspapers such as the *Texas Freeman* and the *Houston Informer*, as well as black Texan church groups and lodges, also denounced segregation and white oppression. Then, during the 1930s, the Association of Southern Women for the Prevention of Lynching, led by Jessie Daniel Ames of Texas, mobilized a strong moral opposition to violence. By then, most church organizations in the state and Congressman Maury Maverick of San Antonio, who later supported a federal antilynching law, were on record as opposing racial violence. In 1942, the last recorded lynching of an African American took place in Texas.

RURAL BLACKS

The African American population in Texas increased from 670,722 in 1900 to 854,964 in 1930. During this period, the majority of blacks stayed in rural areas, where they worked as tenants and farm laborers. As cotton prices fell, their chances to acquire their own farms decreased. Some turned to the Farmers' Improvement Society, first organized by R. L. Smith in the 1890s. The society endorsed the accommodationist philosophy of the nationally famous Booker T. Washington and his Negro Farmers' Congress. Before World War I, that organization spread to other states, advocating self-help through cooperatives, educational fairs, the eschewing of credit, and the improvement of homes and farms.

The burning and mutilation of the body of Jesse Washington following his lynching. *The Texas Collection, Baylor University, Waco, Texas*

The society founded a bank in Waco and sponsored a Women's Auxiliary and a Truck Grower's Union. A Colored Farmers' Educational and Cooperative Union was founded in Dallas in 1905. Other organizations established farmers' institutes and local cooperative associations. Finally, Prairie View Agricultural and Mechanical College held annual Farmers' Congresses to aid black Texans. These organizations all spoke of accommodation and self-help to counteract poverty and segregation. But rural Texans remained poor, and the depth of poverty blacks faced exceeded that of most whites.

BLACK MIGRATION

A number of black Texans sought to escape rural poverty by migrating to urban areas outside the state. Some joined the wave of other black southerners and escaped de jure segregation by moving to northern cities. Still others only went as far as Louisiana or Oklahoma.

In 1914, a few black Texans attempted a return to Africa. Chief Alfred C. Sam, an African, founded the Atkins Trading Company and purchased a ship, the *Liberia*, on which he intended to transport African Americans to new homes in the Gold Coast. The *Liberia* embarked from Galveston, and a small number of black Texans traveled to the Island City to board it. Few, if any, found room on the tiny vessel, and Sam's enterprise never amounted to much. In a similar vein, Marcus Garvey, a Jamaican and the organizer of the Universal Negro Improvement Association (UNIA), advocated black pride, a back-to-Africa movement, and the development of black enterprises. But his attempt to found a local UNIA chapter in Dallas in 1922 met with stern opposition, as had the efforts of Sam, from many black leaders and middle-class African Americans who had no intention of renouncing their U.S. citizenship or leaving their homeland.

In addition to moving out of the state, rural blacks relocated to Texas cities. The percentage of the black population of the state's urban areas grew from 19 percent in 1900 to 32 percent in 1930. Once in the city, blacks tended to settle in black districts and join the workforce by taking largely unskilled jobs. At the behest of white businesspersons and workers, most craft unions excluded blacks from membership. Separate African American unions existed for selected trades such as longshoremen, porters, and switchmen, but these organizations had almost no influence in the State Federation of Labor. Because the dockworkers maintained unions to secure equal pay with whites, the best semi-skilled vocations for blacks were those of longshoreman and stevedore.

In 1900, 57,000 black males in Texas worked in nonagricultural jobs. Nearly 60 percent of them toiled as personal and domestic servants and unskilled laborers. During the next thirty years, the number of African American males employed in urban areas doubled, but 64 percent of them still worked as laborers or as personal servants. The expanding economy of the 1920s did open new employment opportunities for black men as porters and chauffeurs and in building trades and oil refining. The public sector, however, hired few African Americans, except as janitors and manual laborers. Dallas, for example, had no black policemen in 1929; Fort Worth employed two; Houston, five; and San Antonio, four. New industrial expansion opened skilled jobs for whites, leaving for blacks the unskilled work that came with such growth. A higher percentage of black women than white women worked, a phenomenon only encouraged by the limited opportunities for black males. Almost 50 percent of married black women in the five largest Texas cities worked in 1930, as compared to approximately 16 percent of the married white women. Most African American women took jobs as seamstresses, laundresses, personal servants, or otherwise in domestic service.

THE BLACK BOURGEOISIE

The segregated communities also fostered the emergence of a small black bourgeoisie. Ministers and teachers composed the largest occupational group of black professionals in 1930. That year, 205 physicians, 99 dentists, and 20 lawyers statewide served the needs of a segregated society too often ignored by white specialists. African American organizations such as the Lone Star Medical, Dental, and Pharmaceutical Association and the Negro Business League brought leadership and a drive for professionalism to their communities. Texas had only four black-owned banks in 1928, and the shortage of investment capital limited the expansion of black businesses. Most black-owned stores in Texas were mom-and-pop ventures that shared their customers with white retail outlets. Blacks owned 1,736 retail stores in 1929, 53 percent of which were grocery stores, drugstores, and restaurants. The number of black undertakers went from 1 in 1900 to 198 in 1929, and they joined the black bourgeoisie of the period. Most black Texans lacked financial and occupational security, however, and the coming Great Depression would hit them especially hard. One exception, however, was Hobart Taylor, Sr., of Houston, who became a millionaire by investing first in taxicabs, then in an insurance company.

SOCIAL, RELIGIOUS, AND FRATERNAL ORGANIZATIONS

Social activities for African Americans revolved around segregated institutions, especially the church. In 1916, 396,157 blacks belonged to a church; most of these persons were Baptists. As with the general population, the number of church members actually attending services regularly dropped during the 1920s, but churches also served as public forums—for education, social interchange, and the development of African American leadership skills. In addition, all-black chapters of lodges such as the Knights of Pythias (which had 35,000 members in 1921) and the Masons (which had 30,000) offered secular social events in a segregated society. The lodge halls often served the black community as

Tillie Brackenridge in San Antonio, ca. 1900. *The UT Institute of Texas Cultures, No. 85-75, courtesy of Mrs. Charles C. Bush*

schools, recreation sites, churches, and civic centers; the fraternities sometimes offered insurance and banking services to their members. William M. McDonald used his connections with black Masons to convince other fraternal groups in 1912 to help him establish the Fraternal Bank and Trust Company in Fort Worth. In 1930, he sold his controlling interest in the bank to the Masons. His influence in the African American communities of Texas made him perhaps the most important black political leader of the 1920s. In 1905, the Texas Federation of Colored Women's Clubs organized. Each member club provided urban, middle-class black women a forum to discuss reform efforts in addition to opportunities for social activities.

By 1930, black Texans had responded to a racist, segregated society by organizing separate institutions that furnished intellectual and social stimulation apart from white society. These organizations, strong in those urban areas with an increasing black population, schooled the young African Americans who would challenge, and ultimately dismantle, the system of Jim Crow.

EDUCATION

The segregated school system also trained black leaders. The Colored Teachers State Association published the *Texas Standard*, which urged professionalization and new teaching techniques for black teachers. As urban black schools increased in number, parent-teacher organizations and the Interscholastic League of Negro Schools promoted athletic events, academic contests, and school clubs that stimulated youths' social life in the ghetto. School administrators and their counterparts in parent-teacher groups tended to support conservative positions and the status quo, for school funds relied on the support and good will of whites. Black administrators, therefore, dominated these school-related organizations, and they endorsed technical and vocational training at the expense of the liberal arts. Nevertheless, some adminstrators did openly challenge the wisdom of supporting white stereotypes that categorized black Texans as unable to absorb or draw value from any but a technical education.

And slowly, the black school systems did improve. By 1930 illiteracy in the black population had fallen statewide to 13.4 percent, and more black students were attending school, and for longer terms. Comparisons of black to white schools revealed, however, the unfairness of the Jim Crow system. Black students attended school an average of 106 days a year, as compared to 131 days for white students. Black teachers earned on average about $92 per month, as compared to $121 for white teachers. Three-quarters of the black schools were one-teacher, one-room facilities. One study estimated that statewide during the 1920s, per capita spending to educate white children exceeded that spent to educate black children by three times.

The inability of black teachers to attend graduate programs in the white state colleges created problems of competency and professionalism in black education. Prairie View A. and M. offered courses at both the college and high school levels. Its emphases remained on technical, agricultural, and teacher education.

Under the leadership of W. R. Banks, the school established a division of arts and sciences in 1931, but the college offered no graduate courses until the late 1930s and then only in agriculture and home economics. Banks had led the school to accreditation in 1926 and secured some private philanthropic funds for graduate education through the General Education Board, a national organization that gave funds to black colleges. Nevertheless, in the late 1930s, black Texans still had to leave the state to earn a graduate degree in either the liberal arts or education. The private black schools, financed by donations and foundation and church funds, defined their role as primarily training students as teachers and ministers. The shortage of qualified black college students and the growing demands of the black community meant that the private colleges also had to offer some of their student bodies high school level courses. These schools, too, found pressures for providing a technical and vocational education hard to resist. Wiley College, generally considered the best of the black private schools in the state, stressed a general education, but in 1922 it had no choice but to offer some vocational courses and enroll one-half of its student body below the tenth-grade level. Despite the limitations of black education, public and private schools ably prepared many black Texans for leadership in politics, education, and business.

SOCIAL, CULTURAL, AND RECREATIONAL LIFE

The social life of black Texans functioned in a separate sphere from that of whites. Blacks observed Juneteenth as well as the usual state and national holidays. They also held separate county fairs and rodeos, as well as parades, public lectures, picnics, barbecues, and baseball games. In the black sections of some communities, there were separate parks, saloons, dance halls, pool halls, theaters, bowling alleys, and other recreational establishments. In 1920 Andrew "Rube" Foster, a native of Calvert, organized the National Negro Baseball League. These teams toured the South, as did regional, semiprofessional ones. The best-known

black sports hero, Jack Johnson, came from Galveston and held the heavyweight boxing crown from 1908 to 1915. The state legislature banned the showing of films of his fights, arguing that they might inspire "Negroes" to riot.

Fine arts seldom exist in areas of poverty. However, blacks did contribute substantially to American music, which drew on the Texas folk tradition. The vocal and musical style of Texas blues produced the now-famous

Rube Foster. *Johnson Publications*

Blind Lemon Jefferson and Huddie "Leadbelly" Ledbetter, among others. "Leadbelly" composed such well-known songs as "C. C. Rider," "Midnight Special," and "Goodnight Irene." This music, with distinctly rural roots, moved to urban areas with black immigrants, and professional black bands and musicians rose to popularity in the 1930s and 1940s.

At this time, many blacks lacked the educational and cultural opportunities to develop fully a talent for writing. Most of those blacks who did make it as writers reported for or edited black newspapers or wrote religious and educational material. These writings tended to focus on self-help ideology. Yet some used their skills as writers to openly oppose segregation. Carter Wesley, a prominent lawyer and publisher, moved to Houston in 1927. He worked for the *Houston Informer* and later became its publisher. The *Informer*, with a circulation of 45,000, was a crusading voice for equality in a time of segregation. Wesley also published the *Dallas Express*, which, along with the *Informer* chain and the *Galveston New Idea*, gave a long-lasting voice to black writers. Local black newspapers flourished for a while, at least, in Amarillo, Austin, Beaumont, Calvert, Denison, Fort Worth, Port Arthur, San Antonio, San Angelo, and Waco. The best-known black Texas writer, J. Mason Brewer, who won fame as a folklorist, collected his data during this period and published anthologies of black folk tales and poems in the 1930s.

The social, intellectual, and economic life of black Texans thus remained restricted during the early depression years. Despite efforts of a small middle class, blacks had little social or economic influence with which to change the segregated society. Obviously, their political participation, except in selected urban areas, was of limited and negligible influence.

Tejanos

According to recent estimates, some 695,000 Texans of Mexican descent resided in the state as of 1930. Much of the increase was due to the incredible migration of people from Mexico: they were pulled to the state by a demand for cheap labor and pushed from their homeland by the poverty and terror of the revolution that broke out there in 1910. So intense was the migration into rural hamlets and barrios that the newcomers overwhelmed the native Texas Mexican population. In some cases, Tejano communities even came to look toward Mexico for cultural assurance. Not until the 1930s would a "Mexican American Generation" surface to reorient the Tejano community towards the United States.

DISCRIMINATION

Whether native or foreign born, and regardless of social class, most white Texans continued to look upon Hispanics disparagingly as "Mexicans" or "greasers." Lingering racist attitudes from the nineteenth century that marked Mexicans as inferior and ill suited for assimilation into the mainstream of American society were reinforced in the 1920s and 1930s by racist theories that deemed Mexicans inherently "dirty." Mexican Americans, therefore, remained deprived of the full rights of U.S. citizenship. In politics, for example, they faced new hurdles to voting following a series of practices implemented between 1900 and 1920. The 1902 poll-tax requirement and the rule used at the county level by the white men's primary associations barring voters who could not swear to be "a white person and a Democrat," eliminated many Texas Mexican voters. Then, in 1918, a new law prohibited interpreters from translating for voters and election judges from assisting anyone who could not prove that he had been a U.S. citizen for twenty-one years.

Furthermore, Mexican Americans in Texas encountered segregation at every turn. Developers in South Texas laid out new towns with sections specifically intended as "Mexican quarters." When permitted an education, Mexicans attended the "Mexican school," and administrators seldom encouraged them to enter the all-white high schools. Those Tejanos who sought to achieve higher education often left the state to do so, turning to colleges in Rolla, Missouri, New Orleans, or Washington, D.C. Meanwhile, back home in Texas, barber shops, restaurants, and other public places unabashedly displayed signs that read "No Mexicans or Dogs Allowed." In short, white society persistently displayed a repugnance at "mixing with Mexicans."

WORKING CONDITIONS AND ORGANIZED LABOR

As of 1900, 76 percent of Tejanos lived in rural areas. They made their living primarily as agricultural hands: in West Texas, Mexicanos worked in the sheep ranches as *tasinques* (sheepshearers); in South Texas they turned to farm work in *el desenraice* (grubbing) and *la pizca* (cotton picking). In the 1920s, a pattern of migratory labor began that would persist for a half-century thereafter. From the lower Rio Grande Valley, Mexicans pursued the harvest of "King Cotton"; family unit after family unit joined the army of migrant pickers in late summer as it passed through the Corpus Christi area, thence to Central Texas, West Texas, and into North Texas. The "Big Swing" ended as the recruits returned home when the picking season finally ended, in the Panhandle near the start of winter.

Town dwellers coped as best they could in areas often characterized by urban blight and squalor. Barrios in El Paso, San Antonio, and the towns of South Texas swelled with recent arrivals fleeing the Mexican Revolution. In these urban settings, workers turned to public works and mercantile establishments for their livelihoods, though many through necessity joined the migrant cotton stream, returning to their homes following the harvest season to await the start of next year's cycle. New Mexican settlements popped up in cities such as Houston, where Mexicans answered the call for laborers in the construction of railroads and the ship channel. Mexican neighborhoods also sprouted in cities such as Lubbock, where those weary of the "Big Swing" opted to establish new and permanent roots.

While the cotton pickers and other Mexican American *obreros* (laborers) often remained at the mercy of the worst exploitative potentials of the capitalist system, the historical record shows that Mexicans in Texas founded or joined workers' organizations for self-improvement and change. Texas Mexican socialist unions composed of agricultural laborers were active within the cotton-belt area circumscribed by Bexar, Travis, and Victoria Counties as early as the 1910s, for example.

Industrial unionism also surfaced. Among the most prominent labor organizations was Federal Labor Union No. 11,953 of Laredo, which in 1906 gained a wage hike after striking against the Mexican Railway. Other work stoppages marked the first decades of the century. In 1901, 200 Mexican American construction workers struck the El Paso Electric Street Car Company for a salary raise and fringe benefits, as did smelter workers in that city later (1907), both unsuccessfully. When the murder of a Mexican American labor organizer triggered a challenge to the Texas and Pacific Coal Company in Thurber in 1903, 1,600 members of the United Mine Workers, some of whom were Mexican, won both a pay increase and shorter working hours. Onion clippers struck for higher wages in Asherton in 1912. Mexican American clerks in El Paso founded the International Clerks' Protective Association in 1913 and achieved their demand for earlier closing hours. Approximately 300 laundry workers walked off the job in El Paso in 1919 for union recognition, but strikebreakers from Mexico ended that endeavor.

SELF-HELP ORGANIZATIONS

Avenues for self-help took various forms. Though sometimes disfranchised, Tejanos nevertheless found the means of gaining from the extant political structure. In South Texas, where political bosses such as Jim Wells and Manuel Guerra (in Starr County) ruled by their control of the Hispanic vote and access to patronage, Mexicans received numerous social services. These offerings included social-welfare benefits, relief during times of drought, help with legal problems, assistance in marrying, baptizing, or burying a family member, encouragement in improving the lot of talented individuals in the community, and even protection from the persecution of racist members of white society. Sometimes, this standard of living gained the notice of jealous whites. Indeed, many progressive reforms spearheaded by white Texans intended not only to eliminate political machines but also to limit the ability of Tejanos to exploit political contests for their own social advantages.

By the early twentieth century, almost every town in the state had separate Tejano organizations that extended aid to their members and their families and otherwise helped Tejanos survive the difficult living conditions they faced daily. An effort to mobilize these several societies was made on September 14, 1911, at Laredo. Known as *El Primer Congreso Mexicanista* (the First Mexican Congress of Texas), this assemblage considered such issues as unity, cultural nationalism, exploitation in the workplace, educational exclusion, rights of Tejanas, extralegal justice directed at Tejanos, and discrimination. Little, however, resulted from the Congreso meeting, for the individual *mutualistas* (mutual self-help societies) preferred their own independence and control to merging themselves under an umbrella group.

Moreover, the Congreso pursued more "liberal" goals than did the more moderate, and more successful, League of United Latin American Citizens (LULAC) founded in 1929. LULAC's forerunner appears to have been *La Orden Hijos de América* (Order of the Sons of America, or OSA). Organized in San Antonio in 1921 by members of a small but growing Tejano middle class, OSA restricted admission to native-born or naturalized U.S. citizens. Members stressed their Americanism and actively distinguished themselves from recent arrivals from Mexico. They followed an agenda that called for such things as better schooling, an end to segregation, and the right to serve on juries.

When the OSA broke up in the late 1920s, LULAC assumed its mantle. Composed of activist members from a petit bourgeoisie of native-born or U.S.-raised lawyers, doctors, merchants, other professionals, and World War I veterans who represented the emerging "Mexican American Generation" (as opposed to the "Immigrant Generation" of the earlier era) LULAC saw the assimilation into the mainstream as the solution to the problems Mexican Americans faced. Members of LULAC placed great faith in U.S. society's ability to change its racist tendencies and willingness to absorb their race if only Mexicans would adopt the English language and learn other Anglo ways. Once Tejanos altered their "Mexicanness," they could protest to demand their rights as Americans—especially the right to vote. Attacked from its inception as elitist and accommodationist, LULAC nonetheless would prove to have remarkable lasting power.

SOCIAL, CULTURAL, AND RECREATIONAL ACTIVITIES

The social life of Mexican Americans in Texas included traditional Mexican entertainment forms as well as some that reflected Tejano biculturation. Baseball, for example, was a great favorite; the talent many Tejano athletes displayed on local teams with names such as *Los Osos* or *Los Dorados* might well have qualified them, under different circumstances, for participation in minor league outfits. Boxing ranked high on the list as well; numerous young men entered the ring as amateurs and fought with distinction against both black and white opponents.

Mexican Americans observed special days with traditional festivities of various sorts. Religious holy days included commemoration of the date of the apparition of the *Virgen de Guadalupe* to Juan Diego in Mexico City in 1531 (December 12), All Souls' Day (November 2), and Christmas. *Fiestas patrias*, which honored the Mexican historical holidays of independence (*Diez y Seis*, September 16) or the date of the victory at the Battle of Puebla (*Cinco de Mayo*, May 5), were held in almost all Tejano communities. Additionally, Tejanos turned out en masse to attend locally sponsored observances of such distinctly American holidays as George Washington's Birthday or the Fourth of July.

Two members of *Conjunto Alamo:* Leandro Guerro (left) and Frank Corrales. Taken at KCOR radio station, San Antonio, Texas, 1949. *The UT Institute of Texan Cultures, No. 91-147*

The Tejano communities naturally comprised aficionados of music. Through corridos, Tejanos celebrated the brave deeds of Mexican and Mexican American heroes such as Catarino Garza, who had launched the abortive revolution against Porfirio Díaz in the early 1890s; Gregorio Cortez, who had stood up to the authorities following a shootout with a peace officer in Karnes County in 1901; and Jacinto Treviño, who had avenged the death of a brother at the hands of an Anglo in San Benito in 1910—all of whom had fought off the despised *rinches* (Texas Rangers).

Emerging as a working-class favorite by the 1920s was the music played by the *conjunto*, an accordion-led ensemble that popularized the regional music of northern Mexico in Texas. Although members of the Tejano proletariat found conjunto music quite attractive, those of the incipient bourgeoisie identified it with the vulgarity of the masses, the elites preferring more "cultured" musical expressions, such as those of the *orquesta* (orchestra).

Intellectual and artistic expression took a variety of forms. Tent theater and itinerant acting companies staged performances in various parts of South Texas. Indeed, so many of Mexico's best artists and troupes fled to Texas during the revolution that cities such as San Antonio became among the major theatrical centers in the nation. Texas Mexican writers did not often find English-language publishers for their material; consequently, many of their best short stories and poems can be found only in the archived Spanish-language newspapers of the era. Rediscovered in the 1970s, for example, were the works of the poet and activist Sara Estela Ramírez, who penned several literary pieces from Laredo in the early 1900s. In the 1990s, archivists found two novels that Jovita González wrote during the period between the 1920s and 1940s. Historians are only now making use of various memoirs found in manuscript form or in long-neglected books, such as J. Luz Saenz, *Los méxico americanos en la gran guerra* (San Antonio: Artes Gráficas, 1933), which describe Saenz's experiences in World War I.

Other Ethnic Groups

Foreign immigration to Texas continued throughout the early twentieth century. The National Origins Act of 1924 curtailed immigration of peoples from Southern and Eastern Europe, a fact reflected in the 1930 U.S. Census. Nevertheless, the 1920 census reported 360,519 foreign-born Texans, double the number in 1900. These figures did not include indigenous, native-born Texans who continued to preserve their foreign cultural heritage.

These sizeable ethnic communities supported fifty-seven foreign-language newspapers in 1909. The pressures of World War I contributed to a reduction in the number of these publications, but forty of them still ran in 1919. Of these, Spanish-language newspapers, which included six dailies, had a circulation of 88,033. The eleven German-language papers reached at least 25,950 households. In addition, Texas newspapers included Czech-, Polish-, and Swedish-language vehicles.

After Mexicans, Germans constituted the largest white ethnic group in Texas. In most cases, newly arrived immigrants from Germany tended to settle in previously established German "colonies" in Austin, Fayette, Lee, and Washington Counties. From these places, Germans pushed westward and northward to establish "folk islands" scattered throughout McLennan, Bosque, and Coryell Counties and up into the Cross Timbers and due west to the Hill Country. Cotton farming drew the Germans, who in their folk islands tended to retain the indigenous religions, cuisine, and architecture of their homeland. Their institutions and newspapers used their native language and reaffirmed their heritage. The large cities also attracted some German settlers. In 1920, about 1,500 Texans of German descent lived in Dallas and in Galveston, but San Antonio led all other cities, with a population of 3,400 Germans, roughly double the number living in Houston. Urban areas lessened the distinctiveness of European settlers, as they, unlike persons of several other immigrant groups, were not restricted to living in selected wards on account of their skin color. Nevertheless, San Antonio, as well as the Hill Country, retained a quite visibly German culture well past the World War II era.

Other European peoples arrived in Texas as well. Approximately 25,000 Czechs joined the Germans in the folk islands. The same economic forces that drew Germans to these areas also attracted Czechs, both of whom shared a common Eastern European heritage. An estimated 17,000 Polish immigrants settled in a belt extending northwest from Houston, tending to concentrate in the agricultural communities around Marlin and Bremond in Robertson County. By 1890, the state had seventeen Polish Roman Catholic parishes, whose members

Confirmation class of 1905 at Temple B'nai Israel, Galveton, Texas. *Archives of Temple B'nai, Galveston, Texas. The UT Institute of Texan Cultures, No. 73-1096*

had organized National Polish lodges. Meanwhile, approximately 8,000 Italians, mostly from Sicily, came to Texas. Some settled in the Galveston-Houston and Dallas–Fort Worth areas. Some 3,000 Italians migrated to Brazos County, settling along the fertile but often dangerous flood plain of the Brazos River, an area not farmed by older settlers who feared the periodic flood damage. Nevertheless, the Italian population in Brazos County prospered, proudly hosting a visit by the Italian ambassador to the United States in 1905.

Smaller but equally important immigrant groups in Texas included 1,356 Norwegians, who settled in Bosque County in 1900; immigrants from the Netherlands, who founded Nederland in Jefferson County; Lebanese, who settled in Houston and San Antonio; Greeks, who organized the first Greek Orthodox Church in Houston in 1917; Swedes, who migrated to Travis and Williamson Counties; and arrivals from Belgium, Denmark, France, Hungary, Russia, Switzerland, and Great Britain, most of whom went to major cities. Finally, some 1,000 Chinese and a few Japanese chose Texas as their new home, these persons settling mostly along the Rio Grande.

In general, ethnic whites got along well with their Anglo Texan neighbors. The one exception seems to have been during the period of World War I, when the superpatriotism that swept the country sometimes focused on those with foreign-sounding surnames, especially Germans. Indeed, the German Hill Country seemed under particular siege, as neighbor harassed neighbor over actions that some deemed unpatriotic, such as a failure to join the Red Cross or a refusal to endorse the draft.

LITERATURE AND THE ARTS

A rural society rarely produces writers or artists who attempt to explain or to evaluate the contemporary social scene. Early Texas authors tended to write adventure tales or travel accounts that described or drew upon the frontier heritage of the state. Some of these works have lasting value and remain a source for early Texas history, but their importance rests with their topics rather than their literary merit. Among these were John Crittenden Duval's *Early Times in Texas* (1892) and *The Adventures of Big Foot Wallace* (1870), a somewhat exaggerated biography of an early Texas Ranger. Francis R. Lubbock's *Six Decades of Texas* (1900) and John H. Reagan's *Memoirs* (1906) remain valuable accounts of Texas politicians. H. F. McDonield's and N. A. Taylor's *The Coming Empire, or Two Thousand Miles in Texas on Horseback* (1877) might have provided the best travel account of the period.

Some other works concentrated on the recent frontier and its hazards and opportunities for adventure. J. W. Wilbarger wrote *Indian Depredations in Texas* (1889), and James T. DeShields published *Border Wars of Texas* (1912). Neither painted a very positive portrait of Native Americans or took into account American Indian cultures. Cowboys and outlaws earned more favorable literary treatments. Napoleon Augustus Jennings, a New York newspaperman, recounted some of his own experiences in *A Texas Ranger* (1899), as did Charles H. Siringo, in *A Texas Cowboy, or Fifteen Years on the Hurricane Deck of a Spanish Pony* (1885). This book, by a true cowboy, sold thousands of copies and was an American classic, as was the superbly realistic novel of a young man's trail-driving experiences, *The Log of a Cowboy* (1903) by Andy Adams. The outlaws' West was portrayed in William Martin Walton's *The Life and Adventures of Ben Thompson* (1884), Austin's city marshal who was more famous for his brushes with the law than for enforcing it; in Henry C. Fuller's *The Adventures of Bill Longley* (1878); and in the autobiographical *Life of John Wesley Hardin* (1896).

A more reliable history of the state made its appearance during this period in local and county histories. Two amateur historians, John Henry Brown and Anna Pennybacker, each wrote acceptable nineteenth-century accounts of early Texas. Pennybacker, whose work was required reading for several generations of Texas schoolchildren, served as the president of the General Federation of Women's Clubs from 1902 to 1908, campaigned for the United States to join the League of Nations, and sent reports to three Texas newspapers from Geneva, Switzerland, in the early 1920s, keeping Lone Star readers abreast of the proceedings of the League of Nations after the Senate rejected U.S. membership in it.

Meanwhile, professional historians at the University of Texas turned their energies to writing and collecting materials on the state's past. George Pierce Garrison taught the first course in Texas history in 1897. That year he also organized the Texas State Historical Association (TSHA), the first learned society in Texas, which published the *Quarterly of the Texas State Historical Association*, now called the *Southwestern Historical Quarterly* and still a major source of historical information. Joining Garrison at the University of Texas were Herbert E. Bolton, Eugene C. Barker, and Charles W. Ramsdell. Bolton's work on the Spanish settlement, including *Texas in the Middle Eighteenth Century* (1915), made him a founder of the field of Borderlands studies. Barker edited and published the three-volume *Austin Papers* and then wrote the *Life of Stephen F. Austin* (1925) which became a classic. Ramsdell won a lasting reputation as an authority on the South, the Civil War, and Reconstruction. The interest of Texans in their history, now that the frontier was closed, led to the organization of the state archives. In 1891, Caldwell Walton Raines accepted his appointment as history clerk, or state librarian. He edited memoirs and speeches of well-known politicians, including those of James S. Hogg, but probably his most important scholarly endeavor remains his famous *Bibliography of Texas* (1896).

The state produced few authors who won enduring literary fame. Molly E. Moore Davis chose Texas for the setting of *Under the Man-Fig* (1895), an account of the limitations of life and opportunities in a small town. William Sidney Porter (O. Henry) moved from North Carolina to Austin, and his short story collection *Heart of the West* (1913), set mostly in Texas, established him as a master of that genre. Three Texas journalists enjoyed a brief period of national notoriety and popularity. William Cowper Brann published a monthly, the *Iconoclast*, from 1894 to 1898. Located first in Austin and then in Waco, the newspaper aimed at exposing and combating hypocrisy and intolerance. Brann met his death at the hands of a disgruntled reader. *Texas Siftings*, a humor magazine that used the Texas tall tale to entertain its readers, brought Alexander E. Sweet and John Armoy Knox a brief period of fame.

Texas's best-known authors started their work in the 1920s, but their accomplishments really reflected the more modern history of the state. J. Frank Dobie grew up on a ranch in West Texas at the turn of the century. He began his teaching career at the University of Texas in the 1920s. Convinced that southwesterners were unaware of their rich cultural heritage, he turned to folklore, recounting the stories told by the Anglo and Mexican American cowboys and farmers of his boyhood. He edited the Texas Folklore Society's annual publication from 1922 to 1943 and was determined that young Texas writers focus on their own region, rather than on New England or Europe. His efforts, joined by those of his colleagues and contemporaries, including Walter Prescott Webb, who taught history for more than three decades at the University of Texas, and Roy Bedicheck, who for many years directed the University Interscholastic League, dominated Texas literary life from the 1930s through the 1950s. Their influence on young writers who wished to explore the cultural heritage of the state cannot be quantified.

Several other writers who began their work in the 1920s left Texas for more fertile intellectual environs. Katherine Anne Porter, probably Texas's most distinguished fiction writer, was born in Brownwood and grew up in Kyle and San Antonio. In the 1920s, she wrote several short stories set in Texas, "Noon Wine" and "The Fig Tree," for example, which earned her an almost instant national reputation. She lived her life and continued her craft in New York, Paris, and elsewhere. Dorothy Scarborough also went to the East. Her best-known novel, *The Wind* (1925), outraged many West Texans with its unflattering portrait of life in the area. She also wrote sympathetic portraits of East Texas tenant farmers in *The Land of Cotton* (1923) and two lesser novels. Ruth Cross, who landed in Connecticut, published several novels about East Texas dirt farmers, the best of which was *The Golden Cocoon* (1924). Neither Scarborough nor Cross won or deserved the high praise that Porter received. Yet the work of all three women, like that of Webb, Dobie, and Bedicheck, reflected more of Texas's literary future than its past.

Texas poetry had barely begun in the decades preceding the Great Depression. Most Texas poets, like those living in other rural areas, concentrated on sentimental and frequently maudlin subjects, the best of which may be "Cowboy Christmas Ball" by William Lawrence "Larry" Chittenden. General poetry collections included Samuel Houston Dixon's *Poets and Poetry of Texas* (1885) and Francis D. Allan's *Lone Star Ballads* (1874), which included Confederate songs as well as verse. John P. Sjolander, a Swedish American, won a limited national following for his poetry of the Southwest.

The visual arts in Texas did not fare much better. Henry A. McArdle's historic panoramas, which hang in the state capitol, were highly praised. William H. Huddle, a contemporary of McArdle, similarly painted grand historical themes and a number of sought-after portraits. The Onderdonks, Robert Jenkins and his son Julian, won a local following and presently are well known for their painting of the Texas landscape. Frank Reagh's almost miniature impressionistic scenes of longhorns have recently come back into favor. The work of all these artists hang in museum and private collections.

Texas's best-known visual artist of this period was Elisabet Ney, who came to Texas in 1872 with her husband, Dr. Edmund Montgomery. Ney enjoyed an excellent reputation in Europe for the busts she cast of Schopenhauer, Garibaldi, and King William I of Prussia. Once in Texas, she first lived on Liendo plantation in Waller County, purchased from Leonard Groce, but found rural life stifling; after rearing her family, she moved to Austin in 1893. The next twelve years comprised the zenith of her work, as Ney turned out statues of the Texas heroes Austin and Houston and did a tombstone figure of Albert Sidney Johnston. Her best piece, *Lady Macbeth Walking in Her Sleep*, now resides in the National Gallery in Washington, D.C. Eventually, Ney's studio in Austin was purchased by the Texas Fine Arts Association and turned into a museum.

Texas music during this period continued to demonstrate its regional and heterogeneous character. San Antonio, with its large German population, had beer halls and gardens that featured ethnic music, singing societies, and Saengerfests, though German-music performances diminished with the anti-German spirit generated by World War I. The Tuesday music club in San Antonio, Dallas's St. Cecelia Club, and the organization of the Houston Symphony in 1913 all tried to interest their contemporaries in classical music, but with little success. Guest artists toured the state, beginning in 1900 with pianist Ignace Paderewski. Theater facilities in communities not far removed from rural villages remained crude and frequently inadequate; thus, performances were sporadic and mostly located in conveniently reached cities. In 1901, the Metropolitan Opera presented *Lohengrin* in Houston. Several years later, the company visited Dallas, Houston, and San Antonio, but it did not return again to Texas until 1939.

Popular music could be heard in the villages and towns that minstrel and vaudeville troupes visited regularly. In 1905, Karl Hoblitzelle organized the Interstate Circuit, which grew to 175 theaters and attracted well-known vaudeville performers. The advent of nickelodeons cut into the audience for stock companies, and beginning in 1920 the Interstate gradually converted into motion picture houses. This development, plus the increasing popularity of the phonograph after 1910, as well as radio broadcasts, which first started in 1920 with station WRR in Dallas, meant that national live performers and troupes came only to major Texas cities, if at all.

Meanwhile, village audiences enjoyed regional varieties of ethnic music—blues, corridos, Cajun—in addition to the stylings of musicians who played for dances, fairs, parades, and after celebrations. Indeed, local folk music from the southern United States certainly was well loved in Anglo Texas. By this time, the pure "mountain music" had blended with other strains of folk music, including "cowboy songs," the work songs of the same genre as the labor songs of union dissenters or miners. The cowboy songs, in turn, blended with Mexican music, just as cowboys and vaqueros had blended on the range. Clearly, black blues influenced white music, not only rhythmically but also in shared Protestant religious traditions and in the emotional themes of rural life: sadness, death, and poverty.

Out of this eclectic music came what is known as hillbilly music, which current scholars suggest differs from earlier musical forms in that its songs always tell a story and that its devotees took it from the country to the cities of the South. The commercialization of this musical form was only beginning in the 1920s. Radio station WBAP in Fort Worth originated a not-yet-regularly scheduled country music show in 1923, the popularity of which would earn it a regular time slot on Saturday nights. The new availability of phonographs spurred record companies to broaden their repertoire in search of new customers. The first national hillbilly hit, "The Prisoner's Song," resulted from such efforts. Native Texan Vernon Dalhart (he was born Marion T. Sloughtier but combined the names of two Texas towns to form his stage name) recorded the piece in 1924. Later in the decade, Jimmie Rogers, the first nationally known hillbilly singer, began his career. Although not born in Texas (he moved to Kerrville in 1929), Rogers relied heavily on Texas themes and was the first national performer to incorporate the blues into white folk music. Rogers dominated the country charts until his untimely death from tuberculosis in 1933. Like those of other Texas artists of the period, Rogers's career pointed to the future rather than the past. His success represented in a larger sense Texas music, and, for that matter, Texas culture: still rural and provincial, not yet committed to fine arts, it was nevertheless responding to a rapidly developing urban environment.

READINGS

Books

Allen, Ruth A., *The Labor of Women in the Production of Cotton* (Austin: Bulletin No. 3134 of the University of Texas, 1931).

Barksdale, E. C., *The Meat Packers Come to Texas* (Austin: Bureau of Business Research, 1959).

Belleter, Erika, ed., *Images of Mexico: The Contribution of Mexico to Twentieth-Century Art* (Dallas: The Dallas Museum of Art, 1987).

Bryant, Keith, L., Jr., *Arthur Stillwell: Promoter With a Hunch* (Nashville: Vanderbilt University Press, 1971).

Buenger, Walter L., *The Path to a Modern South: Northeast Texas Between Reconstruction and the Great Depression* (Austin: University of Texas Press, 2001).

Carlson, Paul H., *Texas Woollybacks: The Range Sheep and Goat Industry* (College Station: Texas A&M University Press, 1982).

Clark, James A., and Michael Halbouty, *Spindletop* (New York: Random House, 1952).

Cutrer, Emily, F., *The Art of the Woman: The Life and Work of Elisabet Ney* (Lincoln: University of Nebraska Press, 1988).

Davis, Ronald L., *Twentieth Century Cultural Life in Texas* (Boston: American Press, 1981).

De León, Arnoldo, *Mexican Americans in Texas: A Brief History* (2nd ed.; Wheeling, IL: Harlan Davidson, Inc., 1999).

Foley, Neil, *The White Scourge: Mexicans, Blacks, and Poor Whites in Texas Cotton Culture* (Berkeley: University of California Press, 1997).

García, Mario T., *Desert Immigrants: The Mexicans of El Paso, 1880–1920* (New Haven, CT: Yale University Press, 1981).

Hall, Jacquelyn Dowd, *Revolt Against Chivalry: Jessie Daniel Ames and the Women's Campaign Against Lynching* (New York: Columbia University Press, 1979).

Hernández, José Amaro, *Mutual Aid of Survival: The Case of the Mexican American* (Malabar, FL: Krieger Publishing Co., 1983).

Hyman, Harold, *Oleander Odyssey: The Kempners of Galveston, ca. 1850–1987* (College Station: Texas A&M University Press, 1990).

King, John O., *Joseph Stephen Cullinan: A Study of Leadership in the Texas Petroleum Industry, 1897–1937* (Nashville: Vanderbilt University Press, 1970).

Malone, Anne Patton, "Women in Texas History," in *Guide to the History of Texas*, edited by Light Townsend Cummins and Alvin R. Bailey (New York: Greenwood Press, 1987).

Malone, Bill C., *Country Music U.S.A.* (Austin: The University of Texas Press, 1985).

Maxwell, Robert S., *Texas Economic Growth, 1890 to World War II: From Frontier to Industrial Giant* (Boston: American Press, 1981).

McComb, David, *Houston: A History* (Austin: University of Texas Press, 1981).

———, *Galveston: A History* (Austin: University of Texas Press, 1986).

Montejano, David, *Anglos and Mexicans in the Making of Texas, 1836–1986* (Austin: Univeristy of Texas Press, 1987).

Olien, Roger, and Diana Olien, *Wildcatters: Texas Independent Oilmen* (Austin: Texas Monthly Press, 1984).

———, *Oil Booms: Social Change in Five Texas Towns* (Lincoln: University of Nebraska Press, 1982).

Parédes, Américo, *A Texas-Mexican Cancionero: Folksongs of the Lower Border* (Urbana: University of Illinois Press, 1976).

Pate, J'Nell L., *Livestock Legacy: The Fort Worth Stockyards, 1887–1987* (College Station: Texas A&M University Press, 1988).

Peña, Manuel, *The Texas-Mexican Conjunto: History of a Working Class Music* (Austin: The University of Texas Press, 1985).

Pilkington, William T., *Imagining Texas: The Literature of The Lone Star State* (Boston: American Press, 1981).

Rhinehart, Marilyn D., *A Way of Work and a Way of Life: Coal Mining in Thurber Texas, 1888–1926* (College Station: Texas A&M University Press, 1992).

Sharpless, Rebecca, *Fertile Ground, Narrow Choices: Women on Texas Cotton Farms, 1900–1940* (Chapel Hill: University of North Carolina Press, 1999).

Smallwood, James, *The Struggle for Equality: Blacks in Texas* (Boston: American Press 1983).

Winegarten, Ruthe, *Texas Women: A Pictorial History from Indians to Astronauts* (Austin: Eakin Press, 1986).

Woodman, Harold D., *King Cotton and His Retainers: Financing and Marketing the Cotton Crop of the South, 1880–1925* (Lexington: University of Kentucky Press, 1968).

Zamora, Emilio, *World of the Mexican Worker in Texas* (College Station: Texas A&M University Press, 1993).

Articles

Buenger, Walter L. "'This Wonder Age': The Economic Transformation of Northeast Texas, 1900–1930," *Southwestern Historical Quarterly* 98 (April 1995): 519–50.

Cardoso, Lawrence A., "Labor Emigration to the Southwest, 1916 to 1920: Mexican Attitudes and Policy," *Southwestern Historical Quarterly* 79 (1975): 400–16.

Droze, William H., "Rise of the Cotton Mill Industry in Texas, 1850–1933," *Cotton History Review* 2 (1961): 71–84.

Jordan, Terry G., "A Century and a Half of Ethnic Change in Texas, 1836–1986," *Southwestern Historical Quarterly* 89 (1986): 385–423.

King, John O., "The Early Texas Oil Industry: Beginnings at Corisicana, 1894–1900," *Journal of Southern History* 32 (1966): 505–15.

Maroney, James C., "The Galveston Longshoremen's Strike of 1920," *East Texas Historical Journal* 16 (1978): 3.

Márquez, Benjamin, "The Politics of Race and Assimilation: The League of United Latin American Citizens, 1929–1940," *The Western Political Quarterly* 42 (June, 1989).

White, Raymond D., "The Texas Cotton Ginning Industry, 1860–1900," *Texana* 5 (1967): 344–58.

Young, Elliott, "Deconstructing *La Raza*: Identifying the *Gente Decente* of Laredo, 1904–1911" *Southwestern Historical Quarterly* 98 (October 1994): 227–59.

PROGRESSIVISM IN TEXAS

CHAPTER 10

Historians have described the political history of the United States between 1901 and the early 1920s as the Progressive Era. Rapid social and economic change spawned progressivism, as a rising middle class of urban professionals, who wished to create a cohesive community for economic development, joined with agrarian and social reformers. Together, these "progressives" worked to effect good government, end corrupt politics, improve rural life, curtail the influence of large corporations, purify social institutions through laws such as the prohibition of alcohol, and otherwise improve society through prison, educational, social welfare, and suffrage reforms. The progressives stressed that social goals were obtainable through efficient bureaucracy and public education. In short, they believed that through reform they might create an orderly and moral climate, as well as foster industrial and agricultural prosperity.

The Texas brand of progressivism differed from previous reform movements. Unlike Radical Reconstruction, it was an indigenous movement; unlike Populism, it operated within the Democratic party. It also occurred within a shrinking electorate, as African American and lower-class political participation waned. Southern and Texas progressivism aimed for a democratic society for whites only. And all progressives perceived recent immigrants and the uneducated as threats to middle-class, democratic perceptions. Consequently, they saw no clash between social control and social reform. Moreover, Texas progressives remained bound to older agrarian solutions of agricultural efficiency and technical training, and blind to problems of tenant farmers and minority groups. Within these self-imposed limitations, Texas progressivism succeeded.

Texas progressivism carried an inherent anti-eastern bias, which dated back to the Hogg administration and the creation of the Railroad Commission. Texas reformers saw Commission regulations as one way to relieve local businesses from

Above: William Pettus Hobby at the Galveston Convention in 1930 (campaigning for Sterling for governor). *Sterling (Ross S.) Papers, "First Campaign in Photographs" album, 353. The Center for American History, The University of Texas at Austin*

competition with and reliance upon northern financial interests. Therefore, one intent of expanding the power of the Railroad Commission and of state banking and insurance laws was to ensure some protection in the marketplace for local businesspeople. Although Texas progressives did succeed in passing needed regulatory legislation, their attempts to make Texans independent of northern money interests mostly failed.

INTO THE TWENTIETH CENTURY: GOVERNORS SAYERS AND LANHAM

The early years of the twentieth century witnessed a beginning, but not an upsurge, in the progressive movement in Texas. Texas governors Joseph Sayers (1899–1903) and S. W. T. Lanham (1903–1907) were not committed reformers. E. M. House managed both of their campaigns. It was House who persuaded Sayers, a Civil War veteran and former lieutenant governor (1878–1879), to resign from Congress and run for governor. After Sayers's two terms as governor, Lanham, also a Civil War veteran (and the last ex-Confederate to serve as governor), left Congress for the governor's office. Both men were conservative by nature and desired not to upset the favorable business climate, which they credited the developing oil and surging lumber industries with having created. At the same time, the demands for social reforms were lagging, the upheavals of Populism and the Spanish-American War having encouraged a return to the political status quo.

Nevertheless, during the early years of the twentieth century, the state legislature enacted some progressive measures. Some of the legislative proposals for these reforms sprang from the old agrarian coalition of former Governor Hogg, who returned to active political campaigning in 1900 in support of his old friend, incumbent Senator Horace Chilton. Although Chilton's bid for reelection failed, during the campaign Hogg had introduced a reform package calling for three new amendments to the state constitution to counter railroad abuses. While the amendments did not receive favorable legislative support in the 1900 legislature, the efforts of the former Hogg forces signaled an attempt to woo former Populists and old Alliancemen, now active in the Farmers' Union, back into a political coalition. A number of other organizations, including commercial clubs of businesspersons, antiliquor forces, women's clubs, and the State Federation of Labor, joined the appeal for progressive legislation. Much of their efforts centered on election reform, which, ironically, some ex-Populists endorsed as the only method to ensure certain reform goals.

The adoption of the poll tax in 1902 had marked the start of election reform. The poll tax served as a system of voter registration, which made fraud on election day more difficult to perpetrate. The 1905 Terrell Election Law (which superceded a similar but weaker law passed in 1903) furthered the cause of election reform. The law, proposed by senior statesman Alexander W. Terrell, attempted to eliminate election fraud and bring some uniformity into the process of selecting candidates by establishing a modern system of primary elections. Prior to the reform, county nominating conventions were not always called with adequate notice, or were convened at inappropriate times, thus limiting rank-and-file participation. Local political bosses sometimes scheduled conventions to give advantages to certain candidates. In order to prevent such shenanigans, the law guaranteed official secret ballots and prescribed deadlines for the payment of poll taxes. But the centerpiece of the new law was the requirement that all political parties that had polled more than 100,000 votes in the last general election (normally, only the Democrats) would hold primary elections on the fourth Saturday in July. Late July traditionally was a time of agricultural inactivity, and conducting the primary at that time maximized farmers' opportunity to participate in politics. The law further mandated that county and precinct nominees be selected by primary voting returns rather than by convention. Finally, the 1905 law required filed statements of campaign expenses within ten days of a general or primary election and regularized voting qualifications and party governance procedures. Subsequent legislation in 1907, 1913, and 1918 refined the 1905 law.

While the poll tax and the Terrell law did much to clean up elections, the reforms came at the expense of democracy. The poll tax disfranchised large numbers of African Americans who could not afford to pay it. Although the measure may have been undemocratic, progressives still considered the poll tax a reform, for in the 1890s, black votes often had been manipulated by corrupt politicians. Historians have estimated that only between 15,000 and 40,000 of the 160,000 black males over the age of twenty-one in Texas managed to retain the right to vote in the 1920s. The tax also eliminated from the electorate many of the poorest whites—a group that had been all-too-eager to embrace the radical notions of Populism in the 1890s. Progressives were confident that eliminating such "unsavory" elements from politics would go far to clean up the system.

Progressives secured other limited gains during the Sayers and Lanham administrations. Labor unions were exempted from antitrust legislation, fulfilling a major demand of organized labor. Other prolabor measures included limiting the number of consecutive hours railroad trainmen could work to sixteen; increasing safety standards for railroad employees; the outlawing of blacklists, company scrip, and mandatory trading at company stores; and passage of the first law regulating child labor. In practice, some employers ignored this legislation.

Tax reform, long demanded by agrarian interests, also began in this period. In 1905, the legislature raised taxes on intangible assets of corporations and taxed the gross receipts of railroads and insurance corporations. Franchise tax laws, which taxed a company's capital investment, also passed that year, although an attempt to levy additional corporate taxes failed. Backed by the strong progressive leadership of attorney Thomas B. Love of Dallas, the legislature created a commission of insurance and banking; it also initiated a constitutional amendment in 1903 (ratified in 1904) that allowed the chartering of state banks, which had been prohibited by the Constitution of 1876. These laws were designed both to prevent banking abuses and generate local capital investment. The new commission, led by Love, authorized more than 500 banks over the next five years. Other bills that Love and like-minded progressives favored during the governorships of Sayers and Lanham, such as restricting usurious interest rates, creating pure food and drug laws, regulating private banks, raising liquor-license fees, and protecting household furnishings from seizure for debts, all failed.

BAILEYISM AND ANTITRUST

Antitrust suits constituted a major element of progressivism. Progressives believed that restoring competition in the marketplace would attract new industry to Texas and create a favorable business climate for local investors. Texas had a long history of antitrust sentiment, and in 1889 and 1903 the legislature enacted laws restricting trusts. Before World War I, state attorneys prosecuted more than one hundred companies for violating state antitrust laws. Most famous of these antitrust suits was the Waters-Pierce case, which centered on the relationship of U.S. Congressman and later Senator Joseph Weldon Bailey and Henry Clay Pierce, the president of the Waters-Pierce company. In 1897, Attorney General M. M. Crane brought suit against the Waters-Pierce company because it was controlled by the Standard Oil trust of New Jersey. Found in violation of state antimonopoly law, Waters-Pierce was made to forfeit its state charter, at which point Pierce appealed to Bailey for aid. Now, the congressman recommended that the company be reorganized and urged Governor Sayers and other state officials to admit it back into the state. Crane followed Bailey's advice, and the reorganized company, now supposedly devoid of Standard Oil affiliations, once more conducted business within Texas. Then, an investigation in 1905 by the State of Missouri revealed that in contradiction of a 1900 affidavit by company officials, Standard Oil still owned 3,000 shares of Waters-Pierce stock.

Some citizens had always maintained that Bailey's actions had represented a conflict of interest. The Missouri suit seemingly affirmed their charges. Into the public eye came affidavits that tied Bailey to Pierce; the latter employed Bailey as a legal counsel and had loaned him $5000. Later, critics charged Bailey, who by this time was a U.S. Senator, with being compromised by accepting legal fees from both the Standard Oil Company and the Kirby lumber interests. In 1906 Attorney General Robert V. Davidson successfully prosecuted Waters-Pierce: the company was ousted from the state and ultimately paid a $1,808,483.30 fine. While the conflict-of-interest charges leveled at Bailey did not subside, he ran unopposed in the 1906 United States senatorial primary. His opponents urged the state legislature to ignore the primary results and refuse to elect him. For his part, Bailey maintained that his relationship with Standard Oil was a client-lawyer business arrangement and that charges of misconduct against him emanated from political foes. The voters apparently believed him, returning him to the Senate in 1907. Moreover, by that time, both the state senate and house had investigated the charges. The senate exonerated him, while the house sent forth a qualified approval of his conduct. Not satisfied, Bailey determined to make the control of the 1908 Texas delegation to the national Democratic convention a political test of his support; in a scathing campaign, pro-Bailey forces did just that. Two years later, Cone Johnson, an openly anti-Bailey candidate for the Democratic gubernatorial nomination, lost to Oscar Branch Colquitt who got along with Bailey. Nevertheless, Bailey found himself increasingly out of step with progressive Texans. Opposed to prohibition, women's suffrage, and Woodrow Wilson, who received Texas delegation support in 1912 for the presidency, the senator retired to private life in January 1913. Although the issue of Baileyism remained a factor in Texas politics, supporters pressed him to return to the political arena. Consequently, he ran against Pat Neff in the 1920 Democratic primary for governor. He was soundly defeated.

TEXAS IN THE CAMPBELL AND COLQUITT ADMINISTRATIONS

The gubernatorial contest of 1906 featured a campaign in which all the candidates endorsed progressive reform measures. Democrat Thomas M. Campbell, a lawyer from Palestine, received the endorsement of ex-Governor Hogg. Campbell went on to defeat three other candidates in the first primary conducted under the new Terrell Election Law and win the governorship (1907–1911).

The new governor was a genial, pleasant man who believed in prohibition but considered one's use of alcohol a moral choice, one outside the realm of politics. Nevertheless, Campbell and the Thirtieth Legislature formed the most reform-minded government in Texas history. During the Campbell administration, the legislature passed the Hogg antirailroad amendments, which prevented insolvent corporations from operating in Texas, prohibited the wholesale granting of railroad passes, and denied the use of corporate funds for political purposes. Other measures Campbell oversaw included an antinepotism law and strengthened antitrust legislation. The governor responded to demands for tax reform in 1907 with a law aimed at taxing the intangible assets of corporations. This so-called full-rendition law doubled the value of assets on state tax rolls. In 1909 the law was amended, creating a tax board composed of the governor, treasurer, and comptroller to supervise ad valorem taxation. While Campbell failed to convince the legislature to pass a state income tax, he did secure an inheritance tax and higher franchise levies on liquor dealers.

One of the Campbell administration's premiere accomplishments was the Robertson Insurance Law of 1907, which required insurance companies to invest at least 75 percent of their resources drawn from Texas in state real estate and securities. The law also established codes for the various classes of insurance and limited premiums and related charges. Out-of-state insurance companies protested that opportunity for investment in Texas did not merit such a sizable commitment of their funds, and twenty-one of them withdrew from the state. The law had mixed benefits. Certainly, insurance companies previously had invested only a minimum of their funds in state securities, and such investments increased. The state commissioner of insurance and banking modified the regulations, and by 1914, the amount of capital invested in Texas by insurance companies had increased by more than $24 million. On the downside, the law encouraged the development of some "wildcat" companies—that is, local insurance firms that were financially shaky, which created problems for consumers as well as state government. For its part, the insurance lobby continued to fight for modification or repeal of the Robertson law until it was overturned in 1963.

Less controversial was the passage in 1909 of the Bank Deposit Guaranty Act, which created a state insurance program to protect deposits in the newly authorized state banking system. The plan worked well until the 1920s, when the failure of some banks in the economic downturn of that era put stress on the system, as did some mismanagement. The state deposit insurance program was repealed in 1927. Not until the organization of the Federal Deposit Insurance Corporation in 1933 was there similar national legislation.

The Campbell administration supported other legislation that typified southern progressivism: it encouraged an expansion of the Galveston Plan of city government; it responded to agrarian demands by creating a department of agriculture; and appeased urban residents by establishing a state library and a historical commission. Furthermore, Campbell advocated a more direct democracy through the use of initiative, referendum, and recall. Although these procedures did not receive state approval, they were included in certain city charters. And under his tutelage, the prison and public school systems saw reform. In 1907, the legislature strengthened the state's antitrust measures. That year, too, it passed laws extending the eight-hour day to telegraph operators and creating a bureau of labor statistics. Campbell enjoyed fewer successes in his second administration, as prohibition dominated much of the state's political energies after 1908 and crowded out other political issues.

In the gubernatorial election of 1910, Oscar Branch Colquitt, who favored local option in the matter of prohibition, ran as a conservative and aligned himself with the "wet" forces, who opposed statewide prohibition. He won a plurality in the primary and the general election and served as governor from 1911 to 1915. Colquitt was not as committed a progressive as was Campbell. Colquitt's strong antiprohibition stand in the election and his pro-German stance, as World War I neared, alienated him from most progressives. In 1916, he lost in his bid for the U.S. Senate to Charles Culberson and joined a Dallas oil firm. Later, Colquitt bolted the Democratic party and headed the 1928 Hoover Democrats of Texas (who supported the Republican Herbert Hoover for president).

Colquitt's years in office did catalog some progressive achievements. The legislature passed laws regulating child labor, factory safety standards, and the hours of women workers. Furthermore, under Colquitt the first state workmen's compensation legislation was passed, penal reforms continued, and the state built a hospital for tubercular patients, a training school for delinquent children, and allowed counties to create poor farms for the indigent. The governor focused his attention primarily, however, on two pressing problems: the Rio Grande border and the state's finances.

The border problems developed from the 1910 Mexican Revolution, in which insurgent forces ousted the regime of the dictator Porfirio Díaz. As the fighting increased in northern Mexico, the border country from Brownsville to El Paso became the scene of revolutionary activity. The insurrectionists bought arms and equipment from U.S. merchants, recruited freely among South Texas sympathizers of the Revolution, launched guerrilla raids on ranches and farms

Adapted from Lewis L. Gould, Progressives and Prohibitionists: Texas Democrats in the Wilson Era *(Austin: University of Texas Press, 1973), p.33.*

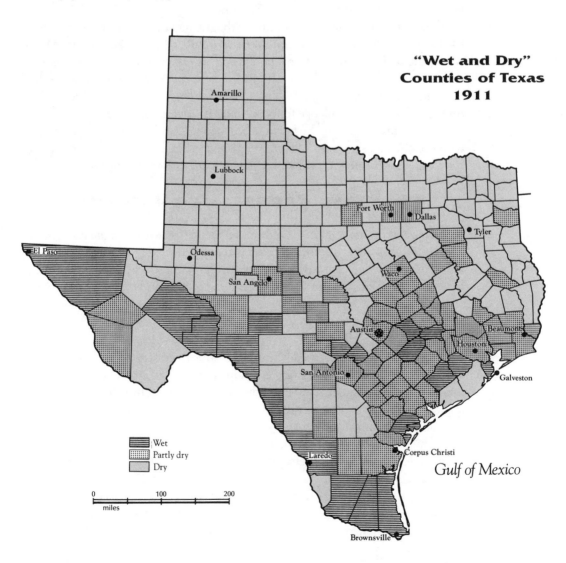

"Wet and Dry" Counties of Texas 1911

to secure needed provisions, sabotaged railroad lines, and in other ways used the Texas side of the border for carrying on the Revolution. Presidents William Howard Taft and Woodrow Wilson sent troops to the border, but they did so with caution and reservations, for both chief executives wished to develop a broader relationship with Mexico as part of their foreign policy. Colquitt, however, responded more boldly to repeated incursions onto Texas soil by ordering the Rangers to the Rio Grande. According to the governor, the move was essential for the protection of the people and the region. In April 1914, following the U.S. occupation of Vera Cruz, Mexico, Colquitt sent part of the Texas National Guard to Brownsville to deter feared attacks by Mexican troops. Colquitt condemned Wilson's policies toward Mexico as weak and urged the president to intervene more directly in the Mexican Revolution. Wilson's refusal to follow the governor's advice led to a division between Colquitt and Texas progressives, who mostly supported Wilson.

Colquitt's other principal irritant was that he had inherited a tax system with too low a tax base. The governor thus faced a state deficit of $1 million. Meanwhile, the new state institutions, public education, prison reform, and bureaucracies in a developing Texas demanded new revenue. State expenses had increased dramatically since 1900, and even though Colquitt campaigned for his second term with a pledge for economies in government, he found it necessary to raise tax rates. Still, he failed to broaden the tax base, and this, combined with the chronic shortage of tax funds, played a central role in Texas politics as state leaders struggled to deal with the emergence of an urban state.

GENERAL PROGRESSIVE REFORMS

Some reform movements could not be identified with a single governor or legislature. A consensus of the Texas citizenry endorsed these institutional reforms, most of which came to fruition in the years after World War I. All of them, however, began at the turn of the twentieth century and typified the progressive spirit.

Educational Reforms

Progressives considered educational reforms necessary both for the sake of their children and for attracting new industry to the South. They built upon a long-term agricultural demand that education include technical training and be made available at no cost to rural citizens. Reformers also wanted to standardize teachers' qualifications, upgrade the quality of the schools, and bring about uniformity and efficiency through a bureaucracy. Although important strides were made in educational reforms, the relative poverty of Texas limited the possible accomplishments.

Nevertheless, between 1890 and 1920, the number of pupils attending Texas public schools increased by 120 percent. About 73 percent of school-age children attended some public school in 1920, with a corresponding drop in illiteracy to 8.3 percent of the population, the lowest in the South. In turn, state expenditure per student, taxation for support of education, and teacher salaries rose. Yet in 1920 an independent survey ranked Texas thirty-ninth nationally in the quality of education offered. One problem in improving Texas's education system was that the tax base and, subsequently, the amount spent per pupil were so low that even dramatic increases in expenditures never matched the amount spent per pupil in most northern and midwestern states.

One general progressive reform was a move to regularize education, so that all school districts might use the same books, offer similar courses, have the same requirements for students and teachers, and resemble one another administratively. Generally, two types of school districts existed: common, which were largely rural; and independent, which usually served incorporated towns. Common schools were administered by trustees, who convened voluntarily to hire teachers and operate and maintain a school. The school district boundaries could change from year to year, but most common school districts comprised a single building that housed all the grades. Independent school districts resembled, for the most part, present-day school systems. Critics of the one-teacher, common schools maintained that rural students received an inferior education. One proposed solution was school consolidation. Under the law of 1909, county lines no longer served as borders for school districts, and in 1914, a majority of voters could consolidate two or more schools. Furthermore, improved transportation and roads allowed the state to provide free transportation for rural students. By 1925, school trustees could mandate consolidation, under certain conditions, and rural students were transported free of charge to their schoolhouses. By 1929, more than 1,500 school consolidations had been accomplished.

Reformers also wanted to issue free textbooks of uniform quality. A 1907 law mandated five-year adoptions for all textbooks, meaning that once chosen, the same title had to be used for the next five years. This requirement provided a measure of uniformity across school districts and prevented schools from merely tailoring requirements to include books that students might happen to own. By 1911, districts could if they wished provide free books; but since few did, a 1918 constitutional amendment mandated that the state issue books. The intense lobbying for selection of a particular company's textbook, and educational reformers' unhappiness with the failure of some publishers to deliver their books on time or at the agreed-upon cost led in 1925 to multiple lists of acceptable books. In 1927, publishing companies wishing to supply Texas schools had to maintain textbook depositories in the state.

Meanwhile, progressives and professional educators fought for compulsory attendance legislation. In 1905, such a bill failed. In 1914, women's clubs, the Texas State Teachers Association (TSTA), the Colored Teachers State Association (CTSA), and other supporters of educational reform pointed out that Texas was one of only five states that had no compulsory school attendance law. The next year, the legislature passed a law requiring that all children between the ages of eight and fourteen attend school for at least a sixty-day term. The school year was to be expanded over the next two years until it comprised at least 100 days. Certain exemptions for students were allowed, however, limiting the impact of the legislation. By 1929, Texas school terms averaged 156 days yearly, the highest in the South and only six days below the national average.

Progressives also wanted to professionalize education by making school administration more efficient and increasing the tax base to provide local schools with sufficient funds to provide a minimum education. The TSTA, CTSA, and women's clubs spearheaded these as well as other educational reforms. Annie Webb Blanton, the first woman president of the TSTA (1916) and the first woman to hold statewide office, superintendent of public instruction (1918–1922), organized the "Better Schools Campaign," which in 1920 helped secure the passage of a constitutional amendment permitting districts to raise school taxes above the original constitutional restrictions.

In 1917, the State Department of Education took over for the University of Texas as the official accrediting agent for high schools, and its powers, as well as those of county school trustees, expanded throughout the period. The State Board of Education, composed of nine members appointed by the governor, replaced the State Department of Education in 1929 and brought bureaucratic efficiency to the state. Its chief duties were to apportion the public school funds, select textbooks, and oversee investments of the permanent school fund and the distribution of funds to rural schools.

The upgrading of teacher qualifications caused reformers great difficulties. As late as 1920, 48 percent of common school teachers in Texas had not graduated from high school. Only 16 percent had graduated from a normal school, and 5 percent from a college or a university. In the case of independent districts, teacher qualifications were considerably better, with 92 percent holding at least a high school certificate, and with over 50 percent having graduated from a normal school, college, or university. But all teachers tended to be transient, with most staying on the job under two years. The state addressed the problems of teacher training as early as 1907 with a conference on education in Texas. One obvious conclusion reached was the need to expand normal-school training for teachers, and by 1911, the state created a Normal School Board of Regents. The legislature authorized the establishment of normal schools at Denton (North Texas Normal, 1899), San Marcos (Southwest Texas Normal, 1899), Alpine (Sul Ross Normal 1917), Commerce (East Texas Normal, 1917), and Nacogdoches (Stephen F. Austin Normal, 1917). Along with the previously established Sam Houston State Normal Institute at Huntsville, in 1923 the legislature designated all of the above as teachers' colleges, giving educators places in which to specialize in teacher training. The state converted South Texas Teachers College in 1929 into the Texas College of Arts and Industries.

As hoped, the availability of higher education and the drive for the professionalization of teaching upgraded the quality of the public schools. By 1929, the number of public school teachers who had graduated from either normal school or college reached 39 percent for common and 73 percent for independent school districts, with 64 percent of all teachers having had four or more years of experience. Nevertheless, the state still confronted overwhelming problems in upgrading teaching staffs. For one thing, teachers were grossly underpaid. In 1920, the average annual salary for a Texas teacher was $615, or about 55 percent of that of the average Texas wage earner. Black teachers earned less than did white ones, and rural teachers earned less than did their urban counterparts. Annie Webb Blanton asked to no avail that the State Industrial Commission set a minimum wage for teachers. Some teachers tried to join or organize unions but met traditional Texas hostility toward such organizations. By 1929, Texas teachers' salaries averaged $924 per year, as compared to the national mark of $1,420.

Texas school districts did come to exercise less control over the social and private life of their employees during the progressive period. Married female teachers found ready employment after World War I. Even with the loosening of restrictions, some rural districts still had rules that forbade teachers to dance in public and established teacher dress codes, which included provisions against bobbed hair. Others, particularly in the years immediately following World War I, forbade teachers from endorsing political candidates. But by 1929, such restrictions were the exception rather than the rule, and by then teaching was gaining the status of a profession.

Possibly, the major impact of progressivism on education was not an improved teaching staff, but rather a change in philosophy. Progressive educators viewed the classroom as a dynamic environment that stimulated learning and was relevant to an individual's life. They supported curriculum changes that took into account the new social science disciplines of psychology and sociology. The changes were far-reaching and included the development of new courses in such fields as economics and business and put less emphasis on rote learning. Progressives also advocated practical training, such as manual, shop, or commercial skills. As more job opportunities opened for women, curriculum expansion included stenography and typewriting, in addition to upgraded home economics courses. Businesspeople, who saw new course offerings as beneficial to the economic well-being of the state, endorsed these reforms, as well as standardized testing and special training in public school administration, which they thought would bring business-like management to the public schools.

The schools broadened their interaction with students to include previously avoided duties. Administrators authorized regular supervised recess periods on the playgrounds. The development of the University Interscholastic League by the University of Texas regularized athletic competitions and instilled a concern for public affairs through declamation and debating contests. Stressing the new-found importance of social adjustment and vocational training for students, administrators advocated the opening of junior high schools, the necessity of attracting more students into high school, and the modernizing of curriculum in order to keep students in school by keeping them interested in their courses. Schools now undertook some health care responsibilities for students, and school nurses visited many of the school districts with regularity. The public health movement sent experts, usually through university extension work, to school-houses to lecture on disease prevention and to aid administrators in maintaining proper sanitation facilities, health and safety standards, and fire control. Teachers were urged to make classrooms more attractive and to update pedagogical technique through visual aids and lesson plans.

Progressive reformers maintained that schools had a responsibility for the improvement of the social order. Schools were called upon to Americanize the foreign born, teach democratic principles, and impart moral values. Civics classes, courses in United States and Texas history, and supervised debates over the character of democracy and citizenship became a regular part of school activities. Some districts created special schools or classes for the foreign born. The increased responsibility of public schools led to the establishment of night schools for immigrants and other adults, so that lessons in democracy and civic responsibility might be extended to those outside the student population. Under progressive guidelines, schools evolved from simple places of learning into social environments that were purveyors of Jeffersonian democracy.

Colleges underwent similar changes. In 1901, the College for Industrial Arts for Women (now Texas Woman's University) was authorized. The legislature added Texas College of Mines (now the University of Texas at El Paso) in 1913 and Texas Technological College (now Texas Tech University) in 1923. Private college education expanded with the creation of Rice Institute (1912) and Southern Methodist (1915), which joined existing church-affiliated schools, Trinity (1869), Southwestern (1873), Baylor (1887), Hardin-Simmons (1891), and Texas Christian (1902). The Baptist state convention expanded its system of higher educational institutions in 1897 with the creation of Mary Hardin Baylor College as a senior school and Howard Payne College, Rusk College, and Decatur College as two-year schools. Other denominations authorized a number of two-year church colleges. Meanwhile, the legislature and cities endorsed the nationwide junior college movement. The state founded junior colleges at Stephenville and Arlington, and cities created seventeen other ones. The junior, or community colleges, were especially significant because they had open-door admissions policies that accepted students of all ages and levels of achievement.

Colleges undertook new roles. Professional education was expanded with the creation of colleges of business, education, engineering, and pharmacy. Various academic disciplines now offered graduate training. Schools of medicine and law were upgraded and new ones were established. Colleges instituted elective course curricula that enabled students to broaden their educations and better prepare for future occupations. By 1930, Texans enjoyed a wide range of options for higher learning at relatively low cost. The expansion and availability of colleges saw student enrollment skyrocket, from 2,148 in 1900 to 23,134 in 1929.

Progressives accepted as axiomatic the Jeffersonian proposition that mass education produced a more responsible citizenry. They expected colleges as well as the public schools to extend that theory to all white citizens. Consequently, university administrators created outreach programs to instruct those Texans who could not enroll on a campus. Agricultural reform, with its long tradition in Texas, fitted nicely within the progressive concept of rebuilding the southern farms through technical expertise offered outside the classroom. The Agricultural and Mechanical College at College Station responded by planting demonstration farms, establishing the Texas Agricultural Experiment Station, and conducting farmer institutes throughout the state. Much of the aid to farmers was designed to foster efficient management. Impressed with Seaman A. Knapp's work on control of the boll weevil, the United States Department of Agriculture (USDA) agreed to establish five demonstration farms on the Gulf Coast. Knapp also started the Home Demonstration Movement in the USDA. By 1912, the Agricultural and Mechanical College was cooperating with the USDA in a variety of programs to teach farmers scientific agriculture and crop diversification. The federal funding of agricultural extension work (Smith-Lever Act, 1914) and agricultural vocational training in public schools (Smith-Hughes Act, 1917) strengthened the college's endeavors.

Southern progressives initiated such agricultural legislation and applauded its efforts. The combined efforts of local, state, and national progressives initiated youth clubs, "Boys Corn Clubs" and "Girls Tomato Clubs," sent educational or demonstration trains to rural areas, and made experts in agriculture available to African American and white farmers. The Agricultural and Mechanical College met specialized needs by sending county agents to solve immediate problems for individual farmers and by allying with agribusiness in studies of new crops, pest control, improved seeds, and other such applied agricultural science. The results of this research were to be transferred to Texas farmers through home demonstrations and county agents. Tenant farmers were omitted from this cycle, however. The Texas legislature talked of an "out of occupancy" tax (tax on absentee owners) to aid tenant farmers, but never seriously considered the proposal. Instead, agricultural and progressive reformers relied mostly on scientific training, new management techniques, and cooperative marketing to revitalize Texas farms.

Other colleges offered services similar to those of agricultural education institutions. Correspondence divisions grew on all campuses. In addition, extension services instructed students in group-study projects by sending out traveling libraries, compiling bibliographies, and furnishing information and printed lectures to debating clubs, women's clubs, labor unions, and other organizations. By 1915, divisions of extension issued bulletins on agricultural cooperation and marketing techniques; school improvement, including information to help upgrade instruction; proper classroom preparation and designs for physical improvements on schoolhouses; and home welfare, which centered on family life, child rearing, and hygiene. Extension directors identified these activities as progressive mandates to serve all the people.

Institutional Reforms

Progressives argued that efficiency in management, scientific investigations and reports, and the recommendations of trained experts could make such institutions as prisons operate better and more humanely. Southern progressives identified the prison system as one of state-run institutions that defined the South as a backward region of the country. In Texas, criminal codes and the legal system still facilitated the county, city, and state governments' use of convicts as a source of labor. The state owned several prison farms, a central plant at Huntsville, and a prison near Rusk that manufactured iron. Progressives and the citizenry wanted these prisons to support themselves. They additionally desired more humane treatment of prisoners and the standardizing of prison administration and the granting of pardons.

A series of newspaper articles in the 1908 and 1909 *San Antonio Express*, the *Galveston News,* and the *Dallas Morning News* exposed the abuses in state facilities and lessee camps. Political graft and the spoils system seemed to dominate the administration and conduct of the penal institutions. Prisoners were overworked, underfed, poorly clothed, and sometimes shot or whipped to death for minor offenses. The lack of sex-segregated facilities and the failure to separate convicts by age and the nature of the crime they had committed led to the sexual abuse of women and juvenile offenders. Basic health and sanitation precautions were simply ignored. The growth rate of the prison population, at twice that of the general population, further complicated the system's problems.

Governor Campbell, who supported prison reform, called a special legislative session to address the issue. The special session stipulated the gradual phasing out of the contract-lease system, established a ten-cent-per-day pay scale for the convict's labor, eliminated the wearing of striped uniforms for prisoners considered not dangerous, mandated segregation and classification of prisoners, and authorized the improvement of prison sanitation and medical services. Although whipping continued, its use was restricted.

But the reform of the prison system continued to generate controversy. Colquitt, for example, publicized the deplorable prison conditions in his successful gubernatorial campaign of 1910. One problem prevailed: elected officials and most citizens still held that the prisons should be self-supporting. The leasing of convicts earned the institutions surplus revenues, but along with that money came the intolerable treatment of human beings. Contract leasing ended in 1912, after which convicts were made to work on state-run farms, a shift intended to generate revenue for a self-sufficient prison system. In boom agricultural years it did so; in the more usual surplus-crop seasons, it operated at a loss. The deficit of the prison system and constant charges of mismanagement of prison facilities and revenues emerged as political controversies regularly from 1913 to 1925. During this period, the state moved to cease iron manufacturing at Rusk prison and sell the state railway that served the factory. A 1925 constitutional amendment provided for the reorganization of the management and supervision of the prison system. In 1927, the legislature created a Texas Prison Board consisting of nine members with staggered, two-year terms. The new board functioned well enough to remove prisons temporarily from political controversy.

Other penal reforms met with mixed success. The state authorized the granting of indeterminate sentences in order to encourage good prisoner behavior in 1883, and it expanded and refined the process in the early twentieth century. It added a suspended-sentence law, a system of parole, for which a prisoner was eligible after having served one-fourth of his or her term, and a concurrent sentence law during the period. Paroles, however, remained under the jurisdiction of the governor and would soon stir up more political controversy. The electric chair replaced hanging as the form of state-mandated execution in 1923. Juvenile offenders began to receive better care when the State Juvenile Training School at Gatesville was transferred to the management of the State Board of Control in 1919, enabling it to emphasize reform and education of the young inmates. The Gainesville State School for Girls was established in 1917. The Gatesville school housed both black and white boys, whereas Gainesville was for white girls only. A similar school for delinquent black girls was authorized but not established. Overall, like the rest of the South, Texas continued to lag behind the more-advanced northeastern states in the utilization of modern penology. Nevertheless, it had undertaken progressive penal reform, and by the early 1920s, its prison system was far more efficient and humane than it had been when the century began.

Progressives also concerned themselves with other wards of the state. The Constitution of 1876 considered care for the poor the responsibility of local government and private charities. The concept that the public domain in a frontier state offered ample opportunity to the displaced poor reinforced this notion. As the population increased and free land dwindled, however, benevolent institutions expanded their care and increased in number. A State Medical Board and a State Department of Health were created. The 1911 legislature authorized commissioners' courts to issue bonds for the maintenance of county poor houses. Local counties and cities could establish hospitals for indigent patients, and the state expanded its services for the mentally ill, the blind, the deaf, orphans, and those suffering from tuberculosis. By 1930, the state had succeeded in making room for most of the white mentally ill in one of four mental hospitals (Austin, San Antonio, Terrell, and Wichita Falls) and for some mentally ill African Americans at Rusk. A psychopathic hospital was authorized at Galveston, and facilities for the mentally ill and epileptics were separated.

In 1919, supported by a study that revealed deplorable conditions in asylums, the legislature created a State Board of Control that had authority over all eleemosynary institutions, which included the State Tuberculosis Sanitorium (near San Angelo), the Texas School for the Blind (Austin), the School for the Deaf (Austin), the Waco State Home for Dependent and Neglected Children, the State Orphan's Home (Corsicana), and, for African Americans, the Texas Blind, Deaf and Orphan School (Austin). Reformers did not, however, gain nearly all that they wished in care for the unfortunate. Both private and public investigating committees throughout the period criticized the condition of the public facilities and deplored their overcrowding. As late as 1929, some of the mentally ill were still confined in jails. Yet the public usually pleaded poverty as a reason not to expand the welfare institutions of the state.

Forest Conservation and Good Roads

The issues of urban progressivism that dominated northern and some western states lacked meaning in much of the South. Southern states usually had no urban political machines and ignored conservation efforts. In Texas, the exceptions to this rule were the conservation of forests and the control of the funds for highway development. The years 1900 to 1910 were banner ones for the Texas lumber industry, but the average cut of more than 2 billion board feet a year alarmed conservationists, who warned that Texas's forests would soon be decimated. W. Goodrich Jones, a bank executive in Temple, crusaded for regulation of the lumber industry and reforestation. In 1908, he attended President Theodore Roosevelt's White House Conference of Governors on Conservation. This experience prompted Jones to organize the Texas Forestry Association, which was committed to a statewide forest conservation plan to prevent lumber barons from completely depleting an area's timber resources and then simply moving on. Jones believed in the conservation of resources for use later, and he worked with lumber tycoons to establish a policy of selective cutting and reforestation that would guarantee future forests as well as profits.

The new association lobbied for the establishment of a department of forestry and the employment of a state forester. The legislature complied in 1915 and created the Texas Department of Forestry, administered as a division of the Agricultural and Mechanical College. The forestry department remained a point of political contention, however, as critics charged it with being too closely linked to timber barons and not committed enough to conservation. Eric O. Siecke took over the agency in 1918, and over the next twenty-five years he did much to stifle political controversy and turn the forestry department into a professional organization. Under his tutelage, the agency established state parks, taught scientific reforesting and selective cutting methods, and developed nurseries for seedlings to replace harvested trees. When World War I pushed the price of lumber up to two to three times its 1912 price, Texas lumber companies flourished. Contrary to the policy in many other states, in Texas no law existed (then or now) mandating that a seedling be replanted for each mature tree cut. The Great War hastened the exploitation of Texas timber resources, and the 1920s witnessed the waning of the bonanza period of the lumber industry. By 1932, the production of Texas lumber was lower than that of any year since 1880. Still, the legislature ignored the appeal of conservationists, and the great old-growth pine forests of East Texas were essentially destroyed. Progressives did endorse

Driver for the Temple Lumber Company, 1927. *Courtesy Houston Metropolitan Research Center, Houston Public Library*

other conservation measures, and under Governor Campbell's direction the legislature passed acts that stimulated reclamation projects in forests and waterways, amended game laws to limit hunting seasons, and expanded the powers of the Texas Wildlife Commission.

The Good Roads Movement emerged around 1910 as the automobile gained popularity in the South. Previously, the coming of the railroads had lessened the demand for well-maintained roads in the South. The Constitution of 1876 deemed the counties responsible for road maintenance, but the widespread use of the personal automobile dramatized the need for a central road authority. At the 1910 state fair, good road enthusiasts held a meeting in which they decided to promote this point. The Texas Good Roads Association organized in 1911 with the intent to educate citizens and the legislature on the need for a central authority to plan and maintain a state highway system. In 1916, Congress enacted legislation offering matching funds for all states that joined a national highway network; the law stipulated that each state must have a central highway planning agency to qualify. The promise of federal funds overrode the objections of those opposed to centralization, and the legislature quickly moved to establish the Texas Highway Department, stipulating that the highway commission should consist of three members appointed by the governor. This highway commission hired a state engineer to consult and advise on plans submitted by the counties for highway construction. But the program floundered from its beginnings; the early commissioners did not cooperate with one another; and counties continued to make plans for roads unilaterally, grant their own contracts for road construction, and apply individually to the state for reimbursement. This lack of cooperation from county to county denied the state a viable highway system. Then, World War I–related activities worsened the roads, while increasing the amount of automobile traffic. The controversy over a state highway system continued into the 1920s, and in 1924, the State Court of Civil Appeals ruled that the legislature should designate the Highway Department sole responsibility for maintaining and building interstate highways. Not long thereafter, in 1925, rumors of mismanagement of the Texas Highway Department were leveled at Governor Miriam Ferguson's appointees to the road commission. In 1926, the U.S. Bureau of Public Roads stopped federal aid for Texas highways pending the outcome of the investigation of the allegations.

Luckily, help was on the way. Incoming Governor Dan Moody personally appealed for and received a continuation of the aid. He reorganized the highway department, selecting for it capable commissioners who hired qualified engineers. Moody appointed a 1928 Citizen's Advisory Commission to formulate a plan for future highway development. As the advisory commission predicted, financing would continue to trouble the drive for the construction of a comprehensive road system. The progressive goal, however, of a professional and efficient highway agency had materialized. In time, an integrated highway system tied together markets and thus validated businesspeople's and farmer's arguments that economic growth depended upon a reliable, modern transportation network.

REFORM INTERRUPTED: THE FERGUSON ADMINISTRATION, 1915–1917

In 1914, a political unknown named James E. Ferguson came to the forefront of Texas politics. His personality and politics partially immobilized reform and remained a political issue for over thirty years. A self-educated lawyer and a banker from Temple, "Farmer Jim" won two terms as governor, was impeached, and then dominated the gubernatorial administrations of his wife (1925–1927, 1933–1935). His race for the governor's office in 1918 and the U.S. Senate in 1922 and Miriam A. "Ma" Ferguson's gubernatorial campaigns in 1926, 1930, and 1940 kept the issue of "Fergusonism" before the Texas electorate. Critics identified the Fergusons with demagoguery and corruption. Supporters lauded them as friends of the oppressed and tenant farmers. Ferguson announced his campaign in 1914 with the statement that Texans were tired of the issue of prohibition. He, therefore, would ignore it and concentrate on more important topics. He campaigned in the poorer agricultural districts, promising to limit the amount of rent that landlords could charge tenant farmers. He defeated Thomas H. Ball from Houston, who advocated prohibition, in the Democratic primary and won the November general election.

Ferguson's first term (1915–1917) garnered a measure of success. His farm tenancy bill capping farm rents passed. Evidently, the state attorney general chose not to enforce it rigorously, and the U.S. Supreme Court declared it unconstitutional in 1921. The governor and the legislature worked harmoniously. He vetoed only five bills, and successful legislation under Ferguson included educational reforms, increased funding for colleges and the University of Texas, and the creation of the State Department of Forestry. Although rumors surfaced concerning malfeasance in government, Ferguson won reelection. His new term witnessed higher appropriations for education, expansion of the college network, a revision of labor laws, and a state highway commission.

Like Colquitt before him, Ferguson had to contend with border problems. Troubles escalated following a series of raids in the lower Rio Grande Valley connected with the *Plan de San Diego*. This radical manifesto, discovered in January 1915 and supposedly written in San Diego (in Duval County), sought to ignite an uprising of Texas Mexicans, sympathizers in Mexico, and other aggrieved minority groups in Texas for the establishment of an independent republic composed of those territories that Mexico had lost to the United States in the Mexican War. With the mounting of hostilities in July, Ferguson ordered all available Texas Ranger companies to the troubled region. The next year, he sent out the Texas National Guard following counter-raids into Texas, even as U.S. Army General John J. Pershing marched into Mexico to capture Pancho Villa, the Mexican rebel leader who had attacked Columbus, New Mexico, on March 9, 1916. Border troubles subsided in late 1916, when both countries assented to allow a joint commission to settle their

differences. Bandit raids, however, continued throughout 1917 and 1918.

Tragically affected by the border troubles were Tejanos in South Texas, whom whites suspected of complicity with the raiders. Texas Rangers, local policemen, and volunteer groups indiscriminately killed and brutalized many Tejanos on various pretexts. A U.S. Senate investigating committee documented the terror, and a legislative investigation led by the Brownsville representative J. T. Canales so implicated the Texas Rangers in the atrocities that the legislature responded by reducing the number of Texas Ranger companies.

Above: James E. Ferguson and Miriam A. Ferguson, ca. 1925. *The UT Institute of Texan Cultures, No. 0002-C, San Antonio Light Collection*

Charges of corruption in the governor's office continued in Ferguson's second term, when they intertwined with his deteriorating relations with the alumni of the University of Texas. As early as 1915, the governor quarreled with W. J. Battle, acting president of the university, over an interpretation of the appropriation law for the university. Ferguson wanted more control over specific items in the school's budget. His detractors said that the governor wished in reality to designate faculty appointments in order to purge the staff of those who politically opposed him. This attack on the University of Texas was complicated by A. and M. College's demand for a share of the Permanent University Fund and the structure of the governing boards of both schools. When the University of Texas board of regents selected Robert E. Vinson as president of the university without consulting the governor, he renewed his attack on the school. Ferguson charged that some faculty members mismanaged state funds and that the university offered an elite and costly education. He threatened to veto the university's appropriation if Vinson and selected faculty members were not fired. When the university regents and the alumni association stood firm against the governor's demands, he made good on his promise and vetoed the appropriation. Now, the regents put out the call for his impeachment.

The Texas Equal Suffrage Association joined the University of Texas supporters in the request. Minnie Fisher Cunningham, president of the association, went to Austin to support the removal of Ferguson because he opposed woman's suffrage. Moreover, Ferguson's defeat of Ball and his refusal even to recognize dry issues united prohibitionists with University of Texas alumni and suffragists. Finally, the seeming intermingling of state revenues with the governor's private funds (including $156,500 in unpaid loans, later discovered to have originated from brewing interests) enlisted progressives, already disenchanted with many of Ferguson's political goals, into the impeachment camp. Since women's reform, progressivism, and prohibition overlapped intellectually and

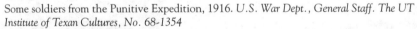

Some soldiers from the Punitive Expedition, 1916. *U.S. War Dept., General Staff. The UT Institute of Texan Cultures, No. 68-1354*

Anti-Ferguson rally at the University of Texas, May 28, 1917. *The Center for American History, The University of Texas at Austin, CN 01027*

politically, their proponents' opposition to the governor should have come as no surprise.

On July 23, 1917, the speaker of the house issued a call for a special legislative session. Although the call did not meet constitutional requirements, Governor Ferguson bowed to the inevitable and legalized it by issuing a summons for a special session. So convened, the legislature drew up a list of twenty-one charges against the governor, of which the senate affirmed ten. Seven of the ten charges involved Ferguson's handling of finances, including the disputed loans and a charge that the governor illegally deposited public funds in the Temple Bank, of which he was a stockholder. On September 2, Ferguson resigned to avoid impeachment. The court of impeachment acted anyway, removing the governor and banning him from holding future state offices.

Amazingly, Ferguson did not quit the political wars; instead he challenged Lieutenant Governor William P. Hobby in the 1918 gubernatorial campaign. Ferguson and his supporters maintained that his resignation had preempted the impeachment proceedings, which, therefore, did not rule out his eligibility for state office. And he attempted to rally voters by continuing his attack on the University of Texas, in particular charging that faculty members were indolent elitists who undertook meaningless and impractical research projects. Hobby defeated Ferguson handily, but "Fergusonism" still did not disappear, as "Pa" Ferguson would soon run for the U.S. Senate, maintaining now that the impeachment limited his eligibility for state, not national, office. Furthermore, "Ma" Ferguson's later political activities kept "Fergusonism" alive, or at least the concept that support or opposition to "Farmer Jim" determined, more than issues of self-interest, how a voter would cast his ballot. Meanwhile, progressives rejoiced over the victory of Will Hobby, who advocated both woman's suffrage and prohibition.

WOODROW WILSON, WILL HOBBY, AND WORLD WAR I, 1917–1919

The United States entered World War I six months before Will Hobby took office as governor of Texas. His election mandate represented a victory for President Woodrow Wilson's policies as well as a rebuff of Ferguson. When Wilson, a Democrat, won the presidency in 1912, his victory signaled a return of the South to national political power, a place relinquished to the political dominance of the Republican party in the aftermath of the Civil War. Texans undertook a major role in Wilson's 1912 nomination and campaign. Thomas B. Love organized the Woodrow Wilson State Democratic League in 1911 and joined with E. M. House, Albert Sidney Burleson, and Thomas Watt Gregory in delivering the forty-man Democratic delegation to the New Jersey governor in the presidential nominating convention of 1912. The unity and morale of the "Immortal Forty," as they called themselves, made them a central element in securing Wilson's nomination. Once in the White House, Wilson repaid the political debt: Burleson served as postmaster general from 1913 to 1921, Gregory was U.S. attorney general from 1914 to 1919 and attended the Peace Conference; House became a special adviser to President Wilson for most of his two terms in office, and Love served as assistant treasury secretary. David Houston, who had been president of both A. and M. College and the University of Texas, was appointed secretary of agriculture. Sam Rayburn began a distinguished career in the House of Representatives in 1913 and earned a reputation as a Wilsonian supporter, as did Morris Sheppard in the Senate. Rayburn fought for national antitrust legislation, and Sheppard introduced the law that became the Eighteenth Amendment (prohibition) .

Texas progressives considered Wilson a beacon to guide their reform efforts, and when the war began they transferred their energies into support of his and the nation's war efforts. The demands on Texans were great. In accordance with the 1917 National Defense Act, 985,571 men registered for the draft, of which 197,789 were Texans who either volunteered or were drafted into the army, navy, or marine corps. In addition, 449 Texas women served in the military as nurses. There were many casualties; 5,170 Texans lost their lives in the Great War, with more than one-third of these deaths the result of the 1918 Spanish influenza epidemic. About 25 percent of the Texans who served in the armed services were African American; nevertheless, tensions between whites and blacks accelerated. A white mob in Huntsville lynched a black man accused of evading the draft and subsequently murdered six members of his family. A riot caused by discrimination in Houston involving the all-black Third Battalion of the Twenty-fourth U.S. Infantry ended with a court-martial that severely punished the soldiers.

Most of the Texas trainees joined other soldiers in four large camps: Bowie, in Fort Worth; Logan, in Houston; McArthur, in Waco; and Travis, in San Antonio. Kelly Field, in San Antonio, offered aviation training. The University of Texas housed a school of military aeronautics for basic flight instruction. Several other training bases for aviators dotted the state, making Texas the national leader in flight training. The U.S. Army Air Force recognized this fact in 1928 with the construction of Randolph Field, "The West Point of the Air," in San Antonio. Other army bases operated in Texas, including an officers training camp at Leon Springs. Concerned with the moral conditions in the civilian areas surrounding the camps, the legislature passed laws prohibiting the sale of alcoholic beverages within ten miles of the camps and an antivice act designed to halt the spread of sexually transmitted disease.

The legislature also responded to the war with acts to compensate people for economic losses incurred by having served in the armed services. One act forbade the forced sale of the property of servicemen until a full year after their discharge. Another omitted penalties for nonpayment of taxes by servicemen, and a third act eliminated poll taxes for servicemen. The state aided returning veterans as well. It urged A. and M. College to grant degrees to juniors and above who had left that institution to join the armed services. A sanatorium at Kerrville was established for veterans. A state service office was designated to assist servicemen or their beneficiaries in obtaining federal government benefits due them. The state gave preference to veterans applying for government employment. And all veterans, including former military nurses, were granted free tuition at state institutions.

In 1916, Congress created the Council of National Defense to mobilize resources to defend the nation. As soon as war erupted, state councils of defense were set up for local mobilization. The Texas Council of Defense comprised ten committees that oversaw the activities of 240 county councils and approximately 15,000 community ones. These councils organized liberty bond and Red Cross drives, encouraged patriotism, publicized the war effort, provided wholesome recreation and morale boosters for servicemen, promoted the various forms of conservation of resources, and stayed alert to any "disloyal" activities in their neighborhoods. After the armistice, the councils helped veterans find employment.

Of all the national agencies in the state, the Federal Food Administration was the most visible. The United States needed to supply food both to its own citizens as well as its allies. This demanded limiting civilians' use of basic foodstuff commodities and increasing the nation's agricultural output. Working with the county councils of defense, agents visited Texas households, going door to door to solicit pledges from families to substitute other foods for wheat, oils, and meat. When the campaign did not succeed, the administration switched its emphasis from housewives to merchants. Now, each seller was asked to conform to the fifty-fifty rule, selling one pound of another cereal grain for each pound of wheat sold. From April 15 to June 15, 1918, the government instituted a "wheat fast" and stopped all shippments of flour into the state. The sale of sugar was also restricted. The administration supervised the price of food and fuel, assessing penalties on violators. It also encouraged volunteerism through "wheatless Mondays" and "meatless Tuesdays" and the planting of vegetable gardens. The Texas experience corresponded to those of other states.

The war induced other important changes in the state. Inflation soared and incomes failed to match it. The cost of government went up, more than doubling as the new progressive institutions, revised school system, and war agencies became functional. As men went off to war, work opportunities for women increased. Not only did women now staff jobs formerly reserved for men, but they undertook significant roles in voluntary agencies and war work. Women's clubs encouraged the propaganda campaign, and women rolled bandages, conserved food and fuel, entertained troops, and engaged in Red Cross and other wartime activities. Their efforts contributed to both the culmination of the woman's suffrage movement and the concept of the "New Woman," or the young, progressive woman who saw other options in life besides marriage and motherhood.

WOMEN IN ACTION

Woman's Suffrage

The woman's suffrage movement had always been intertwined with progressivism. In Texas, women unsuccessfully petitioned the 1868 and 1875 constitutional conventions for the right to vote and founded the Texas Equal Rights Association in 1893. Divisions developed within the National Woman Suffrage Association over whether it should be a limited reform organization for the vote only or a broader movement for women's rights. The split affected the Texas wing of the organization, which lost its momentum. Then, in 1903, the Texas Woman Suffrage Association emerged to seize the mantle of reform. It asked the state legislature in 1915 and 1917 for approval of a constitutional amendment granting woman's suffrage. The political controversy, stirred by the impeachment of Ferguson and sustaining the stern opposition of many men, thwarted the amendment's passage. Nevertheless, Minnie Fisher Cunningham, Annie Webb Blanton, Jessie Daniel Ames, and other women continued to lobby effectively for the cause, and local suffrage associations were up and running in nearly all Texas counties when World War I erupted. The conflict intensified Woodrow Wilson's somewhat unenthusiastic support for a national amendment granting women the right to vote. In a special session in 1918, the state legislature passed an act extending the franchise to women in primary elections. Blanton won the race for state superintendent of education that year, and several other women were elected to local offices. The next year, Governor Hobby requested that the legislature put before the electorate constitutional amendments enfranchising women and denying the vote to the foreign born. Legislators complied, but the voters defeated both measures in an election in which all men in the state, including aliens, could and all women could not cast ballots. Later that same year, however, the legislature ratified the Nineteenth Amendment to the Constitution, which authorized woman's suffrage. Texas was the first southern state and the ninth in the nation to do so.

Women's Organizations

Although the war accelerated the drive for woman's suffrage nationally and locally, the hard work of many women also had fueled it. The women's club movement, regularized with the formation of the Texas Federation of Women's Clubs in 1897, popularized and campaigned for progressive reforms. The federation sponsored many of the state's public libraries and spearheaded drives for creation of public parks, school reform policy, the Texas Woman's College, state eleemosynary institutions, and city beautification movements. Club women worked hard to establish licensing standards for nurses and improved health care facilities. Private Texas organizations of women, such as the National Council of Jewish Women and several women's Protestant groups, endorsed the national movement for settlement houses, the Young Women's Christian Association organization, and other goals of social reform. Women's organizations also worked for specific legislation to aid women in other ways besides removing suffrage restrictions. They met with a measure of success in this endeavor when, in 1913,

Katherine Stinson being sworn in as an airmail pilot by Postmaster George D. Armistad in front of a Wright model "B" airplane, San Antonio, Texas, May 14, 1915. *The UT Institute of Texan Cultures, No. 85-27, San Antonio Light Collection*

the legislature passed an act that defined both separate and community property of husband and wife. Nonetheless, state laws remained restrictive, and married women had limited control of their own property and could not enter into financial contracts or serve on juries until the 1950s.

The obvious need for politically aware and active women led a coalition of women's groups in 1922 to organize the Joint Legislative Council. Over the next year, the League of Women Voters (organized from the Texas Woman Suffrage Association and headed by Ames), the Federation of Women's Clubs, the Congress of Mothers and Parent-Teachers-Associations, the Woman's Christian Temperance Union, and the Texas Federation of Business and Professional Women's Clubs combined forces in this new venture. The "petticoat lobby," as condescending legislators dubbed it, proved remarkably effective. It advocated middle-class, moderate reforms regarding working people, prisons, public health and child welfare, public education, a birth registration program, and the enforcement of prohibition laws.

Prohibition in Texas

The prohibition movement both gained sustenance from and nourished the women's movement. In a period when women were considered keepers of morality and culture, prohibition furnished an issue that allowed them political participation in a reform crusade that did not violate their male-ordained societal role. Moreover, prohibition linked all reformers together. Progressives saw alcohol as a corrupter of democratic society and its sale as a moral evil. In a state nearly bereft of urban reform targets and, except in South Texas, of political bossism, progressives made statewide prohibition their number-one political goal. The presence in the antiprohibition movement of ethnic minorities, Germans and Mexicans in particular, buttressed the identification of dry forces as upholders of Anglo-Saxon democracy. Prohibition thus fit nicely into the progressive's goal of social control.

After 1887, prohibitionists retreated from a strategy of a statewide referendum and concentrated on local-option laws. The Texas Local Option Association organized a campaign in 1903 to dry up North Texas. It furnished speakers and organizers to encourage and abet local-option elections. The powerful Anti-Saloon League entered Texas in 1907 and combined its propaganda and numerical strength with the local-option organization. These separate forces worked within evangelical churches, enlisting preachers, women's groups, progressive politicians, and social reformers into the cause. Dry strength thus centered in North Texas, where a combination of rural voters, the religious press, and Protestant homogeneity contributed to victory after victory for the drys in local-option elections.

Wets met the dry challenge by organizing their own lobbying groups, of which the Texas Brewers' Association, formed in 1901, was the most important; led by the Anheuser-Busch interests, it raised a war chest of $2 million over the next decade. The Retail Liquor Dealers' Association was organized in 1907. Attorney General B. F. Looney demonstrated in 1915 that the brewers association had violated Texas antitrust laws and had illegally contributed to antiprohibition candidates; consequently, the breweries were fined $281,000 and costs. These revelations, plus impeachment proceedings against Governor Jim Ferguson, in which, as mentioned, investigators had accused him of receiving an unsecured loan from the brewers' organization, further wed the drive for prohibition with antitrust movements and besmirched proliquor interests.

By 1908, the issue of prohibition dominated Texas politics. Drys, urged on by the *Baptist Standard* and other religious publications, decided to ask for statewide rather than local-option prohibition legislation, forcing each Democratic primary candidate to declare either for or against prohibition. The issue split the voters almost in half. Drys won narrow victories in the 1908 and 1910 primaries to force the legislature to submit to voters a constitutional amendment outlawing the sale of alcohol. The legislature refused in 1909 by two votes to do so, but relented in 1911, when by a close vote of 231,096 to 237,393, wets defeated a prohibition amendment to the Texas Constitution. Because the wet vote came largely from cities and ethnic and racial minorities, the *Baptist Standard* best expressed the drys' attitude when it declared that prohibition was clearly "an issue of Anglo-Saxon culture" versus the presumably inferior civilization of minorities in urban areas.

The identification of ethnic groups with alcohol paid large dividends to the prohibitionists in Texas and elsewhere during World War I. To not drink alcohol became "patriotic": people did not work well with hangovers, alcohol was needed in the war effort, and saloons corrupted U.S. servicemen. Furthermore, the 1918 law that forbade the sale of liquor within ten miles of military bases practically dried up the state anyway. On February 28, 1918, the Texas legislature approved a national prohibition amendment. The passage of a statewide prohibition law followed shortly, and in January 1920, the Eighteenth Amendment to the U.S. Constitution outlawed the sale of alcoholic beverages.

TEXAS AFTER WORLD WAR I

The same surge of patriotism that identified liquor as un-American in World War I also encouraged a demand for cultural conformity. In an effort to unite a heterogeneous population into a public consensus for a war effort, propaganda committees extolled patriotic goals and middle-class American values. A public suspicion arose of those ideas or people who might not endorse the points of view of the majority. The state and federal governments responded to demands that all join the war effort with legislation designed to enforce patriotism. Texas, for example, made public criticism of the American flag, the war effort, the U.S. government, or soldiers' uniforms a crime punishable by imprisonment. The legislature mandated that public schools teach patriotism, fly the American flag, and, except for foreign-language classes, conduct all studies in English. A legislative committee recommended pulling from circulation in the state library books and periodicals that portrayed Germany or German culture in a favorable light. Election laws were changed to prevent the foreign born from voting. Governor Hobby in 1919 vetoed the state appropriation of money for the German Department of the University of Texas. Sometimes the superpatriotism bordered on silliness: sauerkraut became known instead as "liberty cabbage." Other times it became hysterical and repressive: violent acts such as floggings were used to instill patriotism in those suspected of holding dissenting opinions. In some cases, simply having a foreign-sounding name convinced mobs that one was a potential enemy sympathizer.

The antiforeign hysteria melded into an antiradical crusade after the 1917 Communist revolution in Russia. Now, the state citizenry frequently defined strikes and demands for civil rights as un-American and Bolshevik-inspired. The federal government reinforced such attitudes with the passage of the May 1918 Sedition Act. Consequently, governmental suppression of the American Socialist party leadership and harassment of the editors of the Socialist newspaper, *The Rebel*, destroyed that party in Texas. Minority groups suffered too, as white citizens now greeted demands for civil rights with violence. Race riots occurred in Port Arthur and in Longview in 1919; it took the state militia to restore order in the latter. This fear of radicalism explains passage of a 1923 law that mandated that all teachers in public schools be U.S. citizens and that the study of the constitutions of Texas and the United States be included in the curriculum.

The 1923 legislation was an example of what happened to progressivism in the 1920s. Progressivism did not disappear with the triumph of the Republican party in the 1920 presidential election or with the prosperity of the following decade. Rather, the drive for patriotism in World War I encouraged progressives to stress some goals at the expense of others. Consequently, two strains of progressivism dominated the politics of the 1920s. Since progressives saw no contradiction between reform and social control, they looked to public schools and other state institutions to Americanize foreigners, to inculcate middle-class values, and to protect morality through prohibition. Thus, one faction of progressives actually had no trouble endorsing attempts by a reborn Ku Klux Klan and anti-evolution theory crusaders to exercise social control through enforcing prohibition laws. The other emergent faction embraced "business progressivism," which endeavored to utilize the ideas of efficiency and public service to effect order and prosperity. Business progressives fought for administrative reorganization, good roads, and improved schools and health care; they seemingly ignored the demands of labor unions, tenant farmers, and proponents of civil rights. The social-justice movement, never strong in the South, and the antitrust movement gave way to the two above-mentioned different but not mutually exclusive progressive factions.

THE RETURN OF PROGRESSIVE
ADMINISTRATION: HOBBY (1919–1921)
AND NEFF (1921–1925)

The ascension of William P. Hobby, a business progressive, to the governor's office in 1917, upon Ferguson's resignation, and his subsequent election in 1919 dramatized for progressives the triumphs of Wilson, World War I, and prohibition. Hobby served at a time when the economic downturn of 1920–1921 pulled up and into a boom period that continued through the administration of Hobby's successor, Pat M. Neff. Bountiful crops disguised the economic weakness of Texas farmers by helping to offset falling prices for agricultural commodities. And expanding industry and developing cities absorbed returning veterans and offered new job opportunities for Texas men and women.

Hobby and other business progressives advocated measures to strengthen this growing urban economic network, but their appeals largely fell flat before a reluctant legislature and an unconcerned electorate. In his last term in office, Hobby proposed bills to the legislature that aided education, reorganized the state government, authorized judicial reform, and established a civil-service commission. His only success lay in education.

Pat Neff entered the gubernatorial primary race in 1919 as a prohibitionist who supported Wilson. A devout Christian, a former speaker of the state house of representatives, and prosecuting attorney of McLennan County, Neff espoused progressive goals. Staging a return to politics, Joe Bailey roundly denounced Wilson, prohibition, and almost all of the reforms of the preceding decade as he campaigned against Neff. Naturally, Wilsonian progressives rallied to Neff's cause. Bailey led the first Democratic primary in 1920 but lost the second.

As governor, Neff, as had Hobby, dealt with an unresponsive legislature, which turned down a reorganization of state administrative offices and a proposed constitutional convention. Neff did, however, convince the legislature to consolidate the Pure Food and Drug Department with the Health Department. And the legislature approved the organization of cooperative marketing associations to help farmers sell their commodities as well as the creation of water reclamation and irrigation districts. Governor Neff also worked hard for prison reform, disbanded the board of pardons, and halted the easy granting of paroles, which had been highly visible occurrences under "Farmer Jim" Ferguson's administration. Neff used martial law to quell violence in the railroad strike at Denison and in the turmoil created by the oil discovery near Mexia. His promanagement action in the Federated Shop Craft Union strike led organized labor to oppose his reelection in 1922, but he still won handily. Neff's longest-lasting successes came from his fight for good roads and the initiation of a state park network.

Many of his failures emanated from his attempt to enforce prohibition laws. While governor, Neff described Texas as suffering from the worst "crime wave" in its history and asked the legislature to expand law enforcement agencies and pass more stringent liquor legislation. He wanted an increase in the Ranger force, a repeal of the suspended-sentence law that allowed bootleggers to avoid prison sentences, and a provision for removing local officials who did not vigorously enforce prohibition laws. When the legislature failed to respond, he chided the lawmakers for defending bootleggers, his disparaging remarks causing a rift between his office and the house of representatives. Nonetheless, Neff used his powers as governor and his considerable energy to try to enforce prohibition, dispatching Rangers to areas of suspected bootlegging activity, and taking the lead in publicizing campaigns to eradicate liquor consumption. His successes were slight: an amendment to the Texas prohibition law that made possession of more than a quart of liquor or any material for manufacturing it prima facie evidence of bootlegging. While Neff certainly enjoyed a high measure of support from antiliquor forces, the political divisions over the law continued throughout the 1920s. Indeed, the controversy over enforcement of prohibition laws made Neff reluctant to condemn the Ku Klux Klan. He believed that the Klan's opposition to bootlegging warranted his support of the organization, regardless of its violent tactics.

THE KU KLUX KLAN, FUNDAMENTALISM, AND THE EVOLUTION DEBATE

The general failure of prohibition enforcement brought home to many Texans what they defined as a decline in American morals. The rapidly increasing urbanization seemed to blur what were once clear moral and community values. Migration to the city disrupted the neighborhoods of rural America and, coupled with more and better transportation facilities, broke up the extended family. Historians have cited the urban growth of the United States as creating tensions between rural and urban Americans. This anxiety emanated not only from the countryside, but also from developing southern cities filled with recent foreign immigrants. The anticity focus of rural Texans resulted from their perception of urban areas as hotbeds of disloyal foreigners, religious modernism, illegal speakeasies, organized crime, morally suspicious "New Women," and corrupting modern music. These tensions were further abetted by the post–World War I Red Scare and reinforced by the progressive drive for social control.

The Ku Klux Klan of the 1920s borrowed the name and some of the trappings of the Reconstruction Era organization, but otherwise it was quite different from the original KKK. Founded in 1915 near Atlanta, Georgia, by William Joseph Simmons, an ex-Methodist minister familiar with all types of fraternal orders, the new Klan was to be a secret social organization that would advocate patriotism. Simmons teamed up in 1920 with Edward Young Clarke, who paid field organizers (kleagles) to organize KKK chapters (klaverns) throughout the nation. The organizer received $4 of each $10 initiation fee paid by a prospective inductee, who had to be white, Protestant, and native born. The Klan professed as its goals the preservation of patriotism, the purity of women, white supremacy, and law and order. It opposed radicals, Catholics, Jews, blacks, Mexicans, the wearing by women of short skirts, the consumption of "demon rum," and continued foreign immigration. By 1922, the organization had 700,000 members and by 1925, possibly as many as 5 million. It was strong throughout the South and Midwest, especially in Indiana, Oklahoma, Louisiana, and Texas. Its alleged commitment to the preservation of the social order and its militant fundamentalism seemingly appealed to those in the Bible Belt. The Klan recruited in urban areas of the South, where citizens with rural backgrounds endorsed its professed goals. The organization's ability to enlist the new urban middle class explained Neff's unwillingness to condemn the order and the attitude of other progressives, such as Thomas Love, who described Klan members as good but misguided men.

The Klan came to Texas in 1920. Playing upon white fears engendered by the race riot of 1917, the kleagles made contacts with the better-known citizens of Houston. From contacts with prominent city leaders, the Klan earned enough respectability to recruit extensively in the white middle class. It soon spread across the state, excepting, naturally, those areas with a large Catholic population, such as San Antonio and South Texas. Its core strength lay in the Dallas–Fort Worth area, East Texas, and Central Texas. The motivation behind the Klan in Texas was more the imposition of moral conformity than racism and nativism, and the Klan was willing to use extralegal methods to prevent "moral decay" from spreading throughout the state. Texas newspapers reported eighty incidents of flogging in 1921. Klan victims included doctors accused of perform-

Ku Klux Klan parading, Beaumont, Texas, November 10, 1922. *Courtesy Houston Metropolitan Research Center, Houston Public Library*

ing abortions; businessmen charged with corrupting young women; oil field workers whose rowdy behavior had disturbed the townspeople of Mexia; husbands who abandoned their wives; divorcees who set immoral examples; as well as pimps, prostitutes, gamblers, thieves, and bootleggers. The Klan argued that it existed to enforce law in a time of lawlessness. Governor Neff, who did not belong to the Klan, had buttressed this view by stating—in regard to what he believed to be lax enforcement of prohibition laws—that the period led all other eras of Texas history in lawlessness. Other members of the Texas elite gave tacit support to the clandestine organization. Many Protestant churches endorsed its anti-Semitic and anti-Catholic proclivities. Business leaders feared Klan boycotts. And some in law enforcement agencies winked at Klan flogging and tar-and-feathering expeditions. Evidence indicates that the Klan dominated the Austin, Waco, and Dallas police forces and the Tarrant County Sheriff's Department. Undoubtedly, the Klan emasculated potential opposition by recruiting judges, law enforcement officers, government officials, and newspapermen into the organization.

Some opposition to Klan violence did appear. The *Dallas Morning News,* appalled at the increase in lynching, published editorials in 1921 condemning extralegal use of force, as did the *Houston Chronicle* and the *El Paso Times.* Such well-known Texans as Joseph S. Cullinan of Houston and Maury Maverick of San Antonio denounced the "invisible empire." Some private organizations such as the Chamber of Commerce and the Bar Association requested that Governor Neff condemn Klan violence. He did not. A few local judges and law enforcement officers encouraged grand juries to indict Klansmen for brutal assaults and violent crimes. Others attempted to prevent Klan parades—in which members marched with masks on—or published the names of those who belonged to the organization.

The Klan struck back. It boycotted opposition newspapers; it endorsed political candidates who favored its goals; and its supporters won local offices in 1922 throughout North and East Texas. Klan sympathizers defeated citizen organizations' candidates who opposed the secret society in Beaumont, Fort Worth, Dallas, and Houston. That year the Klan endorsed Earle B. Mayfield for the U.S. Senate, and he defeated James E. Ferguson in the primary and won the general election. Mayfield's victory, however, represented the zenith of Klan popularity.

By 1923, the Klan's increased use of violence had begun to alienate upper- and middle-class white voters. Even if, as Klan officials maintained, there had been no actual Klan participation in floggings and lynchings, the emotionalism of its rallies and its moral fervor certainly helped inspire the hateful acts. Mayfield's election to the Senate convinced many moderates that reasonable people must rally against the Klan. Potential Democratic candidates for president toured the state in 1924 and spoke out against the dangers of the "invisible empire." That year Neff, in a surprise announcement, finally went on record as opposing the organization. The voters nominated Miriam A. Ferguson for governor in 1924 rather than the Klan candidate, Felix D. Robertson of Dallas. Membership in the Klan dropped shortly thereafter, and the organization disappeared toward the end of the decade, but its residue of demands for moral conformity lived on.

Indeed, both private and public agencies worked to establish moral conformity. Their support for uniform behavior codes dovetailed with the early Klan goals of a society that turned back urban sins. Texas teacher organizations passed resolutions demanding that textbooks explain the evils of liquor. Local organizations censored paintings and books they deemed radical or immoral. At various times, club women and ministers attacked indecent dress, excessive drinking, bathing-beauty contests, carnivals, jazz clubs, and dancing. Cities established boards that reviewed motion pictures and approved or disapproved of their contents. Blue laws closed theaters on Sunday. City councils introduced or actually enacted codes that limited flirting, prohibited women from smoking in public, forbade the playing of jazz after midnight, and restricted the brevity of bathing attire. A legislator introduced a bill to ban women's shoes with heels higher than one inch. Clearly, society was changing in the Roaring Twenties, and many Texans knew not how to cope with the new environment.

In the South, much of the demand for conformity and control came with a resurgence of religious fundamentalism. The urbanization of America placed considerable pressure on churches. As upholders and definers of religious faith, churches needed to respond to societal changes and technological advances. Automobiles and roads bypassed rural churches, taking parishioners to urban ones. Radios created ministries with national congregations. Protestant churches, which once focused family entertainment around Wednesday prayer meetings, choir practices, and Sunday schools, now competed with urban activities for their members' time and attention. Not surprisingly, Protestant churches and ministers were the vanguard in the fight to preserve rural values in a time of social change.

Protestant churches directed the religious faith of most Texas churchgoers. Although Catholics (22.6 percent of the state's churchgoers) outnumbered any single Protestant sect, Southern Baptists (19.9 percent), Methodists (17.8 percent) and Baptist Church National Conventionists (16.3 percent) dominated the religious landscape. Of the 1,784,620 church members in Texas in 1916, most attended congregations of fewer than 100 members. These small Protestant churches shared certain characteristics, such as the belief that each person could achieve salvation without direct intervention of a priesthood or an educated ministry. This relatively democratic idea contributed both to religious anarchy and to conformity. Even though each member could read and decide upon the Bible for himself, the scriptures needed a literal rather than exegitical translation to have a direct bearing upon each individual's life. The general assumption of the white population that the Klan attacked vice partly explains why rural Protestants reacted so slowly against the violence of the "invisible empire."

The struggle of fundamentalists to reclaim rural values from urban Texas took place within theological and public frameworks. Organizations such as the Texas Sunday School Association and the Bible-in-the-Public-Schools Association pressured school boards to include some form of religious instruction, such as

Bible readings, during the school day. About 50 percent of the schools complied. The demand for religious orthodoxy soon went to the state legislature, where education bills that mandated morning devotional services, required teachers to take a religious oath, and limited parochial school education all failed. The diversity of the state's population forced legislators from South Texas, the Gulf Coast, and the Hill Country to oppose the bills.

Another effort concentrated on banning the teaching of the theory of human evolution in the public schools. A bill was introduced in 1923 to bar the teaching of evolution in any state-supported educational institution. It passed the house but died in the senate. The next year, another version of the bill, which would have fired teachers who taught evolution and punished members of the state textbook commission who approved books that contained statements supporting the theory that *Homo sapiens* had evolved from othe primate species, lost. Until 1929, similar laws under various guises went to the legislative floor. The state textbook commission did censor textbooks that seemingly treated human evolution as scientific fact. But Texas, unlike five other southern states, passed no antievolution law. The heterogeneity of Texas's population and the strong opposition of legislators from the German Hill Country and the Rio Grande Valley defeated the anti-evolution legislation.

THE WANING OF PROGRESSIVISM, 1925–1931

Miriam A. Ferguson ran for governor in 1924 against the Klan candidate, Felix D. Robertson of Dallas. Part of her campaign focused on opposition to the Klan. Much of her appeal came from the general understanding that her candidacy for governor was a surrogate campaign for her deposed husband. In the second Democratic primary, progressives divided their vote. Some, like Love, campaigned for Robertson on the grounds that the Klan voted dry. Others stayed with Ferguson in reaction to Klan excesses. Mrs. Ferguson defeated Robertson by nearly 100,000 votes in the second primary in a record turnout. Love said Mrs. Ferguson won because progressives hated the Klan violence more than they hated Fergusonism. He led a group of Democratic bolters who fused with the Republican party in an effort to defeat Mrs. Ferguson in the general election. Those who supported fusion chose as their candidate George C. Butte, dean of the University of Texas Law School. Ferguson defeated Butte and his "good government" campaign by 100,000 votes. Her victory in both races rested on rural voting strength. Unlike in "Pa" Ferguson's losing race against Mayfield for the Senate, in this one, "Ma" ran close in or carried the urban Klan strongholds of Texas.

Mrs. Ferguson by no means ran as a reformer, and her gubernatorial administration (1925–1927) boasted of no reforms. It was, as expected, dominated by her husband, who approved appointees and attended all important meetings. The political controversies of the day centered on the Fergusons' liberal policy of pardoning prisoners and the administration of highways by the State Highway Commission composed of Ferguson appointees. One historian best summed up the Fergusons' tenure: "In the murky world of statute books, there may well have been no illegality, but the Fergusons were guilty of a flagrant abuse of the ethical standards of public office." Their chief political antagonist was Dan Moody, the state attorney general. His opposition to the State Highway Commission's method of granting construction contracts to other than the lowest bidders led to a resignation of two Ferguson appointees and the cancellation of several road contracts. Reformers and other enemies of Fergusonism rallied behind the young attorney general, who defeated Mrs. Ferguson in the 1926 gubernatorial race.

In office, Moody, who served as governor from 1927 to 1931, quickly became a spokesman for business progressivism. He urged the state legislature to bring efficiency to government by passing a civil-service law. He advocated new taxation laws, a reorganization of part of the state judiciary, and expanded appointive powers for the governor's office. While the legislature responded negatively to all of these proposals, Moody was able to establish the state auditor's office, which evolved into a modern-day fiscal controller of state agencies. Then Moody and his progressive supporters asked for a commission report on Texas prisons, based on a study of other states' penal facilities. The report effected a compromise between the governor, who wished to expand the powers of the Texas Prison Board, and the legislature. Moody's successes were few, yet national journals cited Moody along with some other southern governors as examples of progressive leaders.

Although Moody triumphed easily over Louis J. Wardlow to win reelection in 1928, the unity of progressive Democrats was shattered that year when Governor Alfred E. Smith of New York, a Catholic and an antiprohibitionist, secured the Democratic nomination for the presidency. Texas Democrats split over support for Smith's candidacy. The Harmony Democrats, who backed Smith, chose Governor Moody to head their state delegation. Thomas Love led the Constitutional Democrats, who pledged to scuttle Smith's bid for the presidential nomination at the national Democratic convention in Houston. The Harmony Democrats prevailed, and Love, ex-Governors Culberson and Colquitt, and other dissident Democrats stormed off to unite with Republicans to support the presidential candidacy of Republican Herbert Hoover.

The dissident Democrats ran their campaign for Hoover much like they had their older prohibitionist ones. Local caucuses featured Protestant ministers and other drys who maintained that the Catholic Smith and his wet supporters betrayed the traditional moral values of Texas. Meanwhile, the leadership of the state Democratic party stayed loyal to the national ticket, their detractors labeling them as "brass collar" Democrats, a sobriquet that still means unbridled loyalty to the party. In November, Texas joined North Carolina and Florida in voting Republican for the first time since Reconstruction. Smith's brashness, urban background, Catholicism, and antiprohibition stand had combined with the relative prosperity of the 1920s to defeat rural loyalties to the Democratic party. The winners of state offices, however, were as usual, Democrats, with Tom Connally defeating Earle B. Mayfield for the U.S. Senate seat.

Moody's first term in office had corresponded to a time of prosperity for the nation and the state. His second term witnessed the stock market collapse of 1929 and the onset of the Great Depression. Now business progressivism, which had solidified with the industrial growth of the 1920s, collapsed with the shattered economy. The rhetoric of business progressivism identified it closely with chambers of commerce and rotary clubs that emphasized efficiency and economic development over the calls for social justice and reform, and efficiency and business profits would hardly play well during the Great Depression. Nevertheless, a residue of Texas progressivism still remains in the popular acceptance of the public-service functions of government.

READINGS

Books and Dissertations

Acheson, Sam Hanna, *Joe Bailey: The Last Democrat* (New York: Macmillan Co., 1982).

Alexander, Charles C., *Crusade for Conformity: The Ku Klux Klan in Texas, 1920–1930* (Houston: Texas Gulf Coast Historical Association, 1962).

Anders, Evan, *Boss Rule in South Texas: The Progressive Era* (Austin: University of Texas Press, 1982).

Bailey, Richard, "Morris Sheppard," in *Profiles in Power: Twentieth-Century Texans in Washington*, eds., Kenneth E. Hendrickson, Jr., and Michael L. Collins (Wheeling, IL: Harlan Davidson, Inc., 1993).

Bernhard, Virginia, Betty Brandon, Elizabeth Fox-Genovese, Theda Purdue, and Elizabeth H. Turner, eds., *Hidden Histories of Women in the New South* (Columbia: University of Missouri Press, 1994).

Brown, Norman D., Hood, *Bonnet and Little Brown Jug: Texas Politics, 1921–1928* (College Station: Texas A&M University Press, 1984).

Bryant, Ira B., *Texas Southern University: Its Antecedents, Political Origin and Future* (Houston: Privately Printed, 1975).

Buenger, Walter L., *The Path to a Modern South: Northeast Texas between Reconstruction and the Great Depression* (Austin: University of Texas Press, 2001).

Clark, James A., and Weldon Hart, *The Tactful Texan: A Biography of Governor Will Hobby* (New York: Random House, 1958).

Coerver, Don M., and Linda B. Hall, *Texas and the Mexican Revolution: A Study in State and National Border Policy, 1910–1920* (San Antonio: Trinity University Press, 1984.)

Furniss, Norman F., *The Fundamentalist Controversy, 1918–1931* (New Haven: Yale University Press, 1954).

Gould Lewis L., *Progressives and Prohibitionists: Texas Democrats in the Wilson Era* (Austin: University of Texas Press, 1973).

Grantham, Dewey W., *Southern Progressivism: The Reconciliation of Progress and Tradition* (Knoxville: The University of Tennessee Press, 1983).

Haynes, Robert V., *Night of Violence: The Houston Riot of 1917* (Baton Rouge: Louisiana State University Press, 1976).

Hilderbrand, Robert C., "Edward M. House," in *Profiles in Power: Twentieth-Century Texans in Washington*, eds., Kenneth E. Hendrickson, Jr., and Michael L. Collins (Wheeling, IL: Harlan Davidson, Inc., 1993).

Hine, Darlene Clark, *Black Victory: The Rise and Fall of the White Primary in Texas* (Millwood, NY: KTO Press, 1979).

Lomax, John A., *Will Hogg: Texan* (Austin: University of Texas Press, 1956).

McCarty, Jeanne Bozzell, *The Struggle for Sobriety: Protestants and Prohibition in Texas, 1919–1935* (El Paso: Texas Western Press, 1980).

Rice, Bradley R., *Progressive Cities: The Commission Government Movement in America* (Austin: University of Texas Press, 1977).

Rocha, Rodolfo, "The Influence of the Mexican Revolution on the Mexico-Texas Border, 1910–1916" (Ph.D. diss., Texas Tech University, 1981).

Tindell, George B., *The Emergence of the New South, 1913–1945* (Baton Rouge: Louisiana State University Press, 1967).

Tinsley, James A. "The Progressive Movement in Texas" (Ph.D. diss., University of Wisconsin, 1953).

Turner, Elizabeth Hayes, *Women, Culture, and Community: Religion and Reform in Galveston, 1880–1920* (Chapel Hill: University of North Carolina Press, 1997).

Webb, Walter Prescott, and Terrell Webb (eds.), *Washington Wife: Journal of Ellen Maury Webb* (New York: Harper and Row, 1963).

Articles

Allen, Lee N., "The Democratic Presidential Primary of 1924 in Texas," *Southwestern Historical Quarterly* 61 (1958): 474–93.

Crane, R. C., "The West Texas Agricultural and Mechanical College Movement and the Founding of Texas Technological College," *West Texas Historical Association Yearbook* 7 (1931): 3–34.

Durham, Kenneth R., "The Longview Race Riot of 1919," *East Texas Historical Journal* 18 (1980): 13–24.

Glad, Paul W., "Progressives and the Business Culture of the 1920s," *Journal of American History* 53 (1966): 75–89.

Gould, Lewis, "The University Becomes Politicized: The War With Jim Ferguson, 1915–1918," *The Southwestern Historical Quarterly* 86 (1982): 255–76.

Hill, Larry D., and Robert A. Calvert, "The University of Texas Extension Services and Progressivism," *Southwestern Historical Quarterly* 86 (1982): 230–54.

Hine, Darlene Clark, "The Elusive Ballot: The Black Struggle Against the Texas Democratic White Primary, 1932–1945," *Southwestern Historical Quarterly* 81 (1978): 371–92.

Ledbetter, Patsy, "Defense of the Faith: J. Frank Norris and Texas Fundamentalism, 1920–1929," *Arizona and the West* 15 (1973): 45–62.

Maxwell, Robert S., "One Man's Legacy: W. Goodrich Jones and Texas Conservation," *Southwestern Historical Quarterly* 77 (1974): 355–80.

Russell, C. Allyn, "J. Frank Norris: Violent Fundamentalist," *Southwestern Historical Quarterly* 75 (1972): 271–302.

Sallee, Shelley, "'The Woman of It,' Governor Miriam Ferguson's 1924 Election," *Southwestern Historical Quarterly* 100 (July 1996): 1–16.

Sorelle, James M. "The 'Waco Horror': The Lynching of Jesse Washington," *Southwestern Historical Quarterly* 86 (1983): 517–36.

Taylor, Elizabeth A., "The Woman Suffrage Movement in Texas," *Journal of Southern History* 17 (1951): 194–215.

Tindall, George B., "Business Progressivism: Southern Politics in the Twenties," *South Atlantic Quarterly* 62 (1963): 92–106.

Tinsley, James A., "Texas Progressives and Insurance Regulation," *Southwestern Social Science Quarterly* 36 (1955): 237–47.

Tuttle, William, "Violence in a 'Heathen' Land: The Longview Race Riot of 1919," *Phylon* 33 (1972): 324–33.

TEXAS AND
THE GREAT DEPRESSION

CHAPTER 11

The prosperity of the 1920s camouflaged serious weaknesses in the U.S. economy. Agriculturists suffered from low prices, a fact that had been mitigated by expanding production. Big business held down wages and increased its profits at the expense of workers and the producers of raw materials. Wealth was unequally distributed: 2 percent of the population controlled 28 percent of the national wealth. The consolidation of money in the hands of the few depressed consumer purchasing power and limited savings, thus weakening most citizens' ability to weather an economic downturn. By the mid-1920s, the railroad, textile, and coal industries were in trouble, and housing starts and automobile purchases had begun to decline. International trade dropped as the U.S. policy of protective tariffs limited the growth of an already weak European economy. Consequently, European nations defaulted on their international debts and withdrew investments from the United States.

Heavy speculation in the stock market in the late 1920s created an illusion of prosperity that disguised both industrial weaknesses and a shaky financial network. Over 7,000 banks closed their doors in that decade, and although only about 2 percent of all Americans owned stock, the market's collapse on October 23, 1929, exposed the nation's economic weaknesses and threw its citizenry into a panic. By 1932, at least one of every four American workers was unemployed, median family income had dropped by 50 percent, a hundred thousand businesses had failed, corporate profits had plummeted from $10 billion to $1 billion, and the gross national product was cut in half. The industrial machine had ground to a halt.

President Herbert Hoover and the Republican party did not cause the Great Depression, but Hoover's unduly optimistic pronouncements promising a rapid return to prosperity, and the fact that he was in office when the depression began, linked him and his party to the downturn in the minds of most Americans. Actually, the president used the powers of the federal government to attack the depression more extensively than had any other chief executive in like situations. He

Ross S. Sterling making his first speech in the 1930 campaign for Texas Governor, Huntsville, Texas. *The Center for American History, The University of Texas at Austin, Ross Sterling Papers, CN-01553*

foresaw as a solution to the depression a cooperative state that would weld together business owners, who promised to keep wages and production levels from falling, workers, who pledged not to strike, and local governments and charities, which dispensed temporary relief. The federal government, meanwhile, would offer loans to agriculture and businesses to enable them to continue producing needed goods and employing laborers. Federal officials, including the president, would create an air of optimism that would prevent panic and restore confidence in the economy. Hoover believed that charities and local governments should provide limited relief to the needy. The dole, he said, diminished a man's character. As the depression worsened, however, many Americans realized that optimism, private charities, and local and state governments could not cope with the impact of the mass unemployment. But in the face of growing public demands for direct relief aid, Hoover held firm to his views, thus appearing heartless and uncaring. Having no choice but to hunt to supplement their diets, rural Americans took to calling rabbits and ground hogs "Hoover hams," and hobo camps that gave temporary shelter to the millions of unemployed became known as "Hoovervilles." In the final analysis, Hoover's policies failed.

By March 1933, the American banking system had collapsed. Texans had returned to the Democratic party the previous November to vote for President Franklin D. Roosevelt, who proclaimed a New Deal for the dispossessed. His decisive action in confronting the bank crisis of 1933 restored a measure of public confidence in the economy. Under FDR's leadership, the federal government accepted responsibility for direct relief for the unemployed and passed measures to stimulate and reform the economy. The economic recovery of the nation moved unsteadily forward until mid-1935. Prosperity and growth seemed assured from 1935 until 1937, when an economic downturn in the fall deepened into a recession that continued throughout most of 1938. Not until the defense buildup of World War II did industrial recovery succeed. As late as 1940, 311,000 Texans were either unemployed or working for a federal relief agency.

An assessment of the New Deal created intellectual challenges for contemporaries and for historians. The New Deal did not work fundamental changes in the capitalist economy or in state politics, nor did it end the depression. It did, however, apply the vast resources of the federal government to attacking the immediate problems of poverty and despair. It would be difficult in retrospect to see how Roosevelt could have acted much differently given the complexities of the economic problems and his and the majority of the New Dealers' commitment to mainstream American values. The president's agenda included neither long-range economic planning nor an abandonment of capitalism. Instead, he advocated a political pragmatism to solve immediate ills and achieve an eventual return to a balanced budget. His charisma and methods captured the hearts of most Texans, if not of the majority of the state's leaders. And, certainly, the citizens of the nation and the state were better off after his administrations than they had been before them.

TEXANS CONFRONT THE DEPRESSION

The immediate impact of the stock-market crash did not affect most Texans. Few had money invested in securities, most lived in rural areas, and, except to tenant farmers, prosperity through agricultural expansion still seemed plausible. Some state leaders even argued that a market collapse would encourage the money formerly siphoned off by stock speculation to return to capital investment in agriculture and manufacturing. The long-standing agrarian hostility toward speculators even encouraged a thinly concealed smugness that the eastern establishment was now receiving its just due. The state press and leadership followed the national pattern in 1929 and 1930 of encouraging confidence in the economy and of pointing out that the present economic downturn represented the historical boom-and-bust cycle. Once the excess waste and inflation were rendered from the economy, they asserted, prosperity would return; meanwhile, private and civic charities should provide for those unfortunate enough to be unemployed. Cities asked community groups to dispense charity through such organizations as the Community Chest, the Red Cross, churches, and the Salvation Army. But these organizations, designed to offer temporary aid to the destitute in good times, could not expand their resources to confront the mass unemployment of the early 1930s. By late 1931, private organizations announced that they were inadequate to the task.

Cities assumed some responsibilities to augment private charities. They used public works to expand job opportunities. Usually, these projects were designed to offer unskilled work to the (presumably) temporarily unemployed, and they included clean-up campaigns and such long-range improvements as widening streets, laying sewer and water lines, and constructing or renovating public parks and buildings. Dallas established the "Committee of 1,000," composed of civic leaders who directed "buy-now" and "hire-the-unemployed" campaigns. Other cities combined this volunteerism, as did Dallas, with offers of free garden spaces, soup kitchens, and the use of public buildings to house transients. Cities in West Texas sponsored rabbit hunts and distributed the animals to the poor. A few civic groups encouraged back-to-the-farm movements or self-sufficiency as an alternative to urban unemployment.

Some local governments took stronger measures. Blacks and Mexican Americans were denied relief in Houston on the grounds that aid to minorities prevented the allotment of resources to deserving whites. Midland and other cities stationed law enforcement officials at train depots to prevent transients from staying in the community. All cities instituted austerity programs; many did so at the expense of women, who were often discharged from city posts to open slots for unemployed males. Public schools frequently refused to hire single women, and they fired women married to other public employees. As the depression worsened, school districts cut teacher salaries and reduced appropriations for public education. Most cities eliminated some urban services and froze employee salaries. Beaumont and Houston cut off either part or all of their street-lights. Dallas reduced its city personnel, eliminated playground supervisors, in-stituted a hiring freeze, and curtailed library services. Most Texas civic leaders warned by 1932 that they could not continue their relief efforts.

STATE POLITICS, 1929–1933

The early reactions of the cities to the Great Depression revealed much about Texans' and Americans' attitudes toward employment. Many believed that government aid sapped the population's willingness to work and weakened the self-help and frontier spirit of the nation. Others believed that once jobs grew scarce, white men should come first.

The demographic composition of the population most affected by the de-pression reflected this attitude. The unskilled and the inexperienced, women, the young, and minorities were the first to be fired and the last to be hired. The rate of unemployment among blacks was double that of whites, and Mexican Americans outnumbered all others in percentage of unemployed. Unemploy-ment had a ripple effect on the economy. Entrepreneurs eliminated proposed or not-yet-completed construction projects. The price of cotton dropped to five cents a pound and that of oil to five cents a barrel. Employers fired workers, who then became nonconsumers. By mid-1932, estimates placed the number of out-of-work Texans at 350,000 to 400,000, with 25 percent of these having no re-sources. Dwindling tax revenues, falling property values, and rural representation in the state legislature limited already short funds for public relief or donations to private charities. As the economic collapse continued, the middle class be-gan to identify with those first beset by poverty, and a consensus for some sort of direct aid to unemployed citizens emerged.

As the depression affected more Texans and revealed the inadequacies of local resources to cope with an economic disaster, the public sought a leader who would take action. Eleven gubernatorial candidates announced in 1930, including "Ma" Ferguson, Earle Mayfield, and Tom Love. Early in the cam-paign, Mrs. Ferguson and Ross S. Sterling emerged as front runners. Gover-nor Moody chose not to run for reelection and left office without really contending with the depression. Sterling, president of Humble Oil and Re-fining (later Exxon) until 1925, had served as Moody's chairman of the State Highway Commission and advertised himself as a business progressive who wanted a bond issue for highway improvements and economies in government. Sterling's personal fortune would decline during the depression, but after his retirement from public office in 1933, he returned to Houston and accrued wealth in real estate and oil investments. His image as a rich man—with a reputed net worth of over $50 million in 1930—did not damage his original appeal to Texans. Although "Ma" led by more than 70,000 votes in the first Democratic primary, Sterling defeated her in the run-off by 90,000 votes. In the general election, Sterling easily defeated the Republican nominee. As the depression continued, however, the stigma of excessive wealth undoubtedly weakened his leadership role.

The Sterling administration (1931–1933) was awash with controversy. The Texas press dubbed the 1931 legislature a "do-nothing" session. A state income tax bill failed, as did a redistricting bill and one that sought to equalize taxes. But even as state revenue fell, the cost of government remained the same. Despite four special sessions, Sterling's term ended with a deficit and without a state relief act. His liberal use of the veto typified the divisions between the governor's office and the legislature. The legislature's unwillingness to provide sources of revenue caused the governor to veto $3 million in appropriations, including monies for summer schools. But the two controversies that marked his administration were in the basic Texas industries of oil and agriculture.

The East Texas Oil Boom

In October 1930, Columbus Marion "Dad" Joiner drilled an oil well near Kilgore. The wildcatter hit oil where the collective wisdom of geologists maintained that none existed, and thus where the major oil companies had not leased extensively. Even after the first couple of East Texas wells came in, the major oil companies ("majors") remained skeptical. The independent oil companies ("independents") did not; they rushed in, and by the time the majors realized the extent of the boom, independents controlled 80 percent of the field. The great East Texas field exceeded the expectations of even the most optimistic oilman. It comprised 140,000 acres in five counties, contained about one-third of the nation's then-known oil reserves, and in 1933, its peak year of production, spewed out 205 million barrels of oil, more than the total production of the rest of the state.

The East Texas oil boom had several economic effects. It helped the poorest part of the state, in which small farmers and sharecroppers composed the majority of the population. As a result of the boom, land leased for as much as $30,000 an acre as new wells were drilled at a rate of one an hour in October 1931. Kilgore became the great boom town of all oil strikes. Prostitutes, gamblers and swindlers mixed with oil-field workers, entrepreneurs, truck drivers, and investors to create an aura of quick wealth and a disregard for law and order. Most of the local residents welcomed the boom, which offered some relief to the chronically depressed area. The immense output of the field drove the price of oil down from a little over a dollar a barrel in 1930 to eight cents a barrel in 1931. The majors asserted that the market for oil could not keep up with the supply. They and conservationists pointed out that rapid drilling and pumping would deplete underground pressure and ruin the field. Some of the independents agreed with the majors, but others with limited capital pumped furiously, sold quickly at whatever the price, maintained their cash flow, and gambled on hitting other wells. Because oil moves underground, as long as one well pumped nonstop, independents felt that all others needed to do so. Also, majors could afford to hold oil reserves until the price of oil went up; their stance, which appeared so sensible, could potentially drive many independents from the only field that they themselves had developed.

The state legislature had earlier authorized the Texas Railroad Commission to prorate oil—that is, establish maximum amounts of oil that wells would be allowed to pump. Progressives had expanded the Commission's powers in 1917 and 1919 to limit production of oil for conservation and environmental purposes, and in both the Yates and Borger fields, the Commission had limited pumping or drilling until immediate problems of transportation or waste had been solved. In East Texas, though, the issue was that the supply of oil exceeded demand, and overproduction rather than conservation was the reason for proration. It was not clear that the Railroad Commission could legally prorate oil for the reason of marketing. In April 1931, the Commission issued its first proration order for East Texas. Some operators promptly procured injunctions to prevent proration; others simply ignored the order.

Majors controlled the refineries in the state. They refused to buy East Texas crude, pointing out that the market had dropped below the 1929 level and that they did not need the oil. Therefore, independents built refineries of their own. Some were substantial operations, but many were "teakettle" refineries, designed to produce a low-grade gasoline that could be sold by independent stations for seven to eight cents a gallon. Fleets of tank trucks carried this East Texas gas and sometimes other petroleum products from one of the eventual ninety-five refineries to independent gas stations. Because these independent trucking firms handled oil pumped above proration levels, their cargo was known as "Hot Oil."

Consequently, the Railroad Commission could not successfully enforce its proration orders. The independent oilmen held a series of meetings but could not agree to curtail production voluntarily. Ultimately, a group of East Texans appealed to the governor for aid. Governor Sterling issued an executive order on August 17, 1931, instructing East Texas producers to cease operation, and dispatched National Guard units, commanded by General Jacob F. Walters, into the East Texas field to enforce the decision. Walters was an attorney for the Texas Company; Sterling, of course, was identified as a friend of Humble Oil and Standard Oil. Understandably, public opinion in East Texas cataloged the governor's actions as an attempt by the majors to freeze out independents. The East Texas field opened again in September and the allowable amount prorated to each well soon dropped to a hundred barrels a day.

Meanwhile, the traffic in Hot Oil increased. Now, illegal pipelines ran to teakettle refineries that sent East Texas gas to independent stations. The market turned to chaos as National Guardsmen met locally with hostility and found it difficult to identify the Hot Oil producers. Because of the secrecy involved, no one knew how much oil was produced, if correct royalties were paid on it, or whether various middlemen were skimming off profits by pumping extra oil and selling it on the side. Sporadic acts of violence occurred in what already had become a boomtown atmosphere in East Texas. The state supreme court in February 1932 ruled that Sterling's declaration of martial law was unconstitutional; however, he left the troops in East Texas until December.

February saw the Commission also lower the allowable oil production rate to seventy-five barrels a day per well. In October, the federal court struck down the Commission's order, on the grounds that it discriminated against wells with high production capabilities. Sterling immediately called a special session of the legislature, which passed a law that specifically authorized the Commission to prorate to market demands. In January 1933, enforcement of proration limits went back to the Commission. At first, the efforts of the Commission failed. Its investigators were poorly trained, frequently took bribes, and were both too few and too timid to face hostile public opinion and shut down Hot Oil operations. Ernest O. Thompson, whom Sterling appointed chairman of the Railroad Commission in 1932, asked for and received a force of Texas Rangers to stop the flow of Hot Oil from the East Texas field. By the end of 1933, a semblance of order had been restored to the area.

Subsequent events also helped bring order to the East Texas field. In 1933, President Franklin Roosevelt placed oil under the production codes of the National Recovery Administration (NRA), and the majors started producing inexpensive gas in order to compete with the East Texas refineries. The majors' stepped-up output drove some of the undercapitalized independents out of the market. The next year, the state enacted legislation to require all refiners to disclose totals of petroleum processed and to account for the sources of supply. When the U.S. Supreme Court struck down the NRA, Congress responded with the Connally Act (named for Texas Senator Tom Connally) which made it illegal to transport Hot Oil across state lines. By 1935, the combination of federal and state laws enforced the powers of the Texas Railroad Commission to prorate oil.

Before the decade closed, the majors owned 80 percent of the East Texas field. The stronger independents survived. Using the vast supplies of East Texas oil, these entrepreneurs went on to amass huge fortunes that led to the stereotyped image of the Texas oilman. The need for East Texas oil outlets caused independents to transfer their offices to Dallas, making it, rather than Tulsa, Oklahoma, the capital of southwestern petroleum money. The boom conditions helped the state survive the depression. Ultimately, the greatest impact of the East Texas field may well have been in forcing the state to limit oil production in order to force up the price of petroleum. The Railroad Commission continued to prorate oil production for the next two decades. For Sterling, however, the crisis in East Texas earned him considerable hostility from the voters of the region.

The Agricultural Depression

The agricultural depression also mired the Sterling administration in controversy. When farmers planted their cotton crop in 1931, the market price of cotton averaged 9 to 10 cents a pound; by harvest time, it had fallen to 5.3 cents a pound, where it remained for the next year. Corn and cattle prices fell to less than one-half of their 1929 levels. Prices for other goods did not drop at the same rate as did those for agricultural commodities. Nor did interest rates fall, because those who loaned money now had less of it to loan. A calculation of the purchase power of cotton with parity (what agricultural commodities could command in other economic sectors, from 1909 to 1914, or a base rate of 100 before World War I) was only 58 in 1932. In simple terms, a farmer needed at least three times the amount of production in 1931 that he had needed in 1928 to pay off the same amount of loan. Small and marginal farmers in North and East Texas suffered the greatest hardship.

Earlier pleas of agricultural reformers to farmers that they voluntarily limit production and diversify crops had failed. Consequently, both the state and federal governments now moved to control the marketing of cotton. In June 1929, Congress passed the Agricultural Marketing Act. It created the Federal Farm Board, which extended loans to agricultural cooperatives to aid them in holding cotton and other crops off the depressed market. As agricultural prices continued to fall and defaults on the loans it had extended seemed probable, in June 1930, the Federal Farm Board organized the Cotton Stabilization Corporation, which directly took over the cooperatives' cotton and held it off the market. The Federal Farm Board had too little capital, however, and there were too few cooperatives to stabilize crop prices. The Texas Marketing Association numbered only 754 cooperatives, with about 47,000 members. The 1931 cotton crop of 17 million bales was the second largest in history, which only added to the existing surplus of 4.5 million bales held over from 1930 production. Now the Farm Board ceased its efforts to prop up the market and returned to volunteerism, urging farmers to diversify crops and "plow up" one-third of the cotton already in the field.

Meanwhile, Texas attempted remedies of its own. Governor Moody proposed that businesspersons buy a bale of cotton in 1930 and hold it until prices increased, but too much cotton made such an appeal ineffective. Then, when farmers asked for a special legislative session to pass a cotton-reduction law, Moody refused to call one, maintaining that legislative action would be futile without a similar response from other cotton-producing states.

Sterling inherited the farm depression. Responding to a joint resolution of the legislature, he called a conference of governors to meet in the summer of 1931 to consider cotton acreage control. Five states sent representatives, who agreed that if Texas restricted production they would, too. But cotton-reduction plans raised national and state opposition from industries that relied on the cotton trade. Shippers, merchants, ginners, and manufacturers, for example, and their employees argued that acreage restrictions would cause a decline in their income. Southern governors and most newspapers reacted negatively to the proposal, except for Huey P. Long of Louisiana, who offered his own "drop a crop" plan. The Louisiana governor proposed that farmers plant no cotton in 1932. His state passed a law to that effect, which it intended to activate as soon as other states enacted similar legislation.

Long's action placed political pressures on Sterling. For the "drop a crop" plan to succeed, Texas would have to curtail its considerable cotton production.

Yet the Texas Cotton Association, an organization of shippers and buyers, and most of the big city dailies opposed Long's idea. Pressure from farmers mounted, and Sterling called a special legislative session in September of 1931. The legislature turned down Long's scheme but passed a measure that limited cotton acreage in 1932 to 30 percent of that cultivated in 1931. A fine for each acre of cotton planted in excess of the allotment was to be levied on offending farmers. Most ignored the law. And only three other southern states passed similar acts. When Long saw that other states would not follow his lead, he repealed the "no cotton" law by executive order. A few days later, in February 1932, the Texas law limiting cotton acreage was ruled unconstitutional. Sterling, who opposed the Long plan, had not been enthusiastic about the Texas legislation.

The Return of "Fergusonism," 1933–1935

The cotton-restriction failure and the issue of having sent troops to the oil field damaged Sterling's reelection campaign. "Ma" Ferguson again challenged him for the Democratic nomination and led all candidates in the first primary. Charges of vote fraud soon emanated from the Sterling camp. In 132 counties, 40,000 more votes were cast than poll taxes paid. Many of these votes came from East Texas, where the Fergusons had strength and Sterling was roundly disliked. Much of the Texas establishment, the other defeated candidates in the first primary, and most of the state press endorsed Sterling in the runoff. In a bitterly fought campaign, Sterling increased his primary votes by over 175,000 but lost by a slim margin of 3,798 ballots. Once again, vote totals exceeded poll-tax receipts. Sterling tried unsuccessfully to get a fourth special session of the legislature to investigate vote fraud. He then filed a suit contesting Mrs. Ferguson's nomination. The Texas Supreme Court ruled that her name should go on the general election ballot, and she defeated Republican Orville Bullington, a Wichita Falls lawyer and businessman, in November.

Sterling always believed that illegal voting in East Texas cost him a return to the governor's chair. He said later that if he had sent the Texas Rangers into those East Texas counties to prevent voter fraud, he would have won. Certainly, Mrs. Ferguson carried those counties in which many poor farmers could not afford to pay their poll taxes, and migrant oil workers made accurate voter roles difficult to keep. The legislature, on the other hand, would have had problems in ascertaining a truly accurate vote count, since a discrepancy between poll taxes paid and ballots cast surfaced in more than 100 counties. Probably, a more accurate estimation of Ferguson's victory lay in the continued support of her husband by poor folks and in the political despair generated by the widening depression. Sterling, like Hoover, received blame for a depression not of his making and for not seeming to care about the less fortunate.

The second Ferguson administration (1933–1935) corresponded to President Franklin Roosevelt's first two years in office. The governor and "Pa" needed to address the financial catastrophe of a $14 million state debt and of a failed welfare system, but New Deal legislation that preempted state economic decisions complicated any local actions. A wary legislature that remembered previous Ferguson administrations' reluctance to pass tax bills also hampered strong executive leadership. Governor Ferguson proposed sales, corporate, and income taxes, but the legislature only enacted a small two-cent levy on each barrel of oil. Partially for revenue purposes, the legislature legalized racetrack gambling and prize fighting. Much of the state attempts to balance the budget centered on economies in government, but the most far-reaching proposal to save money by consolidating state agencies failed. The Graves-Woodruff Reorganization bill, the result of recommendations from a committee appointed by Sterling, would have revamped some state government agencies and higher education. The governor supported the early New Deal legislation, including federal control of the price of oil, and she endorsed a called state election that carried a constitutional amendment authorizing $20 million in relief funds for the unemployed. By executive order, the governor created the Texas Relief Commission to distribute funds from the New Deal's Reconstruction Finance Corporation (RFC). The legislature renamed its agency the Texas Rehabilitation and Relief Commission and authorized it to administer "bread bonds" as well as federal funds available to Texas from the RFC and other New Deal agencies. When the Twenty-first Amendment to the U.S. Constitution ended prohibition, the state authorized a referendum to approve the sale of 3.2 percent (alcohol) beer.

"Ma's" second administration generated less political controversy than did either of the other two tenures of Fergusonism; nevertheless, charges of corruption soon surfaced. Critics complained of a return to her previous policy of the generous pardoning of convicts. Some observers saw her actions as an example of the administration's disdain for law and order that included the dismissal of forty-four Rangers and their replacement by men of dubious character. The governor also issued "Special Ranger" commissions to 2,344 men, thus making the force a venue for political patronage. Finally, political chicanery touched relief agencies as Jim Ferguson oversaw the Texas Rehabilitation and Relief Commission. He and the governor's appointee, Lawrence Westbrook, the head of the Texas Relief Commission, were accused of using relief monies and patronage to build a party machine. A senate investigation forced Westbrook's resignation in 1934. That year the governor announced that she would honor the two-term tradition and not seek reelection.

THE NEW DEAL AND TEXAS

By the time of the 1934 gubernatorial campaign, President Roosevelt and the Democrats controlled Congress. The return of the Democrats to power brought many Texans into national prominence. John Nance Garner, the former Speaker of the House of Representatives, had been mentioned frequently, along with Al Smith and Roosevelt, as a possible front runner for the 1932 Democratic presidential nomination. The Uvalde native's decision to step aside and support Roosevelt won Garner the vice-presidential spot and gave him a lot of political capital to spend with the president. During the president's first term, the vice-president offered him advice on a wide range of matters. Thereafter Garner and FDR gradually split over the New Deal's swing to the left and the president's decision to run for a third term. Nonetheless, the crusty West Texan remained a life-long Democrat, if not a supporter of Roosevelt. Possibly, Jesse H. Jones of Houston, who entered government service as a Hoover appointee to the RFC, exercised more power than did even the vice-president. Roosevelt was impressed by the well-known Houston banker, making Jones chairman of the RFC (1933–1939) and expanding his responsibilities with assignments to the Export-Import Bank (1936–1943), the Federal Loan Agency (1939–1945), and as secretary of commerce (1940–1945). Jones was always more conservative than were most of his New Deal colleagues, and his disagreement with Roosevelt's policies led in 1945 to his break with the Democratic party. During the early New Deal years, though, Washington newspapers hailed Jesse Jones as the most powerful man in the capital.

Some referred to Garner, Jones, and the Texas congressional delegation as a dynasty. Indeed, the congressional seniority system promoted Texans to committee assignments of importance. Nine Texans held chairmanships of permanent committees, including four that were instrumental in passing New Deal legislation: James P. Buchanan, Appropriations; Marvin Jones, Agriculture; Hatton Sumners, Judiciary; and Sam Rayburn, Interstate and Foreign Com-

Franklin D. Roosevelt, Lyndon B. Johnson, Governor James V. Allred, and Mayor of Galveston Adrian Levy during FDR's vist to Galveston, May 1937. *The UT Institute of Texan Cultures, No. 74-1140, courtesy of Helene Levy (Galveston)*

merce. Rayburn went on to become majority leader and Speaker of the House for most of the time from 1940 to 1961. His ability to manipulate legislation and to work out political compromises won him respect on both sides of the House aisle. He endorsed, introduced, and supported most of the New Deal legislation but was usually regarded as a moderate in the Democratic party. Elsewhere in the house, Maury Maverick received national acclaim as a New Deal supporter. After his defeat in the congressional race of 1938, he became mayor of his native city, San Antonio, and then served as an able administrator of wartime mobilization agencies. Wright Patman, the Texarkana congressman, won acclaim as a progressive, particularly concerning bank legislation. Patman, Lyndon Johnson (who went to Congress in 1937), and Rayburn were the most consistent supporters of Roosevelt throughout his administration.

Not all Texas congressmen, however, were ardent New Dealers. Martin Dies of Orange, who later headed the House Un-American Activities Committee, was equally well known as a vigorous opponent of the New Deal. In the Senate, Morris Sheppard, of prohibition fame, usually supported the president. His 1941 replacement, W. Lee O'Daniel, usually did not. Senator Tom Connally, a political moderate and life-long Democrat, aided New Deal legislation in Roosevelt's first term but became personally estranged from the president in 1937. Nevertheless, Connally remained influential in the Senate, and he played a powerful role in the defense build-up of World War II that so aided the state's recovery and economic growth. Probably the majority of Texans endorsed the New Deal with more fervor than did the state's congressional representatives, and their early support of Democratic measures cleared the way for much of the New Deal's legislation.

Reviving the Banking Industry

Roosevelt took office promising relief, recovery, and reform. And his first acts as president were aimed at restoring confidence and starting people working again. He immediately used emergency powers granted in World War I to close the nation's banks for a "bank holiday," a hiatus that stopped runs on banks. When the banks reopened, they fell under government regulations. Under Jesse Jones, the RFC functioned much differently than it had in the Hoover administration. Rather than loaning money to banks and increasing their indebtedness, the RFC bought up their preferred stock, thereby enlarging their capital. Jones consequently propped up the more stable and prosperous banks. The Federal Deposit Insurance Corporation (FDIC) guaranteed deposits up to $5,000 and periodically audited the insured banks. By 1935, the Federal Reserve System controlled interest rates, thereby limiting competition from new (and possibly shaky) banks that might offer more attractive deals to prospective customers. Moreover, government regulations that separated investment and commercial banking mandated careful periodic auditing of banks by various state and federal agencies. These measures restored public confidence in banking.

Jesse Jones, A. J. McKenzie, and Col. W. B. Tuttle at Chamber of Commerce dinner. *The UT Institute of Texan Cultures, No. 0831-A, San Antonio Light Collection*

Jones and his regulatory measures also reduced competition and guaranteed the primacy of national banks. In Texas, banking deposits doubled between 1925 and 1940, and the number of banks decreased from 1,490 (834 state and 656 national ones) to 839 (393 state and 446 national ones). The depression destroyed some of the banks, but the New Deal and Jones, himself a banker, followed a policy that encouraged financial stability through larger, more prosperous institutions. Roosevelt thought that he had saved the financial community, and he expressed surprise that many bankers, including some from Texas, opposed his reelection in 1936.

Recovery and Relief Measures

To begin recovery and relief, Congress enacted the National Industrial Recovery Act (NIRA). It operated through two separate agencies. Title I established price codes through the National Recovery Administration (NRA), allowing industries to set minimum prices for goods or a base price below which competition could not drive it. Industries that participated in the NRA were exempt from antitrust laws. The price codes affected Texas less than they did the more industrialized states, although they were applied to Hot Oil production. Of more significance to Texans, provisions of the NRA set minimum wage standards and guaranteed the right of collective bargaining. After the U.S. Supreme Court struck down the NIRA in 1935, Congress passed the Wagner Act, which threw the powers of the federal government behind the organization of unions by restraining industry from committing unfair labor practices. It guaranteed the right of unions to organize peacefully. Although organized labor never gained a great deal of strength in Texas, federal New Deal legislation spurred its growth. In particular, the collective-bargaining provisions of the law enabled the Congress of Industrial Organizations (CIO) to begin organizing Gulf Coast refineries and unionizing defense industries. Traditional Texan hostility toward unions would recrystallize by the early 1940s, with a spate of state laws designed to restrict their growth.

Title II of the NRA hired the unemployed. It created the Public Works Administration (PWA), an agency that employed workers to build projects of permanent value. Harold Ickes, its director, issued contracts only after extreme care was taken to avoid any hints of waste or corruption, but his caution slowed down the flow of funds at a time when the unemployed needed direct relief. Nonetheless, the PWA operated through 1939, and it began or completed 922 projects in the state, allotting $109,601,943 in public funds. Its varied activities in Texas included the construction of 119 schools, buildings on college campuses, the Fort Worth Public Library, and other civic edifices, as well as parks, sewage plants, bridges, and dams. Roosevelt, however, never believed that public works were quite the right answer for relief. One result was that the early New Deal featured a series of overlapping agencies that fought unemployment, and Ickes's care in dispensing money had encouraged other administrators to find quicker ways to employ the needy.

One immediate problem was combating hunger in the winter of 1932–1933, during which local private and public charities stopped functioning. In May 1933, Congress authorized the Federal Emergency Relief Administration (FERA) and transferred to it $500 million from the RFC. FERA channeled funds through state and local agencies to the unemployed. At first, the states and the cities matched these grants on a one-third local funding requirement, but the emergency soon stopped the matching of funds. By 1937, Texans received $80 million in federal funds and a little under $30 million from state and local matching grants. The agency gave primarily direct-relief funds, although it did offer some programs of work relief. It targeted four areas of emergency relief: public education, college student aid, rural rehabilitation, and aid to transients. It oriented itself toward aid to rural Americans, and by 1935, 298,000 rural Texans received some sort of direct relief from FERA. Additionally, FERA created shelters and relief centers for migrant workers and kept rural schools open by supplementing teachers' salaries and aiding students. From 1933 to 1935, the agency spent $1,595,521 for school aid.

Like others, Roosevelt grew concerned that the careful scrutinizing of contracts by Ickes slowed down the disbursement of relief monies, so in the winter of 1933, the president authorized the creation of the Civil Works Administration (CWA). The CWA was a federal operation with federal payrolls. It took some of its employees from the relief rolls; others were simply the unemployed who could not pass a local means test that would have provided them with direct aid. The CWA employed 239,264 Texans in 1934, with most of them doing repairs on streets and roads. But the alleged waste and extravagance of the agency disillusioned the president. In the spring of 1934, FDR ordered the CWA dismantled.

Instead, he turned to the Works Progress Administration (WPA). This agency was not to compete with private enterprise or take the place of regular government projects, and much of its work took on the character of "make work" projects. The WPA began at the same time that a drought crippled the U.S. farm economy. Food and supplies were dispensed to an average of 70,549 Texas families a month in 1936. That year, in addition, the state ranked eighth in the number of people the WPA employed. Besides construction projects, the WPA hired teachers, researchers for history projects, women for sewing classes, artists through the Federal Theater and Writers' projects, and other white-collar workers. By 1939, the WPA had spent $178,991,802 in Texas.

Other federal legislation targeted specific economic groups. In 1933, Congress created the Civilian Conservation Corps (CCC). This agency, designed to improve transportation facilities, reforest depleted lands, and carry out such conservation measures as flood and erosion control, built camps that housed and employed untrained and unmarried men between the ages of seventeen and twenty-eight. The camps were segregated; 400 black Texans, less than .05 percent of the total number of Texans enrolled, were in the 1935 program. Indeed, in Texas, African Americans were told at first that the camps were for whites only, and this false information held down the number of blacks who participated in the program. All men who did participate received room and board and $30 a month, $25 of which went direclty home to their families. In addition to their salaries, CCC employees could sign up for special educational courses and earn high school diplomas. As of 1936, the federal government spent $41 million in Texas under this program, which continued to operate until 1942.

Numerous other programs touched the lives of Texans. The National Youth Administration (NYA) employed needy high school, undergraduate, and graduate students. Lyndon Johnson headed the NYA in Texas for two years; at the age of twenty-six, he was the youngest NYA director in the nation. The NYA hired between 10,000 and 18,000 students per month in 1935 for clerical or maintenance work. During the summers these young people worked on roads and built recreational facilities. Johnson used only need as a criterion for enrollment, and in 1937, 40 percent of those who qualified for NYA assistance were black. The Home Owners Loan Act created the Home Owners Loan Corporation (HOLC), which refinanced loans at lower payments for needy home owners. It spent $103,068,735 in Texas by 1936 to prevent foreclosures on rural and urban dwellings. The Federal Surplus Relief Corporation distributed surplus agricultural commodities to families on relief. It had the dual purpose of feeding the destitute and holding down farm surpluses, thus increasing agricultural prices. It began in 1933, and as late as 1938, it gave 2,644,976 pounds of food valued at $1,568,000 to 35,849 Texas families and charities.

In addition to temporary relief measures, the national government enacted the Social Security Act in 1935. This measure provided for assistance to the elderly through pensions funded by state and federal taxes or through funds collected by employee and employer contributions. Social security remained a long-lasting contribution of the New Deal to American society, as did those measures that built public buildings, improved roads and the environment, and reforested Texas's depleted timberlands. After 1939, the New Deal relief measures waned, although some Texans remained on relief until 1942; World War II eliminated the need for relief for most of the state's able-bodied citizens. By then, the function of relief had been transferred from the Texas Rehabilitation and Relief Commission to the state welfare department.

New Deal Farm Programs

Most New Dealers thought that the ultimate success or failure of the New Deal would rest with its farm programs. Southern farmers voted for Roosevelt enthusiastically, and he won the support of 89.2 percent of all Texas voters in 1932. His election promised a bold farm program to combat the economic crisis in agriculture. Secretary of Agriculture Henry A. Wallace and his department argued that the lack of purchasing power of farmers thwarted industrial growth, and that the prosperity of the nation consequently rested on restoring disposable farm-family income. Their solutions to farm depressions aimed at reducing production and cutting crop surpluses through government control. To accomplish these goals, Congress passed the 1933 Agricultural Adjustment Act (AAA). The AAA gave direct subsidies to farmers who took land out of production, levied excise taxes on processors (of agricultural goods) to pay for the cost of the program, and authorized marketing agreements among producers' cooperatives, distributors, and processors in order to stabilize prices. The planned agricultural scarcity was coupled with an inflationary monetary policy that included abandoning the gold standard.

The AAA restrictions applied to cotton, wheat, corn, rice, tobacco, dairy products, and hogs; cattle products were soon added to the list. By the time the AAA took effect, many of the year's crops had already been planted, so the agency undertook a "plow-up" campaign, paying farmers $7 to $20 for each planted acre they agreed to plow under. Texas farmers in 1934 and 1935 took between 5.5 and 6 million acres of cotton, wheat, and corn out of production. Some farmers refused the crop-restriction payments and planted anyway, exploiting the increasing price of cotton. Consequently, Congress passed the Bankhead Cotton Control Act in 1934, which specified that all farmers had to accept cotton controls when two-thirds of a county's voters authorized them. Each farmer was assigned a quota allotment based on prior production. If a farmer produced more than that allotment, a prohibitive tax was charged on the excess. Almost all Texas counties complied (237 out of 254) with the control measure. By 1936, Texans had signed twice as many more crop-reduction contracts, more than had the farmers of any other state, when the U.S. Supreme Court declared the AAA unconstitutional. The next year, cotton acreage increased by 20 percent. After new attempts to control cotton acreage failed, Congress passed a new AAA act in 1938, and by the end of that year, Texas cotton farmers had diverted 4 million acres out of production, or three times that of any other state. By 1940, the federal government's agricultural programs paid nearly $3 billion directly to Texas farmers.

In addition, Texas counties received drought relief in 1934 and 1935. Part of this aid came in the purchase of livestock by the AAA. Texans sold over 4 million head of cattle, sheep, and goats to the agency. The federal government spent $27 million to buy these surplus animals, making Texas stockmen by far the largest recipients of this type of aid. Approximately 1,750,000 of the animals were destroyed, with the remainder going to the Federal Surplus Relief Corporation for distribution to the needy. Grain farmers also received drought relief funds. Besides planned shortages, the New Dealers established agencies that loaned money to farmers. The Farm Credit Administration and later the Commodity Credit Corporation pumped $430 million into the rural economy to prevent foreclosures and to make commodity loans available.

Finally, the Rural Electrification Administration (REA) provided low-interest loans and WPA labor to electric cooperatives to lay power lines to rural dwellings. Through these efforts, 17,712 miles of power lines reached 54,000 new customers in Texas at a cost of $16 million. The work of the REA moved Texas farmers into the era of modern amenities and communications and helped break down the isolation of rural dwellers.

The array of New Deal programs sent $716,694,849 into the state economy from March 4, 1933, to January 1, 1938. Only New York, Pennsylvania, and Illinois received more federal monies. The state deficit dropped from $24,102,200 in 1935 to $4,102,000 in 1938. The planned scarcity policy of the AAA increased crop prices until they reached 75 percent of parity in 1939, placing Texas second only to California in value of agricultural products. Undoubtedly, federal assumption of state relief obligations counteracted the potential bankruptcy of Texas and alleviated some of the suffering in the depression.

Minorities and the New Deal

Many of the dispossessed fell between the cracks of the New Deal's poverty floor. Critics charged that the surplus commodities program was more concerned with creating a scarcity of agricultural goods than with feeding the poor. Consequently, few efforts were made to improve the diet and health of the impoverished. For example, a study of aid from the Texas Relief Commission specified that families on relief did not receive enough assistance to maintain an adequate and balanced diet. In particular, the diets of many African American and Mexican American families caused malnutrition. And the same drive for planned scarcity that drove up agricultural prices drove tenants off the farm or into day-laborer jobs. The farm programs encouraged owners to take marginal lands out of production, reduce credit, and turn to mechanization. From 1930 to 1940, the number of African American tenants in Texas decreased from 65,000 to 32,000, while the number of black farm laborers rose by 25,000; some 20,000 other blacks left the state for better job opportunities.

Other critics leveled charges of discrimination at the New Deal. Blacks had a higher percentage of their population on relief and employment rolls than did whites. In Houston, blacks averaged only $12.67 per month in relief payments, compared to $16.86 for whites. The national policy of paying wages for work relief that matched regional compensation scales in private enterprise discriminated against black workers. Local relief agencies also placed blacks only in unskilled jobs. The southern states employed only 11 blacks in 1940 among 10,344 WPA supervisors. Rural blacks faced considerable discrimination in receiving relief aid in East Texas, even though 90 percent of black farm laborers there could find no work in 1935. The Federal Housing Authority (FHA) encouraged segregated housing additions by granting mortgages to blacks only in areas away from white suburbs.

A quiet moment out of the hard life in the barrio. *Russell Lee Photograph Collection, The Center for American History, The University of Texas at Austin, VN14920-33*

But the New Deal did cause a growing political awareness among black people. Although the NAACP had declined in membership in the early 1930s, Antonio Maceo Smith, a black Texan who left the state for an education at Fisk and then New York University, moved to Dallas in 1933 to organize an insurance company. Smith quickly became active in the local chapter of the NAACP and the Progressive League. He then contacted other black leaders in urban areas, who convened a statewide convention in 1937. By this time, the Houston NAACP chapter, with financial support from such wealthy African American businessmen as Hobart T. Taylor, Sr., and Carter W. Wesley, was rejuvenated. Led by the Dallas and Houston chapters, the NAACP decided to challenge Texas's all-white primary law. Lonnie Smith, a black dentist in Houston, agreed to be the plaintiff. The Supreme Court ruled in its 1944 *Smith* v. *Allwright* decision that the white primary was unconstitutional. The newly enabled African American voters identified closely with the national Democratic party that had passed the New Deal relief measures that aided the poor.

The depression years hardened life for Texas Mexicans. Population growth slowed from the pace of the previous two decades. The 1940 census put the figure for U.S. residents of Mexican descent at 484,000. Although this figure is an undercount—much lower than the adjusted totals of 1930—it still represented a decline in immigration. Several factors stifled demographic expansion. In the first place, the economic downturn hardly engendered a climate conducive to immigration. New Deal programs were not as helpful to Mexican Americans as they were to other Americans. Federal relief in the form of employment did not extend to non-citizens, and many Mexican Americans who could not prove their U.S. birth often lost out in openings available in federal projects.

The 1930s, moreover, were years of massive deportation and repatriation for Mexicans in Texas. Extensive repatriation during the depression years, mainly from the rural regions of the state, produced the relocation of an estimated 250,000 Texas Mexicans to Mexico. Many of these persons quickly returned to Texas, and new immigration persisted, although in lower numbers. The Mexican government and many Mexican Americans often helped in repatriation, thinking that those born in Mexico were better off in their native land than they would be in Texas.

Despite the onus of the Great Depression, Texas Mexicans coped, even joining labor unions at a time of intense employer pressure on unskilled employees. In El Paso, Tejanas in 1933 organized the Society of Female Manufacturing Workers to protest subsistence salaries. Tejano pecan shellers led by Emma Tenayuca walked out of west San Antonio plants in a 1938 strike that demanded better wages, improved working conditions, and a ban on child labor. The strike netted some concessions, but the pecan factories soon turned to new machine technology that voided the workers' hard-earned gains. Also in San Antonio, Mexican American women members of the International Ladies Garment Workers' Union (ILGWU) participated in several strikes. In the rural areas, Texas Mexicans working the beet, cotton, onion, and spinach crops took part

Emma Tenayuca, organizer for the Workers Alliance of America, with those protesting alleged beatings by the Border Patrol. *The UT Institute of Texan Cultures, No. 1540-A*

in the 1937 organizing drives of the United Cannery, Agricultural, Packing, and Allied Workers of America (UCAPAWA). In West Texas, 750 Mexican Americans in 1934 joined the Sheep Shearers' Union of North America and asked for increased wages and better working conditions. Threats, arrests, vigilante harassment, and strikebreakers undermined the movement.

Less dramatic but equally bold was the activism of the members of the Tejano community who descended from a group of bicultural, assimilated middle-class men and women whose formative years of Americanization were World War I and the 1920s. This element within the Texas Mexican community had been born or reared in the United States. They thought and perceived of themselves differently than did the "Immigrant Generation," who had arrived in Texas during the turmoil of the Mexican Revolution and still looked to Mexico for cultural and patriotic inspiration in the 1920s. It was this new, "Mexican American Generation" who in 1929 founded LULAC.

Through LULAC, the Mexican American Generation hoped to eliminate racial prejudice, win legal equality, improve educational facilities, and gain a voice in local, state, and national politics. They waged their struggle through strictly legal avenues; LULACers opposed strikes, demonstrations, mass picketing, boycotts, and anything else that might give an impression of disloyalty. They sponsored poll-tax drives, investigated cases of police brutality, undertook efforts to desegregate public places, and dispatched delegations to complain about the second-class status of the Mexican schools. In 1930, LULAC helped fund the first challenge to the segregation of Mexican American schoolchildren in *Del Rio Independent School District* v. *Salvatierra*. In this case, a Texas appellate court held that school authorities could not segregate students merely or solely because they were Mexican American. The school districts of the city successfully argued later that Mexican children's language deficiencies warranted their separate schooling.

Under the New Deal, women encountered discriminatory barriers in employment. Texas officials disapproved of work projects that hired women in nontraditional roles, and WPA officials in the state objected to the employment of married women. The WPA, CWA, and FERA training projects for women were confined to sewing, food processing, domestic service, and health care. And even within those categories, discrimination existed. WPA officials in San Antonio almost always directed black women into vocational schools for domestic service; if they took part in sewing projects, they did so segregated from their white counterparts. Supervisors for all projects tended to be middle-class whites. Moreover, any vocational or educational project assumed that women were only secondary or temporary workers who merited aid in depressed times but who needed no skills for advancement or long-term employment.

STATE POLITICS, 1935–1938

Most of the criticism of the New Deal came not from the left but from the right of the political spectrum. Few such complaints had appeared by the gubernatorial campaign of 1934. By this time, the depression firmly dominated politics, as previous issues of prohibition and Fergusonism disappeared. Seven men announced for the governor's seat. James V. Allred, a lawyer from Wichita Falls and the attorney general (1931–1935), soon claimed the favorite's role. As attorney general, the personable young Allred earned a reputation as an opponent of monopolies and political lobbies. His campaign for governor focused on creating a public utilities commission, restricting lobbies, authorizing a chain-store tax to limit out-of-state competition, and opposing a sales tax. His articulation of these issues and his image as a trust-buster garnered for him a plurality in the first Democratic primary. He won the runoff election by 40,000 votes over Tom F. Hunter, also from Wichita Falls and considered the more liberal of the two politicians. Allred easily triumphed in the general election.

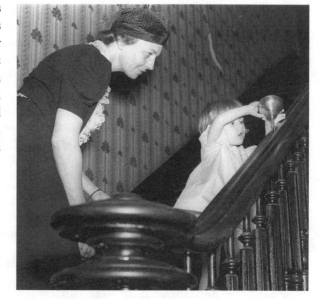

Free Nursery School at 122 Nolan Street, a WPA project. Sallie Schuchard, as a child, oiling a staircase railing as an attendant looks on. *The UT Institute of Texan Cultures, No. 2057-E, San Antonio Light Collection*

The first Allred administration (1935–1937) won attention for its identification with the New Deal. Allred cooperated with the federal programs for combating the depression by establishing the Texas Planning Board (to advise the legislature on the best way to utilize the state's economic resources and coordinate them with the New Deal's relief funds) and by issuing the rest of the "bread bonds." Possibly, his major accomplishment was the reorganization of the Texas Rangers and the Highway Department into the Department of Public Safety (DPS). The abuses of the Ferguson administration concerning Ranger appointments aided Allred's reorganization effort by ensuring some necessary reform of the selection process. The DPS remains the state's most important law enforcement agency.

In 1936, Allred and the state legislature clashed over the issues of taxes, aid to the elderly, and prohibition. In attempting to effect a measure of compromise, the governor called three special sessions of the legislature. Although the legislature did not agree to a significant increase in taxes, in the first of the three special sessions a state tax on chain stores was implemented. More controversial, however, were various issues concerning the repeal of prohibition. In a statewide referendum, the citizens approved of the state going wet, though the referendum did not affect those counties that had been dry prior to the passage of the national prohibition amendment, nor did it approve of the sale of hard liquor. The second special session defined the issues of prohibition, a battle that continued into the 1960s, by outlawing the sale of liquor by the drink, establishing a liquor control board, and approving local-option elections.

The same statewide referendum that addressed the issues of prohibition also contained a resolution for aid to the elderly. The second special session authorized such assistance, but it failed to create taxes or clear-cut guidelines for pension eligibility. The 1935 national Social Security Act mandated that states appropriate matching federal funds to assist the elderly as well as dependent children, the crippled, the blind, and public-health services. Meanwhile, national proposals, such as Louisiana Senator Huey P. Long's "Share Our Wealth" and California reformer Francis E. Townsend's scheme to pay $200 a month to all people over age sixty-five, widened demands in Texas and elsewhere that all elderly people should receive assistance regardless of level of need. Allred argued that aid to all elderly violated provisions of the Social Security Act and would therefore cost the state its federal funds. As the election of 1936 approached, Allred's opponents accused the governor of parsimony toward the elderly and, despite his prohibitionist views, of looking only to liquor taxes as a way to pay for pensions.

Allred won the primary election with 52 percent of the vote. His close identification with the New Deal, Roosevelt's support, and fame associated with having been named the National Chamber of Commerce's Young Man of the Year in 1935 aided his campaign. Between the July primary and the January inauguration, however, the issue of pensions intensified. By September, 81,000 elderly Texans had applied for assistance. The governor called for a third special session of the legislature to appropriate monies for the pension fund. The legislature levied increased taxes on oil, gas, sulfur, carbon black, and other items. Increased taxes on liquor paid much of the cost of the pensions, despite Allred's denial of that intent. Finally, the legislature heeded the governor's charge and tightened provisions for eligibility for aid. In the summer of 1937, 125,000 Texans received such aid, and the issue of Social Security remained a hot political topic.

Allred's second term (1937–1939) enjoyed no relief from financial struggles. A new teacher's retirement system, expanded welfare and social security obligations, and increased funding for public schools all demanded new appropriations, as did financial shortfalls caused by a growth in the prison population and the expensive Texas centennial celebration—in 1932 Texas voters had mandated a celebration of the hundred-year anniversary of independence. The expanded financial demands met with an unresponsive legislature in both the regular and one special session. The legislators did pass bills that addressed the state's problems but had no revenue to support their solutions. Allred used his veto powers liberally. A special session repealed the 1933 law that legalized betting on horse races but did not pass a tax bill. When Allred left office, the state was $3 million in debt.

Late in Allred's second term, President Roosevelt appointed him to a federal judgeship, which he accepted on completion of his stay in office. He resigned from the bench in 1942 to run for the U.S. Senate. After losing that election, he returned to the practice of law. Then in 1949, President Harry S Truman returned him to the federal court.

NATIONAL POLITICS, 1935–1938

By the time of Allred's second race for the governorship, conservatives had begun to rail against the New Deal. Businesspersons had early on expressed reservations over the NRA and the Bankhead Cotton Control Act. Some bankers objected to the coercive powers of the RFC. This unstructured opposition to federal control gained strength with the second phase of the New Deal, which began in March of 1935. That year, New Dealers passed the WPA, social security, the Wagner Act, REA, and measures regulating utilities and banking. Some conservatives claimed that welfare measures, including social security, were brazen tax increases and a violation of traditional American assumptions of self-help and individual responsibility. Indeed, a group of Texas state bankers raised $20,000 to challenge the social security legislation in the courts. Other conservatives decried the increasing power of the federal government. The Wagner Act (barring unfair labor practices) portended the growth of unions in an anti-union state. Despite leftist complaints of the inequities of the New Deal, African Americans received relief aid and switched their votes from the party of Lincoln to the party of Roosevelt. In turn, as blacks moved to urban areas and voted, northern liberals responded more favorably to their grievances. This vague illusion of civil rights permeated the New Deal and alienated racial conservatives. Their anxieties increased when it became clear that northern urban liberals exercised growing powers in the New Deal coalition. These men, such as Senator Robert Wagner of New York, elicited traditional Texas biases toward the Northeast and its big cities.

Roosevelt's popularity discouraged any traditional Texas politician from bolting the Democratic party in 1936. However, other conservatives called a meeting in Detroit, Michigan, to organize anti–New Deal Democrats into a political coalition in opposition to Roosevelt's policies. These Jeffersonian Democrats, as they named themselves, included such prominent Texans as John Kirby, the lumberman; Joseph W. Bailey, Jr., the son of the famous senator and himself a former congressional representative; and J. Evetts Haley, a West Texas rancher and writer. The organization decided that a third party stood little chance of success, so they planned a political strategy aimed at coordinating all groups opposed to the New Deal. The Jeffersonian Democrats seemed to find

ready cooperators in J. S. Cullinan's Constitutional Democrats of Texas and the American Liberty League, a national lobbying group composed of wealthy opponents of the New Deal. Eventually the Jeffersonian Democrats decided that each state organization would use any political tactic conceivable to deny votes to Roosevelt. In Texas, they decided to support selected Democratic candidates for local and statewide offices and to urge voters to support Alf Landon, the Republican candidate, or to "stay home" (not to vote) in the presidential election. Roosevelt won the election handily, however, carrying Texas by 734,485 votes to 103,711 for Landon. The Jeffersonian Democrats exercised little influence in the 1936 election, but they did hammer out a strategy for future conservative politics: support local Democrats, in order to maintain strength within the party, but campaign against the goals of the national party.

Roosevelt used his landslide victory in 1936 to broaden his political aims, which alienated some Texas Democratic leaders and further intensified their suspicions of the New Deal. His attempt, for example, to increase the number of Supreme Court judges and thereby end unfavorable judicial review of New

Above: G. H. Johnson and Gus Brown, officers from the Texas Liquor Control Board, stand beside a captured still. *The UT Institute of Texas Cultures, No. 1541-00, San Antonio Light Collection*

Deal legislation breached his relationship with both Garner and Tom Connally. It was Representative Hatton Sumners of Dallas who bottled up FDR's "court-packing" legislation in the House, stalling it long enough that the president moved the bill to the Senate, where Garner killed it. In the next year, 1937, an antilynching bill threatened traditional southern race relations. It passed the House, despite the best efforts of Sumners to kill it in the judiciary committee, but Connally led a filibuster that defeated it in the Senate. Meanwhile, the sit-down strikes in northern plants, the growing political power of the CIO, and a federal wages-and-hour law reinforced the perception of Texas and southern conservatives that the New Deal was too favorable to labor unions. A decision to combat the economic slump of 1937 with "pump priming" discouraged Garner and other Texans who wanted a balanced budget. Finally, the so-called 1938 purge of Democratic congresspersons who did not support the president failed, but it gave credence to conservative charges that the New Deal represented unwarranted extension of federal powers.

The political battles of the late 1930s stalemated other progressive social legislation. With Garner as its acknowledged leader, a southern Democratic and Republican coalition emerged, and this bloc successfully prevented an expansion of New Deal programs and cut some of those in existence. As World War II neared, foreign policy considerations diverted the president from fighting for domestic programs. Moreover, as prosperity returned to middle-class Texans, they returned to the values of an individualistic, success-oriented society: one that asked for limited government and lower taxes. The earlier consensus supporting direct relief for the poor ceased to exist. Indeed, in 1938 the changing political fortunes of Maverick and Dies might best symbolize changing Texas attitudes. That year, conservatives defeated Maverick, possibly the state's strongest congressional advocate of the New Deal, while Dies assumed the chairmanship of the House Un-American Activities Committee. Dies, an early supporter of Roosevelt and the New Deal, now used his committee to attempt to link FDR and his program to Communist subversion in government and labor unions.

STATE POLITICS, 1938–1944: THE END OF THE NEW DEAL

"Pappy" O'Daniel

The gubernatorial campaign of 1938 typified the confused state of Texas politics. Thirteen candidates announced for the post that Allred vacated. They included Attorney General William McCraw of Dallas, Ernest Thompson, chairman of the Railroad Commission, Tom Hunter, and W. Lee "Pappy" O'Daniel, a flour merchant from Fort Worth. O'Daniel, who was born in Ohio and raised in Kansas, came to Texas in 1925, working first as sales manager then as general manager for Burrus Mills and Elevator Company, which sponsored a radio show that featured O'Daniel and the Light Crust Doughboys, a hillbilly band that for a while included the considerable talents of Bob Wills. During his broadcasts, O'Daniel read some of his own poetry, sang some of his own songs, including "Beautiful Texas," told stories of Texas heroes, and gave listeners advice on family life, child rearing, and business success. The program attracted a sizable following on the three largest radio stations in the state. Its opening phrase, "Please, pass the biscuits, Pappy," may have greeted more listeners than any other in Texas broadcasting history. By 1938, O'Daniel was a very successful businessman who owned his own company, and he enjoyed the status of a Texas folk hero.

On Palm Sunday of 1938, O'Daniel pointed out to his radio audience that every two years he received letters from listeners asking him to run for governor, and he now invited his fans' comments on the idea. Favorable responses deluged the prospective candidate. On his "Hillbilly Flour" program that spring, he announced his candidacy and his platform: the Ten Commandments. He organized his campaign much like a combination of a religious revival meeting and a traveling radio show. "Pappy" toured the state, giving free concerts to everswelling crowds. He dispensed friendly, seemingly off-the-cuff advice on various economic topics, attacked "professional" politicians, told nostalgic stories, recounted homilies, and collected campaign contributions from the crowd by passing among them containers shaped like flour barrels. At first, other contenders ignored O'Daniel's candidacy, regarding it only as an attempt to sell flour. But as they recognized his political threat, they focused on forcing O'Daniel to outline his platform, which grew to list specific planks: abolition of the poll tax (which he had not paid, preventing him from voting) opposition to capital punishment, state assistance for all elderly persons, and a promise of no sales tax. He mixed those proposals with endorsements of mothers' love and the Golden Rule, quotes from the Bible, and the slogan, "Less johnson grass and politicians and more smokestacks and businessmen." O'Daniel won the Democratic primary with no runoff and went on to an easy victory in the general election.

In O'Daniel's first term as governor (1939–1941), his office waged open warfare with the legislature. But abolition of the poll tax and capital punishment seemingly were forgotten. And his campaign promise of aid to elderly persons transformed into a guaranteed stipend of at least $30 a month for the neediest senior citizens. Although a majority of the legislature supported the idea, it failed for lack of appropriations. O'Daniel now proposed that a transaction tax of 1.6 percent be levied to pay for the expanded pension plan. Opponents pointed out that his plan was a thinly disguised sales tax. Dubbing themselves the "Immortal 56"—a reference to the "Immortal 40," who secured the presidential nomination of Woodrow Wilson—a bloc of legislators defeated the transaction-tax bill. The Forty-sixth Legislature closed with no tax bill and a state deficit. The governor refused to call a special session.

O'Daniel ran again in 1940, making the transaction tax, now admittedly called a sales tax, his primary campaign issue. His campaign tactics resembled previous ones. This time, his six Democratic challengers concentrated on the differences between his promises and proposals and his accomplishments. "Ma"

Ferguson announced for the governor's post and aimed her campaign at separating the governor from his rural constituency. And all the major newspapers in the state opposed "Pappy" as an ineffective embarrassment to the state. Nevertheless, O'Daniel won the nomination in the first primary; Thompson, who received most of the editorial endorsements, came in second; Mrs. Ferguson placed fourth and retired from politics. As in 1938, the Republican candidate mounted only token opposition in the general election.

By 1941, the state simply had to address its financial problems. The federal government threatened to withhold payments for the pension plan unless state funds were forthcoming. The deficit in the general fund precluded either state matching funds for teachers' retirement contributions or for needed welfare payments. O'Daniel fought first for the sales tax but eventually compromised on the Morris Omnibus Tax Bill, which increased taxes on oil and gas and levied selective ones on gasoline, tobacco, and the gross receipts of some businesses. It did not address the long-term problem of the source of state revenue. The rather unproductive Forty-seventh Legislature closed on an antiunion note.

Possibly, the governor's only deeply held political conviction was hostility to labor unions. But his views toward organized labor had played no part in his two campaigns. By 1940, however, a strongly antilabor campaign on the state level would dovetail nicely with southern conservative's attacks in Congress on unions. Indeed, Representative Sumners warned of organized labor's threat to the defense industry at about the same time that O'Daniel called a joint session of the legislature to protect war plants by passing a state antiviolence labor law, which led to legislation that outlawed the use of violence or threats of violence to prevent anyone from working. The intent of the law was to keep picketers during labor strikes from denying the entry of strikebreakers into shut-down plants. It seemed unlikely that union membership, which made up less than 15 percent of the nonagricultural workers in Texas, posed any threat to the domestic order of the state. Nevertheless, the act gave O'Daniel a new political issue, with "labor racketeers" replacing "professional politicians" as his chief foes.

Above: "Pappy" O'Daniel campaigning for Governor, 1938. *Jimmie A. Dodd Photograph Collection, The Center for American History, University of Texas at Austin, CN 08129*

O'Daniel's current political stance offered him a new political opportunity when Morris Sheppard, the long-time U.S. senator and New Deal supporter, died in April of 1941. The legislature resolved that the governor should appoint himself to the vacated senate seat, obviously preferring that he be in the national rather than the state capitol. Instead, he appointed Andrew Jackson Houston, the eighty-seven-year-old son of Sam Houston, as senator. The selection was politically astute; clearly the aged and infirm Houston would offer him no challenge in the upcoming special election for the post; indeed, Houston went to Washington, D.C., attended one committee meeting, and died. When the special election drew near, twenty-nine candidates announced for the senatorial vacancy, among them O'Daniel, Martin Dies, the governor, and the young congressman Lyndon B. Johnson.

Johnson began his political career in 1931 as a congressional aide to Congressman Richard Mifflin Kleberg. In 1935, Johnson was, as mentioned, appointed Texas's state administrator of the NYA. In 1937, Johnson won a special election in the Tenth Congressional District to fill the unexpired term of Congressman James Buchanan, who had died while in office.

Now ready to pursue the national office, O'Daniel organized one of his typical campaigns, but in this one he concentrated on the dangers of "labor racketeers" and promised to introduce antistrike legislation once in Congress. He assured his audiences that his bills would mandate a senate roll-call vote on the measure to be broadcast on the radio. That way, he promised, politicians would not dare turn down antiunion measures.

But O'Daniel's old magic seemed to have waned. Fewer crowds turned out for his rallies. Johnson mounted a strong campaign that identified him with the New Deal and Roosevelt. He traveled in rented planes, hired a large, competent staff, used modern techniques of advertising, accrued newspaper endorsements, and claimed the front-runner's spot. On election night, he led by a few thousand votes. Over the next three days, however, returns trickled in from rural East Texas, an area where the O'Daniel candidacy appealed to the poor and to those over age sixty. When "all" the ballots were counted, the governor had defeated the young congressman by a vote of 175,590 to 174,279. Johnson believed that illicit returns cost him the victory, and he decided to distance himself from the New Deal in future campaigns.

O'Daniel announced for reelection to the Senate in 1942. Former governors Allred and Moody stepped up to challenge him for the office. Again, O'Daniel ran as an antiestablishment candidate, telling his audiences, "Washington is the only lunatic asylum in the world run by its inmates." And he accused both Moody and Allred of having received aid from "Communist labor leader racketeers." The first primary vote eliminated Moody, and Allred gained the support of the urban press, New Dealers, younger voters, Johnson, and Connally. The president also offered him an endorsement, but Allred decided that such an accolade would have strengthened O'Daniel's attempt to depict him as a dupe of Washington politicians. Allred lost the runoff by fewer than 20,000 votes.

He blamed his failure on the high preponderance of elderly voters, since many of the nation's young men were abroad in the armed services, and on anti-Roosevelt voters, who were alienated by both the New Deal and wartime controls.

O'Daniel served one regular Senate term. His record as senator was worse than that as governor, where his estranged relations with the legislature saw a record twelve of fifty-seven vetoes overridden. His popularity with Texas voters baffled many of his opponents and much of the press corps. In a way, though, his campaigns, of which he won four in ten years, pointed to the political past as well as the future. His carefully cultivated antiestablishment, country bumpkin image disguised a shrewd businessman who sold himself as a friend of the poor, the elderly, and those who believed that no politician spoke for them. The camp-meeting campaigns called forth religious motifs and emotions, amplified by hillbilly music, that reinforced voters' perceptions of O'Daniel as a good, honest, and down-to-earth man who got on well with the boys at the forks of the creek. Less cynical politicians, such as Hogg or the Populists, used similar campaign tactics. Yet O'Daniel, a college graduate, also was the first gubernatorial candidate to hire a public relations firm and to understand the power of the electronic media, in his case, radio. He capitalized, too, on the vague conservative discontent with organized labor and the New Deal. But by 1948, when his full term in the Senate expired, O'Daniel, realizing that a more urban and cosmopolitan Texas voting public was not likely to return him to office, retired.

READINGS

Books and Dissertations

Allen, Ruth A., and Sam B. Barton, *Wage Earners Meet the Depression*, (Austin: Bureau of Research in the Social Sciences Study, 1935).

Biles, Roger, *The South and the New Deal* (Lexington: University of Kentucky Press, 1991).

Blackwelder, Julia Kirk, *Women of the Depression: Caste and Culture in San Antonio, 1929–1939* (College Station: Texas A&M University Press, 1984).

Briggs, Vernon M., *The Chicano Worker* (Austin: University of Texas Press, 1977).

Brophy, William J., "The Black Texan, 1900–1950" (Ph.D. diss., Vanderbilt University, 1974).

Brown, D. Clayton, "Sam Rayburn," in *Profiles in Power: Twentieth-Century Texans in Washington*, eds. Kenneth E. Hendrickson, Jr., and Michael L. Collins (Wheeling, IL: Harlan Davidson, Inc., 1993).

Buenger, Walter L., "Jesse Jones," in *Profiles in Power: Twentieth-Century Texans in Washington*, eds. Kenneth E. Hendrickson, Jr., and Michael L. Collins (Wheeling, IL: Harlan Davidson, Inc., 1993).

Caro, Robert A., *The Years of Lyndon Johnson, Vol. I, The Path to Power* (New York: Random House, 1982).

Clark, James, and Michael Halbouty, *The Last Boom*. (2nd ed.; New York: Shearer, 1984).

Cotner, Robert C. (ed.), *Texas Cities and the Great Depression* (Austin: Texas Memorial Museum, 1973).

Duke, Escal Franklin, "The Political Career of Morris Sheppard, 1875–1941" (Ph.D. diss., University of Texas, 1958).

Galbraith, Kenneth, *The Great Crash, 1929* (Boston: Houghton Mifflin, 1955).

García, Richard A.,"The Mexican-American Mind: A Product of the 1930s," in *History, Culture, and Society: Chicano Studies in the 1980s,* eds. Mario T. García et al. (Ypsilanti, MI: Bilingual Press, 1983).

Garwood, Ellen Clayton, *Will Clayton: A Short Biography* (Austin: University of Texas Press, 1958).

Glasrud, Bruce Alden, "Black Texans, 1900–1930" (Ph.D. diss., Texas Tech University, 1969).

Green, George N., *A Liberal View of Texas Politics Since the 1930s* (Boston: American Press, 1981).

Hauser, Philip M., *Workers on Relief in the United States in March 1935 Vol. 1, A Census of Unusual Occupations* (Washington, DC: Works Progress Administration, 1935).

Henderson, Richard B., *Maury Maverick, A Political Biography* (Austin: University of Texas Press, 1970).

Hoffsommer, Harold (ed.), *The Social and Economic Significance of Land Tenure in the Southwestern States* (Chapel Hill: University of North Carolina Press, 1950).

Key, V. O., *Southern Politics in State and Nation* (New York: Vintage Books, 1949).

Kilman Edwin J., and Theon Wright, *Hugh Roy Cullen: A Story of American Opportunity* (New York: Prentice Hall, 1954).

Landolt, Robert Garland, "The Mexican-American Workers of San Antonio," in *The Chicano Heritage,* ed. Carlos E. Cortes (New York: Arno, 1976).

May, Irvin, *Marvin Jones* (College Station: Texas A&M University Press, 1984).

McKay, R. Reynolds, "Texas Mexican Repatriation During the Great Depression" (Ph.D. diss., University of Oklahoma, 1982).

McKay, Seth S., *Texas Politics, 1906–1944* (Lubbock: Texas Tech University Press, 1952).

———, *W. Lee O'Daniel and Texas Politics* (Lubbock: Texas Tech University Press, 1944).

McKay, Seth S., and Odie B. Faulk, *Texas After Spindletop* (Austin: Steck-Vaughn, 1965).

Patenaude, Lionel V., *Texas, Politics and the New Deal* (New York: Garland Publishing Inc., 1983).

———, "John Nance Garner," in *Profiles in Power: Twentieth-Century Texans in Washington,* eds. Kenneth E. Hendrickson, Jr., and Michael L. Collins (Wheeling, IL: Harlan Davidson, Inc., 1993).

Rundell, Walter, Jr., *Early Texas Oil Photographic History, 1866–1936* (College Station: Texas A&M University Press, 1977).

Schmelzer, Janet, "Tom Connally," in *Profiles in Power: Twentieth-Century Texans in Washington,* eds. Kenneth E. Hendrickson, Jr., and Michael L. Collins (Wheeling, IL: Harlan Davidson, Inc., 1993).

Smallwood, James, *The Great Recovery: The New Deal in Texas* (Boston: American Press, 1983).

Timmons, Bascom, *Jesse Jones* (New York: Holt Rhinehart & Winston Inc., 1956).

Wisenhunt, Donald W., *The Depression in Texas: The Hoover Years* (New York: Garland Publishing Co., 1983).

———— (ed.), *The Depression in the Southwest* (Port Washington, NY: Kennikat Press, 1980).

Young, Nancy Beck, *Wright Patman: Populism, Liberalism, and the American Dream* (Dallas: Southern Methodist University Press, 2000).

Articles

Ashburn, Karl E., "The Texas Cotton Acreage Law of 1931–1932," *Southwestern Historical Quarterly* 61 (1957): 116–24.

Bilington, Monroe, "Lyndon B. Johnson and Blacks: The Early Years," *Journal of Negro History* 62 (1977): 26–42.

Bourgeois, Christi L., "Stepping Over the Lines: Lyndon Johnson, Black Texans, and the National Youth Administration, 1935–1937," *Southwestern Historical Quarterly* 91 (1987): 149–72.

Cisneros, Victor B. Nelson, "La Clase Trabajadora en Tejas, 1920–1940," *Aztlán: International Journal of Chicano Studies Research* 6 (Summer, 1975).

García, Richard A., "Class Consciousness and Ideology: The Mexican Community of San Antonio," *Aztlán* 9 (1979): 23–69.

Green, George N., "ILGWU in Texas, 1930–1970," *Journal of Mexican American History* 1 (1971): 144–69.

Hendrickson, Kenneth E., Jr., "The National Youth Administration in Texas," Paper presented at the Faculty Forum of Midwestern State University, Wichita Falls, 1983.

McKay, Bob, "The Texas Cotton Acreage Control Law of 1931 and Mexican Repatriation." *West Texas Historical Association Annual Yearbook* 59 (1983): 143–55.

Philips, Edward Hake, "The Sherman Courthouse Riot of 1930," *East Texas Historical Journal* (1987): 12–19.

Sargent, Frederic O., "Economic Adjustment of Negro Farmers in East Texas," *Southwestern Social Science Quarterly* 42 (1961): 32–39.

Sorelle, James M., "'An de po cullard man is in de wuss fix uv awl': Black Occupational Status in Houston Texas, 1920–1940," *Houston Review* 1 (1979): 15–26.

Sparks, Randy J., "'Heavenly Houston' or 'Hellish Houston'?, Black Unemployment and Relief Efforts, 1929–1936," *Southern Studies* (1986): 353–67.

Vargas, Zaragosa, "Tejano Radical: Emma Tenayuca and the San Antonio Labor Movement during the Great Depression," *Pacific Historical Review* LXVI (November 1997).

Volanto, Keith J., "Burying White Gold: The AAA Cotton Plow-Up Campaign in Texas," *Southwestern Historical Quarterly* 103 (January 2000): 327–55.

FROM PEARL HARBOR
THROUGH THE 1960S:
TEXAS AT MIDCENTURY

CHAPTER 12

On December 7, 1941, Texans began their Sunday much as they had any other. By that afternoon, their world had changed forever, for by then they had heard the news that the Japanese had bombed Pearl Harbor in Hawaii. Grim reports of the surprise attack continued into the evening: Japanese aircraft had sunk most of the U.S. Pacific Fleet and had destroyed over 150 American planes. Casualties were heavy: 2,300 servicemen killed and another 1,100 wounded. That night, President Roosevelt called a meeting in which he informed the cabinet and some congressmen of the full extent of the tragedy. The next day, Senator Tom Connally of Texas introduced a resolution declaring war on Japan. Three days later, Germany and Italy honored their treaty commitments to the Japanese and declared war on the United States.

The war was not unexpected. Japan invaded Manchuria in 1931 and gradually pressed into other parts of Asia. The totalitarian dictators Adolf Hitler of Germany and Benito Mussolini of Italy followed by taking similar aggressive actions in Europe and Africa. At first, the United States attempted to remain neutral in the developing world conflict. Then the German invasion of Poland in 1939 caused England and France to go to war against fascist aggression, and the United States began to aid its allies and to prepare for its own defense. Congress passed the Selective Service Act in 1940, sent the Allies needed supplies through the Lend-Lease program, and built defense plants with government subsidies. These war-induced measures turned the national economy and the Texan economy around.

Indeed, a wave of national prosperity continued throughout the next decade. Full employment in wartime suddenly gave many Americans disposable incomes, monies that often could not be spent until peace removed restrictions on the sale of many consumer goods. Even after the end of World War II, the developing Cold War encouraged the buildup of defense industries and the maintenance of a standing army. Government policies accounted partially for the high postwar prices of farm commodities and the demand for petrochemical products. Returning veterans received national and state aid for schooling, housing, and readjustment to civilian life. World War II, then, launched Texas into an in-

Above: Marine Volunteers. *The UT Institute of Texan Cultures, No. 2979, San Antonio Light Collection*

dustrial economy, and postwar changes kept it there. By midcentury, the lives of most Texans were permanently altered.

The census reported a state population growth from 6,414,842 in 1940 to 7,111,194 in 1950, and to 9,579,611 in 1960, and an increase in urban dwellers from 45 to 62.7 to 75 percent. The demographic composition also changed in other ways. By 1960, women outnumbered men in Texas for the first time. The African American population of the state grew in absolute numbers from 924,391 in 1940 to 1,187,125 in 1960, but it declined in proportion to whites from 14 to 12.5 percent. Hispanics, on the other hand, rose from 12 to 15 percent of the state's population, numbering 1,400,000 in 1960. The state's net in-migration in the 1950s accounted for about 6 percent of its growth and counteracted the out-migration of 100,000 black Texans to the western and northern states. Most in-migration came from surrounding states and Mexico. By 1960, 76 percent of the state's residents were native Texans. Of all the states, Texas ranked sixth in population throughout the postwar period.

TEXAS IN WORLD WAR II

Texans reacted quickly to the bombing of Pearl Harbor. Long lines of volunteers gathered at once in front of recruiting offices. The defense department announced in 1942 that Texas furnished proportionally a larger percentage of men and women for military service than did any other state; 750,000 Texans served in World War II, including 12,000 women. Most of these were in the U.S. Army, which at the time included the Air Force, but approximately 185,000 served in the Navy, Marine Corps, and Coast Guard. By the end of the war in August 1945, thirty-six Texans had won the Congressional Medal of Honor. Their number included the two most decorated American servicemen, army Lieutenant Audie Murphy of Farmersville, and navy Commander Samuel Dealey of Dallas, who died in action.

Certain units won reputations as "Texas outfits." The "Lost Battalion" of the Thirty-sixth Division served in Java, and in 1943 the remainder of that unit became the first American troops to land on the European mainland. Other noted Texas units were the 1st Cavalry and the 2nd and 90th Infantry Divisions in the European Theater, and the 112th Cavalry Division and the 103rd Infantry Regiment in the Pacific. Over 150 general officers and twelve admirals either resided or were born in the state. Dwight David Eisenhower, the Allied Supreme Commander in Europe, was born in Denison, and Pacific Fleet Admiral Chester A. Nimitz in Fredericksburg. Other Texans made famous during the war included James Earl Rudder, who led the famed 2nd Ranger Battalion during the 1944 Normandy invasion; Walter Krueger of San Antonio, the Commanding General of the Sixth Army; and Oveta Culp Hobby of Houston, who commanded the Women's Army Corps.

Among the 23,022 Texans who died for freedom overseas were members of minority groups who still faced discrimination in their home state. Nevertheless, Texas Mexicans responded to the crisis of World War II with a patriotic zeal equal to that of any other group. Five of them received the Congressional Medal of Honor. At the battlefront, Tejanos usually fought in integrated companies, although others saw duty in such all–Mexican American army units as Company E of the 141st Regiment of the 36th Division. At home, the call for cooperation with the war effort reached into the barrios and ranchos. Service in combat and in patriotic endeavors threw many Texas Mexicans into a common crisis with Anglos. Racial animosity between the groups softened temporarily as the war united so many in a common cause.

Meanwhile, World War II hardened black Texans' demands for equality. The selective service system registered a total of 257,798 black Texans, about one-third of whom served in segregated outfits usually commanded by white officers. Unfortunately, the wartime treatment of blacks in military service mirrored their condition in American society. The pleasant southern weather and the efforts of southern congressmen secured for the South many of the armed services' training camps. Black troops from all parts of the country who found themselves stationed at these camps were expected to conform to the segregation practices of the local white communities. Training camps in Texas consequently had "little Harlems," which provided separate and inferior facilities for African American soldiers. At Camp Wolters near Mineral Wells, blacks had to erect their own service club because they were denied entrance to white facilities. Base theaters frequently had separate movie showings or separate seating sections for black troops. A backlash against this racial injustice erupted in 1943 in a fight between black and white soldiers at Fort Bliss near El Paso. Meanwhile, black air force cadets trained at Hondo field with integrated dining and recreational facilities but with separate classrooms and barracks. The navy solved the problem of integration by assigning African American sailors to mess duty. Doris Miller of Waco received a Navy Cross for leaving his segregated duties as messman and manning a machine gun at Pearl Harbor, yet he was still a messman when he was killed in action two years later.

Nevertheless, the economic activities generated by the war effort aided all Texans. An estimated 1,250,000 troops trained at fifteen Texas-based army posts. Clear skies and abundant land encouraged the building of forty air bases in Texas, with major ones near Austin, Corpus Christi, Grand Prairie, Houston, Lubbock, Midland, San Angelo, San Marcos, and Wichita Falls. The national headquarters of the Air Force Training Command was located at Fort Worth's Carswell Field. San Antonio continued as the major military center of the state; Randolph Field had been the most important school in the nation for pilots, and nearby Kelly and Brooks Fields added to their capabilities after the war began. San Antonio also served as the headquarters of the Third and Fourth Armies. After the Allied African campaign, the U.S. government located prisoner-of-war camps in Texas. As of June 1944, over thirty base and branch camps held 79,982 German, Italian, and Japanese POWs.

The federal payrolls and the local business generated by servicing military posts spurred economic recovery. In addition, private enterprise expanded. Aircraft factories soon constituted a new industry in the Dallas–Fort Worth area. Shipyards hired large numbers of employees in the Orange–Beaumont–Port Arthur region, as well as at Galveston, Houston, and Corpus Christi. The necessity for new and better refineries to produce fuel for the American and Allied war machine and the development of synthetic rubber turned the Gulf Coast strip near Houston into the largest petrochemical industry in world. Munitions plants were built throughout the state. And steel mills began operation in Daingerfield and Houston. The world's largest tin smelter plant was located at Texas City. Prosperity returned to the oil fields as the wells pumped to full capacity, and the need for paper and lumber products revitalized the East Texas wood-pulp industry. The census recorded the value added by manufacturing for the state as $453,105,423 in 1939 and $1,900,000,000 in 1944. The Great Depression had ended.

The wartime industrial expansion placed a premium on labor. The number of wage earners in the state tripled during the 1940s. As Texans entered military service and defense industries boomed, labor shortages enticed 500,000 Texans from rural areas into cities. The expanding economy opened new work opportunities in particular for minorities and women. Despite wage and price controls, the upsurge in women and minority employment contributed to a higher standard of living for Texas families. Females worked in positions traditionally reserved for males. The song "Rosie the Riveter" hit the airwaves in praise of American women's new roles as pipe fitters, lathe operators, and assembly-line workers. The number of black industrial workers in Texas doubled. However, most of these new hires took unskilled jobs, which left them particularly vulnerable to the effects of postwar demobilization. On the job, blacks faced discrimination in some war plants that segregated their assembly lines, and in

Nurses at the Brooke General Hospital, Fort Sam Houston. *The UT Institute of Texan Cultures, No. 3081-N, San Antonio Light Collection*

others, such as the Baytown oil refineries, that paid higher wages to whites in the same work categories.

Black leaders protested against discrimination in war-related activities, and during the war, the new Fair Employment Practices Commission (FEPC) began to investigate some fifty cities to determine the extent of the unfairness. Federal inquiries exacerbated white anxieties about black migrations to urban areas. In the Beaumont–Port Arthur area, for example, black persons made up one-third of the population in 1940, and in-migration added 20 percent to their numbers over the next three years. The influx put pressure on social services and housing, which, coupled with rumors of FEPC actions concerning equal employment opportunities, intensified racial tension. An unfounded report of the rape of a white woman by a black man in 1943 sent a white mob in Beaumont into the black section of town; local police, the Rangers, and the National Guard restored order only after twenty hours of violence that left three people dead and fifty more injured.

Most Texans, however, cooperated enthusiastically with the war effort. They held scrap drives, bought war bonds and savings stamps, planted "victory gardens," and established civil defense units. The civilian population generally endorsed the National Office of Price Administration's regulation that fixed rents and price ceilings. Although there were rumors of the hoarding of scarce commodities and a black market, Texans, like other Americans, accepted with some grumbling the rationing of sugar, shoes, coffee, meat, canned goods, and, later, gasoline. The popularity of the war and a high level of support of the boys overseas stifled any local dissent such as had appeared during World War I. The side effect of the persecution of ethnic Americans that occurred in Texas during World War I did not reoccur during World War II. Incidents of harassment in the German Hill Country or in Italian American communities were almost negligible. Wartime patriotism emphasized the struggle of all Americans against dictatorships and partially undermined the cultural distinctiveness of European ethnic groups.

The need to supply food to a world at war returned Texas farms to maximum production. The expanded market and the shortage of farm laborers hastened the conversion of many farms to machinery and the growth in farm size. The technology necessary to carry out this economic change in farming had been available since the late 1920s, but it was the impact of the AAA and World War II that made farm owners (facing a shortage of labor) mechanize. The 1945 farm census showed a decrease in the number of farms, an increase in the size and value of them, and a 33 percent increase in the value of machinery per farm. Farm tenancy also declined, from about 244,000 tenants and sharecroppers in 1940, to 169,000 in 1946. Although cotton still led all other Texas crops, it was no longer king. Farmers devoted less acreage to cotton in 1946 than they had in any year since 1895. By war's end, Texas ranked fourth overall in the value of farm commodities, and it led the nation in the production of cattle, goats, sheep, horses, cotton, grain sorghum, tomatoes, onions, spinach, and roses. The

Judy Garland (left) smiles as she waits for parade to start in line-up on Fifth Street, San Antonio. *The UT Institute of Texan Cultures, No. 3082-K, San Antonio Light Collection*

planting of vegetables and specialty crops testified to the new diversification of the state's agriculture. And the trend toward a modern agricultural economy caused a shift in the geographic areas of crop concentrations. New methods of irrigation moved the cotton industry from East and North Texas to the High Plains and South Texas, while East Texas farmers raised more cattle in 1945 than did the West Texas ranchers.

Politics during World War II

Except for the 1942 Senate battle, intrastate politics quieted during World War II. Coke Stevenson, the first person to serve two successive terms as speaker of the state house, won the lieutenant governor's office in 1938 and then succeeded O'Daniel as governor. The highly popular wartime governor never faced a serious gubernatorial challenger, was reelected in 1942 and again in 1944, and served longer in that office than anyone before him. The quiet, pipe-smoking Stevenson exuded an air of poised confidence that matched his personality and political philosophy. He believed in conservative financial policies, which included no tax increases, and limiting the powers of the federal government. He did not see himself as the leader of the state Democratic party, but as a caretaker of the financial stability of the state. His opposition to central planning led him to oppose rationing and the wartime thirty-mile-per-hour speed limit. His distrust of New Deal legislation and his financial policies helped to prevent an expansion of state services.

Stevenson's accomplishments included the funding and improving of the state highway system, raising teachers' salaries, a building program for the University of Texas, and improving public awareness of the need for soil conservation. Exhibiting sympathy for the labor movement, Stevenson, who was not a political extremist, negotiated a no-strike agreement with the labor unions. In 1943, the legislature passed the Manford Act, which stipulated that labor organizers must register with the state and carry identification cards. It forbade unions to make political contributions and required them to post financial and organizational records. The governor let the bill become law without his signature. He showed some concern about discrimination against Mexican Americans in public places, but no similar sympathy for African Americans. He cooperated with the U.S. State Department's Office of Inter-American Affairs in creating a Good Neighbor Commission for Texas that worked to improve relations between Anglos, citizens of Mexico, and Mexican Americans. He took office with a $34 million state debt and left with a $35 million surplus, largely due to wartime prosperity.

The harmony of state politics did not extend to national struggles. Conservative opposition to Roosevelt appeared again in 1940 with the "No-Third-Term Democrats." This political organization hoped to enlist more-traditional Texas Democrats, those who had supported John Nance Garner for the presidential nomination but saw his candidacy collapse with Roosevelt's announcement for an unprecedented third term. Texans and many southern conservatives, moreover, disliked Henry Wallace, who was selected as the vice-presidential nominee after Garner broke with the administration and retired to Uvalde. Some thought the former secretary of agriculture too liberal; others felt his sympathies lay with corn farmers and that his midwestern background had not prepared him to address the problems of southern cotton producers. The No-Third-Term Democrats included many of the old Jeffersonian Democrats and, like them, wanted voters to stay at home or choose Wendell Wilkie, the Republican nominee. As in the past, their strategy aimed at no third party. Nevertheless, Roosevelt won handily, carrying Texas by 905,156 votes to 211,707 for Wilkie. The president garnered about 100,000 fewer votes than did Connally, who won reelection to the Senate.

Texas conservatives opposed to the New Deal wasted no time formulating plans for political actions in 1944. And the conduct of the war enlisted new members to their cause. The wartime controls broadened federal powers and increased conservatives' uneasiness over the expanding central government. *Smith* v. *Allwright* (1944), which, as mentioned, outlawed the all-white primary, and Roosevelt's executive order that forbade discrimination in defense industries and established the committee on fair employment practices threatened the state's segregation patterns. At first, the anti–New Dealers worked to control the state Democratic conventions, send uninstructed delegates to the national convention, and nominate independent presidential electors. When that strategy failed, they bolted the party and organized a third one, the Texas Regulars. Its planks included a return to states' rights "which have been destroyed by the

Communist-controlled New Deal" and a "restoration of the supremacy of the white race. . . ."

Senator O'Daniel spearheaded the Texas Regulars' race. They nominated no candidates, offering instead a list of uncommitted electors to voters. The Republican party and its nominee, Thomas A. Dewey, avoided any unification with the Regulars. Republicans wanted to maintain their separate identity and capitalize in the future on the growing rift in the Democratic party. Traditional conservative Democrats stayed aloof from the Regulars and successfully replaced Wallace with Harry Truman as the party's vice-presidential nominee. Roosevelt won a fourth term, winning 821,605 votes in Texas to Dewey's 191,425 and the Regulars' 135,439. After the election's outcome the Regulars returned to the Democratic party, but their bolt signaled future infighting and state political struggles after the war.

TEXAS INDUSTRIALIZATION

Many Texans never returned to the farm after 1940. Although the state ranked a distant twelfth nationally in manufacturing in 1950, the decade of the forties nevertheless marked the state's transition to an industrial economy. Petroleum fueled the change. By the end of World War II, new technology and advancements in refining, metallurgy, and engineering enabled Texas to replace California as the leading oil producer in the country. Aided by the Railroad Commission's proration policies and favorable federal depletion allowances, the production of crude oil expanded from 755 million barrels in 1945 to 1.5 billion barrels a decade later, though by then the output of the Middle Eastern oil fields threatened to destroy the Commission's ability to control the price of oil. Fortunately for Texas, national legislation established oil import quotas in 1959 and continued the Commission's power to control production, as Texas oil usually accounted for about 40 percent of the nation's total production and 50 percent of its proven reserves. The value of Texas crude and natural gas throughout the 1950s amounted to between $2.5 and $3.2 billion per year. Most of the growth in the oil business came from increased production in older fields, but a major strike brought in new ones in Scurry and Ector Counties in the 1950s, as did the drilling of offshore wells. West Texas became an even more important center of the oil business, as witnessed by the huge population growth of Midland and Odessa.

The Texas Gulf Coast benefited enormously as petroleum became the state's leading export and accounted for 80 percent of the products that went through Texas ports in the 1940s. Texas had no natural deep-water ports, but thirteen have been built over the years, six of which are located from fifteen to fifty miles inland. The Port of Houston, which ranked second nationally in total tonnage handled in 1950, led all others. By the 1960s, petroleum exports continued to dominate port trade, followed by agricultural products and petrochemicals.

Economists generally estimated that for every ten jobs in the oil industry, another thirty-seven appeared in other economic sectors. Manufacturing, for example, employed 119,132 more wage earners in 1962 than it had in 1948, and the total value added of manufacturing rose by $6.18 billion. The transition of Texas to an industrial state brought Texans different kinds of work. Government employment tripled from under 3 percent in 1940 to over 9 percent by 1960. The explanation for the increase lay in the continued operation of military bases, and the continued importance of the defense industry, which increased with the Korean War and throughout most of the Cold War years that followed. The state ranked third nationally in income derived from the federal government. The 1961 location of the manned-spacecraft center near Houston and the 1958 invention of the silicon microchip by Texas Instruments' Jack Kilby stimulated defense spending in the state. Food processing was the third-largest industry in the state, and wholesale and retail trade and financial services employed a quarter of the workforce. Automobile assembly plants and the boat (leisure craft) industry, which did not exist in Texas before 1945, were third in employment and fourth in the value added by manufacturing. The older industries of agriculture, which by this time had less than 8 percent of the workforce, and lumber and wood products, which dropped to eleventh place in value, showed the decline of the older Texas and the rise of the new one.

Oil and its related economic activities placed new pressures on Texas's financial institutions. Lone Star bankers had learned their business before 1945 by lending money to farmers and local merchants. The depression years had reinforced the inherently conservative lending practices of Texas banks, and state regulations that required unit banking had prevented the huge concentrations of capital necessary for funding burgeoning industries. After 1947, major banks, particularly in Dallas and Houston, hired specialists in oil lending to structure loans to drilling and other related enterprises. Texas's bank resources doubled from 1945 to 1960, as the number of wells drilled yearly in the state rose to a level not reached again until the world oil crisis of the 1970s. The linking of interior oil production with Houston cash made that city the center of the oil trade, and particularly vulnerable to fluctuations in petroleum prices, but all of the state's major banks relied on black gold. The deposits in the larger Texas banks never came close to matching the assets of the New York and Chicago institutions, however, and eastern capitalists loaned much of the money for the state's economic growth.

The postwar years also witnessed a continuation of the expansion of Texas's transportation facilities. Even during the depression, the state expanded and attempted to maintain its highway network. The industrial shortages during the war almost halted road construction and created a surplus in the highway funds. A constitutional amendment in 1946 mandated that revenue realized from a tax on gasoline and motor vehicle registration fees be used to construct new roads. In the 1950s, the state highway system expanded at a faster rate than in any other period, and between 1941 and 1963, total highway mileage tripled to over 60,000 miles of maintained roads. The number of motor vehicles registered by Texans went from under 2 million in 1945 to over 5 million in 1962, the new reliance on the private automobile hampering the development of the state's mass transit systems.

The beginning in 1956 of the federal interstate highway system determined the future of many small Texas towns, much as railroads had done in the nineteenth century. Those communities bypassed by interstate highways stagnated, and those served by them grew. The population of Irving, for example, increased from 2,621 in 1950 to 54,985 in 1960.

Now, motor vehicles limited railroad expansion, just as the railroads had replaced earlier forms of transportation. Texas still led the country in miles of track, but that figure declined steadily after 1932. Net profits per mile of track in operation fell, too, as passenger traffic almost ceased to exist and railroads relied on freight revenues to take up the slack.

Air passenger traffic, on the other hand, boomed. In 1945, the legislature created the Texas Aeronautics Commission to stimulate airport and aviation development. By 1951, 638 airports existed in Texas, and eleven airlines enplaned 1.5 million passengers; three times that many boarded planes in 1962, ranking Texas fourth among all the states. Dallas enplaned more than one-third of all passengers, and Braniff Airlines, headquartered there, led the other ten national and three international airlines in passenger service. After declaring bankruptcy in 1982, Braniff underwent a series of reorganizations before ceasing operations completely in 1992.

TEXAS WORKERS AND URBAN GROWTH

The industrialization of Texas continued to spur the migration of its citizens from rural to urban areas. The state grew at a rate of 20 percent in the 1950s, with an out-migration in the economic downturns of 1953–1954 and 1957–1958, and an increase in in-migration of 24 percent during the 1960s. Metropolitan counties received 50 percent of the over 1 million persons who changed residence from 1955 to 1960. Indeed, those areas accounted for over 90 percent of the state's total growth. In 1960, thirty-three Texas cities numbered over 30,000 inhabitants, with Houston (938,219), Dallas (679,684), and San Antonio (587,718) drawing the largest number of intra- and interstate in-migrants. Of the standard metropolitan statistical areas (SMSAs, a census classification of a county or group of contiguous counties that have a population of over 50,000), Houston ranked seventh nationally, Dallas, fourteenth, and San Antonio, seventeenth, and Texas led the nation with twenty-one SMSAs.

Urban growth in the 1950s effected a change in the state's demography. Rural populations became both older and more isolated. The state's median age of twenty-seven was considerably lower than the nation's twenty-nine in 1960, but the age of those in cities of under 2,500 and those on farms exceeded it. Median income totaled $5,693 for white urban families, $4,110 for rural nonfarm families, and $3,201 for rural farm families. Black families ranked significantly lower by earning $2,915, $1,684, and $1,430, respectively. Rural areas, then, still relied on local wholesale and retail trade or on such specialized industries as oil or recreation, and they were marked by an aging population and a declining income. Cheaper land, improved transportation, particularly the trucking industry, communications revolutions, and the nature of Texas industries allowed the growth of commerce in suburban areas. That, coupled with a decrease in transportation time caused by automobiles and highways, saw the migration of a good portion of the population to the suburbs. The collar communities of Dallas, for example, totaled 400,000 inhabitants in 1960. Although both the inner city and the suburbs grew in the 1950s, the suburban population was a year younger on average than that of the downtown core.

Most suburbanites were white, as blacks tended to settle in the central city, where segregated residential patterns and the unskilled jobs they took usually kept them. The mass movement of blacks to cities began in the 1930s and increased during and after the war years. By 1960, 75 percent of black Texans, like whites Texans, lived in urban areas. By this time, the concentration of blacks in East Texas had declined, with no county having a majority black population, while the cities of Dallas, Houston, Fort Worth, and Beaumont all registered more than a 20 percent black population. Meanwhile, school integration mandated by federal courts accelerated "white flight" from the cities in the 1950s and 1960s.

The rapid industrialization of the war years improved the per capita income of southern states, and Texas most of all. The next twenty years witnessed the rise of per capita income in Texas to about 90 percent of the national average, ranking the state twenty-sixth in the nation. Even though the cost of living more than doubled during the inflationary period after World War II and during the Korean War, Texans' real income increased. Of the fifty-seven national cities rated, the cost-of-living index ranked Dallas and Houston in a tie for fiftieth. Per capita income varied sharply throughout the state. Midland topped the national average by 18 percent in 1959, and Dallas, Houston, and Austin exceeded it as well. On the other hand, Brownsville and Laredo fell about 50 percent below the national per capita income. Those counties with high Hispanic populations continued in poverty.

Urbanization, however, proved a watershed in the transformation of the Texas Mexican community. Many Hispanics severed their contacts with rural roots during the post–World War II rise of mass industrialization and consumer culture. By the 1950s, therefore, definite trends of upward mobility, urbanization, acculturation, and social diversification became apparent. At this time, about 25 percent of employed Texas Mexican males worked in middle-class occupational categories, defined as professionals, managers and proprietors, clerks/salesmen, and skilled craftsmen. By 1960, this figure had increased to slightly over 30 percent. With these impressive gains, however, one should take into consideration that the prewar period was a trying one for Texas Mexicans, marked by inflexible Jim Crowism and depression-stimulated repatriation. The economic gains, therefore, represented an increase in opportunities, but they did not conceal for many Hispanics their second-class condition. The per capita income in 1960 was $980 a year for Tejanos, as compared to $1,925 for white Texans. Mexican Americans living in the cities fared only slightly better, with a median income of $1,134 per year.

The same disparity reveals itself in any analysis of the African American community. The median income for black Texans rose from 37 percent of that of white Texans in 1940 to almost 50 percent in 1960. The number of black people classified as professionals by the census also increased dramatically, but the percentage of black Texans in this category ranked significantly below that of white Texans. In 1960, black professionals still served a detached community. The combined forces of urbanization and segregation encouraged the rise of black-owned businesses; more than 75 percent of the black-owned establishments that existed in 1950 had not been in operation in 1940. These enterprises mostly fell into the "mom and pop" categories of grocery stores, general service establishments, restaurants, and amusement businesses that served black neighborhoods.

The lack of capital severely limited the growth of black enterprise in Texas. Few white bankers were willing to loan money to establishments serving a clientele with a low disposable income and who lived in deteriorating neighborhoods with high crime rates; therefore, loans to most black-owned businesses necessarily came from the nine black insurance companies or credit unions that developed in some of the larger cities. Although the Fraternal Bank and Trust of Fort Worth existed in 1950, black banking services were inadequate. Other problems existed for black businesses. They competed with white establishments for black customers. Moreover, ironically, the increasing trend toward manufacturing and industrialization that had brought so many black businesses into being would destroy a lot of them. Few small enterprises could compete successfully with outlets of giant supermarket chains and department stores.

Most of the black workforce continued in unskilled or semiskilled positions. Although Texas industrial workers, with an average income of $88.81 for a forty-one-hour week, earned about as much as their northern counterparts did in 1960, the industries that employed the unskilled continued wage discrepancies. Workers in sawmills and allied lumbering enterprises grossed about 75 percent of the national average for a forty-six-hour week, as compared to those in petroleum, who made twice what unskilled workers took home. Black males earned $1,500 less yearly than did white males ($3,760) in 1953, and white females averaged $1,700 less than white males but grossed $1,000 more than black females. Unskilled and semiskilled jobs offer tenuous employment. In 1960, black male unemployment (7.3 percent) exceeded that of white males (4 percent), white females (4.3 percent) and black females (6.7 percent).

The number of working women grew from 23 percent of the workforce in 1940 to 33 percent, or 1,051,404, in 1960. That year, urban women between the ages of eighteen and twenty-four were more likely to work outside the home than were their rural counterparts. More and better job opportunities continued to draw working women to city life, and older women, typically less burdened with child-care responsibilities, returned to the job market. The percentage of married women in the workforce also grew, with that group being particularly vulnerable to economic cycles. Certain professions remained feminized; one-third of employed women did clerical work, and women dominated the traditional feminine professions of elementary-school teachers, librarians, nurses, and social workers and made up less than 5 percent of lawyers, dentists, and engineers. Hispanic and black women still composed most of the private household laborers. Of the 165,000 black women employed in 1960, 159,000 of them worked in private households, domestic services, or as cooks, bartenders, and food servers.

LABOR UNIONS

Membership in labor organizations grew during the war years from 110,500 in 1939 to 374,800 in 1953. Ten years later, the number had risen by only another 20,000. As it had before, public sentiment in Texas worked against union growth. The opposition stemmed from the traditional hope that outside industries would move to the South to take advantage of cheap labor, from the suspicion that rural populations usually hold for union activity, and from conservatives who saw unions as potential agents for unwanted political and social reforms. The antiunion rhetoric of such politicians as "Pappy" O'Daniel and Martin Dies made union bashing popular in postwar Texas.

The conservatives' fear of unions only mounted with unions' support of Roosevelt and the New Deal and President Harry Truman's subsequent Fair Deal. The opposition to unions brought forth in 1947 a number of state antilabor laws, the most important of which was a right-to-work law that prohibited any requirement that employees join a union. Other acts forbade deducting union dues from wages without the employee's consent; mass picketing, defined as two or more picketers within fifty feet either of a plant entrance or another picketer, (this was struck down by the U.S. Circuit Court of Appeals in 1988); strikes by public employees; secondary boycotts, and the picketing of utilities. Another law made unions subject to antitrust legislation. Finally, that year the Republican-controlled Congress passed the Taft-Hartley Act, which outlawed closed shops and strengthened federal regulation of labor organizations. State restrictions in 1951 further limited labor agreements that might otherwise have required union membership as a condition for employment.

Seventeen other states passed right-to-work laws; most of them were in the South, among which only Texas could claim an industrial base. Union leaders maintained that state restrictions in particular and federal ones in general retarded the growth of labor organizations. The percentage of workers who belonged to unions in Texas never reached national levels, and the state maintained its reputation as hostile toward unions. Other factors contributed to the problems organized labor faced in the state. Service and "high tech" industries, of which Texas had many, expanded faster than did manufacturing, and therefore did not traditionally attract unions. Finally, immigrants from Mexico joined others in the competition for unskilled jobs, depressing wages and further discouraging unionization. The successes that unions did enjoy were greatest along the Gulf Coast, where organized labor's long heritage in the refineries made their members politically important.

TEXAS FARMS

The postwar period from 1945 to 1960 witnessed the transformation of the family farm, with only 10 percent of the population still farming by the end of it. The trend toward larger, mechanized farms had led to the development of professional managers, absentee owners, scientific farming, and a dramatic reduction in the use of farm laborers. The number of farms had dropped to 227,000 by 1960, but over the same period, the size of the average farm had risen from 367 to 630 acres, and the total value of land and buildings per farm had increased five-fold to nearly $50,000. Capital investments to begin farming on this scale were impossible for most family farmers, and the return on investment was higher in most businesses than in farming. The perfection of the mechanical cotton picker revolutionized the cotton farm. It encouraged farming on vast expanses of on flat terrain, spurring the continued movement of cotton and cereal crops to the Rio Grande Valley and the High Plains. Concurrent advances in irrigation techniques and the application of pesticides, herbicides, and fertilizers allowed mass spraying and watering of large contiguous areas. Families that stayed

Recruiters attempt to hire Texan Mexicans for migrant farm work in 1949. *Russell Lee Photograph Collection, The Center for American History, The University of Texas at Austin, VN: IIEF23*

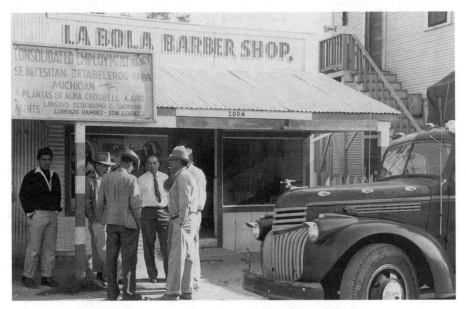

in farming usually converted their operations into corporate entities that stressed efficiency, growth, and entrepreneurialism.

Statistics from 1960 verified the rapid growth of large farms. Texans owned more tractors than farms, led the nation in the number of trucks, and had 40,723 combines. Mechanization completed the labor shift begun during the 1920s: the 1960 census listed no croppers, and it revealed that tenants operated only one-fifth of the farms. Irrigation grew in importance, particularly during 1950–1957, the worst drought in the state's history, and the irrigated acres in 1960 produced 50 percent of the state's cotton and 40 percent of its wheat. The drought prompted the legislature to appoint a committee to look into the problem of water resources in 1956, but legislators never acted on its recommendations; most people did not yet consider water a critical resource. Meanwhile, farmers generated over $2 billion in agricultural revenue in 1960, ranking the state number two, behind California. Texas usually vied with Iowa for second place throughout the period but led the country in 1960 in the production of cotton and cottonseed, grain sorghums, rice, cattle, and sheep.

Economists gave a new name after World War II to the development of commercial agriculture and the supplying, manufacturing, processing, and merchandising industries that serviced it—agribusiness. And agribusiness soon outstripped the gross revenues from the sale of farm and ranch crops. In 1960, farmers spent over $17 million on pesticides, usually DDT, and over $50 million on fertilizers. Feedlots and beef-packing houses dotted the Texas landscape. The agribusiness receipts for $6.2 billion in 1962 testified to the importance of agriculture to the state's economy, as did the ranking of food processing as the leading manufacturing employer.

Agribusiness attracted people to the major agricultural distribution centers of the High Plains and South Texas. The population of cities such as Lubbock actually increased at about the same rate as did the larger metropolitan areas. This meant that Texas urbanization differed from that of the Northeastern United States, where big cities were politically dominant. The widely scattered urban areas of Texas tended to promote their own regional interests. Therefore, Texas cities quarreled over legislative priorities, and their lack of unity allowed representatives of rural areas to dominate the legislature, which ignored urban problems until the late 1960s.

The low pay for agricultural labor and increasing urban job opportunities also lured many minority farm laborers to the city. So, too, did the *Bracero* program, a contract labor agreement between the United States and Mexico between 1947 and 1964, and the rise of corporate, vertically integrated farms that preferred cheap migratory labor from Mexico to a local, permanent workforce. Wildcat strikes led by Mexican Americans in the Rio Grande Valley in the 1960s were, in part, a response to the depersonalization of the workplace.

Furthermore, the Texas Mexican community was subjected to disruptive drives designed to remove Mexican nationals from the state. In July 1954 the Border Patrol, in coordination with police authorities at the local and federal levels, implemented "Operation Wetback" and began roundups of foreign-born

Mexicanos. As in the case of the 1930s repatriation efforts, the operation removed many undocumented workers, and many other immigrants were illegally intimidated into leaving the state for Mexico. The sweeps proved divisive for Tejanos; many complained of the arbitrary nature of the arrests, as some of Texas's Hispanic citizens were illegally detained. Other major organizations, such as LULAC, countenanced the removal on the grounds that "wetback" laborers were exploited and lowered the wage standards for resident laborers.

As farms grew larger and more affluent, the disparity between farm and city living narrowed. By 1960, 98 percent of all Texas households had electricity. The back-breaking work of farm housewives lessened, as many affluent farmers could now afford washing machines and other household appliances. New technology improved the efficiency of and lowered the cost of air conditioners, and Texas summers became nearly bearable. Similarly, the development of improved refrigeration technology allowed for more varied diets through the use of home freezers and regional locker plants.

Farm isolation decreased with the spread of radio and television. By 1955, the state supported 211 AM and 32 FM radio stations. The first television station, WBAP, went into operation outside Fort Worth soon after the war, and by 1950, San Antonio, Dallas, and Houston received television programming. The first public educational television station in the nation began at the University of Houston (KUHT), a 1953 gift of the former facilities of KPRC-TV from the Hobby family. By 1960, antennae dotted the rural landscape and adorned many a suburban roof, with 81 percent of the state's households tuned in. Texas ranked seventh nationally in the number of telephones in 1960, by which time 55.6 percent of all farm houses had their own phones. The revolution in communications and transportation brought all Texans, at least all white Texans, into closer contact with each other and with the dominant value system of the nation.

THE TEXAS FAMILY

Improvement in healthcare facilities and medical science meant that Texans, like all Americans, lived longer. Those born in 1958 had a life expectancy of 73.7 years for white females, 67.2 for white males, and 65.6 and 60.6 for black women and men respectively. Part of the explanation for the newly increased life span lay in the near-eradication of childhood diseases that had plagued prewar Texans. From 1934 to 1954, the percentages of deaths per thousand caused by influenza, measles, and whooping cough, the triple killers of the state's children at midcentury, declined sharply. A corresponding decrease in the number of deaths per thousand for Texas children under one year of age, testified to the postive impact of changes in diet and health care. Despite the improving conditions, the national ranking of Texas for deaths before age one was forty-fifth for whites and thirty-third for blacks in 1950.

The escape from the depression and the impact of the return of veterans from war led to a rise in both marriages and births in the late 1940s and early 1950s, the so-called Baby Boom. American culture of the 1950s celebrated women's return to their traditional roles as wives and mothers and the concept of the stable family. These economic and social pressures helped explain the drop in the median age for marriage in Texas from 24.3 years for males and 21.5 for females in 1940 to 22.8 and 20.3 in 1950, where they remained for ten years. The percentage of married Texans over age the age of fourteen increased from 62 percent of both men and women in 1940 to 70.4 percent for men and 67 for women in 1960.

Nationally, the divorce rate increased each decade, belying the popular image of the stable American family. The percentage of divorced Texans exceeded that of the nation. In 1960, 17 percent of Texas women were divorced, widowed, or separated, and their inability to earn incomes comparable to those of men pushed many in this category below the poverty line. Black Texan women fared worse than did white ones; black women led Texas in 1960 in the percentage of divorces, separations, and widowings and fell below their white counterparts in the percentage (60.2 to 68.8) of married women. The percentage of married white males rose each decade from 1940 to 1960, while that of black males, although higher in 1960 than it had been in 1940, fell in the 1950s. The collapse of the African American family that began in the depression accelerated after the war, as limited job opportunities and discrimination exacted a high psychological toll on black males, particularly on the young who had recently migrated to inner cities. By the middle of the 1960s, 24 percent of all African American families in Texas had female heads of household.

The average family size in the state decreased from 3.74 in 1940 to 3.36 in 1960. Black Texans' families (3.60) were larger than white ones (3.33), but their average household size had remained the same since 1940. The sharpest decline in family size was in rural towns with populations between 1,000 and 2,500, and the largest increase was in the urban fringe areas. The lack of need for children as agricultural laborers probably accounted for the smaller families. The size of African American families in rural farm areas, for example, where blacks owned fewer and poorer farms, was larger than it was in the suburbs, while white population per household in the more-affluent suburbs led all other census classifications. The Baby Boom was ending by 1960, and new problems of a graying nation loomed for the near future.

TEXAS SCHOOLS

The arrival of an urban economy and population accented demands that the state provide better a system of public education. The argument concerning schools that had started with the advent of business progressivism had changed little by the mid-twentieth century: improved schools, reformers urged, would invite new industry into the state by making it more attractive to prospective migrants and by providing a better-educated workforce. These ideas clashed with older demands that taxes be held down at any cost and that teachers should receive minimum pay. Attempts to maintain a segregated system limited school reform, as did the assumption that local communities should retain control over their own school districts.

World War II and urbanization focused these issues for Texans coping with expanding cities and increasing school populations. In 1947, the legislature established a committee to propose revisions in the public education system. Three important laws, sponsored by Representative Claud Gilmer and Senator A. M. Aikin, came out of the recommendations of that committee, which had taken into consideration the facts that most Texas public schools had added a twelfth grade, broadened their curricula to include vocational training and the fine arts, and ranked in the lowest quarter nationally for funding of state school systems. Therefore, the three Gilmer-Aikin laws of 1949 reorganized the public schools. One law established a state board of education, its members elected from each congressional district, that appointed a commissioner to supervise the Texas Education Agency. The other two laws required nine-month school terms for all Texans of school age, set minimum training standards for teachers, mandated improved facilities, and established a formula for minimum teachers' salaries that included shared funding between the state and the local school districts.

These changes produced positive results almost immediately. Teachers went back to school to meet new state certification requirements. Teachers' salaries went up. Black teachers, who had received 79 percent of white teachers' incomes in 1947, now earned equal pay. Special equalization funds to aid poorer school districts were instituted. The expanded powers of the state over administration of local schools hastened the school consolidation movement, as did improved roads and transportation. The 6,409 school districts were reduced to 1,539 in 1960. Now, independent school districts outnumbered those of the common schools, and the one-room school had disappeared. In 1960, Texas ranked third in the nation in public school enrollment.

Nevertheless, critics of the Gilmer-Aikin acts quickly cited their inadequacy. The new legislation was financed by consumer taxes, and insufficient funding would continue to haunt the state's educational system. The minimum salary requirements for teachers were still too low. Moreover, under the new laws, those school districts that made the least effort to raise taxes received the greatest amount of aid from the state. Possibly, the best evaluation of the Gilmer-Aikin acts would be that they at least moved the state educational system into the early twentieth century.

Pressure for other changes in the public school system continued. The Russians' successful launching of *Sputnik I* (the first man-made satellite) in 1957 made Americans suddenly worry that the United States lagged behind the Soviet Union in science teaching and caused some to question the general effectiveness of their educational institutions. Texans, as did most of the nation's citizens, demanded that their schools return to basics and improve academic subjects. The fear that the Soviet Union might outstrip the United States in the struggle for world supremacy prodded the federal government into increasing federal aid for public colleges and secondary schools. The professed need for quality instruction in the state, did not, however, push Texas into the forefront of education. Critics cited the unwillingness of the legislature to appropriate enough money for substantial reform as the reason. Although Texas teachers' salaries rose from an average of $3,231 in 1955 to $5,421 ten years later, as late as 1960, the state ranked twenty-seventh in the level of pay for public school instructors. State per-pupil expense followed a similar pattern; although state appropriations had more than tripled, the state ranking of thirty-two in 1955 dropped to thirty-nine in 1965.

After World War II, higher education in Texas blossomed and became a growth industry of importance to the state economy. Soldiers returning from the war in 1945 for the first time had a government subsidy for a college education. Indeed the "G.I. Bill of Rights" sent so many veterans into the classroom that Texas and national colleges grew rapidly and changed in character. The veterans worked hard, brought a new level of maturity to the classroom, and demanded the offering of new intellectual disciplines of study. Through the efforts primarily of Senator Ralph Yarborough of Texas, the G.I. Bill, with some modifications, was extended to veterans of the Korean War. Another federal government stimulus to higher education was the 1958 National Defense Education Act (NDEA). Passed in response to *Sputnik*, the NDEA loaned money and gave outright grants to college students. These measures began the era of direct aid to students. The government additionally awarded grants to institutions and faculty involved in military and other research projects. The impact of these measures on higher education cannot be overestimated.

The total enrollment in Texas colleges numbered 39,000 in 1940, decreased during the war, then boomed to over 50,000 after the conflict. By 1960, 186,000 students took classes at a Texas institution of higher learning. The Baby Boom and more usual population increases maintained the growth of the student body until the 1980s. The integration of the public schools and an increase in the number of women seeking college degrees also contributed to the university population. The need for new institutions to serve expanding urban areas led to the creation of Lamar State College in 1951, and integration controversies prodded the legislature in 1947 to absorb the private Houston College for Negroes and rename it Texas State University for Negroes, later called Texas Southern University. Expansion of public institutions of higher learning continued, and between 1960 and 1980, the state established thirty new public senior colleges, systems, or branch campuses.

Although private colleges have always played a significant role in the education of Texans, most students chose to attend public institutions. Several factors contributed to this development. The size of the state system allowed students to go far away from home or stay nearby and still attend a public college. By the end of senior and community college expansion in the 1970s, all of the Texas population was estimated to reside within fifty miles of a public college. Tuition for in-state students was a bargain. As late as 1970, 94 percent of those attending a Texas college were born in the state.

The changing economy defined new roles for the state's institutions of higher education. With more demands for technical training and a greater number of older students returning to college, the community college expansion that had started before the war continued thereafter. Most of these colleges separated themselves from public school administrations after World War II. The community colleges changed their curriculums accordingly, their course offerings including technical subjects, and, generally, more closely resembling those of four-year campuses. Four-year institutions, in turn, began to emphasize more research output from their faculties and the granting of more graduate degrees, with the University of Texas leading the way. The new designation of most state colleges as universities signaled this change in emphasis. Private and public universities in 1960 granted about 4,000 graduate degrees. As the drive for graduate education increased the number of new degree programs, in 1965, the legislature authorized the Texas College and University System Coordinating Board. Patterned after the University of California system, the coordinating board's duties included the management of degree programs and long-range educational and financial planning, though political self-interest and regional considerations limited its effectiveness.

Many of the struggles for improvements in education took place against the backdrop of fights to end segregation. In the case of Texas Mexicans, LULAC and the American G.I. Forum led the drive for educational rights. The latter organization grew out of the frustrations experienced by Hispanic World War II veterans who faced difficulties in acquiring financial and medical benefits from the Veterans Administration. Founded in 1948 by Dr. Hector P. García, a Corpus Christi physician and combat veteran in the European Theater, the G.I. Forum gained national notoriety in 1949 when it tangled with a funeral director at Three Rivers, Texas, who refused to handle chapel services for Félix Z. Longoria, a soldier killed in the Philippines during World War II. Though both LULAC and the G.I. Forum fought for similar issues, the latter organization more boldly challenged dominant institutions and white stereotypes about Mexican Americans. Together, the organizations worked with an outstanding group of Texas Mexicans, many of whom belonged to both. Among these professionals were Alonso S. Perales, J. T. Canales, James Tafolla, George I. Sánchez, Carlos E. Castañeda, Hector P. García, Gus C. García, John J. Herrera, Félix Tijerina, and numerous others whose distinction as a group was not rivaled by any other Tejano generation.

The organizations encouraged wider participation in mainstream institutions to ameliorate prejudices toward Mexican Americans. They conducted poll-tax drives to awaken politicians to the demands of Texas Mexicans. They sued in the federal courts for legal and educational rights. In *Delgado v. Bastrop Independent School District* (1948), Texas Mexican lawyers convinced a federal court that segregation of Mexican Americans violated the Fourteenth Amendment. Gus C. García and other distinguished Tejano attorneys won another landmark case in 1954, when the U.S. Supreme Court ruled in *Hernández v. The State of Texas* that qualified Mexican Americans could not be excluded as jurors in their communities of residence.

The organizations combined legal actions with self-help drives for better educational opportunities for Tejanos. They conducted back-to-school drives, held fund-raising dances for scholarships, and pressured local school boards to stop de facto segregation. In 1957, LULAC national president Félix Tijerina of Houston introduced the "Little School of the 400." The project won legislative support in 1959 and may have been the model for the present Head Start program. The activism of LULAC and its liberal allies slowly eroded the old system of race relations. By 1960, schools were legally integrated in theory if not in fact, as were juries. Virulent forms of racism began dissipating in the late 1950s, as court decisions and agitation by labor unionists, minorities, and liberals within the Democratic party fought against prejudice. The election of new leaders to national office, like Ralph Yarborough and Lyndon Baines Johnson, gave new voice to minority complaints. In the state legislature, Henry B. González of San Antonio and Abraham Kazen of Laredo joined other liberals in the fight against institutionalized segregation.

The issue of segregation of public education focused, however, on the African American community. The demand of black leaders for educational equality began during World War II, but integration of the public schools met more white opposition than had the ending of the white primary system. Americans had always believed that the public schools were agents for social advancement, and the possibility of integration conjured up white persons' fears of interracial marriages, moral decay, and collapsing academic standards. Besides, for most white Texans, segregated public institutions validated the presumed inferiority of black persons.

The 1940 convention of the NAACP, which outlined goals of equal suffrage and education for African Americans, knew the attitude of many whites and consequently decided to first sue for the vote and then for desegregation. Thurgood Marshall argued that lawsuits forcing black enrollment in professional and graduate schools would least antagonize whites. After the successful 1944 dismantling of the all-white primary in Marshall, Maceo Smith, Carter Wesley,

Henry B. González (center) conferring with supporters during the 1958 governor's race. *Russell Lee Photograph Collection, The Center for American History, The University of Texas at Austin, DI 237*

and John J. Jones, president of the NAACP, decided to sue the University of Texas for the admission of a black student to its school of law on the grounds that no school in Texas offered black people a law education. Heman Marion Sweatt, a Houston post office employee, agreed to become the plaintiff and seek admittance to U.T.'s law school. The conservative leadership in the state attempted to thwart the suit by broadening educational programs at Prairie View State Normal and Industrial College and changing the name of that institution to Prairie View University, incorporating Texas Southern University into the state system, and establishing an all-black law school in the basement of the state capi-

tol. In response, NAACP attorneys changed their strategy to one that argued that the University of Texas's excellent reputation in law meant that any rival segregated institution necessarily offered an inferior degree. The Supreme Court agreed in the 1950 *Sweatt* v. *Painter* decision and ordered the integration of U.T.'s law school.

Integration of undergraduate education soon followed. Del Mar Junior College, Amarillo College, and a few others integrated in 1952, and by 1955, Texas Western (UTEP) accepted (twelve) black undergraduates; it was the first public four-year college to do so. The University of Texas and Southern Methodist University admitted black undergraduates by 1956, although the dorms and cafeterias at U.T. remained segregated until 1959.

Except for disturbances that prevented black Texans from enrolling at Texarkana Junior College in 1955 and another that failed to do so at Lamar State College in 1956, the integration of the state system of higher education proceeded without a great deal of tension. Still, other black educators and students met other hurdles. Faced with more choices of schools and disparities in tuition costs, black students chose public colleges more often than they did one of the thirteen private black institutions, which consequently suffered a decline in enrollment and increased financial difficulties. New fights for equal status arose over such issues as minority faculty appointments, integrated dormitories, and percentages of minority students in

Above: Heman Sweatt in registration line at the University of Texas. *U.T. Student Publications, Inc. Photographs; The Center for American History, The University of Texas at Austin, CN 00323B*

previously all-white colleges. Those calls would blend with other demands to characterize the turbulent search for reform in the 1960s.

College students and their parents accepted integration with less complaint than did those in the public schools. In *Brown* v. *Topeka Board of Education* (1954), the Supreme Court ruled that segregated schools were inherently unequal and thus unconstitutional. A public opinion poll reported in 1955 that white Texans opposed integration by four to one, whereas black Texans supported desegregation by two to one. Although later polls would show a weakening of white support for Jim Crow schools, the integration process in Texas was both a slow and painful one. Not willing to comply with federal mandates, school districts redrew their boundaries to maintain all-black schools, instituted very gradual methods of integration for black children, and simply appealed the court rulings to keep their institutions segregated as long as possible. By 1957, some 120 school districts had instituted some form of integration. Among those that had not were some in Dallas and Houston. Ten years after the decision in *Brown*, only about 5 percent of the state's black children attended integrated schools—that paltry figure exceeding the percentage in other ex-Confederate states. Although the bitter violence that marked the Deep South's response to the struggle for racial equality mostly bypassed Texas, the maintenance of segregation and the issue of social justice would shape many of the state's political battles in the 1950s and 1960s.

Other issues brought Texas's public educational institutions under attack in the 1950s. Many Texas Regulars, the group that had originated with campaigns against the New Deal and for the endorsement of segregation, thought that university campuses, particularly the University of Texas, harbored faculties who were too liberal. Governors O'Daniel and Stevenson appointed a number of the Regulars and others of similar political persuasion to U.T.'s board of regents. The regents voted in 1942 to fire four economics professors because of their New Deal tendencies, but the president of the university, Homer Price Rainey, refused to do so. In turn, the regents tried to abolish faculty tenure. The conflict between Rainey and the board heated up in 1944 over the regents' demands that John Dos Passos's novel *USA* be removed from the English department's supplemental reading lists. After Rainey denounced this action at a faculty meeting, the board fired him. The controversy spilled over into the political campaign for governor in 1946 when Beauford Jester defeated Rainey in that race. But the issue of academic freedom that the Rainey episode raised continued into the 1950s. On several occasions, the University of Texas Regents censored the *Daily Texan*, a paper edited by Willie Morris, who later achieved some literary fame. The editor responded by printing the paper with blank columns as a protest against censorship. Elsewhere, there seemed a demand for conformity on college campuses that implied that any change or debate threatened society. Conservatives' suspicions of university communities, who in turn doubted the state's commitment to free academic inquiry, pointed the way to the campus battles of the 1960s.

The political conflicts in higher education illustrated a broader problem in society. The Cold War tensions of the late 1940s and early 1950s caused deep anxieties and frustrations in the North American psyche. Despite huge expenditures for national defense, the United States could no longer unilaterally direct international events, and the Soviet Union's acquisition of atomic weapons threatened the very existence of the nation. Senator Joseph McCarthy of Wisconsin rose to national prominence by hurling unsubstantiated allegations of mass subversion of North American institutions by communists, which resulted in the nation's second Red Scare. Quickly, this anti-Communist fervor known as "McCarthyism" dominated much of early postwar politics. The Red Scare merged with societal tensions produced by urbanization and the rise of new groups who openly challenged the old power structure. Consequently, any action that lessened the power of local elites—for example, calls for civil rights, expanded powers of the federal government, and labor union growth—was identified by many as un-American.

In Texas, McCarthyism might have fueled the Red Scare, but W. Lee O'Daniel and Martin Dies had laid the groundwork for militant anti-Communism in the Lone Star State before the end of World War II. And in several of their political races in the 1940s, both Coke Stevenson and Lyndon Johnson campaigned on platforms that accentuated their tough stance against the spread of communism. The anti-Communist hysteria also affected local politics in Dallas, Houston, and San Antonio, where organizations such as the Minute Women crusaded against what they identified as threats to the American way of life. The Minute Women of Houston and their allies forced George W. Ebey, the superintendent of the Houston public schools, out of office. The attack directed at Ebey brought together those who opposed integration, New Deal reforms, and progressive education. Smaller communities and local organizations embraced the Red Scare, too. The drive to stop subversion included removing suspect books from library shelves, not permitting liberal speakers or performers to appear at public forums, purging exhibitions of presumed left-leaning art, and the removal of teachers or texts that had alleged socialist tendencies. A rigorous investigation to rid the state school system of subversive teachers turned up one Communist among 65,000 employees.

McCarthyism faded away in the state and in the nation in the mid-1950s, but the residue of the Red Scare remained. Its militancy framed a pattern of reticence in the public schools that discouraged the discussion of controversial topics or the state adoption of textbooks that contained them. One obvious long-term effect of the Red Scare was that the legislative requirement that students and public employees sign loyalty oaths lasted well into the 1960s.

TEXAS SOCIETY
AND CULTURE AT MIDCENTURY

The pressures that industrialization exerted on society were not apparent to most observers of the 1950s. Most contemporary social commentators wrote of a society that endorsed middle-class values and strove for consensus and conformity. The advent of World War II and the ending of the depression encouraged a search for a consumer culture that an enlarging middle class of the 1950s missed in the recent past. Blue-collar workers and young executives alike returned from work to their suburban homes, changed into leisure clothes, and went out for recreation. In addition, the decline of European immigration by this time added to the sense of a homogenized society. Folk festivals in celebration of the German or Czech roots of Texas communities had become more events of nostalgia than sources of ethnic identification. With at-large voting determining the outcome of most elections for local offices of Texas cities, white elites controlled positions of community power.

Religion

The state retained its Protestant roots. Church attendance fell during the 1930s, but national estimates placed church membership at 60 percent of the population by 1960. Texans undoubtedly matched national averages and probably exceeded them. An unofficial census based on figures some individual denominations provided for the *Texas Almanac* in 1953 verified some trends. The Roman Catholic Church more than doubled in adherents, from 604,000 in 1936 to 1,332,187, and remained the largest single denomination. The Southern Baptists, the fastest-growing Protestant denomination, quadrupled in the same period, to 1,262,451 members. Their number did not include the more than 500,000 African American Baptists, who held similar theological, if not racial, views. Another approximately 100,000 black people belonged to Methodist church bodies, and 679,000 whites cited membership in the Methodist Episcopal Church, South. The Presbyterians at this time claimed 228,000 adherents. The Disciples of Christ, with 74,990 members in 1936, was the fourth-largest white Protestant denomination, with 117,421 members, in 1953. Other Protestant faiths of some size included the Episcopal Church, 94,626, the American Lutherans, 69,042, the Evangelical Lutherans (Missouri synod), 53,302, and The Assemblies of God, 50,000. The number of Jewish congregations fell from 60 to 40 in the period, but the total membership rose to 50,000.

The electronic church, a sobriquet popular in the 1980s, had not such an enthusiastic following in the 1950s. Nevertheless, with the growing influence of television and the radio, evangelical sermons were broadcast throughout Texas. Many of these messages were received by an audience well schooled in fundamentalist values. The growth of the new media pointed toward a change in the political directions of some fundamentalist philosophies. While a blending of fundamentalism and politics was certainly not unknown in Texas history, in the 1960s, new programs such as *Life Line* from Dallas and Billy James Hargis's *Christian Crusade* out of Tulsa flooded the airwaves with anti-Communist rhetoric. The programs turned many of their followers into holy warriors who stood firm against "infidels" advocating any kind of reform. The 1960 presidential election of John F. Kennedy, a Roman Catholic whom many in Texas considered an elitist and a proponent of integration, contributed to the growth in Texas as well as the other Sunbelt states, of what became known as the "religious right."

Leisure Activities

The types of leisure activities undertaken by the more affluent Texans changed with urbanization. There was no state allocation for the Texas Park Board until 1933. But immediately after the war, some 2 million persons visited the 38 state parks, and the advent of tourism had begun. The tourist industry evolved into an important segment of the state's economy by the end of the decade, with San Antonio becoming the leading tourist destination. The motion picture industry that had flourished during the depression continued to attract huge numbers of moviegoers in the 1950s. The state sent its fair share of natives to stardom, including Ginger Rogers, Audie Murphy, Linda Darnell, Gene Autry, Debbie Reynolds, and Ann Sheridan. *The Alamo* and *Giant* were the two best-known pictures filmed in Texas in the 1950s. They captured in a cultural sense the outsiders' view of the state, a land of adventurers and oil moguls.

Another image long held by natives and strangers alike was that in Texas, sports were extremely important, especially Southwest Conference football. In the 1930s, "Slingin'"Sammy Baugh and Davey O'Brien, both of TCU, and "Jarrin'" John Kimbrough of Texas A&M captured the national spotlight. Baugh was an All-American in 1935 and 1936, and then was all-pro six times between 1937 and 1947. O'Brien won the Heisman and Maxwell Trophies in 1938 and led his team to the college national championship. Kimbrough and A&M captured the national title the next year. Not until after World War II, however, did college football win the allegiance of so many Texans. Doak Walker of SMU symbolized the Southwest Conference's national notoriety. The first and only

Recently returned World War II veteran purchasing a shotgun in a general sporting and dry goods store, Azle, Texas, late winter, 1945. *Courtesy of Robert A. Calvert*

Texan named All-American three years in a row, Walker received the Maxwell and the Heisman Trophies in 1948 and was elected to both the college and pro football halls of fame. In 1957, Texas got its third Heisman winner in Texas A&M's John David Crow, who went on to play in four Pro Bowls during his 11-year professional career. But perhaps the Southwest Conference's greatest achievements came during the reign of Darrel Royal, coach of the University of Texas. Royal's teams won eleven conference titles, three national championships (1963, 1969, 1970) and went to sixteen bowl games. Texas Tech and the University of Houston joined the conference after World War II, rounding out its complement.

The 1969 University of Texas team was the last all-white national championship football squad. The tradition-laden Southwest Conference integrated its teams a decade later than did Texas's lesser-known colleges. Abner Haynes entered the football program in 1957 at North Texas State, and his instant success as a running back encouraged other programs to recruit African Americans. Sid Blanks went to Texas A&I in 1958 and led the Javelinas in both rushing and receiving en route to the NAIA national championship in 1962 and All-American honors. The breakthrough for the Southwest Conference came when Jerry LeVias went to SMU in 1965 and took the team to the championship in 1966. The conference nonetheless remained largely lily-white until the 1970s.

Professional football cast its spell on Texans in the 1960s. Dallas tried briefly to support a professional franchise in 1952, but the undercapitalized Dallas Texans moved to Baltimore and were renamed the Colts by the end of the season. Texas millionaires Lamar Hunt and K. S. "Bud" Adams helped found the American Football League in 1960 and secured franchises for Dallas and Houston. That same year, oilman Clint Murchison, Jr., received a National Football League expansion franchise for Dallas, the Cowboys. The recognition that the city could not support two pro teams in 1963 prompted Hunt to move his franchise to Kansas City and rename it the Chiefs. Meanwhile, the Cowboys' organization received accolades for its stable management, and when the team reached the playoffs in 1965, it was the first of twenty consecutive post-season appearances under Coach Tom Landry, who had grown up in Mission and starred at the University of Texas. Houston's AFL team, the Oilers, won the new league's first two championships in 1960 and 1961 behind the quarterbacking of George Blanda. The Oilers lost the 1963 title game to Lamar Hunt's Dallas Texans.

Other professional sports in Texas included a strong minor-league baseball program throughout the twentieth century. The warm and sunny climate made the Texas League an important place for the training of future major leaguers. Other minor leagues also fielded teams in Texas. The late 1940s and the mid-1950s were the heyday of minor league baseball, but the advent of televised major league games cut sharply into attendance at minor league ballparks. Major league baseball arrived in Texas with the Houston Colts, later renamed the Astros, in 1962. In 1964, the Astros moved into the first domed stadium, fittingly named the Astrodome. College baseball also boasted of a

Inside the Astrodome. *Courtesy Houston Metropolitan Research Center, Houston Public Library*

reasonable following in the state, with the University of Texas dominating the Southwest Conference. Several Texas-born players went on to star in the major leagues during this era, including Hall of Famers Frank Robinson and Ernie Banks.

One humorist described basketball as the game Texans play between the end of football season and the beginning of spring training. SMU fielded some nationally competitive basketball teams in the 1950s, but North Texas State, which played in the Missouri Valley Conference and later as an independent, and the University of Houston also received favorable rankings. Elvin Hayes, a product of the latter, may well have been the best-known basketball player until the sport grew in popularity with the advent of television and professional franchises. Texas Western offered athletic scholarships to blacks in 1956 and won the NCAA championship in 1966, the only men's team in Texas ever to do so. Pan American won the NAIA championship in 1962. Professional basketball reached Texas in 1967 with the Dallas Chaparrals of the old American Basketball Association. That club moved to San Antonio and was renamed the Spurs. The Houston Rockets and the Dallas Mavericks rounded out the professional franchises of the state.

The so-called minor sports attracted many Texas athletes, if not spectators. Many hailed Texan Ben Hogan as the best professional golfer of the 1950s. But any list of great Texan golfers must include Jimmy Demaret of the 1940s and 1950s. Sports historians credit Mildred "Babe" Didrikson Zaharias of Beaumont–

Port Arthur as the original driving force behind women's professional golf, and to cite her as the greatest woman athlete ever would be no Texas tall tale. As an amateur, for example, Didrikson set four world records in track and field, and dominated the 1932 Olympics. She also won professional golf tournaments well into the 1940s. Rodeos retained a large following, with major expositions in Fort Worth and Houston, and the growing professionalism of the sport was apparent in the 1950s. Texas has not had much of a boxing tradition. Blacks and whites could not meet in the ring until 1955. Entrepreneurs staged professional bouts without much financial success despite the popularity of welterweight champion Curtis Cokes and 1968 Olympic gold medalist George Foreman, who later went on to win the heavyweight title.

Cultural Activities

Texas may have accrued more fame for its sports than for its artistic endeavors, but along with city living the state acquired desirable urban amenities. The little theater movement that supported numerous local companies statewide in the 1920s lagged in the 1930s. But after World War II, several theatrical groups of note entertained Texas audiences. Paul Baker brought fame to the Baylor University Drama Department when his staging and direction of plays received favorable national commentary. After the university administration objected to Baker's production of Eugene O'Neill's *Long Day's Journey into Night,* Baker went to Trinity University, where he continued to win accolades. Baker staged productions, too, at the Dallas Theater Center in an innovative building designed by Frank Lloyd Wright. Margo Jones of Dallas, until her untimely death in 1955, and Nina Vance, the founder of the Alley Theater in Houston, drew much critical praise for their commitment to staging avant-garde and original works. While Dallas and Houston remained the state's centers of artistic merit, local theater groups proliferated in other major cities and most minor ones.

Although the Great Depression limited the work of artists, by no means did it end work in the visual arts. The Federal Arts Project (1935–1943), a division of the Works Progress Administration, supported needy artists who painted murals and other works of art in Texas and other states. Much of this work is now, unfortunately, lost, but some fine examples of it, particularly of murals, can still be seen on college campuses. The building of the central exposition in Dallas for the 1936 centennial offered employment to some Texas artists. Architect George L. Dahl designed the buildings for the central exposition, and many cited the Hall of State then and now as a prime example of art deco architecture. Tom Lea did some murals for the Hall of State, and the Dallas sculptor José Martin crafted many of the art deco sculptures that decorate the facade of the buildings. The centennial planners went out of state for many artists, turning down bids from the so-called Dallas Nine, who were heavily influenced by Thomas Hart Benton and a movement known as regionalism.

That group as well as other artists continued their work into the postwar period. O'Neil Ford, an important Texas architect who made major contributions to the rise of historic preservation, became well known in the 1950s. Many of the state's artists were probably best recognized for their choice of regional topics, such as José Cisneros, known for his pen and ink illustrations of the Spanish Borderlands, or E. M. "Buck" Schiwetz, who painted watercolors of the Texas landscape. Others possibly earned somewhat more of a national standing—Allie Z. Tennant and sculptors Octavio Medellín and Charles Umlauf—but the move of artists to nonobjective art in the 1950s impressed the faculties of Texas college art departments more than it did general Texas audiences. Nevertheless, Dallasite James Brooks, an important figure in the so-called New York school, and Robert Rauschenburg of Port Arthur left the state and earned national and even international fame. The artists of the 1950s also moved more into a search for their ethnic roots. John Biggers, long-time head of the Art Department at Texas Southern University, went to Africa in 1956 and produced a number of paintings on his experiences there, as well as other works on African Americans.

Texas supported three major symphony orchestras by the 1950s. San Antonio drew upon its broad musical heritage to create a symphony that appealed to mass audiences, featuring guest soloists and providing traditional programs as well as repertoires that resembled those of the Boston Pops. The modern Dallas Orchestra really started in 1945 with the appointment of Antal Dorati as conductor. It has since enjoyed varying degrees of success under a number of talented conductors. The Houston Symphony claimed the greatest prestige of any Texas symphony orchestra. First with conductor Efrem Kurtz and then under John Barbirolli the symphony gained national fame. In the 1963–1964 season, Barbirolli took the orchestra on a tour of the East, becoming the first southwestern symphony to play before eastern audiences. Community symphony orchestras developed throughout the state, drawing on local musicians and guest artists, and those in Austin, Fort Worth, Odessa-Midland, and Amarillo have obtained regional notoriety. The exceptionally strong music programs at the University of North Texas, the University of Houston, and the University of Texas at Austin, as well as very good fine arts programs at many other Texas colleges, added to the availability of serious music for Texans. Two U.T.-trained composers, Tom Jones and Harvey Schmidt, made history on Broadway with their musical *The Fantasticks*, which was the longest-running Broadway show ever.

San Antonio established the state's first resident opera company. Fort Worth soon followed in 1946, and by the late 1950s, the Houston Grand Opera Company and the Dallas Civic Opera had been formed. The Dallas company opened in 1957 with Maria Callas in concert, and by the 1960s it was considered a regional company of national significance. Famed tenor Plácido Domingo is among the international stars who made their American debuts in Dallas. Dallasites could also hear world-class opera; starting in 1939, the Metropolitan Opera's touring company performed in Dallas each spring. All told, if one added the increasing prestige of the Houston Grand Opera, the touring companies, and the development of dance companies—in particular the Houston Ballet—a fair assessment might be that Texas struggled but made significant progress in the fine arts.

Popular music had fewer problems capturing a statewide following. Since World War II, the State Fair of Texas has brought recent Broadway attractions to Dallas (including Texan Mary Martin in 1947). The State Fair extended its control over the Starlight Operetta and put on summer musicals of a similar nature. The Casa Mañana, started by Billy Rose in Fort Worth to celebrate the Texas Centennial, started hosting musicals after the war, as did Houston. By the 1960s, most Texas cities had community theaters, and Dallas and Houston were beginning to attract touring Broadway productions.

The major cities also hosted jazz performamces. The music program at North Texas State University even offered a major in jazz, and the university's official jazz ensemble, the One O'Clock Lab Band, entertained a national following through its tours and records. In addition, students formed local groups that played throughout the area, and some of the young musicians went on to join national orchestras and bands. Although Texas never developed a distinctive "jazz" sound, as did some other southern states, black Texans Ornette Coleman on the saxophone and Teddy Wilson on piano are listed as influential in the development of the genre.

The blues continued its influence on other forms of music, particularly rock and roll, which made Roy Orbison of Wink, Buddy Holly of Lubbock, and Janis Joplin of Port Arthur famous. By the 1950s, most large Texas cities had rhythm-and-blues radio stations that broadcast to white and black audiences, and local

Texas blues great Mance Lipscomb. *The UT Institute of Texan Cultures, No. 77-215*

black Texans performed with regularity at clubs and in concert. Although not as well known as blues musicians of the Deep South, Texans such as Blind Lemon Jefferson, Lightin' Hopkins, Mance Lipscomb, and T-Bone Walker are all famous for their influence over the blues.

Country-and-western music, as it is now called, was the music most identified with the state. Bob Wills, who took Benny Goodman as an example, introduced "western swing" and pioneered the use of a string section as well horns and electric instruments in his band. Wills, along with such singing cowboys as Maurice Woodward "Tex" Ritter, were instrumental in creating the genre called western music, whose lyrics came from Tin-Pan Alley but whose sentiments rested in a nostalgia for an older way of life. Long after the end of prohibition, Texas honky-tonk music thrived in local taverns and received wide play on the radio. New technology and noisy taverns encouraged the electrification of instruments. The country sounds of Texans Ernest Tubb, Ray Price, and George Jones, among others, incorporated all of these traditions, and their music followed southerners to cities and became a national phenomenon.

The contributions of Texas Mexicans to country music had a long historical heritage dating back to the folk music of *vaqueros*. But by the 1960s, such performers as Sunny and the Sunglows, Trini López, René and René, and Sam the Sham and the Pharaohs had hits in mainstream musical circles. However, most Tejano musicians stayed with the traditional forms of music popular in the Mexican American community, primarily the *conjunto* and the *orquesta*. The most acclaimed of the former by the 1960s was Paulino Bernal and his conjunto, and among the most accomplished of the latter was Little Joe y La Familia.

The emergence of new graduate programs at regional state universities and the expansion of existing ones in the 1950s stimulated nonfiction works about Texas history. Recently graduated faculty members frequently chose to publish on Texas topics. They joined writers already working in the field, such as Carlos E. Castañeda, who began his seven-volume *Our Catholic Heritage* in Texas in the 1930s, and Ruben Rendón Lozano, who produced *Viva Tejas* in 1936 to add the story of ethnic groups to the state's history. Business and economic history defined new lines of inquiry, as Joe B. Frantz, *Gail Borden, Dairyman to a Nation* (1951) and John S. Spratt, *The Road to Spindletop* (1957) pointed to new methodological ways to look at economic changes. Ernest Wallace and Rupert Richardson wrote extensively on Indians and the closing of the West. Biographies of major Texans appeared through the efforts of Robert C. Cotner, Llerena Friend, Herbert Gambrell, and Ben Procter. J. Milton Nance wrote a massive two-volume work on the Texas Republic. New approaches to western history came through the work of Frantz, J. Evetts Haley, W. C. Holden, C. L. Sonnichsen, Wayne Gard, and others. Most of these Texas historians, though, continued to be preoccupied with the traditional nineteenth-century topics: the Texas Revolution and Republic, the Civil War, Cowboys, Indians, the "frontier," and biographies of great men. Any significant movement away from the heroic topics and themes would have to wait for a new generation of scholars who began writing in the 1970s.

The decades since World War II offered new outlets for historical scholarship about Texas. The founding of the University of Texas Press in 1950, first directed by Frank Wardlaw, and the publications of the Texas State Historical Association, which include the *Southwestern Historical Quarterly* and *The Handbook of Texas*, guided scholarly interest in the state in the 1950s. Since then, the establishment of the Texas A&M University Press, also first directed by Wardlaw, and the creation of the *East Texas Historical Journal*, the *West Texas Historical Association Year Book*, and the *Journal of South Texas* furnished additional opportunities to publish scholarly writings.

A distance of a generation or so may be necessary for the judgment of literary trends. Nevertheless, as early as the 1970s, scholars asserted certain tenuous evaluations of Texas literature. From the 1930s until their deaths, the work of J. Frank Dobie (1964), Walter Prescott Webb (1963), and Roy Bedichek (1959) cast an aura over Texas literature. Dobie published a number of books—*Coronado's Children* (1931), *The Longhorns* (1941), *Cow People* (1964), for example—that allowed the narrator to tell a somewhat disorganized series of stories sharing a common theme: the search for gold; cattle; Texas ranchers. Although later critics faulted Dobie for his unscientific approach to folklore, his influence in the Texas Folklore Society encouraged the work of William A. Owens, John and Allan Lomax, Mody Boatwright, Wilson Hudson, Francis Abernathy, J. Mason Brewer, and Américo Paredes. Brewer's poetry and work in folklore led the Texas Institute of Letters to elect him as its first black member. Paredes's study of the *corrido,* "*With His Pistol in His Hand*" (1958), told the Texas Mexican view of Gregorio Cortez. Both of these writers, plus the others mentioned above, were more selective and systematic in their treatment of folk tales than was Dobie, and their work and that of younger scholars made the *Publications of the Texas Folklore Society* an important source for the culture of the state.

Webb earned a reputation as an original thinker that caused fellow historians to cite his *The Great Plains* (1931) as one of the two most influential books of the last fifty years. Webb paid as much attention to style as to content, and *The Great Frontier* (1952) and to a lesser extent *The Texas Rangers* (1935) were literature as well as history.

Bedichek kept so busy as the director of the University Interscholastic League that he published *Adventures With a Texas Naturalist* (1947), *Karankaway Country* (1950), and *The Sense of Smell* (1960) after retirement. Most critics considered him the best writer of the three. His works were instantly acclaimed as major observations of the state's plant and animal life. Many rate his first book as a minor classic in the genre of natural history.

The reputations of Dobie, Webb, and Bedichek rested in part on their willingness to turn to Texas subject matter for creative and intellectual stimulation, which gave them a mass following among Texans—many of whom had probably not read their books. This bothered some critics, who felt that the trio's works did not deserve such extravagant praise. Those critics could point to episodes such as the Texas Institute of Letters' decision in 1939 to award its first book award to Dobie for *Apache Gold and Yaqui Silver*, passing over Katherine Ann Porter's nationally acclaimed *Pale Horse, Pale Rider*. The final evaluation of the art of Dobie, Webb, and Bedichek awaits the passage of time, but any writer who turns to the cultural and historical traditions of the state owes all three men an unspoken debt.

Other Texas writers left the state to locate close to the publishing houses of New York or in environments they identified as more conducive to intellectual endeavors. Katherine Ann Porter, who had left Texas in the 1910s, continued to write in the 1940s, 1950s, and 1960s. Her *Collected Stories*, published in 1965, won the National Book Award and the Pulitzer Prize. George Sessions Perry wrote his classic *Hold Autumn in Your Hand* (1941), a sympathetic novel of a Central Texas tenant farmer, before going to Connecticut to pursue a career in journalism; he ended his troubled life in 1952. Edwin Lanham, who also moved to Connecticut, wrote about sharecroppers in *The Stricklands* (1939) and the oil fields in *Thunder in the Earth* (1941). These novels still attract a limited audience. Of those who left the state in the 1950s and 1960s and used their homeland for the setting of their books, William Humphrey of Clarksville and William A. Owens of Pin Hook may be the best known. Humphrey's *Home From the Hill* (1958) and *The Ordways* (1965) rank as major Texas novels. Owens wrote a number of novels, including *Walking on Borrowed Land* (1954), which touched on the very tender nerves of race relations in telling the story of a black principal in the 1930s, but his best work may be nonfiction. His books on Texas music, tales from the oil fields, and *Three Friends: Bedicheck, Dobie and Webb* (1969) all established him as a scholar of note. Most readers will evaluate his autobiographical *This Stubborn Soil* (1966) and *Season of Weathering* (1973) as two of the finer books on growing up in Texas, matched only by such classics as Stanley Walker's *Home to Texas* (1956), Mary Lasswell's *I'll Take Texas* (1958), and Willie Morris's *North Towards Home* (1967) as perceptive comments on life in the state. Other expatriates of note include Terry Southern, Donald Bartheleme, William Goyens, Max Crawford, and Allen Wier.

Some writers stayed with traditional themes and evoked a particular feeling of the state and its geography: John Graves's *Goodbye to a River* (1960) and his later works bring together regrets of a passing Texas with problems created by the emergence of the new one. One might classify in this same vein the important contributions of A. C. Greene and Elroy Bode. Others have turned to historical fiction and written accounts of the West. Tom Lea, a painter as well as a writer, enjoyed wide acceptance for *The Wonderful Country* (1952) and *The Hands of Cantu* (1964). Benjamin Capps's *Trail to Ogallala* (1964) was chosen by other western writers as one of the top twenty-five westerns. Fred Gipson, author of *Dog Man* (1947) and *Old Yeller* (1962), was initially regarded as a storyteller for children but later as a quality writer about Old West.

As the state attracted a more cosmopolitan and heterogeneous population, opportunities for journalists have become more plentiful, and the reflections on Texas of these various writers attracted a wide readership. John Howard Griffin published *Black Like Me* in 1961, a powerful personal account of living in a segregated society. Other reporters, such as Hamilton "Tex" Maule and Dan Jenkins, worked for *Sports Illustrated* and helped change the direction of sports reporting in the 1960s. Edward "Bud" Shrake and Gary Cartwright left the sports pages to write novels and articles for magazines. Other native Texans who acquired a sizable readership from newspapers columns or as freelance journalists included Bill Porterfield, Thomas Thompson, and Larry L. King. King and Willie Morris were but two of the influential Texas writers of the 1950s or 1960s who had served as editors or writers for *The Texas Observer,* a liberal political magazine published in Austin. The *Observer*'s original editor, Ronnie Dugger, went on to write a biography of Lyndon Johnson; another *Observer* editor, Billy Lee Brammer, wrote *The Gay Place,* the best political novel by a Texan. Furthermore, *Observer* editor Lawrence Goodwyn became a well-known historian. The *Observer*'s presence in Austin, along with the University of Texas and the state government, made the capital city the gathering spot for those who wished to evaluate the state.

In the 1960s, a young writer from Houston (by way of Archer City) used his fiction to paint a portrait of life in twentieth-century Texas. Larry McMurtry's first three novels, *Horseman Pass By* (1961), *Leaving Cheyenne* (1963), and *The Last Picture Show* (1966) take place in a small West Texas town that has been decimated by changes wrought by people leaving for the city and the passing of a rural way of life. In a brilliant collection of essays, *In a Narrow Grave* (1968), he explored the changes in Texas and what the end of rural society boded for the state. McMurtry's early works seemed to point Texas literature in a new direction—away from the Texas of cotton and cattle, and toward a more complex and realistic view of the urban present.

READINGS

Books and Dissertations

Allsup, Carl, *The American G.I. Forum: Origins and Evolution,* Center for Mexican American Studies (Austin: University of Texas Press, 1982).

Barnhill, Herschel J., *From Surplus to Substitution: Energy in Texas* (Boston: American Press, 1983).

Buenger, Victoria, and Walter L. Buenger, *Texas Merchant: Marvin Leonard & Fort Worth* (College Station: Texas A&M University Press, 2001).

Carleton, Don, *The Red Scare: Right Wing Hysteria, Fifties Fanaticism and their Legacies in Texas* (Austin: Texas Monthly Press, 1985).

DeMoss, Dorothy D., "Looking Better Every Year: Apparel Manufacturing in Texas," in *Texas: A Sesquicentennial Celebration,* ed. Donald Wisenhunt (Austin: Eakin Press, 1986).

Dugger, Ronnie, Our Invaded Universities (New York: Norton, 1974).

———, *Three Men in Texas: Bedicheck, Webb, & Dobie* (Austin: University of Texas Press, 1967).

Green, Donald E., *Land of the Underground Rain: Irrigation on the Texas High Plains, 1910–1970* (Austin: University of Texas Press, 1973).

Green, George N., "Some Aspects of the Far Right Wing in Texas Politics," in *Essays on Recent Southern Politics*, ed. Harold M. Hollingsworth (Austin: University of Texas Press, 1970).

Heinze, Michael R., *Private Black Colleges in Texas, 1865–1954* (College Station: Texas A&M University Press, 1985).

King, Larry L., *Confessions of a White Racist* (New York: Viking Press, 1971).

Martin, Mary Ellen, "The Impact World War II Had on Women's Employment Patterns" (Master's thesis, University of Texas, 1977).

Moore, Richard R., *West Texas After the Discovery of Oil: A Modern Frontier* (Austin: Jenkins Publishing Co., 1971).

Morris, Willie, *North Towards Home* (Boston: Houghton Mifflin, 1967).

Pennington, *Richard, Breaking the Ice: The Racial Integration of Southwest Conference Football* (Jefferson, NC: McFarland and Co. Inc., 1987).

Ragsdale, Kenneth B., *The Year America Discovered Texas: Centennial '36* (College Station: Texas A&M University Press, 1987).

Rodrigues, Louis J., ed., *Dynamics of Growth: An Economic Profile of Texas* (Austin: Madrona Press, 1978).

San Miguel, Guadalupe, Jr., *"Let All of Them Take Heed": Mexican Americans and the Campaign for Educational Equality in Texas, 1910–1981* (Austin: University of Texas Press, 1987).

Sapper, Neil G., "A Survey of the History of Black People of Texas, 1930–1954" (Ph.D. diss., Texas Tech University, 1972).

Stiles, Jo Ann P., "The Changing Economic and Educational Status of Texas Negroes, 1940–1960" (Master's thesis, University of Texas, 1966).

Woolfolk, George R., *Prairie View: A Study in Public Conscience, 1878–1946* (New York: Pageant, 1962).

Yasbley, Suzzanne, *Texas Quilts, Texas Women* (College Station: Texas A&M University Press, 1984).

Articles

Brophy, William J., "Black Business Development in Texas Cities, 1900–1950," *Red River Valley Historical Review* 6 (1981): 42–55.

Burran, James A., "Violence in an 'Arsenal of Democracy': The Beaumont Race Riot of 1943," *East Texas Historical Journal* 14 (1976): 39–51.

Carleton, Don E., "McCarthyism in Houston," *Southwestern Historical Quarterly* 80 (1976): 163–76.

Gillette, Michael L., "Heman Marion Sweatt: Civil Rights Plaintiff," in *Black Leaders: Texans for Their Times*, edited by Alwyn Barr and Robert A. Calvert, 155–87 (Austin: Texas State Historical Association, 1984).

———, "Blacks Challenge the White University," *Southwestern Historical Quarterly* 86 (1982): 321–44.

Hornsby, Alton, Jr., "The 'Colored Branch University' Issue in Texas—Prelude to Sweatt v. Painter," *Journal of Negro History* 61 (1976): 51–60.

Marcello, Ronald E., "Reluctance versus Reality: The Desegregation of North Texas State College, 1954–1956," *Southwestern Historical Quarterly* 100 (1996): 153–85.

Monahan, Casey, "A Bibliography of Texas Music," *Southwestern Historical Quarterly* 98 (1995): 585–999.

Olson, James S., "The Anatomy of a Race Riot: Beaumont, Texas, 1943," *Texana* 11 (1973): 64–72.

Sapper, Neil, "Black Culture in Urban Texas: A Lone Star Renaissance," *Red River Historical Review* 6 (1981): 56–77.

Story, John W., "Texas Baptist Leadership, the Social Gospel and Race," *Southwestern Historical Quarterly* 83 (1970): 29–46.

THE EMERGENCE OF MODERN TEXAS POLITICS

CHAPTER 13

World War II and the subsequent industrialization of Texas created new problems and exacerbated old ones for a state imbued with rural values. Minorities demanded that institutions and political elites better address their needs; federal legislation and court decisions aided their cause. New feminist awareness, increased entry into the marketplace, and expanded educational opportunities led many women to dispute the traditional roles that men had defined for them. The growing strength of minorities, their liberal allies, and women challenged the white male elite's control of the cities, the state government, and the Democratic party.

The urbanization of Texas put new economic pressures on the Democratic leadership. The state had no choice but to expand its social services, educational institutions, and bureaucracy. These actions necessitated raising taxes and searching for additional revenue sources. The traditional agrarian antipathy toward tax increases and historic assumptions that low taxes and minimum state expenses attracted out-of-state industry reinforced the reluctance of a rural-dominated legislature to accept fiscal responsibility. The oil industry, which had accumulated economic and political power during World War II, remained determined not to have to shoulder any new taxes. Consequently, politicians eventually turned to a sales tax rather than a corporate or state income tax for needed revenue.

The political struggles over taxes and state services encouraged the development of a viable state Republican party. The present-day Republican party in Texas originated with conservative unhappiness over the policies of the national Democratic party. As early as 1940, conservative Democrats had voiced suspicions concerning the New Deal's friendliness toward organized labor and minorities. The Texas Regular bolt of 1944 signaled a division among state Democrats, even though the Regulars garnered few votes. When Harry Truman became president in 1945 after Franklin Roosevelt died, conservatives transferred their animosity toward Truman's Fair Deal. The state Democratic leadership attempted to maintain control of the conservative electorate by divorcing itself from the perceived prolabor

Above: Lyndon Johnson during his 1948 senatorial campaign. *Jimmy A. Dodd Photograph Collection, The Center for American History, The University of Texas at Austin, VN1187/a*

and civil rights stance of the national party. The state Democratic party thus factionalized between those who endorsed national party goals and those who did not. The intraparty warfare increased with the social upheavals of the 1960s.

Texas Republicans, meanwhile, embraced extreme conservative positions, attracting into their party those who opposed new taxes, the expansion of civil rights, and welfare legislation. These issues allowed the Republicans to siphon off former Democrats who were convinced that even the conservative wing of Texas's Democratic party was tainted by its association with national Democratic goals. The clash of liberal and conservative politics produced by industrialization and urbanization unraveled the rigid control of politics that the Democratic party had exercised in the state since the Populist revolt of the late nineteenth century. Although the conservative wing of the Democratic party still controlled state politics at the end of the 1960s, the Republican party was beginning to challenge its hegemony, and new political constituencies forced the Democratic leadership to moderate its political stances.

THE POLITICS OF BEAUFORD JESTER

The gubernatorial election of 1946 occurred amidst national and state turmoil. Headlines trumpeted 331 strikes nationwide, and some politicians charged that communists had infiltrated labor unions. Work stoppages in Texas took place at the General Tire and Rubber plant in Waco and Consolidated Vultee Aircraft in Fort Worth. Police arrested picketing employees at the latter, adding to developing tensions over the political role of labor unions, which had begun drives to encourage workers to pay their poll taxes and vote. Black organizations such as the Progressive Voters League and later the Texas Clubs of Democratic Voters conducted voter registration to exploit the *Smith* v. *Allwright* decision that voided the legality of all-white primaries. The emerging controversy of Heman Sweatt's court suit to enter the University of Texas Law School and the continuing struggle of the anti-Truman Democrats to retain control of the state party machinery intensified political divisions.

The 1946 election for governor saw a number of aspiring politicians announce for the vacancy created by Coke Stevenson's retirement. Homer Rainey, the former president of the University of Texas, was the early front runner. After the board dismissed him from the university because he had opposed the firing of liberal professors, Rainey hosted a radio show in which he defended his actions as president. A groundswell of liberal support encouraged Rainey to announce his candidacy for governor. Other leading candidates were Attorney General Grover Sellers, who was considered a moderate but turned to strident anti-Rainey attacks as the campaign heated up; Lieutenant Governor John Lee Smith, who issued dire warnings of the threat of Communist subversion engendered by integration and corrupt labor unions; and Jerry Sadler, a former member of the Railroad Commission. The political extremism of those three contenders allowed Beauford Jester to consolidate moderate and conservative support for his candidacy. His well-financed campaign included the use of billboards, radio spots, newspaper advertisements, and paid campaign workers. Consequently, Rainey's underfunded race became largely defensive, aimed at refuting charges of personal and political extremism. Jester led the first Democratic primary with 38 percent of the vote to 25 percent for Rainey, forcing a runoff betweent the two men.

Jester went on the attack in the second primary. He secured the endorsement of the defeated candidates, consolidating conservative support. Then he announced his platform: no new taxes, no federal interference with state laws, and firm opposition to labor unions and the PAC-CIO, an organization designed to lobby for candidates and causes endorsed by labor forces. He charged that the primary motive behind Rainey's candidacy was to revenge his firing and warned that if the former university president were elected, he would saddle Texans with

a "new, radical and expensive form of government." Indeed, much of the conservative opposition to Rainey centered on his advocacy of a corporate tax and possibly an income tax. Jester won the runoff with 66 percent of the vote and overwhelmed Republican Eugene Nolte, Jr., in the general election. The other major races recorded victories for Allan Shivers as lieutenant governor, Price Daniel as attorney general, and the reelection of Senator Tom Connally.

The new governor represented a group known as the Texas "Establishment," conservative businessmen and state leaders of the Democratic party. At age fifty-three, the affable and distinguished-looking Jester made friends easily. His background was similar to that of many of the postwar establishment candidates: he had graduated from the University of Texas, practiced law, and made money in the oil business. He was appointed to the University of Texas Board of Regents in 1929 and to the Railroad Commission in 1942, on which he still served during his run for governor. By contrast, Rainey's campaign had brought together an embryonic political coalition in the state. It centered on organized labor, potential minority voters,

Above: Governor Beauford Jester delivers his inaugural address, Austin, Texas, January 22, 1947. *The UT Institute of Texan Cultures, No. 3345-G, San Antonio Light Collection*

those who objected to the Texas Regulars' attacks on the University of Texas, and supporters of the Roosevelt and Truman administrations.

The actions of the Fiftieth Legislature, from January to June of 1947, seemed to verify the worst fears of this liberal coalition. It ignored the backlog of problems that had accumulated during the depression and war years: secondary roads and bridges needed repairs; secondary education and the system of colleges and universities had not been upgraded since the era of business progressivism; eleemosynary institutions and the prison system were in disrepair and controlled by nonprofessionals. Instead of addressing these problems, the legislature turned aside the governor's appeal for a state government board to arbitrate labor disputes and passed nine antilabor bills, including the right-to-work law. The legislature devoted much of its energies to thwarting Heman Sweatt's petition to enter the University of Texas by establishing Texas Southern University, expanding graduate education in teacher training and agriculture at Prairie View A&M College, and authorizing an all-black law school in the basement of the capitol in Austin. After fierce debate, the legislature agreed to instruct a committee to recommend potential changes in the public school system; it also passed some appropriations for secondary-road improvements and cost-of-living increases for state employees.

Jester had not been satisfied with the reluctance of the legislature to address the problems of urban Texas. The virulence of the antiunion propaganda, however, prevented him from modifying the legislature's adamant antiprogressive posture. Nevertheless he and Lieutenant Governor Shivers ran a low-key reelection campaign in 1948 on a plank called "the People's Path," which outlined a program for reform of the public schools and higher appropriations for roads, prisons, colleges, and charitable institutions. They argued that they could effect these changes with no increase in taxes. They defeated handily Roger Q. Evans and Caso March that summer in the Democratic primary and the Republican nominee, Alvin H. Lane, the following November.

The 1948 elections focused Texans' attention not on the gubernatorial campaign but rather on the races for the U.S. presidency and the Senate. The Texas Regulars went on record in 1946 as opposing Truman's renomination as Democratic candidate for president. Later actions by President Truman that included integration of the armed services by executive order and the advocacy of an antilynching bill further outraged the Regulars and their supporters. Jester attacked Truman's stands, charging that the 1948 civil rights plan that the president sent to Congress violated states' rights. Yet the governor did not bolt the party when it renominated Truman that summer. Jester answered those who criticized him by urging conservative Democrats to change the party's direction from within.

Many of the Texas Regulars ignored the governor's plea, and they joined other southern Democratic defectors to form the Dixiecrats, who nominated Governor Strom Thurmond of South Carolina for president. On the national level, some northern Democrats left their party to support Henry Wallace, Roosevelt's former vice-president, on the Progressive party ticket. Wallace and

Lyndon Johnson, Harry Truman, John Nance Garner, and Sam Rayburn. *Sam Rayburn Library; copy from the Institute of Texan Cultures, San Antonio, Texas, 68-7*

his supporters maintained that Truman's containment policy would force the Soviet Union into a confrontation with the United States. Political pundits predicted that the defection of the extreme right and left wings of the Democratic party would assure Republican presidential nominee Thomas Dewey of New York an easy victory in November. But the dogged Harry Truman held on to win in an upset victory. His margin of victory in Texas—1,322,000 votes to Dewey's 304,000 and Thurmond's 114,000—was larger than in any other state. The Dixiecrats did best in East Texas, where the issue of race predominated, but, overall, their poor showing in the state militated against the kind of racial demagoguery that would soon come to characterize politics in other southern states.

The senatorial election of 1948 was even more controversial and heated than was the presidential campaign. Lyndon Johnson still chafed over his questionable loss to "Pappy" Lee O'Daniel in the 1941 senatorial campaign. Johnson had intended to run for the Senate again in 1942, but World War II sidetracked his plans. After the war, he geared up his campaign organization to resume his quest for the Senate in 1948. By this time, Johnson had taken some care to distance himself from what many voters considered his link to the New Deal by voting for the Taft-Hartley Act, campaigning as an anti-Communist, and attacking Truman's civil rights platform. Nevertheless, labor-liberal forces preferred Johnson to former governor Coke Stevenson, who denounced government spending and federal encroachment upon states' rights, and who argued that his anti-Communist sentiments went deeper than Johnson's. O'Daniel, knowing that his reelection chances were slim, chose not to run. His decision aided Johnson, who received "Ma" Ferguson's endorsement and garnered support from many former Ferguson voters in East Texas. The third leading candidate was George Peddy, who also stressed the dangers of communism. Johnson ran a hard-driving, up-to-date, and well-financed campaign that featured whirlwind helicopter tours, a direct-mail blitz, and radio advertising. Stevenson led in the first primary by 477,077 votes to Johnson's 405,617 and Peddy's 237,195.

Johnson won the runoff by 87 votes, and Stevenson immediately charged that Johnson had stolen the election. Much of the following contentiousness concerned Box 13 in Jim Wells County, where returns came in late and favored Johnson by 202 votes to 1. Stevenson contested the vote to the State Democratic Election Committee (SDEC), which upheld the count in Box 13 by a vote of 29 to 28. The state Democratic convention, which featured several fistfights between supporters of the two men, affirmed the SDEC's decision. The convention also saw strong lobbying efforts by former governor James Allred and Johnson's campaign manager, John Connally, to affirm Johnson's nomination and remove Texas Regular delegates who had supported Stevenson, replacing them with Jester/Johnson/Truman loyalists. Thus, the state Democratic party machinery passed into the hands of moderates.

Still smarting, Stevenson went to the U.S. District Court and secured a temporary restraining order to keep Johnson's name off the ballot in the general election. U.S. Supreme Court Justice Hugo Black set aside the restraining order, and the full Court later upheld Black's decision. Johnson won the general election. His rise to power in the Senate would be meteoric, first to minority whip in 1952, and then to majority leader in 1955. Meanwhile, Sam Rayburn retained his House seat and continued as Speaker, a position that he acquired in 1940 and held, except from 1947 to 1949 and 1953 to 1955, until his death in 1961. Together, Rayburn and Johnson would make a formidable legislative team in President Eisenhower's second administration. Nevertheless, the controversy generated by his 1948 victory left an aura of suspicion around Johnson that caused many to characterize the new senator as a wheeler-dealer with a tainted past.

After the 1948 election, Governor Jester turned his attention to Texas politics, and he and Shivers sent to the rural-dominated legislature an agenda that addressed some of the state's problems. An antilynching bill was passed. And in addition to the Gilmer-Aikin Acts, the legislature enacted other educational measures that established Lamar College and appropriated more monies for higher education, including the Texas State University for Negroes. The legislature also voted funds for much-needed repair and expansion of the state highway system, aid for the elderly, and improvement of state hospitals. Formation of a Youth Development Council to oversee three schools for wayward juveniles was authorized.

Jester also met with a legislative committee that issued a damning report on Texas prisons. Aided by a letter-writing campaign by the Texas State Council of Methodist Women, the governor appointed new members to the prison board who favored reform and convinced the legislature to allocate more funds for the overcrowded prison system. The new board hired O. B. Ellis, a reformer, as manager of the Texas Prison System. Under his direction, agricultural experts modernized the prison system's farms, constructed new buildings and renovated old ones, and generally improved conditions for prisoners. The Texas Department of Corrections, as the prison system was renamed in 1957, operated efficiently until Ellis's death in 1961. The number of prisoners increased as the state grew; in the 1960s the federal courts would question the treatment of those incarcerated in Texas and elsewhere, as issues such as the overcrowding of prisons and the civil rights of inmates came under litigation.

The legislature refused to assess additional taxes to support the new reforms. Jester vetoed the second-year appropriations bill, forcing a special session of the legislature in 1950 that would have to consider new revenue measures. Jester died before the special session convened, but his administration had scored some impressive victories. Not only did he guide the passage of some progressive legislation, but he cajoled the legislature into approving constitutional amendments to repeal the poll tax, prohibit discrimination on grand and petit juries, establish civil-service guarantees in counties where voters approved of them, and institute annual sessions of and salaries for the legislature. The voters, however, rejected these proposals in November 1950. Despite the passage of antilabor bills and the requirement of loyalty oaths for students and teachers at public universities, the Jester administration was one of political moderation. Nonetheless, it was the first to address the problems of an urban Texas.

ALLAN SHIVERS AND THE POLITICAL BATTLES OF THE 1950s

After Jester's death, Allan Shivers succeeded to the statehouse. The young, forty-one-year-old governor had served two terms as lieutenant governor and was a former state senator. He hailed from Jefferson County, where he had won a reputation as a prolabor state legislator. As lieutenant governor, he had opposed integration, saying, "I am the kind of Texan who believes colored people do not want to go to school with whites." He also had been the first lieutenant governor actually to influence the state senate by shaping its agenda and controlling committees through appointments. As governor, Shivers directed the creation of the Legislative Council, which researches and drafts bills, and the Legislative Budget Board, which prepares the budget for legislative consideration. Before 1949, the state did not have a budget, rather, each agency submitted a memorandum requesting revenue. The governor, consequently, wielded considerable power in selecting which demands went to the legislature. Ironically, then, although his admirers considered Shivers the strongest of the Texas governors, he effectively weakened the office through his administrative changes, which enlarged the powers of the offices of lieutenant governor and speaker of the house. Future lieutenant governors would emulate Shivers in their control over the senate, and since the chair and the vice-chair of the budget board and the council were the lieutenant governor and the speaker of the house, those offices essentially became rivals of the governorship for power.

Shivers addressed the special session of the legislature in January 1950 with his famous "Goat Speech," in which he pointed out that Texas ranked first in oil and last in mental hospitals; first in cotton and last in care for those ill with tuberculosis; first in goats and last in care for wards of the state. The governor coordinated his call for reform with meetings with lobbyists in which he told them that taxes would have to be levied. The legislature moderately increased taxes and appropriations for colleges and hospitals in that session, and the press praised the governor for his effective leadership.

In the election of 1950, Shivers defeated Caso March and five other candidates in the Democratic primary, and Republican Ralph Currie come November. Two strong supporters of the governor—Ben Ramsey, who became lieutenant governor and won reelection to six terms before going to the Railroad Commission, and John Ben Shepperd, who served first as secretary of state and then in 1952 as attorney general—advised and aided Shivers during his terms in office. The governor continued to exercise strong leadership in the 1951 legislature. A redistricting bill, the first in thirty years, passed, as did one to require state inspection of automobiles and liability insurance for drivers. To finance increased appropriations for roads, eleemosynary institutions, teacher salaries, retirement benefits for public employees, and aid to the elderly, Shivers asked for new taxes on consumer goods. The legislature included in the omnibus tax bill a gathering tax on natural gas pipelines, which Shivers opposed. The Supreme Court declared the law unconstitutional, as it was in effect a levy on interstate commerce. Critics of Shivers maintained that Attorney General Shepperd failed to defend the law with much enthusiasm.

Shivers's successes by 1952 included winning control of the state executive committee of the Democratic party. He then purged from positions of power in the old committee any members of the newly growing liberal wing of the party. Some of the liberal discontent with Shivers came from unions, who objected to his support of antilabor legislation, but most of the liberal objections to Shivers stemmed from his endorsement of Republican Dwight David Eisenhower for the presidency. Conservative Democrats had long been unhappy with the Truman administration. They disliked the president's stand on civil rights and accused him of fighting a "no win" war in Korea, being too soft on communism, and overseeing an administration that tolerated corruption. In Texas, these charges dovetailed nicely with conservatives' accusations that Truman and the national Democratic party intended to deprive the state of its rightful claim to the tidelands.

The tidelands were underwater areas adjacent to the coast. Texas claimed that its historic boundaries as a republic gave the state control of three marine leagues (10.5 miles) of the undersea areas attached to its shoreline. The federal government did not contest the claim until 1937, when Secretary of the Interior Harold Ickes ruled that all of the continental shelf past the three-mile limit belonged to the nation. The issue became more critical after World War II, when it became widely known that the disputed territory held rich deposits of petroleum. In 1946, Congressman Hatton Sumners sponsored a bill that affirmed Texas's claim to the tidelands, but Truman vetoed it. The next year, in a case involving California, the U.S. Supreme Court awarded to the federal government paramount power over disputed territory offshore and the minerals contained therein. U.S. Attorney General Tom Clark, a Texan, nevertheless refused to lease the Texas tidelands to oil companies.

The tidelands controversy carried over into Truman's second administration. Shivers and Sam Rayburn wanted a compromise that allowed the state and national government to split the disputed royalties gained from the leasing of underwater lands. Most Texas oilmen wanted the state to retain total control, since Texas collected 12.5 percent royalties on their profits, as compared to the federal government's likely take of 37.5 percent. The issue was complicated by the fact that royalties collected on the tidelands oil by the state would go into the public school fund. State Attorney General Price Daniel demanded that Texas go before the U.S. Supreme Court and press its historic republic claim. The Court rendered a decision in 1950 similar to its earlier California verdict. Rayburn maneuvered a bill through Congress in 1952 that would have awarded the disputed tidelands to Texas. Truman vetoed that one, too. When Adlai Stevenson, the Democratic nominee for president, would not agree to support Texas's tidelands claims, Shivers decided that he would endorse Republican Dwight D. Eisenhower for president in the 1952 election.

Shivers had constructed a strategy early in 1951 that augured a potential party bolt. That year he supported a state law allowing cross-filing for public office: the listing of the same candidate on both the Democratic- and Republican-party primary ballots. Much of the political maneuverings for the next two years revolved around shifting loyalties to the Democratic party. Although the governor hinted that he intended to support the Democratic party, he made no firm commitment and retained control of the state executive committee. His announcement for Eisenhower consequently surprised few but did persuade liberal Democrats to bolt the state convention and denounce the governor. The Johnson/Rayburn forces held the party line and endorsed Eisenhower's Democratic opponent, Adlai Stevenson, yet they did not campaign vigorously in his behalf. The "Shivercrats," as their opponents labeled those who cross-filed, controlled the 1952 election, in which the governor defeated challenger Ralph Yarborough, a liberal Austin lawyer and ex-judge, by nearly 400,000 votes. Eisenhower, meanwhile, carried the state in the general election, and Republicans nominated few candidates, choosing instead to endorse Democrats who cross-filed on both parties' ballots. Attorney General Price Daniel vanquished liberal Democrat Lindly Beckworth to gain the senatorial seat vacated by Tom Connally.

Texas Politics during the Eisenhower Administration

President Eisenhower fulfilled his campaign promise and signed a quit-claim bill that gave Texas control of the tidelands. Republicans hoped that Ike's actions, coupled with those of Shivers, would lead conservative Democrats into the GOP. Such was not to be. As Shivers pointed out, the president's victory was more of a personal than a party triumph. Other problems affected the relations between Eisenhower and the Texas Republicans. The latter represented the far right, or the Robert Taft wing of the party. Most Texas Republicans had supported Taft for the 1952 nomination and denied the validity of moderate, sometimes called modern, Republicanism. They were uncomfortable with Eisenhower's reluctance to offer his unqualified support to McCarthyism, his sending of troops into Little Rock in 1957 to prevent the Arkansas governor from closing Central High School in opposition to federally mandated integration, and his support of the Civil Rights Act of 1957, which Johnson guided through the Senate.

Moreover, the Republicans lost control of Congress in 1954, and Eisenhower's legislative program depended upon the good will of Senate Majority Leader Lyndon Johnson and Speaker Sam Rayburn. If Eisenhower tried to build a Republican party through patronage and appointments, he would alienate those two powerful Democrats. The president's selection of Texas ad-

Ralph Yarborough campaigning, 1954. *Russell Lee Photograph Collection, The Center for American History, The University of Texas at Austin, CN 08230*

visors consisted of moderates: former Democrats Oveta Culp Hobby as secretary of Health, Education, and Welfare and Dillon Anderson as a consultant to the National Security Council, for example. Even though the president defeated Stevenson once again in 1956, carrying Texas by a larger margin than he had in 1952, state Republicans did not prosper. Cross-filing protected conservative Democratic candidates. Congressman Bruce Alger of Dallas claimed the lone Republican congressional victory in 1956.

If Governor Shivers had decided to retire after the successful campaign of 1952, his good reputation might have remained secure. He had successfully kept the conservatives in control of the Democratic party and had weathered the fight over the tidelands. He had administered a scandal-free administration while expanding state services. Moderate Democrats grew uneasy over his support of cross-filing, but not to the point of advocating an open break with him. Liberal Democrats rallied around Yarborough but had no reason for optimism about gaining control of the party machinery.

The year 1954 began auspiciously for Shivers, as he announced for an unprecedented third full term as governor. Then he met with oilmen and others who warned him that if his administration did not expand state services, Yarborough might win the upcoming election. Now Shivers insisted that higher franchise, beer, and gathering taxes—as opposed to higher taxes on oil and gas—be levied to fund teacher salaries and the construction of new buildings for charitable institutions. The legislature and the lobbies complied with Shivers's request, and his credentials were established for the 1954 campaign.

The contest started slowly but turned into a particularly vitriolic one. Yarborough also proposed new taxes and aid to the public schools, but Shivers had somewhat preempted him on these issues. The challenger then focused upon the scandals that had begun to break in the insurance industry. In the seventeen months preceding the 1954 campaign, seventeen Texas insurance companies had gone bankrupt. Clearly, lobbyists had influenced the insurance commission in its regulatory decisions. It was not clear, however, whether Shivers had known of the developing scandal. Nevertheless, Yarborough's attacks emphasized the governor's lack of control over "influence peddling" and charged that the "Shivercrats" were secret Republicans, narrowing Shivers's eventual victory margin.

Shivers, meanwhile, countercharged that the challenger owed his support to "Communist labor racketeers." Then a strike of CIO retail employees in twenty department stores in Port Arthur exacerbated the issue. Shivers maintained that Communists had inspired the strike, and he appointed an investigating committee to determine the extent of Communist subversive activities on the Gulf Coast. After the committee reported that such a danger did indeed exist, the governor called a special session of the legislature to confront the Red menace. He requested that the legislators pass a bill to make membership in the Communist party punishable by death. The lawmakers did not go that far, but they did make belonging to the Communist party a crime punishable by a

$20,000 fine and twenty years in prison, adding another anti-Communist measure to eight existing antisubversion laws. Later, the investigating committee admitted that it could not actually document any Communist activities in Texas labor unions. But the allegation that unions were running Yarborough's campaign had damaged his chances, particularly with the release of a short commercial entitled "The Port Arthur Story." The film, which was shot at 5 A.M., showed deserted streets and idle refineries as a voice-over narrator warned that all of Texas would resemble Port Arthur if unions won control of the state with a Yarborough victory. Yarborough lost in the second primary by about 80,000 votes, and Shivers defeated Republican Todd R. Adams in the general election.

In the midst of the Democratic primary, the U.S. Supreme Court had announced the *Brown* v. *Board of Education of Topeka* decision, which began the desegregation of U.S. public schools. Yarborough had attempted to hedge on the decision by neither condemning the Court nor endorsing integration. Shivers at first reacted to the decision more moderately than had any other southern governor. But as the race between him and Yarborough tightened, the governor resorted to Negrophobia and charged that Yarborough endorsed a completely integrated society. After his reelection, Shivers persisted in his opposition to the *Brown* decision. He and Attorney General John Ben Shepperd endorsed the doctrine of interposition, or using the powers of the state to block federally mandated integration at the local level. With their support, the July 1956 Democratic primary ballot included three referendums: one opposed compulsory attendance at integrated public schools; another outlawed mixed-race marriages; and a third supported state interposition. Texans approved the measures by a vote of four to one. When a white mob prevented the integration of Mansfield High School that fall, Shivers sent in the Rangers to prevent black students from entering the building. He appointed an Advisory Committee on Segregation in the Public Schools, which he instructed to prevent "forced integration."

In late 1956, the advisory committee reported twenty-one profoundly racist proposals for the consideration of the legislature. One included, for example, the shutting down of the public schools to avoid integration. Ignoring the opposition of the Young Democrats, some white church organizations, and Mexican American legislators, the legislature considered the committee's proposals and passed two bills in 1957. One denied state funds to school districts that integrated without local voters' approval, and another authorized a series of reasons—morality, space, transportation, etc.—that a school district might legally cite as justification for not complying with federal integration orders. After Little Rock, the legislature passed a third bill that closed schools if federal troops were used to integrate them and suspended compulsory attendance laws for children of parents who objected to desegregation. Price Daniel, elected governor in 1956, reluctantly signed the laws, but he made no effort to enforce them. The courts later declared them unconstitutional, but one authority maintained that the laws effectively delayed Texas's progress toward integration for the remainder of the decade.

Besides controversy over integration, scandals rocked the last Shivers administration. The issue of failing insurance companies that arose during the 1954 gubernatorial campaign continued, with the legislature responding by enacting stronger regulatory legislation. The more than twenty laws included one that limited the amount of stock insurance companies could sell, and another that allowed the Board of Insurance Commissioners to investigate and pass judgment on the ability of companies and their officers to do business in the state. Still, more insurance companies folded. In December 1955, U.S. Trust and Guaranty, which controlled seventy-four insurance companies in Texas and twenty-two other states, failed. Indeed, the Lone Star State's regulation of insurance companies was so lax that more of them operated in Texas than in all the other states combined. Another investigation charged some members of the insurance board with gross negligence in accepting gifts from the ICT Insurance Company, which also had gone bankrupt. Ben Jack Cage, ICT's founder, was indicted for bribery and embezzlement. He fled to Brazil. The investigations that continued in 1957 of insurance company failures led Daniel to appoint a totally new commission and propose sixteen new insurance regulatory acts. The investigation also revealed that nine state senators and some house members had accepted legal fees and other gratuities from insurance companies.

Other rumors of wrongdoing surfaced over the conduct of State Land Commissioner Bascom Giles. Giles, Shepperd, and Shivers served on the Veteran's Land Board, created in 1950 to purchase land for resale to veterans at a low rates of interest on forty-year notes. Once a veteran had chosen a site and notified the board of a willingness to purchase a property, an official inspector appraised the value of the parcel and authorized the board to purchase it for resale to the veteran. Giles bypassed these checks on the board by selecting corrupt appraisers to evaluate the land and by having all purchases of large tracts (which were subdivided for sale to veterans) sent directly to his office for approval, bypassing the board altogether. He later added the notice of large-tract purchases to the board's minutes. In collusion with real estate dealers, Giles also authorized inflated prices for land for sale to either nonexistent or defrauded veterans. Journalist Kenneth Towery of the *Cuero Record* received a Pulitzer Prize for his investigative reporting leading to the eventual prosecution of the culprits. Giles pleaded guilty to fraud and received a six-year prison sentence. Since Shivers served on the Veteran's Land Board, many Texans assumed that he and Shepperd should have overseen its conduct more carefully. As a result of these scandals, the governor's popularity in the polls dropped from a 64 percent favorable rating in January 1955 to 22 percent that fall.

The troubles of Governor Shivers's last administration overrode any of its accomplishments. The 1955 session of the legislature once more produced aid for public schools, higher education, and state eleemosynary institutions. Shivers also appointed a citizens' committee to study the impact of the 1950s drought, the worst in the state's history. The legislature empowered a Texas Water Research Committee to look into water problems and authorized more powers for the Board of Water Engineers and the newly created Water Pollution Control Council. These agencies, however, did almost nothing to address the increasingly critical issues of what rights individuals and the state had over the control of water resources. The administration, had, at least, shown some public concern for conservation.

INTO THE 1960s UNDER GOVERNOR DANIEL

Shivers ended his tenure as governor as a somewhat embittered man. Possibly, he had remained governor too long and in seven and one-half years had fought too many political battles. His support of Eisenhower in 1952 and again in 1956 cost him whatever power he might have accumulated in the national Democratic party. His decreasing popularity led him to step aside in 1956, and Senator Price Daniel, with the support of Johnson and Rayburn, announced for governor. Meanwhile, the liberal wing of the state Democratic party was optimistic in 1956, with Yarborough carrying their standard into the campaign. He attempted to tie Daniel to the scandals in Austin, since as attorney general Daniel had also been on the Land Board. J. Evetts Haley, W. Lee O'Daniel, and two others joined the race, too. Yarborough forced Daniel into a second primary, which Daniel won by less than 4,000 of the more than 1,300,000 votes cast.

Unhappy with the press coverage given to Yarborough in the 1954 contest, Frankie Randolph of Houston financed the founding of a liberal-loyalist Democratic paper, the *Texas Observer*, edited by Ronnie Dugger. That group joined with Jerry Holleman of the AFL-CIO in creating the Democrats of Texas (DOT), an organization committed to abolishing the poll tax, broadening liberal influence in the state party, and endorsing national Democratic goals. The DOT supported Yarborough in the special election called to fill Price Daniel's unexpired Senate term. In a winner-take-all race that had no primary, Yarborough garnered 38 percent of the vote to Martin Dies's 29 percent and Republican Thad Hutchinson's 23 percent. Sixteen other candidates split the rest of the vote. Yarborough won a full senatorial term in 1958, defeating William A. Blakley, a rich Dallas businessman who owned Braniff Airlines and whom Shivers had appointed to the Senate to succeed Daniel, in the primary and Republican Ray Wittenburg in the general election. The DOT and Yarborough lost control of the party machinery in 1956, when Johnson/Rayburn/Daniel forces consolidated a hold on the State Democratic Executive Committee and refused to seat liberal delegations to the state convention. The bitterness of liberals towards Johnson would last into the next decade.

Daniel retained the governorship in 1958 with an easy primary victory over state senator Henry B. González of San Antonio, and in a closer race in 1960 over the conservative Jack Cox, who later switched allegiances to the Republican party. Daniel changed from conservative to moderate in his three terms in office, and he was always more popular with the people than he was with the legislature. Some of his problems with the latter came from old Shivers supporters, and some came from combative statements he had made during the legislative battles.

But many of Daniel's problems stemmed from the historic issue of taxes. His first term in office deadlocked over that issue, and the governor never solved the problem. Daniel opposed a general sales tax; he wanted instead a continuation of omnibus tax bills, including so-called sin taxes on tobacco and alcohol, and a larger share of taxes on business interests. Many objected to the sales tax because of its regressive nature—the poor pay a higher percentage of their income in sales taxes than do the middle class and the wealthy. After two special sessions in 1961, the legislature passed a limited sales tax of 2 percent. Daniel refused to sign the bill, and it became law without his signature. The sales tax was a selective one, exempting food, drugs, clothing, farm supplies, and some other items.

The trend throughout the next decade was to broaden the sales tax's coverage and increase its rate. Correspondingly, the rate of business taxes dropped in proportion to revenue earned for the state. The only changes in business taxes were two slight increases in the corporation franchise tax and a slight decrease in the severance tax on sulfur. By 1970, the sales tax generated 62 percent of the state's revenue. Thanks to the sales tax, for the first time the state had some way to predict annual revenue income and maintain a consistent pool of tax monies. Despite Daniel's objection to it, the sales tax was the most significant legislation of his administration.

Texas State Capitol. *Photograph by Bill Wright.*

When Daniel left office in 1962, he listed what he considered his accomplishments, they included: long-range plans for water resources; the construction of over forty dams and reservoirs; pay and curriculum revisions for public schools; a highway expansion program; aid for the elderly; upgraded law enforcement agencies; and improvements in penal and eleemosynary institutions. Two measures Daniel cited—regulation of lobbyists and a code of conduct for state officials—were modified by the legislature until the final acts were almost useless. Nevertheless, these were the first laws in over a quarter of a century to look into legislative misconduct. The governor always supported conservative programs at the state Democratic conventions and thus won few liberal allies. His racial policies, supported by Attorney General Will Wilson, moderated sharply the earlier stands of Shivers and Sheppard. No member of the Texas "Establishment" blocked any school doors to prevent integration. Both Johnson and Yarborough voted for the 1957 Civil Rights Act, and only five of twenty-two Texas congressmen signed the notorious Southern Manifesto, which pledged never to allow integration. During the early 1960s, Texas began to depart from its southern racial heritage.

THE DECADE OF JOHNSON AND CONNALLY

Texas politics in the 1960s focused on the career of Lyndon Baines Johnson, who persuaded the legislature in 1959 to move the primary election to May so that he could simultaneously seek renomination to the Senate as well-as the nomination as the Democratic candidate for the presidency. That accomplished, Johnson maneuvered carefully between controlling the state Democratic convention and convincing the national party that he represented western rather than southern values. Meanwhile, the DOT organization attempted to extract a pledge of loyalty from each convention delegate but only secured a general resolution endorsing loyalty to the national party; conservative Democrats retained the state party machinery.

The 1960 Presidential Election

Johnson campaigned vigorously for the presidential nomination. Sam Rayburn and other Johnson advocates worked to portray LBJ as an experienced statesman who offered wisdom and stability in comparison to his young challenger, Senator John F. Kennedy of Massachusetts. But Kennedy was not to be denied. He projected an image of youth and vitality that many present-day candidates still emulate. Johnson, on the other hand, seemed like an establishment candidate, more at home in the Senate wheeling and dealing than he would be in the Oval Office. At the Democratic national convention in Los Angeles, Kennedy claimed the nomination on the first ballot. Then, to the surprise of the convention delegates, to the consternation of liberals, and to the bewilderment of many of Johnson's supporters, JFK offered the Texas senator the vice-presidential nomination, which Johnson accepted. Nonetheless, conservative

Democrats doubted that they could campaign for a platform that endorsed civil rights and denied right-to-work laws.

Meanwhile, the Republicans nominated two-term vice-president Richard M. Nixon for president and Henry Cabot Lodge III for vice-president. Allan Shivers organized the Democrats for Nixon and joined with a very strong Republican party organization that hoped to duplicate its successes of 1952 and 1956. Both candidates considered Texas's twenty-four electoral votes crucial to their victory. Extreme conservatives decried Kennedy's Catholicism and the civil rights planks of the Democratic platform. Johnson tried both to assuage liberals' doubts about his own beliefs and abilities and to keep Texas Democratic. Then there was the ballot, on which Johnson's name appeared twice: for reelection as senator and for the vice-presidency. The Democrats carried Texas by 45,907 votes of the 2,290,553 cast. The national election was equally close, with the Democrats winning by 118,574 votes out of the 68 million cast. Johnson's efforts and the Mexican American "Viva Kennedy" clubs helped carry Texas for the ticket. The Democratic machine in Illinois secured that state's electoral votes. Nixon's supporters would always argue that dubious votes from South Texas and Chicago had tainted the election. Those contentions never were proven, but Johnson's efforts in the South and in Texas undoubtedly made Kennedy president.

The Texas Republican Party after 1960

The Republicans in Texas looked upon the 1960 loss with some optimism. Nixon and Lodge received more votes in Texas than had any previous Republican candidates. Moreover, the Republican challenger for the Senate, John Tower, garnered over 900,000 votes in his race against Lyndon Johnson, by no means a victory but a strong showing for the Republican nonetheless. Tower had run for the Texas House of Representatives in 1954 and lost, but he remained active in the Republican party and by 1958 was well known as a strong Robert Taft supporter and an opponent of regulation of the oil and gas industries. A former college instructor at Midwestern State University in Wichita Falls, Tower was an unknown to most of the Texas electorate. He ran a spirited race against Johnson, however, capitalizing on Johnson's pursuit of the vice-presidency while simultaneously running for reelection to the Senate. Tower's ability as a campaigner made him a strong contender in the 1961 special election to replace Johnson in the Senate.

After Yarborough's earlier victory, the law had been changed to require runoffs in special elections. Liberals split their vote for senator among Henry B. González of San Antonio, Jim Wright of Fort Worth, and Maury Maverick, Jr., of San Antonio. Republicans voted for Tower and conservative Democrats for William Blakley, once again an interim appointment to the U.S. Senate. In the Blakley-Tower runoff, many liberal Democrats voted Republican or "went fishing." Their argument was that to defeat extreme conservative Democratic candidates in runoffs would force the party to choose moderates, and cause rock-ribbed conservatives to switch to Republicanism. Progressive voters' refusal to support a conservative Democrat may well have determined the election of John Tower as the first Republican U.S. senator from Texas since Reconstruction. Tower went on to win three more Senate terms. In 1966, the *Texas Observer* endorsed Tower over his conservative Democratic opponent, the former attorney general Waggoner Carr. The Nixon landslide of 1972 over George McGovern carried Tower to another victory, and he won a narrow election in 1978. Tower gave the Texas Republicans statewide visibility and credibility.

Despite the contentions of some observers, the state Republican party did not ride on the coattails of Senator Tower. There was a strong grass-roots movement afoot in Texas cities. Women volunteers had organized Republican clubs in 1952 and 1954 in the suburbs of Dallas, Houston, Midland, and San Antonio, as well as some other areas. Some of these clubs had sprung from attempts

to control school boards or oversee the book acquisitions of libraries. The Republican membership dropped after President Eisenhower sent troops to enforce school desegregation at Little Rock, but it rebounded after the 1958 Republican state convention condemned the national party. By 1960, the network of clubs had burgeoned from a dozen to over twenty; by 1963, there were more than one hundred. The growth of these clubs demonstrated that many middle-class whites were moving into the Republican party. The philosophy of these new Republicans even led many of the more-conservative Democrats to switch parties. The Republican party then tilted even farther to the right in the early 1960s. Senator Barry Goldwater of Arizona, whose opposition to federally mandated integration and big government made him the national hero of the Texas Republicans, gave the party strong and unified ideological roots, and he became the GOP's standard bearer in the presidential election of 1964.

Texas under Governor Connally

The Democrats, meanwhile, lay racked with dissension between Johnson and Yarborough forces over control of the state party. The liberals in 1962 supported Houston attorney Don Yarborough (no relation to Ralph Yarborough) for governor. John Connally, closely identified with Lyndon Johnson, vied with Price Daniel for conservative and moderate support. Other candidates included former attorney general Will Wilson and retired U.S. general Edwin A. Walker,

Above: John Tower. *The UT Institute of Texan Cultures, No. 16-309, San Antonio Light Collection*

who flew the American flag upside down in front of his Dallas residence to signal that the country was in danger of collapsing from the central government's policy of forced integration. Connally led in the first primary and Yarborough finished second. The press characterized Daniel's campaign as lackluster, and one burdened by the passage of the sales tax during his administration. In the second primary, Connally defeated the liberal Yarborough by 26,250 votes. Meanwhile, Preston Smith, a West Texan who had served three terms in the state house of representatives and six years in the state senate, led all contenders for lieutenant governor. In November, Connally defeated the ex-Democrat-turned-Republican Jack Cox and was elected governor of Texas. The very conservative Cox, however, won 45.6 percent of the vote, and the Texas GOP added a congressman and won seven legislative contests, six in Dallas and one in Midland. The Republicans eagerly looked ahead to 1964, relishing the opportunity to challenge a divided Democratic party, one that furthermore was led by President Kennedy, a man most Texans perceived as a liberal. Then fate intervened.

In Dallas, on November 22, 1963, Lee Harvey Oswald shot and killed President Kennedy and seriously wounded Governor Connally. The assassin's bullets changed the direction of Texas politics. John Connally, little known to most Texans before 1962, when he won his first elective office, now was unbeatable. He had long been a friend of Johnson, serving as his secretary and organizing the famous 1948 senatorial campaign. In the 1950s, Connally had worked for oilmen Perry Bass and Sid Richardson and had lobbied for the passage of legislation in both the Texas legislature and the U.S. Congress. Connally nominated Johnson at the Democratic convention, campaigned for the ticket, and in return was appointed secretary of the navy. His resignation from that post to campaign for and win the governor's office caught Texans by surprise. As governor, Connally achieved a national reputation and was reelected in 1964 and 1966 with only token opposition. Although he probably could have retained his post in 1968 or been elected to the Senate shortly thereafter, he chose to "retire" from public office. He served subsequently as President Richard Nixon's secretary of the treasury, switched parties, and conducted an unsuccessful campaign for the Republican presidential nomination.

Connally believed, as had the old business progressives, that economic growth came from long-range planning, improved higher education, increased tourism, and attraction of out-of-state industry. He assumed that an active government should pass legislation to secure these goals. His first administration was only moderately successful. By the time of his second, he had survived the assassination attempt and through television had developed a positive image of strength and leadership. By this time, too, Ben Barnes had replaced Byron Tunnell as speaker of the Texas house, after Connally appointed Tunnell to fill a vacancy on the Railroad Commission. The Connally/Barnes team increased faculty salaries and university building programs, created a coordinating board for higher education, a fine arts commission, new intergovernmental agencies for water control and health care, and revised the state penal code. Under Connally, the community college system was upgraded, the University of Houston joined the state system, and San Angelo College became a four-year school. The governor did not enjoy unqualified successes. In Connally's last term, Lieutenant Governor Smith opposed many of his policies in the state senate. The legislature turned down a constitutional revision effort, four-year terms for governors, annual legislative sessions, and legalized gambling on horseracing.

Liberals argued that the governor's vision of economic expansion for Texas was based on regressive taxation and excluded the minorities and the poor. Liberal Democrats also chafed at Governor Connally's control of the state party machinery. In the 1963 congressional debates over what would become the historic Civil Rights Act of 1964, Connally separated himself from the Kennedy administration by opposing the public accommodations section of the bill. Connally later objected to several of the Great Society measures advocated by his good friend Lyndon Johnson. Moderate and conservative Democrats could consequently support the governor with enthusiasm and endorse his hegemony over the state Democratic executive committee. Connally exercised such control over the state Democratic party that he led its delegation to the 1968 national convention even after he had announced he would not seek reelection. The governor's prestige and political philosophy, then, retarded the development of liberalism within the state party and—ironically, given his later conversion to the GOP—lessened the appeal of the Republicans.

The Johnson Presidency

Republicans faced other problems. The assassination of Kennedy sent Johnson to the White House. Now, with a Democratic Texan as president, any Republican hopes for election victories in 1964 seemed dubious. Moreover, the assassination had occurred in Dallas, where *Life Line*, the Red-baiting radio program originated, where Edwin Walker lived, and where Adlai Stevenson, ambassador to the United Nations, had been spat upon and jostled by an angry mob. Dallas, the Republican party's greatest stronghold in Texas in 1964, was a city anxious to claim an image of conservative moderation and escape from a national media image that portrayed it as a city of racists and radical right wingers. Moreover, Johnson brought temporary unity to the Democratic party. He stifled conservative challenges to Senator Yarborough in the primary. He won endorsements by Shivers and Oveta Culp Hobby for his presidential election. Johnson's 1964 presidential campaign successfully identified the Republican presidential candidate, Barry Goldwater, and Texas Republicans with extremism and the radical right. When the ballots were counted, Johnson defeated Goldwater by over 700,000 votes. In Texas, the Republicans lost both of their congressional seats and all but one of their state legislative positions. Furthermore, George H. W. Bush, who had served as congressman from Houston and was considered by many to be the Republican candidate most likely to win a statewide race, failed in his bid to unseat Senator Yarborough.

The Johnsons, Humphreys, Connallys, and Yarboroughs deplaning in Austin, 1964. *Russell Lee Photograph Collection. The Center for American History, The University of Texas at Austin, VN-RY9-64-4-3*

The Johnson triumph did not damage the Republican party in the same way, however, that Franklin Roosevelt's overwhelming victory in 1932 had. Now that Johnson represented a national and not a state constituency, he instituted the Great Society, an expansion of the New Deal/Fair Deal programs that included such measures as Headstart, Medicare (health care for the elderly), and the

Neighborhood Youth Corps. Many conservative Texans and other Americans viewed this and similar legislation with disdain. In addition, by 1967 the nation was sharply divided over the nature of the Vietnam War, the direction of the civil rights movement, and the rise of the youth movement—what became known as the "counterculture"—advocating radical social change. The Republican party seemed a natural home for those who opposed societal changes. For those on the left who saw U.S. involvement in the Vietnam War as a failed Democratic enterprise, the answer was to remove the party's leaders. The ensuing divisions in the national and state Democratic parties would take more than a decade to heal. Johnson announced his decision not to seek renomination on March 31, 1968. The anguish of Vietnam ended his political career.

The 1968 Elections and Their Aftermath

The 1968 announcements by both Johnson and Connally that they would not run for reelection offered opportunities both to conservative and liberal politicians. The Democrats nominated Vice-President Hubert Humphrey for the presidency. Humphrey, however, was not a unanimous choice; antiwar Democrats thought him too closely identified with Johnson, and some conservatives objected to his earlier strong stands for civil rights. Governor George C. Wallace of Alabama ran for the presidency as an independent on the American party ticket. His blatantly racist campaign was aimed at preventing any candidate from receiving a majority in the electoral college. As their candidate, Republicans chose Richard Nixon, now the acknowledged leader of the conservative wing of their party. Connally, Johnson, and Yarborough united their efforts on behalf of Humphrey, who carried Texas by less than 40,000 votes but lost the national election to Nixon. Although Wallace won the electoral votes of five southern states, he polled only 584,000 out of the more than 3 million popular votes cast in the Lone Star State. Texas political issues had obviously severed their southern moorings.

Although cheered by the national victory, state Republicans did not celebrate many victories. Senator Tower and three congressman, including George Bush, constituted the party's national congressional delegation. Eight members of the Texas house and two state senators were Republicans. Liberal Democrats were equally disappointed. Don Yarborough led in the first Democratic gubernatorial primary, but Preston Smith defeated him in the runoff. Smith, in turn, triumphed over Paul Eggars, the Republican nominee closely identified with Tower, by a margin of 57 percent. Speaker of the House Ben Barnes garnered more than 2 million votes in the general election for lieutenant governor, the first Texas politician to poll that many votes. Many observers considered Barnes the heir apparent to the Connally/Johnson mantle and a future national political star.

The conservative Democrats, meanwhile, had adopted a strategy by 1968 that saw them win hard-fought primaries by rallying middle- and high-income voters to edge out candidates supported by African Americans, lower-income whites, and Mexican Americans. After defeating their liberal opponents, conservatives persuaded the traditional Democratic constituency to support them. While some of the higher- and moderate-income voters deserted the conservative Democrats for Republican candidates in the general election, the willingness of the dispossessed and labor unions to support the Democratic party nominees offset these defections. The 1970 election, for example, witnessed the high point of conservative Democratic success in Texas and the shrewdness of its political strategy. Smith coasted to an easy victory over Eggars.More important, Lloyd Bentsen, Jr., a Houston millionaire and former congressman whom Johnson had forced out of the 1964 Democratic senatorial primary, defeated Ralph Yarborough in the primary. Bentsen attacked Senator Yarborough for his "dovishness" on Vietnam and his ties to the national Democratic party. Yarborough defended the national party's stand against vested interests and pointed out his positive accomplishments as a supporter of civil rights and the originator of the G.I. Bill of Rights for Korean and

Vietnam War veterans. But Bentsen prevailed, and after vanquishing Yarborough he turned back George Bush's challenge in the general election by warning labor, African Americans, and Mexican Americans that a second Republican senator would support Nixon's economic policies, which aided the wealthy. As the *Houston Chronicle* pointed out, Bentsen's victory dampened once again liberal Democratic and Republican hopes for a two-party Texas.

CHALLENGES TO THE WHITE MALE ELITE FOR CONTROL OF TEXAS

Forces had risen in Texas by 1970 that both moderated and weakened the grip of white male Texans on the political system of the state. One of the major factors was federal intervention. The U.S. Supreme Court ruled in *Baker* v. *Carr* in 1962 and *Reynolds* v. *Sims* in 1964 that both houses of a state legislature must be regularly reapportioned so that every senator or representative rep-

Above: George H.W. Bush at the University of Texas during his unsuccessful 1970 senatorial campaign. U.T. *Student Publications, Inc. Photographs. The Center for American History, The University of Texas at Austin, DI 00236*

resented roughly the same number of voters. This so-called "one man, one vote" principle altered Texas politics. In 1963, for example, after redistricting to conform with 1960 census figures, 42 percent of the Texas population could elect a majority of the house and 30 percent a majority of the senate. These figures betrayed the fact that rural and small towns, the center of conservative Democratic politics, gave the white elites disproportionate strength in the legislature, even as their role in the direction of the state's economy and society was diminishing. The control of the legislature by rural Texans also discriminated against minorities and Republicans. The inner cities were evolving into mostly ethnic ghettos and the suburbs into middle- and upper-middle-class enclaves. The former supported liberal Democrats and minority candidates, and the latter tended to elect Republicans. Court-ordered redistricting aided the growth of these political groups. Eventually, the concept of one man, one vote necessitated the abolition of multimember congressional districts, and in 1972, court suits restricted countywide legislative races in Bexar and Dallas Counties. Some effects of these redistricting efforts were apparent by that year, as Republicans won seventeen seats in the state house, three in the state senate, and four in Congress.

Another round of federal intervention had begun in 1964, when the states ratified the Twenty-fourth Amendment to the U.S. Constitution, which barred the poll tax as a possible requirement for voting in federal elections. The Texas legislature retained the poll tax as a requirement for voting in state elections (one of only five states to do so) until the U.S. Supreme Court ruled that a poll tax as a prerequisite for any type of voting violated the Fourteenth Amendment. Connally called a special session of the legislature, which passed a voter-registration act that required annual registration by all voters during a four-month period that ended on January 31. This shortened registration period, purposely timed to end a full nine months before election day, was designed to hold down the number of voters. The Court struck down the Texas registration law in 1971 as an unconstitutional deterrent to minority voting. Since then, Texans have been able to register to vote at anytime during the year, have been automatically reregistered by voting, and have been eligible to vote as long as they were registered thirty days before an election. The Twenty-sixth Amendment to the U.S. Constitution in 1971 accorded the right to vote to eighteen-year-old citizens, lowering the minimum-age requirement by three years.

The third round of federal intervention involved controlling state election codes; it was manifested in the Voting Rights Act of 1965. Congress recognized that the low voter turnout among African Americans in the South was due to state or local voting restrictions. The 1965 act outlawed such procedures and provided for federal observers and officials to monitor elections and voter registration. Furthermore, southern states had to submit proposed election procedural changes to the federal government. Congress extended the Voting Rights Act in 1970 and in 1975 broadened it to include Hispanics. It was extended for another twenty-five years in 1982, placing all Texas election procedures under continuing federal scrutiny. The federally mandated changes in election procedures helped explain why the percentage of African Americans of voting age who actually registered to vote in the state grew from 35 percent in 1960 to 56.8 percent in 1970 and to 65 percent in 1976. During the same period, the percentage of whites who registered grew from 42.5 percent to 69 percent.

The lessening of voting restrictions changed the governing of many Texas cities. Ever since the Progressive Era, conservative white business leaders had used a variety of techniques to limit the influence of African Americans and Hispanics in urban politics. One such approach was the use of at-large elections, in which geographic districts or wards are abolished and the entire city is essentially made into one large district. Candidates then run in citywide or countywide races for city council or legislative seats, thus diluting the potential voting strength of racially or ethnically segregated neighborhoods.

Another way that the Establishment sought to limit the influence of the newly enfranchised voters involved the creation of well-organized political "associations," such as the Citizen's Charter Association in Dallas and the Good Government League in San Antonio. By law, city government in most Texas cities was nonpartisan, so in the absence of political parties, these political associations took it upon themselves to recruit and endorse whole slates of candidates and to manage and finance their campaigns. The associations, of course, selected their candidates from among their fellow elites, defending their actions on the grounds that businesspersons could bring disinterested rather than partisan political judgment to the governing of cities.

These practices came under attack, beginning in the 1960s. African Americans, Hispanics, and liberal whites put considerable pressure on cities to modify at-large voting. In several cases, after 1970, these groups instituted legal actions based on the Voting Rights Act that eliminated or modified at-large districts. The Establishment machines also came under, attack. In the early 1970s, the Citizen's Charter Association of Dallas, for example, lost the mayoral election and ceased to exist, and the conservative Good Government League of San Antonio was defeated by a combination of liberal and Mexican American voters. Local political contests became more heated, and blacks and Hispanics won more posts. In 1970, 41 African Americans held local office in Texas, ranking the state nineteenth nationally in total number of offices held by blacks; seven years later, the number more than tripled to 158, for a ranking of fourteenth. In 1970, local elective officials in Texas with Hispanic surnames totaled 723. Clearly, the number of minorities elected to local office did not match the percentages of minorities in the population, but by the 1970s, Texas was overwhelmingly an urban state, and the majority of its citizens resided in areas where municipal governments made decisions each day that affected their lives. These changes and the increase in minority representation in local government were profound.

The Civil Rights Crusade
BLACK TEXANS

White elites did not voluntarily surrender power, nor did the federal government voluntarily decide to advocate minority rights. World War II gave racism a bad name, and struggles during the Cold War in the Third World further encouraged attacks upon segregation at home. The exodus of southern blacks to northern cities made the African American vote the "swing" vote in urban congressional districts and in those states with a large number of electoral votes. Philosophy, pragmatism, and politics combined to encourage national stands against segregation. Black organizations fought for the right to vote and against the segregated society. The Progressive Voters League and the Texas Club of Democratic Voters disseminated information on voter registration and worked otherwise to inform blacks about politics. The NAACP and other organizations

instituted suits against suffrage restrictions and gerrymandered legislative and congressional districts. The successful attacks on voting restrictions sent the first blacks since the nineteenth century to the Texas legislature in 1966: Barbara Jordan to the state senate, and Curtis Graves, a graduate of Texas Southern University, and J. E. Lockridge, an attorney from Dallas, to the house. Jordan, who also graduated from Texas Southern University and held a law degree from Boston University, was the first African American woman to serve in the state senate, the first woman to give a keynote address at a national (Democratic) party convention, and the first African American congresswoman from Texas and the South. Furthermore, Jordan's poise and eloquence as a member of the congressional Judiciary Committee, as it conducted its investigation of the illegal acts of President Richard M. Nixon and his administration (the Watergate hearings), won for her a national following.

Increased political strength for black Texans doomed de jure segregation, just as voting restrictions in the early twentieth century had made de jure segregation possible. Blacks' struggle to reestablish their civil rights, however, included court suits and the direct confrontation of segregated institutions. In 1954 and 1956, the Interstate Commerce Commission and the Supreme Court ruled against segregation on buses. Cafeterias in bus stations, airports, federal buildings, and the offices of municipal agencies desegregated by the early 1960s. Through negotiations with public officials and some court suits, public facili-

Above: Barbara Jordan, U.S. Rep of the 18th Congressional District of Texas, receiving honors after christening the *U.S.S. Miller*, the first U.S. Navy ship named after an African American. *U.S. Dept. of the Navy photograph. The UT Institute of Texan Cultures, No. 73-1032*

ties such as libraries, parks, golf courses, beaches, and the restrooms and eating areas that served them, were integrated during the same period.

The idea of direct confrontation of segregated institutions (rather than relying on lengthy court cases) through nonviolent sit-ins that had begun in 1960 with student protests in Greensboro, North Carolina, spread to Texas. That year, students at Wiley and Bishop Colleges staged nonviolent demonstrations. Protests and demonstrations against segregated theaters and restaurants were carried out by black and white students and their allies nearby the campuses of Texas Southern University, the University of Texas at Austin, North Texas State University, and other schools in 1961. In protest of segregation, the NAACP, the Congress of Racial Equality (CORE), headed by Texan James Farmer, and students at Prairie View A&M and some other colleges led boycotts of merchants in Hempstead, San Antonio, Austin, and Houston, as well as a few other places. Fear of bad publicity or loss of business persuaded most hotels, theaters, and restaurants to desegregate by the early 1960s. The Civil Rights Act of 1964 and five state acts in 1969 that overturned older Jim Crow legislation ended de jure segregation.

Nationally, the nature of the civil rights movement changed after 1965. Young African Americans adopted the slogan "black power," renounced a commitment to nonviolence, and demanded an end to de facto segregation. One result was a series of riots and fires in ghettos that began in the Watts area of Los Angeles in August 1965 and lasted through 1968; another was that the Student Nonviolent Coordinating Committee (SNCC) and CORE abandoned black/white coalitions. In some cases, black power came to mean black separatism, or at least denying whites positions of power in African American organizations.

No ghettos burned in Texas, and only a few violent confrontations between the police and African Americans occurred. At Texas Southern in 1967, African Americans called a meeting to debate grievances over the public schools and police conduct in the ghetto. The arrival of the police called forth a hail of stones and bottles, and the confrontation evolved into an exchange of gunfire between police and students. One police officer was killed, possibly by a ricocheting police bullet, and five black students were indicted for inciting a riot; because of lack of evidence, they were never tried. The People's Party Two, whom the police and the press considered a revolutionary group, and the Houston police engaged in a shoot-out three years later. Carl Hampton, the party chairman, was killed. Black bystanders said that the officers fired first, but the white media and public opinion backed the police. Black persons were similarly suspicious of the nature of justice in Texas when a Dallas court sentenced Ernie McMillan and Matthew Johnson, SNCC leaders, to ten years in jail for a protest that did $211 worth of damage to a ghetto grocery store. Similarly, Lee Otis Johnson, a black activist from Texas Southern University, received thirty years for allegedly passing a marijuana cigarette to an undercover Houston police officer. To African Americans, the sentences seemed too harsh, and good examples of white determination to suppress the black power movement.

By 1971, the backlash had set in. White Texans joined the national consensus that argued that the federal government had gone far enough in correcting societal inequalities with the civil rights acts. The second reconstruction had ended. Pressures from state and federal agencies and infighting within the various movements themselves dissipated much of the reformist energies. Like most other North Americans, blacks had grown weary of the controversies of the 1960s. The decade closed with legal segregation dead but with Texas not entirely desegregated. Many blacks believed that equality before the law simply did not exist and that the problems African Americans faced—rampant unemployment and unequal access to education and certain professions—would persist into the next decades.

Texas Mexicans

The same kind of political activism that swept the African American community activated Texas Mexicans. LULAC and the G.I. Forum remained strong defenders and protectors of the interests of Mexican Americans as the 1960s began, but these organizations resembled the NAACP in that they shied away from active involvement in politics. The election of Raymond Telles as mayor of El Paso in 1957, and especially Henry B. González's campaign for governor in 1958, mobilized the Mexican American community and intensified the political activities of Tejanos. Although the Texas state senator lost the race, he left behind a political organization that plunged into the 1960 presidential campaign of John F. Kennedy. The veterans of the González campaign joined with other politically minded Tejanos, including some members of LULAC and the G.I. Forum, to create the "Viva Kennedy" clubs. The grass-roots movement generated by these organizations did not die after Kennedy's election; rather it worked to keep the political spirit alive, since Kennedy soon defaulted on his promise to appoint Hispanics to federal posts. The result was the founding of the Political Association of Spanish-speaking Organizations (PASO).

PASO endured growing pains in its early years, as moderates and militants argued over what direction the organization should take. The liberal element was in control of PASO by 1963 when, working with the Teamsters, it elected an all Mexican American slate to the city council of Crystal City. The Crystal City revolution was short-lived, however; a new coalition reclaimed the council two years later. But the victory was both symbolic and very important because it notified Anglos that no longer could the white minority in heavily Hispanic South Texas rule unchallenged. Crystal City portended the passing of the old order.

A much broader and more intense political movement that united the various ideological and economic interests of the heterogeneous Texas Mexican community began in the mid-1960s. This groundswell, known as the Chicano movement, paralleled similar social revolts in the nation and in the state. LULAC leaders had opposed protest marches, criticism of mainstream institutions, or dramatic shows of discontent, but by 1965, they also began to adopt the newer strategies of protest marches employed by Mexican American college students, African Americans, women, and antiwar groups. The "movimiento," as its adherents dubbed it, took on its distinctive characteristics with the summer 1966 farm workers' strike and march in the Rio Grande Valley.

The South Texas farm workers toiled under deplorable conditions and without benefit of union representation. PASO members in Starr County had considered striking before 1966, when a wildcat strike against eight major growers occurred almost spontaneously. The strike seemed preordained to fail, and the importation of Mexican laborers and the overt hostility of the Texas Rangers and local Starr County law enforcement officers swiftly broke it. Still determined, the organizers of the strike undertook a march to the state capitol to protest the plight of farm workers and generate sympathy for them. Governor Connally, accompanied by Speaker of the House Ben Barnes and Attorney General Waggoner Carr, met the hundreds of marchers at New Braunfels and informed them that by no means would he call a special session of the legislature or approve or address a Labor Day Rally in Austin to be dedicated to the exploited farm laborers. Now, thousands of sympathizers, including members of LULAC, the G.I. Forum, and PASO, joined the marchers for the last leg of the 290-mile journey. The sixty-five-day march became synonymous with courage, adventure, and justice, and it had only been strengthened by Connally's offering of a cold shoulder to the marchers. The whole affair galvanized the Texas Mexican community, and it catalyzed a militancy that would last until the mid-1970s.

The Chicano movement, so-called by the younger activists who preferred the term *Chicano*, actually comprised several movements, and these different strains clashed ideologically at times over the agenda of reform. The older middle-class organizations, while more outspoken than they had been in the past, still preferred to use mainstream channels to win concessions for their constituents. They instituted court suits, along with the Mexican American Legal Defense and Education Fund (MALDEF) founded in 1968, to desegregate schools and challenge voting inequities. Younger groups, on the other hand, tended to be more militant and engendered more grass-roots support. They prepared for direct confrontations with the Anglo establishment. Through the Mexican American Youth Organization (MAYO) and the Raza Unida Party (RUP), they articulated a militancy that denounced white society for its oppression of Texas Mexicans and accused middle-class Mexican American leaders of being both faint-hearted and accommodationist. The trademarks of the young included the use of the term *Chicano* and the embracing of the fashions of the 1960s (such as the wearing of long hair), pre-Columbian symbols of Mexicanism, proclamations of ethnic integrity, and the need for self-determination.

School boycotts, protest marches, and lawsuits against social inequities marked the movimiento. Politically, RUP offered an alternative to the other two parties, which, RUP members argued, ignored the needs of Mexicanos. Two RUP

416 ❖ The History of Texas

candidates and the party's founder, José Ángel Gutiérrez, won seats in 1970 on the Crystal City school board, implementing a new curriculum and enacting other changes such as a federal free-lunch program. Ramsey Muñiz, the RUP candidate for governor in 1972, polled 6 percent of the popular vote and almost machinated a Republican victory by draining off Democratic voters. The example of Crystal City and the 1972 RUP race inspired similar efforts throughout South Texas. RUP had disappeared by the mid-1970s, having fallen victim to problems common to all third parties: they tended to revolve around a single issue, lacked strong organizational roots, and saw the enthusiasm they generated recede quickly. The 1976 conviction of Muñiz for engaging in a conspiracy to distribute marijuana also lessened RUP's appeal. The movimiento, like black power, moderated in the mid-1970s, but the social protest of the 1960s had dismantled Jim Crow and created a racial pride and awareness that broke old assumptions and the limits of ethnic advancement.

Texas Women

Urbanization and the rise of feminism also challenged the long-held restrictions that men placed on women's role in society. Although they made up a majority of the population, women faced problems in employment and in public affairs similar to those of racial and ethnic minorities. The women's movement of the 1960s and 1970s could build on the failed expectations of women's experiences in the 1950s. In 1950, for example, women earned only 24 percent of degrees awarded nationally in professional studies and the liberal arts; by 1965, the number had grown to over 40 percent. But these new degree earners found that the jobs offered to them were still mostly as salesclerks or secretaries. The 1960s, however, witnessed an increase in women's demands for social and economic opportunity. Young women in Texas were involved in the civil rights movement, worked on such underground newspapers as the *Austin Rag* and Houston's *Space City*, read earlier works by such women as Betty Friedan (who advocated equal wages and equal opportunity for women) and debated what role feminism should have in their lives. The impact of new birth-control techniques (such as the Pill) and the sexual revolution, as well as a willingness on the part of both sexes to delay marriage in order to first achieve a higher degree of financial stability or education, changed the primary goal of women in the 1950s of marrying and quickly rearing a family.

The federal government aided the cause of women. Although women had secured the right to serve on juries in 1954, it was not until after Title VII of the 1964 Civil Rights Act and later court suits that married women gained control of their property and actions were taken against discrimination of women in the workplace. Under Title IX of the Educational Act of 1972, colleges were required to institute affirmative-action programs. That year, too, Sarah Weddington, an attorney from Texas, won a landmark case in the U.S. Supreme Court, *Roe* v. *Wade*, that struck down state laws forbidding abortions during the first three months of pregnancy.

The political and legal activism of women's groups caused the male establishment to take note of their demands. The National Organization for Women (NOW), founded by Friedan to end discrimination in the workplace based on gender, established chapters in Texas in the 1960s. Women's rights advocates in 1971 organized the Texas Women's Political Caucus (TWPC) to promote political activism and participation in party politics. The efforts of these organizations and the Business and Professional Women's Clubs helped secure the 1972 equal legal rights amendment to the state constitution and the 1973 legislative approval of the Equal Rights Amendment (ERA) to the federal Constitution. Moreover, in 1972 Frances (Sissy) Farenthold's unsuccessful but popular campaign for the Democratic nomination for governor made many aware of political opportunities for women.

The women's movement seemed to wane after 1972. Divisions between radical and moderate feminists, plus the inability to expand the movement much outside the middle class, stagnated reform efforts. The ERA failed to achieve national approval. And the very success of NOW and other national organizations in changing abortion laws called forth a tremendous negative reaction among Catholics and fundamentalist Protestants. Texas now has a law banning third-trimester abortions. The emergence of the religious right, organized around a "right to life" crusade, pointed toward a political ideology that stressed the virtues of home, motherhood, and what its adherents described as traditional "family values." It seemed opposed to many of the feminist aspirations of the late 1960s and early 1970s.

But the apparent decline of the women's movement was misleading, as it continued long after the militant rhetoric of the 1960s had softened. Women entered the workplace in the next decades in increasing numbers. Whether by choice or by necessity, two-income households became the norm rather than the exception, and that fact modified traditional gender roles and childbearing practices. Women as a majority of the population introduced new issues that politicians could not ignore. Consequently, a rather quiet revolution took place. Texas cities subsidized rape crisis centers and shelters for battered women, and national campaigns endorsed daycare centers and other issues of importance to working women. The state legislature, for example, enacted a spousal rape law in 1986.

Moreover, women entered politics more frequently and with more success. Women won 698 public offices in 1982, including the election of Ann Richards as state treasurer. Richards was the first woman to hold a statewide office in fifty years. Furthermore, she gave the keynote address at the 1988 Democratic nominating convention and was elected governor of Texas in 1990. Three women served in the state senate in 1987 and thirteen in the house, and Mayor Kathy Whitmire of Houston and Mayor Annette Straus of Dallas led the two largest cities in the state. The urbanization that produced new jobs and the feminism that demanded an increased role for women was finally eroding, albeit gradually, the prewar image of a macho Texas.

SHARPSTOWN
AND THE END OF AN ERA

The impact of minorities and women on Texas politics was not readily apparent in the administration of Governor Preston Smith. He advocated a moderate conservative stance that differed but little from that of the previous administration. Given his conservative philosophy, that moderation alone made his administration somewhat surprising. The governor himself, however, sharply contrasted with John Connally: Smith was not as articulate, nor did he present as attractive a figure on television. Smith represented West Texas, and his political support came from rural areas and small cities, not from suburbs, middle-class voters, or the urban business community. He encountered additional difficulties in that the public perceived of him as something of a political accident. Although he won two comparatively easy victories, many saw those as resulting from the weakness of liberal challengers, and they consequently saw Smith's administration as one in a holding pattern, waiting for Barnes to claim the governorship. Lieutenant Governor Barnes, handsome and articulate (a national magazine ranked him as a leading young politician with the potential to become a U.S. senator and possibly president), stood in the wings and weakened the governor's political clout.

Smith's two terms reflected his ambivalence about how forcefully a governor should push a program through the legislature, as well as the weakness of his political position vis-à-vis the state senate. Moreover, Speaker Gus Mutscher ran the house, and he held in disdain any legislation that hinted at reform. Ultimately, the governor's program met mixed success. He secured a minimum-wage law, development of medical schools in Houston and Lubbock, and spending for vocational education. The legislature turned down his request for a slight increase in taxes. The governor tentatively endorsed a 1969 Barnes/Mutscher proposal that would have eliminated the sales-tax exemption on food, but he then was embarrassed when a "housewives' revolt" forced the house to unanimously kill the bill. Urban voters rejected a water proposal that favored West Texas and seemed very expensive. The electorate also had turned down a proposed increase in legislative salaries, but it approved of lowering the voting age to eighteen and the legal sale of liquor by the drink.

Smith won in 1970 by a smaller percentage over his Republican opponent, Paul Eggars, than he had garnered in 1968. Some maintained that the Bush race against Bentsen, who had defeated Yarborough in the Democratic primary, turned out more Republican voters, while Smith's administration and Bentsen's victory convinced liberals to "stay home." Many viewed the second Smith administration as a lame-duck one before it even began, citing the assumed challenge of Barnes in 1972. But political arguments and personal ambitions gave way in 1971 to scandals that implicated or besmirched a number of the members of the legislature, dominated the governor's last term in office, and torpedoed Barnes's political career.

The federal Securities and Exchange Commission (SEC) announced in 1971 a probe of Texas officials and some businessmen who allegedly profited from illegal manipulation of stock-market transactions. In a special session in 1969, a banking bill that would have exempted state banks from the regulation of the Federal Deposit Insurance Corporation was guided through the legislature by Gus Mutscher. Frank Sharp, who controlled the National Bankers Life Insurance Company and the Sharpstown State Bank, was the lobbyist and chief advocate of the measure. While Sharp lobbied for the bill, several legislative leaders bought stock in his life insurance company with money from unsecured loans from his bank. The officeholders then sold their stock to a Jesuit organization, which took Sharp's advice and paid over-the-market price for the shares. Smith and Dr. Elmer Baum, chairman of the state Democratic Executive Committee, netted about $125,000 from the transaction. Mutscher, two of his aides, and some other legislators also attempted to profit from the scheme. Smith, explaining that he had not understood the legislation, vetoed the bill. Sharp's empire promptly collapsed, the Jesuits lost their stock investment, and the SEC moved in to investigate the scandal.

Despite the charges of malfeasance, Mutscher attempted to retain his rigid control of the house. He appointed a committee of his friends to investigate the charges, and its report exonerated those accused. Nevertheless, a coalition of liberals, Republicans, and mavericks nicknamed "the Dirty Thirty" joined to denounce the speaker and the report and proceeded to rebell against Mutscher's heavy-handed tactics. The speaker in turn picked a committee to redistrict the house based upon the 1970 census. The 1971 plan drew most of the Dirty Thirty into districts in which they would have to run against each other or in which they could not win. A federal district court overturned the Mutscher plan in January 1972, but by that time the speaker and two of his legislative henchmen had been indicted by a Travis County grand jury. They were convicted on charges of conspiracy and bribery in Abilene in March 1972.

The turmoil of the scandal, dubbed "Sharpstown," led to a groundswell for reform. The 1972 election, consequently, sent seventy-two new members to the house and fifteen to the senate. Mutscher, who ran for reelection despite his conviction, lost. So did Smith, who ran fourth in the primary. But to the surprise of many political observers, Barnes placed third. Although he had not been implicated in the scandal, the lieutenant governor had borrowed money from Sharp's bank and fell victim to the anti-incumbent fervor. Frances "Sissy" Farenthold, a member of the Dirty Thirty, placed second, and Dolph Briscoe, a millionaire rancher and former state legislator from 1947 to 1957, led the first primary.

Farenthold's campaign was a fitting final hurrah for the 1960s. She spoke on college campuses to jubilant student audiences. She proposed that the state pass corporate taxes, increase social services, consider a gun-control law, and upgrade education. Her volunteers knocked on doors, posted placards, and campaigned zealously. Her campaign lacked adequate financing, however. Business and financial interests rallied to Briscoe, who defeated Farenthold by 1,095,168 to 884,594. In the general election, Briscoe won over Republican Hank Grover by a little under 100,000 votes. Ramsey Muñiz, La Raza party candidate, collected 214,118 votes. Finally, 1972 saw President Richard Nixon trounce the Democratic nominee, George McGovern, by over 1 million ballots nationwide. The president's landslide helped win for Senator Tower a 300,000-vote margin over moderate Democrat Barefoot Sanders, who had derailed Ralph Yarborough's comeback attempt in the Democratic primary.

Overall, the Sharpstown scandal wrought fewer changes than observers supposed it might. New and open politics did not come to Texas, although the next session of the legislature in 1973 did adopt some reforms, including registration of lobbyists, requirements for open public meetings of most state agencies, reports on campaign financing, and a law requiring state officials to disclose their sources of income. But the election of 1972 did symbolize the end of an era. Barnes was the last candidate of the Johnson/Connally mold. Although the Establishment would find new candidates, they were more moderate than those before them. Briscoe ran open conventions and generally had good relations with labor organizations. Indeed, one of the reasons why the Farenthold campaign was underfinanced was that union leaders failed to endorse her. They saw Briscoe as no threat, and the slight division between organized labor and Farenthold represented a problem with the liberal/labor alliance. Labor had never been comfortable with liberal votes for Republicans over their conservative Democratic opponents. Neither had many minority voters who identified the Democrats as the party of civil rights. Briscoe, for example, included Tejanos in his administration and got along reasonably well with the Mexican American community. The shrillness of the previous Democratic infighting passed with La Raza and the Farenthold campaign. Her race against Briscoe in 1974 failed to generate the enthusiasm of the previous quest. Democratic politics of the 1970s and 1980s would stress party harmony, moderation, and the inclusion of minorities—both to ameliorate the tensions of the 1960s and to beat back the growing Republican challenge.

Readings

Books and Dissertations

Atkinson, Gene, "James V. Allred" (Ph.D. diss., Texas Christian University, 1979).

Bainbridge, John, *Super-Americans* (Garden City, NY: Doubleday, 1961).

Banks, Jimmy, *Money, Marbles, and Chalk* (Austin: Texas Publishing Co., 1971).

Bartley, Earnest R., *The Texas Tidelands Controversy: A Legal and Historical Analysis* (Austin: University of Texas Press, 1953).

Bartley, Numan V., *Massive Resistance: Race and Politics in the South During the 1950s* (Baton Rouge: Louisiana State University Press, 1969).

Bryant, Ira B., *Barbara Charline Jordan: From the Ghetto to the Capitol* (Houston: D. Armstrong, 1977).

Champagne, Anthony, *Congressman Sam Rayburn* (New Brunswick, NJ: Rutgers University Press, 1984).

Collins, Michael L., "Ralph Yarborough," in *Profiles in Power: Twentieth-Century Texans in Washington,* eds. Kenneth E. Hendrickson, Jr., and Michael L. Collins (Wheeling, IL: Harlan Davidson, Inc., 1993).

Conkin, Paul, *Big Daddy from the Pedernales: Lyndon Baines Johnson* (Boston: Twayne and G. K. Hall, 1986).

Crawford, Ann Fears, and Jack Keever, *John B. Connally: Portrait in Power* (Austin: Perkins Publishing Co., 1973).

Deaton, Charles, *The Year They Threw the Rascals Out* (Austin: Shoal Creek Publishers, 1973).

Devine, Robert A., ed., *Exploring the Johnson Years* (Austin: University of Texas Press, 1981).

Dugger, Ronnie, *The Politician: The Life and Times of Lyndon B. Johnson* (New York: W. W. Norton and Co., 1982).

Engler, Robert, *The Politics of Oil: A Study of Private Power & the Public Interest* (2nd ed.; Chicago: University of Chicago Press, 1976).

Foley, Douglas E., et al., *From Peones to Politicos: Ethnic Relations in a South Texas Town, 1900–1977* (Center for Mexican American Studies; Austin: University of Texas Press, 1977).

Garson, Robert, *The Democratic Party and the Politics of Sectionalism, 1941–1948* (Baton Rouge: Louisiana State University Press, 1974).

Gellerman, William, *Martin Dies* (New York: John Day Press, 1944).

Green, George Norris, *The Establishment in Texas Politics* (Westport, CT: Greenwood Press, 1979).

Green, George N., and John J. Kushma, "John Tower," in *Profiles in Power: Twentieth-Century Texans in Washington,* eds. Kenneth E. Hendrickson, Jr., and Michael L. Collins (Wheeling, IL: Harlan Davidson, Inc., 1993).

Hardeman, Dorsey B., and Donald C. Bacon, *Rayburn: A Biography* (Austin: Texas Monthly Press, 1987).

Hendrickson, Kenneth E., Jr., "Lyndon Baines Johnson," in *Profiles in Power: Twentieth-Century Texans in Washington,* eds. Kenneth E. Hendrickson, Jr., and Michael L. Collins (Wheeling, IL: Harlan Davidson, Inc., 1993).

Jordan, Barbara, and Shelby Hearon, *Barbara Jordan: A Self Portrait* (Garden City, NY: Doubleday, 1979).

Kearns, Doris, *Lyndon Baines Johnson and the American Dream* (New York: Harper & Row, Publishers Inc., 1976).

Kinch, Sam, Jr., and Stuart Long, *Allan Shivers* (Austin: Shoal Creek Publishers, 1973).

Kinch, Sam, Jr., and Ben Procter, *Texas Under a Cloud* (Austin: Pemberton Press, 1972).

Ladino, Robin Duff, *Desegregating Texas Schools: Eisenhower, Shivers, and the Crisis at Mansfield High* (Austin: University of Texas Press, 1996).

McBee, Ronald Lee "Beauford Jester"(Master's thesis, University of Houston, 1952).

McCroskey, Vista, "Barbara Jordan," in *Profiles in Power: Twentieth-Century Texans in Washington,* eds. Kenneth E. Hendrickson, Jr., and Michael L. Collins (Wheeling, IL: Harlan Davidson, Inc., 1993).

McKay, Seth S., *Texas and the Fair Deal* (San Antonio: Naylor Press, 1954).

Morehead, Richard, *Fifty Years in Texas Politics* (Burnett: Eakin Press, 1982).

Navarro, Armando, *The Cristal Experiment: A Chicano Struggle for Community Control* (Madison: University of Wisconsin Press, 1998).

Olien, Roger M., *From Token to Triumph: The Texas Republicans Since 1920* (Dallas: Southern Methodist University Press, 1982).

Pack, Leslie, "The Political Aspects of the Texas Tidelands Oil Controversy" (Ph.D. diss., Texas A&M University, 1979).

Philips, William, *Yarborough* (Washington: Acropolis Books, 1969).

Shockley, John S., *Chicano Revolt in a Texas Town* (Notre Dame: University of Notre Dame Press, 1974).

Soukup, James R., et al., *Party and Factional Division in Texas* (Austin: University of Texas Press, 1964).

Steinberg, *Alfred, Sam Rayburn* (New York: Hawthorn Books, 1968).

Wolff, Nelson, *Challenge of Change* (San Antonio: Naylor Press, 1975).

TEXAS IN TRANSITION

CHAPTER 14

The past thirty years have both reaffirmed historic Texas traditions and pointed the way to important changes for the state's future. In the 1970s, oil prices shot up, bringing jobs, immigrants, and prosperity to the state. Boom turned to bust in the mid-1980s, however, as world oil prices plummeted. When the state's economy entered a severe recession, all but the strongest oil-related companies collapsed, followed by hundreds of banks and other financial institutions. Hard times forced the state government to raise taxes and cut services. Population growth slowed.

The state slowly recovered in the 1990s. Texas emerged from the oil-bust years with a more diversified economy. Strong population growth resumed as well, and by the year 2000, Texas had passed New York to become the nation's second-largest state, with nearly 21 million people. Demographically, several trends stood out. The number of Hispanics, children, and elderly persons in Texas grew significantly, and foreign immigration accelerated.

In state politics, the 1970s and 1980s marked a transition in which conservative voters began to leave the Democratic party. In the 1990s, the Republicans emerged triumphant; the GOP won every statewide race in 1998, and two years later the popular Texas governor, George W. Bush, captured the United States presidency. However, the state's Republican leadership continues to wrestle with many of the same issues that earlier faced Democrats, including education, prisons, environmental policies, and the tax system.

Texans enter the new millennium optimistic, but they face serious challenges. A population with burgeoning numbers of children and elderly persons will place unprecedented burdens on the education system and social services. Despite strong economic growth in the 1990s, the gap has widened between well-educated, affluent Texans who command high wages in the "new economy," and poorer, less-educated people laboring in low-paying service jobs. Sections of the state that remain dependent on agriculture, such as parts of West Texas and the Rio Grande Valley, have not prospered to the degree that have most urban areas.

Above: Governor Rick Perry. *Courtesy of the Office of the Governor*

Demographers predict that by 2005, whites will be a minority of the state's population—a development that will have unpredictable, but undoubtedly far-reaching, consequences. However, if current trends continue, it seems certain that in the twenty-first century, Texas will more closely resemble the nation than the unique place that many Texans nostalgically remember.

THE TEXAS POPULATION IN TRANSITION

The migration to Texas of people seeking employment modified the state's traditional population configuration. In 1970, 71 percent of Texans were natives of the state; by 1994 the figure was only 65 percent. New Anglo Texans tended to come from the Midwest, breaking the older in-migration pattern of whites from southern states. About 12 percent of the population in Texas was African American in 2000, close to the national figure. The Hispanic population grew from a little under 20 percent in 1970 to 32 percent in 2000, and Asian Americans increased to nearly 3 percent. Demographers predict a continued increase in the non-white population. Indeed, in the year 2000, the combined population of African Americans, Hispanics, and Asians living in Texas already had reached nearly 48 percent of the state's population.

The most significant change in the Texas population in recent years has been the dramatic increase in the number of Hispanics. Several factors account for this rise. Hispanics have a higher percentage of people of childbearing age and a higher fertility rate than whites or blacks. Then there is the proximity of Texas to Mexico. The Rio Grande has always been a false border in terms of cultural heritage, and despite increased efforts to prevent illegal immigration, the border remains porous for Texas-bound immigrants. The Immigration Reform and Control Act of 1986 offered amnesty to those Hispanics living illegally in this country before January 1, 1982. As of the summer of 1988, more than 330,000 undocumented workers in Texas had applied for amnesty.

In the 1990s, immigrants continued to arrive in Texas from Mexico—and increasingly from other Latin American countries—both legally and illegally. The Immigration Act of 1990 boosted total immigration into the United States by 40 percent, with most of the increase going to family members of resident aliens already legally in the country and to skilled workers and professionals. At the same time, the Border Patrol intensified its policing of the Rio Grande, but such efforts did little to stop the flood of immigration. The federal government estimated that 700,000 illegal immigrants were living in Texas as of October 1996, a number surpassed only by California's 2 million. That same year, legal permanent resident immigrants in Texas numbered 825,000. Since then, as policing techniques have grown more effective in border cities, an increasing number of illegal immigrants have resorted to crossing the river at isolated points, thereby undertaking a perilous trek across hundreds of miles of desert; many have not survived the journey. Despite the dangers, as long as there are plentiful jobs in Texas, it seems unlikely that immigration, legal or otherwise, will decline any time soon.

Estimates vary, but experts generally agree on what the state will look like in the next decade: the population of Hispanic immigrants (as well as immigrants from Asian and African countries) will continue to grow, as the proportions of blacks and whites stabilize. One can argue, then, that today the state is witnessing a Texas Revolution in reverse: economic conditions in the 1830s pushed and pulled Anglo settlers into Mexican territory, where they promulgated a war for independence and spread Anglo-American culture. In recent decades, economic and social conditions in this country and south of the border have attracted millions of immigrants from Mexico and other Latin American countries. The political and cultural changes that are likely to occur as a result of this Hispanicization of Texas may in some respects rival those that took place as a consequence of the first Texas Revolution.

These changes in population explain, in part, why Texas has had so little success in solving the problem of poverty. In 1980, 2 million Texans (15 percent of the population) lived below the poverty line—a rate worse than the national average. By 1993 (with the poverty line calculated at $12,675 annual income for a family of three), the figure had grown to 18 percent. The economic recovery of the late 1990s improved things somewhat; only 16 percent of Texans lived below the poverty line in 1998. But Texas remained among the ten worst states in the proportion of its population classified as poor.

As has long been the case, poverty remained closely associated with race, ethnicity, and age. Poverty rates show a disproportionate percentage of people of color below the poverty line—14 percent of whites, compared to 31 percent of blacks and 33 percent of Hispanics. Twenty-four percent of the state's children live in poverty, most of these in single-parent households. Although Texas ranked among the twenty best states with regard to infant mortality (6.3 percent in 1998), the rate for blacks doubled that of whites. In inner-city minority neighborhoods and in the Rio Grande Valley, infant mortality rates approached those of some Third World countries.

Historically, the conservative Texas political Establishment has sought to minimize state funding for poverty programs. In the 1960s, President Johnson's "war on poverty" created "welfare" programs such as Aid to Families with Dependent Children (AFDC), Medicaid, and Food Stamps, which replaced the minimal aid that the poor had previously received through Social Security. In the late 1960s, the U.S. Supreme Court forced states to relax eligibility requirements for these programs, and the numbers on Texas welfare rolls exploded. AFDC caseloads went up 400 percent; families getting AFDC rose from 23,507 in 1967 to 120,245 in 1973. But in 1974, Texas still ranked near the bottom—forty-first-in per capita aid for all categories of public assistance from state and local governments. That year a state legislative committee issued a report entitled "The Poverty Cycle in Texas," which recommended that state leaders abandon their frontier beliefs about public welfare and provide for the needs of the less fortunate. But traditional values prevailed, and the legislature failed to act on the recommendations.

Since then, Texas-style politics as usual has largely prevailed. While the 1982–1983 legislature did increase AFDC payments, mandate provisions for health care for farm workers and the elderly, and pass an Omnibus Hunger Act, it failed to levy any new taxes to fund the measures properly. In 1995, a proposed state budget left health and human service spending about $1 billion shy of needed funding. At the same time, Congress moved toward revising federal entitlement programs and cutting their funding. The resulting welfare reform bill, signed into law by President Bill Clinton in 1996, ended AFDC and replaced it with block grants to the states. The states, in turn, were ordered to cut welfare rolls in half by 2002 and place a five-year lifetime benefits cap on most recipients. By late 2000, the welfare roles in Texas had indeed been reduced by half, the number of food-stamp recipients had dropped by 46 percent, and state enrollment in Medicaid (the government health-insurance program for the poor) had declined by 20 percent.

In 1993, Texas ranked forty-sixth among the states in the amount spent on public welfare, forty-eighth in AFDC payments to children, forty-ninth in aid to the mentally ill, and dead last in immunizations provided for children and the number of citizens with health insurance. These trends continued in the aftermath of the 1996 welfare reforms. In 2000, a federal judge ruled that more than a million low-income children in Texas were not receiving the medical care they deserved, in part because state Medicaid officials had failed to inform many parents that their children qualified for the program. A state senate committee found that 1.4 million Texas children in 2000 lacked health insurance, and that about 600,000 of them were eligible for Medicaid but not enrolled in it. Acting on the committee's recommendations, the legislature began implementing plans to increase awareness and accessibility to assistance programs. It is too early to judge whether welfare reform will prove effective. Clearly, though, the state's overall approach to the problem of poverty has been consistent with the individualistic, limited-government philosophy that so many Texans continue to hold dear.

Nevertheless, the issue of social services looms large for the future, primarily because so many Texans are young. The in-migration of the last three decades kept the median age of Texans (32.7 years as of 1997) beneath the national average, largely because of the continuing arrivals of Hispanics, whose birthrates in 2000 were nearly 50 percent higher than those of Anglos. And the state's median age would have been even lower if not for the migration of so many retirees to Texas. People over the age of sixty still constitute only 3 percent of recent in-migrants to Texas, but that figure ignores the "snowbirds," Midwesterners who live in South Texas during the winter. In 1997, snowbirds numbered 1.3 million and spent an estimated $992 million in the state. In any case, Texas will not escape the national phenomenon of people living longer. By 1998, life expectancy for Texans had risen to 80 for women and 74 for men, both three years longer than in 1979.

These population trends, in which the numbers of both the very young and the very old are rising, signal some sobering realities for Texas in the coming years. As the Baby Boomers begin to retire around 2010, there will be fewer productive workers to support them during their retirement. Those dwindling numbers of workers will also be supporting a much larger population of children, many of them poor and Hispanic. Experts predict a growing competition between the young and the elderly for available tax resource expenditures. If political decisions hinge on whether to aid a youthful ethnic population that wishes to obtain educational or job training, or a graying Anglo population that wants lower taxes and better medical care, the problem of setting the state's priorities could become even more acute.

THE TEXAS ECONOMY IN TRANSITION

Those people entering Texas in the 1970s and the early 1980s followed the state's transition into a modern industrial state. The domestic price per barrel for Texas crude oil stayed at around $3 until the Organization of Petroleum Exporting Countries (OPEC) gained control over the international price of oil in the early 1970s. The 1973 Arab oil embargo ended the stability in oil prices that had existed for the previous twenty-five years. As a result, the price of crude quadrupled and held firm through 1979. With the Iranian revolution, the subsequent Iranian-Iraqi War, and cutbacks in Saudi Arabian production, oil prices doubled again in 1979–1980, briefly reaching $40 a barrel before stabilizing at $34 in October 1981.

The sudden increase in energy prices came at a time when the nation suffered from stagflation, that is, a combination of high inflation and high unemployment. The energy crisis had two powerful effects on the state. Texans, like all Americans, naturally suffered from inflation and rising energy costs, but the money flowing into Texas from the escalating price of oil created a sense of exuberance about the state's economic future. Workers arrived in Texas in droves, and the unemployment level was less than half the national level. Banks, which scurried to loan money to energy-related companies, grew in number and more than tripled in total resources from 1974 to 1986. Real estate prices and the number of construction firms skyrocketed. Construction contracts totaled $1.75 billion in 1975 and $4.80 billion ten years later (urban wags joked that the state bird of Texas was the crane). Some argued that low taxes and antiunion laws had created a favorable business climate, which in turn made the economic boom possible. Others credited the frontier spirit of self-reliance and the Texas entrepreneurial character, prompting editors of out-of-state newspapers to groan about what they considered stereotypical Texas braggadocio.

Unfortunately for Texas, the inflated oil prices that had really created the boom failed to hold. Conservation measures, increases in non-OPEC oil sources, and the failure of OPEC nations to obey the cartel's production quotas caused oil prices to tumble, starting in 1983. When OPEC suspended all production controls in 1986, oil prices collapsed. That summer, the price of oil briefly fell below $10 a barrel. A gradual upward trend began in 1987, and from 1989 to 1999, the price fluctuated in the range of $17–$22.

The economic hangover from the bust of the mid-1980s quickly set in. Oil and gas production provided 28 percent of the state revenue in 1981, but not quite 12 percent at the close of 1994. Energy-related industries employed one out of twelve nonfarm workers in 1982. By 1989, those industries had lost 282,000 jobs, and by 2001, only about 158,000 Texans worked in oil-related occupations. Economists speculated that for each drop of $1 in the price of a barrel of oil, 25,000 jobs and $1 million in state and local tax revenues were lost. The 1987–1988 legislature passed a $5.7 billion tax bill, the largest of any state in history up to that time. Outstanding real estate and energy loans caused many banks to fail.

Indeed, the banking industry lost nearly $4 billion in the late 1980s, and the number of banks in Texas declined from nearly 2,000 in 1986 to 1,091 in 1992. Among those to go under was the state's largest bank holding company, InterFirst Corporation of Dallas. The 1980s savings-and-loan scandals only complicated the problem of collapsing financial institutions. The number of savings and loans (S&Ls) in Texas decreased from 318 in 1980 to 64 in 1992. Many of these S&Ls would have failed in any case, due to collapsing real estate prices, but a relaxation of regulatory practices had led to reckless lending practices. And in more than a few cases, fraud by S&L executives compounded the problem. By December 1993, the federal government had spent $21 billion to bail out depositors and investors in insolvent Texas savings and loans—71 percent of the national total. With banks failing left and right, the 1986 legislature rewrote banking laws to allow out-of-state holding companies to purchase Texas banks, and by 1990, out-of-state banks owned the ten largest Texas institutions.

The oil bust of the 1980s cast a dark cloud over the Texas economy, but that cloud had a silver lining. In the years following the oil bust, the state's economy diversified and matured. After a brief but painful national recession in the early 1990s, Texas led all states in the number of new jobs created. Of the nine largest states during the 1990s, Texas's economy grew the fastest. By the end of the century, most major sectors of the state's economy—manufacturing, transportation, utilities, financial services, communications, transportation, oil, construction, wholesale and retail trade—were enjoying robust growth. Falling interest rates made it easier for businesses to raise capital and for individuals to finance houses and consumer goods. In addition, the U.S. Senate ratified the North American Free Trade Agreement (NAFTA) in 1993, removing most trade barriers between the United States, Mexico, and Canada. Although controversial, the treaty spurred the growth of manufacturing, construction, and trade along the Mexican border. Texas triples the next-closest state, California, in income realized from trade with Mexico, and in 1999 that trade generated nearly $35 billion for the Lone Star State. Oil no longer dominates economic growth in

Turning basin of the Houston Ship Channel. The fifty-five mile long canal helped make Houston an important center in the world oil-petrochemical industry. *Courtesy Houston Metropolitan Research Center, Houston Public Library*

the state, as it did for most of the twentieth century. Alaska replaced Texas in 1988 as the nation's top oil-producing state, and in 1999, Texas produced only one-third as much oil as it had in 1972.

The major growth in job opportunities in Texas during the 1990s was in the service sector, with particular growth in the retail trade, telecommunications, and health services. By 2001, three-quarters of all non-agricultural Texas jobs were in the "service-producing" (as opposed to "goods-producing") category. Nevertheless, manufacturing did well in the 1990s, as Texas added nearly 100,000 jobs in that sector, more than any other state. One out of every four new manufacturing jobs was in computer-related industries, making Texas one of the leaders of the nation's "high-tech" revolution. By 2001, the world's two largest manufacturers of personal computers—Dell and Compaq—were Texas-based companies. The growth of service-sector jobs and high-tech manufacturing has further weakened labor unions nationally and in the state. In 2000, about 505,000 Texans belonged to a labor union, or roughly 6 percent of the workforce—less than half of the 1965 figure.

Military-related employment entered a long period of decline when the Cold War ended. Between 1991 and 1999, the number of people employed directly by the military fell nearly 30 percent, from 321,000 to 233,000. However, defense contractors such as Lockheed-Martin and Raytheon continued to play an important role in the state's economy, providing some of the best-paying jobs. After suffering the highest unemployment in the nation in the early 1990s, Texas saw its jobless rate drop and then hover in the 4-5 percent range from 1998 to 2001.

Despite the general impression of Texas wealth, the per capita income of the state only reached the national average for the first time in 1981, an achievement that the oil bust promptly reversed. After bottoming out in the early 1990s, Texans' income rebounded significantly—to an average of $26,858 in 1999—but that figure still placed Texas behind twenty-seven other states. Per capita income varied throughout the state; affluent metropolitan areas like Dallas–Fort Worth boasted per-capita incomes over $32,000, whereas income for the five southernmost counties along the Rio Grande averaged barely $12,000, making South Texas one of the poorest regions in the nation. Growth also has eluded much of deep East Texas and far West Texas, places that have traditionally depended on farming and other raw-material production (including oil). The primary industrial and business development of Texas has occurred in a triangle defined by Dallas on the north, Houston on the south, and Austin/San Antonio on the west. Despite sharp variations along racial, ethnic, and gender lines, this core region has generally prospered.

TEXAS FARMERS: THE END OF A DREAM?

As the urban, industrial economy grew and matured in the late twentieth century, agriculture struggled to remain profitable. The kinds of crops grown and animals raised by Texas farmers and ranchers changed little between 1970 and 2000. Livestock (mainly cattle) consistently accounted for nearly 70 percent of the total value of the state's agricultural output. Cotton remained the single most valuable cultivated crop, about 10 percent of the agricultural total, but the value of all grain crops combined surpassed that of cotton, totaling about 14 percent of agricultural products. Nursery and greenhouse crops quadrupled from 1969 to 1997, reflecting an urban and suburban demand for landscaping plants and exotic fruits and vegetables. Overall, about 100,000 fewer acres of land are devoted to agriculture than were in 1970, a consequence of "urban sprawl" and economic hard times for farmers.

Serious trouble in the agricultural sector began in the mid-1970s, as overproduction and foreign competition drove down farm prices. Federal assistance to farmers sunk to historic lows from 1974 to 1977, and high interest rates made it difficult for farmers to finance their operations. In addition, prices of fertilizers, pesticides, fuel, and electricity rose by 63 percent between 1975 and 1981, driving many small operators into bankruptcy. In the late 1980s, prices and income began a modest recovery, which continued into the early 1990s. Average farm income for the years 1990–1994 was more than double that of 1985–1989, but in the second half of the 1990s, the recovery stalled, due in part to severe drought conditions over large portions of the state in 1996, 1998, 1999, and 2000. In both 1996 and 1998, crop and livestock losses exceeded $2 billion. To make matters worse, even as farmers struggled with their third year of drought in 1999, the prices of cattle, cotton, and grain dropped to their lowest levels in more than ten years. Not surprisingly, farm income for the rough years of the late 1990s was down 30 percent from the good years earlier in the decade.

The federal government has long played a major role in determining the fate of Texas farmers and ranchers. Since the 1960s, direct government assistance payments to Texas farmers and ranchers have averaged $733 million a year, with large fluctuations from year to year, depending on growing conditions, commodity prices, and the political climate. Historically, government subsidies, crop insurance, loan programs, and disaster relief did not bear much relationship to which political party was in power: both major parties supported federal farm programs. The most significant departure from the policies of the previous forty years came in 1996, at the hands of a Republican-dominated Congress and a Democratic presidential administration. Named the "Freedom to Farm Act," the bill lifted many of the regulations that controlled supply (and thus propped up prices) for agricultural products. The bill was designed to wean farmers off federal assistance, but it could not have anticipated the drought of the late 1990s. As world supply of agricultural products expanded and Texas crops withered, farmers again teetered on the brink of insolvency. Pressured by farm-state representatives, Congress in 1998 enacted massive drought-relief legislation. The ironic consequence was that federal aid to Texas farmers reached its highest level in history in 1999: $1.9 billion.

The ups and downs of recent years show how farmers today, not unlike farmers in the 1890s, are tied to a market over which they have little control, as well as how vulnerable farmers' incomes can be to international market forces and changes in government policy. A global economy, coupled with an urban electorate reluctant to grant farmers protection against foreign competition, gives farmers and ranchers little cause for optimism.

As many novels and films since World War II have reflected, the passing of the family farm evokes nostalgia from many Americans. Deep within both the North American and Texas psyches there still resides a Jeffersonian-like belief that family farms preserve republican values. But economic and political change in the nation and the world has made the small family farm an endangered species. Today, less than 3 percent of all employed adult Texans work in agriculture (including forestry and fisheries). In short, the concept of Texas as an agrarian state is no more. Nevertheless, the state still leads the nation in arable land, a renewable resource. And for an economy in transition to succeed, Texas agriculture cannot not be ignored.

THE CHANGING FACE OF URBAN TEXAS

Those who left farms since the 1970s moved, as had those of the previous thirty years, to Texas cities. The urban population of the state in 1980 was 81.2 percent of the total, which actually exceeded the national average. By 1999, it had grown to 84.6 percent. Demographers expect the urban-to-rural ratio to stabilize in the near future, mainly because so many Texans are choosing to live in rural areas adjacent to cities and commute to work. In the most remote rural counties, however, the exodus from farm to city continues. In the 1990s, seventy of the most isolated Texas counties actually lost population, with West Texas and the Panhandle hardest hit. A USDA classification system aptly described these as "lonely counties."

Texas cities, on the other hand, have seen dramatic growth in recent years. In 2000, twenty-five Texas metropolitan areas numbered more than 100,000 people, more than double the number in 1970. The greater Dallas–Fort Worth metropolitan area is now the state's largest (and nation's ninth-largest), with 5.2 million people—larger than 31 U.S. states. The Houston-Galveston-Brazoria metropolitan area ranked second in the state, with a population of 4.7 million; San Antonio ranked third, with 1.6 million. Three individual Texas cities (as opposed to metropolitan areas) now rank in the top ten nationally: Houston (fourth, with 2 million), Dallas (eighth, with 1.2 million), and San Antonio (ninth, with 1.1 million).

Not only did Texas cities grow in the 1990s, but they were among the fastest-growing cities in the nation. Texas boasted three of the country's ten fastest-growing metropolitan areas in 2000: the growth of McAllen-Edinburg-Mission ranked fourth nationally, that of Austin–San Marcos fifth, and that of Laredo ninth. In Texas's largest cities, an explosive increase in the suburban population fueled growth. Collin County in suburban North Dallas grew to 492,000 people in the 1990s, nearly doubling its population and making it the eighth-fastest growing county in the nation.

Several factors underlay this dynamic urban growth. Open spaces once surrounded all Texas cities, and these inexpensive collars of land easily became suburbs. Furthermore, the state's proximity to Mexico made Texas cities natural destinations for Mexican immigrants seeking jobs; new international air connections encouraged immigration from overseas; and the warm climate gave Texas cities an advantage over their northern counterparts. The ample availability of land, coupled with a lack of urban planning and Texans' traditional laissez-faire attitudes toward development, led Texas cities to grow out rather than up. The consequence was urban sprawl, with superhighways cutting through and virtually destroying older neighborhoods in order to link central cities with their immediate ring of suburbs. By the 1970s, urban highways had become the principal corridors of growth; strip malls and frontage-road office centers usurped the functions of many downtown buildings. By the 1990s, with little land left to develop in the central cities and suburbs, the urban sprawl had begun to absorb the rural farming communities beyond the original suburban rings. Towns like Pflugerville and Cedar Park north of Austin, or Flower Mound and Frisco north of Dallas, all tripled or quadrupled their populations between 1990 and 2000, as they became the so-called bedroom communities for their neighboring cities.

The central cities also have continued to grow—just not as fast as the suburbs. As they had since 1945, the inner cities attracted a larger minority population. In 2000, the census reported that Anglos constituted 73 percent of the state's suburban population, while they composed only 46 percent of the central-city population. Anglos are now a minority within the city limits of Houston, Dallas, San Antonio, and Fort Worth, with Hispanics comprising at least 30 percent of the population in all four. Far from being the "melting pot" of legend, Texas urban areas are better described as "salad bowls," sprawling hodgepodges of neighborhoods heavily segregated along racial, ethnic, and economic lines.

While urban growth in Texas has been impressive, in order for growth to continue—and for the quality of urban life to improve at the same time—other issues must be addressed, one of the most important of which is the transportation system. Historically, Texans have loved their automobiles. This, along with a suspicion of comprehensive urban planning and the desire to keep taxes low,

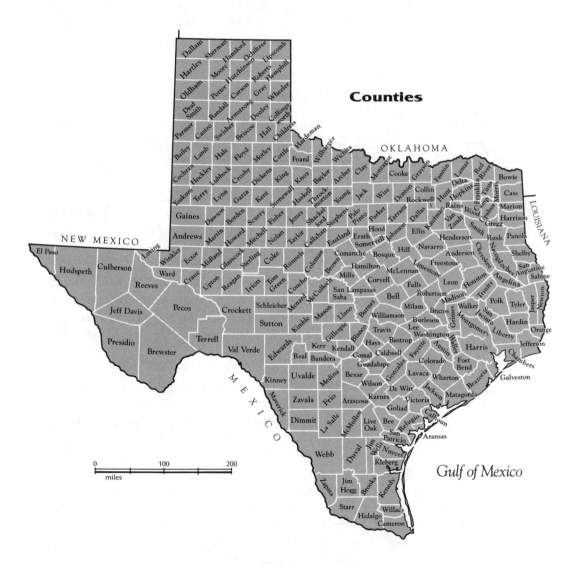

Counties

has made cars and freeways the primary means of getting around Texas cities. Unfortunately, Texans only began to realize the need for alternative, more economical forms of transportation at a time when federal largess for urban mass-transit systems had largely ended. Thus, Texas cities got a late start in dealing constructively with the problems of urban transportation, with seriously detrimental consequences: according to the Texas Transportation Institute, in the year 2000, urban congestion cost the state $5 billion annually. In the state's cities and suburbs, drive-time delays were 200 percent longer than they were in the 1980s.

Recognizing the need to modernize urban mass transit, the legislature in the 1970s authorized cities to create metropolitan transit authorities (MTAs) and allowed them to fund their operations with sales taxes. All of the state's largest cities eventually took advantage of this source of funding. Despite these developments, ridership on the main form of public mass transit—city buses—continued to decrease. In 1990, only about 2 percent of urban commuters used public transportation. In the late 1990s, though, ridership began to increase, as cities improved their mass-transit systems and traffic gridlock made mass transit more attractive to commuters.

Many saw commuter- and light-rail systems as the long-term solution to the urban transportation problem. In 1984, the Dallas Area Rapid Transit system (DART) was created to build a light-rail system for that city. For years thereafter, however, suburban–inner city rivalries and budgetary concerns stalled actual construction. Critics argued that light rail was impractical in spread-out Texas cities and that ridership would never make a dent in the traffic problem. But when the first twenty-six-mile phase of the system was completed in 1996, the public's response was enthusiastic, and ridership has grown each year. DART recorded 95 million passenger trips in 2000, and suburbs that only a few years ago actively had opposed the creation of the system suddenly began clamoring for the lines to be extended to their communities.

Despite the Dallas success, voters in San Antonio and Austin defeated light-rail projects in 2000. In Houston, the MTA opted to build a short, seven-mile line that would only serve the central city—a plan that required no referendum since existing funds would finance it. Even this modest proposal met opposition from limited-government "property-rights" groups, who filed suit to stop it, and from Republican Congressman Tom DeLay, who sought to block federal funding for the project. Nevertheless, construction finally began in 2001, with transit officials hoping that the popularity of the central-city line will convince voters to support the building of actual commuter lines in the future. Plans to link Texas's major cities together with high-speed "bullet trains" such as those in Europe and Japan have met similar opposition, often with financing and lobbyists provided by commuter airlines. Consequently, severe traffic congestion—once a phenomenon limited to urban freeways—has become a common problem even on rural highways, especially on the state's busiest interstate, the Dallas-Austin-San Antonio stretch of I-35.

Texas's commercial transportation system, however, is healthy and has contributed to economic growth. The state is either first or second in the nation in a number of transportation indicators, such as railroad-track mileage, paved mileage of highways and rural roads, the number of motor vehicles, and the number of aircraft. DFW airport was the third busiest in the country in 1998, behind only Atlanta's Hartsfield and Chicago's O'Hare. Texas's ports handled 427 million tons of cargo in 1998, almost double the amount of just ten years earlier. The Port of Houston led all other ports nationally in foreign waterborne commerce and ranked second in total tonnage. The transportation systems connected Texas to a thriving tourist industry. Texas attracted 169 million visitors in 1995, second only to California. In 1999, travelers spent $36.7 billion in Texas. According to industry spokespersons, 470,000 Texans owe their jobs to tourism, and tourists generated $623 million in local tax revenue and $2 billion for the state treasury.

One good way to increase the vitality of a city and add to its tourist-dollar appeal is to improve its offering of fine-arts institutions. Unfortunately, Texas lagged behind the nation in aid to the arts, ranking always among the bottom-five states. Yet many urban areas have instituted bond drives for the building of downtown art districts, focusing upon constructing performing-arts centers and museums. The Texas frontier tradition discourages tax expenditures for cultural development, even if business progressives argue that money spent for cultural enhancement will bring a net profit in the attraction of visitors, new industries, and new residents. For example, when Dallas lost out to Chicago in a highly publicized competition to lure the Boeing aircraft corporation's headquarters to the Metroplex in 2001, company officials said they based their decision in part on the superior cultural attractions of Chicago's downtown. The experience prompted much public debate and handwringing by city leaders over whether Dallas should spend more on such things as museums and parks. While observers will draw differing conclusions about such episodes, it seems safe to predict that conflicts over how to spend available urban resources will not disappear.

RELIGION IN TEXAS: A FORCE FOR TRADITION

By most measures, Texans are a very religious people. In 1990 Texas led the nation in the number of churches (16,961) and church members (5,282,341). Nearly 65 percent of Texans said that they regularly attend church—10 percent more than the national average. Measured by the number of adherents (rather than full church members), the largest religious group overall was the Baptists, followed by the Catholics, Methodists, Churches of Christ, Lutherans, and Presbyterians.

The greatest single statistical change in religion in Texas since the 1970s has been the increase in the number of Catholics. Between 1980 and 1990, Roman Catholics (3.6 million adherents) passed Southern Baptists (3.3 adherents) as the largest individual denomination in the state, although when Southern Baptists are combined with the state's 816,000 Black Baptists and other smaller

A statue of Our Lady of Fatima in Buddhist-like pose in present-day Port Arthur. *Courtesy of Robert A. Calvert*

Baptist groups, they still outnumbered the Catholics. The increase in the number of Catholics is mainly due to the growth of the Hispanic population.

Among Protestants, evangelical denominations and congregations have grown faster than have mainline Protestant churches, in which membership and attendance has been mostly stagnant. Ironically, evangelical churches, which tend to be very conservative or fundamentalist in their theological orientation, have often been the quickest to embrace nontraditional modes of worship, such as the use of electronic musical instruments and televised services. Statistically, most Texas congregations (and especially evangelical ones) remain small, with fewer than 100 members. But a few evangelical churches in big cities have become "megachuches," such as Houston's Lakewood Church, a non-denominational congregation that in 2001 claimed weekly attendance of nearly 30,000. Usually led by a charismatic preacher exercising strong authority, these urban congregations have enjoyed rapid growth by featuring enthusiastic "praise services" backed by orchestras or rock bands, as well as by offering a wide range of other attractions and services, such as schools, child care, and recreational facilities. While the megachurches appear to have been somewhat more successful than mainline churches in attracting a diverse body of worshipers, overall the old saying remains true in Texas: Sunday morning is the most segregated time of the week.

Texas churches since the 1970s have endured wrenching political and ideological controversies, primarily over the issues of fundamentalism and modernism. The fundamentalist upsurge in Texas churches coincided with the rise of the political right in the Reagan era, when opposition to abortion, homosexuality, and feminism became the hallmarks of the so-called "religious right." Harkening back to the fundamentalist crusades of the 1920s, modern fundamentalists proclaimed the Bible to be the inerrant word of God, literally true in all matters of science and history as well as theology. In their view, homosexuality, abortion, and feminism should be condemned as sin. All of the state's traditional Christian denominations have wrestled with these issues, but none more so than those of Texas's largest Protestant denomination, the Southern Baptists.

Beginning in 1979, fundamentalists in the Southern Baptist Convention (SBC), who explicitly identified themselves as conservatives in both politics and theology, mounted a concerted campaign to purge all nonfundamentalist perspectives from the denomination nationwide. Engineered primarily by two Texans—Paul Pressler, a Houston judge and former legislator, and Paige Patterson, a minister from a prominent Texas Baptist family—the fundamentalists' takeover of the SBC was virtually complete by the early 1990s. In the process, nonfundamentalist faculty and administrators at Baptist seminaries were fired, and the SBC adopted new creedal statements condemning homosexuality and abortion and instructing women to "submit" themselves "graciously" to the leadership of their husbands. However, a sizeable majority of Texas Baptists, and their state-level organization, the Baptist General Convention of Texas (BGCT), fell into the "moderate" camp, and thus vigorously opposed the fundamentalist takeover. The Baptist moderates (who always claimed to be theologically conservative) fought back in a number of ways. In 1990, Baylor University, concerned that fundamentalists might gain control of the BGCT as they had the SBC, removed itself from the control of BGCT. Four years later, after the fundamentalist takeover of the state's leading Baptist seminary, Southwestern Theological Seminary in Fort Worth, Baylor opened its own school of theology and hired the recently fired president of Southwestern, Russell Dilday, as a distinguished professor. Many Texas Baptists have ceased giving financial support to the SBC, and some congregations have formally severed all ties with the national Convention. It is too early to say whether conflicts like the one plaguing Texas Baptists will cause a long-term splintering and decline in the traditional Protestant denominations in Texas, but many observers think it probable.

As the case of the Baptists illustrates, the line between religion and politics has become increasingly blurred. And since the 1970s, Protestant fundamentalists and other religious conservatives have increasingly identified with the Republican party. Their religious views led them, as in the 1920s, to oppose the teaching of the theory of evolution in the public schools, to advocate school prayer, to oppose the ordination of women and gay persons as ministers, and to condemn abortion. As the state became more Republican, their influence grew. The state legislature restricted abortion in the third trimester of pregnancy in 1987 for the first time since *Roe* v. *Wade*. In 1999, Governor George W. Bush signed a law requiring parental notification before a minor can obtain an abortion. Throughout the 1990s, the Christian Coalition organized local campaigns to elect school board candidates and to endorse local Republican office seekers, apparently with considerable success. State Republican platforms have subsequently shown the influence of the religious right, endorsing anti-abortion measures, school prayer, education vouchers, and other causes that religious conservatives describe as embodying "family values."

The continuing influence of religion—and its strong conservative bent—suggests that religion has been a major force in upholding Texas tradition. However, as the state becomes more diverse, this may change; today, in all of Texas's major cities, the number of Muslim mosques, Buddhist temples, and other non-Christian houses of worship is rapidly growing. The Census Bureau estimated that in 1998 there were 124,000 Jews in Texas, and the number of Mormons grew from an estimated 111,000 in 1990 to 198,000 in 1999. Ethnic Christian congregations, from Korean Baptists to Mexican Assemblies of God to Chinese Lutherans, have enjoyed rapid growth along with the immigrant population. Religious people often bemoan the decline of morality in the modern world, but if churchgoing is any indicator of moral fiber, then Texans may still fairly claim to be an upstanding people.

ONTO A WORLD STAGE: TEXAS CULTURE IN THE MODERN ERA

With the rising prosperity of the late twentieth century, cultural life in the Lone Star State entered a new phase of its history. The days when Texas took a cultural back-seat to the East or West Coast were largely gone; in essence, the state became the "Third Coast," with music, theater, film, art, and literature that could rival those of other states and regions.

In classical music, the symphony orchestras of Houston, Dallas, and San Antonio built upon the foundations laid in earlier decades. Following the hard times of the 1980s, the Houston Symphony reclaimed its standing as a nationally renowned orchestra under the leadership of Christoph Eschenbach, who became its music director in 1988. By 1995, the orchestra boasted an annual budget of $17 million and employed 98 full-time musicians, presenting 200 performances each year. The Dallas Symphony grew in size and quality as well, especially after the completion in 1989 of the Meyerson Symphony Center, a spectacular hall designed by architect I. M. Pei and built by the City of Dallas at a cost of $81.5 million. The Fort Worth Symphony benefited from the exposure it received as host orchestra for the acclaimed Van Cliburn International Piano Competition and from its new home, the $67-million Bass Performance Hall, completed in 1998.

Texas opera and ballet companies were somewhat slower to achieve national stature, but by the 1970s, companies existed in the state's major cities. Under the leadership of John Herbert, the Houston Grand Opera earned a reputation for staging seldom-heard European works and for its innovative revivals of Scott Joplin's *Treemonisha* and the Gershwins' (George and Ira) *Porgy and Bess*. The company moved into the magnificent Wortham Center in 1995, and its annual budget topped $14 million. The Dallas Opera likewise earned acclaim, staging the state's first complete cycle of Wagner's *Ring des Nibelungen* in the early 1980s and hosting the world premiere of Dominick Argento's *The Aspern Papers* in 1988. Houston also developed the state's premier ballet company. Under the artistic direction of English dancer Ben Stevenson, the Houston Ballet grew from a 28-dancer regional ensemble to one of the nation's largest and most critically acclaimed ballets, with 52 dancers and a worldwide reputation. By contrast, ballet in Dallas struggled in the 1980s and 1990s, with two local companies folding. Finally, in 1994, Dallas arts patrons formed a joint venture with the Fort Worth Ballet to form the Fort Worth–Dallas Ballet—one performing company with governing boards and performances in each city.

As in the case of opera and ballet, Houston has led the way in theater. By the early 1970s, that city's Alley Theater had moved into its new downtown home, and it had helped to promote the careers of American playwrights such as Eugene O'Neill, Arthur Miller, and Edward Albee. In 1996 the Alley received a special Tony Award for Outstanding and Sustained Achievement by a Regional Professional Theatre, and in 1999, two Alley productions—*Not About Nightingales* and *The Civil War*—debuted on Broadway and were both were nominated for Tonys. The Dallas Theater Center produced a wide variety of plays, including Texas playwright Preston Jones's *Texas Trilogy*, which went on to the Kennedy Center and Broadway. By the end of the 1980s, the Dallas Theater Center rivaled the Alley as the state's best resident company. In the mid-1990s, there were some 300 producing theater companies in Texas. Experts credit the state's University Interscholastic League (UIL) one-act play contest, which for decades has exposed thousands of Texas high school students to drama, as perhaps the single most important factor in making Texas a state in which the theater has flourished.

Individual Texans also have made their mark on the world of drama. Edward Albee, who lived in Houston and was associated with both the University of Houston and the Alley Theater, continued to write plays in the 1970s, 1980s, and 1990s, two of which won the Pulitzer Prize. Wharton-born Horton Foote, who had risen to prominence as a playwright and screenwriter in the 1960s, remained productive, writing the screenplays for the films *Tender Mercies* (1983) and *The Trip to Bountiful* (1985) and winning a Pulitzer for his play *The Young Man from Atlanta* in 1995. Texan Larry L. King wrote several dramatic works, but he is best known for the story that became the 1977 Broadway smash, *The Best Little Whorehouse in Texas*, which enjoyed a run of 1,703 performances. In one of Broadway's most versatile careers, dancer-singer-choreographer-director Tommy Tune of Houston won nine Tony Awards—the only person in theatrical history to win a Tony in four different categories.

Achievements in classical music, dance, and drama notwithstanding, popular music is the area in which Texas has made its greatest mark in recent decades. By the end of the 1960s, the genre of popular music most associated with Texas—country-and-western—stood at a crossroads. Throughout the 1960s, rock-and-roll had taken the nation by storm. At this time, virtually all commercial country music was produced and recorded in a handful of Nashville studios, and to an urban nation in turmoil, that music seemed increasingly formulaic, corny, and largely irrelevant. Moreover, breaking into the Nashville scene and becoming

Willie Nelson sings at Farm-Aid, September 1985. *Corbis*

a recording star was nearly impossible—even for those with real talent—as a young Texas singer-songwriter named Willie Nelson discovered.

In 1970, after ten frustrating years in Nashville, Nelson moved to Austin, where he grew his hair long, dressed in faded jeans, and began making music his own way. His early Austin albums made him something of a cult figure in the nascent Austin counterculture, although the music was mostly traditional country and honky-tonk, shorn of the slick orchestration that had come to characterize the "Nashville Sound" of that era. In 1973, as his popularity grew, Nelson began hosting annual Fourth of July "Picnics," rowdy, all-day outdoor music festivals that attracted tens of thousand of fans. In 1985, he founded Farm-Aid, a nationally broadcast, all-day benefit concert for family farmers.

The music scene that began to coalesce in Austin in the early 1970s attracted other self-styled musical "outlaws," among them Waylon Jennings, a singer-songwriter from Littlefield who had played bass for Buddy Holly, and New Yorker Jerry Jeff Walker, whose 1973 album *Viva Terlingua*, recorded live in the Hill-Country hamlet of Luckenbach, became the signature album for the entire genre. Other important figures in the movement's early days included Guy Clark, Gary P. Nunn, Billy Joe Shaver, Michael Murphey, and a western swing band called Asleep at the Wheel, which introduced a new generation to the music of Bob Wills. Ground zero for the Austin music scene was a club in a converted National Guard armory, the Armadillo World Headquarters, which opened its doors in 1970.

"Progressive country," as the new Austin music was being called, remained a well-kept secret nationally until 1975, when Nelson's *Red-Headed Stranger* album, a collection of sparsely arranged ballads, rocketed to the top of the country *and* pop charts—the first country album ever to do so. A second album the following year, a collaboration with Waylon Jennings entitled *Wanted: The Outlaws*, became the best-selling country album in history. The Austin music scene also received national exposure from the PBS television program "Austin City Limits," founded in 1974. By 1990, 280 television stations broadcast this program. Austin was beginning to attract singers and songwriters from all over the state and beyond, artists who played much more than just country music. Joe Ely, Butch Hancock, and Jimmy Dale Gilmore all gravitated to Austin from Lubbock, bringing a harder-edged rockabilly sound to Texas music. Dallas's Stevie Ray Vaughan moved to Austin, and by the time a helicopter crash claimed his life in 1990, he had almost single-handedly ignited a blues revival with his virtuosity on the electric guitar. By the 1990s, Austin could boast more live music performances on any given night than could Nashville. Since 1972, Texas singers and songwriters have also showcased their talents at the annual Kerrville Folk Festival, which lasts eighteen days and attracts over a hundred artists each year. The South by Southwest Music and Media Festival, held in Austin each March since 1987, now features a thousand musical acts on forty downtown stages.

While Texas became a center of music performance and recording, some Texans continued to make their musical mark in Nashville. George Jones and Ray Price, prominent since the 1950s, were still making hits in the 1970s and beyond. In 1972, Tanya Tucker of Seminole scored her first country hit at the age of thirteen, and over the next three decades she recorded thirty albums and twenty-nine top-ten singles. Even more successful during the same era was Houston-born Kenny Rogers, who recorded 58 country-pop albums and sold over 100

Indoor shot of the Armadillo World Headquarters, the place many consider the birthplace of Texas rock music. *Photograph by Burton Wilson, The Center for American History, The University of Texas at Austin, CN 05147*

million records worldwide, making him one of the most popular American entertainers of the twentieth century.

Another Texas singer, George Strait, pointed country music in a new direction in the 1980s. Eschewing both the counterculture trappings of a Willie Nelson and the pop tunes of a Kenny Rogers, the clean-cut son of a South Texas rancher appeared onstage wearing immaculate boots, cowboy hats, pressed jeans, and button-down western shirts, and recorded songs in both the classic honky-tonk and western-swing styles. In the process, Strait almost single-handedly inaugurated the so-called New Traditionalist movement in country music. He scored his first top-ten hit in 1980, and by the mid-1990s he had recorded thirty-one No. 1 country songs.

Although Texas is best known for country music, the state has also produced its share of pop and rock stars since the 1960s. Houston's ZZ Top began gaining a local and statewide following with their gritty, blues-influenced rock tunes in the early 1970s, and they continued to tour and produce albums and videos into the twenty-first century. Rivaling ZZ Top's success was the Steve Miller Band, fronted by Dallas-raised Steve Miller, whose catchy pop-rock albums and singles topped the charts several times. However, the best-selling American rock act of all in the 1970s was the Eagles, led by Don Henley, who grew up in the small East Texas town of Linden and attended North Texas State University. The Eagles sold over 100 million albums and won 4 Grammy awards, and their greatest-hits collection was the best-selling album of all time in the United States. Following the group's breakup in the 1980s, Henley enjoyed a successful solo career and returned to Texas, taking up residence in Dallas.

Tejano artists also have made their mark on modern Texas music. In the 1970s, Freddie Fender and Johnny Rodríguez topped the country charts with tunes sung in both Spanish and English, but most Tejano musicians catered to the demands of the Mexican American community, with *conjunto* and *orquesta* remaining the most popular musical forms. However, by the 1990s, Texas-Mexican radio stations had appeared in major urban areas, and Spanish-language TV reached almost all households. Soon, a new group of young recording stars had emerged, including Selena, a native of Lake Jackson. At the time of her tragic murder in 1995, she had just wrapped up her first English-language album; released posthumously, it became the first Tejano album to reach No. 1 on the pop charts.

In the 1970s, Texans continued to build on the state's storied reputation as a producer of jazz artists. As one of the creators of "free jazz" in the late 1950s, Fort Worth's Ornette Coleman was credited with liberating jazz from the prevailing conventions of harmony, rhythm, and melody. This towering figure in the jazz world continued to make innovative music in the 1970s, 1980s, and 1990s, traveling and studying in Africa, recording with stars such as guitarist Pat Metheny and the Grateful Dead's Jerry Garcia, writing a critically acclaimed ballet (*Architecture in Motion*), and composing the soundtracks for films such as *Naked Lunch* and *Philadelphia*. Coleman's contributions earned him a prestigious

MacArthur fellowship in 1994. A number of his Texas protégés also earned national reputations as jazz artists, including tenor saxophonist Dewey Redman, drummers Charles Moffett and Ronald Shannon Jackson, alto saxophonist Prince Lasha, and reedman Julius Hemphill—all of whom, like Coleman, hailed from Fort Worth. Another Fort Worth jazz artist influenced by Coleman was clarinetist John Carter, who was credited with restoring the clarinet to prominence as a jazz instrument. But Carter is perhaps even better known for his five-album recording, made in the 1980s, entitled *Roots and Folklore: Episodes in the Development of American Folk Music*, which traced African American history through jazz. Jazz appeared to grow in popularity in the 1990s, as the number of jazz clubs multiplied in the larger cities. Several universities offered formal programs of study in jazz, led by the nationally ranked graduate program at the University of North Texas.

Texas long had provided popular subject matter for television and film, a trend that continued into the modern era. In the 1970s, the nighttime soap opera *Dallas* took the country by storm, as the devious Texas oil tycoon, J. R. Ewing (played by Weatherford native Larry Hagman) became the villain that everyone loved to hate. The series became a sensation internationally as well, and when the 1980 season finale ended with a cliffhanger shooting of the main character, the show's ratings were the highest in history. The amazing popularity of the program served to reinforce a whole set of Texas stereotypes in the eyes of the world; the men were all cowboy boot-and-hat-wearing oil millionaires, the women as beautiful as supermodels, and nearly everyone owned ranches and shopped at Neiman-Marcus. In the late 1980s, Larry McMurtry's sprawling cowboy saga *Lonesome Dove* was made into a critically acclaimed TV miniseries, co-starring the Oscar- and Emmy-winning native of San Saba, Texas, Tommy Lee Jones. In the 1990s, martial-arts star Chuck Norris, who himself had moved to Texas, starred in one of that decade's longest-running shows, *Walker, Texas Ranger*. Texas, its seems, might have left its mythic nineteenth-century past behind, but the rest of the world was still eager to see it as the land of larger-than-life rugged individualists.

Recent films have presented a somewhat more sophisticated view of the state, although they, too, have sometimes perpetuated stereotypes. In 1980, the Paramount film *Urban Cowboy* touched off a national craze for country-and-western music, country dancing, cowboy clothing, and honky-tonk culture. The film, which was actually about the lives of oil-industry workers, further served to bring Texas into the national spotlight, and for a while made "Texas chic" an identifiable fashion trend.

Movies about Texas, or with a Texas setting, are too numerous to mention individually. A short list would include *Tender Mercies* (1983), about a down-and-out country singer from a small Texas town—for which Texas playwright Horton Foote won a best-screenplay Oscar, and director John Sayles's *Lone Star* (1996), which starred Brownsville-born Kris Kristofferson in a suspenseful drama about racial tensions on the Texas-Mexico border. Several of Larry McMurtry's novels have been made into successful feature films, including *The Last Picture Show* (1971) and *Terms of Endearment* (1983), which together won seven Oscars. Since the 1970s, Texas has become an important center for filmmaking. In 1995, the state was the site of 69 major film projects, with budgets totaling $330 million. Between 1991 and 2000, 240 feature films, 62 made-for-TV movies, and 61 national TV series were produced in Texas. Since 1971, a state agency, the Texas Film Commission, has offered a variety of free services designed to encourage and assist film-production in the state. The annual South By Southwest music festival in Austin added a film and multimedia festival to its slate of activities in 1994, and it is considered one of the nation's best today.

Texas has also come into its own in the visual arts. By the 1970s, Texas artists worked in so many diverse styles and media that short categories would not do their efforts justice. By this time, however, changes in the concept of how museums should be operated allowed Texans to judge for themselves the major artists and artistic trends. The Texan of recent years has had art-viewing opportunities that simply did not exist prior to the 1960s. The major Texas cities have built new museums or renovated old ones to accommodate their expanded collections as well as traveling exhibitions. The Menil Collection in Houston, the Edward Larabee Barnes-designed Dallas Museum of Art, and Fort Worth's Kimbell Art Museum, designed by Louis I. Kahn, are all considered world-class museums for their collections as well as for their buildings. But these institutions now focus on national and international trends, rather than on Texas regionalism and the showcasing of local artists.

Texas's mark on the literary world since the 1960s has been significant, if uneven. Poets generally have not flourished on Texas soil. In the 1990s, the Texas Review Press at Sam Houston State University was the only Texas press routinely publishing book-length collections of poetry. A handful of modern Texas poets established national reputations, including William Barney of Fort Worth, Vassar Miller of Houston, and several poets affiliated with university creative-writing programs: Texas Tech's Walt McDonald, Robert Phillips of the University of Houston, and R. S. Gwynn of Lamar University. However, the quality of most Texas poets' work still awaits judgment. The Poetry Society of Texas, headquartered in Dallas, had 600 members in 25 chapters across the state by 1994, suggesting that there are sizeable numbers of poets and poetry lovers in Texas.

In fiction, as in so many other facets of Texas life in the late twentieth century, Texas's distinctiveness began to fade. Being a "Texas writer," like being a Texas poet or artist, no longer automatically meant dealing with the rural, regional themes so long associated with the state. Of course, some writers continued to do work that was clearly "Texan" in theme. Novelist Elmer Kelton of San Angelo, who had written popular cowboy novels since the 1950s, began to write more "serious" fiction in the 1970s. Works such as *The Day the Cowboys Quit* (1971), *The Time It Never Rained* (1973), *The Good Old Boys* (1978), and *The Wolf and the Buffalo* (1980) won critical acclaim and numerous awards, and by the 1990s, Kelton enjoyed a national following. Another admired Texas novelist was Cormac McCarthy, a Rhode Island–born writer who made his home in El Paso since 1976. Although they dealt with ostensibly "western" themes, his novels, such as *Blood Meridian* (1985), and the "Border Trilogy" of *All the Pretty Horses* (1992), *The Crossing* (1994), and *Cities of the Plain* (1998), had a complex, brooding, and often nightmarish quality that set them apart from conventional western literature.

Possibly the most important change in Texas literature has been the growing importance of Latino writers. A number of Tejanos emerged from the Chicano movement of the 1960s to become major figures in the Chicano Literary Renaissance. Tomás Rivera's 1971 novel, *Y no se lo tragó la tierra* (*And the Earth Did Not Devour Him*), established him as one of the nation's leading Hispanic writers. The Crystal City–born writer went on to serve as chief executive officer of the University of Texas at El Paso and the University of California at Riverside before his death in 1984. Rolando Hinojosa of Mercedes has been one of the most prolific Tejano novelists, publishing a dozen novels set in the lower Rio Grande Valley since the early 1970s, including the acclaimed multinovel *Klail City Death Trip* series. Tejana poet-playwright-novelist Estela Portillo Trambley, who died in 1998, was one of the pioneering women in the Chicano Literary Renaissance. The older tradition of Texas literature, and nonfiction, written to reflect only an Anglo past, is clearly passing.

Larry McMurtry, the state's best-known writer, can possibly serve as an example of the state's transition from a rural to an urban society, and of a writer who grappled with the impact of that transition on people's lives. While McMurtry's novels of the 1960s had been set in rural and small-town Texas, in the 1970s his work began to focus on urban themes. In a trilogy consisting of *Moving On* (1970), *All My Friends Are Going to Be Strangers* (1972), and *Terms of Endearment* (1975) he created a group of interlocking characters from Houston who dealt with the vicissitudes of urban living. Then, in something of a literary surprise, McMurtry published *Lonesome Dove* (1985), a long, Pulitzer-Prize-winning novel about two ex-Rangers on an epic cattle drive. McMurtry subsequently wrote books on such Old West topics as Billy the Kid, Calamity Jane, and Crazy Horse, as well as a sequel to Lonesome Dove, confounding literary critics who had applauded his earlier calls for Texas writers to abandon Old West themes and confront Texas's urban present. His literary odyssey perhaps embodies the story of Texas literature as a whole in the late twentieth century— a moving away from the traditional regional themes, but at the same time, a lingering fascination with the state's frontier past.

Nonfiction by Texans, or about Texas, has endured numerous changes since the 1960s. In the newspaper business, the major trend has been toward consolidation, often in the hands of out-of-state corporations. In 1965 there were 114 daily newspapers in Texas, 62 of which were family-owned concerns, 59 of which were owned by eleven Texas-based chains, and only 3 of which were owned by out-of-state chains. By 2001, Texas had fewer daily papers, 92, only 9 of which were family owned; all the others belonged to one of some 20 corporate chains, many of which were out-of-state companies. Atlanta-based Community Newspaper Holdings, Inc., owned the most Texas papers, 19. Two national media conglomerates, Hearst Corporation and Cox Enterprises, owned the papers of Houston, San Antonio, Austin, Midland, Beaumont, Waco, Laredo, Longview, Nacogdoches, Longview, Lufkin, and Marshall, plus 17 weekly papers. The growth of multiple ownership can be attributed largely to efforts to cope with the economics of newspaper publishing and the need for a number of suburban dailies within large metropolitan areas. The trend toward consolidation was particularly striking in the big-city dailies. Houston, Dallas, and San Antonio all began the 1990s with two major papers; by 1995, each city had only one. Faithful readers mourned the passing of their favorite papers, reporters and columnists scrambled to find jobs with their former competitors, and consumer advocates worried that the lack of competition would drive up prices and stifle freedom of expression.

The magazine industry experienced similar trends. In the 1970s and 1980s, local and regional magazines flourished. Most of the state's larger cities boasted at least one slick, city-based magazine that covered stories of local interest and provided movie, restaurant, and music reviews. Increasing publication costs, the oil bust of the mid-1980s, and the proliferation of alternative media sources such as the Internet spelled the demise of most such city magazines. Of these publications by the end of the 1990s, only Dallas's *D Magazine* survived. However, the pioneering state-level features-and-culture magazine, Austin-based *Texas Monthly*, proved very successful and provided an outlet for the writing of many of the state's most talented print journalists. In Austin and the other large cities, so-called "alternative" newspapers such as the *Houston Press*, the *Dallas Observer*, and the *Austin Chronicle* filled some of the void left by the departure of the city magazines and the second dailies.

Several Texans established national reputations as journalists in the last decades of the twentieth century. Longtime CBS news anchor Walter Cronkite retired in 1981 and passed the torch to another Houstonian, Dan Rather. Beaumont's Jim Lehrer anchored the highly respected *Newshour* on PBS and moderated several important presidential debates. After serving as Lyndon Johnson's press secretary, Bill Moyers of Marshall had a long and distinguished career, especially as a producer of public-television documentaries. NBC's Sam Donaldson, who began his career as a teenage disc jockey in El Paso, became a high-profile member of the White House press corps and a fixture on Sunday-morning TV talk shows. Liberal syndicated columnist Molly Ivins acquired a national following for her barbed political columns and books, especially those aimed at George W. Bush. In addition, Larry L. King, Edwin "Bud" Shrake, William Broyles, Jr., Gary Cartwright, and Stephen Harrigan all made national reputations as Texas magazine journalists before writing best-selling books. In the 1990s, former state land commissioner Jim Hightower hosted a liberal radio talk show that was syndicated on over 100 stations nationwide.

Historians, in and out of academia, also contributed to the growing body of Texan-produced nonfiction. Before the 1970s, the University of Texas boasted the only history department in the state with much of a national reputation. In the decades since, other history programs have improved dramatically. A nation-wide glut of Ph.D.s allowed Texas A&M, the University of Houston, Texas Tech, and the University of North Texas to begin filling their faculty ranks with professors holding terminal degrees from nationally prominent programs. The same held true at Rice, TCU, SMU, and Baylor. In the 1990s, U.T.-Arlington, U.T.-El Paso, and SMU inaugurated new doctoral programs in history. By the end of the century, historians working at Texas universities were producing monographs in the full range of historical fields.

In the field of Texas history, historians began moving away from the uncritical celebrations of the frontier past. That meant, among other things, that Texas history would cease to be told exclusively from the Anglo, male perspective. In the 1970s, young scholars such as Alwyn Barr and Arnoldo De León produced seminal works on blacks and Hispanics in Texas. Paul D. Lack, Walter L. Buenger, Carl H. Moneyhon, Alwyn Barr, Lewis L. Gould, Norman D. Brown, and George Norris Green all produced new syntheses of specific eras of Texas politics; many of their books showed the influence of the liberal trends that had swept the American academic world in the 1960s. By the 1990s, more quality historical studies of Texas women were being written, including books by Elizabeth Hayes Turner, Rebecca Sharpless, and Elizabeth York Enstam. Randolph B. Campbell produced the first modern scholarly study of slavery in Texas, and Donald L. Chipman wrote a new general history of Spanish Texas. Increasingly, scholars de-emphasized Texas exceptionalism and instead placed Texas history in regional or national contexts: books by Lawrence Goodwyn on Populism, Elizabeth A. H. John on Indians, and David Weber on the Spanish borderlands are good examples. Scholars also applied the techniques of the so-called New Social History to re-examine the histories of specific Texas communities. The result has been community-studies such as the work of Jesús F. de la Teja on San Antonio, Gilberto Hinojosa on Laredo, and Randolph B. Campell on Harrison County. A few independent scholars not affiliated with a university also produced cutting-edge historical works, including Jack Jackson and Robert Weddle, both of whom wrote on Spanish Texas. Historian Dan L. Flores, journalist Stephen Harrigan, and naturalist Joe C. Truett wrote books in the tradition of John Graves, blending history, natural history, and personal memoir. By and large, though, the public has been slow to embrace the new approaches to Texas history. Works on traditional topics like the Texas Revolution and biographies of great men continued to garner the most popular attention. Texans still love reading about their heroic frontier past. For example, T. R. Fehrenbach's popular history of Texas, *Lone Star*, first published in 1968, remains the most popular general history of the state and was re-issued in 2000.

Public history organizations have had to navigate the sometimes-treacherous waters of academic and popular history with care. The Texas State Historical Association enjoyed strong growth in the last three decades of the twentieth century and emerged as arguably the best-run state historical society in the nation. It was more successful than most such organizations at reconciling the tastes and interests of academic and amateur historians. Its most ambitious project, the

New Handbook of Texas (1996), took fourteen years to complete, at a cost of over $5 million. With some 23,000 entries by 3,000 authors, the *Handbook*, which the TSHA made accessible via the Internet in 1999, was deservedly hailed as the most comprehensive state-level historical reference work ever written. The new Bob Bullock Texas History Museum in Austin opened its doors to favorable public reaction in 2001, and several of the state's important historical museums and sites received major renovations and restorations, including the Sam Houston Memorial Museum, the San Jacinto Museum, the Star of the Republic Museum, and the Texas State Cemetery. In each case, as in the magnificent $98-million restoration of the State Capitol building in the 1990s, the public enthusiastically supported the project and for the most part seemed not to object to the expenditure of public dollars.

TEXANS AT PLAY: SPORTS AND LEISURE

The post–World War II trends toward greater leisure time and a wider variety of ways to spend it continued in the last three decades of the twentieth century. Sports continued to be more of a religion than a pastime for millions of Texans, and for many of them, *sports* was synonymous with *football*.

After becoming competitive under Coach Tom Landry in the 1960s, the Dallas Cowboys of the NFL entered a golden age in the 1970s, during which the team played in five Super Bowls, winning two (1972, 1978). During Landry's twenty-five years as head coach, the Cowboys won thirteen division championships. The team's twenty consecutive winning seasons (1966–1985) remains an NFL record. Even in down years, the Cowboys remain among the most successful pro sports franchises of all time, consistently at or near the top in television revenues and sales of team apparel and memorabilia. In the late 1980s, the Cowboys' on-field fortunes declined, and in 1989, the team was sold to Arkansas oilman Jerry Jones, who dismissed Landry and hired Port Arthur native Jimmy Johnson as the Cowboys' new head coach. Johnson led the Cowboys back to prominence, winning Super Bowls in 1993 and 1994. A rift between the coach and owner led Johnson to leave the team in 1994, and Jones replaced him with Barry Switzer, who led the team to its fifth Super Bowl win in the 1996 game.

Pro football in Houston never enjoyed the success of the Cowboys. From 1970 to 1977, the Houston Oilers managed just two winning seasons. In the late 1970s, however, under the coaching of O. A. "Bum" Phillips and the bruising running of University of Texas Heisman Trophy winner Earl Campbell, the team had its run of glory, making the playoffs in 1978, 1979, and 1980. But the Oilers never reached a Super Bowl, and the team lapsed into mediocrity before owner Bud Adams moved the franchise to Tennessee in 1997. Houston went several years without a team, but the city was granted an expansion franchise beginning with the 2002 season.

Texas's two major league baseball franchises have enjoyed only limited success on the field. The Texas Rangers joined the American League when the

Enron Field. *Courtesy Houston Astros Baseball Club*

Washington Senators were moved to the Dallas–Fort Worth Metroplex in 1972. Only in 1996, after moving into its state-of-the-art stadium, the Ballpark in Arlington, did the team finally win a divisional title, a feat it repeated in 1998 and 1999. Each time the Rangers lost in the first round of the playoffs. Houston's pro team, the Astros, followed a similar trajectory, wining its first divisional title in 1980, followed by four more in 1997, 1998, 1999, and 2001, each time failing to advance past the first round of the playoffs. Perhaps the greatest moment in Texas pro baseball history came at the hands of a player who was born and raised in Texas and who played for both of the state's teams. On May 1, 1991, forty-four-year-old Alvin native Nolan Ryan, whom the Rangers had signed away from the Astros as a free agent two years earlier, pitched a major-league record seventh no-hitter in Arlington—a record that many baseball experts believe may stand forever.

By the 1970s, Houston, San Antonio, and Dallas all had professional basketball teams. In the mid-1990s, the Houston Rockets won back-to-back NBA titles. The San Antonio Spurs won five divisional titles in the 1970s and 1980s, and the team went on to win the NBA championship in 2000. Women's pro basketball came to Texas in 1997 in the guise of the WNBA, and Houston's team, the Comets, won the new league's first four championships.

New stadiums and arenas for pro teams—funded in part by tax dollars—have become major public issues in Texas, as in the nation. In the early 1990s, Mayor

Henry Cisneros pushed the City of San Antonio to build the Alamodome, arguing that a major city needed a first-class stadium. About the same time, the city of Arlington funded the construction of the Rangers' new stadium, the Ballpark at Arlington. Not to be outdone, Houston taxpayers helped to finance the construction of the Astros' Enron Field (completed in 2000) and also approved public funding of new stadiums for the Rockets and the city's NFL expansion team, the Texans. In 2001, the publicly financed arena in Dallas for the Mavericks and Stars (the American Airlines Center) opened for business, and construction began in San Antonio for the Spurs' new facility (the SBC Center). That same year, Cowboys owner Jerry Jones announced his intention to seek public assistance for the construction of a new stadium and entertainment complex in one of the Metroplex cities. Critics cried that public funding for such projects amounted to "corporate welfare" and that other, more pressing needs such as public transportation and city schools went neglected, but owners argued that the cost of modern professional sports required help from the public sector and that the new facilities would increase city revenues.

Ice hockey was slow to catch on in Texas. However, in 1993 Minnesota's NHL team, the North Stars, moved to Dallas, where they were renamed the Stars and became a consistent winner, culminating in a Stanley Cup championship in 1999. Before long, a dozen Texas cities boasted minor-league hockey teams, and with the growth of club- and school-sponsored hockey, there are now opportunities for amateurs across the Lone Star State to learn the game.

Once considered exclusively country-club sports, golf and tennis both enjoyed phenomenal growth in Texas since the 1960s. By the start of the twenty-first century, there were nearly 900 golf courses in the state, and most high schools and colleges fielded golf teams. The Byron Nelson (Dallas) and the Colonial (Fort Worth) are considered among the most prestigious tournaments on the PGA tour. Numerous Texas golfers since 1970 have become major stars. El Paso's Lee Trevino dominated the tour in the early 1970s, winning the U.S. Open once, the PGA twice, and the British Open twice. Ben Crenshaw won the Masters title twice; Payne Stewart captured the U.S. Open twice; and Charles Coody, Tom Kite, and Justin Leonard won the Masters, the U.S. Open, and the British Open, respectively. Texas produced three standouts in women's golf: Monahans-born Kathy Whitworth recorded 88 career wins, more than any pro golfer in history, male or female; Dallas's Sandra Haynie and Midland's Judy Rankin recorded 42 and 26 LPGA tour victories, respectively. Famed Austin golf teacher Harvey Penick collected his tips and tales in his 1992 work, *Harvey Penick's Little Red Book,* the best-selling sports book of all time.

Tennis rivaled golf in popularity and growth as a participant sport. One of tennis's most famous events took place in the Astrodome in 1973, when female star Billie Jean King played Bobby Riggs in a much-hyped "Battle of the Sexes" match. Riggs, a fifty-five-year-old former pro player, had disparaged the abilities of women on the court and boasted that even at his age, he could beat the world's best female player. Before a national prime-time television audience, King proved Riggs wrong, winning in straight sets. Although largely a publicity stunt, the match brought tennis to a whole new audience, especially women. Since then, Texas has produced few major pro stars, but the 1990 Wimbledon women's finals had a distinctly Texas flavor, pitting Houstonian Zina Garrison against Martina Navratilova, a Czech native who made her home in the Dallas–Fort Worth area after immigrating to the United States in the 1970s. Navratilova won the 1990 match, one of 56 lifetime Grand-Slam titles, making her arguably the greatest female tennis player of all time.

Other sports have enjoyed more limited popularity in Texas in recent decades. Rodeo remains popular at both the amateur and professional levels. The greatest individual star of rodeo, Ty Murray of Stephenville, won pro rodeo's all-around championship seven times, an all-time record. Houston boxer George Foreman proved to be one of that sport's most durable stars, winning the gold medal at the 1968 Olympics, capturing the world heavyweight championship in 1973, and then reclaiming it in 1993 at the age of forty-five. In track-and-field, the Texas Relays in Austin rated as one of the major events in the country. In 2001—its 74th year—the meet attracted over 5,000 high school and collegiate athletes, including many Olympians. Cycling has grown in popularity, aided by the celebrity of three-time Tour de France winner Lance Armstrong of Austin. Houston and Dallas both had pro teams in the North American Soccer League, but soccer was slow to catch on with the public as a spectator sport, and the league itself folded in the 1980s. In 1996, Dallas acquired a franchise,

Rodeo Rider. *Courtesy Frederick Baldwin and Wendy Watriss*

the Burn, in the newly created Major League Soccer. As a participant sport, soccer now rivals little-league baseball in popularity among school-age children of both sexes, and the flood of immigrants from soccer-playing countries, including Mexico, bodes well for the game's future in Texas.

High school and collegiate sports continue to draw more participants and spectators than do pro sports. High school football remains king in Texas, followed by basketball, track, and baseball. Perhaps the most important recent development in Texas sports has been the rise of women's sports. By the 1960s, women's programs were appearing on college and high school campuses, and they were an important part of university life by the 1980s. The University of Texas won the women's NCAA basketball championship in 1986, and Texas Tech duplicated that feat in 1993. The rise in women's participation (sometimes accompanied by a loss of programs for men) owed much to a 1972 federal law known as Title IX, which required equal funding for men's and women's sports. Today, in many smaller towns, girls' high school basketball rivals the traditional male sports in popularity.

Men's college basketball in Texas has never achieved the fanatical following that the sport enjoys in the Midwest or the East Coast. The University of Houston probably sent the most high-quality players to the pro ranks, including NBA greats Elvin Hayes, Otis Birdsong, Clyde Drexler, and Hakeem Olajuwon. But college basketball fans have been disappointed by the performances of their teams nationally. No Texas team has made it to the men's NCAA Final Four since the University of Houston's three consecutive trips in 1982, 1983, and 1984.

College baseball has been a considerably brighter story. The University of Texas holds the NCAA record with 27 appearances in the College World Series, and the team won national titles in 1975 and 1983. Numerous Texas high school and college ballplayers since the 1960s have gone on to star in the major leagues, including Austin's Don Baylor, who played 19 seasons in the big leagues before becoming a successful professional manager; five-time Cy Young winner Roger Clemens, who played at U.T.; and all-time strike-out king Nolan Ryan.

But football still rules Texas college sports. Since 1970, Texas teams have finished in the Associated Press Top Twenty list 54 times: 16 times each for Texas A&M and the University of Texas; 10 times for the University of Houston; 5 times for SMU; 4 times for Baylor; and 3 times for Texas Tech. No Texas Division I team has won a national championship in that time, although U.T. and SMU have both finished second. Three players at Texas colleges have won the Heisman Trophy since 1970: U.T.'s Earl Campbell (1977) and Ricky Williams (1998), and the University of Houston's Andre Ware (1989). In small-college divisions since 1970, national championships have been won by Texas A&I (5 times); Southwest Texas State and Abilene Christian (twice each); and Angelo State, East Texas State, and Austin College (once each).

The 1980s and 1990s were times of upheaval in Texas college football. After decades of prominence, the Southwest Conference entered a period of decline in the 1980s. Part of the problem was scandal, as the NCAA placed several teams on probation for recruiting violations, paying players, or other rules infractions. Most famous was the case involving Southern Methodist University. In 1987, the NCAA learned that SMU boosters, including Governor Bill Clements, had regularly paid players. The NCAA gave the school the first-ever "death penalty," which forced SMU to abolish its football program for two years. Scandals such as this tarnished the conference's image nationally, and contributed (along with the intense competition for high school players) to the decline in its competitiveness. In an era when college football was a multimillion-dollar industry, the large schools suffered financially by having to play private schools such as Rice and TCU, which were rarely competitive and thus had difficulty drawing a television audience. In 1990, the University of Arkansas left the Southwest Conference for the Southeastern Conference, and soon U.T. and A&M were searching for a new home as well. In 1994, according to a report by the *San Antonio Express-News*, Lieutenant Governor Bob Bullock, who held degrees from both Baylor and Texas Tech, and Lubbock's John Montford, who chaired the senate finance committee, helped to broker a deal that brought U.T., A&M, Texas Tech, and Baylor into the Big 8 (which became the Big 12), and the Southwest Conference ceased to exist. TCU, SMU, and Rice ended up in the Western Athletic Conference, and the University of Houston went to Conference USA.

When Texans were not watching or playing sports, they spent much of their leisure time pursuing other recreational activities. In 2000, there were more than 6.25 million paid visits to Texas's 76 state parks. Hunting is still a principal fall and wintertime activity for millions of Texans, and thanks to the state's warm climate, those who love to fish have the opportunity to do so year round—both in fresh and salt water. Since wagering on horseraces became legal in 1987, those who like to play the ponies may do so at tracks in Houston, Dallas, and San Antonio. In 1997, the Texas Motor Speedway, which can accommodate over 200,000 spectators, was completed near Fort Worth, bringing professional auto racing to the Lone Star. The nation's largest open-air flea market, First Monday Trade Days in Canton, attracted an estimated 100,000 buyers, sellers, and browsers each month. On any given weekend, Texans could attend a plethora of yearly events—everything from the Renaissance Festival in Magnolia to the Black-Eyed Pea Festival in Athens to the Mosquito Festival in Clute. The variety of leisure activities illustrates how much things have changed since the days when attending a church ice-cream social, fishing in a local creek, or watching a Friday night high school football game were about the only available means of relaxing after a hard week's work.

THE PARADOX OF TEXAS POLITICS

Texas politics since 1970 have been paradoxical. On one hand, the era witnessed the end of a century of Democratic dominance and, for a while, a seemingly competitive party system in statewide races. In five consecutive gubernatorial races (1978 to 1994) the party in power lost the governor's office to the party that had been out of power. Yet this apparent competitiveness was deceptive. During all this time, Texas never ceased being a conservative state; it merely took some years for conservative voters to find their new political home. In the end, Texas was once again primarily a one-party state dominated by conservatives.

Since the days of the Shivercrats in the 1950s, the Republican party had sought to sell itself to Texans as the party of conservatism. The liberalism of Lyndon Johnson's presidency, with its embrace of civil rights and its war on poverty, frightened conservative Democrats and made the Republican party look increasingly attractive.

The 1978 elections demonstrated the strength that grassroots Republicanism had obtained. Governor Dolph Briscoe, a traditional conservative Democrat, announced for a third term, but in a surprising primary, he lost to the moderately liberal attorney general John Hill. The Republicans nominated Dallas oilman William P. Clements, Jr. For his part, Hill ran a complacent campaign, confident in the belief that Republicans simply did not win Texas governors' races. When November arrived, the unthinkable occurred: thanks to a well-organized and lavishly funded campaign, Clements beat Hill by a razor-thin margin to become the first Republican governor since Reconstruction. This major political upset refurbished the Republican party of Texas, as did the winning presidential ticket of Ronald Reagan and George Bush in 1980, which carried on its coattails 35 Republicans to the Texas state house, 8 to the state senate, 166 to county and district offices, and 5 to the U.S. Congress.

Clements's first term in office was only a moderate success for Republicans. His relations with his own party were harmonious, but his frank and sometimes abrasive manner alienated Democratic legislators and many prospective independent voters. Although Clements had mixed success with the legislature in pursuing his conservative agenda, which stressed tougher law enforcement and reducing the size of state government, most observers believed that he would easily be reelected. The 1982 campaign once again proved the experts wrong.

For governor, the Democrats nominated Secretary of State Mark White, a Briscoe ally with a conservative political record. Lloyd Bentsen announced for reelection as U.S. senator, as did Lieutenant Governor Bill Hobby. They campaigned vigorously for a ticket that included four liberals: Jim Hightower for commissioner of agriculture, Ann Richards for state treasurer, Jim Mattox for attorney general, and Gary Mauro for land commissioner. Clements spent $13 million on his campaign, twice the amount spent by White. Meanwhile, the economy had begun its slide, and by November the unemployment rate of over 6 percent dampened voters' enthusiasm for Clements. White won with 54 percent of the vote, aided by high minority turnout. Even more surprising was the fact that the full slate of Democratic candidates won, including the four liberals.

White soon confounded most predictions that he would be another conservative Democrat in the Briscoe mold. His administration secured health care for the indigent, a mandatory seatbelt law, workers' compensation and unemployment insurance for farm workers, tougher pesticide regulations, a state ethics advisory commission, health insurance for retired teachers, higher nursing-home standards, and major education reforms. The *Texas Observer* described the governor as the most liberal chief executive of the last fifty years. But White's administration soon encountered political difficulties. The economic downturn became a depression in Texas; schoolteachers quarreled over education reforms; and the prison system continued to be a political hot potato. Despite White's progressive bent, minorities expressed discontent with his administration. Polls reported that many Texans questioned his leadership in a time of crisis, particularly when it came to taxes. Both Clements and White announced for governor in 1986.

This time, White lost to Clements. Observers credited White's defeat to low turnout in rural areas and among minority voters, particularly Mexican Americans. Clements's victory solidified the Reagan sweep of 1984, when the popular Republican president carried the state by over 1 million votes. The Republicans also gained legislative and congressional seats that year, and elected former Democratic congressman-turned-Republican Phil Gramm to replace retiring senator John Tower. The Clements victory retained these Republicans and increased the number of local office holders to 504. While Democrats captured all the other statewide offices below the gubernatorial level, it was becoming clearer that Republicans now stood a chance of attracting over the traditional Democratic small-town voters, who joined many suburban voters in pulling straight Republican-party tickets. The Democratic party found itself at a crossroads: it needed its traditional white East Texas voters, but at the same time it also needed to mobilize voter turnout in the minority and low-income precincts, where social issues were important concerns. Whether such a coalition could be forged and then maintained was problematic, to say the least.

The 1988 presidential election fully revealed the Democrats' problems. The party nominated Massachusetts governor Michael S. Dukakis for president and Texas's own Senator Lloyd Bentsen for vice-president. Texas Democrats pinned their hopes on the theory that the conservative Bentsen might be able to bring back to the party those Democrats from rural areas and small towns who had voted for President Reagan in 1980 and 1984. However, the Republican national ticket also included a Texan, presidential nominee George Bush, who had been Reagan's vice-president. Helped by a tough campaign run by prominent Houston lawyer James A. Baker III, Bush easily won, carrying 56 percent of the vote in Texas. Moreover, the Republicans won their first down-ballot races since Reconstruction, electing three state supreme court justices and one railroad commissioner. Republicans predicted that soon theirs would be the majority party in Texas.

Meanwhile, Bill Clements was halfway through his second stint in the governor's office (1987–1991). This term was not as contentious as his first. The state's political energies were sapped by a depression and the need to settle the issue of court-ordered prison reform. Clements, nonetheless, vetoed a record fifty-five bills in his two terms as governor, and the divisions between his office and the Democratic legislature prevented any overall legislative agenda. Attempts to modify the Mark White education reforms failed, and Texans legalized wagering on horseracing. Clements said early on that he would not stand for reelection in 1990.

On the Democratic side, the gubernatorial race was a donnybrook, with the liberal state treasurer, Ann Richards, emerging victorious in the primaries over Attorney General Jim Mattox and former governor White. After the exceptionally nasty primaries, in which White and Richards had traded accusations of corruption and drug abuse, most pundits predicted an easy win for the Republicans. The Democratic party seemed divided, and many voters expressed disgust over the way the Democrats had conducted their primary campaigns. It also appeared that the Republicans had picked a winner in Clayton Williams, a rancher and oilman from Midland. Williams had the advantage of being a political outsider in a time of increasing voter dissatisfaction with career politicians. He was also rich, having already spent $9 million in winning the Republican primary. At the general election's onset, he led Richards by twenty points in the opinion polls.

Throughout the campaign, Williams portrayed himself as the stereotypical Texas rancher, a successful businessman who would return the state to the good old days. But his campaign soon turned into a shambles, as he made numerous political gaffes, including publicly telling a joke about rape, refusing to shake Richards's hands after a state-televised debate, and admitting that he had paid no income tax in 1986. Richards won the election, even carrying many of the traditionally Republican urban counties. Most credited her victory to Williams's blunders, which alienated suburban women voters, driving many of them into the Richards camp.

Republicans had expected to win some top offices in the state, perhaps even the legislature. They got part of what they wanted. Senator Gramm easily won reelection and fellow Republican Kay Bailey Hutchison was elected state treasurer. In the agriculture commissioner's race, Republican Rick Perry defeated liberal Democratic incumbent Jim Hightower. But for the first time since 1974, the Republican party did not gain any seats in the legislature. Also, the Democrats mustered some able candidates besides Ann Richards. Former State Comptroller Bob Bullock handily won the powerful lieutenant governor's post; Dan Morales, a legislator from San Antonio, was elected attorney general, becoming the first Hispanic to win a statewide elected executive office. Gary Mauro retained his post as land commissioner.

As governor of Texas, Ann Richards rose to national political stardom. Economic growth started in 1990 and continued throughout the next several years,

Above: Former governor Ann Richards. *Courtesy Ann Richards*

and her approval rate soared to over 60 percent. Governor Richards appeared around the nation and on television lauding the state and its advantages. She ably chaired the 1992 Democratic presidential convention, thereby gaining more national exposure and popularity. The governor seemed to epitomize the arrival of women in national politics. Some critics argued, however, that she did not exert strong executive leadership at home. During her tenure in office, the fiscally-conservative Democratic lieutenant governor, Bob Bullock, largely ran the legislature, but with tight budgets, little happened legislatively except for the establishment of a state lottery and the continued building of prisons. Richards's legacy lay not in legislation but in her fulfillment of campaign promises to make state government reflect the diversity of the state's people. The governor appoints about 4,000 persons to terms on boards and commissions; 48 percent of Richards's appointees were women, 25 percent were Hispanic, and 12 percent were African American, ending decades of mostly-white, mostly-male governance.

Texans continued to play important roles in presidential politics. In 1992, the big political news was that Ross Perot, the Dallas billionaire, would challenge President Bush and Arkansas Governor Bill Clinton for the presidency. Perot's only real political experience had been as chair of the committee that designed the Mark White education reforms. Championing a balanced budget and opposing NAFTA, the eccentric Perot proved to be the sensation of the 1992 campaign. In the end, though, his only real impact may have been to cost Bush the election and, indirectly, to give Texas another Republican senator. After defeating Bush, President Clinton tapped Senator Lloyd Bentsen for the office of treasury secretary. Kay Bailey Hutchison won the special election to fill the vacant Senate seat, and Texas now had *two* Republicans in the U.S. Senate.

In 1994, the Republicans felt that Governor Richards was vulnerable and rallied around George W. Bush, a co-owner of the Texas Rangers baseball team and son of the former president. This time, Richards's campaign did not go well. She was perceived of as running a negative campaign and as being soft on crime, despite having added 75,000 new beds to the state's prisons. Bush ran an excellent campaign, taking no controversial stands and depicting himself as a successful businessman who wanted local control of schools. He won an easy victory, with 53.4 percent of the vote.

Bush's confident, noncontroversial campaigning style carried over into his administration as governor. Having run as an educational reformer, he successfully pursued his plans for standardized testing and charter schools. He bolstered his standing with the right wing of the Republican party by championing such issues as support of the death penalty and school vouchers. Although the legislature defeated vouchers and his most ambitious program—a wholesale restructuring of the state tax system—he succeeded in winning a modest reduction in home-owners' property taxes. When he ran for reelection in 1998, the state's economy was booming and Bush's approval ratings were high. The elections would confirm the Republican party's arrival as the majority party in Texas.

This time, Bush ran against the only real liberal left in statewide office, Land Commissioner Gary Mauro. The outcome was a foregone conclusion, as Bush won 69 percent of the vote. But what was truly significant was the party's showing statewide: for the first time, Republicans swept all fourteen statewide elections. They now held every one of the twenty-nine offices elected by statewide vote, including all eighteen judgeships on the state supreme court and the court of criminal appeals. Only in the state house of representatives did Democrats maintain a semblance of power at the state level. There, a 78-72 Democratic margin enabled the popular conservative Democrat Pete Laney, a Panhandle cotton farmer, to retain his powerful position as speaker of the house. But the days of Democrats in any positions of leadership in Austin seemed clearly numbered.

Bush's landslide reelection as governor of Texas positioned him for a presidential run. He fended off a strong challenge by Arizona senator John McCain in the 2000 Republican primaries, aided by a campaign organization that shattered all fundraising records. Bush also benefited from his good relations with the late Democratic lieutenant governor, Bob Bullock, who had become something of a political mentor to Bush and crossed party lines to endorse Bush's candidacy. On the campaign trail, Bush repeatedly cited their relationship as proof that he could work with Democrats—a quality voters found appealing after the vitriolic partisanship of the Clinton years. Meanwhile, Clinton's vice-president, Al Gore, captured the Democratic nomination but had to work hard to distance himself from the personal scandals of Clinton while at the same time

George W. Bush taking the oath of office as governor of Texas, 1/17/95. *Texas State Library & Archives Commission*

taking his share of credit for the robust national economy during the eight years of the Clinton administration.

In the November 2000 election, Bush lost the popular vote to Gore by some 500,000 votes, but, following a protracted and controversial vote recount in Florida and a favorable ruling by the U.S. Supreme Court, the Texas governor was declared the winner of the electoral vote and became president. It was an inauspicious start, but Bush was eager to get to work. Bush brought many Texans to Washington with him to serve in his administration, and Texas Republicans also occupied prominent positions in Congress, including House Majority Leader Dick Armey of Irving and Majority Whip Tom DeLay of Houston. In Texas, Lieutenant Governor Rick Perry, a Democrat-turned-Republican who had come up through the ranks of the state government, succeeded to the governorship.

Texas Democrats may have a very difficult time reclaiming their majority status. Since the 1970s, the Democratic party in Texas has increasingly become the party of inner-city and minority voters, while the Republicans have swept the suburbs and West Texas and have made major inroads into the rural East Texas vote. One of the Democrats' biggest problems has been voter turnout; African American and Hispanic turnout tends to be significantly lower than that of whites. Democrats also have been frustrated by their inability to forge strong coalitions across racial and ethnic lines, as black and Hispanic political interests have tended to evolve along separate paths.

In the 1970s and 1980s, Hispanic political power had grown, almost always operating within the liberal wing of the Democratic party. The number of Hispanics registered to vote increased from 488,000 in 1976 to over 1.3 million in 1995, and that year voters elected 2,215 Hispanics to public office. That number included twenty-five state legislators and Attorney General Dan Morales. Texas sent five Tejanos to Congress, led by longtime San Antonio congressman Henry B. Gonzalez, who chaired the powerful House Banking Committee and retired in 1998 after a thirty-seven-year career in the House. An alliance between sympathetic Anglos and middle-class Hispanics had shaped the new ethnic politics, and the best-known Hispanic politician became Henry Cisneros, who had served as mayor of San Antonio during the 1980s without overtly using his ethnicity to win office. Increasingly, middle-class whites (as well as blacks) found they could support Hispanic politicians when the issues involved concerns that affected all urban citizens—law enforcement, better streets and highways, education, economic development, and the like. Thus, political activism among Hispanics in the 1980s and 1990s represented a return to the mainstream and a move away from the militancy of the 1960s. Indeed, Republicans like George W. Bush even made some inroads into the Hispanic vote; Bush, who frequently addressed Hispanic audiences in Spanish, got between 37 and 39 percent of the Hispanic vote in 1998, and 35 percent nationwide in the 2000 presidential race. Hispanics in the 1990s also were hurt by the withdrawal from public life of two of their highest-profile leaders: Henry Cisneros, who resigned from his position as housing secretary in the Clinton administration following a scandal; and state attorney general Dan Morales, who voluntarily retired from politics.

Black voters remained more wedded than Hispanics to the Democratic party in the 1990s, with only 10 percent of them indicating a Republican-party preference. The number of black elected officials in the state in 1992 was 472, including 2 U.S. congressional representatives, 2 state senators, and 14 members of the house. By 2000, about 11 percent of all registered voters in Texas were African American and 19 percent were Hispanic. Democrats still controlled about 4,000 of the 5,000 county-level offices in Texas, and it is here that black political power is most influential. George W. Bush often spoke of reaching out to African Americans, but his standing with them was injured by his refusal as governor to sign the James Byrd Hate-Crimes Act, a bill named for a black man from Jasper who in 1998 was abducted by three white supremacists, chained to a pickup truck, and dragged to his death. After Bush's move to the White House, Governor Rick Perry in 2001 reluctantly signed the bill, which toughened penalties for crimes committed because of the victim's race, religion, color, gender, disability, sexual preference, age, national origin, or ancestry.

Black political power has been most strongly evinced in city politics, especially in Dallas and Houston. There, the dynamics have been similar to Tejano politics in San Antonio. In the 1990s, black mayors Ron Kirk in Dallas and Lee Brown in Houston succeeded in building coalitions across racial lines around issues such as city services and economic development, sometimes butting heads with more traditional minority politicians who had come to politics through the civil rights movement of the 1960s.

In summary, Texas politics since 1970 has been a roller-coaster ride, with plenty of excitement, controversy, and colorful personalities. But none of this should conceal the fundamental reality of political life as the Lone Star State enters the new millennium: Texas remains true to its conservative political heritage. Party labels may change, and in time, demographic change may make the election of liberals once again possible. But for the foreseeable future, Texas will continue to be a state dominated by conservative voters.

Historic Assumptions in Transition

In the late twentieth century, Texans found many of their institutions and policies inadequate or ill-suited to the needs of a diverse, modern, urban, and industrial state. Among these are such fundamental matters as public and higher education, the criminal justice system, the water supply, environmental protection, and the tax system. Long-held assumptions about how best to deal with these issues have, for the most part, determined policy and budgetary decisions. But these assumptions may have to change if the state is to meet the challenges of the future.

Public Education:
An Ideological and Financial Battleground

Since the 1980s, there has been a widespread perception that the state's system of public education needs reforming. There, however, the consensus ends; few issues in recent times have evoked as strong opinions, heated emotions, and conflicting ideas as the question of what to do about the public schools of Texas. Disagreements generally revolve around three related issues: 1) How can the quality of education be improved?; 2) How should the system be funded?; and 3) How can a high-quality education be made available to all Texas children?

The first issue—how to improve the quality of instruction—has been the source of much ideological disagreement. The state government had grappled with educational inadequacies since the 1960s. Between 1969 and 1975, the legislature sought to improve the system in piecemeal fashion, extending the school year to 180 days, buttressing special-education programs, creating bilingual programs, and increasing state funding for teachers' salaries, school operating expenses, and student transportation costs. Although the state tinkered with methods of state funding to school districts several times between 1977 and 1981, it still ranked thirtieth nationally in pay to teachers in 1980 and thirty-eighth in expenditures per pupil. Texas was also near the bottom on Scholastic Achievement Test scores.

In 1984, the concern over education led Governor Mark White, with a strong push from Lieutenant Governor Bill Hobby, to appoint a committee on school reform, headed by Dallas billionaire Ross Perot. The committee's recommendations led to House Bill 72 (HB 72), which enacted school reforms at a cost of $2.8 billion.

Among the many provisions of HB 72 were higher salaries and competency testing for teachers, stricter teacher-certification rules, and the requirement that secondary-school teachers get degrees in specific academic subjects rather than in education. But the most controversial aspect of the law was actually one of its minor components, the so-called "no-pass, no-play" rule. HB 72 raised the minimum passing grade to 70; students failing to make that mark in any required course would not be eligible to participate in extracurricular activities, including sports, unless the next six-weeks grade report showed a passing grade. Despite widespread praise, some parents and coaches organized campaigns to modify no-pass, no-play. (In 1995, the legislature watered down the rule, cutting the suspension period from six weeks to three and allowing students to continue to practice but not participate in interscholastic competition.) Voters also demanded that the appointed school board be made elective, despite opposition from major newspapers, Lieutenant Governor Hobby, and Ross Perot. Otherwise, the reforms stayed in place; most Texans approved of their general parameters.

By the mid-1990s, there was a widespread perception that the education reforms of the 1980s had not solved the problem. The new Republican governor, George W. Bush, ran for office in 1994 as an education reformer. At his urging, when the legislature convened the following year, it enacted the Public

Schools Reform Act. The centerpiece of the bill was a school accountability system, under which schools and districts received ratings based on their students' performance on a statewide standardized test, the Texas Assessment of Academic Skills (TAAS). Schools were required to meet minimum standards on TAAS and to lower dropout rates. Another reform was the charter-school program, which allowed the creation of public schools that are exempted from many state regulations, allowing them to be more innovative in both educational and administrative matters. By 2001, the state had 163 operational charter schools, with more slated to open soon. As another component in its "school-choice" philosophy, the Bush administration also supported the idea of school vouchers, which would allow parents to use a proportion of state education dollars to pay the cost of tuition at a private school. However, a small-scale voucher bill failed in the House in 1999, and it was not a priority of the new administration of Governor Rick Perry in 2001.

The Bush reforms had their share of critics. Opponents of standardized testing complained that students and teachers have become slaves to TAAS, with students and teachers devoting far too much classroom time to prepping for the yearly test. Likewise, critics branded the charter-school program a failure, citing lower-than-average TAAS scores at those schools and a few well-publicized examples of malfeasance at individual campuses. Enemies of vouchers depicted them as the first step toward abolishing the system of public education. Whether these ideas will prove successful in the long run remains an open question. However, George W. Bush touted these ideas in his successful 2000 presidential campaign as a model for the nation to follow.

The issue of education reform can never be separated from questions regarding funding. Even as the state wrestled with the 1984 reforms, a group of poor school districts, represented by the Mexican American Legal Defense Fund (MALDEF), sued the state, contending that its method of financing public schools was unconstitutional. In the Texas system, local property taxes paid for nearly half of the cost of public education, and, as everyone knew, property in affluent areas produced far more tax revenue than property in poor areas. As a consequence, the 100 wealthiest of the state's 1,086 school districts spent $7,233 per pupil in 1986, while the poorest 100 spent $2,978. A state court ruled in favor of the plaintiffs, and the state supreme court upheld the ruling in 1989.

Facing a court-ordered deadline after several failed efforts to address the issue in the early 1990s, in 1993 the legislature passed a law that took a share of property taxes from the 100 high-property-wealth districts to balance the overall funding. Dubbed the "Robin Hood" bill, the law was upheld by the Texas Supreme Court in 1995, but it has faced widespread criticism and legal challenges from wealthier districts that are forced to send millions of dollars to the state, which in turn redistributes the funds to poorer districts. Leaders from both parties acknowledge that the structure of the present funding system must be fundamentally changed, but when the 2001 legislative session ended, all efforts to do so had failed. At the beginning of the twenty-first century, Texas remains below the national average in per-capita spending on public education, placing the state below the national average, and local property taxes continue to finance nearly half of the total cost.

The inequities in public education have grown more pronounced because of the changes in the state's population. The Dallas school system in 2001 was 52 percent Hispanic, 37 percent African American, 9 percent white, and 2 percent Asian American. Houston's statistics were similar. Giving up on ever achieving racial balance in schools, city leaders in the 1980s and 1990s began to stress the need to improve minority academic performance and reduce the dropout rates, whatever the racial balance of a particular school or district. In recent times, Republican proponents of school-choice measures and standardized testing sometimes found allies in the minority community, where failing schools were a source of much concern. On the other hand, urban parents and school officials clamored for the state to commit significantly more financial resources overall to public education, something the legislatures of the late 1990s and early 2000s have been loathe to do. In the final analysis, despite many efforts to make public education more effective and accessible to all, long-held assumptions about the proper role of the state in achieving these goals continue to hold sway. Most observers believe that these assumptions simply have to change if Texas is to meet the challenges of the new century.

Higher Education: A World-Class System?

Since the 1970s, enrollments in state institutions of higher education have grown slowly but steadily. A total of 966,840 students attended Texas's 101 public and 39 private colleges and universities in the fall of 1999. Approximately 90 percent of them attended state-supported institutions; nearly half (412,684) were enrolled in the state's fifty public community-college districts. The gender makeup of the campus populations has changed. In Texas, as in the nation, more females than males now attend institutions of higher learning. Although certain degree programs remain feminized, the numbers of women enrolled in the sciences, business schools, and masters of arts programs are all now roughly equal to those of males. Men still dominated Ph.D. programs in 2001. However, by the 1980s, professional programs such as law and veterinary science were no longer the male preserves that they once had been. In the 1990s, nearly 42 percent of new faculty hired were women, although, overall, male professors still outnumbered females by 3 to 1. The college population has aged slightly since the 1970s, partially because of the growth of community colleges and the number of students who are working. Compared to thirty years ago, the average student now takes longer to graduate, with most of them requiring more than five years to do so. The student bodies have also turned toward political conservatism and occupational pragmatism (trends that largely began in the 1980s); one-third of all Texas college students major in business. The past three decades, then, have witnessed major changes on the Texas campuses that will shape the state in the twenty-first century.

One such change since the 1970s has been the effort to increase racial and ethnic diversity on college campuses. In 1983, the state implemented the first of several Equal Educational Opportunity Plans for Higher Education. These were five-year affirmative-action plans aimed at increasing the enrollment of minorities at Texas's major universities. Under these plans, universities undertook extensive minority recruiting and retention programs and made efforts to increase the diversity of faculty. A second five-year plan was initiated by Governor Bill Clements in 1989, and a third by Governor Ann Richards in 1994. These plans produced modest results. By 1992, African Americans accounted for about 9 percent of state university students (up about one percentage point from 1989), and Hispanics comprised 16 percent (up two percentage points). Of the 2,000 doctoral degrees conferred in 1991, only 72 went to blacks and 56 went to Hispanics.

In 1996, a landmark court case brought a major policy shift. Denied admission to the University of Texas Law School, four white applicants sued the state of Texas, claiming that the university had violated the equal protection clause of the Fourteenth Amendment when it used racial preferences in making admission decisions. The Fifth Circuit Court of Appeals found in favor of the plaintiffs, and Texas Attorney General Dan Morales soon ruled that the decision, *Hopwood* v. *State of Texas*, required all of the state's universities to administer admissions, financial aid, and student retention programs on a race-neutral basis.

The *Hopwood* case and its aftermath have had mixed effects. Overall, minority enrollments at state universities did not decline significantly—in large part because U.T. and A&M were the only state institutions that openly used race or ethnicity as an admissions factor. Those two institutions immediately saw significant decreases in the numbers of blacks and Hispanics enrolled. By 2001, however, minority enrollments at the two flagship universities had essentially returned to pre-*Hopwood* levels, in part because of a bill passed in 1997 (HB 588) that provided automatic admission at Texas public universities to any student in the top 10 percent of his or her high school class. Nationally, the laws concerning affirmative action remain in flux; *Hopwood* was upheld by the U.S. Supreme Court in June 2001, but other similar cases are still winding their way through the lower courts, and experts believe that the high court has yet to issue the definitive decision on affirmative action in college admissions.

A different sort of equal-access issue has involved the geographic availability of higher education. In 1987, MALDEF filed a suit on behalf of LULAC (League of United Latin American Citizens) against the state, charging that the lack of graduate and professional programs in South Texas constituted discrimination against Mexican Americans. After a lower court ruled in favor of the plaintiffs, the legislature created the South Texas Initiative, which allocated millions of extra dollars to the nine state universities in San Antonio, Corpus Christi, Kingsville, and along the Rio Grande. Nearly 100 new academic programs were created. Although the state supreme court eventually overturned the lower court's decision and ruled that the state had not intentionally discriminated against border residents, the Initiative continued. In 1993 alone, the Initiative pumped $460 million into the South Texas schools. The additions in 1989 of the Brownsville and Edinburg campuses to the U.T. System, and the Laredo, Kingsville, and Corpus Christi schools to the A&M system, were another part of the overall effort to improve the quality of higher education in South Texas.

As in the case of the public schools, the fate of higher education in Texas has depended, in large measure, on money. Funding for Texas colleges and universities traditionally came from two sources: general tax revenue and the Permanent University Fund (PUF). In any given year, over 90 percent of the funds that state-supported colleges and universities receive from the state government comes from general tax revenues; the PUF endowment accounts for the rest. Since 1931, Texas A&M and the University of Texas have shared PUF funding, with A&M receiving one-third of the revenues and U.T. two-thirds. On an inflation-adjusted basis, state spending on higher education (apart from the PUF) has remained virtually unchanged since the mid-1980s.

The PUF, the value of which was pushed up by the oil boom to more than $2 billion in 1986, had long created a general feeling that the university system discriminated between the haves (the University of Texas and Texas A&M) and the have-nots. In 1984, voters ratified a constitutional amendment allowing the other member schools of the U.T. and A&M systems to draw upon PUF funds—the first major change in PUF rules in half a century. The following year, in an effort to secure more dependable funding for the schools outside the A&M and U.T. systems, the state created the Higher Education Assistance Fund (HEAF) to pay for capital improvements on the other campuses. Since the mid-1990s, the legislature has earmarked $50 million annually to be placed in a permanent endowment for HEAF, with the goal of eventually making HEAF a self-sustaining fund like the PUF. To counteract rising costs and declining revenues, the legislature raised resident tuition in 1985 for the first time in three decades; it has increased steadily ever since, from $4 per semester hour in 1985 to $42 in 2001. Nonetheless, higher education is still a bargain in Texas. Of the fifteen largest states in 1999–2000, ten charged higher tuition and fees than did Texas.

For many decades, Texans believed that the two flagship universities, plus a few other second-tier universities and teachers' colleges, would be adequate to meet the state's higher-education needs. Since the 1970s, however, the realization has been slowly growing that a world-class system of higher education is not a luxury but a necessity if Texas is to make a successful transition to the twenty-first century. A mediocre university system eventually will mean lower wages and incomes, depressed tax revenues, and a loss of good-paying "new-economy" jobs to those states that *have* invested adequately in higher education. But universities will have to compete with prisons, public schools, health care, and other programs for their share of the state's budget. When Governor Rick Perry took office in 2001, he placed higher education at the top of his list of priorities and singled out three specific areas on which his administration would concentrate: making a college education accessible to more students, boosting funding for research, and recruiting top-caliber faculty. The question remains whether any one governor or legislature—especially if the economy slows and budgets tighten—will be able to deliver on such promises.

The Challenges of Criminal Justice

In 1972, Texas inmate David Ruiz filed a handwritten lawsuit against the director of the Texas Department of Corrections (TDC), W. J. Estelle, in the court of U.S. District Judge William Wayne Justice of Tyler. Ruiz charged that conditions in the prison at Huntsville violated inmates' civil rights. *Ruiz* v. *Estelle* went to trial in 1978, and Judge Justice's ruling in 1980 ordered the state to clean up the problems of prison overcrowding, inmate brutality, and other shortcomings. The ordered changes were expensive as well as broad, and they could not be made overnight. In 1983, the legislature appropriated $750 million to build new units and upgrade older ones. Failure to hold the prison population below the court-ordered 95 percent of capacity led the state to refuse to admit some prisoners, overcrowding county jails and prompting the early release of some inmates. In December 1986, Judge Justice found the TDC in contempt of court and threatened to fine the state up to $24 million per month until the prison system's inadequacies were rectified.

By 1990, the situation had improved, and federal supervision of the prison system had been relaxed somewhat. But the issues of overcrowded prisons and high rates of crime persisted well into the 1990s. The prison population grew from 18,151 in 1975 to 92,000 at the end of 1994. When the crime rate continued to climb in the 1990s, the state embarked on the largest prison-expansion program ever. Between 1990 and 1998, the state spent over $2.3 billion on new prisons. By August 2000, the Texas Department of Criminal Justice, or TDCJ (as it had been renamed in 1989), was operating 51 prison units and 9 other assorted facilities, and the inmate population had grown to 133,000—second only to that of California.

The crime rate in most categories had dropped by the end of the 1990s. The rate of recidivism (when a felon commits another felony after release from prison) also fell, from 52 percent in 1992 to 31 percent in 2000, a ten-year low. Some credited longer prison terms for these improvements in crime statistics, while others argued that the improvement was simply due to the long economic expansion of the 1990s. In 2001, Judge Justice pronounced Texas prisons "vastly improved" and removed most remaining federal supervision of Texas prisons.

The presidential campaign of George W. Bush focused national attention on the Texas prison system. The Bush campaign touted the fact that crime had declined during his tenure as governor, suggesting that tougher sentencing had worked in Texas. Opponents focused on the death penalty, which Texas has used liberally. Between 1976 and February 2001, the state executed 242 inmates; 152 of these executions occurred during Bush's tenure as governor, including a record 40 executions in 2000. A total of 448 condemned criminals sat on Texas's death row at the beginning of 2001, 63 percent of whom were black or Hispanic. In recent years, Texas had carried out nearly half of the executions in the nation. On the campaign trail, Bush repeatedly responded to criticism by asserting that the death penalty was applied fairly in Texas and that the state had never executed an innocent person. A poll conducted in 2000 revealed that nearly three-quarters of Texans supported capital punishment, but more than half of them also believed the state had indeed executed innocent people. In 2001, after Rick Perry succeeded George W. Bush in the governor's office, legislators debated two highly publicized bills regarding the death penalty. One would have instituted a moratorium on executions while the system was reassessed, and the other would outlaw the execution of the mentally retarded. The first failed in the legislature; Governor Perry vetoed the other.

With the incarcerated population now the equivalent of a city the size of Abilene, observers on all sides of the criminal-justice issue are beginning to agree that changes must be made in the way Texas deals with crime and criminals. Of those in prison in 1994, 85 percent were high school dropouts, 45 percent were illiterate, 80 percent were drug or alcohol abusers; and 12 percent were incarcerated for drug-related offenses. An improved education system, better substance-abuse programs, new in-prison rehabilitation programs, and a rethinking of issues relating to sentencing and parole will become increasingly urgent priorities in the coming years.

The Water Dilemma

Well-meaning people may disagree on the need for more prisons, but everybody agrees on the need for more water. But where adequate water supplies will come from, and how that water will be paid for, are among the thorniest questions facing Texans in the new century.

Texas water comes from two sources, surface water (rivers and lakes) and the state's seven major and sixteen minor underground aquifers. In the 1990s, underground water (or groundwater) accounted for more than half of all water used in the state; nearly three-quarters of it was used for agricultural irrigation. Many small and medium-sized Texas cities, and some large ones (including San Antonio), also get most of their municipal water from underground sources. Since most Texas rivers are small and often dry for part of the year, and since there are no natural lakes within the borders of the state, surface water mostly comes from man-made reservoirs.

In Texas law, the state holds all surface water in trust for the people and regulates its use through the issuance of permits. Underground water, on the other hand, historically has been governed by an entirely different law: the "rule of capture," which allows landowners to pump unlimited amounts of water from wells on their land. Aquifers recharge from surface water percolating down through the ground, but at varying rates. Some, like the giant Ogallala Aquifer that underlies most of the Panhandle and contains 90 percent of the state's groundwater, recharge so slowly that pumping them is basically a mining operation. The dual legal system, then, means that the most renewable part of the state's water supply—surface water—can be regulated, while the least-renewable part—the underground aquifers—has been left in the hands of individuals with little personal incentive to practice conservation. With so much of the state dependent on groundwater, and with the demands rapidly growing as the population expands, the need for some sort of effective, comprehensive water plan has become increasingly urgent.

In the years since World War II, a bewildering array of state agencies, often with overlapping or conflicting jurisdictions, has attempted to exert authority over sources of water. The growth of cities and the demands of modern agriculture have led to intense regional and rural-urban conflicts over this vital resource.

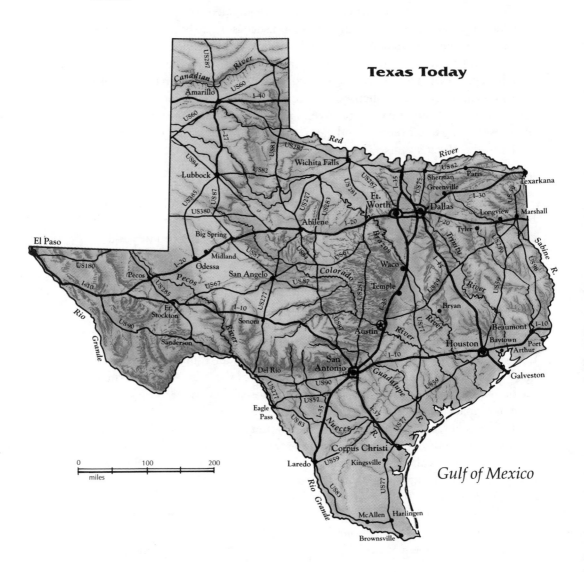

In the late 1940s, concerns in the High Plains over depletion of the mammoth Ogallala Aquifer—and fear that the state government might take matters into its own hands and start regulating groundwater from Austin—led Panhandle leaders to lobby for the creation of groundwater districts. The lobbying succeeded, and in 1949, the Ground Water District Act provided for the creation of local regulatory agencies with the power to regulate the spacing of wells and the amount of water pumped from aquifers. The High Plains Underground Water Conservation District was the first groundwater district created under the law's provisions. By 1992, thirty-four groundwater districts had been established.

The record of these districts has been mixed. Some, like the High Plains district, have enjoyed modest success in slowing the depletion of aquifers. Others, like the Edwards district, which is supposed to conserve the Edwards Aquifer in the Austin–San Antonio area, have been caught up in a battle between urban and agricultural interests and have proven largely ineffective. Overall, since the 1980s Texas has been using groundwater at about double the rate that it naturally recharges.

Every Texas governor since Price Daniel has acknowledged the need for a comprehensive water plan, but all their efforts have failed, due either to opposition from powerful interest groups or the seemingly prohibitive cost of such projects. In 1969, West Texans and their allies pushed through the Texas Water Plan, a constitutional amendment that authorized the transfer of water from the Mississippi River to the High Plains. The project was both costly and environmentally unsound. The legislature submitted the proposed amendment to the voters, who turned it down by a narrow margin. West Texas remained dependent on underground water.

In 1997, the legislature created sixteen regional groups to provide more comprehensive planning for both surface and groundwater resources. The groups soon identified nearly $17 billion in new water-project needs, plus $80–$100 billion in needs for repair and replacement of existing water-related infrastructure. A bill proposed in the 2001 legislative session was intended to fund $200 million per year of these needs, but by the time the bill passed, opponents had stripped it of its funding. In short, Texas enters the new millennium with the state's water needs growing more serious by the year and with no comprehensive plan for meeting them.

No single solution will solve the water dilemma. Building more dams on the state's rivers reduces flows to farmers and to cities below the dams. Drawing too much water from rivers also reduces the flow into the Gulf of Mexico, which can damage the fishing and shrimping industries in coastal bays and lead to the intrusion of salt water into environmentally-sensitive wetlands. Drawing water from aquifers lowers the water table, often reducing or ending the flow of springs that feed rivers. Limiting the amount of water that can be drawn from aquifers hurts farmers, which in turn injures the rural economy and drives up food prices. Clearly, an intelligent, coordinated plan that combines new surface-water projects with innovative conservation measures in all areas holds the key to the future. Whether the state will succeed in implementing such a plan before matters reach crisis levels remains to be seen. In water, as in so many other areas, Texans are still struggling to reconcile their frontier values of limited government and private property rights with the needs of a modern, urban, industrial state.

Protecting the Texas Environment

For many years, Texans thought of pollution as something that happened in Los Angeles or the industrial cities of the North. The relatively small size of Texas cities, the relative lack of heavy industry, and the state's wide-open spaces allowed people to adopt a laissez-faire attitude toward environmental protection. The assumption that the natural environment could take care of itself went virtually unchallenged until the 1960s, and for many years thereafter it remained very low on the priority list of most Texans.

Between the 1960s and 1990s, a crazy-quilt of state agencies was charged with protecting water quality: first the Texas Water Pollution Control Board, then the Texas Water Quality Board, then the Texas Department of Water Resources, later the Texas Water Commission, and finally the Texas Natural Resources Conservation Commission (TNRCC). Air pollution control followed a similar trajectory. The state's first Air Control Board was appointed in 1966; in 1993, along with the Water Commission, it was consolidated into the TNRCC, which would have jurisdiction over all air, water, and solid-waste regulatory programs. These agencies expanded over time, primarily because of federal mandates imposed by the various Clean Air and Clean Water acts of the past four decades.

By most standards, these state agencies and their efforts were inadequate. In 1990, Texas ranked worst among all fifty states in carbon dioxide emissions, a principal component in air pollution and a widely suspected cause of global warming. In 1992, the EPA identified twenty-eight hazardous-waste sites in Texas bad enough to entitle them to cleanup under the federal Superfund program. By the end of the century, pollution in Texas had gotten worse. Texas released more ozone-producing chemicals into the air, produced more carcinogenic benzene and vinyl chloride, and operated more hazardous-waste incinerators than any other state. In 1999, Houston passed Los Angeles as the city with the nation's worst air quality. Health alerts due to smog became common in the late 1990s in Houston, Dallas, and Austin.

In the 2000 presidential race, George W. Bush defended the state's environmental record, citing a bill that allowed nearly a thousand aging industrial plants built before 1971 to reduce emissions voluntarily. Critics pointed out that as governor, Bush had blocked stronger legislation that would have *forced* these plants to cut emissions. Indeed, at the beginning of 2000, only about 15 percent of the plants had agreed to the voluntary reductions.

No part of Texas has faced greater environmental challenges than the Texas-Mexican border region. As the *maquiladoras*—U.S.-owned factories built to take advantage of cheap labor—proliferated on the Mexican side of the border in the 1980s and 1990s, the region's population grew dramatically, with negative effects on the local environment. Demands for water at times reduced the flow of the Rio Grande to a trickle, and it became one of North America's most polluted rivers. Smog became a visible problem even in Big Bend National Park. Mexico's poverty made it hard for that nation to enforce its already-inadequate environmental laws. Soon after becoming president in 2001, Bush met with his Mexican counterpart, President Vicente Fox, and secured Fox's assurances that Mexico would begin to abide by international agreements on water use. Time will tell whether a new spirit of international cooperation will lead to a cleaner future for the people of the border region.

Issues of pollution and development have increasingly led to conflicts among state and federal regulators, lawmakers, and private citizens over efforts to protect endangered species. Since the 1970s, Texas has been the scene of some notable successes in rescuing some animals from the brink of extinction. Most famous has been the ongoing program at the Aransas National Wildlife Refuge near Corpus Christi to save the whooping crane. Bald eagles and wild turkeys have returned to sections of the state from which they had virtually vanished. Efforts to save other, less glamorous species have run afoul of property-rights advocates who object to state or federal intrusion on their land or interference with agriculture or development. For example, the extremely rare Texas Blind Salamander, which is found only in underground water in the Edwards Aquifer near San Marcos, faces possible extinction as wells draw down the level of the aquifer to meet the water needs of the Austin–San Antonio area. In the Hill Country, the golden-cheeked warbler faces pressure as development in the hills west of Austin reduces its habitat.

Efforts to protect the environment, then, have shared much in common with attempts to improve education, water supplies, or prisons. Texans' historic suspicions of government, combined with the desire for low taxes and economic growth, have limited the effectiveness of environmental-protection programs. Nevertheless, attitudes seem to be changing. A 1999 poll revealed that more than half of Texans considered urban sprawl a significant problem. In Houston, a city long noted for its pro-growth attitudes, environmentalists defeated a proposal to build a new airport on the Katy Prairie west of town, an environmentally sensitive wetland. Support for clean energy sources such as wind power is growing. Despite signs of change, a consensus has yet to emerge regarding the proper roles of the state and the private sector in keeping Texas both safe and beautiful for future generations.

Taxes: A Decision Deferred?

Few assumptions have been as firmly rooted in the Texan mindset as the proposition that low taxes bring economic growth. Texas's tax structure, consequently, has evolved in an almost topsy-turvy manner. The state raises revenue through a franchise tax on corporations; various "sin taxes" (taxes on cigarettes, alcohol, etc.); excise taxes; gasoline and motor-vehicle taxes; severance taxes on oil and natural gas; local property taxes; and, since 1962, a general sales tax. Since then, when taxes have had to be raised, the sales tax has been a handy choice. During the 1970s and early 1980s, Governors Smith, Briscoe, and Clements all promised not to raise taxes and to raise revenue instead through economic growth.

The population swell of the 1970s and 1980s put pressure on schools and other institutions and necessitated increased appropriations. But rising oil prices boosted revenue from the severance tax, so the state once again could avoid raising taxes—unless, of course, government services needed to be expanded, which the legislature was reluctant to do. Critics of the tax system pointed out other problems. Although food purchases were exempted from it, the sales tax fell hardest on those who could least afford it. The *Dallas Morning News* estimated in 1988 that low-income and middle-income Texans paid, respectively, five times and three times more proportionally of their earnings in taxes than did the wealthy. The franchise tax applied only to about 15 percent of the businesses in the state, and, since it taxed investment rather than profits, it actually discouraged economic growth.

When oil prices collapsed in the 1980s, so did 25 percent of the state's revenue. In 1982, severance taxes on oil provided 30 percent of the state's revenue; by 1988, this proportion had fallen to 8 percent. Since the state constitution mandated a balanced budget, the legislature had to raise taxes in 1984, 1986, 1988, 1990, and 1991. The largest of these, the $5.7 billion hike of 1987, raised various sin taxes and fees, increased the franchise tax, and boosted the state's share of the sales tax from 5.25 percent to 6 percent. This occurred at the same time that the federal government declared state sales taxes nondeductible from federal income taxes. A smaller $528 million tax increase in 1990 raised the sales tax again, this time to 6.25 percent, the third-highest in the country. It also raised the state tax on cigarettes from 26 to 41 cents per pack, the highest in the nation. The 1991 tax bill raised gasoline taxes from 15 to 20 cents per gallon. Because such taxes fall disproportionately on the poor, they made the system even more regressive than before.

The 1987 deficit led the legislature and Governor Clements to create a Select Committee on Tax Equity. Although it did not make actual recommendations, in 1988 the committee issued a report that unmistakably implied that Texas needed to restructure its tax system radically. First, it suggested that the state should change the antiquated 1907 franchise tax, so that businesses making money in the new service economy would pay their fair share. The other major recommendation suggested the unthinkable: a personal income tax. Lieutenant Governor Bill Hobby (who was not seeking reelection) and state comptroller Bob Bullock both endorsed an income tax in 1989. Negative public reaction was swift, and almost all candidates in the elections of 1990—and in all major races since then—promised to oppose it. As a consequence, the state never acted on the 1988 report, except for an important restructuring of the franchise tax in 1991 to tax business incomes as well as assets. A state personal income tax remains taboo. At the close of the twentieth century, Texans still paid among the lowest state taxes in the nation. In 1999, Texas taxes were the lowest of the fifteen-largest states, and the state ranked forty-seventh in state taxes paid per capita. The sales tax generated 55 percent of all state tax revenue. Without a state income tax, property taxes in Texas are among the highest in the nation, with home- and business-owners shouldering more than 40 percent of the state's tax burden. There is widespread agreement that both property and sales taxes have reached the maximum limits that the economy can stand and that citizens will tolerate.

Governor Bush in 1997 proposed the most sweeping structural changes in the state's tax code in thirty years. The centerpiece was a $2.8 billion reduction in property taxes and the elimination of the franchise tax, to be financed by higher sales taxes and a new, broader tax on businesses. But when his proposals emerged from the legislature, all that remained was a modest increase in the homestead exemption—the equivalent of about $140 per year in savings to the average homeowner—which voters approved.

The state's system of taxation overall remains heavily regressive; a nonpartisan tax research group estimated that in 1998 the poorest 20 percent of Texans spent 16 percent of their income paying state and local taxes, while the wealthiest 20 percent spent less than 4 percent of theirs. George W. Bush's unsuccessful attempt to restructure the tax system demonstrated how resistant it is to change. Experts predict that unless fundamental changes are made to the state's system of taxation, built-in budget deficits in the range of 8 percent per year can be expected by 2007, assuming no changes in the level of state services. Whether those changes will be along the lines of those recommended by Hobby and Bullock in the 1980s, Bush in the 1990s, or some yet-to-be-proposed plan, remains to be seen. But almost all of the challenges facing Texans in the twenty-first century will hinge upon a rethinking of how they will pay for state and local government

CONCLUSION

The historical trends since 1970 have made Texas more like the rest of the nation. Despite the decline of oil revenue, personal incomes have moved closer to the national average. The migration into Texas of many Hispanics and the enfranchisement of minorities have moderated the Democratic party by making it less politically conservative and replacing rural leaders with those from urban areas. Meanwhile, the Republican party in Texas, as elsewhere in the South, seems to have won the majority of the white voters' loyalties and now represents conservative political values. The state clearly has left its older economic reliance on a boom-or-bust raw-material economy. Although Texans and other North Americans may still think of the Lone Star State as the domain of cowboys and oil tycoons, its inhabitants more closely resemble those of other urban states in transition to a service economy. Future prosperity is likely to depend on electronics, telecommunications, high-tech manufacturing, and business services.

Ingrained problems remain. The new urban leadership must find ways to extend economic opportunity to all citizens. That means solving such problems as high minority unemployment, a relatively low number of minority high school and college graduates, fewer jobs in minority neighborhoods, tense minority-police relations, and the flight of the affluent to the suburbs. These problems, too, may be national as well as local and may force Texans to think less in terms of frontier-style self-reliance and more in terms of intra- and interstate cooperation. Whichever party becomes the majority one, its leaders will have to address issues of education, water, transportation, and an inadequate taxing system.

The concerns faced by Texans today are not particularly new ones. Texas has wrestled with the dilemmas of taxation, education, a shifting heterogeneous population, and cyclical economic prosperity and recession since the founding of the Republic. These issues seemed more critical at the beginning of the twenty-first century, however, as a dynamic global economy bombarded the state and the nation with problems and opportunities that could not be addressed from simply a parochial or even a national perspective. The impact of these new forces clearly has compelled the citizenry to contemplate their declining resources in an increasingly competitive national and international marketplace.

The leaders of the state and the nation must face the issue of extending opportunities to all citizens without destroying the social fabric or the natural environment. It seems critical, therefore, that a state with its eyes on the twenty-first century also look back to the past to try to understand how and why the state's citizens behave as they do, and to determine what changes need to be made in order to survive in and contribute positively to the modern world.

READINGS

Books

Buenger, Walter, and Joe Pratt, *But Also Good Business: Texas Commerce Banks and the Financing of Houston and Texas* (College Station: Texas A&M University Press, 1986).

Bullard, Robert D., *Invisible Houston: The Black Experience in Boom and Bust* (College Station: Texas A&M University Press, 1987).

Champagne, Anthony, and Edward Hapham, *Texas at the Crossroads: People, Politics and Policy* (College Station: Texas A&M University Press, 1987).

Downs, Fane, "Texas Women at Work," in *Texas: Sesquicentennial Celebration*, ed. Donald Wisenhunt (Austin: Eakin Press, 1986).

Feagin, Joe R., *Free Enterprise City: Houston in Political-Economic Perspective* (New Brunswick, NJ: Rutgers University Press, 1988)

Fletcher, Jesse C., *The Southern Baptist Convention: A Sesquicentennial History* (Nashville: Broadman & Holman, 1994).

Knaggs, John R., *Two Party Texas: The John Tower Era, 1961–1984* (Austin: Eakin Press, 1986).

Miller, Char, and Heywood T. Sanders (eds.), *Urban Texas: Politics and Development* (College Station: Texas A&M University, 1989).

Minutaglio, *Bill, First Son: George W. Bush and the Bush Family Dynasty* (New York: Times Books, 1999).

Montejano, David, *Anglos and Mexicans in the Making of Texas, 1836–1986* (Austin: University of Texas Press, 1987).

Norman, Mary Anne, *The Texas Economy since World War II* (Boston: American Press, 1983).

Platt, Howard, *City Building in the New South* (Philadelphia: Temple University Press, 1983).

Pratt, Joseph A., *The Growth of a Refining Region* (Greenwich, CT: JAI Press, 1980).

Quinn, Bernard, *Churches and Church Membership in the United States, 1980* (Washington, DC: Glenmary Research Center, 1982).

Sherrill, Robert, *The Oil Follies of 1970–1980* (Garden City, NY: Anchor Press, 1983).

Smallwood, J. B., Jr., "Conservation and Environmental Development in Texas," in *Texas: Sesquicentennial Celebration*, ed. Donald Wisenhunt (Austin: Eakin Press, 1986).

Story, John, *Texas Baptist Leadership and Social Christianity* (College Station: Texas A&M University Press, 1986).

Tolleson-Rhinehart, Sue, and Jeanie R. Stanley, *Claytie and the Lady: Ann Richards, Gender, and Politics in Texas* (Austin: University of Texas Press, 1994).

United Way of Texas, *With a View to the Future* (Austin: United Way, 1989).

Wisenhunt, Donald W., *The Development of Higher Education in Texas* (Boston: American Press, 1983).

Articles

Burka, Paul, "The Year Everything Changed," *Texas Monthly* 11 (1983): 100-109.

Davies, Christopher S., "Life at the Edge: Urban and Industrial Evolution of Texas, Frontier Wilderness-Frontier Space, 1836–1986," *Southwestern Historical Quarterly* (1986): 443–554.

Day, Barbara Thompson, "The Heart of Houston: The Early History of the Houston Council on Human Relations, 1958–1972," *Houston Review* 7 (1986): 1-32.

Goldberg, Robert A., "Racial Change on the Southern Periphery: The Case of San Antonio, Texas," *Journal of Southern History* 49 (1983): 349–74.

Loewenstein, Gaither, and Lytlleton T. Sanders, "Bloc Voting, Rainbow Coalitions and the Jackson Presidential Candidacy: A View from Southeast Texas," *Journal of Black Studies* 18 (1987): 86–96.

Plaut, Thomas R., "The Texas Economy," *Texas Business Review* (1983): 15–20.

Rice Center, "Houston Population and Employment Forecasts," *Research Summary Rice Center*: 1–4.

APPENDIX

Provincial Governors of Texas

Antonio Martínez, 1817–22
José Félix Trespalacios, 1822–23
Luciano García, 1823

Governors of Coahuila y Texas

Rafael González, 1824–26
José Ignacio de Arizpe, 1826
Victor Blanco, 1826–27
José Ignacio de Arizpe, 1827
José María Viesca (provisional)
Victor Blanco, 1827
José María Viesca, 1827–30
Rafael Eca y Músquiz, 1830–31
José María Viesca, 1831
José María de Letona, 1831–32
Rafael Eca y Músquiz, 1832–33
Juan Martín de Veramendi, 1833
Francisco Vidaurri y Villaseñor, 1833–34
Juan José Elguezábal, 1834–35
José María Cantú, 1835
Marciel Borrego, 1835
Agustín Viesca, 1835
Miguel Falcón, 1835
Bartolomé de Cárdenas, 1835
Rafael Eca y Músquiz 1835
Henry Smith, Nov. 14, 1835—March 1, 1836 (Provisional during
  Texas War for Independence)

Presidents of Texas

David G. Burnet	March 17, 1836–Oct. 22, 1836
Sam Houston	Oct. 22, 1836–Dec. 10, 1838
Mirabeau B. Lamar	Dec. 10, 1838–Dec. 13, 1841
Sam Houston	Dec. 13, 1841–Dec. 9, 1844
Anson Jones	Dec. 9, 1844–Feb. 19, 1846

Governors Of Texas

J. Pinckney Henderson	Feb. 19, 1846–Dec. 21, 1847
George T. Wood	Dec. 21, 1847–Dec. 21, 1849
P. Hansborough Bell	Dec. 21, 1849–Nov. 23, 1853
J. W. Henderson	Nov. 23, 1853–Dec. 21, 1853
Elisha M. Pease	Dec. 21, 1853–Dec. 21, 1857
Hardin R. Runnels	Dec. 21, 1857–Dec. 21, 1859
Sam Houston	Dec. 21, 1859–March 16, 1861
Edward Clark	March 16, 1861–Nov. 7, 1861
Francis R. Lubbock	Nov. 7, 1861–Nov. 5, 1863
Pendleton Murrah	Nov. 5, 1863–June 17, 1865
Andrew J. Hamilton	June 17, 1865–Aug. 9, 1866 Provisional
James W. Throckmorton	Aug. 9, 1866—Aug. 8, 1867
Elisha M. Pease	Aug. 8, 1867–Sept. 30, 1869 Provisional
Edmund J. Davis	Jan. 8, 1870–April 28, 1870 Provisional
Edmund J. Davis	April 28, 1870–Jan. 15, 1874
Richard Coke	Jan. 15, 1874–Dec. 1, 1876
Richard B. Hubbard	Dec. 1, 1876–Jan. 21, 1879
Oran M. Roberts	Jan. 21, 1879–Jan 16, 1883
John Ireland	Jan. 16, 1883–Jan. 18 1887
Lawrence Sullivan Ross	Jan. 18, 1887–Jan. 20, 1891
James Stephen Hogg	Jan. 20, 1891–Jan. 15, 1895
Charles A. Culberson	Jan. 15, 1895–Jan. 17, 1899
Joseph D. Sayers	Jan. 17, 1899–Jan. 20, 1903
S. W. T. Lanham	Jan. 20, 1903–Jan. 15, 1907
Thomas M. Campbell	Jan. 15, 1907–Jan. 17, 1911
Oscar Branch Colquitt	Jan. 17, 1911–Jan. 19, 1915
James E. Ferguson	Jan. 19, 1915–Sept. 25, 1917
William Pettus Hobby	Sept. 25, 1917–Jan. 18, 1921
Pat Morris Neff	Jan. 18, 1921–Jan. 20, 1925
Miriam A. Ferguson	Jan. 20, 1925–Jan. 18, 1927
Dan Moody	Jan. 18, 1927–Jan. 20, 1931
Ross S. Sterling	Jan. 20, 1931–Jan. 17, 1933

Miriam A. Ferguson	Jan. 17, 1933–Jan. 15, 1935
James V. Allred	Jan. 15, 1935–Jan. 15, 1939
W. Lee O'Daniel	Jan. 15, 1939–Aug. 4, 1941
Coke R. Stevenson	Aug. 4, 1941–Jan. 21, 1947
Beauford H. Jester	Jan. 21, 1947–July 11, 1949
Allan Shivers	July 11, 1949–Jan. 15, 1957
Price Daniel	Jan. 15, 1957–Jan. 15, 1963
John Connally	Jan. 15, 1963–Jan. 21, 1969
Preston Smith	Jan. 21, 1969–Jan. 16, 1973
Dolph Briscoe	Jan. 16, 1973–Jan. 16, 1979
William Clements	Jan. 16, 1979–Jan. 18, 1983
Mark White	Jan. 18, 1983–Jan. 20, 1987
William P. Clements, Jr.	Jan. 20, 1987–Jan. 15, 1991
Ann Richards	Jan. 15, 1991–Jan. 17, 1995
George W. Bush	Jan. 17, 1995–Jan. 17, 2000
Rick Perry	Jan. 17, 2000–

United States Senators

Sam Houston	Feb. 21, 1846–March 4, 1859
Thomas J. Rusk	Feb. 21, 1846–July 29, 1857
J. Pinckney Henderson	Nov. 9, 1857–June 4, 1858
Matthias Ward	Sept. 29, 1858–Dec. 5, 1859
John Hemphill	March 4, 1859–July 11, 1861
Louis T. Wigfall	1859–1861 (Went to Confederate Senate)
Morgan C. Hamilton	Feb. 22, 1870–March 3, 1877
James W. Flanagan	Feb. 22, 1870–March 3, 1875
Samuel B. Maxey	March 3, 1875–March 3, 1887
Richard Coke	March 3, 1877–March 3, 1895
John H. Reagan	March 3, 1887–June 10, 1891
Horace Chilton	Dec. 7, 1891–March 30, 1892
Roger Q. Mills	March 30, 1892–March 3, 1899
Horace Chilton	March 3, 1895–March 3, 1901
Charles A. Culberson	March 3, 1899–March 4, 1923
Joseph W. Bailey	March 3, 1901–Jan. 8, 1913
R. M. Johnson	Jan. 8, 1913–Feb. 3, 1913
Morris Sheppard	Feb. 13, 1913–April 9, 1941
Earle B. Mayfield	March 4, 1923–March 4, 1929
Tom Connally	March 4, 1929–Jan. 3, 1953
Andrew Jackson Houston	April 21, 1941–June 26, 1941
W. Lee O'Daniel	Aug. 4, 1941–Jan. 3, 1949
Lyndon B. Johnson	Jan. 3, 1949–Jan. 20, 1961
Price Daniel	Jan. 3, 1953–Jan. 15, 1957

William A. Blakley	Jan. 13, 1957–April 19, 1957
Ralph W. Yarborough	April 19, 1957–Jan. 12, 1971
William A. Blakley	Jan. 20, 1961–June 15, 1961
John G. Tower	June 15, 1961–Jan. 21, 1985
Lloyd Bentsen	Jan. 12, 1971–Jan. 20, 1993
Phil Gramm	Jan. 21, 1985–
Robert Krueger	Jan. 20, 1993–June 14, 1993
Kay Bailey Hutchison	June 14, 1993–

INDEX

The History of Texas, Third Edition

Developmental editor and copy editor: Andrew J. Davidson

Production editor: Lucy Herz

Proofreader: Claudia Siler

Cartographers: Jim Bier and Jane Domier

Cover designer: DePinto Graphic Design

Printer: Versa Press

UNITED STATES OF AMERICA

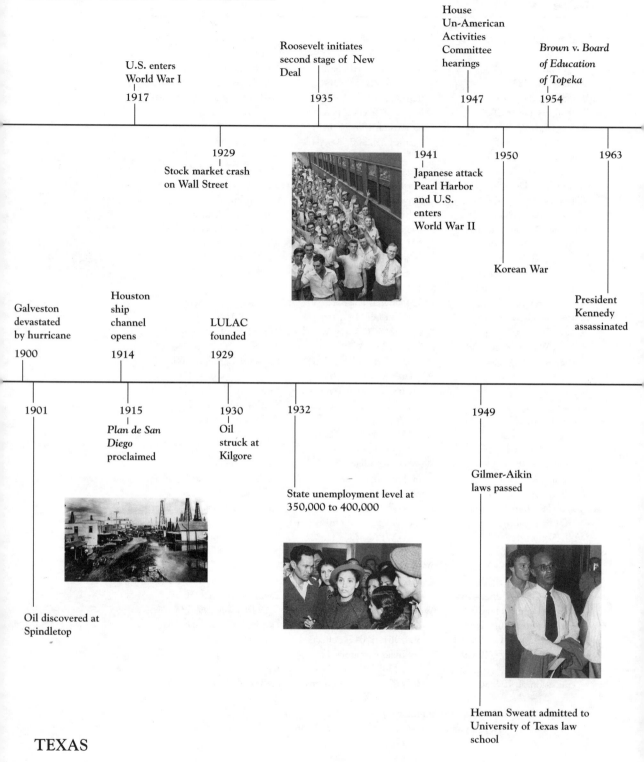

U.S. enters
World War I
1917

Roosevelt initiates
second stage of New
Deal
1935

House
Un-American
Activities
Committee
hearings
1947

*Brown v. Board
of Education
of Topeka*
1954

1929
Stock market crash
on Wall Street

1941
Japanese attack
Pearl Harbor
and U.S.
enters
World War II

1950

1963

Korean War

President
Kennedy
assassinated

Galveston
devastated
by hurricane
1900

Houston
ship
channel
opens
1914

LULAC
founded
1929

1901

1915
*Plan de San
Diego*
proclaimed

1930
Oil
struck at
Kilgore

1932

1949

Gilmer-Aikin
laws passed

State unemployment level at
350,000 to 400,000

Oil discovered at
Spindletop

Heman Sweatt admitted to
University of Texas law
school

TEXAS